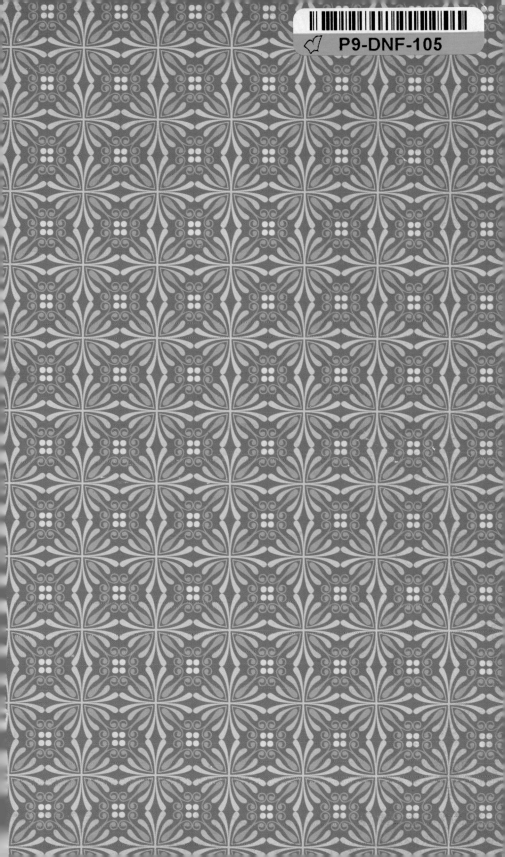

The Book of

The Truth
Behind the Story

Publications International, Ltd.

Contributing writer: Lisa Brooks

Cover and interior art: Art Explosion, Clipart.com, Getty, Shutterstock.com

Interior illustrations and photography © Art Explosion, Artville, Jupiterimages, NASA, Shutterstock.com, Thinkstock

Louis Weber, CEO
Publications International, Ltd.
8140 Lehigh Avenue
Morton Grove, IL 60053

Permission is never granted for commercial purposes.

ISBN: 978-1-68022-755-0

Manufactured in China.

8 7 6 5 4 3 2 1

Contents

✳ ✳ ✳ ✳

Chapter 1

The Story Behind History

Stormy Weather

Noah's ark is one of the best-known stories from the book of Genesis. Could it have really happened?

✳ ✳ ✳ ✳

SHIPBUILDING IS AN important profession, yet most shipbuilders live and die in anonymity. (Raise your hand if you know who designed the *Titanic*. Yeah, didn't think so.) It's a different story, of course, if your name is Noah and your boss is God—then your accomplishments will become one of the most fascinating tales in the Old Testament.

Indeed, practically everyone is familiar with the story of Noah's ark, perhaps the most famous floating menagerie in history. But many people are a little light on the details, so let's take a closer look.

Wickedness Punished

The whole thing started because God was angry. He took a look around and saw only wickedness and violence, so he decided to wipe the earth clean with a global flood and basically start over. Not everyone was wicked, however. God found one righteous man—Noah—and instructed him to build a massive ship out of wood, which he was then to fill with a mated pair of every kind of bird and animal. Noah was also instructed to stock food for all the animals as well as for himself and his family, which included his wife, three sons, and their wives.

The ark itself, as designed by God, was to be 300 cubits long, 50 cubits wide, and 30 cubits high. A cubit is around 17.5 inches, though an Egyptian royal cubit was a little longer, around 20.5 inches. (Noah went to school in Egypt, so he may have used this particular measurement.) As a result, the ark was between 437 and 512 feet long and nearly three stories high—a pretty good-size vessel for the day.

Time-Consuming Project

Building the ark wasn't some weekend project. In fact, if one takes the Bible literally, Noah spent around 120 years constructing it—he was 480 years old when God first spoke to him and 600 when the flood finally occurred. (People lived a *lot* longer back then.)

The flood that followed was a horrifying event. God produced torrential rains for 40 days and 40 nights, enough to flood the entire planet past the mountaintops and kill everyone and everything on it. As the waters receded, the ark came to rest on the mountains of Ararat. However, it took several months more for the world to dry. When finally invited by God to exit the ark, Noah immediately built an altar and worshipped God with burnt offerings. God was pleased, and he promised never to destroy the earth by flood again.

It's a remarkable story, but one that begs a lot of questions. How did Noah fit thousands of birds and animals—plus their food—into the ark? And what about their waste? Feeding the animals and cleaning up after them must have been a Herculean task. The simplest answer, of course, is that God took care of it. After all, the entire event was supernatural in origin, from God instructing Noah on what to do and how to do it to the flood itself.

Fact or Fiction?

Whether the story of Noah's ark is true or not has been the subject of debate for centuries. Some theologians believe it literally, while others posit that the flood did occur, but that it was regional rather than global. And some believe the story is more allegory than fact—a fable designed to illustrate God's intolerance toward wickedness and sin.

Interestingly, some explorers believe that Noah's Ark still rests atop Mount Ararat in eastern Turkey. Over the years, several expeditions have searched the mountain looking for concrete proof of the vessel, though nothing conclusive has been found.

Early Reading

The Dead Sea Scrolls provide a remarkable glimpse into the creation and history of the Old Testament.

✳ ✳ ✳ ✳

I N 1946, A couple of Bedouin shepherds looking for a stray goat stumbled upon some ancient desert caves near the shore of the Dead Sea in Israel. They returned with what would turn out to be one of the world's most important archaeological finds—the oldest biblical and extra-biblical documents ever uncovered.

In the following years, nearly 900 manuscripts were recovered from 11 caves in the ancient settlement of Qumran, about 13 miles east of Jerusalem. Known as the Dead Sea Scrolls, the documents, many of which are fragments, have provided astounding insight into ancient Hebrew life and the contents of the Bible.

Biblical Cornucopia

The scrolls are believed to date from the third century B.C. to A.D. 68 and are written in Hebrew, Aramaic, and Greek. They have been divided into two categories: biblical and non-biblical. The documents in the biblical category include fragments from every book of the Old Testament except for the book of Esther. Included among them are 19 copies of the book of Isaiah, 25 copies of Deuteronomy, and 30 copies of the book of Psalms. The documents also contained some surprises, including prophecies by Ezekiel, Jeremiah, and Daniel not found in the Bible, as well as previously unseen psalms attributed to King David and Joshua.

Of equal interest are the documents that do not pertain to the Bible. Many deal with common life and Jewish law, and they include rule books for the community, war conduct, hymnic compositions, and writings of wisdom. Perhaps most intriguing, however, was what has come to be known as the Copper Scroll, found in cave three. It features a list of 64 underground hiding places throughout Israel said to contain gold, silver, aromatics, and manuscripts. Some scholars believe that these deposits, if they still exist, may be treasures from the temple of Jerusalem that were hidden for safekeeping.

Authors Unknown

Following the discovery of the scrolls, archaeologists were understandably eager to learn who created them and hid them in the protective caves. Archaeologists excavated the Qumran ruin, a series of structures located on a terrace between the Dead Sea and the caves where the scrolls were found, but they learned little. The excavation did shed some light on life in ancient times but provided little additional information regarding the amazingly preserved manuscripts.

The biggest question, of course, was why the keepers of the scrolls, believed by some to be a Jewish sect known as the Essenes, felt it necessary to hide the documents. Some scholars believe the scrolls were hidden away during the First Jewish Revolt between A.D. 66–70 to protect them from advancing Roman forces sent to hunt down rebel Jews. There is some debate about this, however, and the controversy continues.

Time has taken a toll on the documents, which today are extremely fragile, but so did their discovery. Muhammed edh-Dhib, the Bedouin who found the first scrolls, hung them from a tent pole while he tried to decide what to do with them, taking them down occasionally to show people. The documents passed through many hands before finally being placed under the protection of the Israel Antiquities Authority. In March 1948, the Arab-Israeli War prompted officials to temporarily relocate the invaluable scrolls to Beirut, Lebanon; they were returned when the conflict ended.

Solving the Puzzle

Researchers have been poring over the Dead Sea Scrolls for more than 50 years, attempting to learn as much as they can about their contents, their significance in regard to Judaic and Christian history, and the people who created and later hid them. Detailed photographs of a large percentage of the intact scrolls and fragments have been made to give scholars around the world greater access.

The importance of the Dead Sea Scrolls cannot be overstated. Until their discovery, the oldest Hebrew manuscripts of the Bible dated back only to ninth century A.D. The scrolls pushed that date back another thousand years, while simultaneously providing scholars with astounding new insight into one of the most influential texts in human history.

Fresh Ingredients for the Melting Pot

This is the story of how foreigners built the United States.

✳   ✳   ✳   ✳

FOUNDED AS A nation of immigrants, the United States has seen four major waves of immigration that have shaped its history. Like ocean waves devouring a shoreline—chewing up the existing landscape, only to leave behind new sand and soil in its place—the tides of demographics left their mark on America.

First Wave: Western Europe and Africa

The first major influx to North America began long before

the nation's founding. From the early 1600s until about 1820, immigration came predominantly from colonial powers. England was the major contributor to what would become the United States of America, though the other mercantile and colonial powers—France and Holland, in particular—would enrich the new nation's settlements as well.

What drove these Europeans to the New World's coasts? Dreams of land ownership, freedom from religious and political persecution, and a chance to break loose from the caste system that characterized Europe in one form or another since the end of the Dark Ages. In the late 1700s, as democracy shook Europe's established kingdoms, newcomers also included French families, many of whom found their way to New Orleans, forming a colorful part of the Deep South's culture.

By the early 1800s, New York City began overtaking Philadelphia as the nation's premier city and became a major entry point for immigrants—though major eastern seaports from Newport to Savannah also brought in would-be citizens by the thousands. North and south of the forbidding Appalachian Mountains, the hardiest of these immigrants pushed westward in search of land on which to build new lives.

The major exception to this trend was, of course, the African slave trade. Africans kidnapped and brought to the United States formed a substantial minority whose numbers (together with their U.S.-born children) grew from nearly 750,000 in 1790 (the first year of the U.S. census) to a little more than 1.1 million by 1808, the year the slave trade was officially abolished. As Thomas Jefferson and other founding fathers foresaw, the problem of slavery would grow exponentially every decade, as the slave population multiplied throughout the east and south.

Second Wave: Central Europe and China
The next wave spanned the period from 1830 to about 1870, when the nation's growth beckoned to men and women of

northern and central Europe. In a 20-year period, some 2.5 million people came to the United States; about a third were Irish nationals who came to escape a terrible potato famine that condemned many of their countrymen to starvation. Because the Irish immigrants generally had little money when they arrived, they tended to remain in eastern cities such as New York and Boston. More affluent immigrants, such as Germans and Scandinavians, tended to move west in a band running from central Pennsylvania to the Dakotas and Great Plains.

By the time Manifest Destiny brought the United States to the Pacific shores at the end of the Mexican–American War, immigrants began coming in from the other direction—the Far East. Exaggerated tales of California gold prompted many young Chinese men to embark for America. Though the majority of them took their earnings back to China, some established small businesses along the western seaboard or worked in the mining and rail industries. Their numbers grew until 1882, when Congress passed the Chinese Exclusion Act, which all but prohibited Chinese immigration for the next 80 years.

Third Wave: Eastern and Southern Europe

From the 1870s through the early 1920s, America found a new source of fresh blood. Wars of liberation and nationalization forced legions of immigrants across the ocean on a growing network of transatlantic steamship lines. Between 1870 and 1900, approximately 12 million immigrants entered the United States, creating chaos among states that were charged with regulating immigration. To oversee this influx, the United States established a federal immigration facility on New York's Ellis Island. This new gateway to America opened for business on January 1, 1892.

One of the largest groups of "new" immigrants hailed from Italy, a nation reeling from poor harvests, disease, and the economic and political aftershocks of the wars of unification. From

1880 to 1900, America's Italian population increased tenfold, from around 44,000 in 1880 to more than 484,000 in 1900. Hailing from rural areas of Italy, they quickly adjusted to urban life, forming rich, distinctive "Little Italy" communities in many American cities.

In addition to national groups, Jews fleeing persecution in Russia, Germany, and other Eastern European nations brought new talents to the nation's shores. Between 1880 and the early 1920s, about two million Jews left their homelands to come to America.

When the United States slumped into the Great Depression and World War II recalled millions of citizens to the colors of their motherlands, immigration trailed off.

Fourth Wave: Far East and Latin America

The mid-1960s saw the start of a new immigration wave that continues today. Communist revolutions in Eastern Europe and Southeast Asia and an economic boom in the United States coincided with a removal of legal immigration quotas to produce the largest wave of immigration ever seen. This latest round of mass immigration was driven by conditions in Asia, Africa, and Latin America, three regions whose numbers of emigrants to the United States grew almost tenfold between 1960 and 1990.

What About the Football Game?

Most people were taught that Thanksgiving originated with the Pilgrims when they invited local Native Americans to celebrate the first successful harvest. Here's what really happened.

✳   ✳   ✳   ✳

THERE ARE ONLY two original accounts of the event we think of as the first Thanksgiving, both very brief. In the fall of 1621, the Pilgrims, having barely survived their first arduous year, managed to bring in a modest harvest. They celebrated with a traditional English harvest feast, with food, dancing, and games. The local Wampanoag Indians were there, and both groups demonstrated their skill at musketry and archery.

So that was the first Thanksgiving, right? Not exactly. To the Pilgrims, a thanksgiving day was a special religious holiday that consisted of prayer, fasting, and praise—not at all like the party atmosphere that accompanied a harvest feast.

Our modern Thanksgiving, which combines the concepts of harvest feast and a day of thanksgiving, is actually a nine-teenth-century development. In the decades after the Pilgrims, national days of thanksgiving were decreed on various occasions, and some states celebrated a holiday for thanksgiving annually. But there was no recurring national holiday until 1863, when a woman named Sarah Josepha Hale launched a campaign for an annual celebration that would "greatly aid and strengthen public harmony of feeling."

Such sentiments were sorely needed in a nation torn apart by the Civil War. So in the aftermath of the bloody Battle of Gettysburg, President Lincoln decreed a national day of thanksgiving that would fall on the last Thursday in November, probably to coincide with the anniversary of the Pilgrims' landing at Plymouth. The date was later shifted to the third Thursday in November, simply to give retailers a longer Christmas shopping season.

Jive Turkey

Did the Pilgrims start a tradition by eating turkey at the first Thanksgiving—or was that Tiny Tim's doing?

✳ ✳ ✳ ✳

Which came first, the turkey or Thanksgiving? Governor William Bradley's journal from around that time indicates that "besides waterfowl there was great store of wild turkeys, of which they took many." Another record notes that "our governor sent four men on fowling…they four in one day killed as much fowl, as with a little help beside, served the company almost a week."

Of course, "fowl" doesn't necessarily mean turkey, so the best we can say is that the Pilgrims may have eaten it. The only food we know for certain they ate was venison, and that was provided by their guests, the Native Americans (who may have been a little surprised by the meager spread their hosts had laid out). They probably also ate codfish, goose, and lobster, but not a lot of vegetables—you can catch fish and fowl, but it takes time to grow crops. And mashed potatoes? Nope—potatoes hadn't yet been introduced to New England.

So how did the gobbler become the centerpiece of Thanksgiving celebrations? It may have had something to do with the prevalent diet at the time the national holiday was founded in 1863. Beef and chicken were too expensive to serve to a crowd, and even if you had your own farm, you needed the animals' continuous supply of milk and eggs. Venison was an option, but you couldn't always count on bagging a deer in time for the holiday. Turkey was readily available, not too expensive, and very popular, perhaps in part due to the scene at the end of Charles Dickens's *A Christmas Carol* in which Scrooge buys "the prize turkey" for Bob Cratchit's family. The novel, published in 1843, was immensely popular in America and may have secured the humble fowl's center-stage spot on the Thanksgiving table.

The Wives of Henry VIII

England's Henry VIII is famous for having six wives. But how much do you know about those ladies themselves?

✳   ✳   ✳   ✳

A TRUE RENAISSANCE MAN and child of privilege, Henry VIII spent his youth enjoying life's finer pursuits, learning about music, languages, the arts, sports, poetry, and architecture. During these years, he also picked up a penchant for vice, earning a steadfast reputation as a gambler and, most notably, a womanizer. Although Henry was second in line to succeed his father as King of England and Lord of Ireland, his elder brother's death left the position open. Henry took over the monarchy just shy of his 18th birthday, but he was more interested in entertainment than politics. The new king took a few years to get settled into the business of running England, but he was quickly thrust into his first marriage. Undeserved as his lecherous reputation might be—monarchs were expected to play the part of the playboy—Henry certainly did run up quite a collection of wives: a total of six by the time of his death in 1547 at age 55.

Catherine of Aragon

Marriage to wife number one, Catherine of Aragon, was an arrangement pushed by her father, King Ferdinand II of Spain, and Henry's own father, Henry VII. Catherine had been married to Henry's older brother Arthur for only a few months, and upon his passing, Henry was betrothed to the widow. In this way, the fathers were guaranteeing an ongoing union between England and Spain. It took Henry nearly a quarter of a century to end this marriage of convenience, but he was finally granted an annulment on the grounds that Catherine had once been married to his brother. The pope refused to grant this annulment, so Henry arranged to receive it from the archbishop of Canterbury. This severely damaged

Henry's—and England's—relationship with the Roman Catholic Church. Three years later, Henry closed Catholic monasteries and abbeys.

Anne Boleyn

Anne Boleyn, marchioness of Pembroke, was a lady-in-waiting who became the other woman. Anne was an English noble, educated in France, who provided reputable servitude to Queen Catherine. During her period of personal assistance, Anne and Henry began their affair, with Henry proposing marriage roughly six years prior to his annulment from Catherine. An argument has been made that the pair did not consummate their affair until Henry's annulment was final (although others claim she was pregnant when she married). According to the theory, Anne was not so moralistic that she wouldn't engage with a married man—she had simply seen the fate that befell her sister Mary when she carried on with Henry. When Mary Boleyn finally gave in and consummated her affair with the king, she was rewarded with a pink slip and sent packing. It turns out that Mary was the luckier of the two, being simply sent away. Anne, on the other hand, after failing to produce a male heir, was beheaded on charges of adultery and witchcraft.

Jane Seymour

Apparently, Henry viewed his wives' ladies-in-waiting as his own personal marriage buffet. Upon Queen Anne's passing, he plucked his third wife, Jane Seymour, from Anne's group of attendants. Of course, it has been suggested that Henry's interest in Jane was the true reason he had Anne killed—not the six fingers he accused her of having (which was seen as the mark of the devil). Unfortunately, Jane only lasted a year as Henry's wife. Although she finally brought Henry a legitimate male heir, Edward, Jane succumbed to a fever caused from complications of childbirth.

Anne of Cleves

On the market yet again, Henry once more tried his hand at

an arranged marriage. Following his chancellor's advice, Henry agreed to marry Anne of Cleves for her family's advantageous political ties to both the Catholic Church and the Protestant Reformation. With the nuptials already scheduled, Henry was said to have voiced his misgivings upon finally meeting his bride-to-be. Although striking in personality, Anne was not as agreeable in appearance as the king had hoped: He likened Anne's visage to that of a horse. Although he followed through with the vows, Anne—dubbed "Flanders Mare" by Henry— was released from her role as queen through an annulment. But at least she got a generous settlement for her troubles.

Catherine Howard

The tables were turned on the adulterous King Henry by his fifth wife, Catherine Howard, a woman who was known to engage in illicit affairs of her own. Even before settling down with the king, Catherine—who was Anne Boleyn's first cousin—was intimately involved with many men about town. Soon after they were wed, the king discovered that his bride was still sowing her oats with other suitors. Apparently, what's good for the gander was most certainly not good for the goose, for Henry said, "Off with her head!" and Catherine was no more.

Catherine Parr

Henry's sixth and final wife, Catherine Parr, was famous for her own lengthy list of marriages. With two marriages before Henry and one after, Catherine holds the record for the most-married queen in English history. She is also the only one of Henry's six brides to make it out of her marriage alive and without an annulment. Only four years after their wedding, Henry died at age 55 from obesity-related complications. Catherine escaped the fates of Henry's first five wives and survived as a widow free to marry one last time—to Thomas Seymour, Jane Seymour's brother.

Henry VIII's Tower of London Victims

* Queen Catherine Howard, Henry's fifth wife, was beheaded for adultery on the Tower Green. With her went her lovers, Thomas Culpepper and Francis Dereham, and her lady-in-waiting Jane Rochford.

* Jane Rochford was instrumental in the downfall of two queens. She arranged trysts for Catherine Howard, for which both were executed, and she had previously testified against her husband, George Boleyn, and sister-in-law Queen Anne, helping them to their graves by accusing them of incest.

* Desperate to marry Jane Seymour, Henry had his second queen, Anne Boleyn, executed on trumped-up charges of adultery and witchcraft. Accused and killed with her were her brother George, as well as Henry Norris, Francis Weston, and William Brereton, who had been close friends with the king. Anne's musician, Mark Smeaton, was also executed for supposed adultery with the queen.

* The royal House of Plantagenet nearly became extinct under Henry's rule. The Plantagenets were descended from earlier kings of England, primarily the profligate Edward III, and possibly had a better claim to the throne than the Tudors. Those who made this assertion publicly were often executed on petty or unfounded charges.

* Edward Stafford, Third Duke of Buckingham, was beheaded for being the leader of nobles who were openly resentful of Henry's reliance on low-born ministers such as Cardinal Wolsey, the son of a butcher. Many historians

believe he was also killed because he was part of the royal Plantagenet family and had bragged that his family was more royal than Henry's.

✳ King Henry's paranoia grew as he edged closer to death, and Henry Howard, Earl of Surrey and son of the Duke of Norfolk, was one of those who paid the price. The king became convinced that Norfolk and Surrey were planning to grab the throne from Henry's son Edward when he died, so both were sent to the Tower. Surrey was beheaded, but his father was saved, only because Henry died the day before he was to be executed.

✳ Thomas Howard, Third Duke of Norfolk, narrowly avoided losing his head when Henry VIII died the day before he was to sign the duke's death warrant. He was released in 1553 by Mary I.

✳ Margaret Pole, the 67-year-old Countess of Salisbury, suffered one of the most gruesome beheadings on record. She refused to put her head on the block, saying that she was no traitor, and therefore had to be forced down. The executioner's first blow struck her shoulder. According to some accounts, she then jumped up and ran from the executioner, who struck her 11 times before she finally died.

✳ The longest-serving prisoner of the Tudor reign was Sir William de la Pole, who sat in the Tower of London for 37 years. Sir William was arrested by Henry VII for suspicion of treason because he was a Plantagenet and he and his brother were Yorkist heirs, the leading contenders for the English throne. Henry VIII had Sir William executed in 1513.

✳ Being Henry's most trusted minister provided no protection from the executioner. Thomas Cromwell rose to power in 1532 and was a major figure in the English Reformation.

Like many of Henry's advisors, his fall was caused by his support for one of Henry's wives—in this case, his arrangement of the king's marriage to Anne of Cleves, whom Henry despised. Cromwell was sent to the block in 1540.

* Anne Askew's execution proved that Henry considered Protestants to be heretics. She had been arrested for preaching Protestant views and was cruelly racked to get the names of other prominent reformists. Queen Katherine Parr was nearly arrested after pleading for mercy for Anne, but her plea was rejected and Anne burned at the stake.

Topping Off the Capitol

As the Civil War raged on, the uncompleted dome on the U.S. Capitol became a symbol of a country fighting to remain united.

※　　※　　※　　※

THE U.S. CAPITOL in Washington, D.C., was originally topped with a short copper dome. A new, more majestic dome was approved in 1855 with an estimated cost of $100,000. That price tag rose exponentially over the next decade, rising to a final total of $1,047,291.

Starting, Stopping, and Starting Again

Work began in 1856 and mostly continued smoothly. That changed with the Civil War, however. One month after war broke out, construction ceased. Congress decided that the funds should be used for the war rather than the Capitol. The building was even used as a temporary barracks for troops stationed in Washington, D.C., to protect the city.

The order to stop construction left the contractor, James, Fowler, Kirtland, and Company, with 1.3 million pounds of iron onsite. Worried about keeping their business afloat, they decided to continue with the dome construction on their own.

At this point, the line between reality and myth becomes blurred. Some sources suggest that Lincoln used the contractor's decision to his advantage, while others claim that it was always his intention to finish the dome for the sake of the country. According to Lincoln biographer Carl Sandburg, the President said, "If people see the Capitol going on, it is a sign we intend the Union shall go on."

As the exterior of the dome neared completion on December 2, 1863, crowds gathered on Pennsylvania Avenue to watch. After the years and months of construction and a war that was tearing the country apart, the great dome over the Capitol at last appeared to be finished. One can only imagine the emotion felt when the 19.5-foot-tall statue of Freedom was hoisted atop the immense dome.

Cherokee: The Trail of Tears

Yet another example of America's sad history with the First Nation Tribes.

❋ ❋ ❋ ❋

IN 1830, THE U.S. Congress passed the Indian Removal Act, which forced the resettlement of most Cherokee from their homes in the southeastern United States to land west of the Mississippi River. Those Cherokee who refused to go were arrested by the U.S. Army between 1838 and 1839 and sent to an area that was then called "Indian Territory" (now Oklahoma). Of the 15,000 Cherokee who set out on the journey, more than 4,000 died along the way. Edward Wilkerson Bushyhead was seven years old when he moved with his family. Later in his life he traveled to California, where he became a sheriff, then served as chief of police, and eventually owned a newspaper. When he died at age 75 in 1907, he was believed to be the last survivor of the Trail of Tears.

The Cherokee Nation Treaty of 1866

The Cherokee Nation is one of the largest First Nation groups in the history of the United States. Many members now live in poverty, but at one time it was a wealthy nation.

✻   ✻   ✻   ✻

BEFORE THE CIVIL War, some Cherokee had southern plantations that held as many as one hundred African slaves. When the Civil War began, the Cherokee officially sided with the Confederacy (though thousands fled and fought with the Union Army); this made all previous treaties between the Cherokee and the U.S. government null and void.

After the war, new treaties were drawn up. As part of the Cherokee Nation Treaty of 1866, the Cherokee guaranteed newly freed slaves citizenship in the Cherokee Nation. However, few African American freedmen were embraced by the Cherokee, and even today many of their descendants struggle for full acceptance.

The last surviving Native American signatory to the Treaty of 1866 was Chief Samuel Houston Benge. Benge fought for the Union during the Civil War and achieved the rank of lieutenant. He died at his farm on October 23, 1902, at age 70. He is buried at Fort Gibson National Cemetery in Oklahoma.

The Dawes Commission

Who is considered a citizen of the Cherokee Nation today? Anyone who can prove they are descended from a person listed on the Dawes Rolls. These rolls are lists of people accepted by the Dawes Commission between 1898 and 1914 as members of the Cherokee (and four other nations). The Dawes Commission was formed to divide tribal land into plots, which were then divided among tribal members.

The Mason-Dixon Line Surveyors

Who knew it was the British that divided the southerners from the northerners?

* * * *

A DISPUTE AROSE IN the 1700s between the colonies of Maryland and Pennsylvania over the boundary line between their lands. The proprietors of each colony, the Penns of Pennsylvania and the Calverts of Maryland, took their argument to the British courts for resolution. In 1750, England's chief justice declared that a line of demarcation should run between southern Pennsylvania and northern Maryland at a point 15 miles south of Philadelphia. At the shared expense of both controlling families, British experts were hired to create this line.

A decade after the ruling, astronomer Charles Mason and surveyor Jeremiah Dixon began creating the line of demarcation. Their undertaking was a formidable one, and it took them five years to survey the 230 miles of land. In addition to the technical difficulties of establishing a reliable tangent line, the duo faced the potential hostilities of Native Americans who inhabited the area. The team planted a limestone marker at each mile point. These stones had an M on one side and a P on the other, and each was about three and a half feet long and weighed about 300 pounds. More ornate stones, featuring the Penn and Calvert coats of arms, were positioned at every fifth mile.

Far more than a boundary separating Pennsylvania and Maryland, the Mason-Dixon Line served to divide the North from the South in the years to come. To this day, original stone markers can still be found along the route.

Mason outlived his colleague Dixon by nine years, and was the last survivor of the Mason-Dixon Line surveyors when he died in 1786.

Secret Service Agents— the President's Guards *and* Counterfeiter Fighters?

Two roles that fall under the umbrella of the United States Secret Service are protecting the president and fighting counterfeiters. What's the connection?

✳   ✳   ✳   ✳

THE CONNECTION GOES back to 1876, when the newly formed Secret Service was investigating a group of counterfeiters in Chicago, Illinois. A Secret Service informant began frequenting the Hub, a saloon that was the counterfeiters' regular hangout. Four counterfeiters hatched a plan to spring their talented buddy, Benjamin Boyd (an engraver), out of the Joliet penitentiary. They planned to steal Lincoln's body from Oak Ridge Cemetery in Springfield and demand Boyd's freedom as ransom. When one counterfeiter dropped out, the other three felt they still needed another participant. Unfortunately for them, they approached the informant, Lewis C. Swegles, who promptly told his boss—Patrick D. Tyrrell, the chief of the regional office of the Secret Service.

The night the counterfeiters went to the cemetery to carry out their plan, Secret Service agents were waiting for them. The counterfeiters bungled their mission in an amazing fashion, and Lincoln's body was never touched. The counterfeiters fled the scene but went right back to the Hub, where they were promptly arrested. After this event, the Secret Service gradually began protecting presidents, in addition to their original role of fighting counterfeiters.

Joseph Smith Founds a New Church

The story of Mormonism.

✳ ✳ ✳ ✳

When Joseph Smith was 14 years old, he struggled over which church to join. His mother attended a local church, but his father did not. Not sure what to do, he began to pray about it. According to Smith, one day as he was praying, God and Jesus appeared and told him that all existing churches had deviated too much from Jesus' original teachings. A few years later, an angel named Moroni appeared to Smith and told him about a set of gold plates that contained a record of ancient Americans who were visited by Christ after his resurrection. Smith found the plates buried near his family farm, and four years later the angel helped him translate them. Smith published the *Book of Mormon* in 1830. Today the sacred text steers Mormon followers who believe that their church is the authentic restoration of the church established by Jesus Christ during New Testament times.

The Joseph Smith Murder

After founding the Mormon Church in 1830, Joseph Smith searched for a peaceful place to settle down with his followers. But wherever they went, trouble followed.

First they settled in Kirtland, Ohio. By 1838, the other residents of that city were resentful of the Mormons and their increasing numbers, and Smith and his followers moved to Far West, Missouri. They were there less than a year before opposition rose up. They fled to Commerce, Illinois, and renamed the town Nauvoo (Hebrew for "beautiful place"). This settlement was peaceful for several years, and the town became powerful; it was the second largest city in the state after Chicago. It was during this time that the Mormons began to practice polygamy, and this—together with their growing numbers and power—again aroused resentment from neighboring communities.

Smith served as mayor and chief judge in Nauvoo, and when a community newspaper published an article critical of the Mormons, Smith ordered the newspaper's offices shut down. This action sparked outrage and riots. Authorities from nearby Carthage arrested Smith and his brother Hyrum and charged them with inciting a riot. On June 27, 1844, a large mob attacked the Smith brothers and supporters John Taylor (1808–87) and Dr. Willard Richards (1804–54) at the Carthage jail. Hyrum was shot in the face and died instantly; Joseph was shot multiple times and died as he tried to escape through a second-story window. The last of the four men was Taylor, who was shot four times but survived. In 1880, after the death of Brigham Young, Taylor became the third president of the Mormon Church. He died in 1887 at age 78.

Justifying Polygamy: Joseph Smith justified the practice of polygamy by pointing to the figure of Abraham in the Old Testament. Smith is believed to have had nearly 30 wives, though he claimed to have only one.

Last Attempt: In April 1844, Joseph Smith announced his candidacy for the office of president of the United States. He was killed two months later.

The Brigham Young Party

In 1846, Brigham Young led Mormon settlers on a 1,500-mile westward migration. After halting for the winter of 1846–47, Young continued west with an advance party of 148 people. On July 24, 1847, he arrived at the mouth of Emigration Canyon. Here, he declared, "This is the right place," and continued down the valley to establish the permanent settlement of Salt Lake City.

Making the Grade

Methods of evaluating student work have changed with the times, and the A–F grading system in the United States is a recent phenomenon.

✳ ✳ ✳ ✳

Grading Before Grades

BEFORE THE ERA of standardized tests, report cards, and voluminous grade books, most schools in the United States were rural one-room schoolhouses. Student evaluation consisted of qualitative descriptions of the student's progress and was the prerogative of the individual schoolmaster. The earliest schools to establish a consistent grading system were the first universities, including Harvard, Yale, and the College of William and Mary. Before grading systems became standardized, entrance to these colleges was based mostly on social class, reputation, social networking, and the scattered reports of childhood tutors.

As the American population grew, it became difficult for college professors to send detailed descriptions of each student's work to so many parents. In the late-eighteenth century, Yale began to evaluate its students by four discrete categories, marked by Latin adjectives: Optimi, second Optimi, Inferiores, and Pejores. The four-point system—still in use today as the basis of GPA calculations—can also be traced to Yale: The four descriptive adjectives were matched up with the numbers 1–4.

The first numerical system at Harvard was based on a 20-point format, which is popular today in many countries. This was eventually replaced by a 100-point system, which was then adopted by other universities. The point system was often criticized as being too specific, so sometimes a range of points would be matched up with words or divisions. For example, in 1877, Harvard divided its students into six divisions, with Division One receiving between 90–100 points, and so on.

The first time that a modern letter grade was correlated with a range of numbers was at Harvard in 1883, when one report card referenced a *B* grade. The first all-out *A–F* grading system— implemented at Mount Holyoke College in Massachusetts in 1897—was based on a 100-point system that would strike fear in the hearts of modern students: An *A* was 95–100, and anything below a 75 meant failure, which at that time was denoted by the now not-so-dreaded *E*.

Grading the Grading System

It wasn't until the rapid urbanization of the mid-nineteenth century that a consistent grading system became necessary outside of the university environment. Education came under the auspices of public funding; education bureaucrats experimented with different systems and tried to make schools in the same city practice the same system.

These early systems borrowed from the various conventions that were already popular at the major universities. The trendy letter system of this time period was quite different than the one that is in use today. The letters were based on descriptive adjectives rather than numeric ranges: *E* for Excellent, *S* for Satisfactory, *N* for Needs Improvement, and *U* for Unsatisfactory. This system is still used in primary education. It is likely that the disappearance of the *E* as a failing grade resulted from confusion with the *E* for Excellent.

The current *A–F* method became popular in the mid-twentieth century and is based on the "tens" system: 90–100 is an *A*, 80–89 is a *B*, and so on. A survey conducted by Georgia State University found it is practiced by 90 percent of colleges nationwide. The system is often criticized, as an *A* can mean different things to different schools and different teachers. A handful of universities have replaced grades with the qualitative descriptions of yore, but it seems the current system is in for the long haul.

Banking's Crumple Zone: The Federal Reserve

The United States' first century was marked by periodic financial panics. The Federal Reserve System grew out of a need to weather them. Today, when the chairman of the Federal Reserve Board speaks, tremors ripple through the global economy.

✳ ✳ ✳ ✳

Raison d'être

ANYONE WITH A bank account can understand the problem that led to the Federal Reserve System (Fed). Say you have $1,000; you can keep it under a mattress or in a bank. The mattress method earns you no interest, but your access to the money is unquestioned. On the other hand, if you were sure you could withdraw your money on demand, you'd prefer to earn interest on it, so you'd deposit it.

However, the minute you suspect that your withdrawal privileges are endangered, you'll be at the teller's window to withdraw it all, right doggone now. Everyone tends to do that at once. When they do, it creates a run on banks—a panic. The antidote to panics is to assure the public that their deposits are safe and can be withdrawn at any time. Assured of that, the public doesn't withdraw cash en masse, and there's no crisis.

In the nineteenth century, the United States mostly lacked a central reserve bank and blundered along with a topsy-turvy monetary system; periodic panics demonstrated the need for reform. But it wasn't just about bank runs. If a central bank could easily contract or expand the money supply, government could moderate dizzy growth or meet liquidity needs. In the 1800s, many banks issued their own banknotes, which fell in value with distance from the bank's flagpole. Bank failures were unknown in Canada, eh, with its far more resilient monetary system.

Panic of 1907

The U.S. stock market went seriously south in 1906. This led to tighter credit and a run on trust companies—quasi-banks engaged in riskier investments and market manipulations than conventional banks. When one bank stopped cashing checks drawn on the Knickerbocker Trust Company of New York, the dam burst. Soon everyone wanted their money out of the trusts. Only the intervention of J. P. Morgan, who formed a consortium to lend the trusts money—a move supported by Congress' Aldrich–Vreeland Act, which created emergency money, essentially doing what the Fed would later do—stemmed the tide of red ink.

Shhhh . . . It's at Jekyll Island

In 1910, the nation's banking kahunas met in secret at Jekyll Island, Georgia, to napkin-sketch what would become the Federal Reserve Act of 1913. This act created a Federal Reserve Board of Governors in Washington, D.C., supervising 12 regional Federal Reserve Banks (FRB). Banks would become shareholders of the Federal Reserve System, depositing cash in return for FRB stock. Fed branches would be able to lend banks money in a crisis.

World War I Crisis

The Fed began operations in November 1914, shortly after World War I began, but just a little too late to stem the financial crisis caused when the British began demanding loan payments in specie (gold). Although an extension of the Aldrich–Vreeland Act cushioned the blow, the lesson was clear: A central bank—the Federal Reserve System—was necessary for the financial stability of America.

Postwar

For the Fed, the postwar period was a time of learning by doing, as well as a time of shakeout: What could it legally do, and who would direct its actions? With banks failing all over, the Depression gave the Fed a full-immersion baptism in monetary policy. Also helping alleviate that situation was the Federal Deposit Insurance Corporation (FDIC), created to increase confidence in the banking system. The Fed and FDIC remain the primary bulwarks of public confidence in banking to this day.

The Fall of the Crooked E: Who Killed Enron?

For a company that seemed to have everything going its way, the end sure came quickly.

✳ ✳ ✳ ✳

IN THE 1990S, the U.S. Congress passed legislation deregulating the sale of electricity, as it had done for natural gas some years earlier. The result made it possible for energy trading companies, including Enron, to thrive. In effect, the law allowed a highly profitable market to develop between energy producers and those local governments that buy electricity—a system kept in place because of aggressive lobbying by Enron and other such firms. By the turn of the twenty-first century, Enron stock was trading for $80 to $90 a share.

Trouble in the Waters

All was not smooth sailing, however, for the energy giant. Its new broadband communications trading division was running into difficulties, its power project in India was behind schedule and over budget, and its role in the California power crisis of 2000–2001 was being scrutinized. Then, on August 14, 2001, CEO Jeffrey Skilling announced he was resigning after only six months in his position. He also sold off 450,000 shares of Enron stock for $33 million.

Ken Lay, the chairman at Enron, affirmed that there was "absolutely no accounting issue, no trading issue, no reserve issue, no previously unknown problem" that prompted Skilling's departure. He further asserted that there would be "no change or outlook in the performance of the company going forward." Though he did admit that falling stock prices were a factor behind Skilling's departure, Lay decided to assume the CEO position.

Don't Worry, Everything's Under Control

Enron's financial statements were so confusing because of the company's tax strategies and position-hedging, as well as its use of "related-party transactions," that Enron's leadership assumed no one would be able to analyze its finances. A particularly troubling aspect was that several of the "related-party" entities were, or had been, controlled by Enron CFO Andrew Fastow (who may or may not have realized that he was being groomed as a scapegoat).

Sound confusing? Good, then the plan worked. And if all this could confuse government regulatory agencies, think of how investors must have felt. Stock prices slowly started sliding from their highs at the beginning of 2001, but as the year went on, the tumble picked up speed. On October 22, for instance, the share price of Enron dropped $5.40 in one day to $20.65. After Enron officials started talking about such things as "share settled costless collar arrangements" and "derivative instruments which eliminated the contingent nature of restricted forward contracts," the Securities and Exchange Commission (SEC) had a quote of its own: "There is the appearance that you are hiding something."

Things Fall Apart

The landslide had begun. On October 24, Lay removed Fastow as CFO. Stock was trading at $16.41. On October 27, Enron began buying back all of its shares (valued around $3.3 billion). It financed this purchase by emptying its lines of credit at several banks.

On October 30, in response to concerns that Enron might try a further $1–2 billion refinancing due to having insufficient cash on hand, Enron's credit rating was dropped to near junk-bond status. Enron did secure an additional billion dollars, but it had to sell its valuable natural gas pipeline to do so.

Enron desperately needed either new investment or an outright buyout. On the night of November 7, Houston-based energy trader Dynegy voted to acquire Enron at a fire-sale price of $8 billion in stock. It wasn't enough.

The sale lagged, and Standard & Poor's index determined that if it didn't go through, Enron's bonds would be rated as junk. The word was out that Lay and other officials had sold off hundreds of millions of dollars of their own stock before the crisis and that Lay stood to receive $60 million dollars if the Dynegy sale went through. But the last, worst straw was that Enron employees saw their retirement accounts—largely based on Enron stock—wiped out.

By November 7, after the company announced that all the money it had borrowed (about $5 billion) had been exhausted in 50 days, Enron stock was down to $7.00 a share. The SEC filed civil fraud complaints against Arthur Andersen, Enron's auditor. And on November 28, the sky fell in: Dynegy backed out of the deal to acquire Enron, and Enron's stock hit junk-bond status. On December 2, 2001, Enron sought Chapter 11 protection as it filed for the biggest bankruptcy in U.S. history. Around 4,000 employees lost their jobs.

So Who Killed Enron?

* Ken Lay and Jeffrey Skilling were indicted for securities and wire fraud. Lay was convicted on 6 of 6 counts, and Skilling on 19 of 28. Skilling was sentenced to 24 years and 4 months in prison. Lay avoided prison time by dying of a heart attack before he was sentenced.

* Arthur Andersen accountants signed off on this fraud. Why? They were getting a million dollars a week for their accounting services. The firm was convicted of obstruction of justice for shredding documents related to the Enron audit and

surrendered its licenses and right to practice. From a high of more than 100,000 employees, Arthur Andersen is now down to around 200. Most of them are handling lawsuits.

* Investors bought stock in a company they didn't understand for the greedy promise of quick money.

* Stock-ratings companies said it was a great investment, even though they had no idea what shape Enron was in.

* Investment bankers who knew that Enron was shaky bought in for a shot at quick and easy profits.

History's Most Idiosyncratic VIPs

High-level dignitaries should demonstrate dignified behavior— and yet, the annals of history show a litany of idiosyncratic elite. Whether it was a tendency toward eccentricity that suited them to politics and social status or, rather, the privileged position itself that drove them kooky, odd conduct by high-powered bigwigs has always been around.

✳   ✳   ✳   ✳

His Royal Snobbery

CONSIDER CHARLES SEYMOUR, the sixth Duke of Somerset and Baron of Trowbridge. This historical figure is often referred to as the "Proud Duke," but a more fitting nickname might be the "Pompous Duke." Baron Thomas Babington Macaulay, a nineteenth-century poet and politician, once quipped that Seymour's "pride of birth and rank amounted almost to a disease." So snobbish was the duke that he wouldn't lower himself to the level of his servants by uttering even a single word to them. Instead, he enlisted sign language to communicate his needs and desires. He preferred not to mingle with the general masses, either—he had private homes built along his travel routes from Somerset to London so that he could remain isolated from lower-class travelers who used inns.

Hungarian Bloodletter

Countess Elizabeth Bathory of Hungary is another historical figure who displayed some notable eccentricities. Her odd
behavior, however, was of a more criminal nature. A raven-
haired beauty with smooth ivory skin, Bathory, along with a
team of cohorts that included a dwarf named Ficzko, tricked
hundreds of young maidens into her home, Cachtice Castle,
enticing them with hopes of well-paid work, only to brutally
torture and murder them. According to some accounts, the
countess sought their virginal blood for rejuvenating baths.
Apparently, skin care in sixteenth- and seventeenth-century
Hungary wasn't up to snuff. Also known as the "Bloody
Countess" for her particularly disturbing behavior, Bathory was
imprisoned in a fortress and lived for four years trapped behind
a wall of stones, with meals slipped to her through the cracks.
She died behind those walls.

Slippery Cal

Calvin Coolidge, the 30th president of the United States,
also had a strange personal grooming regimen. Thankfully, his
product of choice was not the blood of young virgins, but the
more easily accessible petroleum jelly. Coolidge was dubbed
"Silent Cal" for his introverted disposition and tendency
toward taciturnity. Alice Roosevelt Longworth, Theodore
Roosevelt's eldest daughter, famously described Coolidge as
looking "as if he had been weaned on a pickle." With that image
in mind, consider Coolidge's strangest habit: In bed, whilst
eating his typical morning breakfast of boiled wheat and rye,
he enjoyed having his head massaged with Vaseline. Pair that
odd picture with another of his strange eccentricities, his
regular exercise routine—atop the electric horse that he kept
in the White House—and you have one idiosyncratic national
leader, indeed.

Dinner Goes to the Dogs

Another odd aristocrat, the eighth Earl of Bridgewater, Sir
Francis Henry Egerton, was a lonely sort who nursed a peculiar

penchant for a few of his prized possessions, namely his pet dogs and his enormous collection of shoes—he had a pair for each day of the year. Egerton, who lived in the late eighteenth and early nineteenth centuries, was known for hosting fantastic dinner parties in which he demanded only the finest decorum from his guests. Instead of hosting humans, though, his table was set for his brood of pet pups. Dressed in the most exquisite fashions of the day, and with first-rate, handmade leather shoes to rival his own, the dogs' necks were adorned with crisp linen napkins. If a dog deviated from what Egerton considered acceptable table manners, it was exiled to the kitchen for a lonely week of solitary meals.

Wearers Beware

Instead of requiring particular dress from his subjects, as his near-contemporary Egerton did with his dogs, idiosyncratic Czar Paul I of St. Petersburg strictly forbade specific articles of clothing for all of the inhabitants of his land. The czar associated round hats, sleeveless vests, pantaloons, laced shoes, and top boots with French revolutionaries, so he passed a law decreeing the wearing of these items unconstitutional. Hundreds of armed troops were unleashed on the streets to ambush those frocked hooligans, who were then stripped of the undesirable garb. One boot-wearing lawbreaker even watched as authorities snipped his too-tall boots down to shoe shape.

Crime and Punishment

Austrian Empress Maria Theresa was known for her exemplary and visionary leadership skills in the eighteenth century, but she also had a few strange tendencies on her rap sheet. After dealing with rumors of her own husband's supposed infidelities, Maria became staunch in her distaste for all indecent behaviors. The empress sought to weed out sinners by forming a task force to locate and punish adulterers, prostitutes, and other unseemly sorts. Prostitutes, for instance, were exiled to isolated regions of the country—creating, in essence, sinner suburbs. Stranger than these organized witch hunts, though, is the legend related to the birth of her daughter, Marie Antoinette. The empress seized the opportunity of her imminent labor to attend to another medical need. Since she was already in pain anyway, she figured she'd have her dentist pull out that pesky bad tooth. Now that's multitasking!

Written in the Stars

Some modern leaders have had a few eccentric habits, as well. Take Ronald Reagan, the 40th U.S. president. Early in their marriage, he and his wife Nancy developed a strong dependency on astrology, which guided them through many of his important leadership decisions. Feeling particularly vulnerable after a 1981 assassination attempt, the Reagans enlisted the help of famous astrologists to draw up the appropriate charts to see what the stars had in store for them, and then they used the charts to plan the president's calendar. The determinations they came to through the guidance of astrology affected the bombing of Libya, the invasion of Grenada, and the launch of the *Challenger.*

Women Break the Atmosphere Ceiling

The first U.S. astronauts were the renowned Mercury 7. But they were followed fairly quickly by the Mercury 13. Never heard of them? Here's the lowdown on women in the U.S. space program.

✳   ✳   ✳   ✳

IN 1960, DR. William R. Lovelace II, who helped develop the training regimen for NASA's male astronauts, decided he would extend the system of NASA fitness tests to women. He invited Geraldyn "Jerrie" Cobb, an accomplished pilot, to take them; she passed easily. Then, with financing from world-famous pilot Jacqueline Cochran (who didn't participate herself because she was considered too old), he brought together a group of 13 women—the First Lady Astronaut Trainees, or FLATs. The 13 were Cobb, Myrtle Cagle, sisters Jan and Marion Dietrich, Wally Funk, Jane Hart, Jean Hixson, Gene Nora Stumbough, Irene Leverton, Bernice Steadman, Sarah Gorelick, Jerri Sloan, and Rhea Hurrle.

The Not-So-Friendly Skies

The 13 were serious about becoming astronauts, but they ran into a wall of bureaucratic prejudice. (This was two years before the Civil Rights Act of 1964.) One of the most significant was NASA's requirement that astronauts have engineering degrees and be graduates of military jet test-piloting programs that were only open to men. NASA wasn't about to bend those rules. Some officials appeared sympathetic to the women's argument, but behind closed doors, it was a different story. At the bottom of a letter on the subject, Vice President Lyndon Johnson wrote, "Let's stop this now."

In 1963, Russian cosmonaut Valentina Tereshkova became the first woman in space. No female astronauts were selected until 1978.

A New Generation

The new astronaut recruits in 1978 were called NASA Group 8. Their selection had been based on two directives. NASA needed personnel for space shuttles—pilots, engineers, and scientist astronauts—but there was also a need to create a diverse astronaut corps, so NASA recruited women and minorities. Out of 8,079 applicants in all, a mere 208 were given tests and interviewed. On January 16, 1978, the 35 members of NASA Group 8 were formally announced. Of those, six were women, three were African American, and one was Asian American. These new astronaut candidates were nicknamed the "Thirty-Five New Guys" (or TFNG, an acronym that has a less respectable military meaning, as well).

The women of Group 8 were all officially mission specialist astronauts, as opposed to their male counterparts, many of whom were pilot astronauts. This raised a few eyebrows because of a general belief that women tended to have faster reflexes than men—science fiction authors had been writing about female space pilots for decades. The women of Group 8 left their mark on NASA:

* Dr. Sally Ride, a physician, was the first American woman to go into space, on June 18, 1983.

* Dr. Shannon Lucid was a biochemist who at one time held the record for the longest mission by a woman—188 days— serving on the Mir space station.

* Dr. Kathy Sullivan, a geologist, was the first American woman to walk in space.

* Dr. Judith Resnick, an engineer, died in 1986 aboard *Challenger*. Three other Group 8 astronauts—Ronald McNair, Ellison Oni-zuka, and Dick Scobee—died with her.

* Dr. Margaret Rhea Seddon, physician, participated in two Spacelab missions aboard the space shuttle *Columbia* focusing on the study of biology and life sciences.

* Dr. Anna Fisher, a physician, participated in the first space salvage mission in 1984, bringing back satellites from space. Her second scheduled space mission was canceled after the *Challenger* tragedy.

* Mission specialist requirements are a bachelor's degree in engineering, physical sciences, biological sciences, or mathematics, and at least three years of related experience or an advanced degree. The physical requirements are as follows: vision of minimum $^{20}/_{150}$ uncorrected, but $^{20}/_{20}$ corrected; maximum sitting blood pressure of $^{140}/_{90}$; and height between 150 and 193 cm.

Women Gain Influence

Women have gone on to play a major role in the American space program. Astronaut Dr. Kathryn Thornton, aboard the *Discovery* on a secret mission in November 1989, became the first woman to fly on a military flight. In 1992, Dr. Mae Jemison became the first African American woman in space. In 1995, Eileen Collins became the first woman to pilot a shuttle. In 1999, she became the first female space shuttle commander.

In 1996, Group 8 alum Lucid spent six months aboard the Russian space station Mir. Susan Helms became the first female crew member of the International Space Station in 2001. And in 2002, biochemist Dr. Peggy Whitson became the station's first resident science officer. On August 16, 2002, she spent four hours and 25 minutes on a space walk installing micrometeoroid shielding for the space station.

On a more somber note, teacher Christa McAuliffe, selected from among 11,000 applicants to receive training as a mission specialist, died along with Resnick and the rest of the *Challenger* crew on January 28, 1986, when the shuttle exploded during liftoff. And on February 1, 2003, Dr. Kalpana Chawla and Dr. Laurel Clark were aboard the shuttle *Columbia* when it broke up over Texas. The entire crew of seven died.

Of the original six female astronauts, Ride (two flights; 344 space hours) founded her own company, Sally Ride Science, to motivate girls and young women to pursue careers in science, math, and technology; she has also written science books for children. After serving as NASA's chief scientist at the Washington, D.C., headquarters, Lucid (five flights; 5,354 space hours) has resumed duties at the Johnson Space Center in Houston. Seddon (three flights; 722 space hours) retired from NASA in 1997 and moved to the Vanderbilt Medical Group in Nashville, Tennessee. Sullivan (three flights; 532 space hours) went on to serve as president and CEO of the

Center of Science & Industry in Columbus, Ohio. Fisher (one flight; 192 space hours) was assigned to the Shuttle Branch while awaiting assignment either as a space shuttle crew member or aboard the International Space Station. After her death aboard the *Challenger*, Resnick (two flights; 144 space hours) was posthumously awarded the Congressional Space Medal of Honor.

Happy Birthday, Dear Valentine?

Why do we celebrate St. Valentine's birthday? We don't. Instead, we commemorate his martyrdom.

✳ ✳ ✳ ✳

Who was St. Valentine? The Catholic Church says there were actually three St. Valentines, and all were martyrs. So which one does Valentine's Day honor? The most likely candidate was a Roman priest during the reign of Claudius II, emperor of Rome from A.D. 268 to 270. Desperate for men to fight his wars, Claudius forbade soldiers to marry. According to the legend, young lovers came to Valentine to be married, and these unauthorized marriages led to his imprisonment. While awaiting his execution, he fell in love with his jailer's daughter. Shortly before his death on February 14, he wrote her a letter and signed it "From Your Valentine."

The problem is that there's no proof any of this actually happened. Valentine's name is not on the earliest list of Roman martyrs, and there's no evidence that he was put to death on February 14. In fact, in 1969, the Catholic Church removed Valentine's Day from the list of official holy days.

How did Valentine become associated with a celebration of love? It may be that February 14 was chosen by the early Church to replace a Roman fertility festival called Lupercalia, which fell on the same date. Another explanation is that the sentimentality of Valentine's Day can be traced to the Middle

Ages, an era fixated on romantic love. It was popularly believed that birds chose their mates on February 14, a legend Geoffrey Chaucer referenced in his poem "Parliament of Foules": "For this was on St. Valentine's Day, when every fowl cometh there to chooses his mate."

What about all the flowers and chocolates? These fairly recent additions to the Valentine story have more to do with the power of retailers than the passion of romance.

Cleopatra's Death

Cleopatra is one of history's most exotic and mystifying rulers, but perhaps more intriguing than her life is her death. Here is why Cleopatra really committed suicide.

✳ ✳ ✳ ✳

REMEMBER THE ILLUSTRIOUS movie *Cleopatra?* Let's revisit the death scene: Roman general Mark Antony (Richard Burton) falls on his sword and dies in the arms of Cleopatra (Elizabeth Taylor). With her lover dead, Cleopatra allows an asp to bite and kill her. How intense, how romantic, how… untrue.

Antony and Cleopatra were indeed lovers. But the greatest love of her life was Egypt, and she took tremendous pride in being its ruler. If Antony had died but Egypt had survived, it's doubtful that Cleopatra would have killed herself.

For one thing, she had three children by Antony (and one son by Julius Caesar). Cleopatra persuaded Antony to part ways with his Roman partner-turned-nemesis Octavian, and he then agreed to her request that Egypt remain independent rather than become a Roman province. Under her influence, Antony also declared Cleopatra Queen of Kings and Queen of Egypt, to rule with her son by Caesar. He also distributed the kingdoms of Armenia, Parthia, Libya, and Syria among their three children.

Rome considered these acts treasonous, and in 31 B.C., Octavian destroyed Cleopatra's and Antony's navy in the Battle of Actium. In 30 B.C., Octavian refused Antony's resignation and attacked Egypt. Antony, who had no means of escape and possibly believed that Cleopatra was already dead, killed himself. However, Cleopatra did not consider suicide yet.

Instead she locked herself in her mausoleum and refused food. Octavian threatened to harm her children if she died, so she began to eat again. Octavian then planned to send her to Rome to be led as a captive in the procession celebrating his triumph, and it was at this point that she reached for the snake. The fear of public humiliation was the determining factor in Cleopatra's suicide.

Wyatt Earp

Movies, books, and legends have surrounded one of the Old West's most famous names with a cloud of gunsmoke. Was he was a hardened killer who took advantage of his job title? On the contrary, Wyatt Earp was a good cop.

✳ ✳ ✳ ✳

EVEN IN ROUGH towns, most citizens wanted law and order. Only the criminals wanted lawlessness, and they weren't the majority even in Tombstone, Dodge City, or Wichita—three places Wyatt Earp wore a badge.

Earp earned a reputation for firm law enforcement. Everyone made the same claim: If you were breaking the law, Earp would surely make you stop. He didn't care how big the gang was, but he also didn't want innocent civilians getting involved—for their own safety. Most westerners had heard of Wyatt Earp and didn't want trouble with him. His reputation helped keep things dull, in the best of ways.

Earp avoided excessive force. He preferred using a pistol-barrel crack to the noggin followed by an arrest, and he kept the hammer on an empty chamber. The first time Earp actually killed anyone was during the gunfight at the OK Corral, when he shot Frank McLaury. The incident itself was a lawful arrest resisted by known felons who were using deadly force against legally appointed officers.

When Earp finally cut loose, it was only after serious personal provocation. Within a few months of the OK Corral incident, Wyatt's brothers were brutally ambushed—Virgil was seriously wounded and Morgan died. Wyatt tried to resign from his police position, but his superiors refused the resignation. He then went on a rampage against his brothers' attackers, hunting them down and killing them. Wrong as that was, Earp never undertook the revenge ride under pretense of legal policing.

Lindbergh's Historic Flight

Acclaimed aviator Charles Augustus Lindbergh became famous for his historic flight in the Spirit of St. Louis, but he was not the first to fly nonstop across the Atlantic.

✳   ✳   ✳   ✳

ON MAY 21, 1927, the airplane *Spirit of St. Louis* touched down in Paris, France, having just made a nonstop flight from Long Island, New York. Undertaken by Charles Lindbergh (who was affectionately known by the nicknames "Lucky Lindy" and "The Lone Eagle"), the 3,610-mile flight was indeed a first in aviation history and catapulted Lindbergh to international celebrity. But it was not the first nonstop flight across the Atlantic Ocean. That feat was accomplished by two British pilots, Captain John William Alcock and Lieutenant Arthur Whitten Brown. On June 15, 1919, they successfully flew their modified bomber aircraft from St. John's, Newfoundland, to Galway, Ireland. Although the aircraft crash-landed in a bog near the town of Clifden, the flight stands as the first nonstop transatlantic crossing.

By the time Lindbergh emulated Alcock and Brown's achievement in the *Spirit of St. Louis* nearly eight years later, at least 81 people had already made the trip. What sets Lindbergh apart is that he was the first to fly *solo* across the Atlantic without stopping. He took off from the Roosevelt Airfield in Garden City on May 20 and arrived at Le Bourget Airport in Paris 33.5 hours later.

✴ Lindbergh's daring solo achievement earned him the $25,000 Orteig Prize offered by New York hotelier Raymond Orteig, a ticker-tape parade along New York's 5th Avenue, the Distinguished Flying Cross, and eventually a Medal of Honor. The former Minnesota farm boy's accomplishment also boosted the public's interest in flying, a phenomenon referred to as the "Lindbergh Boom." For the first time, people began to view air travel as a safe, reliable means of transportation.

The Panama Canal

The treaty granting the United States the right to build the Panama Canal also gave the U.S. complete control over the canal's operation; over the years Panamanian citizens began to resent this arrangement. After decades of negotiations, the canal was finally given over to Panamanian control in 1999 (although the United States reserved the right of military intervention if the waterway's security was ever threatened). Since then the canal has been ably managed by the Panama Canal Authority (PCA), which has increased traffic and reduced both accidents and the average transit time for ships.

Seeking to further improve the canal's usefulness to world trade, the PCA has completed an ambitious expansion plan to allow the canal to handle more traffic and larger ships. In 2011, nearly 40 percent of ships were too large to fit through the Panama Canal. These so called "post-Panamax" ships (a ship that just fits through the canal is called a "Panamax" ship) had to dock at West Coast ports; cargo was then carried to the East Coast via truck or rail. The expansion was completed June of 2016.

Before the Panama Canal

Before the Panama Canal, ships had to travel around Cape Horn at the southern tip of South America to go from the Atlantic to the Pacific. The great distance posed one obstacle, but the treacherous waters around the Horn were the real threat. Heavy storms, ever-changing and violent winds, limited visibility, and the threat of icebergs make this one of the most feared routes on the high seas.

The Attack on the HMS *Gaspee*

Eighteen months before the Boston Tea Party, the British revenue schooner HMS *Gaspee* was burned by American patriots near Providence, Rhode Island. The central motive behind the attack was resentment and distrust of British efforts to regulate trade—it came on the heels of a series of taxes put into effect by the British in 1764.

The *Gaspee*, moored in Narragansett Bay, was seen by the colonists as a symbol of British heavy-handedness. Sent to enforce customs collections and to inspect vessels operated by colonists, the ship provoked immediate resentment. On June 9, the *Gaspee* grounded as it chased a ship; the colonists knew the *Gaspee* would be stuck where it was until high tide, and they took full advantage of the situation. Under the canopy of a moonless night, a group of angry patriots boarded the ship.

In the ensuing scuffle, the ship's commander, William Dudingston, was wounded by musket fire and forced to surrender his vessel. Dudingston was placed on a rowboat, and he and his crew went ashore. The colonists then burned the *Gaspee* within full sight of cheering colonists gathered along the shoreline. No one was killed in the *Gaspee* incident, which is a testament to the colonists' good faith. Theirs was simply a symbolic act against a system they felt was unfair.

During the aftermath, a British commission of inquiry attempted to round up those suspected of involvement. Their intention was to bring the suspects to England for trial, but the colonists strongly objected because the suspects would have zero chance of getting a fair trial in England. When the Rhode Islanders displayed a lack of memory regarding the incident, the Crown realized that a sea change had indeed occurred. In a statement that proved telling, the British collector of customs for Rhode Island offered, "There's an end to collecting a revenue and enforcing the acts of trade."

The *Gaspee* Affair served as a precursor to the American Revolution. American Colonel Ephraim Bowen (1753–1841) was the last surviving participant in the attack. Bowen was born in 1753 in Providence, Rhode Island, to Lydia Mawrey and R. Ephraim Bowen, a doctor. During the *Gaspee* incident, Bowen helped John Mawney, a medical student, attend to the wounded William Dudingston. Bowen went on to serve as a deputy quartermaster general during the Revolutionary War, and after the war, he opened a rum distillery in Pawtuxet. In 1838, he wrote a statement about the *Gaspee* incident. Bowen died in 1841.

La Amistad

In 1839, hundreds of Africans were captured near Sierra Leone and sold as slaves. They were boarded onto a slave ship and brought to Cuba. Once there, they were falsely classified as native Cuban-born slaves; the slave trade was technically illegal in Cuba at the time, but individuals who had been slaves for a long time could still be traded.

A Portuguese trader bought 36 of the slaves, and he had them boarded onto the schooner *La Amistad* to transport them to another port. Three days into the journey, the slaves broke free of their chains and attacked the crew. They spared two Cuban slavers aboard the ship because the Cubans agreed to steer the ship back to Africa. The Cubans initially headed toward Africa, but once it became dark, they gradually turned and headed for the United States.

More than a month later, the ship was found off Long Island by the U.S. Coastal Survey. The Cubans immediately claimed that the Africans were slaves and their property. The Spanish ambassador became involved and demanded the ship be returned to Spain. Abolitionists became involved as well and arranged for a translator to give the Africans' side of the story. The Africans told the translator that they had recently been kidnapped in Africa. The judge decided that the Africans should be freed. The case was appealed, and John Quincy Adams argued the Africans' case before the Supreme Court. He used the principle of habeas corpus in their defense. He argued that if the United States were to turn the Africans over to Spain, it would set a precedent that would threaten the freedom of all. His argument convinced the court, and it ruled in the Africans' favor.

Tiananmen Square

When protestors took to Peking's Tiananmen Square demanding an end to political corruption in April 1989, not many people noticed. The group, comprised heavily of students, assembled peaceably to push for democratic reform from a government it viewed as corrupt. Over time, however, the crowd grew in volume. By May, there were approximately one million people in the square, with countless more staging protests on the city's streets. People from all walks of life were standing beside the students in solidarity against the government. Fearing a civil war, Deng Xiaoping sent in the military to break up the demonstration. His efforts failed. An uneasy standoff persisted for the rest of the month.

On June 4, the situation turned deadly. The army opened fire on unarmed protestors in the streets. No one knows for certain what triggered the violence, but an estimated 3,000 people were killed during the massacre, with an additional 10,000 sustaining injuries. Opinion is divided on Xiaoping's role in the incident. Some claim that the leader issued a "no shoot" order to his soldiers, while others—including former premier Li Peng (who himself has been blamed for the slaughter)—maintained that Xiaoping thought the actions were necessary to maintain control. Due to global media coverage, China's heavy-handed actions were condemned by nations across the world.

America at Its Best

All but forgotten by a twenty-first-century public that depends on the information highway to stay informed, the Chautauqua of the nineteenth century was a traveling mode of education that circulated through the actual byways of America to edify, entertain, and enlighten.

The term *Chautauqua* actually refers to three types of educational organizations. The original Chautauqua Sunday School Assembly was founded in August 1874 by John H. Vincent, a Methodist clergyman, and Lewis Miller, a businessman, as a summer school for Sunday school teachers in Chautauqua Lake, New York. Over the next few years, the Chautauqua expanded into a lyceum and general amusement series, which included schools for languages and theology, as well as refresher courses for schoolteachers. Young students who wanted to broaden their cultural horizons joined clubs specializing in reading, music, the arts, physical education, and religion. The Chautauqua Institution still exists as a resort area with a summer program dedicated to the arts.

The Chautauqua Institution inspired the Chautauqua Literary and Scientific Circle, a correspondence school with courses in history, science, and the arts. Established in 1878, it still flourishes as a legitimate form of adult education.

Tent Chautauquas began around 1903, borrowing their name from the original institution though they had no official connection to the school. They traveled around America during the summers, setting up in tents on the outskirts of small towns for a few weeks, giving lectures, concerts, and recitals for adults. The tent Chautauquas survived until around 1930, when more pervasive forms of entertainment and popular culture, such as the cinema and radio, began to dominate the attention and leisure time of the public.

Origins: The History of Things

These intriguing stories offer insight into the history of some everyday items, expressions, and endeavors—stuff you never think to think about.

✳ ✳ ✳ ✳

The Latin Alphabet

PEOPLE HAD BEEN writing hieroglyphics (symbols that stood for objects such as *dog, reed,* or *pyramid*) for at least a millennium before the first glimmer of an actual alphabet appeared. Around 2000 B.C., a group of Egyptian slaves (the Semitics) figured out how to communicate with one another using symbols that represented sounds, not just things. From this system, we eventually got the Phoenician and Aramaic alphabets, as well as the Greek and Latin alphabets. Early Greek was written right to left, before the "ox-turning" method (in which the direction of writing changed with every line) was adopted. By the fifth century B.C., the left-to-right method was in place.

The Evil Eye

The language of superstition is universal. From Europe to the Middle East, from Mexico to Scandinavia, folktales have long warned people against the power of the "evil eye." Essentially, the evil eye is an unintentional look of envy from a person who covets what the recipient possesses. At the very least, it's plain old bad vibes; at its most potent, the evil eye is blamed for bad luck, disease, and even death for the person who receives the look. Cultures that fear the evil eye have developed various means of protection: A common European custom is to wear a locket containing a prayer. In India, small mirrors are sewn into clothing to deflect an evil gaze and reflect it to the person who gave it; similarly, the Chinese use a six-sided mirror called a *pa kua.* The Italians have developed various hand gestures for protection. Sometimes the defense is more elaborate: Folk healers in Mexico smear raw chicken eggs over someone's body to keep him or her safe from the evil eye. In this case, the person might just get a plain old dirty look.

The Jump Rope

Skipping and jumping are natural movements of the body (especially for kids), and the inclusion of a rope in these activities dates back to A.D. 1600, when Egyptian children jumped over vines as play. Early Dutch settlers brought the game to North America, where it flourished and evolved from a simple motion into the often elaborate form prevalent today: Double Dutch. With two people turning two ropes simultaneously, a third, and then fourth, participant jumps in, often reciting rhymes. Jumping techniques have become so complex that there are now worldwide organizations that sponsor Double Dutch competitions.

Quiche

Although similar concoctions date back to ancient Roman cheesecakes and medieval European tarts and pies, the modern quiche recipe comes from the Lorraine region of France. The original quiche Lorraine was an open-face pie filled with eggs, cream, and bacon. Cheese was later incorporated, along with any number of additions, from shallots to shellfish, depending on one's preference. In North America, quiche enjoyed its greatest popularity as a trendy 1970s food, joined by other notable offerings such as fondue and Caesar salad.

Taxicabs

Think of Cleopatra being carted around on a sedan chair, and you have the origins of the modern-day taxicab. Rickshaws replaced sedan chairs as a means of transporting people from one place to another, followed by horse-drawn carriages, which finally gave us poor humans a rest. At the end of the nineteenth century, automobiles started to fill the streets, and with the invention of the *taximeter* (an instrument that measures both the time and distance a vehicle has traveled), transport by cab became increasingly popular. Throughout the world, cab companies have painted their taxis particular colors, both for identification purposes and to cut down on the number of unofficial drivers. Today in New York City alone, taxis transport more than 200 million passengers almost 800 million miles every year.

Where Did the U.S. Flag Salute Begin?

The Salute began along with the Pledge of Allegiance. Was it developed by the D.A.R. to make patriotic hearts swell with pride? Nah. Truth being stranger than fiction, it started as a magazine's marketing gimmick.

❋　❋　❋　❋

The Youth's Companion

FROM 1827 THROUGH 1929 (YES, 102 years), a magazine called *The Youth's Companion* (TYC) saw print. Somewhat similar to today's *Reader's Digest*, TYC meant to reinforce wholesome values like conformity, patriotism, and Christianity.

TYC used premium incentives to build its subscriber base. Here's how: Suppose your daughter sold subscriptions, if she sold a few, she could earn a watch; if she sold more, she could get a sewing machine, maybe even a piano. This brilliant scheme turned young customers into energetic salespeople and helps explain why half a million U.S. households took *TYC*—thus putting them squarely in the path of any new marketing pitch the magazine might try.

Francis Bellamy

Reverend Francis Bellamy, the Salute's actual author, was an interesting fellow: a Freemason, a Baptist minister, and a Christian Socialist. A lot of modern Masons, Baptists, ministers, Christians, and socialists might find the combination odd, but Bellamy didn't. Even Masonic Baptist Christian Socialists have to make a living, and in the 1890s, Bellamy got a job in *TYC's* premium department. That department's boss, James Upham, would play a key role in how the rest of the story played out.

His Salute

TYC advanced the view that all schools should fly the U.S. flag. Naturally, the magazine sold flags. The premium department hit on the idea of sending schoolchildren flag cards, each to be sold for a dime apiece and representing 1 percent of a school flag. Sell a hundred cards, get your school a flag! Then Upham thought: *What if we came up with something for kids to actually do with the flag besides just fly it—perhaps say a daily salute and loyalty oath?* He tasked Bellamy with inventing a pledge and salute.

The Bellamy Salute, as historians now call it, began with a military salute: right hand touching forehead, palm down. Where they said "... to my Flag," the kids extended the arm gracefully toward the Colors. Of course, careful readers have noticed an oddity in that wording. In 1923, to thwart immigrants from the verbal equivalent of crossing their fingers during the Pledge, the National Flag Conference changed "... to my Flag" (which might as well refer to Denmark's or Italy's) to "... to the Flag of the United States of America ..." The hand now began over the heart but still extended at the correct time. Bellamy complained but to no avail.

There were, of course, local variations on the Salute. Not everyone adopted the 1923 changes or even had a flag salute or flag. Some never extended the arm to begin with.

Achtung!

TYC merged with another youth magazine in 1929. Bellamy died in 1931, never living to see Germany dominated by fascist racists usurping his salute. The Nazi-sympathizing German-American Bund quickly noticed that they could salute the U.S. flag and that of Adolf's Third Reich with the same motion. As early as 1935, Americans—having seen newsreel footage of vast Nazi rallies—expressed discomfort with the similarity. In 1939, Hitler went to war with Poland, France, and Britain; the United States remained neutral.

By 1942, the United States was at war with Germany. Even though the U.S. usage of the Salute predated Hitler's by 30 years, it still looked lousy for American schoolkids to start class each day looking like a Reichstag session. That year, Congress formally enacted the Salute we know today: hand over the heart.

Marcus Garvey

Jamaican-born activist Marcus Garvey came to the United States to pursue his campaign for black rights worldwide.

✳   ✳   ✳   ✳

A Strong Start

WHEN HE ARRIVED in New York in 1916, Marcus Garvey wasted little time in moving into action. He soon began recruiting members for the Universal Negro Improvement Association (UNIA), speaking first on street corners in Harlem, then in black churches. Garvey was a gifted orator, and blacks responded eagerly to his message of self-reliance and pride. The UNIA provided more than a sense of community and a slogan. Decades before the Civil Rights movement, what the group accomplished was astonishing: Local branches helped launch small businesses, sold affordable insurance to their members, and acted as mutual aid societies. The Negro Factories Corporation, the financial arm of the UNIA, owned grocery stores, restaurants, a laundry, a fleet of moving vans, and a printing press. By 1920, the UNIA had nearly 1,000 branches around the world.

All Aboard the Black Star Line

In 1919, Garvey began his most daring project: a steamship company called the Black Star Line. Garvey envisioned Black Star ships transporting goods between black-owned businesses in North America, the Caribbean, and Africa. Shares were sold for five dollars at UNIA meetings. Garvey's followers eagerly bought more than $600,000 worth of shares.

On August 1, 1920, more than 25,000 of Garvey's followers gathered at Madison Square Garden to hear his opening address for the UNIA's First International Convention of the Negro Peoples of the World. Two-thousand delegates from 22 countries attended the monthlong convention. Garvey, wearing an elaborate uniform with a plumed hat, was elected the "Provisional President of Africa." But the convention was not all grandiose titles and ornate clothing—delegates presented complaints about the treatment of blacks worldwide and proposed specific remedies, summarized in the Declaration of Rights of the Negro Peoples of the World.

Trouble in Mind

Ultimately, the triumph of the convention masked the beginnings of trouble. The Black Star Line was a powerful symbol but a financial disaster, and the U.S. government was investigating Garvey. Meanwhile, Garvey's insistence on separatism rather than integration had alienated activists who were interested in equality and an integrated America. In June 1922, the black press blasted its own leader for meeting with the Ku Klux Klan. "I regard the Klan, the Anglo-Saxon clubs and White

American societies, as far as the Negro is concerned, as better friends of the race than all other groups of hypocritical whites put together," said Garvey. The headlines on the black-owned newspaper *The Messenger* demanded, "Garvey must go."

In early 1923, Garvey was indicted on charges of mail fraud related to the sale of stock in the Black Star Line. The government's case was shaky: Company records showed serious mismanagement but no signs of fraud. During trial, the prosecutor ended his summation by asking the jury, "Gentlemen, will you let the tiger loose?"

Aftermath and Legacy

Nevertheless, Garvey was convicted and after serving half of a five-year term, he was deported to Jamaica. Garvey continued working for the rights of blacks, first in Jamaica and then in London, but he never regained the influence he enjoyed before his conviction. Already ill, Garvey died of a stroke on June 10, 1940, after reading false notices of his death in newspapers.

In 1964, Garvey's body was returned to Jamaica, where he was declared the country's first national hero. Upon visiting Garvey's grave in Jamaica, Dr. Martin Luther King Jr. remarked that Garvey "gave millions of Negroes a sense of dignity and destiny and made the Negro feel that he was somebody."

Holy Matrimony!

Marriage is a sacred institution. Unfortunately, it's also often described as an expensive, fleeting institution. Here are some statistics about holy matrimony.

❋　❋　❋　❋

Average cost of wedding in 2009, United States: $19,000

Average cost of wedding in 1945, United States: $2,240

Cost of average 1945 wedding, in today's terms: $26,902

Most Expensive Wedding in History: $60 million. In 2004, billionaire steel magnate L. N. Mittal dropped $60 million on his daughter's wedding to an investment banker. The wedding included a party at Versailles, a reception at a castle built especially for the occasion, and a $1.5 million wine tab.

Average Age at First Marriage Americans are waiting longer than ever to get married for the first time. Meanwhile, the gap between the average ages of men and women at their first marriage is dwindling (men are listed first; women second):

1900: 25.9, 21.9

1950: 22.8, 20.3

2000: 26.8, 25.1

More Marital Statistics

* Country with highest average age at first marriage for men: **Dominica, 35.4**

* Country with highest average age at first marriage for women: **Jamaica, 33.1**

* Country with lowest average age at first marriage for men: **Nepal, 22.0**

* Country with lowest average age at first marriage for women: **Chad, 18.0**

* Divorce rate in Massachusetts, prior to legalizing gay marriage in 2004: **2.2 of every 1,000 total population**

* Divorce rate in Massachusetts in 2008: **2.0 of every 1,000**

Highest and Lowest Divorce Rates, by Country:

The United States has one of the highest divorce rates in the entire world. Whether this is due to our marriage laws or our quickly shortening attention spans is up for debate. Here are the countries with the highest divorce rates (as of 2007), as a percentage of total marriages:

1. Sweden—54.9

2. United States—54.8

3. Belarus—52.9

✳ **And the lowest:**

1. India—1.1

2. Sri Lanka—1.5

3. Japan—1.9

✳ **Divorce rates among religious groups:** According to religious leaders, couples who "pray together, stay together." However, this is not borne out by the facts. Here are the results of a 1999 study of some 4,000 Americans conducted by the Barna Research Group about divorce rates among religious (and nonreligious) folks:

1. Nondenominational Evangelical Christians: 34 percent

2. Baptists: 29 percent

3. Protestants: 25 percent

4. Mormons: 24 percent

5. Catholics: 21 percent

6. Lutherans: 21 percent

7. Atheists: 21 percent

The USPS: The Check Is in the Mail

What is now known as the United States Postal Service was established in 1775 by the Continental Congress, which also appointed Benjamin Franklin the first postmaster general. It was a job with which Franklin had some experience—he worked as postmaster of Philadelphia under the British Parliamentary Post and later as one of two deputy postmasters of North America.

❋ ❋ ❋ ❋

Through Rain and Sleet...

THERE ARE 32,741 POST offices throughout the United States. Combined, they employ 656,000 career employees and manage 221,000 vehicles—the largest civilian fleet in the world. Here's more:

46 million: the number of address changes processed each year

8.5 million: the number of passport applications accepted in 2008

597,000: the average number of postal service money orders issued daily

300: the number of "employee heroes" recognized by the postal service in 2008 for saving the lives of customers on their routes

For Your Protection

* The Postal Inspection Service is one of the oldest federal law enforcement agencies and was the first to offer federal agent careers to women.

* More than 9,000 suspects were arrested in 2008 for crimes involving the mail or for crimes against the postal service.

* Postal inspectors prevented 800,000 fake checks—worth an estimated $2.7 billion—from entering the United States in 2008.

Mail by the Numbers

203 billion: pieces of mail processed in 2008

667 million: the approximate number of mail pieces processed each day

28 million: pieces of mail processed each hour (on average)

463,000: pieces of mail processed each minute (on average)

36.6 million: the number of stamps printed in 2008

$62 million: the amount of money raised for breast cancer research since July 1998 through the sale of the Breast Cancer Research Semi-Postal Stamp

1963: the year the Zoning Improvement Plan (ZIP) Code was launched

What Is that Written on Your Dollar Bill?

Money is hard to come by these days. But that hasn't stopped artists from drawing, writing, and painting on dollar bills. Just ask all those poor George Washingtons wearing hats, fake mustaches, and glasses as they pass through drive-through windows and dollar-store cash registers.

✳   ✳   ✳   ✳

Where's George?

Hank Eskin may be responsible, at least indirectly, for defacing more dollar bills than any one person. Eskin is the founder of the Where's George website, which since 1998, has allowed visitors to enter their local zip code along with the serial number of their dollar bills to track where those bills have traveled. As of June 2010, the site was actively tracking more than 173 million bills (not just $1 bills) with a total value of more than $937 million.

Where's George used to sell rubber stamps advertising the website, which people then used to stamp their dollars. It's not unusual to find dollar bills today with some form of www.wheresgeorge.com stamped on them. However, the website stopped selling the stamps in 2000 following an investigation by the U.S. Secret Service. The agency informed the site's administrators that the stamps constituted a form of advertising on U.S. currency—something that is illegal.

Defacing Currency With Joe D

Who is Joe D? He's one of the busiest dollar-bill—any bill, actually—defacers today. The mysterious Joe D runs his own Flickr site, which catalogues his currency artwork. Some of his most famous work includes an extremely politically incorrect $5 bill that's been altered to show the left side of Lincoln's head being blown out by a gunshot and a $1 bill in which George Washington has been turned into Darth Vader—all with the skillful use of a ballpoint pen. Joe D's site also features George Washingtons that have been turned into red devils and green-haired Jokers of Batman fame, as well as a rather cute Abraham Lincoln who has been turned into a dead ringer for Mario of Nintendo video game fame.

Making a Statement

Some money doodlers seem to have a sense of humor. Several websites feature a dollar bill with the timeless question "Do you like root beer?" while another recommends simply if inelegantly "Write anything on more bills." Finally, if you ever end up with the dollar bill advising "If you see any writing on this bill call 1–800–5187," don't bother picking up the phone. There are three numbers missing from that phone number. And for the animal lovers out there, you have to appreciate the sentiment behind "Free the werewolves," another message printed on yet another dollar bill.

Money on the Wall

Some bar and restaurant owners have the right idea: They

encourage their patrons to write silly messages on dollar bills and then stick them to the walls of their establishments. The messages may not always be clever, but it's not a bad way for a bar owner to make a few extra bucks.

* The average dollar bill lasts a little less than two years before it's worn out and pulled from circulation.
* An individual dollar bill weighs a gram, as does a five-dollar bill. A 10-, 20-, 50-, and a 100-dollar bill are likewise one gram.

Cash Curiosities

Beyond the standard money lore—that it's the root of all evil, makes the world go round, and (sadly) never grows on trees— there's a wealth of monetary trivia.

* Beginning around 9000 B.C., cattle were used as a form of money. The animals had consistent value, so it was simple to "spend" them.
* The original currency was the cowrie shell, first used in China around 1200 B.C.
* Before the American Civil War, banks—not the government—printed their own paper currency.
* The Treasury Department issued the first $1 bill in 1862. It featured a portrait of Treasury Secretary Salmon P. Chase. George Washington took his place in 1869.
* In 1934 and 1935, the United States printed $100,000 notes, the largest bill to date. They featured a portrait of Woodrow Wilson and were only used in transactions between Federal Reserve banks.
* In a typical year, 95 percent of new notes are printed to replace worn-out money.
* The average life expectancy of a $1 bill is 21 months, while $100 bills typically last 89 months.

* In the 2008 fiscal year, the U.S. Mint produced more than 10 billion coins, half of which were pennies.

* In 2008, it cost 1.67 cents to make one penny. Taxpayers spent more than $130 million making pennies that were worth $80 million.

* The $ sign likely originated on old pesos, which included a P and an S that eventually merged and evolved into the $ sign.

Scenes From a Mall

What's more American than baseball? Try shopping malls. From Main Street to megaplex, and from city to suburb, Americans have always heeded the call of the mall.

✳   ✳   ✳   ✳

1920s: Starter Strip

THE PRECURSOR TO the modern mall debuted in 1922, courtesy of J. C. Nichols and his Country Club Plaza in Kansas City. Built near a residential development on the city's edge, the Plaza was the first shopping district set away from a downtown area.

As automobile traffic and urban congestion continued to drive families out of cities and into the suburbs, more shopping centers popped up. They all followed the same "strip" format: A line of convenience shops (anchored by a grocery or pharmacy) with a single parking lot out front.

1930s–1940s: Main Street in a Box

With the decline of urban Main Streets—typically lined with specialty stores such as jewelers, clothiers, and cobblers—came the rise of the department store, which housed all of these specialties under one roof.

Meanwhile, shopping centers continued to evolve as surrogate town squares, offering community activities and entertainment such as firework displays and live music. In 1949, the Town and Country Shopping Center in Columbus, Ohio, introduced nighttime shopping with performances by Grandma Carver—a woman who dove from a height of 90 feet into a small pool of flaming water.

1950s–1960s: A Mall Is Born

The post-World War II era saw the marriage of department stores and strip centers (it sounds sexier than it actually was). In 1950, Northgate in Seattle opened as the first shopping center to have two parallel rows of stores facing each other with a pedestrian walkway in between. These walkways were originally called "malls," hence the name.

The following year, the first two-level shopping center opened in Framingham, Massachusetts. In 1956, an Austrian architect named Victor Gruen fully modernized malls with the opening of the first fully enclosed, two-level, climate-controlled shopping center in Edina, Minnesota—Southdale Center—which ultimately became the blueprint for all modern malls. By 1964, America was home to 7,600 of them.

1970s: Festival Fever and Vertical Velocity

By 1972, there were 13,174 suburban malls. Not to be "malled" by the competition, cities responded with their own take on the suburban staple. In 1976, two new models made the scene: Boston introduced Faneuil Hall Marketplace as the first "festival marketplace" (an historic site rehabbed into a shopping destination), while Water Tower Place in Chicago debuted as the first "vertical mall" (suburban sprawl squeezed into skyscraper form).

1980s-1990s: Malls Get Mega

Between 1980 and 1990, more than 16,000 new shopping centers cropped up from coast to coast. Also on the rise: factory outlet stores and "category killers"—big-box retailers such as Toys "R" Us and Office Depot that specialize in just one thing. The shopping mall took a serious hit in the 1990s with the advent of the Home Shopping Network and the internet. The solution? "Shoppertainment," which transformed shopping into a full-on "experience" with amusement parks, restaurants, movie theaters, miniature golf, and, oh yeah, stores. The first megamall, Mall of America in Bloomington, Minnesota, opened in 1992 and remains the nation's largest mall at 4.2 million square feet.

2000 and Beyond: A Return to Main Street

Today's mall is going back to where it started—only better. The latest trend combines the ambience of old-time Main Street with megamall experiences (restaurants and multiplexes) and strip-mall convenience (parallel layouts and out-front parking). Dubbed "lifestyle centers," the new malls promise to provide something for everyone. Perhaps it is a mall world after all.

The Great Dwarf Wedding (of Peter the Great)

If you've ever been in a wedding, spent time with someone who is about to be wed, or have gotten married, you know that the wedding process can be kind of a circus. But Russian Tsar Peter the Great took it to a whole new level.

✳ ✳ ✳ ✳

Peter's Peculiar Pastimes

FOR 43 YEARS BEGINNING in 1682, Pyotr Alexeyevich Romanov (let's call him Peter for short) ruled the land of Russia. He took the tsarist empire into a new, expanded era, which resulted in more power and influence across the country and indeed around the world. It wasn't an easy task, and Peter wasn't a hero in everyone's eyes—millions of people died due to his actions. He's remembered not only for his strong-willed political victories but also for being a tyrant.

Perhaps all the pressure heaped on him is why the infamous leader had a fondness for spectacle and humor in his downtime—think practical jokes, elaborate gifts, and Peter's "monsters." This was a pre-PC time, and the tsar's "monsters" were dwarfs (what we'd now call little people), giants, and malformed humans that Peter took to arranging in carnivalesque weddings and funerals.

Though it makes most people uncomfortable to think about today, in Peter's time the practice of putting dwarves on display or "keeping a buffoon" was considered typical entertainment. Peter took the pastime further than most, largely because he could afford it. He sent a decree across the land that anyone who sent a malformed human "marvel" to St. Petersburg would receive 100 rubles. With his ever-expanding cast of characters, Peter set about designing events to showcase them.

A Double Wedding

In 1710, Peter's niece Anna was wed to Frederick William, whose uncle was the Duke of Prussia. The wedding, like most at the time, was arranged for political reasons. Peter had a hand in organizing the wedding festivities, because he had a secret plan in mind: Several days after the feasting and celebrations for the happy couple were over, a second wedding was held, this one between two dwarfs. From the bride's dress and the food served, to the nuptials and the grounds decorations, all of it was modeled exactly after the wedding of Anna and Frederick.

More than 70 dwarves were gathered for the event. Peter himself presided over parts of the ceremony, and chairs were set up around the perimeter of the room for the court to watch. After the wedding (which was sped up, just as Anna and Frederick's had been), the audience watched the dwarfs enjoy a banquet. It was all very amusing to the crowd, especially since many of the dwarves were peasants and spoke in a coarse vernacular, or were hunchbacked from working in the fields all their lives. The dwarves got drunk and fights broke out. The guests spilled food and generally caused chaos. While all this was happening, Peter and his retinue looked on, laughing and applauding the ridiculous antics of the dwarves.

Looking at Peter's callous dwarf spectacles, a modern person's sensibilities are likely offended. But was Peter solely crass or was he making a comment on the largely out-of-touch lifestyle of the wealthy? Either the dwarf wedding was a big joke on the people watching and laughing, or it was a cruel display of a marginalized portion of eighteenth-century Russia. Perhaps it was purely a way to pass the time in between wars and political upheaval, or perhaps the tsar simply had too much money on his hands. It's probably safe to assume that for Peter the Great, one of history's most intriguing leaders, it was a little bit of everything.

Life (and Death) at the Hotel Chelsea

While many celebs have stayed there, some who have left in body bags may still be hanging around.

❊   ❊   ❊   ❊

I T IS THE place where poet Dylan Thomas was staying when he died, where author Charles R. Jackson committed suicide, where Sex Pistol Sid Vicious may have murdered his girlfriend, and where singer-songwriter Bob Dylan composed part of *Blonde on Blonde.* "Beat" icon Jack Kerouac penned *On the Road* there, novelist Arthur C. Clarke wrote *2001: A Space Odyssey* within the Chelsea's walls, and avant-garde filmmaker Andy Warhol shot much of *Chelsea Girls* there (before he himself was shot nearby).

Many other famous people have stayed at the Chelsea over the years: Mark Twain, Eugene O'Neill, Thomas Wolfe, and Tennessee Williams; William Burroughs, Willem de Kooning, Madonna, and Arthur Miller; Edith Piaf, Jane Fonda, Jimi Hendrix, and Janis Joplin; Leonard Cohen, Allen Ginsberg, and the Grateful Dead.

Today, the Hotel Chelsea, once the creative hub and long-term residence of so many artists, has a policy that limits the short-term visitors who occupy 40 percent of its 240 apartments (the other suites are residential) to stays of no longer than three weeks.

Glory and Ruin

The Chelsea, which proclaims itself the first New York City structure to be listed as a historic building and cultural preservation site, started life in 1883 as a luxury apartment cooperative designed in the Queen Anne style. An impressive 12 stories high, it was Manhattan's tallest structure until the completion of the 20-story World Building in 1890.

Back then, the building's address, 222 West 23rd Street, was in the heart of the city's thriving theater district, yet by 1903 the apartment was bankrupt due to high overhead and the relocation of many theaters. The place was closed, and when it reopened a couple of years later, it was as a hotel.

18 Straight Whiskies

Over the years, many people residing behind the red-brick walls and wrought-iron balconies have elected not to observe house rules requiring them to behave with decorum and to clean up before they leave. The poet Dylan Thomas, for example, returned to his room at the Chelsea on the night of November 3, 1953, following a boozy session at the White Horse Tavern in Greenwich Village. He purportedly exclaimed, "I've had 18 straight whiskies, I think that is a record." Whether or not he was exaggerating, the noted Welsh imbiber had a monster hangover the next morning, but he managed to put himself back together and return to the White Horse for more hooch. Shortly after midnight on November 5, Thomas (by now back at the hotel again) slipped into a coma caused by pneumonia complicated by acute alcoholism. He was transported from the Chelsea to St. Vincent's Hospital, where he died four days later.

Writer Charles R. Jackson, whose semiautobiographical novel *The Lost Weekend* helped Ray Milland snag a Best Actor Oscar after the book was filmed in 1945, was another tormented soul given to binge drinking. Although heavily involved with Alcoholics Anonymous, Jackson continued to struggle with alcohol before committing suicide in his room at the Chelsea on September 21, 1968.

Punk Mayhem

Ten years later, Nancy Spungen apparently had little say in her death, which came in Room 100 after months of drug abuse and domestic violence at the hands of her boyfriend, punk rocker Sid Vicious. Their clashes seemed to climax with Nancy's death from a stab wound to the abdomen on October 12, 1978. The injury was linked to a knife owned by Vicious, who confessed (later retracted) to the murder. Vicious, of course, was no more serene emotionally than his deceased gal pal, and he died from a heroin overdose just three months later.

The fact that Vicious never stood trial encouraged speculation that Spungen was killed by a burglar or drug dealer who entered the room while Sid was in a junk-induced stupor. *Well, New Yorkers seemed to say, anything is possible at the Chelsea.*

Not every Chelsea tale is a sad one. Before the artist Alphaeus Cole passed away at the hotel on November 25, 1988, he was, at 112 years and 136 days, verified as the world's oldest living man. Since Cole had resided at the hotel for the last 35 years of his life, the place evidently had an invigorating effect on him, and the same can be said for many others who have passed through the Chelsea's doors.

The Chelsea on Film

Still, the who's who of Chelsea guests and a what's what of their colorful indiscretions have given rise to much speculation along the lines of "If only these walls could talk!" Andy Warhol's 1966 movie *Chelsea Girls* firmly established the hotel in pop culture legend. Yet, even though that rambling, three-hour-plus, underground film (codirected by Paul Morrissey) focused on the radical lives of several of its residents—including Warhol "superstars" Nico, Ondine, legit actress Mary Woronov, Ingrid Superstar, International Velvet, and Brigid Berlin—the only cast member who actually lived there was poet René Ricard. Banned upon its release in Chicago and Boston, *Chelsea Girls* was a hit in New York and stands as the only Warhol cinematic effort to have achieved any kind of mainstream acceptance.

The Dead Don't Sleep Easily

These days, the hotel lobby is decorated with the artwork of former residents, yet the Chelsea rarely accepts paintings as a form of payment. And maybe that's why this onetime mecca of bohemians, oddballs, and assorted fringe characters is reputedly haunted by many of their ghosts. The phantom of Sid Vicious has allegedly been spotted in the elevator, while a stop with Sid on the eighth floor may lead to an encounter with the ectoplasmic presence of novelist Thomas Wolfe, who wrote *Look Homeward, Angel* and *The Web and the Rock* while residing at the Chelsea. According to some of the hotel's residents, it is artistic spirits such as these that inspire creativity in the living.

Diggin' Dirt!

Many of the nation's juiciest scandals have sprung from the Big Apple. Here is a notorious quartet.

✳ ✳ ✳ ✳

NEW YORK CITY is no stranger to scandal. In fact, over the centuries it probably ranks second only to Chicago in terms of politicians who get caught in compromising positions, the public revelation of high society's dirty little secrets, and assorted other embarrassments. Here are some highlights from among New York's worst scandals.

Eliot Spitzer's sexual shenanigans. Spitzer was the governor of New York and a promising up-and-comer in the Democratic Party until 2008, when he was fingered in a federal investigation that publicly revealed his penchant for high-priced call girls. Eliot!

The revelation had a devastating effect on Spitzer's political career, which had been built on his reputation as a squeaky-clean foe of organized crime and political corruption. The fact that the governor had been cheating on his wife was bad enough, political analysts noted, but more damning was the obvious fact that he was a bald-faced hypocrite.

Caught red-handed, Spitzer may have felt he had no choice but to resign as governor. After more than a year of lying low, he reentered the public eye as a political commentator. Observers' opinions are mixed as to whether he might one day seek political office again.

Miss America's political downfall. In 1945, Bess Myerson broke barriers as the first Jewish Miss America. Forty-two years later, the Bronx-born beauty was forced to resign from her job as New York City's commissioner of cultural affairs under a dark cloud of scandal. Among the allegations: that Myerson had used her political clout and winning personality to sway the judge overseeing the divorce of her paramour, Andy Capasso, a business executive 21 years her junior. Capasso, a wealthy sewer contractor, was later convicted of tax evasion and sentenced to four years in a federal prison.

According to an investigative report leaked to the *Village Voice*, Myerson, who was appointed by Mayor Ed Koch in 1983, manipulated Judge Hortense Gabel by placing that jurist's emotionally disturbed daughter, Sukhreet, on the city payroll as her assistant. Once Gabel had ruled in Capasso's favor, the newspaper reported, Myerson fired Sukhreet, initiated a cover-up, and lied about the entire affair. It was a sad end to the career of a woman who had given the city so much.

The Queen of Mean takes a fall. Everyone loves it when the obnoxiously rich fall from grace, and few wealthy New Yorkers have fallen as hard as hotel magnate Leona Helmsley. The wife of billionaire Harry Helmsley, who owned the lease on the Empire State Building, among other holdings, Leona Helmsley was convicted of tax evasion and sentenced to prison in 1989 following a widely publicized trial. Among the revelations: that she often terrorized her employees and routinely tried to stiff those who did work for her, including the contractors who renovated the couple's Connecticut mansion.

Perhaps most damning of all, however, was the testimony of a housekeeper who told the jury she had heard Helmsley comment, "We don't pay taxes. Only the little people pay taxes." Helmsley denied making such a statement but was never able to live it down. She died in 2007.

The humiliation of the *New York Times*. Since its founding in 1851, the *New York Times* has enjoyed a reputation as the newspaper of record. But that reputation received a vicious black eye in 2003 when it was revealed that one of its star reporters, Jayson Blair, was guilty of plagiarism and of making up many of the stories he filed.

Blair was a promising young journalist when he joined the *Times* as an intern in 1998. However, within two years he had been repeatedly called on the carpet by his editors for making too many errors in his reporting. Nonetheless, Blair was promoted to the national desk in 2002. A year later, Blair's conduct as a reporter had became so egregious that the *Times* was forced to conduct its own investigation, which found numerous instances of plagiarism, falsification of information, and outright lying. As a result, Blair was let go, and the *Times* published a 7,239-word mea culpa detailing Blair's errors and the newspaper's response.

Fast Facts

❈ Of the classical Greek city-states, Sparta gets the women's rights prize (such as it might be). Sparta was the only city to mandate public education for girls, and only in Sparta did women strip for athletics, just as all Greek men did.

❈ What kind of a guy was Socrates? He wandered around barefoot and shirtless, dependent upon handouts from friends. He never had a real job to speak of.

❈ The ancient Olympics weren't always a fun time. The heat was miserable, the site was buggy, and the concessions served shabby, overpriced food. Sanitation was minimal. A slave-owner once threatened to send an errant charge to the Games as punishment.

❈ All those splendid Greek statues you see in off-white marble? Most used to be painted in realistic colors. We know because tiny bits of paint remain embedded in nooks and crannies.

❈ The pigtail common to Chinese peasant men until early in the twentieth century dated back to a Manchu emperor in the 1600s. Enforcing this Manchu style on the Chinese served as a constant reminder of Manchu overlordship.

❈ Footbinding—the deformation of girls' feet into barely walkable little triangles—began in China around A.D. 1000. It took hundreds of years for this painful, crippling practice to die out.

❈ Those who attended Genghis Khan's burial (A.D. 1227)—all 2,900 of them—were executed. Evidently the Mongols were fairly sure someone would try to plunder the grave.

❈ Ancient Chinese used ants to kill citrus pests.

❈ Early medieval European monarchs had outstanding names. Who can resist Charles the Bald (reigned 823–877), Louis the Stammerer (877–879), Charles the Fat (881–887), Louis the Blind (901–905), or Charles the Simple (893–922)?

Chapter 2

Culture—From Low to High Society

Thumbs Up: A Sign of Life or Death

An ancient hand gesture earned new meaning during an era of strife and confrontation.

✳ ✳ ✳ ✳

THE THUMBS-UP GESTURE supposedly originated in the arenas of ancient Rome, where spectators would use it to signal whether they wanted a vanquished opponent to be spared or put to death. The Latin term for the gesture—*pollice verso*—means "with a turned thumb." But when a gladiator found himself looking up at the business end of a foe's sword, a sea of spectators' thumbs pointing upward was the last thing he wanted. In the Coliseum, thumbs-up was a signal to the victorious warrior that he should put the other combatant to death, whereas a raised fist with the thumb concealed was an indication to show mercy.

The gesture was resurrected and given an entirely opposite connotation by American pilots during World War II. The flyboys adopted the signal because they needed a nonverbal cue to indicate to ground crews that they were ready to take off. But it was the media that established it among the civilian population back home. Photos of daring young flyers—grinning confidently from their cockpits before takeoff, their thumbs held high—saturated American newspapers, magazines, and newsreels during the war. As a result, the public, eager for good news and encouragement during those dark days, heartily embraced the gesture. The thumbs-up sign fell from favor with the youth generation of the 1960s, who disdained its militaristic origins and preferred the peace sign instead. But the wildly popular television show *Happy Days* brought it back in the 1970s; it was the signature gesture of the sitcom's iconic character, The Fonz. Be careful where you use it, however; in countries such as Iran and Greece, a thumbs-up is considered extremely rude.

Watching Through the Night

Watch Night introduced a different way to celebrate a familiar holiday.

✻　✻　✻　✻

IN ONE SENSE, New Year's Eve may be the most universal of holidays, as virtually every culture on the planet has some way of marking the passing of one era and the start of another. Of course, each culture celebrates at its own time of year and with its own set of traditions. For most Americans, December 31 is a time for counting down and drinking up, and January 1 is a time of empty resolutions and epic hangovers. But even in America there are alternative ways to mark the passing of an old year and the coming of a new one.

For many black Americans, the New Year's holiday centers around one of the most meaningful and popular religious services of the year: Watch Night. Throngs of people gather in churches on New Year's Eve for a long evening of song, reflection, celebration, and prayer in a ceremony that can fluctuate between pious and raucous.

Holy Origins

Watch Night originated with the Moravians, Christians whose roots trace back to the present-day Czech Republic. The first such services likely took place in Germany in 1733. In 1777, Methodism founder John Wesley brought the practice to the states, calling for his followers to renew their covenant with God in a monthly vigil that corresponded to the full moon.

Where Legend Meets Fact

It is commonly believed that the tradition of celebrating Watch Night on New Year's Eve dates to the American South during the days of slavery. This much is true. But why? Some sources claim that slave families gathered to pray together on New Year's Eve because they feared it would be their last night together. Many slaves saw their families broken up after New Year's when individuals were sold to raise funds to settle outstanding debts. But this explanation falls short. The most significant evidence against this theory is that Southern businessmen were unlikely to conduct business on New Year's Day.

Let Freedom Ring!

What is known is that Watch Night became an important African American celebration during the Civil War, as slaves and free blacks across the country gathered in their churches on New Year's Eve 1862 to await a watershed moment in United States history. The next day, January 1, 1963, President Abraham Lincoln was scheduled to—and did—sign the Emancipation Proclamation. This simple but eloquent 725-word document freed everyone held in slavery in the Confederate States and declared all of them eligible for military service in the Union. Then and now, the document was criticized for having freed only those slaves residing in states that were in rebellion, but it irrevocably committed the federal government to abolishing slavery throughout the entire country.

The Watch Night tradition continued in black congregations for decades as a celebration of hard-won freedom and then waned in the early years of the twentieth century. The practice was reinvigorated in the 1960s as part of the Civil Rights Movement and continues to this day, serving as a powerful reminder and celebration of one of the most pivotal moments in American history. Celebrations vary from church to church, but there are many commonalities. Services typically begin late, around 10 P.M., and continue until shortly after midnight, though some groups stay throughout the night and celebrate until dawn. One congregation will often host another, so that members of both churches can share the night together. There's usually a sermon, or the pastor may read the official church record from the year that's ending. Members of the church will often give spontaneous testimonials of the trials they've faced and the blessings they've received, putting the former behind them and expressing gratitude for the latter. The service sometimes includes a candlelight procession and is always interspersed with joyful singing. Just before midnight, worshippers crowd together around the altar and fall to their knees to pray in a moving scene that dedicates the start of the year to God. And so continues the Methodist notion of renewing one's covenant at New Year's.

Clubs & Organizations Down on the Farm

A rural youth group helped to revolutionize agricultural practices.

✳   ✳   ✳   ✳

IN THE UNITED States, 4-H Clubs have been an inspirational and educational presence for more than a century. Ohio school superintendent A. B. Graham is generally credited with starting the first 4-H Club in the United States in 1902. The federal government even got involved, with Congress creating and funding the Cooperative Extension Service, of which 4-H remains a part.

In the early years, the organization had more on its mind than developing the skills of rural youth. The U.S. Department of Agriculture and other organizations faced difficulty getting many farmers to adopt the latest scientific advances in farming. They found that children, on the other hand, were eager to experiment with new ideas. The 4-H Clubs were intended, at least in part, to get the current generation of farmers to accept these new ideas by seeing their children succeed with them.

Over time, the organization grew in scope and redefined its focus. In the 1940s and 1950s, 4-H introduced international exchange programs, and clubs increasingly began to participate in scientific research. Local chapters carefully gathered and documented data on new kinds of livestock feed or planting practices, sharing the information with scientists. Clubs also spread to urban areas. Over the next several decades, emphasis gradually shifted to broader life skills, such as leadership, community involvement, reading, and math.

So, what does "4-H" stand for? Well, originally there were only three H's—Head, Heart, and Hands. In 1911, one club organizer suggested adding a fourth H to represent "Hustle." But at some point, the last H came to stand for "Health" instead.

Cutting the Red Tape

Everyone hates it; Dr. Seuss helped the government reduce it.

✳   ✳   ✳   ✳

Q: Where did the term *red tape* originate?

A: Actual red tape originated as an antifraud measure, similar to wax seals in ancient times. The goal was to ensure that a document received by its intended recipient was the exact same one sent by its author or authors. So it had to be secured in such a way that any tampering would be revealed. Anyone seeking to alter an official document would have to break the wax seal and untie the red tape.

The Vatican archives preserve about 85 copies of Henry VIII's petition to Pope Clement VII for a divorce from his first wife, Catherine of Aragon, wrapped with official red tape. But red tape was probably in use for many, many years before that. The Vatican itself used red tape, as did the British Parliament and other European chanceries and courts.

Q: So what happened next in this "tacky" story? Why did the term stick?

A: Around 1736, *red tape* became synonymous with pointless bureaucratic procedure and obstruction. Some scholars suggest that frustratingly hard-to-access American Civil War veterans' records were bound in red tape. Today, red tape is alleged to frustrate scientists, keep economies from achieving their potential, prevent start-up companies from succeeding, and block the efforts of charities. All politicians campaign against it. All officials promise to cut it—at least until some of them are accused of fostering it. Red tape, it seems, is an evil growth, entwining and frustrating everyone's best efforts.

Q: What does Dr. Seuss have to do with any of this?

A: During World War II, newspapers published a series of articles dubbed the "Society of Red Tape Cutters." The intention was to commend those individuals who kept bureaucracy (red tape) from deterring the war effort. Theodor Geisel (a.k.a. Dr. Seuss) illustrated the certificate for the award, which went to such notables as Franklin D. Roosevelt, Harry S. Truman, and Admiral Chester W. Nimitz. Since then, other groups have taken the same name, including a Society of Red Tape Cutters in Northfield, Illinois, that consists of volunteers who help senior citizens get government services.

The Tonys

The Tony Awards, which recognize excellence in the theater, were first given in 1947. Of the six people who won major acting awards, Patricia Neal was the only one still alive in 2009.

✳   ✳   ✳   ✳

BORN PATSY LOUISE Neal in Knoxville, Tennessee, in 1926, Neal became interested in performing after appearing in functions at her local church. She attended Northwestern University for two years and then moved to New York. After settling in there, she began calling herself Patricia. She got her start performing on stage then began appearing in movies.

She married writer Roald Dahl in 1953 (they divorced in 1983). Patricia Neal is an esteemed actress, but she also became noted for her resilience after experiencing several personal tragedies. An accident forced her son, Theo, to undergo intense rehabilitation while he was still just an infant. Neal and Dahl lost their oldest daughter, Olivia, when she contracted measles encephalitis at just seven years old. At age 39 in 1965, Neal suffered three debilitating strokes. Her husband coached her through her rehabilitation, and she eventually returned to acting.

The following were the first Tony Award winners:

✳ Actor (dramatic): Fredric March (1897–1975), for *Years Ago*

✳ Actress (dramatic): Ingrid Bergman (1915–82), for *Joan of Lorraine*

✳ Actor (dramatic): Jose Ferrer (1909–92), for *Cyrano de Bergerac*

✳ Actress (dramatic): Helen Hayes (1900–93), for *Happy Birthday*

✳ Actor, supporting or featured (musical): David Wayne (1914–95), for *Finian's Rainbow*

✳ Actress, supporting or featured (dramatic): Patricia Neal (1926–2010), for *Another Part of the Forest*

Inspiration Station

Napoleon Dynamite: Based On a True Story?

For all you liger-loving folks out there who connected with the painfully nerdy hero of the 2004 indie blockbuster *Napoleon Dynamite,* take heart: Truth is just as strange as fiction. Many of the eccentric details that made Napoleon so endearingly weird was inspired by the experience of director Jared Hess. The llama, the martial-arts obsession, the uncle's online purchase of a time machine—those details came straight from the life of either Hess or his friends and family, many of whom live in small-town Idaho. The film was originally a short feature, filmed on a budget of $200,000. Fox Searchlight pictures picked up the story for $4 million and a bespectacled legend was born.

V.I.P. Muse: Francesca da Rimini

Should you ever find yourself forced into an arranged marriage, here's a silver lining: If your story is tragic enough, you might become the subject of artistic masterpieces for centuries to come. Anyway, that's how it went for Francesca da Rimini, a young Italian woman in the thirteenth century. Her father wanted to marry Francesca off to Giovanni Malatesta, the lame and disfigured son of an ex-rival. Knowing that Francesca would never agree to it, her father arranged for a switcheroo, thus "marrying" his clueless daughter to the handsome younger son Paolo (but really to Giovanni). Once Francesca figured out that she'd been fooled into marrying Giovanni, she began a steamy affair with Paolo. Giovanni found out, however, and murdered the pair.

The story has inspired countless artists, including Dante, who included the couple in parts of his *Divine Comedy;* Auguste Rodin, who sculpted *The Kiss* in 1888–89, used the lovers as his subject; Tchaikovsky wrote a poem about Francesca and Paolo; and Rachmaninoff dedicated an entire opera to the couple, called simply, *Francesca.*

Smoke 'Em If You Got 'Em

Back in the days when smoking was fashionable, these now-defunct cigarette brands could light up a room. Today, most of these tobacco manufacturers are remembered through their highly collectible premium inserts, including pin-back buttons and cards featuring baseball players. Here are a few worth revisiting.

✳   ✳   ✳   ✳

Chesterfield Cigarettes

A MAINSTAY OF THE 1950s scene, the company featured advertisements by such luminaries as Lucille Ball, Dean Martin and Jerry Lewis, Ronald Reagan, and Rod Serling, and was once a sponsor of the police drama *Dragnet*. The brand is still manufactured but hasn't been advertised in the United States for several years. Dogged by declining sales, the product may soon join the ranks of the forever forgotten.

Duke Cigarettes

Extra Credit! The company was owned by industrialist James Buchanan Duke, whose establishment of The Duke Endowment encouraged a Durham, North Carolina, college to change its name to Duke University in honor of Duke's deceased father.

Fatima Cigarettes

This brand was a staple advertiser of 1940s radio programs, including *Dragnet*, with star Jack Webb appearing in several print and radio ads for the company. It was also purported to be the favorite of actress Jean Harlow.

Old Judge Cigarettes

Old Judge is best known by collectors for introducing the first major set of baseball cards in the late 1880s.

Other Brands of Days Past Include:

* Admiral Cigarettes
* American Beauty Cigarettes
* Broadleaf Cigarettes
* Champ's Cigarettes
* Clix Cigarettes
* Contentnea Cigarettes
* Cycle Cigarettes
* Emblem Cigarettes
* Gypsy Queen Cigarettes
* Hassan Cigarettes
* Hindu Cigarettes
* Kotton Cigarettes
* Lenox Mouthpiece Cigarettes
* Lloyd's Cigarettes
* Lord Salisbury Cigarettes
* Marvels Cigarettes
* Mino Cigarettes
* Mogul Cigarettes
* Mono Cigarettes
* Murad Cigarettes
* Obak Cigarettes
* Ogden's Cigarettes
* Old Mill Cigarettes
* Paul Jones Cigarettes

* Pet Cigarettes
* Picayune Cigarettes
* Pirate Cigarettes
* Player's Cigarettes
* Polar Tobacco
* Red Sun Cigarettes
* Turf Cigarettes
* Turkey Red Cigarettes
* Twenty Grand Cigarettes
* Wings Cigarettes
* Zira Cigarettes

How It All Began

Air Flair

Necessity, they say, is the mother of invention. In the case of Doc Marten work boots (aka DMs), it's also the doctor.

In 1945, Dr. Klaus Maertens hurt his foot skiing in Bavaria and needed a shoe with some cushioning. Inspired by the auto industry's use of compressed air, he cut up some old tires and sewed them to his shoes. It didn't quite work.

Maertens tapped his electrical-engineer friend, Dr. Herbert Funck, to figure out how to trap air inside a shoe sole. Instead of tires, Funck molded raw PVC rubber to form air pockets, and DM's trademark "air-cushioned sole" was born. The shoes were initially marketed only to soldiers, but eventually mine and factory workers caught on as well.

To expedite production of DMs—and hopefully popularize them beyond Germany—Maertens and Funck began searching for an industrial partner. They teamed up with British manufacturer R. Griggs in 1959. Griggs, who was already known for producing quality work boots, purchased the patent for Doc Maertens and changed the spelling to "Martens" for broader audience appeal. On April 1, 1960, Griggs distributed the first pair of cherry-red, eight-eyelet, air-cushioned work boots, named 1460 in honor of the date. Today, the 1460 model remains the company's top seller.

Star Power

One of the best-selling shoes of all time is the Converse All Star, the brainchild of Marquis M. Converse. In 1908, he launched the Converse Rubber Shoe Company in Malden, Massachusetts, specializing in winter boots. He soon realized he could make more money if he produced shoes for all seasons, so in 1912 or 1915 (sources vary), Converse introduced a canvas sneaker. This was followed in 1917 by the high-top Converse All Star, a sneaker specifically designed for the new sport of basketball.

From there, much of the shoe's success goes to pro player Chuck Taylor, who began wearing the shoes in 1918. He became such a fan that he joined the Converse sales force in 1921, promoting both his sport and his shoe. When basketball debuted in the 1936 Olympics, so did the Converse All Star; by World War II, the All Star was the official shoe of U.S. soldiers, who wore them during training exercises. Today, the iconic shoe has managed to keep its footing and remains on the market.

Inspiration Station

Monet's Water Lilies

It might seem obvious that Claude Monet's famous paintings of water lilies were inspired by, well, water lilies; but the flowers he immortalized on canvas floated unnoticed by Monet for some time before he was inspired to paint them.

In the late 1800s, the painter designed and built a water garden full of water lilies near his house in Giverny, France. The pond's landscaping was inspired by Japanese gardens and design, with irregular contours and integrated features of the surrounding area. Monet said, "I planted my water lilies for pleasure; I cultivated them without thinking of painting them. And then suddenly, I had the revelation of the magic of my pond." Until his death in 1926, the lilies he had randomly planted in the water garden remained Monet's favorite theme. "I perhaps owe having become a painter to flowers," he remarked.

Shabby Chic: How Secondhand Became First Class

If you're a fan of the interior design style known as "shabby chic," then you know that one man's dusty old armoire is another man's pride and joy. Defined by heavily painted, chipped wood furniture, threadbare rugs and carpets, antique pictures, decorative accents such as quilts, and pretty much anything in a pastel color, shabby chic is a style inspired by hand-me-downs.

It all began when wealthy folks in Great Britain would move their old furniture into their summer cottages, in order to make room for newer, posher stuff. Their secondhand, well-loved, and mismatched furniture was often given a coat of white or pastel paint to spruce it up, creating a cozy, lived-in feel. The term "shabby chic" was coined in the 1980s by a style magazine and an interior design trend was born. These days, the shabby chic look is featured in home decorating magazines and Web sites, where readers can find tips to make brand-new furniture look tattered and old on purpose.

Finnegan Would Be Proud

Thorton Wilder reportedly was inspired to write the Pulitzer Prize winning play, *The Skin of Our Teeth*, after a prop rubber chicken fell from the stage into his lap during a performance of the hit Broadway revue *Hellzapoppin*. But that's just one theory as to how Wilder's bizarre modern allegory (which blended Bible stories, dinosaurs, and the Miss America Pageant, among other things) came to be. Most scholars understand that Wilder was directly inspired by James Joyce's experimental novel, *Finnegan's Wake*, and wrote the play as a response. Some people believe the similarities between the two expressionist works are a little too close for comfort, claiming that of the two epic cyclical histories, Joyce's is the true avant-garde example.

Prince, *The Godfather*, and Apollonia

The brilliant and ever-eclectic (and eccentric) musician Prince was always able to find inspiration everywhere he went, including the movies. In the early 1980s, Prince held auditions to find a singer for an all-female pop group; Spanish-Italian model and vocalist Patricia Kotero got the job. In order to add more sass to her image, however, a name change was in order. Prince had recently seen Francis Ford Coppola's *The Godfather* and was inspired by the character of Apollonia, the beautiful, doomed Italian woman Michael Corleone marries while he's hiding in Italy. Kotero was renamed Apollonia and went on to star opposite Prince in the hit movie *Purple Rain*.

The Two Towers: King and Browning

To the frustration of fans worldwide, horror maven Stephen King's seven-part series *The Dark Tower* has been written and published separately over a period of 22 years, starting in 1970. At age 19, King came across a poem by Robert Browning titled, "Childe Rowland to the Dark Tower Came," and found in it inspiration for his own epic journey. Inspired by Tolkien's *Lord of the Rings* saga, the series follows the hero, Roland, on his quest to the literal and figurative Dark Tower. *The Dark Tower* story has been made into films and graphic novels, and the characters in the story have gone on to inspire musicians and writers to create related works.

Why You Buy

Supermarkets have gone to great lengths to make you think that an "impulse" buy really was an impulse.

✳ ✳ ✳ ✳

End Caps

THE "END CAPS"—THE shelves at the outer ends of each aisle—are the equivalent of beach-front property. Studies have shown that placing items on end caps can boost their sales by as much as a third. By giving items their own little plot of land, supermarkets convey the impression that they are special or that they are a good deal. Not necessarily. Just because something is on the end cap doesn't mean it's on sale. Worse, supermarkets sometimes use the end caps to move product that hasn't been selling that well—meaning those Little Debbie snack cakes you just threw into your cart might be expiring any day now.

Ambience

Mood lighting. Sample counters. Espresso bars. These days, high-end grocery stores like Whole Foods more closely resemble Macy's or Nordstrom than a traditional supermarket. That's because retailers know that the more welcoming you can make an environment—and the longer people spend in a store—the more people will buy (this is also the theory behind Wal-Mart's greeters).

But it's not just lighting and music. Supermarkets also use aromas to get you in the mood to shop. That's why you'll find the rotisserie chicken roasting near the entrance to many grocery stores.

Changing Locations of Items

For many people, the grocery store becomes routine—they purchase the same staples each week, and after a while, shoppers on autopilot begin to ignore the other items in the store.

To combat this, grocery stores will constantly rotate stock. By shifting items—even within the same aisle—supermarkets can force shoppers to consider new—and hopefully more expensive—items.

Product Placement on Shelves

It's one of the fundamentals of marketing: People are lazy. But just how lazy is surprising. Study after study has shown that the average grocery shopper can't even be bothered to look at anything beyond eye level. Some supermarkets take advantage of this by putting the most expensive items on eye-level shelves in the aisles, while others charge suppliers a hefty fee for a spot there. Consumer experts suggest better deals can be found by simply checking out the items on the bottom or top shelves.

Putting Promotional Displays or Nonfood Items at the Entrance

When's the last time you walked into a grocery story and saw what you needed at the entrance? Probably never. Consumer psychologists have found that shoppers need a little time to get into the shopping mind-set. As a result, the entrance of grocery stores are known as something of a dead zone, sales-wise. That's why you'll often find magazines, books, and the flower department near the front of the store—anything to get the shopper into a more relaxed state of mind.

Advertising Non-sale Items in the Sale Flyers

Savvy grocery shoppers in search of the best deal head straight for the flyer rack when they enter a supermarket. Little do they know that those "sale flyers" are littered with non-sale items. Advertising items at their regular price alongside items that are actually on sale creates the illusion that the regularly priced items are a great buy.

By the Numbers

$820 billion: total annual U.S. sales of grocery industry (approximate)

$328 billion: total spent by shoppers on unintended grocery purchases, according to a 2008 survey

$98 billion: total spent by shoppers on groceries that go to waste, average year

Great Ad Campaigns That Made Us Buy

There are a lot of people who want you to buy something, and when the advertising industry is on, the ads they come up with can sure be effective.

✳   ✳   ✳   ✳

COULD A SIMPLE soft drink unite those embroiled in a state of hostility? Bill Backer, an advertising representative for the Coca-Cola account, believed Coke could do just that when he brainstormed an anthem of peace to air alongside a pack of Coke-adoring pacifists. The song's lyrics—about the act of singing itself—insisted that buying a Coke would keep the world in perfect harmony. Sappy as the image may have been, Coca-Cola calculated that about 4,000 pieces of fan mail were sent the week the commercial debuted.

If a schmaltzy song can sell soda, perhaps an animated, life-size faux-food product could accomplish a similar trick. Enter Twinkie the Kid. This Hostess mascot was a cowboy by trade but was equally adept at saving sponge-cake-loving children from peril.

How Much Would That Cost?

In the 1990s, MasterCard claimed that so many special moments are "priceless"—but for those items that can be purchased, you should use your credit card. Combined visions—one part life's happy happenstance and one part purchased goods—all brought forth the same conclusion: Memories are invaluable, but you have to spend some dough to fuel them with consumer goods.

For those times when fast cash can't save the day, though, how about an intervening breath mint? Mentos, aka the "fresh-maker," was up for almost any face-saving endeavor. Just ask that poor schmuck who sat on a freshly painted park bench in his neatly pressed suit. Thanks to the salvation of the roll of Mentos that he found in his pocket, he was able to see the bright side of his situation: a newly pin-striped suit, instead of ruined workday garb.

At least with a campaign such as the ever-evolving "Got Milk" onslaught, the product is actually used to hawk itself. Now, if only the ad industry didn't insist on doing so with that messy moo juice adorning the drinker's lips.

National Department Stores

Among the founders of the best-known U.S. department stores still successful in the early twenty-first century, Samuel M. "Sam" Walton was the last to survive. He passed away in 1992 at age 74. Walton opened his first department store in 1962; it would become part of one of the world's largest chains of retail stores—Wal-Mart.

✳   ✳   ✳   ✳

WALTON GREW UP in Oklahoma and Missouri during the Great Depression. He began his retail career at JCPenney in Iowa, and in 1944, he opened a deep-discount Ben Franklin store in Newport, Arkansas. His strategy: Buy super cheap, sell cheap. The store was so successful that in 1950 the landlord wouldn't renew Walton's lease (he wanted to give the cash cow to his son). But Walton didn't go away empty handed: The discounting and land ownership lessons he learned would become the core of his future business model.

Next, Walton bought a five-and-dime in Bentonville, Arkansas. By 1962, with more than a dozen five-and-dimes operating profitably, he was ready for department stores. When the first

Wal-Mart opened in Rogers, Arkansas, Walton stuck to several key principles: property ownership, no unions, low prices, low costs, and austerity. Manufacturers had to let Wal-Mart reps investigate their operations for ways to cut costs and give Wal-Mart a better price. His method worked—and continues to work—because his customer base cares about lower prices above all.

Other national department store founders include:

* Rowland Hussey Macy (died 1877) started Macy's in 1851.

* Marshall Field (died 1906) bought his first store in 1865.

* Richard W. Sears (died 1914) and Alvah C. Roebuck (died 1948) founded Sears, Roebuck and Co. in 1893.

* Sebastian S. Kresge (died 1966) opened S. S. Kresge in 1899; it became Kmart in 1977.

* James Cash Penney (died 1971) started JCPenney in 1907.

The Comforting Idea of the Lost Cause

After the war, many Southerners turned to a much-needed belief system to make sense of their experience.

* * * *

AS THE CIVIL War ended, large parts of the South were left desolated. In order to cope with the difficulties of the war's aftermath, many Southerners needed to feel that, despite its outcome, the struggle had been worthwhile. As a way to fill that need, the concept of *The Lost Cause* was born. Arising after the war, this is a view of the antebellum South that romanticizes plantation life and whitewashes the evils of slavery. From this point of view, the Confederate cause was just and necessary.

Origins of the Idea

The term *lost cause* first appeared in 1866, just one year after the end of the war, in Edward Pollard's *The Lost Cause: A New Southern History of the War of the Confederates*. At the heart of the idea of the *lost cause* is an idealized image of the prewar South. The vision of the *lost* cause has been so successful that its point of view continues to color our current understanding of antebellum Southern life. Visions of a magnolia-lined driveway opening onto the porch of a towering Georgian mansion; a delicate Southern lady fanning herself on the porch; the happy, smiling slave serving her genteel mistress a glass of sweet tea—all of these images fit into the typical lost cause revisionist scenario. *Gone With the Wind*, the 1939 movie adaptation of Margaret Mitchell's novel, is probably the most enduring and well-known example of the *lost cause* tradition.

The Perfection of Plantation Life

For those who were left to rebuild their shattered lives and culture, imagining the peace and prosperity of plantation life was a comforting distraction from the reality of post-war defeat, destruction, and occupation of the South. This culture of the plantation was as close as America has come to having an aristocratic class—in fact, many of those who made up the functional ruling class of early America were Southerners. Before the Civil War, Virginia was home to more presidents and military leaders than any other state. Four of the first five presidents—George Washington, Thomas Jefferson, James Madison, and James Monroe—were Virginians.

Foremost among these Virginians was Jefferson, whose philosophy of agricultural life defined the Southern worldview and provided the romanticized version of the region after the war. Jeffersonian notions of freedom—that is, the freedom to own and work the land—took root in the South, but new economic forces were gaining strength in the North. Part of the Northern industrial makeover included the concept of freedom more and more being tied to the right to work for wages.

Industrialization and the factory-wage system were seen as a threat to the Southern way of life. As some historians see it, the impersonal industrial might of the North threatened Southern culture even before the first gunshots were fired.

A Vital Idea

The image of the happy slave was crucial to this concept of Southern civilization. Plantation life rested on several assumptions about the ethics of slavery. It was not viewed as a necessary evil but instead as beneficial to the black race. Looking back at the peculiar institution, proponents of the lost cause believed that blacks were inherently suited to slavery, which next led to the assumption that blacks had been happy with their enslavement and desired to be loyal to their white masters. In keeping with this theory, Southern masters saw themselves as kind and compassionate to their docile servants, certainly more so than Northern factory bosses could be. Southern slaveowners wanted to believe themselves to be like fathers to their chattel, but factory bosses could never share that kind of paternalistic relationship with their employees, black or white.

In support of this view, Jefferson Davis wrote a post-war memoir in which he glowingly expounded on slavery in the South: "Their servile instincts rendered them contented with their lot, and their patient toil blessed the land of their abode with unmeasured riches. Their strong local and personal attachment secured faithful service... Never was there happier dependence of labor and capital on each other. The tempter came, like the serpent of Eden, and decoyed them with the magic word of 'freedom.'"

"Mr. Lincoln's War"

Even though a sanitized version of slavery is a large part of this worldview, the *lost cause* concept does not accept that slavery caused the war. Davis also wrote in his memoir that slavery "was in no wise the cause of the conflict, but only an incident." According to Davis, the Civil War was merely the Southern defense of the homeland against the "tremendous and sweeping usurpation" and "the unlimited, despotic power" of the federal government. It is little wonder, then, why so many Southerners referred to the conflict not as the Civil War, but as "The War of Northern Aggression" or, more pointedly, as "Mr. Lincoln's War."

The war itself, however, played a great role in defining how the *lost cause* came to be understood. Besides casting the North as antagonistic, the believers in the lost cause largely focused on Southern heroism. Many Southerners saw the perfect embodiment of bravery, honor, and manliness in the figure of General Robert E. Lee. Even the fact that the South lost didn't weaken the legitimacy of the Southern cause. Edward Pollard, who gave the concept its name, noted that although the South lost on the battlefield, it would ultimately win the "war of ideas." And unfortunately, Pollard was right to some degree, at least until the Civil Rights movement (often called the "Second Reconstruction") rooted out the last residue of state-sponsored white supremacy.

Keepers of the Cause

After the war ended, various organizations such as the United Confederate Veterans (later Sons of Confederate Veterans), the United Daughters of the Confederacy, and the Southern Historical Society made sure that history wouldn't be written entirely by the victors. Many of these organizations lobbied local, state, and national governments for money to build Confederate monuments, and their efforts were quite successful.

Through movies, the idea of the *lost cause* has shaped the American memory of the Civil War. Two phenomenally successful films— *The Birth of a Nation* in 1915 and *Gone With the Wind* in 1939—bore the marks of *lost cause* revisionism: white superiority, glorification of plantation life, and the infantilization and demonization of blacks. The success of these two movies wasn't just limited to the South—it was nationwide, which is a testament to the widespread acceptance of the lost cause narrative. Indeed, after seeing *The Birth of a Nation* at a special White House screening, President Woodrow Wilson is reported to have re-marked: "It is like writing history with lightning, and my only regret is that it is all so terribly true." In a way, it could be argued that it wasn't the Northern victory but the *lost cause* that unified the nation after the war.

The Impressionists

How did a group of painters come to be called "Impressionists"?

✳   ✳   ✳   ✳

HEADS WILL NOD in synchronous unison when you comment on a painting's Impressionistic aspects. Impressionism began in France in the mid-1800s. A group of artists, including Claude Monet and Pierre-Auguste Renoir, joined together after their works were repeatedly rejected for exhibition at the prestigious Salon in Paris. The artists staged their own exhibition in 1874.

Impression: Sunrise, a painting of Monet's that was exhibited at the separate exhibition, garnered particular scorn from critics; they derided its "unfinished" appearance. The artists were gratified by this scorn because they felt that what they were doing was new, different, and exciting. They began to call themselves "Impressionists" (after the Monet painting) to show that they were going to continue to innovate rather than give in to the critics.

Instead of describing a scene precisely, Impressionists tended to focus on the sensation the scene conveyed. Some instructors of Impressionistic painting teach the acronym ELBOW:

* E: Everyday life—no contrived or ornate scenes

* L: Light—specifically, sunlight

* B: Brushstrokes—small and subtle, in primary colors

* O: Outdoor—Impressionists painted outside to capture L and W

* W: Weather and atmosphere—these elements create the overall *impression*, hence the name

The last living Impressionist was Claude Monet, who died on December 5, 1926, outliving Mary Cassatt by fewer than six months.

The following artists are also considered major Impressionists:

* Edouard Manet (1832–83)

* Berthe Morisot (1841–95)

* Alfred Sisley (1839–99)

* Camille Pissarro (1830–1903)

* Edgar Degas (1834–1917)

* Pierre-Auguste Renoir (1841–1919)

* Mary Cassatt (1844–1926)

* Claude Monet (1840–1926)

A Portrait of Oils

The unique characteristics of oil paint contributed to the accomplishments of the Renaissance—and still inspire artists today.

✳ ✳ ✳ ✳

PAINTINGS ARE AMONG the most ancient of artworks. More than 30,000 years ago, Neolithic painters decorated caves with patterns and images of animals. All paints include two elements: pigment and a liquid binder. Pigments from charred wood and colored minerals are ground into a fine powder. Then they are mixed into the binder; linseed oil is the most popular, but other oils, including walnut oil, are common.

The idea of using oil as a binder for pigment is very old, but oil paints as we know them are relatively modern. In the twelfth century, a German monk named Theophilus wrote about oil paint in his *Schoedula Diversarum Artium* and warned against paint recipes using olive oil because they required excessively long drying times. The Italian painter and writer Cennino Cennini described the technique of oil painting in his encyclo-pedic *Book of Art*. Oil paints came into general use in northern Europe, in the area of the Netherlands, by the fifteenth century and, from there, spread southward into Italy. Oils remained the medium of choice for most painters until the mid-twentieth century.

Oil paintings are usually done on wood panels or canvas, although paintings on stone and specialty paper are not uncom-mon. In any case, the support material is usually prepared with a ground to which oil paint easily adheres. Oil paints dry slowly, an advantage to artists, who adjust their compositions as they work. When the painting is done, a protective layer of varnish is often applied. In the nineteenth century, oil paint in tubes simplified the painter's work. A rainbow of innova-tive, synthetic colors contributed to the emergence of new approaches to art and, in particular, modern abstract painting.

Something Old, Something New

The Art Deco style perfectly captured the excitement and energy of a new century.

* * * *

THE PERIOD BETWEEN the two world wars was one of dramatic social, political, and technological change throughout the Western world. The old empires and aristocracies of the preceding five centuries had all but fallen away, replaced by democratic governments and a much looser, more egalitarian social order. The chasm between rich and poor narrowed dramatically, as the middle class grew and as entry to the wealthiest upper circles became easier through success in business and industry. New inventions allowed more leisure time for everyone; population centers shifted rapidly from rural areas to fast-paced urban settings; and prudish Victorian notions of morality were replaced by the fast and easy lifestyle of the Jazz Age. It was almost as if the entire world had been completely reinvented in a radical and exciting new way.

A Breath of Fresh Air

Inspired by this dizzying, liberating change, artists and designers attempted to reflect and represent their new, distinctly modern world while retaining what they found of value from the past. They embraced sleek, clean designs that combined geometric patterns and machine-tooled lines with traditional motifs, such as the female form and floral patterns. Artists combined natural materials such as jade, ivory, and chrome with new materials such as plastic, ferroconcrete, and vita glass. They merged elements of cutting-edge art movements such as Cubism and Bauhaus with traditional Greek, Roman, Egyptian, and Native American styles. And they applied their creation to all areas of this new modern world: buildings, fashion, posters, advertising, appliances, and furniture. The result was a sleek, elegant, sophisticated, and luxurious style now known as Art Deco.

Exposition Internationale des Arts Décoratifs

The trend toward this modern new world—and the graphic style that so perfectly represented it—developed gradually in the first two decades of the twentieth century. Art Deco saw its formal debut in 1925 at an exhibit held in Paris called the *Exposition Internationale des Arts Décoratifs et Industriels Moderne.* Designers and crafters from 23 countries displayed a breathtaking array of artifacts that together captured all that was innovative and exciting about the twentieth century. At the time, the movement was generally referred to as *style moderne;* it wasn't until decades later that the term *Art Deco*—derived from the name of the Paris exhibition—came into use.

The Movement Hits the States

Though the United States did not participate in the 1925 show, the country quickly became an influential force in the Art Deco movement. The style swept across America and figured prominently in Hollywood movies. Studios were quick to see that Art Deco offered an ideal visual shorthand for conveying sophistication, wealth, and elegance. Through the efforts of costumers, set designers, and prop masters, the movement soon became a familiar backdrop against which Greta Garbo, Bette Davis, William Powell, and Fred Astaire played out the fantasies of the nation on the silver screen. Even the grand movie palaces built in the 1920s and 1930s fully embraced the style, and the few that remain today offer excellent examples of the movement's influence on interior design. While Hollywood stars did little to define and shape the Art Deco style, they probably did more than anyone to popularize it, not only in the United States but also in Europe, where American films were screened regularly.

The American Quilt

Whether you curl up for a nap under your grandmother's quilt or do a little quilting yourself, rest assured, your interest in this beloved bedding is steeped in tradition.

✳　✳　✳　✳

The First Few Stitches

QUILTING IS THE process of sewing together layers of fabric and filler. The bottom layer is called the *backing,* the middle layer is the filling or *batting*, and the top layer is called, well, the *top*. The layers are sewn together to create cozy bedding or clothing.

People have been quilting—but not necessarily making quilted blankets—for a long time. An ivory carving from around 3600 B.C. depicts a king in a quilted cloak. Excavation of a Mongolian cave revealed a quilted linen carpet, and a pair of quilted slippers found near the Russia/China border was probably from the eighth or ninth century.

Patchwork, the process of piecing together scraps of fabric to make a larger whole, was widely practiced in Europe through the 1600s because it was economical. Old clothes and blankets were often recycled into something entirely new.

Early Amish Influence

The roots of the traditional quilt began to take hold in Europe and the United States in the eighteenth century. The oldest existing piece is the Saltonstall quilt. It was made in Massachusetts in 1704 and, though tattered, provides a window into the quilt-making styles of the era.

Amish settlers arrived in Pennsylvania in the early 1700s, and their quilts, known for jewel-toned fabrics and striking geometric patterns, surfaced in the 1800s. Our concept of patchwork quilts, patterns, and blocks has been greatly influenced by Amish quilters.

An Industrial Revolution

By the end of the eighteenth century, the textile industry in England had been fully mechanized, and the French were coming up with better, faster, and cleaner ways to dye fabric. Large quantities of colorfast, printed cottons became readily available, much to the delight of people everywhere.

By the time the War of Independence rolled around, the vast English textile industry was exporting thousands of tons of cotton to America. These fabrics made up the majority of the clothes and quilts of the era.

Social Hour

It's a misconception that people made quilts just for practical purposes. In fact, most quilters engaged in the hobby because they loved the craft—not because they needed a blanket. By 1820, sewing groups were widespread, allowing people to work together to sew quilts that were pulled across large frames. Many of the close-knit community sewing bees (or sewing circles) of yesterday still function as quilting guilds and clubs today.

Patterns and Designs

Though some quilters specialize in whole-cloth quilts, most of the quilts made today are of the patchwork variety. Pieces of fabric are sewn together to make a single block; multiple blocks are then stitched to each other, creating the quilt top.

One of the most admired quilt styles comes from Hawaii. These quilts incorporate just two colors—usually red and white—and one large cutout design sewn directly onto the quilt top. The striking geometric shapes and intricate stitching have made Hawaiian quilts popular among quilters and quilt admirers for two centuries.

Modern-Day Quilts

Quilting in the United States experienced a revival in the 1970s, largely due to the country's 200th birthday. As part of the celebration, women and men alike took a renewed interest in quilting and in folk art and crafts in general.

The surge in the popularity of quilting turned this humble pastime into the $3.3-billion-a-year industry it is today. The current movement toward more simple, eco-friendly lifestyles will likely keep quilting alive for years to come.

Inspiration Station

"Hi, I'm Alice. As in Wonderland."

Charles Dodgson, more commonly known by his pen name, Lewis Carroll, wrote *Alice's Adventures in Wonderland* in 1865. The story, as most people know, is a fantastical one, full of talking animals, bizarre circumstances, and one special little girl named Alice. The pipe-smoking caterpillar might have come from the recesses of Carroll's imagination, but the story's heroine was actually inspired by a real girl named Alice Liddell. Carroll was a friend of the Liddell family, and he met Alice when she was about four years old. Carroll often entertained the Liddell children with his wild tales. One day in 1862, Carroll was on a boating day trip with a reverend and the Liddell girls. Little Alice asked him for a story "with lots of nonsense in it." Carroll began making up a tale on the spot, and he placed Alice at the center of the story. Alice liked it so much, she asked Carroll to write it down; the rest is English literature history.

You Know You Love It: The Scoop on the Macarena

When Spanish singing duo Los Del Rio went to Caracas, Venezuela, in the early 1990s, they had no idea that the trip would result in a song that would soon be on the lips (and hips) of millions. According to the band, Antonio Romero and his singing partner Rafael Ruiz were watching an exceptionally talented flamenco dancer perform in a club in Caracas; the woman, whose name was Macarena, was so gifted that Romero was moved to blurt out, "Give your body joy, Macarena, that your body is to give joy and good things!" The duo put the words to music, added some backstory for their character, and called the piece "The Macarena."

The song was released in 1993 and became a hit in South America and on cruise ships. Then a couple of DJs known as The Bayside Boys got a hold of the track and made a club remix. The infectious song, with its Latin beat and unintelligible (for many people) lyrics, spread like wildfire across the United States and around the world. These days, no office Christmas party, wedding reception, or bar mitzvah is complete without a rousing group dance to "The Macarena."

Classy Chapeau

The pillbox hat, like the container from which it borrows its name, is compact, classy, and simple.

❋ ❋ ❋ ❋

HISTORICALLY, THE PILLBOX hat was first worn as a ceremonial military accessory, especially in Commonwealth countries. The Royal Canadian Military College, located in Kingston, Ontario, made the pillbox hat and accompanying chinstrap an essential element of the institution's dress uniform in 1878.

But it wasn't until the early 1960s—when Jacqueline Kennedy, the elegant wife of President John F. Kennedy, made it her chapeau of choice—that the hat's popularity soared. When Mrs. Kennedy wore a light-colored pillbox hat to her husband's inauguration ceremony in January 1961, American women flocked to the department stores in search of similar styles. Bob Dylan, the generation's most influential musician and spokesman of the street, heralded the hat in his song "Leopard-Skin Pill-Box Hat," off his multimillion-selling album *Blonde on Blonde*.

Much of the revival in pillbox popularity can be credited to renowned stylist Oleg Cassini, the man Mrs. Kennedy selected to design her extravagant gowns and complementary accessories. A couture designer famous for his millinery style, Cassini created the pillbox hats the First Lady wore so gracefully. Unfortunately, Mrs. Kennedy was also wearing a pillbox hat on November 22, 1963, when her husband was assassinated and died in her arms. The popularity of the pillbox hat declined sharply after that tragic day in Dallas, and the fashion has never regained the status held during the Kennedys' Camelot.

Toy Story

For almost 150 years, FAO Schwarz has been the first name in fun.

✳ ✳ ✳ ✳

N O NAME IS as synonymous with toys as FAO Schwarz. This paragon of playtime may be a New York institution, but it actually got its start in Baltimore.

The four Schwarz brothers left Germany for America in the mid-1800s. They settled in Baltimore, where they worked for Theodore Schwerdtmann, owner of a retail store for imported goods. Henry and younger brother Frederick August Otto (the "F.A.O." in FAO Schwarz) imported toys from other countries, including Germany, France, and Switzerland for Schwerdtmann & Co, which became Schwerdtmann & Schwarz in 1871. In 1870, Frederick left to open another branch, the Schwarz Toy Bazaar, in New York. Henry took over Schwerdtmann & Schwarz in 1872, and brothers Gustave and Richard ran their own toy stores in Philadelphia and Boston.

The brothers pooled their purchasing power to bring a wide variety of European toys and trinkets to American stores. At the time, stores that sold only toys were all but nonexistent. Most Americans gave their children handmade toys rather than store-bought playthings. There was no Toys "R" Us; instead, toys cropped up on a shelf or two at local general stores. Baltimore, however, was another story. A disproportionately large population of German immigrants lived in the shipping center. As the Schwarz clan tapped directly into that market, demand spread.

Frederick would often request specific changes from European manufacturers, making many of the toys on FAO's shelves

Schwarz exclusives. This practice became a tradition, as evidenced by the unique and lavish displays in the stores, particularly the giant keyboard made famous by Tom Hanks in the 1988 movie *Big*.

The venerable American toy icon experienced financial woes at the turn of the twenty-first century and changed ownership several times, but its flagship New York store continues to be a must-see attraction for tourists and toy enthusiasts alike.

The Story Behind *TIME*

Henry R. Luce spent his early years in China, where his parents worked as missionaries. Briton Hadden, the son of a stockbroker, grew up in Brooklyn. The two met at Connecticut's Hotchkiss School. Both went on to Yale, where they worked on the student newspaper, the *Yale Daily News*, and joined the secret society Skull and Bones. Though they had opposite personalities, they also had common literary interests. After struggling in journalism jobs after graduation, they agreed to collaborate on a news magazine. They approached fellow Bonesmen for funding and published the first issue of *TIME* in 1923. The erratic Hadden was the magazine's primary innovator, promoting the smug, reader-magnetic "we know everything" writing style that became known as "*TIME*style."

A mere two weeks after Hadden's untimely death in 1929, Luce took Hadden's name off *TIME*'s masthead. Hadden's will left his *TIME* stock to his family and stipulated that it was not to be sold for 49 years, but Luce had control of it within a year. His friends called him "Father *TIME*"; others called him "Il Luce," in reference to Italian dictator Benito Mussolini, who was called "Il Duce."

During and after World War II, Luce lost some of his journalistic balance and began yielding to propaganda. He was anticommunist and anti-isolationist, convinced that the United States must accept the mantle as the free world's bastion against the Red Menace. Though his prediction for the Cold War came true, the shift of focus in Luce's publications toward his political agenda was noted by readers and was not universally approved.

Luce also founded *Fortune* and *Sports Illustrated* and purchased and reinvented *Life* magazine. By the 1960s, he controlled the largest publishing empire in the United States. Luce's editorial reign at *TIME* lasted until his retirement in 1964, and he passed away in 1967.

From the Vaults of History

A Family That Stays Together...

In the long list of infamous criminals, few surpass the grisly accomplishments of Alexander "Sawney" Bean. Bean was the renowned head of a 48-member clan in sixteenth-century Scotland who has been accused of murdering and cannibalizing more than 40 people. While many historians claim that Bean never existed, his reputation for ambushing and eating innocent victims after hauling them back to his cave has fueled the Edinburgh tourism industry for hundreds of years.

According to legend, Bean and his family would ambush small groups of travelers. They would then rob and murder the victims, afterward dismembering and cannibalizing them. The leftovers were then carelessly tossed into the sea from the door of their secret cave. Eventually, the bodies would wash up on shore. The Beans' crime spree continued until they were captured alive and convicted of high crimes against humanity. The men were drawn and quartered and the women were burned at the stake. The story of the Beans has been made into a number of movies including Wes Craven's *The Hills Have Eyes*, Gary Sherman's *Death Line*, and Christian Viel's *Evil Breed*.

A Magnificent Mind

As a painter, Leonardo da Vinci is world renowned for his ability to inject life and emotion into his subjects, but surprisingly, he was not a proliferate painter—he painted only 31 pieces in his lifetime. Not to mention that one painting, *Virgin of the Rock* took more than 25 years to complete.

What undoubtedly consumed Leonardo's time were his interests as an Italian polymath, writer, architect, inventor, engineer, musician, painter, botanist, anatomist, and sculptor. He is credited with designing the first armored car in 1485, as well as the machine gun, the bicycle, glider, turnspit (for roasting meat), concave mirrors, water pump, movable bridge, parachute, the revolving stage, and even the first inflatable tube. Leonardo is also noted for his thorough study into the flight of birds as well as for his accurate drawings of human anatomy. One of the reasons historians have had a difficult time interpreting Leonardo's work is that he wrote all of his notes backward as mirror images.

Rope: A Year Tied at the Waist

Ever feel like you're tied down to your significant other? In 1983, two performance artists decided to take the idea to a literal extreme.

✳ ✳ ✳ ✳

The Inspiration

IT's EASY TO feel like you're attached at the hip to someone you see all the time. For Linda Montano and Tehching Hsieh, though, it was more than just a feeling. Montano (a female) and Hsieh (a male) actually had never met until she saw some examples of his work. A dialogue started, and they began to discuss a mutual project: a yearlong collaboration connecting art and life—literally.

In 1983, the performance artists decided to create an exhibit in which they would remain tied together by an eight-foot rope attached to their waists for exactly one year. The ground rules were simple: They would always be together, never remove the rope, and never touch. The artists say their inspiration came from the concept of communication and people's struggle to connect. As you can imagine, things got interesting.

The Routine

An average day started with Montano waking first and meditating, exercising, or watching television until her attached associate awoke. Once they were both up, they'd run or walk Linda's dog, do some work, then go sit back-to-back at their respective desks and think for five hours.

As far as going to the bathroom, the two say it was usually a rushed affair. Part of the deal required them to always be in the same room if they were indoors, so privacy was out of the question.

The Sex

The other common subject of question, sex, was also crossed off the list. By virtue of the "no-touch" rule, the artists agreed to abstain from any sexual contact for the entire yearlong period. Even though they could have theoretically touched other people (that wasn't disallowed), they decided it would only be an escape, and so it was banned.

Montano explained it best in a 1984 magazine interview: "I believe that in the next 200 years, we will all be in outer space, so why not practice outer-space sex now by letting astral bodies merge."

Uh, yeah.

The Danger

Our dynamic duo had only two close calls they can remember: the elevator incident and the tripping trouble. In the first, Hsieh walked into an elevator and the doors closed before his companion followed. He was able to hit the "door open" button just in time, but Montano said she had nightmares of being sliced in half for days. In the second scare, a passerby ran between the two on a crowded street and was almost clothes-lined. Once again though, disaster was averted. The only other physical danger the two reported revolved around their bike riding trips, when they rode in a single file fashion, artfully avoiding becoming tangled and/or mangled.

The Struggles

According to Montano and Hsieh, their relationship evolved over the months and brought about many less threatening challenges than one would think. In the early weeks, they spoke for hours every day. Eventually, they began getting annoyed with each other and pulled on the rope, leading to further anger. Next came the silent phase, when they would only gesture to indicate a need for food or bathroom. That led to an era of grunts and unintelligible noises—a time the artists referred to as a "beautiful regression."

It's worth noting that during the same period, Montano worked on a few other performance art pieces on her own: wearing only monochromatic clothes, listening to one note for seven hours every day, staying in a colored space for three hours a day, and starting to speak in a different accent every year. We couldn't make this stuff up if we tried.

Things You Don't Know (And Didn't Need to Know) About ... Donald Duck

Why does Donald Duck wear a shirt but no pants? We don't have the answer to that one, but we've covered just about everything else!

✳ ✳ ✳ ✳

✳ Donald Duck made his 1934 film debut in a cartoon about hens. You might not recognize him, though; he had a skinny neck, a longer bill, over-exaggerated feet, and a thicker body. A makeover in 1940 made him the duck he is today.

* Donald's middle name is Fauntleroy. His official birthday is June 9, 1934.

* Walt Disney discovered Clarence "Ducky" Nash (who created Donald's voice) on the radio. Nash was using that distinctive voice to act as a spokesman for a local business.

* Donna Duck was Donald's first girlfriend (1937). Ever the romantic, Donald's suave pick-up line was "Hiya, Toots!" He dumped Donna for Daisy Duck in 1940.

* Daisy is obviously very patient. She and Donald have been an item for 60 years but have never married . . . although they came close in 1954's *Donald's Diary*.

* Donald's uncle, Scrooge McDuck, was once listed in *Forbes* as the second wealthiest fictional character, with a net worth of just over $29 billion.

* It's easy to tell Donald Duck's nephews apart. Starting with *Duck Tales*, Huey wore red, Dewey wore blue, and Louie wore green.

* In some cartoon panels, Donald has *four* nephews, Huey, Dewey, Louie, and the one most widely called Phooey. Cartoon conspiracy theorists admit that the duckling's presence may have been a mistake or a misunderstanding.

* Though Donald is always basically a good-intentioned guy, he is known for his occasional outbursts. At least once, he was accused of profanity, causing a cartoon video to be pulled from shelves. Ain't that just ducky?

Behind the Best-Selling Posters of All Time

No teenager's room is complete without a poster or two. You remember your own favorites. You might even have them rolled up in your attic. But did you know...?

✳   ✳   ✳   ✳

✳ The photographer behind Farrah Fawcett's iconic, number-one-selling poster was hired to do a bikini shot with the actress. Fawcett didn't bring a bikini, but she had this red swimsuit, and the photographer had a Mexican blanket to use as a background. Sales: as high as 12 million copies.

✳ Actresses can be directed, snakes cannot. Thus, the famous poster image of Nastassja Kinski wearing a boa constrictor took over two hours to capture while the photographer waited for the snake to cooperate. Kinski lay naked on the cement the entire time until the snake finally slithered over the proper parts for the right shot. Sales: unknown.

✳ The famous poster of Marilyn Monroe with a billowing white dress wasn't originally intended to become a poster. Monroe was filmed walking over a subway grating in *The Seven Year Itch*; the shot was turned into a picture that still graces walls and halls. Sales: millions of copies.

✳ Bo Derek's romp on the beach in a Blake Edwards movie was another shot that wasn't originally meant as a poster. Bo Derek posters from her movies *Bolero* and *Tarzan the Ape Man* were also best-sellers. Sales: way more than 10.

✳ A fortuitous out-of-this-world photograph resulted in another of the best-selling posters of all time. NASA's *Apollo 17* astronauts snapped a picture of Earth from the vantage point of space to result in the famous so-called "Blue Marble" poster. Sales: unknown.

Santa, Is that You?

America's Santa Claus owes a big thank-you to a German artist.

* * * *

THOMAS NAST IS famous in American history as the cartoonist whose drawings brought down Boss Tweed. Less well known is that jolly ol' Santa Claus might look very different today if it wasn't for Nast.

Ho, Ho, Er . . . Who Are You?

Initially Santa's image followed his origins as St. Nicholas, and he was often depicted as a stern, lean, patriarchal figure in flowing religious robes. Around the year 1300, however, St. Nicholas adopted the flowing white beard of the Northern European god Odin. Years passed, and once across the Atlantic Ocean (and in America), Nicholas began to look more like a gnome. He shrunk in size, often smoked a Dutch-style pipe, and dressed in various styles of clothing that made him seem like anything from a secondhand-store fugitive to a character from *1001 Arabian Nights*. One eerie 1837 picture shows him with baleful, beady black eyes and an evil smirk.

Santa Savior

Into this muddled situation stepped Nast. As a cartoonist for the national newspaper *Harper's Weekly*, the Bavarian-born Nast often depicted grim subjects such as war and death. When given the option to draw St. Nicholas, he jumped at the opportunity to do something joyful. His first Santa Claus cartoon appeared in January 1863, and he continued to produce them for more than two decades.

Nast put a twinkle in Santa's eye, increased his stature to full-size and round-bellied, and gave him a jolly temperament. Nast's Santa ran a workshop at the North Pole, wore a red suit trimmed in white, and carried around a list of good and bad children.

Nast surrounded Santa Claus with symbols of Christmas: toys, holly, mistletoe, wishful children, a reindeer-drawn sleigh on a snowy roof, and stockings hung by the fireplace. Nast tied all these previously disparate images together to form a complete picture of Santa and Christmas. Other artists later refined Santa Claus, but it was Thomas Nast who first made Santa into a Christmas story.

Things You Don't Know (And Didn't Need to Know) About… Barbie

"Born" in 1959 and sold worldwide, Barbara Millicent Roberts is one of the most popular dolls ever. The average American girl has ten of them. But what do you really know about Barbie? Read on…

✳   ✳   ✳   ✳

✳ Barbie is a Leo. Her parents' names are George and Margaret. She grew up in Willows, Wisconsin, and graduated from Willows High School. While there is no mention of higher education, she has had more than 100 different careers. Model seems to be the main one.

✳ Barbie sported a ponytail for the first two years of her career. She got her first new 'do in 1961, when she started wearing a bubble cut. Two years later, she got wigs. She decided to grow her hair out in 1967 and has kept it long ever since.

✳ While Barbie was meant, in part, as a toy to inspire little girls to "do anything," Barbie had self-esteem issues of her own. Until Malibu Barbie hit the scene in 1971 (with her forward-friendly eye contact), Barbie could only manage demure, sidelong glances.

✳ Maybe the problem stemmed from her dieting habits.

Included with the outfit for Barbie Baby Sits was a book called *How to Lose Weight* with the advice "Don't eat." To underscore that, Barbie Slumber Party included a scale that only went up to 110 pounds.

* Barbie got her first house in 1962. Perhaps because it was mostly cardboard (as was the furniture), Barbie and her many pals continued to live half-naked beneath countless little girls' beds.

* Barbie was blissfully single until 1961, when Ken Carson came into her life. They broke up on Valentine's Day 2004. She kept the house. They're still friends.

* When Twist 'N Turn Barbie was introduced in 1967, Mattel offered the new doll at reduced prices with the trade-in of an older Barbie. The old dolls—undoubtedly worth a lot now—were donated to charity. That Barbie! She's such a doll!

Inspiration Station

Painting a Play

August Wilson's ten-play epic, *Pittsburgh Cycle*, depicts the experiences of Black America in each decade of the twentieth century. The installment set in the 1930s, *The Piano Lesson*, won Wilson his second Pulitzer Prize and is regarded as one of his finest works. What some people don't know is that the play was inspired by a painting of the same name by artist Romare Bearden. The story goes that Wilson was viewing the painting when he suddenly turned to a friend and announced, "This is my next play." Wilson, who wrote *The Piano Lesson* in 1989 and passed away in 2005, said, "In Bearden I found my artistic mentor and sought, and still aspire, to make my plays the equal of his canvasses."

The Weirder, the Better

Pretty pictures of idyllic landscapes, tidy portraits of good-looking people—this was not the stuff that moved legendary photographer Diane Arbus to take pictures. Instead, Arbus was inspired by what society deemed ugly and captured the image with a camera that inspired her, as well. Fascinated by the "freaks" exhibited at circus sideshows and the down-and-out characters that lurked in New York's seedy Bowery district, Arbus treated all of her ragged subjects with awed respect and referred to them as aristocrats. "I really believe there are things nobody would see if I didn't photograph them," she said.

In 1962, Arbus found inspiration in the tool she used to make the art itself: She swapped her old Nikon for a larger-format camera that produced large, square negatives and finished prints that made everyone (even conventionally attractive celebrities like Mae West) look grotesque and stark. The result was arresting. The images inspire in the viewer a range of feelings, everything from fear to pity, from reverence to love.

Men's Societies

A fraternal organization is a group of men who bond through rituals, handshakes, and sometimes uniforms. They usually have overlapping missions, whether emphasizing fellowship, patriotism, religion, or philanthropy, and most are particularly active in community service. Here are some of the most recognizable, along with notable members past and present.

✳ ✳ ✳ ✳

Moose International, Inc.: Founded in 1913, the Family Fraternity, often called the Loyal Order of Moose (and Women of the Moose), is a nonsectarian and nonpolitical organization. Moose International headquarters, in Mooseheart, Illinois, oversees 2,000 lodges, 1,600 chapters, and approximately 1.5 million members throughout the United States, Canada, Great Britain, and Bermuda. According to the group's mission statement, the moose was selected as the namesake animal because "it is a large, powerful animal, but one which is a protector, not a predator."

Moose members are active in their communities, contributing nearly $90 million worth of service every year to charities and social causes in their hometowns.

Famous Moose: Presidents Franklin D. Roosevelt and Harry S. Truman, actor Jimmy Stewart, athletes Arnold Palmer and Cal Ripken Sr., and U.S. Supreme Court Chief Justice Earl Warren.

The Benevolent and Protective Order of Elks of the United States of America: This organization was founded in 1868, making it one of the oldest fraternal organizations in the country. The order has more than 1 million members working in some 2,100 communities, with headquarters in Chicago. The Elks' mission is to promote the principles of charity, justice, brotherly love, and fidelity; encourage belief in God; support members' welfare and enhance their happiness; bolster patriotism; cultivate good fellowship; and actively support community charities and activities. A major component of the Elks' mission is working with and mentoring youngsters.

Famous Elks: Presidents John F. Kennedy and Gerald Ford, actor Clint Eastwood, football coach Vince Lombardi, and baseball greats Casey Stengel and Mickey Mantle.

Lions Clubs International: The world's largest service organization, Lions Clubs International includes some 45,000 clubs and 1.3 million members in 200 countries around the world. The international headquarters is in Oak Brook, Illinois. The organization was founded in 1917 in the United States and became international in 1920 when the first Canadian club was established in Windsor, Ontario. All funds raised from the general public are used for charitable purposes, and members pay all administrative costs. Since the Lions Clubs International Foundation began in 1968, it has awarded nearly 8,000 grants (totaling $566 million) to assist victims of natural disasters, fight physical and mental disabilities, and serve youth causes.

Famous Lions: President Jimmy Carter, racecar driver Johnny Ruterford, explorer Admiral Richard Byrd, and basketball star Larry Byrd.

Masons: The Freemasons belong to the oldest fraternal organization in the world. Today, there are more than 2 million Freemasons in North America. Freemasonry, or Masonry, is dedicated to the "Brotherhood of Man under the Fatherhood of God." Masonry's principal purpose is "to make good men better." No one knows exactly how old the movement is, but many historians believe it arose from the powerful guilds of stonemasons of the Middle Ages. In 1717, Masonry became a formal organization when four lodges in London formed England's first Grand Lodge. The oldest jurisdiction on the European continent is the Grand Orient de France, founded in 1728.

Famous Masons: George Washington, James Monroe, Wolfgang A. Mozart, John Glenn, and Harry Houdini.

The National Geographic Society

Ah, for the days when knowledge was hip. On January 13, 1888, an impressive group of people met in Washington, D.C., to consider a new project. Pooling their curiosity about the world and its peoples, they launched an organization devoted to advancing geographical knowledge: the National Geographic Society. You might recognize the names of some of those founders, especially telephone inventor Alexander Graham Bell.

About six months after its founding, the society started a semi-scholarly journal. Anyone who's ever waited in a dentist's office has seen *National Geographic* magazine. Vol. I, #1 contained a message from the society president, geographic and geological studies, notes on a recent storm, and the society by-laws. Judging by the first issue's membership list, most early members worked for the U.S. Geological Survey or the U.S. Coast & Geodetic Survey.

Today the society is one of the most visible nonprofit research organizations in the world, a font of captivating photography and geographic journalism. The youngest founder was 23-year-old geologist Robert Muldrow II. A decade later, he would become the first to measure Mount McKinley's altitude by instrument. The last surviving founding member of the National Geographic Society, he died July 28, 1950, age 86.

The Intelligence on IQ Tests

IQ scores are best known as quantitative representations of a person's intelligence. Yet the original IQ test was intended to predict future scholastic achievement, not intelligence.

✳   ✳   ✳   ✳

Relatively Smart?

THE FAMED DUMBBELL Forrest Gump had an IQ of 75, but he did pretty well for himself. He was a military hero, savvy businessman, exceptional table tennis player, and beloved son, husband, and father. An IQ test is supposed to measure intelligence, but there is much debate over what an IQ score actually means.

A person's intelligence quotient is calculated according to his or her performance on a standardized test. This means that the score is not derived from how many questions are answered correctly but on how many the person gets right relative to others who have taken the same test. IQ tests are usually standardized so that 100 is the mean score, and half of the scores lie within 10 points of the mean—so half the population has an IQ between 90 and 110. "IQ test" actually refers to a number of popular tests that are standardized in a similar fashion, such as the Wechsler or Stanford-Binet tests.

The first IQ test was developed in the late 1800s, hand-in-hand with the appearance of special-education programs in schools. Administrators needed a reliable way to identify those who were unable to learn as easily or quickly as others. From the beginning, then, IQ tests were meant to measure one's ability to perform academic tasks; this is not necessarily synonymous with intelligence.

Kinds of Smart

IQ test questions measure such functions as short-term memory, vocabulary, perceptual speed, and visual-spatial reasoning. These are all skills that help a person succeed in a school, work, or even social environment. Not surprisingly, high IQ scores are positively correlated with one's future academic success. They are also correlated, though not as strongly, with the socioeconomic status of one's parents, as well as on future income and future job performance.

Many researchers have pointed out that IQ tests neglect to calculate many types of talent that could also fall under the "intelligence" heading. Psychologist Howard Gardner developed his theory of multiple intelligences, which include linguistic, logical-mathematical, spatial, bodily-kinesthetic, musical, interpersonal, intrapersonal, and naturalist. Many multiple-intelligence tests try to include indicators of "books smarts," "street smarts," and "creativity smarts."

Testing IQ Tests

The reliability of IQ tests as meters of intelligence is also suspect because, on average, African American, Native American, and other minority or immigrant populations score lower than populations of Euro-American descent. These minority groups tend to come from areas where there is a high dropout rate and limited access to quality education. IQ tests are administered in standard English, which partly accounts for the low scores (especially in the verbal section) among people who speak other dialects of English or English as a second language.

The Ku Klux Klan: A Southern Phenomenon?

Since the first Ku Klux Klan formed in Tennessee in 1865, the white sheet and hood have symbolized intimidation and ethnic hatred. Although the Klan was born in Dixie, many of its power bases have been—and remain— far outside the former Confederacy.

✳ ✳ ✳ ✳

The First Klan: Politics by Other Means

To UNDERSTAND THE first Ku Klux Klan, one must understand the times. The same year that Robert E. Lee surrendered to Ulysses S. Grant, numerous former Confederate citizens decided that if they couldn't have their old status quo on paper, they'd have it in practice. This meant keeping the Democratic Party in state and local power, which would occur only if Republican-sympathizing African Americans didn't vote. The Ku Klux Klan's primary aim was to suppress black voting.

The first KKK was less a centralized organization than a handy label adopted by ad hoc local political terrorists and racists. Those types also existed in non-Southern states but were less likely to call themselves Klansmen. General public revulsion at Klan tactics led to the Ku Klux Klan Act of 1871, which started sending members to jail for civil-rights violations. Membership waned to a few die-hards.

The Second Klan: Loyal Order of Hoodlums in Hoods

This Klan, born from the general hoopla over the 1915 film sensation *Birth of a Nation*, soon went mainstream and national. Its focus was anti-Catholic, anti-Communist, anti-immigrant, anti-Semitic, and anti-African American. Some KKK members lynched and burned, but for most it was a social pastime much like a fraternal lodge. This Klan boasted millions of members.

Politically and numerically, the Klan was strongest in Illinois, Indiana, and Michigan, with lesser power bases in California, Oregon, and the South. Woodrow Wilson praised it, and evidence indicates that Warren G. Harding joined it. Its downfall began with a 1925 violent-assault scandal, then accelerated with the onset of the Depression and the rise of Hitler in Germany. This was the deepest KKK penetration of government and society, but it was more Midwestern than Southern; by World War II, it had subsided to a few thousand hardcore bigots.

The Civil Rights–Era Klan: White Supremacy

The 1950s brought a national movement toward any good Klansman's worst nightmare: African Americans as equal participants in society. Again the Klan rose, though in nothing resembling the numbers of the 1920s. This version was much like the first Klan—mostly Southern, with tentacles in other regions, balkanized into numerous groups competing for the sympathies of militant racists.

This time the atrocities occurred in the light of modern mass media, as the nation watched Klan violence on the nightly news. Anyone trying to excuse the Ku Klux Klan as a harmless social club looked delusional, and in the mainstream American psyche, the Klan bedsheet came to emblemize terrorism. After losing the war against the civil-rights movement, the Klan once again receded to several thousand members.

The Modern Klan: Stolen Thunder

By the 1980s, the Klan had become a minor player in racist subculture. Christian identity, neo-Nazism, and the skinhead movement attracted many who would have raided their linen closets in another era. In the past, police had at least attempted to protect civil-rights demonstrators from Klan violence; now angry crowds rained scorn on KKK rallies. Only police protection shielded Klansmen from the brand of violence their ideological forebears used to dish out.

By 2006, the Ku Klux Klan consisted of scattered islets dotting the map from Maine to Louisiana to California. Thus, the Klan does have Southern roots and a Southern presence, but it has often taken on a decidedly Northern and Western character.

Things to Do at Carnaval

Carnaval, thought to come from the Latin carne and vale, which literally translates to "goodbye meat," is a four-day pre-Lent party held throughout Brazil with dancing, music, and elaborate destaques (costumes).

✳ ✳ ✳ ✳

THOSE LUCKY ENOUGH to experience Carnaval should be sure to add the following to their to-do list:

Enjoy the taste of fresh acai: This wonder berry is just beginning to be touted by the health conscious in the rest of the world for its amazing antioxidants, omegas, and nutrients. Brazilians have enjoyed the chocolate and tart berry taste of *acai* for years. It's usually mixed with guarana, an energy-boosting berry. The taste is unusual for first-timers, but after a few rounds of this power-packed combo, they have energy to spare.

Join a samba school: Samba, the sexy hip-shaking moves that pulse through *Carnaval*, is taken seriously in Brazil. Those thousands of dancers aren't just drunk locals, they're part of various samba schools throughout Rio de Janeiro. The point of all the over-the-top costumes, singing, and displays is to win votes. The parade in the Sambodromo arena is actually a competition, and schools practice year-round to be crowned winner of Carnaval.

For much-needed financial support, schools let in a few outsiders to learn the samba and the school's theme song. While no one expects an outsider to be a *passissta* (the best dancers and often the most scantily clad), the schools are being judged throughout the chaos, and one misplaced feather or sloppy hip shake could cost vital points. Visitors should bring their A-game if they hope to participate in the true spirit and intensity of Carnaval.

Skip Rio and do Carnaval in Bahia: Brazil's strong African roots are most present in the region of Bahia. Here, Carnaval takes place in Salvador. The dancing is just as zesty, but costuming is less significant, and the music is performed by bands atop slowly moving trucks. Depending on whom you ask, many consider this to be the best Carnaval celebration in all of Brazil.

Oddball Beauty Pageants

Not all contests are only skin deep.

✳   ✳   ✳   ✳

THERE ARE AS many kinds of beauty pageants as there are hobbies, sports, and cultural obsessions. If you're a Star Trek fan, a beach bum with an artistic bent, or the proud owner of a bushy beard or moustache, these are for you.

Klingon Nation

Every year, Trekkies (or, as they prefer to be called, "Trekkers") gather in Atlanta for a Star Trek Convention that includes the Miss Klingon Empire Beauty Pageant. Contestants can compete as established female Klingon characters, or if they prefer, they can invent their own original characters. Contestants are judged on beauty, personality, and talent, but they are warned on the official website that the talent portion should not get too wild and crazy: "no flaming *bat'leth* twirling."

Shell Games

Hermit crabs may not be known for their beauty, but don't tell that to the organizers of the Miss Curvaceous Crustacean Beauty Pageant in Virginia Beach, Virginia. It isn't the crabs so much as their themed habitats that are judged in this annual beachfront event, and there seems to be no end to the unique ideas that contestants dream up as they surround their hermit crabs with elaborate environments. Past winners had such themes as "Hermit the Hulk," "Spider Crab," and "Beauty and the Crab."

It'll Grow on You

At the Annual World Beard and Moustache Championship, held in the past in both America and Europe, Germans usually take the top honors, but American contestants are muscling in. There may be other changes coming soon, as well: In 2003, a bearded woman became the first female to join the National Beard Registry, an Internet facial hair group, and some feel that it's only a matter of time before a bearded lady will join the men as a winner.

Night Flight

Muhammad was just another guy running a caravan business. Then, in A.D. 610, the angel Gabriel came calling with news that Muhammad had been chosen to spread the word of God.

✳   ✳   ✳   ✳

(Editor's note: This story has many variations. This is one of them.)

THE QUR'AN TELLS the story of the miracle of Muhammad's trip from Mecca to Jerusalem to heaven and back to Mecca—all in a single night. Often referred to as "Muhammad's Night Flight," or the "Night of Ascension," this tale starts with Muhammad receiving a visit from the angel Gabriel on the twenty-seventh night of Rajab (the seventh lunar month of the Islamic calendar) in A.D. 621. To prepare for his trip, Gabriel cut open Muhammad's chest, washed his heart to purify it, then emptied a powder into his chest to increase his wisdom and strengthen his faith.

Gabriel also provided a special means of transportation for Muhammad called al-Buraq, a magical white horse with a stride as far as the eye could see. Mounting the creature, Muhammad and Gabriel began their journey.

The Good, the Bad, and the Ugly

During the trip to Jerusalem, the prophet saw people who were planting and harvesting in just two days. Gabriel explained that they were being rewarded for fighting for Allah. When they rode by people whose lips and tongues were pinched shut with scissors of fire, Gabriel explained that they were being punished for lying. Muhammad also saw angels using stones to repeatedly crush people's heads; these people would regain their shape only to be smashed again. According to Gabriel, these people were being punished for not praying before sleeping.

With prayer stops at Mt. Sinai and Bethlehem, Muhammad and Gabriel made it to Jerusalem. There, waiting for them at the Temple Mount, were all of the previous prophets of God. Because God held Muhammad in higher regard than the others, he was chosen to lead the other prophets in salat (ritual prayer).

All Prophets Go to Heaven

Then it was time for Muhammad to ascend to heaven on a staircase of alternating steps of gold and silver. Muhammad and Gabriel entered the first level of heaven and journeyed through all seven levels, meeting such prophets as John, Jesus, Joseph, Idris, Aaron, Moses, and Abraham. Each prophet gave Muhammad their blessing to become the last prophet of Allah.

From the seven levels, Muhammad went on to paradise, witnessing the favors that God had for the faithful including the Hurul'In, women created by Allah who were neither human or jinn (creatures created from a smokeless flame), and the *wildan ul-mukhalladun*, very beautiful servants of the inhabitants of paradise. It was promised that even the person who had the least status in paradise would have 10,000 *wildan ul-mukhalla-*

dun to serve him, each carrying a tray of gold and a tray of silver.

Muhammad then ascended past paradise to meet Allah, who told Muhammad to command the faithful to pray 50 times a day. Moses, concerned that the faithful would not keep to God's commandment, convinced Muhammad to return to the presence of Allah repeatedly to reduce the number of daily requirements. Eventually, God reduced the requirement of daily prayer to five.

There and Back Again

Heading back to Jerusalem via the gold and silver stairway, Muhammad rode his magical horse back to Mecca. Many people questioned his story the next day, but Muhammad described every aspect of the mosque in Jerusalem and also said that he noticed on his way back to Mecca where their sheep were grazing and described shepherds looking for a lost camel. Muhammad even described the camel in detail; his description was confirmed when the shepherds returned from the fields.

Although some assert that Muhammad's journey was spiritual, most of the faithful believe it was a physical journey. The Night of Ascension is usually celebrated with prayers, the lighting of cities with electric lights and candles, and readings of the legend, called Laylat al-Mi'raj ("Night of the Ascension").

The Bunny Hype

Everyone knows that rabbits do not lay eggs. So how did a colored-egg-toting bunny become associated with Easter?

✳   ✳   ✳   ✳

IT IS SOMETIMES claimed that rabbits and eggs are fertility symbols associated with springtime, and their connection to Easter is a simple derivation of ancient pagan practices. Not so fast. Rabbits are indeed a symbol of fertility, because they reproduce like—well, rabbits. And it makes sense that ancient pagans associated the advent of spring—the time of rebirth, renewal, and new life—with rabbits and eggs.

Why decorate hard-boiled eggs for Easter? This custom may have originated among Christians in the Middle Ages, when eating eggs was prohibited during Lent, the 40 days leading up to Easter. The faithful broke the Lenten fast with an Easter celebration that included feasting on brightly colored hard-boiled eggs—which were probably plentiful by that time.

Where did the idea of an egg-carrying rabbit come from? One theory points to hares' tendency to overbuild when it comes to home construction. Hares raise their young in hollows in the ground and sometimes separate them into multiple nests for safety's sake. People hunting for eggs may have found them near, or even in, an unused hare's nest—appropriated by some resourceful bird—and came to the mistaken conclusion that the hares had laid eggs.

This confusion may have become the foundation for an old German myth about "Oschter haws" (Easter hare), which laid eggs in gardens for good children to find. German immigrants brought the legend of the Easter hare to America (along with the story about a shadow-sighting groundhog). In the United States, rabbits are more plentiful than hares, and the egg-bearing bunny soon became part of the folklore of Easter.

Things You Don't Know (And Didn't Need to Know) About... Bugs Bunny

Shhhhhh. Be vewy, vewy quiet. We're hunting wabbit twivia. We know it's awound here somewhewh.

✳ ✳ ✳ ✳

✳ The Oscar-winning rabbit made his unofficial debut in 1938 in *Porky's Hare Hunt*, a Porky Pig cartoon. He was eventually named by accident: Because the director of that cartoon, Ben Hardaway, was nicknamed "Bugs," preliminary sketches were identified as "Bugs' bunny."

* Had director Fred "Tex" Avery (who is widely given credit for creating the Bugs we know) had his way, Bugs would've been called Jack E. Rabbit.

* The familiar "What's Up, Doc?" came from Avery, who'd spent his teen years hearing the question from neighbors and high school classmates. Since 1940, almost every Bugs Bunny cartoon has included those three words (or a variation thereof).

* There was a Mrs. Bugs Bunny—at least for a few minutes. The little, uh, woman appeared in 1942's *Hold the Lion, Please!* Later comic books gave Bugs a girlfriend named Honey Bunny.

* Broccoli and celery growers once begged Warner Bros. (Bugs's studio) to allow the Wascally Wabbit to replace the carrot by sampling their crops too. The studio said no. Mel Blanc, the voice behind Bugs Bunny, was not allergic to carrots, by the way. He reportedly just didn't like them.

* Blanc was also the voice of Barney Rubble, Daffy Duck, Mr. Spacely on *The Jetsons*, Twiki on *Buck Rogers in the 25th Century*, and some 400 other characters.

* Bugs Bunny has his own star on Hollywood's Walk of Fame. He appeared on a U.S. postage stamp in 1998. And yes, he really did win an Oscar in 1958.

* Th-th-th-th-th-that's all, folks!

In Defense of Animal Rights

For centuries, everyone from farmers to philosophers had argued over the concept of cruelty toward animals. In 1824, an Irish politician finally took steps to make it stop.

✳   ✳   ✳

ODAY, THE SOCIETY for the Prevention of Cruelty to Animals is an international organization. It began, however, with a bill in the English Parliament in 1822. The sponsor of the bill was Colonel Richard "Humanity Dick" Martin, scion of a prominent Irish family and a member of Parliament from Galway. "Martin's Act," as it was known, was intended to "Prevent the Cruel and Improper Treatment of Cattle" and applied to all livestock, including "Horses, Mares, Geldings, Mules, Asses, Cows, Heifers, Steers, Oxen, Sheep, and other Cattle." Individuals convicted of perpetrating such abuse were to pay a fine "not exceeding five pounds, not less than ten shillings" or "be committed to the House of Correction or some other prison . . . for any time not exceeding three months."

Early Efforts to Protect Animals

The earliest laws protecting animals date to the seventeenth century. A 1635 law in Ireland made it an offense to pull wool from a sheep or to attach a plough to a horse's tail. In 1641, the Massachusetts Bay Colony decreed "No man shall exercise any tirrany or crueltie toward any bruite creature which are usualie kept for man's use." During the government of Oliver Cromwell in England, the Puritans opposed blood sports like cockfighting and bull baiting. Citing the Old Testament book of Genesis, they argued that God made men responsible for the welfare of animals but did not make men their owners.

The SPCA in Great Britain and the United States

Martin convened a meeting with fellow animal rights activists and in 1824 formed the Society for the Prevention of Cruelty to Animals (SPCA). The SPCA sent inspectors to slaughterhouses to ensure that animals were held and killed humanely. Inspectors also monitored the treatment that carriage horses received from coachmen and cab drivers. In 1840, the organization was granted a royal charter by Queen Victoria and became the Royal Society for the Prevention of Cruelty to Animals (RSPCA).

In 1866, Henry Bergh founded the American Society for the Prevention of Cruelty to Animals (ASPCA). Bergh was incensed by the ill treatment of animals he witnessed while working as a diplomat in Russia. With the assistance of the RSPCA in London, he successfully lobbied for anticruelty laws in New York State and persuaded the state to give the ASPCA the authority to enforce the laws.

Bergh earned the moniker "The Great Meddler" for his efforts on behalf of what he called "these mute servants of mankind." As Bergh wrote in a letter to a reporter after the creation of the ASPCA, "Day after day I am in slaughterhouses, or lying in wait at midnight with a squad of police near some dog pit. Lifting a fallen horse to his feet, penetrating buildings where I inspect collars and saddles for raw flesh, then lecturing in public schools to children, and again to adult societies. Thus my whole life is spent."

The ASPCA did not ignore the welfare of cats and dogs. According to the information in its first annual report in 1867, one David Heath was sentenced to ten days in prison for beating a cat to death. When the judge read his verdict, Heath was reported as saying "the arresting officer ought to be disemboweled." For that remark, Heath received an additional penalty of $25.

Bergh's concern for helpless creatures did not stop with livestock and pets. In 1874, he and others from the ASPCA rescued a little girl named Mary Ellen, the victim of vicious abuse in the aptly named New York neighborhood, Hell's Kitchen. Bergh's efforts led to the founding of the New York Society for the Prevention of Cruelty to Children in 1875.

※ Chapter 3

The Cycles of War, Revolution, & Justice

Famous Revolutionary Organizations: Where There's a Will, There's a Warrior

Since time began, people have formed organizations that espouse their political, social, cultural, or nationalistic ideas. These groups come from every walk of life, every continent, and every era. The only commonality they share is their passion for what they believe—ideas for which they will give anything, including their lives.

※　※　※　※

Carbonari

WHILE IT IS unknown whether the group originally developed in France or Italy, the Carbonari, or "charcoal burners," derived their philosophy from the ideals of the French Revolution and the Enlightenment. Primarily a political organization, the Carbonari opposed absolutism and desired the establishment of a republic or, second-best, a constitutional monarchy in Italy. The society had a clearly delineated, hierarchical structure, not unlike that of the Freemasons. Like many other revolutionary organizations, the Carbonari were not averse to using violence to achieve their goals.

Black Hand

While this underground sect, whose more official name is Unification or Death, is sometimes grouped with secret societies, it is more often defined as a terrorist organization. Established in 1911 in Serbia from the remnants of the more mainstream pan-slavic organization National Defense, the Black Hand was dedicated to forming a greater Serbia. Violence was the group's primary tool. A member of the Black Hand assassinated Archduke Franz Ferdinand in 1914. The fallout from this act resulted in World War I.

The Fenians

Even before the Norman Conquest, the Irish struggled to assert their independence from English influence. In the mid-1850s, a more organized resistance to English rule began to develop in the form of the Fenian Brotherhood. The name comes from the *Fianna*, legendary soldiers of Ireland. Although the term *Fenian* applies to the broader movement, most Fenians belonged to the Irish Republican Brotherhood—which actually originated in the United States in 1858. The revolutionary group saw armed conflict as the primary tool for achieving independence from England.

Satyagraha

Indian independence leader Mohandas Gandhi originated a philosophy of social action called *satyagraha*. It was derived, in part, from the Hindu concept of *ahimsa*, a principle of non-injury. *Satyagraha* further developed into a campaign of civil disobedience and non-violent resistance as the people of India agitated for freedom from British rule. The Indian National Congress, the oldest political organization in India and a major force in the crusade to free India, adopted *satyagraha* under Gandhi's leadership in the 1920s. Satyagraha helped lead to the eventual independence of India in 1947 and influenced numerous other nonviolent struggles throughout the world, including the American civil rights movement of the 1960s.

Tongmenghui

Founded in Tokyo in 1905, Tongmenghui was also called the Chinese United League or the Chinese Revolutionary Alliance. Led by Sun Yat-Sen and Song Jiaoren, the secret organization was designed to unify the disparate antimonarchy forces within China. It encompassed republicans, nationalists, and socialists. In addition to governmental change, Tongmenghui also sought social revolution with the reestablishment of Chinese culture and agricultural revolution in the form of land redistribution.

The Bolsheviks

Their name derived from the Russian word for "majority," the Bolsheviks were a splinter group from the more mainstream Social Democratic Labor party. With Vladimir Lenin as their leader, the Bolshevik faction argued that the agrarian class should be the power base for the impending Marxist revolution, while their opponents (later called the Menshevik, or "minority," by Lenin) believed that anyone committed to Marxist ideals should be included. The more extreme view of the Bolsheviks eventually won the day; they became the ruling Communist party of Russia in March 1918.

Mutiny on the *Potemkin*

At the beginning of 1905, the Russian empire was in a state of flux. The populace churned with discontent, and the autocratic power of Czar Nicholas II was in danger of collapse. At the time, the average worker in the Russian industrial complex labored a punishing 11-hour workday, with the slight break of a 10-hour workday on Saturday. Worker safety was not a high priority; conditions were extremely poor. Unrest was spreading throughout Russia.

✳ ✳ ✳ ✳

STRIKE!

IN JANUARY 1905, four members of the Assembly of Russian Workers were unfairly dismissed from their jobs at the

Putilov Iron Works in St. Petersburg, resulting in a general strike. The strike was organized by Father George Gapon, the founder of the labor union and a Russian Orthodox priest. Eventually, more than 100,000 people refused to return to work. Within a week, business and daily life in St. Petersburg had ground to a halt—the city had no electricity or gas to stand against the brutal Russian winter, no newspapers were being printed, and public areas were closed.

Gapon decided to make a personal appeal to the czar. On January 22, having received 135,000 signatures on a petition demanding a shorter workday, increased wages, and better working conditions, he led a large group of unarmed workers and their wives and children to present the petition to Czar Nicholas II. As the crowd neared the palace, the police and the czar's Cossack soldiers opened fire, killing and wounding scores of laborers and their families. The incident would come to be known as Bloody Sunday.

The exact number of casualties is unknown. The official count produced by the government listed 96 killed and 300 injured, but labor groups claimed that up to 4,000 had been killed or wounded. Lenin would later comment that, on the day after the violence, "St. Petersburg looked like a city just conquered by an enemy." News of Bloody Sunday spread throughout the Russian Empire, exacerbating the already strained relationship between the czar's government and the populace. Labor unions went on strike in response to the news; renters attacked their property owners and refused to pay their rents.

In addition to the strain of Bloody Sunday, the Russian Empire had been locked in bitter conflict with the Japanese regarding Manchuria and Korea since February 1904. The relatively younger and inexperienced Japanese army had gained a number of decisive victories over the Russians, and by the middle of 1905, the Russian navy was devastated and broken. The conflict culminated in May 1905 with the Battle of Tsushima, which left the Baltic Sea and Eastern fleets destroyed; only the Black Sea Fleet remained.

Unrest at Sea

In June 1905, morale in the Black Sea Fleet was at an all-time low. The Central Committee of the Social Democratic Organization of the Black Sea Fleet was planning a simultaneous uprising on all ships to occur sometime in the autumn. Aboard the *Potemkin*, one of the most advanced ships in the fleet, trouble was brewing. Weeks of poor food and cruel treatment at the hands of the ship's officers had created resentment among the enlisted men. However, the *Potemkin* was isolated from the rest of the fleet on artillery drill orders at Tendra Island in the Black Sea, and the crew was unaware of the planned fleetwide mutiny.

Discontent among the crew came to a boil when the ship took on meat containing maggots. The crew complained and refused to eat the putrid meat. The ship's medical officer pronounced the meat suitable for consumption, claiming the maggots were dead and would cause no harm. A borscht was made from the rotten meat. The crew protested, refusing to eat the borscht, and purchased food from the ship's store, instead. When the second in command of the ship, Ippolit Giliarovsky, became aware of this, he ordered 12 of the men who had refused to eat the stew be executed at random.

As men were chosen and armed marines prepared to fire, a sailor named Afanasy Matushenko, who served as the ship's torpedo quartermaster, spoke up. "Comrades," he said, "don't forget your oath! Don't shoot at our own men!"

The marines did not fire. Instead, acting on Matushenko's orders, the sailors took up arms against the officers who had oppressed them. In moments, seven officers lay dead. Some accounts suggest that Matushenko was the one who shot Giliarovsky. The medical officer who had declared the meat suitable for human consumption was also killed in the uprising.

One sailor, Grigory Vakulinchuk, was mortally wounded. The bodies of the officers were thrown overboard, and the officers who had not been killed in the mutiny were driven overboard themselves.

Arriving in Odessa

That evening, the *Potemkin* arrived at the port of Odessa, where a general strike was already under way. The authorities in the port city refused to refuel and resupply the ship, but they did allow Vakulinchuk's body to be brought ashore. The following day, his funeral procession became a political event, with many of the striking populace turning out to support the crew of the *Potemkin*. Some accounts of the event report that police and soldiers opened fire on the crowd, killing as many as 2,000. The *Potemkin* left port.

Showdown

Two squadrons of the Black Sea fleet were dispatched to apprehend the *Potemkin*. The joint squadron gathered at Tendra Island and bore down on the mutinous ship. However, placing faith in their comrades among the squadron, the *Potemkin* sailed straight into and through the line of ships and emerged on the other side unscathed.

The *Potemkin* sailed to the Romanian port of Constanta, where the crew attempted to restock. The authorities, however, refused to resupply the ship. Desperately in need of fuel and food, the ship sailed for the Russian port of Theodosia but received a similarly cold reception there. Eventually, it returned to Constanta, where the *Potemkin* surrendered to Romanian authorities on July 8, 1905.

Although the crew of the *Potemkin* did not succeed in defeating the czarist regime, a revolutionary seed had been planted in the Russian navy. Sailors were involved in mutinies up to and after the decisive revolution of 1917. Lenin would later write that the *Potemkin* uprising had been the first attempt at creating "the nucleus of a revolutionary military force."

The *Potemkin* mutiny is also notable for the film it inspired. Sergei Eisenstein's *The Battleship Potemkin* is widely regarded as one of the most influential films of all time. It is most famous for the sequence on the Odessa steps; this confrontation forms the climax of Eisenstein's film. That scene has been re-created in homage by several filmmakers, most notably by director Brian De Palma in the film *The Untouchables* and Francis Ford Coppola in *The Godfather*.

The IRA and Sinn Féin

The Irish Republican Army (IRA) and its political body, Sinn Féin, are two of the most controversial institutions in Ireland. Deciphering their history is like trying to trace the lineages of the old European monarchies—there are countless crossbreedings, divergences, and circuitously snaking twists along the way.

✳   ✳   ✳   ✳

Back to the Beginning

THE ENGLISH INFILTRATION of Ireland began in A.D. 1170, when the Normans, who had already colonized England, decided to make Ireland a part of their kingdom. In the following centuries, the Irish increasingly adopted the customs, system of government, and language of their English neighbors. For the Irish clans that continued to rule and practice their customs, English dominion was a constant threat.

Since the northern tip of Ireland is the farthest from England, the population there retained a culture distinct from the southern areas of the island. But in the early 1600s, Queen Elizabeth I established the Plantation of Ulster in Northern Ireland, and colonists from England, Scotland, and Wales flooded the land. The native Irish Catholics in Ulster were forced to the margins of society.

Thus began the sectarian struggle in Northern Ireland that continued for centuries. The largely Protestant descendants of

the colonization of Ulster fought—militarily, culturally, ideo-
logically—with the largely Catholic descendants of the area's
original inhabitants. It was within this inflammatory context
that the IRA and Sinn Féin emerged.

The Early Days of Sinn Féin and the IRA

According to Irish political lingo, those who seek a united
Ireland free from English rule are called nationalists, while
those who desire continued political allegiance with England
are called unionists. Sinn Féin was founded as a political party
in 1905 by a nationalist who wanted Ireland to establish its
own monarchy. During this same period, a group of young
revolutionary nationalists sought to establish a socialist democracy in Ireland. They built up an army and staged the famous
Easter Rising of 1916. Although the rebellion was quickly
suppressed, supporters of the nationalist movement formed
the Irish Republican Army in the following years. The political
party Sinn Féin had been mistakenly credited with the Easter
Rising, so from that point on, it was considered the political
arm of the IRA.

The Irish War of Independence, which consisted of bloody
guerrilla warfare between England and the IRA, was fought
between 1919 and 1921. The Anglo-Irish treaty of 1922 officially liberated the southern 26 counties of Ireland from
English rule but kept the 6 counties of Northern Ireland under
English control. Sinn Féin negotiated the treaty, but some party
members were none too happy with the decision to divide
Ireland. When the agreement was ratified, many members of
Sinn Féin defected, taking with them the anti-treaty contingent
of the IRA.

Civil war ensued. The pro-treaty forces in Ireland, assisted
by the English, won the war. The Irish Free State (now the
Republic of Ireland) gained its independence, while Northern
Ireland remained part of the United Kingdom.

Schism in the Party

After the end of the civil war, Sinn Féin split. Some members founded the new Free State's political parties, while those opposing the government became a radical political party that would not participate in the parliament. The IRA became a fringe paramilitary group, also consisting of those who refused to accept the existence of the Free State or acknowledge that Northern Ireland was part of the United Kingdom. During the 1940s, 1950s, and 1960s, the IRA carried out attacks on police stations in Northern Ireland and staged political assassinations and intermittent bombings.

During the 1960s, many members of Sinn Féin adopted a more Marxist outlook. They began to denounce the bloody tactics of the IRA. At the same time, violence and rioting continued in Northern Ireland, where nationalists and Catholics protested the civil rights abuses that were practiced against them by Protestants and unionists.

In an attempt to abstain from violence, the IRA failed to protect the Catholic communities of Northern Ireland and the group splintered. The Official IRA and the Official Sinn Féin favored a peaceful approach to securing a united Ireland. The Provisional IRA and Provisional Sinn Féin, however, believed that violence was the answer. They also continued to abstain from parliamentary politics. The Official Sinn Féin has since morphed into other Irish leftist parties, such as the Labour Party and the Workers Party. The IRA and Sinn Féin of today are descendants of the Provisional IRA and Sinn Féin.

The Troubled Pathway to Peace

In 1972, British paratroopers killed 14 unarmed demonstrators in what became known as the Bloody Sunday massacre. In the aftermath of this event, IRA membership dramatically increased. The IRA became a clandestine operation with a complex and ambiguous network of terrorist cells, while Sinn Féin sought to establish itself as a legitimate political party. The

British government suppressed the IRA and its sympathizers: During the 1970s and 1980s, thousands of political prisoners were arrested. Meanwhile, the IRA terrorized communities in Northern Ireland, murdering or torturing civilians suspected of being informants. They also started bombing England.

The popularity of Sinn Féin was jeopardized by the unpopularity of the IRA. Most nationalists in Northern Ireland, while sympathetic to the IRA, preferred a peaceful approach to negotiations with England. In 1986, Sinn Féin leader Gerry Adams sought to bring the party into mainstream politics, while a group led by Ruairí Ó Brádaigh refused to do so until a united, free Ireland was established. The latter group broke off to form the radical Republican Sinn Féin.

Progress at Last

Adams's Sinn Féin is now a major player in Irish politics. In 1997, an IRA cease-fire was declared. In 1998, the monumental Belfast Agreement paved the way for self-determination for Northern Ireland. Yet the implementation of the agreement remains troubled. One provision was that the IRA decommission all of its weapons, and indeed this qualification has been met. Sinn Féin denies any connection with violence instigated by those claiming affiliation with the IRA, but allegations have been made against top Sinn Féin officials regarding their continued involvement. Moreover, some Sinn Féin officials have been accused of being double agents for the UK.

As for the IRA, violence continues under the auspices of newly created fringe groups such as the "Real IRA." Sinn Féin's connection with the IRA remains ambiguous, yet its popularity has grown substantially due to its involvement in the peace process and its support of reforms in areas such as health care and minority rights. Sinn Féin is now the largest nationalist party in Ireland.

The Hundred Years War Lasted How Long?

The answer is complicated—the Hundred Years War lasted both more and less than 100 years, depending on how you look at it.

✳ ✳ ✳ ✳

THE HUNDRED YEARS War was an extraordinarily complicated conflict with far-reaching effects. Piecing together its history requires tracing the tangled genealogy of the royal houses of England and France, not to mention sorting out shifting allegiances, territorial rights, and interspersed civil wars.

The conflict's name is a confusing misnomer. If you tally time from the day war was declared in 1337 to the date of the final treaty that ended it in 1453, the war lasted 116 years. The actual conflict was not continuous, however. There were several periods of declared peace when there were years between active campaigns. If you add up the times of actual fighting, the war lasted only 81 years.

The Fight Explained

This time the two nations weren't fighting over just territory; the prize was the throne of France itself. The last king who ruled France's House of Capet died without a son, and two royal families vied for the open crown.

The House of Valois was a junior line of the royal Capets—it descended from the younger brother of King Philip IV. The House of Plantagenet, the ruling family of England, held its primary claim to the French throne through English King Edward II's queen, Isabella of France, who was Philip IV's only daughter. When she married Edward, a clause in her marriage contract stated that her sons would be in line to inherit both the French and English crowns. When her last brother, Charles IV, died without a son, Isabella claimed France for her son, Edward III, by right of this contract—as Philip IV's grandson, he was the only male directly descended from the House of Capet's senior line. The French weren't keen on a foreign king, however, and they resisted, citing ancient Salic law, which prohibited women from inheriting the throne or anyone from inheriting the crown *through* a female. Instead of accepting Edward, they crowned Philip of Valois, Charles's cousin through his father's younger brother.

A War in Phases

The first phase of the war was initiated in 1337 by England's Edward III, who invaded after the French refused him the throne. Edward's campaigns were interrupted several times by delays and the intervening Breton War of Succession, but they were able to deal the French several devastating defeats. At Poitiers, the French king was captured and the country fell into chaos, but Edward was unable to take Paris and negotiated the Treaty of Bretigny in 1360.

Nine years later, France's Charles V resumed hostilities. Over the next 20 years, the French managed to regain much of their lost territory before making peace with Richard II in 1389. England was kept busy with civil strife until 1415, when Henry V invaded, determined to take the French crown. He was stunningly successful, especially at the Battle of Agincourt, and he forced a treaty that gained him significant territory and the French king's daughter. Although they officially named their future sons as heirs to the French throne, Henry's gains didn't last long after his death.

France finally gained the upper hand in 1429, when Joan of Arc, supposedly following the word of God, led a relief force that helped the French defeat the English during the siege of Orleans. Over the next quarter century, France continued to see victory after victory, until the English were finally forced to abandon all of France except for the region around Calais.

Legally Speaking

Every day, in addition to the thousands of people who deliberately and maliciously perform illegal acts, there are thousands more who inadvertently break laws and statutes that are outdated, outlandish, and somewhat amusing—but still on the books. These are America's forgotten laws. What's not so funny is that most are still enforceable.

✳ ✳ ✳ ✳

✳ Kentucky's 100-year-old "Infidel" law effectively bans any non-Christian religious publication from public schools— and most public schools across the state have reinforced the ban in their policy manuals. One old Kentucky law that should be enforced is the statute that requires all residents of the state to bathe once a year.

✳ In Los Angeles, it's unlawful to bathe two babies in the same bathtub simultaneously.

✳ Maine has a law that bans the sale of cars on Sunday. (Does Detroit know about this?)

✳ You can go to jail for taking a bite out of someone else's hamburger in Oklahoma. You'll also be violating the law of the Sooner State if you make faces at a dog.

✳ In Boston, it's okay to kiss in public—as long as it isn't in front of a church or on Sunday: That's the day when all displays of public affection are against the law.

✳ If you're planning on going to a movie in Gary, Indiana, watch what you eat. It's illegal to go to a theater within four hours of eating garlic.

✳ It's illegal to tie a giraffe to a telephone pole in Atlanta.

✳ If you put a penny in your ear, you're in violation of Hawaiian law.

* Several states have laws that only allow sex between heterosexuals—and only in the missionary position.

* In Port Arthur, Texas, it's against the law to emit any obnoxious odor in an elevator.

Fast Facts

* The oldest military medal? Probably the Gold of Valor. It was awarded by the Egyptian pharaohs around 1500 B.C.

* What's with General George Patton's ivory-handled revolvers? He started carrying revolvers in 1916 after he nearly blew his own leg off with the Army's newfangled automatic pistol.

* The last soldier of World War II, Japan's Lieutenant Hiroo Onoda, didn't surrender until 1974, having fought a guerilla war on the Philippine island of Lubang since early 1945. For 29 years, he refused to be fooled by ridiculous Allied stories about the war ending in 1945 and only gave up the fight after his old unit commander was flown to the Philippines and ordered him to lay down his arms.

* Sailing into space: Pieces of Germany's High Seas Fleet, scuttled off Scotland at the end of World War I, have been used to build deep-space probes.

* The longest-running mercenary contract belongs to the world's smallest standing army—the Vatican's Swiss Guards, a 100-man company first hired by Pope Julius II in 1506.

* Britain's early twentieth-century super-weapon, the battleship H.M.S. *Dreadnought*, was fitted with ultramodern weapons, so her builders naturally omitted the ancient ram from her design. Her only kill was a submarine, which she sunk by ramming it.

* During his invasion of England in 1014, King Olaf's fleet of Viking ships managed to pull down London's wooden Thames River bridge. (Hence, the children's song "London Bridge Is Falling Down.")

Medievally Executed

In contrast to popular belief and medieval myth, crime and punishment in the days of yore wasn't all guts and gore.

✳   ✳   ✳   ✳

ALTHOUGH EXECUTIONS MAY be uncommon these days, they were regular events until the late twentieth century. Humankind even invented "humane" ways of sending a convicted criminal to the eternal prison, methods that include the gas chamber, electric chair, and lethal injection. Culprits from medieval times were escorted off this mortal coil by more macabre methods, none of which could be considered morally acceptable by today's standards. Here's the story behind the history.

Lightweight Laws

Common criminals weren't drawn and quartered for petty insults, nor were they sentenced for their transgressions by mob justice without the benefit of a formal inquiry. There were judges and there were trials, and though justice was swift, it was rarely sudden. Hearings lasted less than half an hour, and judges often deliberated and delivered the verdict themselves. In today's system, prison terms are handed out like traffic tickets, but offenders in medieval times were subjected to a "three strikes" policy. If a person was caught committing a crime for a third time, he or she was ushered out of town, which kept the jails uncluttered and the streets safe. The malcontent was sent elsewhere to transgress in a new location. Banishment, not beheading, was the rule of the day. Considering that most common people spent their entire lives within 10 to 15 miles of where they'd been born, being sent away from everything they'd ever known was serious punishment.

Sentences Fit the Crimes

Significant offenses such as murder and arson were treated seriously, often resulting in capital punishment. Most of these wrongdoers met their fate at the end of a rope, which was the preferred method of execution.

Being burned at the stake was the designated demise for pagans and heretics. It was a common punishment in the earlier years of the Protestant Reformation, and the definition of a heretic changed depending on who was in power. In England, Henry VIII split from the Catholic Church, but he still burned Protestants such as Anne Askew. His son, Edward VI, was a devout Protestant, however, and being Catholic during his reign could lead one to the stake. This Catholic/Protestant persecution switched once more after Mary I was crowned, and then back again with Elizabeth I.

The rack was one of the stake's partners in criminal justice. It was used to extract confessions and to persuade those already judged guilty to accuse others. Being put to the rack was a torment for commoners only, since it was considered uncouth to torture a member of the nobility. However, jailers had few compunctions about racking a commoner in order to get him to implicate a noble.

Nobles convicted of high treason were spared the traditional drawing and quartering. Instead, they were beheaded—having one's head lopped off with a swift swipe of the blade was considered a "privileged" way to die. The honor was dubious, though, since the ax was usually dull, and it often took several swings before the head was severed.

The Opium War

Contrary to popular belief, the Anglo-Chinese War, otherwise known as the Opium War, was not waged to keep China from exporting opium to Britain.

✳ ✳ ✳ ✳

BETWEEN 1839 AND 1842, Britain and China fought the Opium War to prevent widespread British trafficking of the illegal drug into China. The war resulted in a decisive defeat for China, which was forced to import British shipments of the narcotic.

Britain's Drug Trade

In the early nineteenth century, Britain was the world's largest trafficker of illegal drugs, dwarfing the activity of any of today's South American drug cartels. It shipped tons of opium annually from its plantations in India to Canton, China, in exchange for Chinese goods such as tea. This was despite the fact that the trade and consumption of opium was illegal in Britain because of its harmful effects. The trade had a devastating impact on Chinese society—an estimated 27 percent of the adult male population was addicted to the drug by 1906.

Opposition to Opium

In 1836, the imperial Chinese government made opium illegal and started closing down the vast number of opium dens that littered the country. British trade in the drug continued, however, thanks to widespread bribery and corruption. In 1839, when the morally resolute Lin Tse-hsu became Imperial Commissioner at Canton, he had the British stores of opium destroyed and requested that Britain's Queen Victoria cease trade in the drug. When Chinese boats attempted to prevent English merchant vessels from entering Canton in November 1839, war broke out and the British immediately deployed warships to the area. The Chinese suffered humiliating defeats to the technologically superior British and were forced to agree to the Treaty of Nanking. This gave Britain control of Hong Kong, and over the next 30 years, opium trade to China more than doubled.

The Colorado Coal Field War

During the early 1900s, Colorado Fuel & Iron (CF&I), owned by John D. Rockefeller Jr. dominated mining in Colorado's Southern Coal Field. Miners were paid per ton of coal mined, so they received no payment for mine repair or maintenance work. Since the company owned all rental housing and shops, the system simply recycled wage dollars through the company's coffers.

In August 1913, Southern Coal Field miners went on strike to demand union recognition, eight-hour days, hourly pay, and the right to trade and live anywhere they wished. Company police evicted all strikers from company property, so the families moved to tent cities organized to defend against strikebreakers. The strikebreakers marauded with searchlights, random beatings, and occasional machine-gun hosings from the "Death Special"—a primitive armored car.

Soon CF&I executives asked themselves: "Why spend money on thugs? That's what the Colorado National Guard is for!" The governor obliged; the Guard arrived in October. Neutral at first, the Guard soon continued the terror. On April 20, 1914—just after Easter celebrations—the Guard assaulted, machine-gunned, sacked, and burned a camp at Ludlow. There were 21 fatalities, more than half of whom were women and children. The miners shot back at the Guard and began wrecking mines. Only the arrival of federal troops ended the "Ten-Day War." The strike finally ended in December 1914.

The miners lost the shooting war but won the PR war. Upton Sinclair led demonstrations against Rockefeller in New York and excoriated the media for covering up the ugly truth. Within a few years, the companies met most union demands.

The Coal Field War's last known survivor was Mary Benich McCleary, an 18-month-old tot on April 20. In the midst of the attack on that day, a teenage boy scooped up baby Mary in his jacket and ran, saving her life. Ms. McCleary passed away on June 28, 2007, at age 94.

The Battle of Lake Erie

On September 10, 1813, an American flotilla under Commodore Oliver H. Perry faced a British flotilla off modern Sandusky, Ohio, for control of the Great Lakes. The fleets were tiny, but neither side had anything larger available in Lake Erie.

The Americans' shorter-range but heavier cannon dictated the need to fight the British at close quarters. Perry's flagship, USS *Lawrence*, ran a gauntlet of British cannon fire to close with HMS *Detroit*, while her comrade USS *Niagara* at first failed to close with her own designated target, HMS *Queen Charlotte*. When *Lawrence* was beaten to a pulp, Perry transferred his flag to *Niagara*. Crashing the British line in *Niagara*, Perry cut loose with both broadsides. *Queen Charlotte* and *Detroit* collided in the confusion, hampering their ability to return effective fire. After three hours of battle, the British struck their colors and were captured.

The Battle of Lake Erie was a major victory on the northern front in the War of 1812. It led to the recapture of Detroit (which had been taken by the British in August 1812) and forced the combined British and Native American forces (led by British General Procter and the Shawnee Chief Tecumseh) to flee to Canada.

The Battle of the Alamo

The siege of Alamo Mission, San Antonio de Valero, Republic of Texas, from February 23 to March 6, 1836, was part of Mexico's effort to subdue an insurgency. The Alamo Mission itself wasn't much of a fort, but General Antonio López de Santa Anna had to capture it if he wished to put down the Texan rebellion. Some 180 or so defenders, plus noncombatant women and children, holed up in the mission under Colonel William Travis, who hoped for reinforcements but got none.

On March 6, Santa Anna's numerically superior forces stormed the Alamo Mission, capturing it within three hours and ultimately killing (in some cases, executing) all its defenders, including Davy Crockett and Jim Bowie. The exact number of Mexican casualties is unknown but is estimated to have been about triple the Texan losses. The battle became one of history's great rallying cries, especially for the Texans, who avenged the Alamo six weeks later in the surprise attack at San Jacinto.

Order of Sons of America

The struggle for civil rights in Texas often focused on Mexican Americans. One organization came together to join the battle.

✳   ✳   ✳   ✳

I N THE EARLY twentieth century, Mexican Americans were subject to prejudice, abuse, and mistreatment by American citizens. Many felt that this was their lot in life—an unchangeable constant they'd simply have to endure. Historical journals are rife with factual accounts of prejudices and mistreatments visited upon Mexicans by the very group with whom they wished to assimilate. Like any minority lacking for power, most who suffered through such hardships kept their heads down and prayed for the best. More often than not, however, their prayers went unanswered. A smaller number of individuals took a more proactive approach. And a select few of these managed to change the world. Thirty-seven men bonded together to form the Mexican American civil rights organization Orden Hijos de America (Order of Sons of America). Texas would never be the same.

A Grand Stand

In the early 1920s, Ramon H. Carvajal operated a barbershop in San Antonio. As in other such establishments, banter of all types was casually traded back and forth. A favored topic among haircutters and customers was politics. While many Mexican Americans differed on the preferred path toward their emancipation, most agreed that something had to be done.

Rather than merely dream of pie in the sky, one group of determined men decided to take concrete steps to aid their people. On October 13, 1921, they banded together to form a new Hispanic civil rights organization that became one of only a handful of such groups then operating in Texas. The Order of Sons of America (OSA) would meet Hispanic oppressors head on, fighting the good fight against anything or anyone that it deemed abusive.

This was no small task, of course. Bigotry, ignorance, and preconceived notions about Hispanics had a firm grip on many Texans. A change in accepted norms would require a stiff, uphill battle.

The Prevailing Climate

To appreciate what the OSA was up against, it helps to have a feel for the period. Texas during the 1920s was a land fraught with divisiveness and distrust. A mighty wave of some 219,000 Mexican immigrants arrived in the United States between 1910 and 1920, doubling the state's Hispanic population. These people came predominantly for the mining, railroad, and agriculture work that was being offered in the Southwestern states. The intense demand for low-wage physical labor offered an answer to hungry Mexicans fleeing a country rife with economic instability.

When World War I drew to a close at the end of the decade, however, an economic recession produced a severe backlash against Mexican immigration. With only so many jobs to go around, newcomers were sometimes viewed as interlopers. And Mexican immigrants were no exception. Serving to inflame the situation, an estimated 500,000 Mexicans entered the United States during the mid-1920s. Like the group who had come before them, the majority found jobs in physical labor. Not surprisingly, long-brewing resentments soon reached a fever pitch.

A Mob Mentality

A number of Texans feeling displaced and powerless by the

ever-increasing migration north decided to push back. And push they did. Ethnic slurs against Mexican Americans became commonplace. Mob violence and intimidation increased sharply. By the late 1920s, an estimated 600 Mexican immigrants had been lynched.

Even the Texas Rangers played a role in the repression of Mexican Americans. It is estimated that hundreds, if not thousands, were killed outright by the famous law-enforcement agency. And such abuses had a snowball effect. Mexican Americans were quickly losing whatever small significance they had, becoming politically disenfranchised from the land that they'd hoped to call their home. Clearly, something needed to be done.

The Seed Grows

Founders John C. Solis, Francisco and Melchor Leyton, and Santiago G. Tafolla Sr. turned their idea of establishing a political organization into reality by first obtaining a state charter in January 1922. The OSA pledged to use its "influence in all fields of social, economic, and political action in order to realize the greatest enjoyment possible of all the rights and privileges and prerogatives extended by the American Constitution."

A charter, first drawn up in English and later in Spanish, added that the OSA would function as a mutual aid society, a civic group, and a pro-labor machine. Chapters began to spring up in numerous Texas towns, with each concentrating in specific areas of expertise. The Corpus Christi and San Antonio chapters, for instance, were most active in civil rights activities.

The OSA quickly went to work righting wrongs. In Corpus Christi, it fought to erect a new Mexican school. As a direct result of its efforts, the Cheston L. Heath School opened in September 1925. In 1926, the organization helped desegregate the all-white Palace Bath House. In 1927, it managed to seat the first Mexican American on a jury in Nueces County. Later that year it won the right to remove a blatantly prejudicial "No

Mexicans Allowed" sign from North Beach. There seemed to be precious little that the OSA couldn't accomplish when its members put their minds to it. But their days were numbered. Change was blowing in the air.

The OSA's Legacy

Despite winning scores of battles for Mexican American citizens, however, the OSA was short-lived. Splinter groups that began forming only a few years after the OSA's inception would eventually weaken it by siphoning off key members. By 1929, Orden Hijos de America had all but dissolved. Eventually, it would be displaced entirely by other civil rights organizations, the majority of which would morph into the League of United Latin-American Citizens, commonly known as LULAC. That organization, more than 150,000 strong, thrives to this very day. It owes its existence to the Order of Sons of America and those 37 brave souls who had the audacity to proclaim "enough is enough."

✳ The earliest Spanish-language newspaper definitively known to have been published in Texas was the *Nacogdoches Mexican Advocate* in 1929. One side was printed in Spanish, with English on the other.

The Bombardment of Fort Sumter

The first assault of the Civil War, lasting more than 34 hours, was launched after months of standoff.

✳   ✳   ✳   ✳

O N DECEMBER 26, 1860, Major Robert Anderson and 70 Federals under his command rowed from their garrison at South Carolina's Fort Moultrie to the more secure Fort Sumter in Charleston Harbor. After South Carolina's secession from the Union six days earlier, Anderson—a Southerner loyal to the Union—felt the move to the more defensible fort was necessary to ensure the safety of his soldiers.

Starting the War

Fort Sumter offered little strategic value, but it meant everything to both sides. To the North, it symbolized the United States. To the South, it represented the right to leave that Union.

Although President Abraham Lincoln, newly inaugurated in March 1861, swore to defend federal property within the seceded states, he also pledged that the Union wouldn't fire the first shot. He announced plans to send supply boats to bring "food for hungry men." Confederate President Jefferson Davis, however, decided to wage war anyway. On April 12, 1861, four Confederate emissaries rowed to Fort Sumter and called for surrender. Anderson refused, and the Confederates opened fire around 4:30 A.M.

The South Wins the First Battle

After more than a day of shelling leveled part of the fort and set the interior afire, Anderson realized further defense was futile. He evacuated the fort, and the Confederates allowed him to return North.

Like Dominoes Falling on the River

Forts Henry and Donelson, guarding strategic rivers in Confederate territory, held the key to success for an ailing federal army.

✳ ✳ ✳ ✳

CIGAR-CHOMPING UNION GENERAL Ulysses S. Grant was courageous and aggressive, but in 1862 he needed a second chance to prove his leadership. He had left the army back in 1854 only to go on to a succession of failed business ventures.

At the same time, the Union as a whole needed a second chance—an opportunity to prove that it could turn its industrial superiority and the numerical advantage of its soldiers into significant battlefield victories. So far, after almost a year of war, the Federals had not proven themselves to be a fine fighting machine.

Action in the West

In February 1862, the highly strategic Confederate Forts Henry and Donelson in northwestern Tennessee provided both Grant and the Union military the opportunities they were looking for.

Fort Henry sat on the Tennessee River. Though the river offered an ideal invasion route into the South, Union generals were unsure about attacking the haphazardly defended fort. Not Grant, though. He and Commodore Andrew H. Foote proposed a joint land-water assault on Henry, which was finally approved by their superiors.

A Naval Operation

Army and navy were intended to attack together, but when cold, wet, and muddy conditions delayed Grant, Foote started without him. On February 6, his force of ironclads and wooden gunboats began shelling the fort heavily. Confederate General Lloyd Tilghman and his soldiers fiercely fought back as long as they could, but Tilghman finally surrendered to Foote just before Grant's mud-caked troops arrived on the scene. It soon became evident that, amazingly, there had only been about 100 soldiers in this rebel force—Tilghman had ordered the bulk of his troops to Fort Donelson 12 miles east, while he stayed behind to defend Henry.

Onto the Next Stop

Fort Donelson was next on Grant's list. A military prize, it lay on the Cumberland River leading directly into Nashville, an industrial center and Confederate state capital. What's more, Donelson's commanding officer was General John Floyd, a former U.S. secretary of war who was wanted by the federal authorities for allegedly having transferred arms to the South.

Grant and Foote attacked on February 13 and soon had Fort

Donelson in a choke hold, squeezed by land troops on three sides and floating artillery on the fourth. Somehow, two days later, the rebels broke out of one side and drove the Union forces back a mile—but the Union pushed back and forced the Confederates back into the fort.

That night, General Floyd and General Gideon J. Pillow passed command of Donelson to General Simon Boliver Buckner and fled, taking some troops with them. Ironically, Buckner was a friend of Grant who had loaned him money during his "down-and-out" period in the 1850s. No one knows if that act of friendship was on his mind when he sent Grant a request for terms of surrender.

Unconditional Surrender

Grant may not have realized that Buckner was now in command of the fort, but if he did, sentiment apparently had no effect on him. His response was, "No terms except unconditional and immediate surrender can be accepted."

Capturing Henry and Donelson was a rewarding victory for the Federals. They took control of most of Kentucky and Tennessee, used the Tennessee and Cumberland rivers as supply lines, and made Nashville a supply center for the Union army in the West.

Fire on the Waters

The battle for the Mississippi River was a make-or-break effort for both North and South.

✳   ✳   ✳   ✳

AFTER WINFIELD SCOTT's blockade of Confederate ports went into effect in 1861, the only unfettered trade route left open to the Confederacy came through Mexico. To reach the South's mills and armies, that route had to cross the Mississippi River. If the Union could take control of the Mississippi, it would cut the Confederacy in two, and the

South's trade with the rest of the world would effectively be over.

Taking Charge in New Orleans

One end of the Mississippi, New Orleans, swiftly fell to the Union navy, but to control the waters further north, river navies would be necessary, and both sides began in earnest. With shipbuilding centers in St. Louis, Louisville, and Cincinnati, the Union had a definite edge, and soon a fleet of ironclads, gunboats, and transports were fighting their way south toward Vicksburg. On July 1, 1862, two pincers closed in on that river city, but the Union didn't control the water just yet.

Confederate Resistance

The South fought back, building makeshift warships in local boat-yards. When the powerful Confederate ironclad *Arkansas*, under construction at Memphis, was moved to the headwaters of the Yazoo River just above Vicksburg for completion, Admiral David Glasgow Farragut sent the Union ironclad *Carondelet*, the gun-boat *Tyler*, and the ram *Queen of the West* up the Yazoo to find her in mid-July. He discovered the *Arkansas* was far stronger than he'd expected. The Confederate ironclad badly damaged the *Carondelet* and chased the other two boats away, and then it approached Vicksburg without warning. No Union vessel had steam up, so the *Arkansas* chugged past, exchanging fire with 20 Union ships, devastating three of them and disabling the ram *Lancaster*. But the *Arkansas* was damaged as well, losing an eighth of its crew. In a dramatic moment following the clash, as the ship sailed alongside the Vicksburg waterfront, cheering spectators saw how badly it had been damaged and fell silent.

Farragut ordered the *Essex* and the *Queen of the West* to attack the *Arkansas* at its moorings. The *Essex* ran aground, and for ten minutes the two ships blasted away at one another, their heavy armor protecting them from fatal damage. Losing power, the *Essex* floated away downstream. The *Queen of the West* rammed the *Arkansas* but did no great damage, leaving the *Arkansas* a still-potent threat.

Further Down the River

Downstream at Baton Rouge, Confederate General John C. Breckinridge attacked the Union troops who, with the aid of the *Essex* and two gunboats, were holding the city. The Confederates had counted on the *Arkansas* coming to help them, but it had not arrived.

Unbeknownst to Breckinridge, the *Arkansas*, which had not been fully repaired, had broken down just north of Baton Rouge. Seeing her smoke, the *Essex* sailed to investigate. Under intense fire from the *Essex*, the *Arkansas* ran aground and, set afire by her crew, exploded and sank.

Switching Sides

The *Arkansas* had died nobly, but the game was not yet over. Southerners were still shipping supplies from Louisiana, so in February 1863, Admiral David Dixon Porter sent the *Queen of the West* down to blockade the Red River. Unfortunately, the ram came under fire from shore batteries, was hit and, ultimately, captured by the Confederates. While the Southerners repaired the *Queen*, Porter, unaware of what had happened, sent the new ironclad *Indianola* down to join it. When the *Indianola's* skipper, George Brown, saw the *Queen of the West* coming toward him in the company of the rebel ram *Webb* and two Confederate gunboats, he tried to flee up the Mississippi, but the rebels caught the *Indianola* and drove it ashore.

Psych!

Admiral Porter, realizing that the *Indianola* was in enemy hands but not knowing its condition, plotted to delay any potential salvage the Confederates might have planned. Using an abandoned flatboat, he built a dummy ironclad and set it adrift. With smoke-pots in her "smokestacks," she looked like the South's worst nightmare. When the crews attempting to salvage the *Indianola* saw this formidable monster coming, they panicked, burned the *Indianola*, and fled. Union forces reached the *Indianola* in enough time, however, that they put the fire out and reclaimed the ironclad without too much damage.

The Mississippi finally came under complete Union control a few months later. On July 4, 1863, after dozens of river and land battles, Vicksburg finally surrendered. As Lincoln declared, "The Father of Waters once more goes unvexed to the sea."

The Oddness of Stonewall Jackson

Despite his reputation as a great warrior for the South, Stonewall Jackson was one of the Confederacy's quirkiest heroes.

✳   ✳   ✳   ✳

THOMAS J. JACKSON had far more than his fair share of oddities and strange habits. From a young age, he was plagued by numerous illnesses—many of which were likely psychosomatic. He was a tremendous hypochondriac who complained of failing vision, poor hearing, stomach pains, and constant aching in his joints, muscles, and nerves. Many of these maladies may have been the result of his insatiable curiosity. In researching medicine and anatomy in an attempt to diagnose himself, he would convince himself that he suffered from the conditions he was reading about.

Once Jackson was finished diagnosing himself, he decided to set up his own treatment. After consulting numerous doctors—many of whom were outright quacks—he subjected himself to dozens of unnecessary and highly questionable treatments, such as ingesting or inhaling concoctions of silver nitrate and glycerin, convinced that they were having a positive effect on his health. Once a problem "cleared up," he wasted no time in dreaming up new and even more improbable sicknesses he might be experiencing. His constant exploration of medicines and therapies led him to many popular fads of the time, such as hydropathy. Proponents of hydropathy extolled the virtues of swimming in mineral waters or hot springs, claiming that the natural essence of the water healed all illnesses. Jackson jumped in with both feet and would often incorporate soothing baths into his daily exercise.

Exercising to a Fault

Ahead of his time in some ways, Jackson had a devotion to exercise that was considered strange by his contemporaries. He embraced calisthenics and regular exercise decades before most Americans would see them as a part of a healthy and fit lifestyle. Jackson, to the bemusement of other pedestrians and onlookers, could often be seen engaging in brisk walks. He would hold his long cane aloft, batting away tree branches or other obstacles that might get in his way. Moving quickly with an exceptionally long stride, he wasn't quite running, exactly, but his loping and hopping down various roads and paths might be considered a precursor to modern jogging.

A Man of Deep Faith

Stonewall was also a very religious man, holding fast to his beliefs with a fervor and intensity that raised eyebrows even in a time of great piety. Many viewed him as a fanatic. He believed in the literal interpretation of the Bible and held it as the true letter of the law. He usually refused to work and disrupt his rest on Sundays, in observance of the Sabbath, making an exception only during the war. Religion often clouded his wartime judgment: He promoted observant Protestants over capable—but less pious—military men and believed that he and his cause would be protected by the divine.

Ridiculed by Students

Jackson's eccentricities were a bit of a hindrance in the early part of his career. As a professor at Virginia Military Institute, he was not a beloved teacher—in fact, his students gave him the nickname "Tom Fool." At one point, an alumni campaign attempted to have him removed from his position. The issue was dismissed by his superiors in 1856, however, and he remained at VMI until the outbreak of the war.

Jackson's wartime success quickly set aside concern over his peculiarities, but they continued to be noticed. Once, several soldiers noticed him raising his arm straight up into the air and occasionally lifting his leg slightly off the ground. When they asked what signal he meant to give them with that display, he informed them that one of his arms and one of his legs were each heavier than the other arm and leg, and in order to help his blood flow properly to and from his extremities, he had to raise his limbs in this fashion.

Firepower and Progress

Throughout the Civil War, armies struggled to keep up with military technology.

✳   ✳   ✳   ✳

PROVIDING A RAPIDLY growing army with sufficient arms to conduct a war was the primary responsibility of the Federal Ordinance Department in the spring and summer of 1861. The regular Army's stockpile of arms was insufficient to meet the needs of thousands of volunteer troops, especially after state militias on both sides of the Mason-Dixon Line had raided government arsenals and taken whatever rifles and cannons they could find.

Colonel Henry Knox Craig was appointed head of the Ordnance Department in 1851, and he used his position to fight any attempt to modernize the arms used by the regular Army. It took the intervention of sitting U.S. Secretary of War Jefferson Davis to convince Craig to begin ordering .58 caliber rifles in place of .69 caliber smoothbore muskets. The .58 caliber rifle was a big step forward, providing much more accuracy at longer distances.

To Breech or Not to Breech

Colonel James Ripley, a 67-year-old veteran and West Point graduate, replaced Craig when war broke out in April 1861. One of Ripley's first acts was to perform an inventory of federal arsenals, in which he discovered that many had been all but emptied by state forces. Through a combination of government manufacture and private sources and overseas purchases, Ripley was able to rebuild the federal stockpile and provide much-needed rifles and artillery to the armies forming across the Union. This helped restore order to a department that had been ineffective in its preparation for war. Ripley also worked to standardize ammunition and weapons, making resupply in the field more efficient.

Like his predecessor in the office, however, Ripley was resistant to change, especially when it came to technological advances in warfare. For instance, he rejected the purchase of breech-loading carbines for the infantry, as well as of weapons that used magazines able to fire multiple rounds before reloading. More interested in saving ammunition than in saving lives, Ripley believed that it was more efficient for infantry soldiers to load single bullets one at a time down the muzzle and to take careful aim before firing. This wasted less ammunition but also lowered firepower in battle. Breech loaders, he further reasoned, were not as accurate and were more expensive. They required more maintenance and were heavier than muzzle loaders, as well.

President Lincoln was interested in testing and supporting new weapons, such as the Henry Rifle, but Ripley refused to test or purchase this gun. The Henry had a 15-round magazine that enabled the user to fire several rounds per minute. The Ordnance Department purchased only about 1,700 Henry Rifles during the war, but state governments and regimental commanders bought more than 10,000.

Had to Let Him Go

After several disagreements with Lincoln and Secretary of War Edwin Stanton, Ripley was finally replaced in September 1863. It was said that "instead of seeking out better designs, [Ripley] applied his ingenuity, which was considerable, to fighting them off." He was replaced by Brigadier General George Ramsay, who was willing to purchase new technology but later had his own feud with Stanton. He was relieved of his post in September 1864.

A Singular Woman

Mary Walker received a Medal of Honor, had it revoked, and then got it back posthumously. She never wavered in her belief that she'd earned it.

✳   ✳   ✳   ✳

ONLY ONE WOMAN has received the Medal of Honor—Dr. Mary Walker, in 1866. A medical doctor, she insisted her skills matched those of any male physician, but the army refused to accept her as a surgeon. She signed on as a nurse, working her way up to assistant surgeon for an Ohio regiment.

Experiences in War

Working as a battlefield doctor, Walker was captured by the Confederates and held for four months. After the war, she felt she deserved some recognition. Since she was civilian medical personnel, there were only a limited number of official honors available to her, so she lobbied Congress for a Medal of Honor. Her citation was longer than most, explaining that she partly received the medal because, "by reason of her not being a commissioned officer in the military service, a brevet or honorary rank cannot, under existing laws, be conferred upon her." Uncertain of what honor they could legally bestow, Congress decided to give her this one.

Taken Back

Around the time of World War I, Congress changed the rules for the Medal of Honor to strictly recognize valor in combat by military personnel. The medal had been handed out casually, and Congress decided to rescind more than 900. Although a battlefield doctor, Walker wasn't military and never experienced combat, so the government asked for the medal back. She refused and broke the law by publicly wearing her no-longer-valid medal. She died two years later in 1919, the medal still in her possession. After a few decades, her relatives lobbied for the medal to be restored, and in 1977 President Jimmy Carter signed legislation reinstating it.

Paying for the War

Bullets cost money. Bandages cost money. Horses cost money. No matter which side you're on, war costs money. How did the Union and the Confederacy pay for their Civil War?

✳ ✳ ✳ ✳

The Union:

Had the advantage of an established Treasury Department.
A national apparatus was in place for raising and spending money, but even so, a recent depression had resulted in lower tariffs on foreign goods, which in turn dropped Northern revenues by nearly 30 percent. Meanwhile, the federal budget suffered from four years of deficit spending between 1858 and 1861. The South's secession caused a new panic in the North, making the war even less affordable.

Had a secretary of the Treasury with no prior experience in finance. Secretary of the Treasury Salmon P. Chase had been a lawyer, the governor of Ohio, and a U.S. senator. But even without banking or finance knowledge, Chase kept the North solvent by offering short-term bank loans at 7.3 percent. Chase also developed the now-common practice of selling bonds to the public, with some as small as $50. Banks also bought long-term bonds at a rate of 6 percent, bringing the government more than $1 billion between the two sales. The North actually financed more than 66 percent of the war this way.

Had a solid tax base to draw from. In August 1861, the North had the dubious distinction of enacting the first federal income tax in U.S. history. Up until that time, the developing war had depended on receiving its financing from the lowered tariffs for foreign goods. Once the income tax was in place, however, the Union received more than 20 percent of its war funding from the new source of revenue. The subsequent Internal Revenue Act of 1862 covered everything from liquor and tobacco to professional licenses and inheritances.

Relied on actual gold to back up the bonds that were sold. When early Northern failures on the battlefields led to another financial panic, gold supplies dropped to dangerous levels by the end of 1861. Without gold, the United States couldn't pay for supplies—it couldn't even pay its own army. The result was an innovative bill that introduced the concept of "legal tender," or paper money backed by U.S. reserve gold. The Legal Tender Act became law in February 1862 and created the "greenback."

Enacted the National Banking Act in February 1863. This legislation federalized banks of a certain stature, allowing them to issue the "greenback" as legal U.S. currency. The measure also allowed hundreds of banks to do away with their own proprietary banknotes. State banks issuing their own notes were eventually driven to federal compliance by 1865 and were forced to pay a 10 percent tax on all paper issued.

The Confederacy:
Did not have much available capital with which to begin a war. Most of the South's wealth was represented by land and slaves, which made up 30 percent of the area's financial assets. However, the South held only 12 percent of the currency in circulation and just over 20 percent in bank holdings. Many Southern cotton plantations were heavily indebted to Northern

bankers and merchants. When the Confederate Congress tried to force debt payment in exchange for Confederate bonds in May 1861, Southern debtors surrendered a mere 5 percent of what they owed.

Lacked tax savvy. The Confederate States of America, being a new governmental machine, did not have an active Treasury Department and had no economic devices such as taxation and collection. In fact, when the South tried to enact a direct property tax at the state level, only one state actually collected it.

Had a false sense of security. The South would eventually print more than $1.5 billion in paper currency, to be redeemed in gold within two years of the war's end—so strong was the South's faith in being victorious. In many cases, states, cities, and some businesses generated their own "money" by actually printing it themselves, without having anything to back it.

Issued bonds that no one could afford to buy. The Confederate Congress issued $100 million of Confederate bonds in 1861 at 8 percent interest. The trouble was, even those Southerners who had extra money to invest had to think twice, especially when the inflation rate soared to 12 percent per month by the end of 1861, which meant that the bonds were actually losing money.

Saw pricing controls go through the roof. The cost of living in the South became too great for many families. For example, the price of common salt—used by many farms and homes to preserve meat—increased from $2 per bag to more than $60 per bag by the end of 1862.

Had fiscal responsibilities that did not end when Lee surrendered to Grant in April 1865. According to a 1947 national news magazine article, Southern states were still paying out more than $3 million in pensions to veterans and their surviving dependents—more than 82 years after the end of the Civil War!

Badger Ingenuity: Damming the Red River

In 1864, during the Civil War, a combination of homegrown Wisconsin ingenuity and sheer brawn saved the day for Union soldiers stuck in an embarrassing jam on Louisiana's Red River.

✳ ✳ ✳ ✳

Mind Over Matter

GREAT BATTLES ARE decided in many different ways. Acts of bravery and courage under fire often determine the outcome of armed conflict. Other struggles end in defeat through the folly or indecision of a commander. Only 14 people were given the official Thanks of Congress for their services to the Union during the Civil War, and all but one—Lieutenant Colonel Joseph Bailey of Wisconsin—were commanders in the armed forces. As the chief engineer of the 19th Corps, Bailey saved a Union gunboat fleet trapped on Louisiana's Red River in May 1864 using a single formidable weapon—his brain.

Revered River

The Red River, a tributary of the Mississippi, was highly prized by Union forces as a channel by which to capture Shreveport and establish its control over northern Louisiana. The plan was that Shreveport and the surrounding area would then serve as a springboard for launching excursions into Texas and Arkansas. In April 1864, General Nathaniel Banks led a Union force of 32,000 soldiers and 13 gunboats, including 6 formidable ironclads, northward up the Red River.

Stuck in the Mud

A series of skirmishes with a determined Confederate opposition slowed the Union advance. At Alexandria, Confederate defenders had been busy digging channels to divert the river. They succeeded in lowering the water level to a depth of less than four feet, which created quite a problem for the Northern fleet. The smallest Union gunboats required seven feet of water to travel, and the larger craft needed a depth of more than ten feet.

The Union advance was stalled. The gunboats were at risk of becoming stranded on the river as the waters continued to recede, which would make them sitting ducks for either capture or destruction by Confederate artillery. On May 1, Chief Engineer Bailey was authorized to take any actions necessary to free the boats and permit the advance to continue. To the amazement and consternation of the Union leadership, he resolved to build a dam.

Dam It All

Bailey had worked in the Wisconsin woods in his youth, and he sought out lumbering experience among the approximately 3,500 soldiers he had at his disposal. He then directed the felling of hundreds of trees in the Red River's adjacent forests and had the cut timber fashioned into cribbing. Other soldiers were detailed to gather rock and earth to fill the cribbing that would be used in the makeshift dam. All the while, Bailey's lumberjacks and laborers were subject to continuous Confederate sniper fire.

To complete the dam, Bailey intended to have four barges deliberately overloaded and sunk midstream above the rapids. He would then connect the cribs to the barges, creating two 300-foot wing dams jutting into the river from each bank. This backup would force the water level up to a point at which the gunboats could maneuver down the river. The remaining open water in the middle of the river would form an ingenious spillway through which the gunboats could pass over the rapids.

Cleverness Lauded

In just ten days, the dam was built. The Red River water level rose to almost 13 feet because of Bailey's dam, which allowed the gunboats safe passage into navigable water. The last boat passed over just as the dam itself was breaking due to the water pressure in the river. In his report to the War Department, General Banks lauded Chief Engineer Bailey as the person who both saved a Union fleet worth more than $2 million (a value of approximately $200 million today) and permitted the Red River Campaign to continue.

During the Civil War, the Iron Brigade's proud Badgers wore a black campaign hat similar to an Aussie hat (with one side turned up) as a distinctive emblem. It was one of the most dreaded sights for Confederate soldiers, who knew that these Yanks had never run from a fight.

To replenish the Iron Brigade's appalling Gettysburg losses, the generals assigned to it a mutinous Pennsylvania conscript regiment, the 167th. The mutiny ended when Colonel Rufus Dawes ordered the 6th Wisconsin to form line, load, and aim at the Easterners. Fortunately, the command of "Fire" was not necessary.

The 32nd Infantry Division of the Wisconsin National Guard, known as Les Terribles (a French compliment for its World War I valor) and the "Red Arrow" Division (for its patch). It helped invade New Guinea and the Philippines in World War II and its soldiers earned eleven Medals of Honor in that conflict.

World War II was tough on Janesville. Ninety-four Janesville men, all of Company A of the 192nd Tank Battalion, became prisoners at Bataan in 1942. Because of the Bataan Death March and a brutal POW camp regime, barely a third ever saw home again.

Wake Island: Alamo Of The Pacific

On December 11, 1941, the Marines on the beaches of Wake Island witnessed an imposing sight: the approach of three cruisers, six destroyers, and two troop transports, all flying the ensign of the invincible Empire of Japan. Pearl Harbor had been smashed, the Philippines was under invasion, and the largest British warships in the area had been sent to the bottom by Japanese bombers. Now, the Marines knew, it was their turn.

* * * *

WAKE ISLAND IS a three-island coral atoll some 2,300 miles southwest of Hawaii, part of a chain of defensive U.S. bases that ran from Hawaii to the Philippines. Home to an airstrip, 523 Marines and sailors, and another 1,200 civilian contractors, Wake Island was a perfect staging area for raids against the Japanese Mandate Islands, which included the critical Marshall and Marianas island chains.

Throwing Back the Invaders

Flushed with smashing successes throughout the Pacific, the unbeaten Japanese Navy decided to capture Wake and rid itself of a potential aerial threat. Because Wake and its connected islands, Peale and Wilkes islands, possessed few natural defenses and only a dozen F4F Wildcat fighters, the Japanese high command was confident that a relatively small invasion force, preceded by its vaunted tactical bomber service, would get the job done quickly and easily.

But they neglected to plan for the determination and skill of the defending Marines. Although the bombing campaign on December 8th killed scores of Marines and reduced the Wildcat squadron from 12 to 4 flyable planes, on December 11, when the Japanese flotilla appeared on the horizon, Marine gunners were waiting for them. After enduring a savage shelling from the light cruisers and destroyers that escorted a 450-man Special Naval Landing Force detachment, the Marines waited until the transports were close in, then let loose with their coastal batteries. On Peacock Point, at the southern tip of Wake Island, gunners scored four hits on the cruiser *Yubari*, flagship of Rear Admiral Sadamichi Kajioka, and minor hits on several other ships. Their counterparts on Peale Island wasted no time in sending the destroyer *Hayate* to the bottom, while lucky strafing runs from the Wildcats managed to detonate a rack of depth charges at the stern of the destroyer *Kisaragi*, putting her out of action for good.

With his force reeling from the violent, unexpected resistance, Rear Admiral Kajioka postponed the invasion to wait for reinforcements, and the cheering men on Wake Island became the only island defenders to throw back an amphibious invasion—a feat all the more impressive because the garrison started the war with only enough personnel to man about half the island's defense guns.

An Island Alone

But the ordeal was not over. While naval commanders in Hawaii made plans to relieve the island, they fretted over scarce resources. The U.S. Navy had few aircraft carriers and virtually no battleships to defend the Pacific Ocean, and naval commanders were wary of sending their precious flattops into a potential trap. The Navy dispatched the seaplane tender *Tangier* to Wake carrying batteries from the 4th Marine Defense Battalion, supplies, and ammunition. Shortly afterward, it ordered the carrier *Saratoga* and the slow-sailing *Task Force 14* to escort the relief effort. The carrier *Lexington* was sent belatedly to support *Task Force 14*, but the relief effort dispatched December 15 was too little, too late.

The Japanese enjoyed the crucial advantage of air bases within striking distance of Wake Island, and land- and sea-based bombers pounded the defenders daily after December 11, knocking out two of four Wildcats and repeatedly demolishing unsalvageable fighters rolled into the open as decoys. The last two Wildcats were brought down by fighters from the heavy carriers *Soryu* and *Hiryu* on December 22. With news of the two carriers in the vicinity, U.S. fleet commanders changed the *Tangier*'s orders from reinforcement to evacuation. But on December 23, with the task force still about 430 miles from Wake, a thousand-man battalion of Japanese soldiers stormed the island before daybreak. Seventy defending Marines on Wilkes Island delayed the landing there, but the defenders of Wake Island were overwhelmed. Before midday on December 23, Wake was in Japanese hands.

The loss of Wake Island was a bitter blow to the U.S. Navy, which had suffered a string of disasters since December 7. But in the dark days of December 1941, Navy planners decided that their only line of defense—their few precious carriers plying the Pacific's waters—could not be risked for the island.

The U.S. never attempted to retake Wake Island. Vengeance would have to wait until the Battle of Midway the following June. Meanwhile, Wake remained in Japanese hands until September 1945, nearly a month after Japan's surrender.

"The Snake Will Smoke"— The Curious History Of The Brazilian Expeditionary Force

The land of Carnival and bossa nova fielded one of the conflict's fiercest fighting units and became the only South American country to fight in the war.

✳   ✳   ✳   ✳

BRAZIL'S FAILURE TO commit troops during the First World War led to a joke: One was more likely to see a snake smoke than to see Brazilians fighting in Europe. But from 1944–1945 the soldiers of the Força Expedicionária Brasileira (FEB, "Brazilian Expeditionary Force") were proud to display the insignia patch of a green snake smoking a pipe as they trudged through the mountains of Italy, beating back the Fascist forces and playing a significant role in breaking the so-called Gothic Line defending the Po Valley.

At the outset of the war, Brazil, ruled by dictator Getúlio Vargas, was neutral and maintained strong economic ties with both the United States and Germany. However, Brazil's eventual cooperation was strategically important to the Allies for several reasons:

* The northeastern coast of the country was considered the most likely spot for a German invasion of the Western Hemisphere.

* The United States needed a base in Brazil from which to supply the African campaign.

* German submarines off the South American coast were wreaking havoc on Allied shipping.

* After Pearl Harbor, Vargas sensed an opportunity to obtain favorable treatment from the United States and joined the Allied powers. In exchange for a naval and air base at Natal on Brazil's northeast coast, the United States provided technical advice to build the Volta Redonda steel mill. The Natal base proved the perfect springboard for operations in Africa and Italy, and regular patrols soon began to thwart the U-boat menace.

* Initially there was no expectation that Brazil would participate in the war. But in a 1943 meeting at Natal, Franklin Roosevelt encouraged Vargas and his government to commit troops; the Brazilians didn't need much convincing.

* The country's military commanders wanted to participate in the fighting to avenge German submarine raids in the South Atlantic.

* Vargas wished to buy time to build a populist base.

* Vargas's opponents within the government believed (rightly, it turned out) that soldiers who fought Fascism abroad would demand democracy at home.

So, while maintaining a domestic force to guard the border with Argentina, the government assembled the FEB. Reaching 25,334 troops at its peak, the FEB was made up of police and all who would volunteer. When no more volunteered, the government conscripted men for the army. The last time Brazilian forces had fought outside their own country's borders had been the 1865–70 war against Paraguay. The regular army was still using surplus equipment supplied by the French after the First World War, including 25-year-old tins of rations.

The FEB was initially slated for action in Africa, but by the time it was ready to deploy, the Germans had been expelled from that continent. Instead, the Brazilian troops were sent to the mountains of Italy, where they suffered in the unfamiliar terrain and cold. Though they operated as an autonomous force, the Brazilians attached themselves willingly to the depleted American IV Corps of 5th Army, in whose service they soon saw heavy combat. In one of the FEB's initial actions it fought seasoned German troops at close range until forced to retreat due to lack of ammunition.

One German officer is said to have exclaimed that the Brazilian troops fought like devils without regard to their own safety. Soon after the FEB's arrival, German propaganda pamphlets and radio broadcasts appeared in Portuguese—a testament to the unit's effectiveness. The FEB's most glorious moment came when, after four months of heavy fighting, it seized the heavily defended summit of Monte Castello. Its heaviest action, however, was during a grueling four-day battle to take the town of Montese, where the FEB suffered 426 casualties in four days of fighting.

Before any battle, the Brazilian troops were heard to say, "The snake will smoke."

Half Fish And Half Nuts: Frogmen Of World War II

Before there were Navy SEALs, there were Underwater Demolition Teams—squads that specialized in scouting and clearing underwater obstacles for troops landing on beaches in Europe and the Pacific.

✳ ✳ ✳ ✳

Frogman: A swimmer provided with breathing apparatus and other equipment to execute underwater maneuvers, especially military maneuvers.

From Boatmen to Swimmers

More amphibious assaults occurred during World War II than in any conflict prior or any since. Attacking a fortified enemy beach from the sea, however, is a high-risk operation. The disastrous landing at Gallipoli during World War I had proven that to succeed, an attacking force needed to have thorough knowledge of the terrain as well as an opportunity to disable enemy obstacles before storming the beach. The U.S. Navy now had to consider planning an invasion of France and an island-hopping campaign in the Pacific. This led to the creation of the Scouts and Raiders unit in the summer of 1942. These special units would scout enemy beaches and destroy obstacles before the landings. Recruits were put through a rigorous training program designed to weed out weaker members.

Initially the group's objective was to destroy enemy obstacles using specially designed explosives. The men were trained to use rubber boats to work the shallows near the beach. It was assumed that the Scouts and Raiders would spend all their time in the boats and, as such, each soldier wore full Navy fatigues, a life jacket, and a steel helmet. Their training placed very little emphasis on swimming. All of that changed during the days leading up to the invasion of the South Pacific Island of Kwajalein atoll during the Marshall Islands campaign in early 1944.

Lewis Luehrs and Bill Acheson, two members of the Scouts and Raiders, sat in a small rubber boat bobbing in the waves beyond the coral reef surrounding Kwajalein. They had a problem.

Their mission: to get as close to the beach as possible and note any Japanese defense obstacles that would impede the imminent landing by the 5th Amphibious Force. The 5th's commander, Admiral Turner, was apprehensive about the operation and had ordered the daylight reconnaissance mission by the Scouts and Raiders—though the unit was accustomed to working under the cover of darkness. Daylight or not, Luehrs and Acheson could not proceed farther than the reef without being detected, but they were still too far out to accurately observe the Japanese defenses. Cognizant of the importance of their mission, the two men stripped down to their underwear and swam to the beach.

They found beach gun embankment locations and a submerged log wall. Underwater reconnaissance was born.

Training of Underwater Demolition Teams (UDTs) began in earnest in February 1944, and after April, UDT operations became a priority facet of atoll landing operations. UDT members, swimming without lifelines and clad only in trunks, masks, and flippers, were nicknamed the "Naked Warriors," and were fondly described by landing crews as "half fish and half nuts."

The group's opinion was so respected by the end of the war that when 23-year-old UDT member Don Lumsden suggested a change in the invasion plan for the landings on Borneo, General Douglas MacArthur promptly implemented the suggestion without question. Thirty-four operations UDTs would eventually clear safe paths in every major Pacific landing, including Eniwetok, Saipan, Guam, Tinian, Peleliu, Leyte, and Iwo Jima.

Normandy

The Allied invasion of France remains the single largest amphibious assault in history. It was rife with challenges: The Germans had studded the beach with explosive-tipped steel posts, and the surf was littered with large steel barricades. The elite members of the Navy's UDT were to arrive in the second wave after the enemy gun emplacements and bunkers had been cleared by tanks and troop carriers from the first wave. This would allow the subsequent waves to move unimpeded and secure the beachhead. A strong tide on the day of the landing, however, pushed many of the UDT units ahead of the first wave, and the team was at the mercy of German machine guns and mortars before they could reach the beach. At Utah beach, at least 23 were killed and 60 wounded out of a force of 175 men. Those who reached the shallows were able to destroy some of the obstacles with explosives. In the confusion, some American soldiers from the first wave took shelter behind obstacles that were rigged to detonate. Enemy fire, however, forced the soldiers to abandon their dangerous cover before it exploded.

UDT Warfare at its Peak—Okinawa

The most extensive use of UDTs occurred at Okinawa. On March 29, 1945, three days before the scheduled main assault, 1,000 UDT swimmers were dropped by landing craft 500 yards from shore. Each swimmer was covered in silver camouflage paint and carried a reel of fishing line knotted at 25-yard intervals, a length of sounding line with an attached lead weight, a stylus, and a sheet of Plexiglas wrapped around their forearms. Under the cover of naval bombardment, they set out to scout out the reefs and defenses guarding the Okinawa beachheads.

Upon reaching the reef, each swimmer, working in concert with the others, began by tying one end of the fishing line to the seaward edge of the reef. They then swam across the reef toward the shore, unwinding the reel and stopping every 25 yards when a knot appeared to take a sounding with the lead weight. Each time, the swimmers would use the stylus to write down their measurements on the Plexiglas sheet, along with the location of safe channels and information of other obstacles or defenses.

For the duration of their scouting mission, the swimmers faced the risk of being hit by errant American cover fire or gunfire by the Japanese, as well as hypothermia and cramping. Within an hour, the reef was scoped, and the UDTs returned. They reported no mines, but did discover hundreds of poles threaded with barbed wire. The next day, the swimmers headed for the reef again, this time armed with small explosive charges. After setting the timed fuses, the UDTs witnessed a thunderous chain explosion that cleared a safe assault path to the beaches.

More UDT operations followed after Okinawa, but never again on such a scale. UDTs were later used during the Korean War before being reorganized as the SEALs in 1962.

Pushing The Nuclear Button

Truman's "decision was one of noninterference—basically a decision not to upset the existing plan."

—General Leslie R. Groves on President Harry Truman's decision to drop an atomic bomb on Japan

✳ ✳ ✳ ✳

PRIOR TO TAKING office as president in April 1945, Truman knew nothing of the Manhattan Project. He had served only 83 days as vice president, during which his time with Roosevelt was limited. The bomb had never been mentioned to him, nor had many of Roosevelt's intentions about foreign policy. Truman had a lot to catch up on. He worked with Roosevelt's trusted military, scientific, diplomatic, and political advisers to learn in days what had taken years of planning and research.

Option A: Invasion

As early as 1943, the United States had begun to make plans for invading Japan. When Germany surrendered in the spring of 1945, attention shifted to subduing the Japanese home islands, which were defended by some two million soldiers. The plan for invasion was called Operation Downfall. The first stage, Operation Olympic, would require roughly 767,000 Allied soldiers to invade Kyushu, Japan's large southern island, on November 1, 1945. Olympic would be followed by Operation Coronet in March 1946, an invasion of Honshu, Japan's largest island, which would require some 28 divisions.

Truman worried that Operation Downfall would result in "an Okinawa from one end of Japan to the other." He later claimed that the United States might sustain as many as one million casualties—to say nothing of the loss of Japanese lives. Meanwhile, Japan would continue the fight with its army of three million men stationed throughout China, destroying thousands of Chinese, Japanese, and Soviet lives on Asia's mainland.

Option B: Stay the Course

On the other hand, Truman considered that perhaps more of the same could force Japan to surrender. Firebombing of Japanese cities by American B-29s had leveled many of Japan's major cities with a force far greater than the estimated power of the atomic bomb. Air and sea power might work. But despite the repeated raids, so far Japan had remained defiant.

Option C: Rely on Russia

If the Soviet Union entered the war against Japan, Truman felt that Emperor Hirohito might persuade his cabinet warmongers that unconditional surrender was preferable to conventional destruction by the two emerging superpowers. However, discussions at the Potsdam Conference in July had revealed disagreements and tensions between the Big Three over control of Europe and policy with Japan.

Option D: Drop the Bomb

Political and moral considerations weighed heavily on the decision to use atomic weapons. Influential scientists petitioned Truman not to use the atomic bomb, predicting erosion of U.S. moral authority if it became the first nation to unleash nuclear destruction. Conversely, more than $2 billion had already been spent developing the weapons, and the momentum for using them was in place. Some hoped the bombs' power could be used as a demonstration against Japan. Yet with only two live bombs in stock in July 1945 and with the technology still uncertain, the risk of a dud or the loss of one operational bomb was judged too great for the demonstration approach. The plan for a drop proceeded.

The United States, Britain, and China issued an ultimatum to Japan on July 26, 1945, demanding unconditional surrender under threat of "prompt and utter destruction." In the end, Japan remained outwardly unmoved by the Allied ultimatum, and Truman refused to alter existing plans to use the atomic bomb. He knew that using the bomb would end the lives of many Japanese citizens. But not using it would condemn many more citizens—of many countries—to more traditional deaths.

Comanche Code Talkers

Most people associate code talkers with World War II, but the system was actually first used in World War I. While soldiers from the 142nd Infantry Regiment were fighting with the French Army against the Germans in northern France in 1918, Allied leaders had become suspicious that the Germans were intercepting their communications; the leaders were frustrated and trying to come up with a solution to this vexing problem. When one American captain overheard two of his soldiers having a discussion in their native Choctaw language, he thought of a plan. Allied forces began experimenting with a new code based on the Choctaw language, and it was wonderfully successful—the Germans never broke it.

Inspired by Choctaw code talkers' successes in World War I, the U.S. military again used Native American languages for battlefield communication during World War II. Fourteen Comanche speakers landed at Utah Beach at Normandy on D-Day, and eight Meskwaki from Iowa became code talkers in North Africa.

The Marines ran the largest code talker program, utilizing some 400 Diné (Navajo) speakers in the Pacific. Marine code talkers didn't simply speak Diné, they used a Diné-based code that only a Diné speaker could learn. None of the codes were ever broken. Non-code talking Diné POWs could tell that the words were Diné but couldn't tell what the messages meant.

The last surviving Comanche code talker, Charles Chibitty, died July 20, 2005, at age 83. Chibitty was born Near Medicine Park, Oklahoma, in 1921. He enlisted in 1941 and trained at Fort Benning in Georgia. At a 2002 meeting with Pentagon officials, Chibitty gave some examples of how certain words and phrases would be translated: A tank was a "turtle," and a machine gun was a "sewing machine." In a touch of sagacious comedy, Adolf Hitler was *posah-tai-vo* ("crazy white man").

Miranda Warning

The violation of one man's rights becomes a warning to us all.

✳   ✳   ✳   ✳

MOST OF US have never heard of Ernesto Miranda. Yet in 1963, this faceless man would prompt the passage of a law that has become an integral part of all arrests. Here's how it came to pass.

You Have the Right to Remain Silent

In 1963, following his arrest for the kidnapping and rape of an 18-year-old woman, Ernesto Miranda was arrested and placed in a Phoenix, Arizona, police lineup. When he stepped down from the gallery of suspects, Miranda asked the officers about the charges against him. His police captors implied that he had been positively identified as the kidnapper and rapist of a young woman. After two hours of interrogation, Miranda confessed.

Miranda signed a confession that included a typed paragraph indicating that his statement had been voluntary and that he had been fully aware of his legal rights.

But there was one problem: At no time during his interrogation had Miranda actually been advised of his rights. The wheels of justice had been set in motion on a highly unbalanced axle.

Anything You Say Can and Will Be Used Against You in a Court of Law

When appealing Miranda's conviction, his attorney attempted to have the confession thrown out on the grounds that his client hadn't been advised of his rights. The motion was over-ruled. Eventually, Miranda would be convicted on both rape and kidnapping charges and sentenced to 20 to 30 years in prison. It seemed like the end of the road for Miranda—but it was just the beginning.

You Have the Right to an Attorney

Miranda requested that his case be heard by the U.S. Supreme Court. His attorney, John J. Flynn, submitted a 2,000-word petition for a writ of *certiorari* (judicial review), arguing that Miranda's Fifth Amendment rights had been violated. In November 1965, the Supreme Court agreed to hear Miranda's case. The tide was about to turn.

A Law Is Born

After much debate among Miranda's attorneys and the state, a decision in Miranda's favor was rendered. Chief Justice Earl Warren wrote in his *Miranda v. Arizona* opinion, "The person in custody must, prior to interrogation, be clearly informed that he has the right to remain silent, and that anything he says will be used against him in court; he must be clearly informed that he has the right to consult with a lawyer and to have the lawyer with him during interrogation, and that, if he is indigent, a lawyer will be appointed to represent him."

Aftermath

In the wake of the U.S. Supreme Court's ruling, police departments across the nation began to issue the "Miranda warning." As for Miranda himself, his freedom was short-lived. He would be sentenced to 11 years in prison at a second trial that did not include his prior confession as evidence. Miranda was released in 1972, and he bounced in and out of jail for various offenses over the next few years. On January 31, 1976, Miranda was stabbed to death during a Phoenix bar fight. The suspect received his Miranda warning from the arresting police officers and opted to remain silent. Due to insufficient evidence, he would not be prosecuted for Ernesto Miranda's murder.

Chapter 4

Politicians & Their Politics

The News Is What the President Says It Is

When it comes to Lincoln's repression of newspapers, rumors battle with the truth.

✳ ✳ ✳ ✳

POLITICIANS OFTEN CITE the actions of their historical forebears to justify their own indiscretions. Abraham Lincoln,
for example, is said to have suppressed civil rights during the
Civil War, so he occasionally gets referenced when a modern
politician wants to do the same thing. Today's official might
say, "Lincoln suppressed newspapers during the Civil War, so
I should be able to meddle with a few civil liberties, too." But
did Lincoln really work to curtail freedom of the press? It's not
quite so clear cut.

Freedom of the Press?

A handful of cases are frequently cited to portray Lincoln as
opposed to a free press. In June 1863, the editor of the *Chicago
Times* wrote inflammatory antiwar articles that attacked
the efforts of Lincoln and the Republicans. Union General
Ambrose Burnside, who was in command of the Department
of the Ohio at the time, was alarmed at what he considered the
Times's "repeated expression of disloyal and incendiary sentiments." The general had the editor arrested and the paper shut
down. Although Lincoln had suspended habeas corpus in areas

where he feared physical unrest, he was troubled by Burnside's actions and consulted his Cabinet for a response. They agreed that the editor's arrest had been improper, so Lincoln freed him and allowed the *Chicago Times* to return to press. When people asked Lincoln why he hadn't supported the closure of the newspaper that had been so critical of him, he wrote that those with such a question did "not fully comprehend the dangers of abridging the liberties of the people." That doesn't sound like something a hater of the press would write!

Lies Instead of News

President Lincoln wasn't completely above shutting down a printing press if he thought it was necessary. On May 18, 1864, the *New York World* and the *Journal of Commerce* each published a forged presidential proclamation calling for a new draft of 400,000 troops. Once these papers were on the street, the administration wasted no time in going after them. Lincoln himself ordered General John A. Dix to arrest the publishers and editors and to seize their presses. When further investigation determined that the journalists had been taken in by the forgery themselves and had never intended to convey false information, the journalists were released and allowed to resume publication.

In his telegram to Dix releasing the journalists, Secretary of War Edwin Stanton wrote of President Lincoln, "He directs me to say that while, in his opinion, the editors, proprietors, and publishers of the *World* and *Journal of Commerce* are responsible for what appears in their papers injurious to the public service, and have no right to shield themselves behind a plea of ignorance or want of criminal intent, yet he is not disposed to visit them with vindictive punishment."

The People Have Spoken

Official action from the government wasn't the only sort of suppression that affected newspapers. In March 1863, the 2nd

Ohio Cavalry was camped outside of Columbus, Ohio. After the local newspaper, *The Crisis*, printed antiarmy stories—including the wish that no member of the 2nd Ohio return from the war alive—the soldiers ransacked its offices. *The Crisis* continued publication, however. The next year, its editor was indicted by a federal grand jury and arrested for conspiracy. He died in November before he could go on trial.

Although Lincoln wasn't afraid to take action when he felt it necessary, he was keenly aware of the danger in restricting civil rights and did so only after careful consideration. Those wishing to use him as a role model for their actions against free speech should perhaps take a closer look.

Return to Sender

Kids who procrastinate on homework projects like to justify the delay by recalling that Abraham Lincoln scribbled the Gettysburg Address on the back of an envelope shortly before he gave the speech. Well, those same kids are about to get schooled.

✳ ✳ ✳ ✳

THE GETTYSBURG ADDRESS, given by Lincoln at the dedication of Gettysburg National Cemetery on November 19, 1863, is considered by most historians to be one of the greatest pieces of oratory ever presented by a president. Almost everyone knows at least the opening line, even if they don't know how many years "four score and seven" equals (it's 87, in case you're curious).

Presidential Procrastination?

One of the most enduring myths surrounding the Gettysburg Address is that Lincoln wrote it on the back of a used envelope as he rode a train from Washington, D.C., to the Pennsylvania cemetery. It's definitely a great story, but historians agree that it's not true.

To Lincoln, the Gettysburg speech was a minor effort, a necessary honorific that he assumed would quickly be forgotten. Nonetheless, he did spend some time on its creation, writing at least two drafts and changing the speech slightly as he gave it.

Short and Sweet

During the dedication, the speaker at the podium just before Lincoln, a man named Edward Everett, spent two hours recounting the Battle of Gettysburg in excruciating detail. The audience was exhausted by the time Lincoln finally took the dais, not to mention a little startled when his speech lasted only two minutes. In fact, some people were confused when Lincoln sat down, unsure that the speech was actually over. Silence followed, and Lincoln later confided to a friend that he felt the speech, in its brevity, had disappointed people. Of course, he couldn't have been more wrong about one of history's most noble expressions of democracy.

The Guy Who Killed the Guy Who Killed Abraham Lincoln

What's it take to bring down an assassin? Sharp-shooting skills and a story of your own.

✳ ✳ ✳ ✳

The Mad Hatter

YOU MIGHT FIGURE that a guy who takes down a presidential assassin is a stand-up sort of fellow. But according to legend, Thomas "Boston" Corbett, the man who shot Lincoln's assassin, John Wilkes Booth, was a few bullets shy of a full round.

Born in London in 1832, Thomas Corbett moved with his parents to Troy, New York, in 1839. As a young man, he became a hat maker and was exposed to the dangerous chemicals involved, included mercurious nitrate, which was used in curing felt. Long-term exposure would more than likely turn him into a certified "mad" hatter. After losing his first wife and child during childbirth, Corbett turned to the bottle. Later, however, he turned to Jesus Christ and moved to Boston. It was here that he rechristened himself as "Boston."

Described as a religious fanatic, an account from a Massachusetts hospital states that Corbett cut off his own testes after reading from the Bible the book of Matthew chapters 18 and 19 (which discuss removing offending body parts) and being approached by prostitutes on the city streets. After removing his offending body part, he apparently attended church and ate dinner at home before calling the doctor.

A Bullet for Booth

In 1861, Corbett enlisted as a private in Company I, 12th New York Militia. After several years in service, he found himself with a group on the hunt for the infamous assassin John Wilkes Booth. And though the cavalry was instructed to bring Booth in alive, it's generally accepted that Corbett shot him while Booth was surrounded in a burning barn. Given the chaos, the distance, and the smoke, it's surprising that the bullet even hit Booth.

Fifteen Minutes of Fame

Corbett wasn't punished for shooting Booth. In fact, he received a share of the reward money, totaling $1,653.85. For a short period of time, Corbett was considered a hero and even signed autographs for his fans.

Afterward, Corbett moved around for a few years and eventually settled in Concordia, Kansas, where, in 1887, he was elected as the assistant doorkeeper to the Kansas House of Representatives. He lived as a bit of a hermit, but he preached at the Methodist Episcopal Church and became known as something of a loudmouth evangelist. Then one day in the winter of 1887, Corbett threatened to shoot people over an argument on the floor of the House of Representatives. He was quickly arrested, determined to be unstable, and booked for a permanent vacation to a psych hospital.

Loose Ends

That wasn't the last America would hear from Boston Corbett. He escaped from the hospital on his second attempt in May 1888, stole a pony that was tied up in front of the hospital, and high-tailed it out of there. He reappeared one week later in Neodesha, Kansas, and was said to have later headed to Mexico.

Corbett seemed to have disappeared, though sightings were reported far and wide. As with everything surrounding the Lincoln assassination, there are plenty of conspiracy theories regarding Corbett: There are some who say that Corbett wasn't the one who shot Booth. Others say that it was not actually Booth who Corbett shot, and that Corbett later traveled to Enid, Kansas, to meet a man claiming to be Booth.

What is known about Corbett is that before he disappeared, he made a dugout home near Concordia, Kansas. Today, a stone marker between two trees in the middle of a pasture stands as a monument to the guy who killed the guy who killed the sixteenth president of the United States.

Crossing Swords

Confederate General Robert E. Lee's surrender to Union Lieutenant General Ulysses S. Grant on April 9, 1865, marked the end of the Civil War. For such an important moment in American history, though, the event is shrouded in misconceptions.

✻　✻　✻　✻

THE SURRENDER TOOK place in a private home in a town called Appomattox Court House, not in the courthouse of the town of Appomattox. It's easy to see how this misconception arose. There is a town in Virginia named Appomattox, and it does have a courthouse. But it was the private home of Wilmer McLean in the town of Appomattox Court House, Virginia, that housed the historic meeting.

At no time did Robert E. Lee surrender his ceremonial sword to Grant, only to have the Union leader magnanimously return it. General Lee did arrive in full military uniform, which included his ceremonial sword. General Grant, on the other hand, arrived wearing only a dirty private's uniform. In Grant's own words: "The much repeated talk of the surrendering of Lee's sword and my handing it back . . . is the purest romance. The word *sword* or *sidearms* was not mentioned by either of us until I wrote it in the terms." These terms were written during the meeting in Appomattox Court House, but they did allow the Confederate officers to keep their sidearms. The misconception surrounding the sword could have arisen after a different magnanimous act by Grant. As General Lee left McLean's house after surrendering, Grant's men outside cheered in celebration. Grant immediately ordered the cheering to stop. "The Confederates were now our prisoners," he said later, "and we did not want to exult over their downfall."

By all accounts, Lee greatly appreciated Grant's behavior during the surrender, and the site is now appropriately part of a national historic park. But there is still no sign of a courthouse.

What Caliber Were Beecher's Bibles?

Although his moral light faded in later years, Henry Ward Beecher continues to be remembered for abolitionist work and his power in the pulpit.

✳ ✳ ✳ ✳

ENRY WARD BEECHER became one of the best-known and most influential men in America during the mid-1800s. His family's legacy, his oratorical skills as a preacher, and his moral authority as a moderate abolitionist brought him fame and large audiences. He was so famous that at one point his name was borrowed for rifles used to fight the forces of slavery in Kansas. But his legacy became somewhat compromised by positions he took in post-war politics and by a love affair that went public toward the end of his life.

Beecher's Beginnings

Born in Litchfield, Connecticut, Henry was the son of Lyman Beecher, a prominent religious leader. The elder Beecher later headed Lane Seminary in Cincinnati, which exposed Henry to activity at a key stop on the Underground Railroad. His sister, Harriet Beecher Stowe, penned the famous antislavery novel *Uncle Tom's Cabin*. Henry was critical of slavery and actively spread the message of emancipation. He attended Amherst College and Lane Seminary to prepare for a life in the church. By 1837, Beecher had joined the ministry, gotten married, and started preaching at a small Presbyterian church in Lawrenceburg, Indiana.

A Preacher's Life

Beecher quickly advanced within his profession, moving to a larger church in Indianapolis and then on to New York. He also earned a reputation on the speakers' circuit. In Brooklyn, Beecher served Plymouth Church and delivered a series of speeches entitled "Lectures to Young Men" that gained great popularity. His message both from his pulpit and while on tour was keeping moral values, with emphasis on the sins to be avoided. Each week, hundreds of young men came to hear him. By the end of the 1850s, Beecher's church regularly filled to capacity. He also learned to use the growing press, writing books and regular newspaper columns.

Political Pursuits

Beecher's efforts to emancipate slaves went beyond the moral message from his rostrum and into the political arena. He was an early backer of the Republicans and an ardent supporter of abolitionism. As the sectional conflict heightened and as abolitionists and proslavery transients flooded into Bloody Kansas to stack the vote on slavery, Beecher raised money to send 25 guns and just as many Bibles in with abolitionist immigrants. These guns, and soon any others used in the conflict, became known as "Beecher's Bibles," an ironic reference to a unique form of moral persuasion.

Soon after Congressman Preston Brooks of South Carolina clubbed abolitionist Senator Charles Sumner of Massachusetts in the Capitol, Beecher joined the controversy and painted Sumner as a martyr in the fight to rid the country of slavery. In similar fashion, he branded Brooks a villain, comparing his physical assault on Sumner to attacking a blind man, and sarcastically noting the Southern "chivalry of the man Brooks." He publicly wondered if Brooks might also enter "the sleeping room of a woman" to "bludgeon" her to death.

Taking Up the Union Cause

Once the actual war broke out, Beecher took the side of the Union, supported Lincoln, and traveled to England to persuade British audiences and the government not to side with the Confederacy. On more than one occasion he held slave auctions at his church to purchase the freedom of slaves. After introducing one chattel for sale, he asked, "May she read liberty in your eyes? Shall she go free? Let the plates be passed and we will see." Those in the congregation wept and donated to the cause.

Though he and Lincoln did not see eye to eye throughout the war, Beecher gained greater respect for the president after he issued the Emancipation Proclamation. Lincoln recalled Beecher's efforts in England and asked him to deliver a commemorative address at Fort Sumter after the war's end.

Postwar Positions

During Reconstruction, Beecher did not always agree with the reigning radical Republicans in terms of suppressing the South and the civil rights of freed slaves. He opposed federal protection of blacks and wanted instead to persuade Southern public opinion to move in favor of equal treatment of former slaves. Also, though many public figures saw the appointment as an abomination, Beecher supported Confederate General Robert E. Lee's selection as president of Washington College in Lexington, Virginia, asking, "When war ceased, and he laid down his arms...who could have been more modest, more manly, more true to his own word and honor than he was?" Beecher felt political practicality should replace radicalism and that the Christian approach was to accept Southerners as brothers. This position brought him great criticism from Northerners and Republicans alike.

A Legacy Tarnished

Beecher joined other religious movements in the latter half of the century and took moderate positions on temperance, women's rights, and evolution. His final days, however, are remembered for something else altogether. Beecher's national reputation as a civic leader and moral authority began to fade after Theodore Tilton, a radical writer and editor and friend of Beecher, accused the preacher of having an affair with his wife, Elizabeth. Elizabeth Tilton confessed to the affair and recanted several times, and a church trial in 1874 and a civil suit in 1875 made it a giant media event, well catalogued in the *New York Times* and other urban newspapers. Beecher's church twice exonerated him, and the civil trial ended in a hung jury, but his reputation was sullied. Henry Ward Beecher died in 1887 at age 73 of a cerebral hemorrhage. More than 40,000 mourners came to pay their respects as he lay in state.

Napoleon

Napoleon was born in 1769 on the Mediterranean island of Corsica, which had recently fallen under the control of France. As a young man, he excelled in science and mathematics. He joined the French armed forces and studied military history and theory during the tumultuous years of the French Revolution. When members of the royal family threatened to restore the monarchy, Napoleon took advantage of the popularity he had earned through successful military campaigns to take control of the government as part of a three-person council. He quickly pushed out the other two leaders and built a French Empire that redefined the national boundaries of Europe. Other nations formed coalitions to challenge Napoleon on the battlefield, but all crumbled before the great general. A man of simple tastes but great ego, he died in 1821 while exiled on the island of St. Helena, six years after being forced from power.

Napoleon's Ministers

Napoleon was Emperor of France from 1804 through 1814 and part of 1815. Étienne-Denis Pasquier was born two years before Napoleon on April 21, 1767, and was the last remaining of Emperor Napoleon's ministers. Pasquier served the emperor as councilor of state and prefect of police. After Napoleon's defeat, Pasquier continued to play important roles in the French government, becoming chancellor of France in 1837. Pasquier died in 1862 at age 95.

The French Government Under Napoleon

The French Revolution of 1789 replaced the authority of the nation's monarchy with promises of democracy and equality, but a decade of squabbling among social and political groups left the country with no stable government. When Napoleon stepped into the void, he spoke of the liberal ideals of the revolution but established a far stronger dictatorship than most French kings ever enjoyed. He allowed elections for local government, but these offices were all answerable to the authority of prefects appointed to each region by the emperor. He also established the Napoleonic Code, which granted some civil rights and allowed for the rise of a true middle class, but also favored business interests and protected the property rights of the wealthy. After Napoleon's defeat at Waterloo, the nation lurched from one form of government to another for more than 50 years—a restored but weakened monarchy, a short-lived republic, and another empire headed by Napoleon's nephew—before establishing a modern democracy in 1870. Many of the institutions established by Napoleon, such as the prefects, survived it all and remain part of French government today.

The Significance of Waterloo

The Battle of Waterloo occurred near Brussels between French forces under Napoleon and combined British, Belgian, Dutch, German, and Prussian armies led by the British Duke of Wellington. The day began with Wellington and Napoleon facing each other across the field of battle after a night of heavy rain. The French leader delayed his attack until noon to allow the field to dry so that his artillery and cavalry could move more freely. French forces unsuccessfully attacked Wellington's center throughout the afternoon. Their early evening attack broke their opponent's center, but by then Prussian forces had assaulted the French flank, drawing critical resources away from the main fight. Wellington regrouped, drove the French back, and then advanced forcefully. Beset on two sides, the once-feared French army retreated. Over the preceding 20 years, Napoleon had established himself as one of the most powerful rulers and most successful military strategists since the days of the Roman Empire. His defeat at Waterloo ended once and for all his rule of France and his great influence over the affairs of Europe.

Air Force One

According to the official White House website for *Air Force One*, Franklin Roosevelt was the first U.S. president to travel extensively by air. His trips to the Yalta Conference and other destinations in Europe were an essential part of the World War II effort, but left his staff scrambling to find ways to ensure his safety and security as well as to keep the nation running while he was abroad. His successor, Harry Truman, also flew frequently, but it wasn't until the final years of Truman's administration that the name *Air Force One* came into use. The term is actually a call sign rather than the name of a specific aircraft and is only used to identify the aircraft when the president is on board. Each president since Roosevelt has had a dedicated airplane at his disposal, but any Air Force jet that has a sitting president as a passenger uses the call sign *Air Force One*.

Specifications of Current *Air Force One* Aircraft

* Model: Boeing 747–200B

* Engine thrust rating: 56,700 pounds

* Fuel capacity: 53,611 gallons

* Range: 7,800 miles

* Wing span: 195 feet, 8 inches

* Length: 231 feet, 10 inches

* Height: 63 feet, 5 inches

* Maximum altitude: 45,100 feet

* Interior floor space: 4,000 square feet

Special Amenities of Current *Air Force One* Aircraft

* Exercise room

* Full medical facility

* Retractable stairways

* Two galleys with capacity to prepare 100 meals in one sitting

* Shielded wiring to protect from electromagnetic pulses

* Classified defensive countermeasures technology

* In-flight refueling capability

* Safe for storing nuclear launch codes

* Two private bathrooms with showers

* Number of telephones: 85

* Number of televisions: 19

Ten Really Embarrassing Things U.S. Presidents Have Done in Public

Just because you're the leader of the free world doesn't mean you're perfect!

✳ ✳ ✳ ✳

1. **Flaunting a mistress:** John F. Kennedy—Perhaps booking your alleged mistress, Marilyn Monroe, as a performer at your birthday party is not such a good idea.

2. **Mistreatment of an animal:** Lyndon B. Johnson—Note to future leaders: Even if you love your beagle do not pick him up by the ears in front of the press.

3. **Oversharing:** Lyndon B. Johnson—LBJ made the list twice! This time he flashed his scar while recovering from gallbladder surgery.

4. **Bumbling:** Gerald R. Ford—Parodied by *Saturday Night Live* as a bumbler, Ford was actually a football star at the University of Michigan in the 1930s. Yet that didn't stop him from slipping down the steps of *Air Force One* or shooting his golf ball into a crowd of spectators more than once. News cameras were always there to capture the action.

5. **More animal mistreatment:** Jimmy Carter—It was supposed to be a private fishing excursion in Georgia. Unfortunately, a nearby cameraman photographed Carter as he battled an attacking swamp rabbit that tried to board his boat.

6. **Adultery of the heart:** Jimmy Carter—Carter had a run-in with a rabbit of the Playboy variety prior to the 1976 election when he admitted to having "committed adul-

tery in [his] heart many times."

7. Illness: George H. W. Bush—What does protocol say about vomiting on the lap of the Japanese prime minister?

8. Infidelity: Bill Clinton—Does an impeachment trial count? And let's not forget that dress!

9. Poor grammar: George W. Bush—There are many "Bush-isms" that would fit this category, but among the best entries was a comment delivered on the 2000 campaign trail: "Rarely is the question asked—Is our children learning?"

10. Trapped: George W. Bush—Another two-time mention. After abruptly ending a press conference in China, the president exited stage right—only to find his escape hampered by a locked door. Despite his tugging at the door and mugging for the cameras, Bush was at a loss until an aide escorted him from the room.

"The nine most terrifying words in the English language are: 'I'm from the government and I'm here to help.'"

—RONALD REAGAN

It's Not True, by George!

George Washington is known for a great many things, some of which are true (he was the only president to be elected unanimously) and many others that are imagined. Here are some of the latter.

✳ ✳ ✳ ✳

Washington wore wooden dentures. It's common knowledge that Washington had gnawing dental problems. This brought the leader much pain and sent him in search of relief. Over time, each of Washington's teeth had to be extracted and replaced with dentures. Legend holds that these dental appliances were fashioned from wood, which (some say) could account for Washington's "wooden" smile.

In fact, Washington's false teeth were made from hippopotamus and elephant ivory, as well as human teeth that were not his own. During his lifetime, Washington used several sets of falsies. Most were ill-fitting and therefore contorted his expression, but none were made from wood.

Washington threw a silver dollar across the Potomac River. George was a tall (6'2"), athletic man, but he certainly wasn't a good enough throw to hurl a silver dollar all the way across the Potomac River, which is close to a mile wide at Mount Vernon, Maryland (site of the president's home). There is evidence that, as a boy, he tossed something across the Rappahannock River in Fredericksburg, Virginia (near his childhood home). If that's the case, though, that "something" certainly wasn't a silver dollar, because the coins didn't even exist when Washington was young.

Washington wore a wig. Despite the fact that it was all the rage for men to sport a powdery hair hat in the late 1700s, George would go only so far to fit in. He kept his brownish-red hair at a length that allowed him to tie it back in a braid, and then he'd ocasionally give it a good dusting of powder just for the sake of fashion.

Washington's Tab

Some people believe that as commander in chief of the Continental Army, General George Washington "selflessly" refused a salary in favor of an expense account. Talk about shrewd moves.

✳   ✳   ✳   ✳

WHEN WASHINGTON TOOK over leadership of the Continental Army in 1775, he refused to accept a salary. Perhaps he did so to demonstrate sacrifice and to forge solidarity with the "have-nots," a group that included soldiers under his command. Many applauded Washington for his noble gesture without knowing that the general had just been granted carte blanche to use and perhaps even abuse government funds.

From September 1775 to March 1776, Washington spent more than $6,000 on alcohol alone. And during the harsh Valley Forge winter of 1777–1778, when his weary troops were perishing from hunger and exposure, Washington indulged his appetite for extravagant foods. An expense-account entry included "geese, mutton, fowls, turkey, veal, butter, turnips, potatoes, carrots, and cabbage."

By 1783, Washington had spent almost $450,000 on food, saddles, clothing, accommodations, and sundries. In today's dollars, that's nearly $5 million. When he became president, Washington again gallantly offered to waive his salary in favor of an expense account. The offer was politely refused, and he was paid a $25,000 stipend. It seems America could no longer afford the general's brand of sacrifice.

A Pox on Your House... of Commons

It was a sordid little 1963 drama so outrageous it would have played well on the big screen. The players included a top official in English government, a beautiful showgirl/call girl, a prominent medical man, and a military member of the Communist Party. When it was all over, the outrage accelerated the paranoia of the Cold War and threatened the national security of Britain—not to mention the rest of the world.

✳   ✳   ✳   ✳

The Cast Members

JOHN PROFUMO WAS the secretary of state for war under Harold Macmillan, England's prime minister for the Conservative Party in the early 1960s. Profumo was married to a beautiful movie actress named Valerie Hobson, whose biggest role was starring in *The Bride of Frankenstein*.

Christine Keeler was a young, vivacious model and topless showgirl in the Soho area of London, where she often posed for noted osteopath Stephen Ward, who fancied himself a sketch artist as well as a socialite. Ward had introduced Keeler, along with fellow showgirl Mandy Rice-Davies, to the world of the rich and famous.

Yevgeny Ivanov was a Soviet naval officer based at the Russian Embassy in London. He was acquainted with Dr. Ward. The British security service MI5 had tagged Ivanov as a KGB agent and had asked Ward to work on getting Ivanov to shift his allegiance to the West. With just a little prodding, they reasoned, Ivanov could be persuaded to join their side.

The Story Unfolds

All of these characters found themselves under one enormous roof in July 1961. Ward was throwing a party at Cliveden, the Buckinghamshire mansion of England's Lord Astor. Profumo was immediately attracted to Keeler and began seeing her after the party. But, on the quiet advice of a government official, Profumo called off the affair just a few months later.

What Profumo didn't know, however, was that Keeler had also been sleeping with Ivanov. Indeed, Christine Keeler was playing both sides of the Iron Curtain.

The Plot Thickens

This might have been the end of the story. But Keeler had also been involved with two other men, Aloysius "Lucky" Gordon and Johnny Edgecombe, who got into a bloody brawl over Keeler at a club in Soho. In December 1962, Keeler was at Ward's house visiting Mandy Rice-Davies when Edgecombe showed up. Keeler refused to let him in, so Edgecombe shot at the door, attracting the attention of police and blowing the whole story wide open.

In the end, Keeler served nine months for committing perjury in a trial involving "Lucky" Gordon. Ward was charged with living off the "earnings of prostitutes"—namely Keeler and Rice-Davies. On the final day of the trial, Dr. Ward cheated the Royal Courts of their justice by committing suicide. The ensuing publicity brought Profumo's name to light, suggesting an affair with Keeler.

The Climax

Profumo intensified his troubles and broke the scandal wide open in March 1963 by lying to the House of Commons. He claimed that his relationship with Keeler involved "no impropriety whatever." But his story didn't hold water, and he admitted his indiscretions only two months later. The facts of Keeler's two-timing affair with Profumo and Ivanov became public, along with Keeler's assertions that both Ward and Ivanov had asked her to pump Profumo for information regarding the transport of American nuclear missiles to what was then West Germany.

The implications of this—in a time of heightened Cold War paranoia—led to Profumo's resignation in early June.

The scandal also led to the resignation of Prime Minister Harold Macmillan several months later. Although he claimed ill health, the real reason was clear—the breach of security had occurred during his watch, even though no exchange of sensitive data had actually occurred.

The Epilogue

The aftermath of the Profumo Affair was a curious one. In disgrace, the former Parliament secretary wound up as a janitor for a London settlement house. On the upside, his wife forgave his transgressions. And in the end, his ability as a charity fundraiser led Queen Elizabeth II to award him Commander of the British Empire (CBE) in 1975.

Christine Keeler sold her story to a London tabloid for tens of thousands of dollars. She starred as herself in a British/Danish film called, appropriately, *The Keeler Affair*. In a photo shoot for the film, Keeler posed naked in a strategically positioned chair in what would become a famous and often copied image.

In 2001, Keeler published a tell-all autobiography entitled *The Truth at Last: My Story*, which made some wild and unsubstantiated claims about Profumo, Ward, and the British government. Ultimately, British intelligence and the FBI were unable to prove that Ivanov had tried to use Keeler to get information from Profumo.

Good Foreign Policies, Happy Endings

In some circles, diplomacy and foreign policy may be thought of as negative terms, but when they're effective, great things can happen.

✳   ✳   ✳   ✳

IN TODAY'S WORLD, it seems as though the overriding philosophy is "every country for itself": protecting the resources of the land, the people, and the country as a whole. Taking care of one's own surely isn't all bad, but whatever happened to goodwill? Yes, altruism, clearly, is less of a priority—taking its place is a bombastic ethnocentrism that is eroding that old-fashioned optimistic ideal of humanity. But for all the pessimism involving foreign relations in the last century, the U.S. government is still slipping in some good deeds here and there.

USAID

There's USAID, a foreign assistance agency with roots that go back to World War II. The organization was founded on the belief that, in order to achieve democracy and a global free market, the entire world must develop sustainable economic growth. In Brazil, for instance, where youth unemployment is high and electrical power availability is low, USAID found a way to address the problems together for a better outcome. Between 10 and 20 million poor Brazilians lack access to power grids, so USAID recruited groups of unemployed 16- to 24-year-olds to participate in their training program. In learning how to utilize renewable energy sources and rely less on the nation's power grid, young people who would have otherwise faltered in the job market now have marketable skills. Additionally, a more ecologically sound energy sector is emerging in Brazil as a result.

The World Bank

The World Bank, established in 1944 to encourage postwar global rebuilding, is doing its part, too. Once a mere lending institution, it has evolved into an elaborate consortium set to alleviate the pressures of worldwide poverty. With this goal in mind, the World Bank, unlike typical financial institutions, provides more than just monetary assistance to those in need. A World Bank program in Bolivia, the Bolivia Land for Agricultural Development Project, began in late 2007 to bring land to poor farmers by providing them with revolving credit and then finding third parties to match funds. Ongoing technical assistance and monitoring is also given through the World Bank to ensure success for the previously landless farmers.

The Peace Corps

Initiated by President John F. Kennedy and established in 1961, the Peace Corps was built with the intent of bringing peace to the world through volunteer service. A lofty goal, for sure, but through the many participants in its history and the programs pressed forth by them, it is a goal that can be met. Take the Kenyan Sign Language project: In 2002, while already in Kenya providing volunteer service to the community through the Peace Corps, a group noticed the lack of aid for hearing-impaired Kenyans. Few written materials in Kenyan Sign Language existed. Due to lack of funding, Kenyans with hearing impairments were neglected at schools, and in some cases, even their own family members had difficulty communicating with them. During a period of roughly 18 months, the Peace Corps created a software program to fill in this gap. Once finished, they worked with donor organizations to get the computers that the Kenyans needed to run the program.

Food for Peace

Helping out on the food front is Food for Peace, a USAID program put together during the Eisenhower administration, which funnels U.S. food overseas to fight malnutrition and starvation worldwide, while encouraging global agricultural development. In Zimbabwe, a country with a staggeringly high unemployment rate of roughly 80 percent in 2007 and ever-worsening drought conditions, the people rely heavily on staple foods, such as grains. These are inexpensive and relatively easy to grow. With the ongoing economic deterioration of the land, the poor people in urban areas of Zimbabwe have suffered greatly. By bringing sorghum, a nutritionally sound grass cereal, into the area for farming and trade, Food for Peace has helped citizens of Bulawayo (Zimbabwe's second-largest city) establish a model for consumer trade while providing sustenance to its people. Better yet, sorghum suits the dry climate of the region much better than the corn that was previously planted there.

The Carter Center

Another do-good group, the Carter Center—created in 1982 by former President Jimmy Carter and his wife, Rosalynn—was established in an effort to improve human existence the world over. With projects in 72 countries, the organization is making a difference. For example, in Chad—a country with ongoing internal unrest and poor economic development—*dracunculiasis*, or guinea worm disease, plagued the region (and the intestines of its people) for years. The Carter Center took on the challenge in 1986 and seriously arrested the pandemic by 1998 through water-safety education and assistance with larvicidal treatments.

Operation Provide Hope

Since 1992, Operation Provide Hope, a U.S. State Department program, has been donating medical supplies to the former Soviet Union. The incentive was initially established to help the region segue into a freer democratic state. In addition to the supplies, the program has built medical facilities and trained local people to make the facilities sustainable. In this region, prior to Operation Provide Hope, even a minor infection could turn into a major problem. Since implementation of the program, though, the line between life and death has become more distinct.

Clearly, while one hand of a government tends to its own flock, the other hand can still lend help to those in need of a good deed.

Alexander Hamilton's Pecuniary Success

Have you ever wondered why Alexander Hamilton—who was never a U.S. president—is on the ten-dollar bill? Most of us know of Hamilton because of his duel with Aaron Burr at the end of his life. But before that fateful day, the statesman influenced important policy in the brand new United States and assured a lasting legacy.

✳ ✳ ✳ ✳

IN 1773, HAMILTON entered King's College in New York—now known as Columbia University—as the country was gearing up for revolution against the British. This is where he began a foray into the world of politics, anonymously writing pamphlets that supported the idea of revolution and criticizing Loyalist ideas.

When the Revolutionary War began, Hamilton joined a volunteer militia. He took the initiative to teach himself about military history and strategy, and soon, high-ranking military officials began to take notice. One of those officials was none other than George Washington, who was so impressed with the young Hamilton that he made him a lieutenant colonel in the Continental Army. Hamilton became one of Washington's most trusted aides, and left the general with a lasting impression. Washington would not soon forget Alexander Hamilton, and the end of the war would not be the end of the association between the two men.

After the war, Hamilton was appointed to Congress as a New York representative, then resigned a year later to practice law. Interestingly, although he supported the revolutionary cause during the war, he specialized in defending Loyalists and British subjects, believing America should foster friendly relations with the British. This belief would come to shape many of his future ideas, and it made him a bit of a controversial figure in the new country.

While practicing law in New York City, Hamilton took advantage of the city's status as the up-and-coming financial center of the new country. In 1784 he founded the Bank of New York, which, amazingly, stayed in business for 223 years. In 2007, the bank merged with Mellon Financial Corporation and is now known as the Bank of New York Mellon.

The Constitutional Convention

Several years later, in 1787, Hamilton's father-in-law, New York State Senator Philip Schuyler, chose him as a delegate for the Constitutional Convention. The Convention began with the intention to strengthen the existing Articles of Confederation, but ultimately resulted in the creation of the U.S. Constitution, effectively creating a new government. During debates over the new document, Hamilton once again expressed his idea that the British model of government was one of the best in the world, and the U.S. would be smart to emulate it. He even suggested electing a president who would remain in office for life, but most of his fellow delegates didn't appreciate the idea of an American "monarch."

So while he was not utterly content with the final document, Hamilton still considered it an improvement over the Articles of Confederation, and became a vocal proponent of its ratification. In October 1787, Hamilton, and fellow founding fathers John Jay and James Madison, authored *The Federalist Papers*. Hamilton wrote fifty-one of the series of the eighty-five essays, which defended the new Constitution.

In 1788, Hamilton's former commander, George Washington, received several packages at his Mount Vernon home containing all eighty-five essays. Hamilton had written his essays anonymously, under the penname "Publius," but eventually he admitted to Washington that he was one of the authors. He also admitted that he had sent *The Federalist Papers* to Washington in an attempt to convince him to be the first president of the new United States.

The First Secretary of the Treasury

Thanks in part to Hamilton's persuasive essays, the Constitution was ratified on June 21, 1788. George Washington, at first reluctant to leave the peace and quiet of Mount Vernon, finally agreed to be the first president. One of the problems he immediately faced in office was the mountain of debt the new country owed after the Revolutionary War. Needing a good advisor to help sort out the issue, Washington appointed his old trusted aide, Alexander Hamilton, to Secretary of the Treasury.

Some of the new government officials wanted to cancel the debt facing the country, but Hamilton argued that paying it off would earn the new United States more respect. In the First Report on the Public Credit he submitted to Congress, Hamilton called for the national government to assume the states' debt. He proposed that all debt be consolidated and distributed among the states, and he suggested taxes to help pay off the debt. This was not a popular idea, and it was debated for months between Hamilton, Thomas Jefferson, and James Madison. Most Southern states had already paid off their debt, and they resented having to pay taxes to help the Northern states. The disagreement finally led to what became known as the Compromise of 1790: Jefferson and Madison agreed to Hamilton's idea, but in return, the U.S. capital was relocated from its temporary northern locations in New York and Philadelphia to the permanent southern location of the District of Columbia. This helped to appease the Southern states.

Hamilton's Second Report on the Public Credit outlined his ideas for establishing a national bank, which he believed to be another crucial step in creating a stable nation. Once again, Madison opposed his idea, saying the Constitution did not expressly permit the creation of such an institution. In Madison's opinion, anything the Constitution did not specifically allow was not to be permitted. But Hamilton argued that unless the Constitution specifically forbade the creation of a bank, it should be permitted. Thus began the never-ending debates over Constitutional interpretation!

But in the end, drawing upon his experience with creating the Bank of New York, Hamilton helped to establish the First Bank of the United States. The bank was owned by both the government and private investors, with the majority of the stock held by investors.

While promoting the formation of the bank, Hamilton also submitted another proposal: he suggested the establishment of a U.S. Mint. Up until this time, the currency used in America was a hodgepodge of coinage. Spanish, Portuguese, and French coins had all found their way into circulation. Hamilton believed it best if the U.S. had its own, uniform currency. So in 1792, Congress passed the Coinage Act, which created the United States Mint in Philadelphia. Hamilton proposed adopting the dollar as the basic monetary unit in the country, with a decimal system and fractional coins for smaller transactions.

It's easy to see that Hamilton was immensely influential in the creation of the United States. He not only helped to ratify the document that created a new government, but thanks to his fiscal policies, the country was able to pay off interest on public debt, fund an army and navy, and balance the budget. Hamilton laid the groundwork for the strong economic power the country enjoys today. He is often considered the "father of the federal government" and the author of capitalism in America. Woodrow Wilson once stated, "We think of Mr. Hamilton rather than of President Washington when we look back to the policy of the first administration." Today, Hamilton's many contributions are honored in the Museum of American Finance in New York City. Fittingly, the museum is located at 48 Wall Street—the exact location that Hamilton's Bank of New York first conducted business.

The Burr-Hamilton Duel

On July 11, 1804, U.S. Vice President Aaron Burr mortally wounded former Secretary of the Treasury Alexander Hamilton during a duel at Weehawken, New Jersey. Bitter differences between the two men can be traced to their philosophical stances (Burr was a Democratic-Republican, Hamilton a Federalist) as well as pivotal events that had pushed both to the breaking point.

✳ ✳ ✳ ✳

TENSIONS BEGAN WHEN Burr snatched a U.S. Senate seat away from Hamilton's father-in-law, Philip Schuyler. Hamilton also held a grudge against Burr for obtaining and publishing one of his private papers. In the document, Hamilton was highly critical of President John Adams, also a Federalist. The ensuing publicity proved embarrassing to Hamilton and widened rifts in the Federalist Party.

Burr blamed Hamilton for his defeat in the race for governor of New York in 1804. Burr had switched parties and run as a Federalist, but Hamilton urged New York Federalists not to support him. When Burr learned that Hamilton had also defamed him at a society dinner, he challenged him to a duel.

When the two faced off, each managed to squeeze off a round. Burr emerged unscathed but Hamilton wasn't so lucky. A bullet ripped through his spine and proved fatal. Some witnesses claim that Hamilton intentionally aimed into the air, not at his nemesis. Some also stated that Burr's manner immediately following the shooting suggested regret. Burr was indicted for murder in New York and New Jersey but was never tried. After the duel, Burr's political career went down in ruins.

Several years after the incident, Burr was tried for treason for attempting to start a new republic in the Southwest, but he was acquitted. When Burr died on September 14, 1836, at age 80, he was the last surviving participant of the 1804 duel.

The Posthumous Life of Alexander Hamilton

The duel between Alexander Hamilton and Aaron Burr is one of the most famous—if not the most famous—duels in American history. We may never know which duelist shot first or what their intentions truly were. But we do know a bit about what happened to Hamilton and his legacy after those fateful shots rang out.

✳   ✳   ✳   ✳

THE BULLET FROM Burr's pistol hit Hamilton in the lower right abdomen. It ricocheted off his ribcage, grievously damaging his liver and diaphragm, and finally came to rest within his lumbar vertebrae. According to witnesses, Hamilton immediately collapsed, having been paralyzed by the bullet. A short distance away from the clearing of the dueling ground, Hamilton's family physician, Dr. David Hosack, was waiting in the woods to attend to any injuries. Sadly, Dr. Hosack was the same doctor who treated Hamilton's son, Philip, after he was fatally shot in a duel just three years earlier. No doubt the family doctor was hoping that his services would not once again be required; but after the two gunshots echoed through the trees, Dr. Hosack heard someone frantically calling his name.

The doctor wrote an account of his experience about a month after the deadly duel. He described how he entered the clearing where the duel had taken place and saw Hamilton on the ground, held by his friend and second, Judge Nathaniel Pendleton. When the doctor approached the two men, Hamilton managed to weakly proclaim, "This is a mortal wound, doctor." Soon after, Hamilton passed out, his vital signs so feeble that Dr. Hosack wasn't certain he could be revived. Pendleton and the doctor rushed to ferry the lifeless Hamilton across the Hudson River to the Greenwich Village home of his friend William Bayard Jr., where the statesman would spend the last hours of his life.

On the way, the doctor rubbed Hamilton's face and hands with smelling salts. This apparently helped to temporarily reinvigorate the wounded man, and he opened his eyes, telling the doctor, "my vision is indistinct." But once he awoke and his pulse became stronger, he was able to see his pistol lying nearby. Hamilton told the doctor, "Take care of that pistol; it is undischarged, and still cocked; it may go off and do harm. Pendleton knows that I did not intend to fire at him." This is interesting to note, as it seems to imply that Hamilton didn't even realize his pistol had fired, into the air or otherwise.

After these few short exchanges, the doctor reported that Hamilton said little else, except to say that he was unable to feel his legs and to acknowledge the fact that he knew he would probably not live much longer.

Another account of Hamilton's final hours was written by the Rt. Rev. Benjamin Moore, the rector of Trinity Church and

Bishop of New York. According to Rev. Moore, Hamilton requested to receive communion as he lay upon his deathbed in Bayard's home. Moore was hesitant to oblige, as he considered participating in a duel to be a mortal sin. So he asked Hamilton if, in the event he recovered, he would use his influence to denounce the "barbarous custom" of dueling. Hamilton replied, "That, sir, is my deliberate intention." Rev. Moore also stated that Hamilton claimed he held no resentment toward Burr, and, in fact, forgave him for the fatal shot.

Hamilton died on July 12, 1804, about thirty-six hours after the duel, with his wife, Elizabeth Schuyler Hamilton, by his side. Today, Bayard's home, located at 80–82 Jane St. in Manhattan, is marked with a plaque which reads, "Where Alexander Hamilton, first Secretary of the Treasury, died after his duel with Aaron Burr." Interestingly, Hamilton's death actually helped him keep his promise to Rev. Moore: in the months following the duel, an anti-dueling movement began to pick up momentum in New York state. Although the southern states wouldn't embrace the practice until after the Civil War, the Burr-Hamilton duel signaled a dueling decline in the North.

Of course, this was not the end of Hamilton's legacy in America. In fact, the country we know today is still very similar to the nation that Hamilton envisioned more than two hundred years ago. He believed the country should have a strong, centralized government, while still allowing states individuality. And he posited a government with three branches—the executive, the judicial, and the legislative—which became a foundation of our political structure.

Hamilton took his ideas and helped to found the Federalist Party, which is considered the first political party in America. Just like Republicans and Democrats are alternately praised and vilified by citizens and the press, the Federalists were criticized by some, and embraced by others. They supported a strong national government and a strong economy. They also believed the country should foster friendly relations with Great Britain, which was a less-than-popular idea when the War of 1812 erupted. By the end of the war, American patriotism was high, and the Federalist Party began to fade away. But the vision of Hamilton and his party took hold, and the idea of a strong government and economy have stood the test of time.

Hamilton's influence has not only been felt in Washington, D.C., but also in a most unlikely arena—Broadway. In 2004, author Ron Chernow published Alexander Hamilton, a biography of the statesman which spent three months on the *New York Times* Best Seller list. A few years later, actor and composer Lin-Manuel Miranda happened to pick up the book at the airport. His perusal of the story inspired him to write *Hamilton*, a unique Broadway musical that juxtaposes the eighteenth-century life of Hamilton with modern-day rap and hip-hop. The show was nominated for a record-breaking sixteen Tony Awards, and won eleven, including Best Musical of 2016. Even with all of Hamilton's innovative ideas, could he ever have envisioned sell-out crowds waiting in line to see a stage version of his life? Perhaps it's only now, in modern times, that it's easy to see that the Burr-Hamilton duel was only the beginning of Alexander Hamilton's intriguing story.

Dunkin' the Doughnut Myth

It's well known that President John F. Kennedy had an affinity for sweet things (ahem). What isn't true is that he referred to himself as a jelly doughnut in a landmark speech.

When JFK journeyed to Berlin in the summer of 1963, his administration had already survived the debacle of the Bay of Pigs and withstood the anxiety of the Cuban Missile Crisis— all while maneuvering through the frigid waters of the Cold War. His trip to West Germany was seen as an endorsement of both democracy and détente, and the speech he was scheduled to deliver to the German people was expected to be one of the most influential of his presidency. When he concluded his commentary with the words "I am a Berliner" in the native language of his listeners, it was regarded as a key moment in his thousand days in office.

The text of Kennedy's speech was a plea for the freedom of all people, and he used Berlin as a symbol of that freedom. To emphasize the point, he used the phrase *"Ich bin ein Berliner"* in an attempt to convey his unity with the people of Berlin. What he didn't realize is that the word *Berliner* could also be used as the word for *jelly doughnut*. By using the phrase the way he did, Kennedy could be accused of indicating that he was a jam-filled pastry rather than a participant in the city's struggle for freedom.

The words were scripted for Kennedy by a respected interpreter, Robert H. Lochner, who was carefully tutored on the proper phrasing. Lochner was informed that while a citizen of Berlin would say, *"Ich bin Berliner,"* that would not be the correct terminology for Kennedy—a non-citizen—to use. This is why the preposition "ein" was added to the text, even though it could be loosely construed as a denotation of a doughy delicacy.

The First United Nations

When a group of nations band together for collective security, it's an alliance or coalition. When a great many nations band together for global security, it's the United Nations (UN). But there was a UN before the UN: the League of Nations.

✳ ✳ ✳ ✳

Genesis

FOUNDED IN 1919 AND now almost forgotten, the League of Nations was the UN's forerunner. World War I's devastation suggested that the next war would be even bloodier; might it obliterate all civilization? Forty-four nations banded together to form the League, which was headquartered in Geneva, Switzerland. The League sought to influence nations to take the following actions (and failed because):

* Stop arming themselves to the teeth. (If someone wouldn't disarm, and the League couldn't or wouldn't arm to disarm them, so much for disarmament.)

* Let peoples govern themselves as they chose. (Unless they chose Communism, which left out the Soviet Union—a rather big puzzle piece.)

* Abandon sleazy secret maneuvers in favor of open international dialogue. (Fine, provided nations stopped doing sneaky things. They didn't.)

* Trust the League for security rather than military power blocs. (A military is needed for authentic security, and the League had none.)

When it came to keeping the peace, humanity talked a better game than it played. The League faltered when authoritarian nations rearmed, suppressed national self-determination, began secret political maneuvering, and forged military power blocs.

Exodus

The United States never joined the League. Domestic "it's not our problem" sentiment disappointed President Woodrow Wilson, who pinned all his personal prestige on the League's promise. The League ebbed into a genteel, useless debate club as other powers withdrew:

* Japan invaded Manchuria in 1931. Fed up with lectures, resurgent Japan left the League in 1933 and invaded China proper in 1937. Little was done.

* The League fidgeted but did little as Hitler remilitarized the Rhineland, slurped up Austria, browbeat Czechoslovakia out of existence, and started the Holocaust.

* Mussolini's Italy used chemical weapons against Abyssinia (Ethiopia). Lectured but not thwarted, Italy quit the League in 1937.

* In 1939, the League expelled the Soviet Union (which had finally been admitted in 1934) for invading Finland. Stalin didn't care. He'd only joined to annoy Hitler anyway.

World War II came, and its death toll of 72 million confirmed the League's founding fears while standing as a tombstone for its failures. The League's rump membership took the organization behind an Alp and euthanized it in 1946. The Palace of Nations, its Geneva HQ, later became a UN office.

Legacy

The League wasn't all failure. It reduced slavery, aided POW repatriation, developed passports for stateless persons, and ran other errands of mercy. It resolved some dangerous regional conflicts. It established that larger and wealthier nations should help improve the world, while giving smaller and poorer nations a voice. Despite the League's glaring failures, humanity needed an international peace and humanitarian organization. Another would come.

Successor

At the height of World War II, Franklin D. Roosevelt and Winston Churchill first used "United Nations" as a synonym for "The Allies." The United Nations agreed not to seek or accept separate peaces with the Axis (Germany, Italy, Japan, and minor allies) and kept that commitment. After the war (1945), the United Nations became a formal, funded organization.

After the lessons from the League's experience, the UN has compiled a better track record. While it obviously didn't eliminate regional power blocs, there hasn't been a WWIII, and most people think that's good. The UN's six official languages (Arabic, Chinese, English, French, Russian, and Spanish) better reflect the world than did the League's French, English, and

Spanish. Major powers understand that if they quit the UN in a huff, the remaining membership will simply decide without them. It's imperfect, but it has seen its 60th anniversary. Its ancestor, the League of Nations, never celebrated a 30th.

Continuing to Work Together

As of this writing, 193 member states represent virtually all recognized independent nations. The first session of the general assembly convened January 10, 1946, in the Westminster Central Hall in London under the auspices of acting Secretary-General Gladwyn Jebb, a prominent British diplomat. On February 1, Norway's Trygve Lie was chosen to be the United Nations' first secretary-general. The secretary general is appointed for a renewable five-year term; to date no secretary general has served more than two terms.

Today the United Nations is headquartered at an 18-acre site on New York's Manhattan Island. The land was purchased in 1946 through a donation from John D. Rockefeller Jr.; even though it's physically located in New York City, it is considered international territory. The United Nations is comprised of six principal operating organs: the General Assembly, the Security Council, the Economic and Social Council, the Secretariat, the International Court of Justice, and the Trusteeship Council. The General Assembly operates on a one-state-one-vote system, and a two-thirds majority is required to pass many resolutions. The organization has twice been honored with the Nobel Peace Prize.

Chapter 5

The Background Behind Your Surroundings

Washington, D.C.: The Official Story

First, let's put a myth to rest: The District of Columbia was not wrested from swampland back in the 1790s. It only feels that way. The temperature, officially designated as "sub-tropical," averages 86 degrees during the summer, and it rains approximately 115 days per year. (The record high, by the way, was 106 degrees on July 20, 1930.)

✳   ✳   ✳   ✳

THE CITY ITSELF was built mostly on farm and forestland on the north bank of the Potomac River and encompasses 68.3 square miles, including 6.9 square miles of water and 13.25 square miles of parkland, making Washington one of the greenest cities in America. That's good news for the 591,833 residents who are packed in at a density of 9,639 people per square mile. Washington is currently the 27th most populous city in the United States, slightly behind Nashville and a little ahead of Las Vegas.

Approximately one-fifth of D.C.'s population is younger than 18. More than a quarter of the population is between ages 18 and 34, and a little more than a tenth is older than 65.

Nearly half of the city's adults, or about 243,000 people, work for the federal government. And they're a well-educated bunch. Almost 40 percent have a bachelor's degree or higher, compared to 24 percent of all Americans. As of 2008, their annual median income hovered around a whopping $50,000.

What will that salary get you, though? A home in Georgetown, D.C.'s priciest neighborhood, will set you back an average of $3 million. Condos in trendy Dupont Circle go for around $1 million and a *pied-a-terre* in bohemian Adams Morgan costs a mere $650,000.

Of course, Washingtonians don't always stay home even when they can afford one. The city's culture-vultures and socialites help keep the 106.3-mile Metro Rail subway system one of the busiest in the nation, carrying 215 million passengers per year.

If they're not going to work, Washingtonians might be headed to one of the capital's 30+ professional theaters, 40 museums, or going out to eat, perhaps at Citronelle on fashionable M Street. Welcome to Washington, D.C., and bon appétit!

Yellowstone: A Ticking Time Bomb

This beloved national park is actually a giant volcano, which means that it's only a matter of time before the whole place blows sky-high.

✳ ✳ ✳ ✳

Not What It Appears

ABOUT THREE MILLION people visit Yellowstone National Park each year. They do a little hiking, maybe some fishing. They admire the majesty of the mountains and antagonize a few bears for the sake of an interesting picture. And, of course, they visit the geysers. Hordes of tourists sit and wait patiently for Old Faithful to do its thing every ninety minutes or so. When it finally blows, they break into applause as if they've just seen Carol Channing belt out "Hello, Dolly." And then they go home.

Few of these tourists give much thought to what is going on below their feet while they are at Yellowstone. Geologists, however, have known for years that some sort of volcanic activity is responsible for the park's strange, volatile, steamy landscape. Just one problem: They couldn't find evidence of an actual volcano—the familiar cone-shaped mountain that tells to us in no uncertain terms that a huge explosion once took place on that spot.

In the 1960s, NASA took pictures of Yellowstone from outer space. When geologists got their hands on these pictures, they understood why they couldn't spot the volcano: It was far too vast for them to see. The crater of the Yellowstone volcano includes practically the entire park, covering about 2.2 million acres. Obviously, we're not talking about your typical, garden-variety volcano. Yellowstone is what is known as a supervolcano.

It's Already Erupted a Bunch of Times

There is no recorded history of any supervolcano eruptions, so we can only use normal volcanic activity as a measuring stick. Geologists believe that Yellowstone has erupted about 140 times in the past 16 million years. The most recent blast was about 100,000 times more powerful than the 1980 eruption of Mount St. Helens in Washington, and it spread ash over almost the entire area of the United States west of the Mississippi River. Some of the previous Yellowstone eruptions were many times more destructive than that.

And here's some interesting news: In the past 20 years or so, geologists have detected significant activity in the molten rock and boiling water below Yellowstone. in other words, the surface is shifting.

Nearby, the Teton Range has gotten a little shorter. Scientists have calculated that Yellowstone erupts about every 600,000 years. And get this: The last Yellowstone eruption took place about 640,000 years ago.

There's No Need to Worry... Yet

Before you go scrambling for the Atlantic Ocean, screaming and waving your arms in the air, know that the friendly folks who run Yellowstone National Park assure us that an eruption is not likely to happen for at least another 1,000 years. And even then, any eruption would be preceded by weeks, months, or perhaps even years of telltale volcanic weirdness.

The Fountain of Youth

It's been an obsession of explorers for centuries, but no one has been able to find the magic elixir.

✳ ✳ ✳ ✳

SPANISH EXPLORER JUAN Ponce de León was supposedly searching for the fabled fountain of youth when he discovered Florida. However, it wasn't until after his death in 1521 that he became linked with the fountain.

The first published reference associating Ponce de León with the fountain of youth was the *Historia General y Natural de las Indias*, by Gonzalo Fernandez de Oviedo in 1535. The author cited the explorer's search for a fountain of restorative water to cure his impotence, but the veracity of this account is questionable since Ponce de León had children at the time of his 1513 voyage and didn't even mention the fountain in his travel notes.

Moreover, the fountain of youth legend predates Ponce de León. In Arabic versions of the *Alexander Romance*, a collection of myths about Alexander the Great, the Macedonian king and his troops cross a desert and come to a fountain in which they bathe to regain strength and youth. This story was translated to French in the thirteenth century and was well known among Europeans.

If a fountain of youth actually exists, no one has found it in any of its supposed locations, which are most typically cited as Florida, the Bahamas, or the Bay of Honduras. It may turn out, however, that a fountain of youth exists in science. David Sinclair, a Harvard University professor and the founder of Sirtris Pharmaceuticals, discovered in 2003 that the molecule resveratrol could extend the lifespan of worms and fruit flies. In 2006, Italian researchers prolonged the life of the fish *Nothobranchius furzeri* with resveratrol.

Drugs that are based on this research could be on shelves soon, though initially they will be designed only to aid diabetics. It's not quite eternal life—it's basically just extended fitness. But that's more than Ponce de León found.

Strange Structures

Humans have the capacity to achieve great things, conquer the seemingly impossible, and invent wonders that make our world a better place. However, sometimes they just like to build things that are big, tall, or strange.

✳ ✳ ✳ ✳

Personal Vanity Gets Etched in Stone

SOUTH DAKOTA HAS Mount Rushmore, but nestled in the Catskill Mountains is the town of Prattsville, New York, which features Pratt Rocks—a set of relief carvings begun 84 years before its famous western counterpart. Zadock Pratt, who founded the world's largest tannery in the 1830s, commissioned a local sculptor to immortalize his visage high up on a mountainside. The numerous stone carvings include a coat of arms, Pratt's own bust, his business milestones, and even his personal accomplishments, such as his two terms in the U.S. House of Representatives. Carvings also include a shrine to

Pratt's son George, who was killed during the Civil War. But the strangest bit found at this site is a recessed tomb that was intended to house Pratt's decaying corpse for eternity. It leaked, Pratt balked, and the chamber remains empty.

Mega-Megaliths

The offbeat dream of Bill Cohea, Jr., and Frederick Lindkvist, two highly spiritual fellows, Columcille was designed to resemble an ancient Scottish religious retreat located on the Isle of Iona. More than 80 oblong stones are "planted" in a Bangor, Pennsylvania, field to approximate the ancient site, a place where some say "the veil is thin between worlds." In addition to the megaliths, Columcille has enchanting chapels, altars, bell towers, cairns, and gates—enough features to lure Harry Potter fans into an entire day of exploration. Cohea and Lindkvist began their ever-evolving project as a spiritual retreat in 1978. They encourage everyone to visit their nondenominational mystical park. Their request? Simply "be."

Stacked Really High

It's quite surprising to encounter a 1,216-foot-tall smokestack, especially when that chimney is located in a rural town deep in western Pennsylvania. Homer City Generating Station produces electricity by burning coal. But the process has one troubling side effect: Its effluence can be toxic in certain quantities. The super-tall smokestack's purpose is to harmlessly disperse this undesirable by-product, thereby rendering it safe. It does this by releasing the agents high up in the atmosphere where they (theoretically) have ample time to dilute before falling back to Earth. At present, this soaring chunk of steel-reinforced concrete ranks as the third tallest in the world, just behind a 1,250-foot-tall smokestack located in Canada and a 1,377-foot-tall monster over in Kazakhstan.

Fee! Fie! Foe! Fum!

A drive through Staunton, Virginia, may leave some wondering if they've mistakenly entered the land of the giants. After all, an 18-foot-tall watering can and a six-foot-tall flowerpot are displayed on the main boulevard. But fear not. It's no giant who dwells in this hamlet but rather an average-size gent named Willie Ferguson. A large concentration of this metal fabricator's giant works can be seen on the grounds of his sculpture studio. At this metal "imaginarium," visitors will find a six-foot-long dagger, a ten-foot-long set of crutches, a six-foot-tall work boot—everything, it seems, but the proverbial beanstalk.

Cross with Caution

If you've crossed Vermont's Brookfield Floating Bridge by car, you're aware of its treachery. If you tried it on a motorcycle, you probably took an unplanned swim. That's because the lake that the bridge is supposed to cross occasionally crosses it. The 320-foot-long all-wooden Brookfield Bridge rests on 380 tarred, oaken barrels that were designed to adjust to the level of Sunset Lake and keep the bridge deck high and dry. But more often than not, they allow the bridge to sink several inches below the surface. Why does this bridge float in the first place? Sunset Lake is too deep to support a traditional, pillared span, so since 1820, impromptu "water ballet" maneuvers have been taking place as vehicles amble across.

Tower City

As drivers creep along I-76 just west of Philadelphia, they witness a stand of super-tall broadcasting masts towering over a suburban neighborhood. The Roxborough Antenna Farm is to broadcasting towers what New York City is to skyscrapers. In the land of broadcasting, height equals might, so the higher the tower, the better the signal strength. With eight TV/FM masts jutting above the 1,000-foot mark (the tallest stretches to 1,276 feet), the array easily outclasses most skyscrapers in height. The reason these big sticks exist in such a concentrated area? Location, location, location. The Roxborough site is a unique setting that features geographical height, proper zoning clearances, and favorable proximity to the city—a trifecta by industry standards.

Glacial Lake Missoula

Around 13,000 B.C., in what is today the Pacific Northwest of the United States, geologic time was measured in hours and days— with all the devastation you'd expect from such sudden geology. One minute there was a lake, then someone pulled the plug and released a flood.

✳   ✳   ✳   ✳

Glacial Floods and Lakes

A GLACIAL FLOOD OCCURS when a large glacial meltwater lake gets loose. When the continental two-mile-thick glaciers of the Cordilleran ice sheet released an icy clasp on North America, they left large lakes at the glaciers' melting edges. Glacial Lake Missoula was roughly the size of Connecticut and about 2,000 feet deep. It contained 500 cubic miles of water, about the volume of Lake Ontario, perched in the northern Montana Rockies. If it still existed today, it would be the 11th largest lake on Earth in terms of water volume.

Not the Most Glamorous Name . . .

Geologists named the ice dam (a finger of the ice sheet that holds back the entire lake) the Purcell Trench Lobe. If the ice dam were to fail, the water could only go west because of the Rockies. No one is sure if the water undermined the dam's base, spilled over the top, or physically floated the dam like a big iceberg, but the dam definitely failed, and when it did, Glacial Lake Missoula headed for the Pacific Ocean at speeds approaching 80 miles per hour.

Big Lake, Big Baggage

You probably know that rivers transport sand and pebbles. Glacial Lake Missoula transported rocks the size of large cars; they're still lying around Palouse Country, in eastern Washington state. The entire lake, full of icebergs and all the forest and animal debris in the path of the water, spread out to cover the southeastern portion of Washington—about a hundred miles across. Today, this long-lost body of water is called Lake Lewis, and its high-water marks can be seen far up on the region's hillsides.

It Has to Go Somewhere!

The water had only one outlet: the mile-wide canyon at Wallula Gap near the Washington–Oregon boundary. Beginning at Idaho and going west, the interstate border is a straight line until it hits the Columbia River. Wallula Gap is a brief hike from that spot.

Don't Hold Your Breath

Multiple glacial floods hit the young Columbia Basin as the ice dam re-formed and failed again. Each flood took about a week to run its course. Nobody is sure how long the re-forming took, but geologists believe there may have been more than 100 such cycles.

Gangster's Paradise

Throughout the 1920s and 1930s, Wisconsin's Northwoods were the place for bad guys looking to escape the heat—literally and figuratively—of Chicago. After the Chicago & North Western Railroad expanded due north into Wisconsin's wooden hinterlands, Chicagoland's elite came to vacation on the crystal-clear lakes. But they didn't come alone. For gangsters and their henchmen, the Northwoods were both a summer playground and a year-round hideout. Today, numerous communities have their own stories of gangster legend and lore.

✳ ✳ ✳ ✳

Public Enemy No. 1

AFTER SERVING EIGHT-AND-A-HALF years for robbery and assault, John Dillinger took off on a ten-month crime spree that earned him the title "Public Enemy No. 1." He and his gang rampaged across the Upper Midwest, busting cronies out of the slammer, robbing banks, murdering lawmen, and escaping from the FBI each time. Possibly needing a quiet vacation, Dillinger and accomplices headed to northern Wisconsin. On Friday, April 20, 1934, they showed up at Little Bohemia in Manitowish Waters.

The owner of a nearby resort tipped off the feds, and G-men headed north. But what happened just two days later would disgrace the Bureau. Driving into the resort, headlights off, the lawmen met some Civilian Conservation Corps workers who were leaving the resort after dinner. Figuring Dillinger and his partner-in-crime, Baby Face Nelson, were inside the car, the lawmen called for the driver to stop. Unable to hear the order, the car didn't stop and the lawmen opened fire, killing one of the innocents. When Dillinger and his band heard the gunfire, they made a hasty escape. Nelson, in a nearby cabin, escaped along the shoreline of Star Lake. Both parties forced nearby neighbors to provide getaway cars.

Both Dillinger and Nelson were killed within the year. But Little Bohemia Lodge remains on Highway 51, the main thoroughfare to and through the Northwoods. It still serves breakfast, lunch, and dinner, with a heaping helping of history.

The Capones

"Big Al" Capone turned 21 the day after the Volstead Act, the legislation that made alcohol illegal, went into effect. This seems like an ironic twist for someone who would go down in history known as a bootlegger, gangster, and criminal mastermind.

The Northwoods wasn't a temporary escape for Big Al, as it served as his permanent getaway. He didn't even try to cover up this fact, dubbing his Couderay retreat "The Hideout." His home on the shores of Cranberry Lake came complete with a gun turret alongside the driveway, openings in the stone walls for machine guns, and a personal jail. Booze runners from Canada would land their planes on the lake, and Capone's gang then took care of the distribution.

Al's older brother, Ralph "Bottles" Capone, was the director of liquor sales for the mob and covered his tracks by operating Waukesha Waters, a distribution company for Waukesha Springs mineral water. But Ralph had another passion: bookmaking. Ralph was less vicious than his brother, but bookmaking got him into trouble. He landed in prison in the early 1930s for tax evasion, coincidentally the same charge that sent Al to Alcatraz, where he was imprisoned for seven-and-a-half years. When Big Al was released in November 1939, he was so stricken with syphilis that he was unseated as leader of the criminal underworld. He died seven years later.

Later, Ralph lived in Mercer, from 1943 until his death on November 22, 1974. He managed the Rex Hotel and Billy's Bar and owned a house that had previously belonged to his brother. Ralph sponsored community Christmas parties, donated food and gifts to the needy, contributed to churches, and financed high school class trips. Despite his criminal history, locals remember him mostly for his kindness and charity. He also earned at least $20,000 a year from an Illinois cigarette vending machine business and was repeatedly investigated by the Internal Revenue Service. After 1951, Ralph Capone didn't even bother to file tax returns. At the time of his death he owed $210,715 in back taxes.

The Most Vicious

Few gangster aficionados know the story of John Henry Seadlund, dubbed "The World's Most Vicious Criminal" by FBI director J. Edgar Hoover. A loafer from Minnesota, Seadlund turned to crime after a chance meeting with Tommy Carroll, a veteran of Dillinger's gang. To make fast cash as a new criminal, Seadlund considered kidnapping wealthy Chicagoans vacationing in the Northwoods and demanding ransom. But after joining with a new lowlife, James Atwood Gray, Seadlund's kidnapping plot expanded to include a professional baseball player. The plan was to kidnap the St. Louis Cardinals' star pitcher Dizzy Dean, but Seadlund gave up when he realized how hard it might be to get ransom from Dean's ballclub.

Kidnapping ballplayers didn't pan out, so Seadlund abducted a retired greeting card company executive while heading out of Illinois in September 1937. After getting ransom, he exacted a kidnapping and murder scheme on the retiree, leaving him and accomplice Gray dead in a dugout near Spooner. He was caught when marked bills from the ransom were used at a racetrack the following January.

Beyond Bigwigs
Northwoods legend and lore extends beyond the mob's biggest names. During Prohibition, federal agents found and confiscated major gang-run stills in towns across Wisconsin's northern third. Elcho was the purported home to a mob doctor who traded bullet removal for booze, and Hurley was a gangster hot spot, as it was a "wide-open" town that flouted Prohibition and laws against prostitution. Wisconsin's Northwoods mob stories are as big as its fish tales.

Wisconsin Symbols Say It All

What makes Wisconsin unique? What sets it apart? Cheese, cows, and lakes are some things that come to mind. But more importantly, what does Wisconsin want people to remember? Well, just like every other state, Wisconsin has a long list of state symbols and emblems—things that Wisconsinites think represent the state best. Do Wisconsinites know there is a state soil? Did anyone know there is a state soil? Read on.

✳   ✳   ✳   ✳

✳ **State Animal:** You wouldn't be a Badger fan if you get this one wrong. Yup, it's the badger, and there are plenty of them throughout the state, although you don't often see them. These nocturnal creatures are a bit shy, hiding in their dens during the day and hunting at night.

* **State Nickname:** Wisconsin is "The Badger State." This wasn't a trick question, although you might get the second part of the question wrong. Does the nickname come from the state animal? Nope. In fact, the state animal probably came about after the nickname. Wisconsin has been known as the Badger State since the 1830s, when miners dug tunnels into the hillsides to search for lead and stay warm in the cold Wisconsin winters—just like the animals.

* **State Wildlife Animal:** How many state animals can one state have? The Wisconsin wildlife animal is the white-tailed deer. You've probably seen them along the side of the road.

* **State Domesticated Animal:** In America's Dairyland, what else could it be? The dairy cow, of course. Officially named in 1971, this animal represents the importance of the dairy industry to Wisconsin's economy.

* **Name for Wisconsin Residents:** Wisconsinites

* **State Mineral:** Illinois might have a quaint little town called Galena, but Wisconsin has an abundance of the mineral of the same name, also known as lead sulphite.

* **State Grain:** Knee-high by the Fourth of July, the favorite grain is corn. It is used for livestock feed and ethanol fuel—and who can resist a good Sweet Corn Festival in early August?

* **State Nicknames:** Oops. Didn't we already have this one? Over the years, Wisconsin has also been known as the Cheese State, the Dairy State, America's Dairyland, and the Copper State.

* **State Dog:** Named in 1985, the American Water Spaniel represents hunting and water sports in Wisconsin. But does anyone know someone who actually has one?

* **State Tree:** An 1893 vote among the children of Wisconsin made the sugar maple the official tree. A second vote was

held in 1948, but the sugar maple prevailed once again and it was made official once more in 1949. Maybe the beautiful red-orange autumn leaves and the delicious syrup made from its sap have something to do with this tree's popularity among residents and tourists alike.

* **State Soil:** What? There's a state soil? Yes, it's Antigo Silt Loam. If you forget the name—which you probably will—just remember that this silty soil was created by the glaciers that once covered much of the state. It's good for dairy farming, growing potatoes, and raising timber.

* **State Fish:** Its official name is the muskellunge, but most anglers know it as the musky—a large fish found in the lakes of northern Wisconsin.

* **State Motto:** Adopted in 1851, the motto, "Forward," represents Wisconsin's drive to be a national leader.

* **State Bird:** The robin won the title by a margin of 2–1 over the nearest competitor in a vote of schoolchildren in 1927. The robin usually leaves for warmer climates in October, and its familiar red breast marks the unofficial start of spring when it returns.

* **State Symbol of Peace:** Losing out to the robin for state bird, the mourning dove got its own designation in 1971.

* **State Dance:** It's the polka! This one was honored in 1993, representing the state's German, Czech, and Polish heritage. Even if you've never taken a whirl around the dance floor, you'll probably recognize "The Beer Barrel Polka," a popular tune in Milwaukee.

* **State Beverage:** Some may guess beer, but in keeping with the title of America's Dairyland, the real state beverage is milk.

- ✳ **State Song:** "On, Wisconsin!" What else could it be?

- ✳ **State Flower:** The wood violet got the nod from Wisconsin's schoolchildren in 1909. In 1948, it was discovered that the designation had never been made official and it was put to the legislature, who sealed the deal in 1949.

- ✳ **The State Seal:** In an attempt to include everything Wisconsin, the state seal is a bit complicated. Industry is represented by a pick and shovel, arm and hammer, and anchor. Thirteen vertical stripes and the motto "E Pluribus Unum" show Wisconsin's dedication to the Union. A sailor and yeoman symbolize the state's land- and water-based workforce. Lead ingots and a cornucopia highlight state resources. The seal is rounded out by a badger over the shield and the state motto: "Forward."

- ✳ **The Wisconsin State Flag:** When soldiers wanted a state flag to fly during the Civil War, legislators created one by highlighting the state seal on a blue background. In 1979, the word *Wisconsin* was added in white letters across the top to make it more easily recognizable.

- ✳ **The State Quarter:** With so many symbols to choose from, it was almost impossible to decide which one should grace Wisconsin's contribution to the 50 State Quarters Program. Six concepts were chosen from a pool of almost 10,000 entries. A statewide vote narrowed it to three, and residents ultimately picked the Agriculture Dairy Barns theme to represent Wisconsin's quarter, issued in 2004. A cow, cheese, and an ear of corn are featured along with the word *forward* and the year Wisconsin became a state—1848.

Aldo Leopold: Friend of the Environment

This wildlife ecology wunderkind made Wisconsin's lands his laboratory.

✳ ✳ ✳ ✳

Inspired by Nature

IT MIGHT BE a stretch to call Aldo Leopold a god—or a poet, for that matter. But there's no denying that the man who is now considered the father of wildlife ecology was a creator. And as anyone can tell you who has been moved by the poetic musings of his book *A Sand County Almanac*, his opus about the changing land around his Wisconsin farm, what Leopold created—a national transformation in thinking about the relationship between man and nature—was nothing short of poetic.

Rand Aldo Leopold, born in 1887, grew up in Iowa and—ironically perhaps—was a hunter. With an aim to ensure that wildlife remained wild (and likewise, fruitful for hunters), Leopold joined the U.S. Forest Service shortly after graduating from Yale. His first assignment? Managing the Arizona territories, including its timber and what he then called "varmints"—wolves, coyotes, and other predatory animals that preyed on valuable livestock and game. His attitude was in line with the common thinking of the time: Wildlife had to be controlled in order to protect the interests of man.

A Major Attitude Adjustment

It's possible that a long bout of nephritis—which struck Leopold after being caught in a flood and blizzard in 1913—gave him time to reflect. Perhaps the crisis of World War I broadened his view. Whatever the impetus, Leopold, who had married and become a father, recovered his health, and resumed his work with the Forest Service, began to see conservation as more than a matter of economics.

It was in Wisconsin that the seeds of Leopold's brave new thinking took root and blossomed. As a professor of game management at the University of Wisconsin-Madison, Leopold penned the revolutionary book *Game Management* which was published in 1933. Part philosophy and part how-to manual of skill and technique, Leopold's book began shaping the conservation ethic—the notion that humans and wilderness exist in a state of mutual interdependence and that it is a privilege, not an obligation, to bend the earth to people's will.

But was it too late? Could humans undo what damage had already been done? In 1935, Leopold was determined to find out. He purchased a small square of worn-out former farmland alongside the Wisconsin River near Baraboo. On the grounds were the remains of a dilapidated old chicken coop, where Leopold, his wife, Estella, and their five children would stay during their visits. Though the family fixed it up, the coop's nickname—"The Shack"—remained. The family retreated to the land on weekends and school vacations to relax, explore, and, in typical Leopold fashion, to experiment.

Working in the World's Biggest Laboratory

Leopold saw the exhausted land as an outdoor laboratory, a living workshop in which he could test his ideas about restoring health to the depleted earth. He and his family enriched the soil, built a garden, cut firewood, fought drought, and planted prairie grasses, flowers, hardwoods, and conifers—nearly 40,000 pines alone.

This life-size and lifelong test of Leopold's land proved fruitful. He eventually transformed the farm into a healthy, thriving landscape and in the process helped shape many of the environmental restoration techniques used today. Sadly, Leopold didn't live to see all that his little plot of land on the Wisconsin River would come to mean to the world; he died of a heart attack while struggling to fight a brush fire that was encroaching on his land in 1948.

Eden in Wisconsin

North of La Crosse, in Galesville, near the Mississippi River, is an imposing statue of the Reverend David O. Van Slyke, an itinerant nineteenth-century preacher and Methodist missionary. His flowing cape is caught, frozen in the wind, and in one hand he holds a book; in the other an apple. Here is a man who must have had something to say to the ages. And so he did. In 1886, Van Slyke published news of a remarkable discovery that, he noted, he had arrived at by entirely scientific methods: Galesville, he claimed, was at the center of the Biblical Garden of Eden. Really.

✳   ✳   ✳   ✳

In Love with Nature

DAVID O. VAN Slyke was born in 1818. At age 44, he enlisted in the 30th Wisconsin Infantry to serve as a chaplain in the Civil War. At the end of the war, he returned home to Galesville to do missionary work. He built a house and started a farm. And he became increasingly bewitched by the area's natural beauty, especially its rivers and high bluffs.

"I, as a matter of pleasantry, used occasionally to say to my friends, this is the Garden of Eden," Van Slyke recalled. "At this suggestion I smiled."

After a time, however, he came to look at the bluffs framing his pleasant garden valley as a wall. He noticed that the whole region between La Crosse and Winona, Minnesota, was bracketed and contained. Biblical scholars had long been disappointed in trying to find a real location for Eden in the arid Middle East. Perhaps there might be clues, which if carefully sifted, could provide actual, scientific proof that Galesville was in fact the biblical birthplace of humanity!

Finding Proof Everywhere

Van Slyke was not disappointed in his search. Nearly everywhere he looked, he was able to find proof of his theory. His starting point was Genesis 2:8–14, which noted that although four rivers ran into Eden, only one ran out. That described Trempealeau County, making the Mississippi into the Bible's Euphrates River. In fact, where else on the planet, he wondered, was there such a compact yet complex water system?

Well-traveled visitors passing through by steamboat often told Van Slyke that the area was the most beautiful they had ever seen. Among the bluffs one must also "look out for snakes, for how could you have such a garden without a 'serpent'?" Van Slyke noted that the region "has been notorious for rattlesnakes from time immemorial." He said, in fact, that the bluffs were known to Native Americans as "Rattlesnake Hills."

The preacher began to share his developing theory in a series of columns in the *Galesville Independent*, "to invite general inspection and criticism." More discoveries followed.

The climate was neither too warm nor too cold. Yes, it could be a struggle during the winter, but surely a wise creator put gentle impediments in the way of humanity's growth. Also, the area was seemingly protected from tornadoes and "yet so free from malaria." Also, it was obviously a land of milk and honey. For example, butter from the nearby towns of Arcadia and Alma had just won first and second place in an international competition at St. Louis.

Yes, it was a large area for just Adam and Eve to roam, but "did you ever think how long they lived, how many children they probably had, what a numerous family before the first pair died, numbering into the thousands?" By contrast, across the Mississippi Van Slyke observed that the farms of Minnesota were "rough and rugged" and home to "Fallen Humanity." Van Slyke concluded that the great flood must have come, and Noah and his family rode the ark from Galesville around the world, finally landing on top of Mount Ararat in Turkey.

Spreading the News

In 1886, Van Slyke collected his research in a lengthy pamphlet entitled "Found At Last: the veritable Garden of Eden, or a place that answers the Bible description of that notable spot better than anything yet discovered." Somewhat unfortunately, his book carries one additional, idiosyncratic proof: The creator would surely have placed Eden at the center of the earth—and Galesville is in the central time zone!

Van Slyke was mocked, of course, but he retained a good sense of humor about it. Why, of course the clues were perhaps a bit obscure! Did his detractors expect Eden to be marked by a sign? If so, they would be disappointed. "Evidently not a Lo here, or a Lo there," he sniffed.

In the end, however, Van Slyke's main argument was simply that "the scenery is simply GRAND." So, Eden must be located roughly between La Crosse and Bluff Siding, Wisconsin. "We CAN and HAVE proven it, on scientific principles."

Van Slyke died in 1890, but his booklet is often reprinted by Galesville merchants to promote the idyllic qualities of their town. Whether or not Galesville was Eden, Van Slyke was not the last resident to compare it to paradise. Visitors can judge for themselves—but remember to look out for rattlesnakes.

＊ The Gideons, of hotel Bible fame, got started in Boscobel. Traveling salesmen John Nicholson and Sam Hill first shared a room there of necessity in 1898 and realized their religious commonality. They met again the next year and founded the Gideons in Janesville—to provide lodgers with wholesome reading.

＊ The Cistercian monks of Sparta support their abbey by refilling ink and toner cartridges. If you think about it, it's an ingenious way to keep the place fiscally sound. The business is called LaserMonks, and its slogan is "Commerce with Compassion." You go, brothers!

Legendary Lake Mills

Along the interstate between Madison and Milwaukee is the small town that dubbed itself "Legendary Lake Mills." It's legendary, indeed, and controversial too.

✳ ✳ ✳ ✳

An Underwater Mystery

SINCE THE 1840S, locals have buzzed about "stone tepees" standing at the bottom of Rock Lake. The idea seems plausible. Less than three miles due east is Aztalan State Park, an archeological site where the ancient remains of a Middle-Mississippian village, temple mounds, and ceremonial complex have been restored.

But Native American legend and local folklore, combined with years of third-party research, have not been enough to persuade top scientists that there are pyramids beneath Rock Lake's waters. In fact, the phenomena has been dubbed "North America's most controversial underwater archeological discovery of the twentieth century."

One theory holds that Ancient Aztecs believed that their ancestors hailed from a land far north of Mexico, called Aztalan. The legend goes that in 1066, the Aztalans of Lake Mills appealed to the gods for relief from a long drought by building sacrificial pyramids. Rain came down, creating a beautiful lake and submerging the pyramids. They named the lake *Tyranena*, meaning "sparkling waters."

Fast-forward 800 years. When the first white settlers set up camp along Tyranena's banks in the 1830s, the resident Winnebago people shared the story of Tyranena with them. But even the Winnebago didn't quite understand the story, as it came from a "foreign tribe." The lore remained as elusive as the small islands that settlers reported as floating above the water.

Soon after the settlers arrived, a sawmill and a gristmill were built on the lake's edge, subsequently raising the water level. What little was left to see of the supposed pyramids was submerged.

Doubt and Circumstance

Over the next 200 years, the lake would be caught up in a continuous cycle of sensationalism and doubt, false starts, and circumstance. In the early 1900s, two brothers, Claude and Lee Wilson, went out duck hunting one hot, clear day during a drought and were able to reach down and touch the so-called pyramid's apex with an oar. Local residents would find the pyramid again the next day, but by the time a reporter got onto the lake a week later rain had fallen, ending the drought and raising the water level. Through the decades, anglers would declare their belief in the structures when they snagged their lines and nets, but interest waned.

The lore was rekindled in the 1930s when a local school-teacher, Victor Taylor, took it upon himself to canvass residents and dive over the pyramids, without diving equipment. He described four conical underwater structures. With this "evidence," state and national agencies threw money into the effort, even hiring professional divers to explore the underwater structures. But these divers were literally mired by the lake's deteriorating, muddy bottom, mucking up belief in the pyramids once again.

Eventually the controversy would reach an MIT engineer, Max Nohl, the man who invented the first scuba-type device. A master excavator, Nohl made it his personal mission to uncover the truth beneath the lake. He rekindled the town's pyramid fever with his extensive dives and written accounts with detailed measurements.

Debunked?

While Nohl successfully made his case, the curious fact remained that no professional archeologist wanted to be associated with Rock Lake. The establishment theory contends that the lake bottom anomalies are merely glacial castoffs from the last Ice Age. In an article in the September 1962 issue of *The Wisconsin Archeologist*, the pyramids were wholly debunked by the state's academes, who alleged that Native Americans didn't work in stone and that mound-building only began 2,000 years prior, whereas Rock Lake was at least 10,000 years old.

In July 1967, Jack Kennedy, a professional diver from Illinois, was sport diving with friends on Rock Lake. Near the end of the day, after all of his comrades had run out of air, Kennedy took one last dive... over a pyramid. Shocked at his discovery, he removed three rocks from its wall. Further analysis revealed the rocks were made of quartzite from a riverbed. The first concrete evidence was now in hand.

Kennedy continued to dive at Rock Lake, eventually making a sketch of a structure 70 feet long, 30 feet wide, and 15 feet tall, which appeared in *Skin Diver* magazine. His discovery led to a resurgence in the exploration of Rock Lake, a summer haven for leisure boaters and beach-goers. Explorers have documented stone rings, tombs, curiously long rock bars, and pyramidal structures in dives, sonic sonar, and aerial photography. In 1998, two Rock Lake enthusiasts, Archie Eschborn and Jack LeTourneau, formed Rock Lake Research Society to "document and help preserve these archeological treasures that could rewrite North American history... and persuade state officials to declare Rock Lake a historical site."

History Still Unwritten

Does the Aztalan connection hold water? How does glacial activity fit in the picture?

To date, Rock Lake remains just that, a lake, which is still unprotected as a historical site. But locals continue to believe, if not for the archeological and anthropological truth, then for the opportunities the lore and legend provide. In Lake Mills, you can stay at the Pyramid Motel or throw back a Stone

Tepee Pale Ale, made by the city's resident Tyranena Brewing Company. Or perhaps you can head to one of the city's three beaches and try your hand at uncovering the mysteries of the "sparkling waters" yourself.

Aztalan: A Prehistoric Puzzle

A millennium ago, Wisconsin ruled the north.

✳   ✳   ✳   ✳

A Mysterious Site

AZTALAN IS A fortified settlement of mysterious outsiders who worshiped the sun. The Middle Mississippian culture erected stepped pyramids, may have practiced cannibalism, and enjoyed coast-to-coast trade. Some have linked the Mississippians to the Aztecs and even to the legendary city of Atlantis. All that is truly certain is that they lived at Aztalan for 150 years. Then they disappeared.

Aztalan, near present-day Lake Mills, is now a state park and, in fact, a National Historic Landmark. Still, what happened at Aztalan and the truth about the people who lived there are among the greatest archaeological puzzles in the world.

Aztalan is ancient. During the period when it was settled, sometime between A.D. 1050 and 1100, a time when gunpowder was invented in China, Macbeth ruled Scotland, and the Orthodox and Roman Catholic churches split. In America, across the Mississippi from St. Louis in what is now Illinois, there was a strange, 2,000-acre city of earthen pyramids later dubbed "Cahokia." Its population was roughly 20,000—more than London at that time.

Aztalan appears to be the northern outpost of the Cahokia peoples. Because of location, archaeologists call their civilization Middle Mississippian. They are distinct from the Woodland peoples, who were there first and remained afterward. The Mississippians were quite enamored with the sun, and at Cahokia, residents erected wooden solar observatories, similar to Britain's Stonehenge.

Like Cahokia, Aztalan was a truly weird place: 22 acres surrounded by a stockade with 32 watch towers, all made from heavy timbers and then covered with hard clay. Inside, pyramidal mounds stood as high as 16 feet. Outside the fortifications, crops were planted. According to Cahokia experts, the Mississippians are the ones who introduced corn to North America.

Today, Aztalan looks much different than it did at its peak. The mounds remain, and part of the stockade has been rebuilt. Also, the Friends of Aztalan group is trying to recreate antique agriculture with a small garden of gourds, squash, sunflowers, and an early type of corn, all planted just as the Mississippians would have.

In addition to vegetables, the Mississippian diet may have included some more interesting dishes—namely human flesh. At Cahokia there's evidence of human sacrifice, and since the time of Aztalan's discovery by whites in 1836, it has been thought that its residents practiced at least some sort of cannibalism. But science and interpretations change with time. There is speculation that the so-called "cannibalism" could have simply been a ceremonial or funerary practice that had nothing to do with eating human flesh.

Gone Without a Trace

Another puzzle is why the Mississippians suddenly vanished from the Midwest sometime between A.D. 1200 and 1300. Author Frank Joseph has taken the folklore of three continents and made a case linking Atlantis, Aztalan, and the Aztecs in his books, *The Lost Pyramids of Rock Lake* and *Atlantis in Wisconsin*. Joseph's theory is that the people of Atlantis founded Cahokia and Aztalan, mined copper, cast it into ingots, and shipped it back, fueling Europe's Bronze Age. After a cataclysm destroyed their Mediterranean island empire, leaderless survivors in the Wisconsin settlement migrated south. They created a new Aztalan in Mexico and became the Aztecs.

The Aztecs themselves referred to their far-away, long-ago homeland—wherever it was—as "Aztlan." However, scholars deny that residents of Aztalan ever used that name. It was merely a fanciful label applied by European settlers.

Joseph's evidence is circumstantial but intriguing. One of the great mysteries of Europe's Bronze Age is where all the necessary copper came from (bronze is made of copper and tin). Known low-grade deposits in Great Britain and Spain would have been quickly exhausted. Yet Lake Superior's shores have, and had, the only known workable virgin, native copper deposits in the world.

The Mississippians certainly knew that—they mined Michigan's Upper Peninsula. Meanwhile, according to legend, Atlantis was reigning supreme, enjoying great wealth derived from its trade throughout the known world of precious metals, especially copper. The Lake Superior mines closed precisely when Europe's Bronze Age ended. Coincidentally, or perhaps not, it was at this time that Atlantis supposedly sank and disappeared forever. Many more answers about the Mississippian culture are yet be found. According to the Cahokia Mounds Museum Society, archaeologists have explored only 1 percent of the site. Could the decisive link to Atlantis or the Aztecs still be buried beneath the grounds of Cahokia or Aztalan? Only time will tell.

As the name suggests, Mississippian culture spanned the length of the Mississippi River, including areas in what are now the states of Mississippi, Georgia, Alabama, Missouri, Arkansas, Illinois, Indiana, Kentucky, Ohio, Wisconsin, and Minnesota. It must have been desirable real estate! While Aztalan is usually considered to be a Mississippian settlement, there are many artifacts at the site from other groups of people that predate their arrival.

- For many years before it was studied and preserved, the area of Aztalan was plowed for farming; pottery and other artifacts were carted away by souvenir hunters.

- Aztalan became a National Historic Landmark in 1964 and was added to the National Register of Historic Places in 1966.

- There is speculation that some of the mounds at Aztalan could have been used for astronomical purposes.

- It is believed that Aztalan was a planned community with spaces for the general public, ceremonial locations, residential areas, and sections designated for elite individuals.

- Based on the artifacts unearthed at Aztalan, it appears that the people living there were skilled at farming, hunting, and fishing.

Some Current States and Their Early Names

- Delaware—Lower Counties on Delaware

- Connecticut—Connecticut Colony

- Rhode Island—Colony of Rhode Island and Providence Plantations

- Vermont—Province of New York and New Hampshire Grants

- Kentucky—Virginia (Kentucky County)

- Ohio—Northwest Territory

- Maine—Massachusetts

- Texas—Republic of Texas

- California—California Republic

- Oregon—Oregon Territory

- Hawaii—Kingdom of Hawaii, Republic of Hawaii

Going to Hell (Michigan)

When it comes to capitalizing on an interesting name, the residents of Hell, Michigan, have a helluva talent.

✳ ✳ ✳ ✳

Welcome to Hell

SOME PEOPLE CLAIM to have gone through Hell; other people (approximately 266 of them) actually live there. The tiny unincorporated community in southeast Michigan attracts many visitors each year who are determined to have a "Hell of a time"—or at least leave with some memorable souvenirs. Fortunately, local residents (known as Hellions) have embraced their town's name and are happy to deliver the kitsch. Visitors can purchase a souvenir baseball bat, otherwise known as "A Bat Outta Hell," or an "Official Deed" to own one square inch of Hell. Among the town's hot attractions are Screams Ice Cream Parlor and Hell's Wedding Chapel. There's even a "fully non-accredited" school called Damnation University that provides souvenir diplomas.

Despite its name, the community of Hell is actually a serene place situated among hills and creeks. In the 1830s, a pioneer named George Reeves recognized its beauty and decided to settle there. He operated a dam and mill on what is now Hell Creek, and he also built a distillery, where he made whiskey out of excess wheat. Local farmers took a liking to the whiskey, and Reeves became a popular guy among other pioneers who came to Hell to "drink in the beauty."

To Hell and Back

There are different theories about the origin of the name. In one, a couple of German travelers arrived to the lovely landscape and said *"So schoene hell,"* which roughly translates to "So bright and beautiful." In another, state officials asked Reeves what the town should be named, and he supposedly responded, "You can name it Hell for all I care." Another theory is that the area, swampy and full of bugs, created a miserable experience for settlers, who deemed it Hell. Either way, thanks to some creative decision-maker, everyone with an interest in kitschy vacation destinations can now claim they've been "To Hell and back."

Going Underground in Indiana

In the late 1970s, Vic Cook was busy working as a high school music teacher and musician in Indiana. Unlike many of us, however, he was also busy dreaming of living a Walden-like existence in a low-cost, energy-efficient home in the woods.

While giving a guitar lesson one day, Cook told his student that he wanted to build a monument to nature but feared that the state's building codes would prevent it from happening. The student mentioned that his sister was trying to sell some wooded land in Pendleton, Indiana. Two weeks later, Cook purchased the land and had a site for his dream house. When he found an 1890s stove at a yard sale, he was on his way. Then he started digging.

Digging Deep

Cook eventually dug 22 feet down into the earth. He erected the walls of his house, each made from six inches of solid wood, which would also act as natural insulation for the house with the heat of the earth doing the rest. The result was that the house stays around 68 degrees year-round, although a small kerosene heater is needed on rare occasions.

When it came to the roof and the structure that would be visible above ground, Cook wanted to make sure they were aesthetically pleasing and, more importantly, blended well with the natural environment. The roof, which includes solar panels, was designed to be aerodynamic, making it able to withstand winds of 200 miles per hour. The panels use sunlight to power six solar batteries, which are capable of storing up to a month's supply of electricity for the entire house. A generator is kept on hand, though, just in case the sun decides not to make an appearance for several days.

All the Comforts of Home

Cook found his makeshift refrigerator one day when he came across a log in the woods. For the next six weeks, he worked on the refrigerator, hollowing it out, lining it with insulation, and adding a solar battery to it. The battery supposedly helps pull cool air out of the earth and into the log. Cook even added a freezer, which uses nothing more than a microchip to cool down the earth's air.

The next comfort of home that Cook added to his house was running water. Obviously, he wasn't going to be able to get city water out in the woods and he wasn't keen on digging a well. Instead, he designed special tanks for the roof that could catch rainwater. Gravity is all it takes to give Cook running water in the kitchen and bathroom. In keeping with the theme of the house being one with nature, Cook opted to go the composting route with his bathroom.

The most amazing thing of all is that Cook spends only about $30 each month on utilities, and because the house has no utility hookups, his property taxes are extremely low.

The Giant

Considering that the house has literally become one with the earth, Cook decided to name his labor of love the Earthship. Over the years, though, the house has acquired a nickname— the Giant—after Neil Armstrong's famous line about his "one giant leap for mankind." The line also reflects Cook's leap of faith into a one-man home-building project with a budget of less than $8,000.

All in all, Cook has spent more than a decade and 26,000 hours building his dream home. And he's always happy to show it off. Beginning each spring, Cook offers tours of the Earthship, welcoming the chance to inspire people to follow their dreams.

From Desert Watering Hole to Sin City

Two events and three men combined to create Las Vegas and its glittering strip of fantasy-themed casino resorts. Now it's one of the world's top gambling and tourist destinations.

✳   ✳   ✳   ✳

THERE'S REALLY NO place in the world like Las Vegas. It's a world-renowned mecca for gaming, entertainment, and shopping. Once a mobster paradise, the city now bills itself as the Entertainment Capital of the World, and it's still a place where one can get into trouble without actually getting into *trouble*.

Before all the lights and splendor, however, Las Vegas wasn't much of anything. It began as a nineteenth-century pioneer trail outpost where desert-weary California-bound settlers drew fresh water from the artesian wells in the surrounding Las Vegas Valley.

No Gambling? No Dice!

In 1905, Las Vegas became a railroad town (incorporated as the City of Las Vegas in 1911) with service facilities, supply stores, and saloons. But Vegas's growth was stunted for the next two decades when in 1909, the Nevada legislature killed the best thing the town had going for it: legalized gambling.

The Appeal of the Gambling Repeal

In 1931, Nevada repealed the ban on gambling, ostensibly to raise tax money to fund its public school system but also to undermine the state's thriving illegal gambling industry. Soon downtown Las Vegas became host to a slew of roughneck casinos sporting a few slot machines, gaming tables, and—in some cases—sawdust floors.

That same year, construction began on the Hoover Dam

34 miles south of Las Vegas, bringing an unprecedented influx of workers and tourists to southern Nevada. But with nothing to do in nearby Boulder City (the town built by the federal government for dam workers where alcohol and gaming remained illegal), workers and tourists alike streamed north along Highway 91, heading to Vegas to find their fun.

The Strip Is Born

One man, Thomas Hull (owner of the California-based El Rancho motel chain), noticed the busy traffic—particularly the heavy flow of Vegas-bound travelers from Los Angeles. Seeking to attract their business, Hull opened the El Rancho Vegas in April 1941 on a stretch of Highway 91 just south of Vegas city limits. This area eventually morphed into the famous Las Vegas Strip.

The El Rancho wasn't your typical Vegas gaming joint. The sprawling Spanish mission–style complex featured a main casino building surrounded by such welcoming amenities as 65 guest cottages, a swimming pool, a nightclub, a steakhouse, retail shopping, and recreation areas. It had a casual "boots and jeans" ambience that placed an emphasis on comfort and pleasure. The El Rancho brought gambling and vacationing together in Vegas's first casino resort and became the model for future casino development.

Observing the success of the El Rancho, movie theater mogul R. E. Griffith emulated Hull's model and added a new dimension. In October 1942, Griffith opened the Hotel Last Frontier on the site of the old Pair-O-Dice nightclub near the El Rancho. Aiming to trump the El Rancho, Griffith designed the Last Frontier around an authentic Old West theme, featuring frontier-style decor, genuine historical artifacts, and costumed employees. Griffith thus introduced the fantasy theme concept to Vegas.

Consequently, the stage was set for the notorious Benjamin "Bugsy" Siegel, who in 1946, with the opening of the

Mafia-bankrolled Flamingo down the road from the Last Frontier, elevated Hull's and Griffith's prototypes to new heights. Siegel spared no expense in creating an ultra-glitzy, ultra-glamorous "carpet joint" (to use his words) designed to lure the wealthy Hollywood set. His loose spending of mob money—combined with his girlfriend's penchant for skimming Flamingo cash—eventually cost Siegel his life. But Siegel established the trend of over-the-top luxury casino resorts that define Vegas today, and he brought an alluring mob mystique to Vegas that put the city on the map for good.

Get Savvy on the Seas

Many people fall (overboard) for some of the most enduring myths about the largest area of our world—the oceans.

✳ ✳ ✳ ✳

Myth: Oceans don't freeze solid because of deep currents.

Fact: Although the water around the Arctic and Antarctica is freezing cold, oceans don't freeze solid for several reasons. Oceans contain a lot of water, which circulates around the world. Water from warmer oceans and from underground volcanoes flows into the Arctic, which warms it up a bit. But the main reason oceans don't go into a deep freeze is the salt in the water. The freezing point of saltwater is lower than that of freshwater, and as ocean water reaches the freezing point, the salt crystals interfere with the formation of ice crystals. This water is also more dense and therefore sinks, allowing warmer water to come up to the top—below the surface ice. The surface ice actually insulates the warmer water in the same way an igloo insulates the air inside it. The ice also reflects the sun's rays, and this helps warm the surface and prevents the ice from thickening further. Nearly all the ice in the Antarctic is "seasonal," which means it melts and reforms annually.

Myth: Icebergs are made of frozen seawater.

Fact: This seems like common sense because icebergs float in seawater, but many natural phenomena defy common sense. Oceanographers agree that icebergs are made of freshwater—in the form of snow—that has compacted over hundreds or thousands of years. True icebergs are huge pieces of ice that have broken off from the glaciers that make up the continental ice sheets (as found in Antarctica or Greenland). Seawater, with its salt content, doesn't mix with the freshwater of the iceberg. To test this theory at home, put saltwater and freshwater in the freezer at the same time—and see which solidifies faster.

Flag, You're It!

Ohio's distinctively shaped flag has a unique history.

✳ ✳ ✳ ✳

IN 1901, AMIDST America's mania for world's fairs, an architect named John Eisenmann designed a flag representing Ohio for the Pan-American Exposition held in Buffalo, New York. A year later, it became the official flag of the state. Eisenmann's design was unique: The official name for the triangular, "swallowtail" cut of the flag is a *burgee*, and it's the only state flag in the country in this style.

Representing Ohio

Flags aren't just pretty decorations; they have a special language that deems each element representational. Each part of the Ohio state flag symbolizes an Ohio quality or landmark. On the side closest to the flagpole rests a large blue triangle, which represents Ohio's lush hills and valleys. The stripes that emanate from the triangle call to mind the vast roads and waterways of the state. Thirteen stars dot the inside of the triangle to symbolize the first 13 states of the union, while the four other stars up by the triangle's peak were added to symbolize that Ohio was the 17th state admitted to the Union.

Aside from its special burgee cut, the showstopper of the Ohio flag is the white circle with the red center, located in the middle of the triangle. Not only does this circle represent the O in Ohio, but it also recalls Ohio's famous nickname, "The Buckeye State."

In 2005, a local Boy Scout invented a way to fold his state's flag in 17 moves, representing Ohio's order of admittance to the Union. The scout saw his flag-folding technique passed by the Ohio State General Assembly in 2005 as the official Ohio flag-folding method.

Bragging Rights

Ohio has more than a few things to brag about.

✳   ✳   ✳

✳ Ohio is home to one of the first traffic lights in the United States. The signal went up in Cleveland on August 5, 1914, at East 105th Street and Euclid Avenue. The Honorable A. A. Benesch, director of public safety, put them into operation at exactly 5 P.M.—rush hour! Thirty-three years later, the first pedestrian button was installed at the same intersection.

✳ Ohio invented the automobile accident. So far as it is known, the first car wreck in history occurred in Ohio City in 1891, when local resident John Lambert—who designed and built his own automobile—lost control of his ride and smashed into a hitching post.

✳ Ohio was home to the country's first full-time car shop, opened in 1899.

✳ It could be said that pretty much everything cool about cars was invented in Ohio—including automatic windshield wipers, developed by William M. and Fred Folberth of Cleveland.

✳ The world's fastest electric car has "Buckeye" in its name.

The Buckeye Bullet, designed by students at Ohio State University, broke international speed records in 2004 when it revved up to 271 miles per hour and broke the national speed record at 314 miles per hour, in two separate trials.

* Ohio was home to the first ambulance service. Back in the day, ambulance services were run by local funeral homes (which no doubt gave a scare to everyone they picked up). But in 1865, Cincinnati General Hospital instituted the first true municipal ambulance service, which operated out of the city's fire department.

* Emergency bragging rights don't end there: Cincinnati is credited with being the first American city to have its own professional fire department.

* More rubber is produced in the town of Akron than anywhere else in America.

* More greenhouse and nursery plants come from Ohio than from any other state.

Ohioans, Pre-Ohio

Before Ohio, and even before "The Ohio Territory," Native Americans roamed the great Midwest. The most prominent Pre-Columbian cultures of Ohio were decimated and scattered by European guns and infectious disease, but so far as archaeology and history can tell, these are the earliest groups to call Ohio home.

* * * *

The Adena Culture, 800 B.C.–A.D. 200

NOMADIC CULTURES WERE present in Ohio millennia before the Adena, but this culture boasts some of the earliest evidence of sedentary settlement in Ohio. The Adena were predominantly in southern Ohio, where they left behind

earthwork mounds for posterity's sake. ("Earthwork mo
is archaeologist-speak for conical mounds of earth plac..
over burial structures.) The Adena are well-known for these
funeral mounds, with the largest, Grave Creek Mound of
West Virginia, measuring 70 feet tall and 300 feet in diameter. Even though Adena archaeological sites have been found
in Kentucky, Indiana, West Virginia, Pennsylvania, and New
York, they were definitely Ohioans at heart—300 Adena sites
have been uncovered in Ohio, and only 200 in all the other
states combined.

The Hopewell Culture, 100 B.C.–A.D. 500

"Hopewell" is actually a catchall term for a conglomeration of
cultures that once flourished in the Northeast and Midwest.
They were connected by the Hopewell Exchange System,
a sophisticated network of trade between distant villages
throughout the contemporary United States and possibly
into Mexico. Many scholars believe the Hopewell descended
directly from the Adena culture and thus derived from southern Ohio. As with the Adena, the most conspicuous remains of
the Hopewell culture are the many mounds they left behind,
though the Hopewell mounds were even bigger and more
elaborate. The largest collection of Hopewell burial mounds
are the Mound City Group in Chillicothe. This and two other
Hopewell sites in Ohio are National Historic Landmarks and
are being considered for nomination as World Heritage sites.

The Mississippi Culture, A.D. 800–1600

The mounds just keep getting bigger. This new constellation
of Native American cultures didn't just build mounds, they
built temples on top of the mounds (they're also known as the
Temple Mound Builders), suggesting a more stratified class
structure with priests and chiefs. They were skilled crafts-
people and farmers who set up a trade network that extended
throughout the Mississippi valley, the southern United
States, and into Mexico. Unlike the Adena and Hopewell, the
Mississippi culture did not radiate from Ohio, although many

villages in Ohio were part of the Mississippi culture. The largest Mississippi structure, located in southern Illinois, is known as Monk's Mound and is considered the largest ceremonial structure of the Pre-Columbian inhabitants of the United States. It is 100 feet high, 955 feet long, and 775 feet wide.

The Erie Culture, unknown–A.D. 1680

This may be one of the only modern Ohio cultures that can clearly trace its history to Pre-Columbian groups. The Erie lived in northern Ohio and into Pennsylvania and western New York. They apparently made their homes in scattered villages throughout the region both before and after European contact. In early colonial times, the Erie were known for resisting relationships with European traders, and therefore their history has been reconstructed through remaining oral histories. Since the Erie had so little contact with Europeans, they never bought guns. In 1656, the well-armed Iroquois nearly wiped out the defenseless Erie. The last Erie group surrendered in 1680, and the remaining Erie were taken up into other tribes. This last great native tribe of Ohio has been immortalized as the namesake of one of the Great Lakes.

＊ Legendary frontiersman Daniel Boone was kidnapped by the Shawnee in Kentucky and taken to Ohio in February of 1778. He managed to escape in June of the same year.

The City of the Dead

An archaeological site with burial mounds used by Ohio's earliest settlers holds more questions than answers.

＊ ＊ ＊ ＊

THE AREA REFERRED to as the City of the Dead is actually five separate locations throughout Ross County in central

Ohio. Beginning in roughly A.D. 100, a group of people known as the Hopewell culture came into the lush, green plains and ample water supply of the Ohio River Valley. They built up earthworks and enclosures, and soon the area was crawling with life.

The Mysterious Mounds

The Hopewell Culture was a collection of different Native American groups, gaining the name Hopewell simply because that was the last name of the farmer who owned the land where the first mound was discovered. Each group brought unique building skills to the area. The Ohio Valley was filled not only with mounds but also earthen walls that took on varying shapes.

The City of the Dead lies along the Scioto River near Chillicothe. In this area, there are more than 23 earthen mounds. Sadly, during World War I, the U.S. Army created Camp Sherman over the mounds, destroying many of them. After the war, the Army destroyed much of the camp and attempted to rebuild the mounds, which makes dating them quite difficult.

However, excavations of the mounds themselves shed some light on why they were created. During excavation, it was discovered that within each mound was something resembling a charnel house—a small structure into which human remains would be placed as well as personal belongings and artifacts. It appears as though the remains and belongings were placed inside the structure and then it was lit on fire. When the fire had burned out, dirt was brought in, and mounds were constructed over the burned remains. The city is open to visitors and, questions aside, is the most revealing look at Hopewell culture that the public can get.

Crater of Light

James Turrell's Roden Crater is an epic earthwork-in-progress.

❋   ❋   ❋   ❋

O N THE WESTERN edge of the Painted Desert northeast of Flagstaff, Arizona, a dormant volcano is the setting for an elaborate art project. Quaker artist James Turrell purchased the 400,000-year-old, two-mile crater in 1979, and since then he has been carving out tunnels, rooms, and circular openings that allow in light and a view of the sky. But when will Roden Crater be completed and visitors let in? That's a question Turrell fans—and others who "dig" land art installations—have been asking for years.

Digging a Hole

Throughout his artistic career, Turrell has played with space, light, and perspective. In fact, some people call him a "sculptor of light." He designed the Live Oak Meeting House in Houston, Texas, for the Society of Friends. It features what he calls a "skyspace," a square in the roof that opens to sky, creating (according to Turrell, speaking on a PBS program) "a light that inhabits space, so that you feel light to be physically present." Skyspaces pop up in other works by Turrell—such as a hotel and art gallery he codesigned on Japan's Benesse Island—and their particular shapes and angles allow light to enter in stunning ways.

Turrell spotted Roden Crater while he was working as an aerial cartographer. At the time, he was interested in land art, and he envisioned a series of tunnels and light-filled chambers inside the volcano. The entire place would function as a kind of naked-eye observatory in which visitors could observe the sun, moon, stars, clouds, and amazing celestial events. With its low light pollution and warm, clear climate, Arizona is perfectly suited to this kind of observation.

Time and Money

Using grants from the prestigious Guggenheim Foundation and the Dia Art Foundation, Turrell purchased the crater and got to work moving tons of earth to fulfill his artistic vision. This has been an architectural project as much as an artistic one. It turns out that moving tons of earth takes a lot of effort ... and money. But the artist did not want to scale back his plans. When certain funding sources dried up, Turrell had to look elsewhere for help, such as the Macarthur Foundation and the Santa Fe-based Lannan Foundation.

What's Inside?

Although Roden Crater is unfinished, there are certain completed features, including a long tunnel through the heart of the volcano and a pair of breathtaking skyspaces that frame the Arizona sky above. According to Turrell, the completed art piece will include more than 1,000 feet of tunnels and seven viewing rooms, as well as a feature called "The Eye of the Crater," situated 38 feet below the volcano's center.

Meanwhile, Turrell's admirers can't wait to see the finished product. Some people have snuck onto the site to see the work-in-progress and snap some pictures. A few art critics and VIPs have been invited inside the crater. Roden Crater was featured on a show in the UK called *Sculpture Diaries* and on the PBS program *Art: 21*. In 2007, it was the subject of a *New York Times* article in which the reporter, Jori Finkel, stressed just how highly anticipated it is: The crater, she said, "is one of the hottest tickets around. Writers have compared it to Stonehenge and the Mexican pyramids." Others have predicted that the cinder cone will be the "Sistine Chapel" of the United States or one of our newest "Wonders of the World."

Once open, no doubt Roden Crater will be recognized as something spectacular—a blend of art and architecture that, by placing light at the center, will seem effortless in its construction, even though it took years to complete.

Big American Cities With the Worst Infrastructures

Year by year, our nation's infrastructure falls into deeper disrepair. Once viewed as the model of modernity, America's vital network of roads, bridges, utilities, and waterways has reached an alarming state. Limited funding and continued backbiting add to the dilemma. One thing seems certain: If you live in one of the following cities, you may want to be extra careful.

✳ ✳ ✳ ✳

Minneapolis, Minnesota

The August 1, 2007, collapse of the I-35 bridge signaled a growing infrastructure crisis in the United States. When the span suddenly gave way, it swept away the lives of 13 people. Previous and subsequent checks have turned up problems with many of the city's spans. As is often the case with infrastructure in need of repair, funding stands as a near-immovable roadblock.

Atlanta, Georgia

When a drought hit Atlanta in 2007, the city's aging plumbing added to the crisis. Leaky pipes buried below the streets hemorrhaged as much as 18 percent of the city's water. But rotting municipal pipes aren't exclusive to this bustling Southern city. Sadly, the situation plays out clear across the United States.

New Orleans, Louisiana

Each year, 20 million tons of cargo move through the city's Industrial Canal Lock, a passage that leads to the Gulf Intracoastal Waterway. This vital commercial link is critical to the nation's economy, yet its 1921 design has rendered it nearly obsolete. At certain times, the undersized lock detains ships for up to 36 hours. Congress authorized the lock's replacement in 1956, but a mountain of red tape, including plan changes and community concerns, placed the project on indefinite hold.

Work finally commenced in 2002 but was slowed when a judge ruled that the Army Corps of Engineers had failed to prepare a proper environmental study. No completion date has been issued, but the project is expected to cost nearly $1.3 billion.

New York, New York

The Brooklyn Bridge is among a growing number of crumbling spans and rotting roadways. With rusting structural steel and rotting road decks bearing testament to its neglect, the 1883 icon has been listed as "structurally deficient" by America's federal rating system. Repairs began in 2010 and are expected to continue with two more waves of consturction until 2022.

Nashville, Tennessee

In addition to its own infrastructure concerns, Nashville has another worry—and it's a big one. If Kentucky's 55-year-old Wolf Creek Dam should burst—a very real possibility given its current horrendous state—the country music giant could be playing a sad tune. The mile-long structure impounds the largest artificial reservoir east of the Mississippi. When seepage holes were discovered along the reservoir's foundation, engineers dropped the dam's water level. The action offered a quick fix for a looming problem. If the dam should break, many cities along the Cumberland River, including Nashville, would be inundated.

Sacramento, California

In 2007, the Army Corps of Engineers cited 122 American levees that were "at risk of failure." A disproportionate 19 were located along the Sacramento River. The Natomas Levee, in particular, poses an ominous threat. If it were to fail, its surging waters would place 70,000 area residents in deadly peril and would put the ARCO Arena and Sacramento International Airport under an estimated 20 feet of water.

Seattle, Washington

Like far too many American cities, Seattle is dogged by decaying infrastructure. Unlike most, however, the city is situated in an active earthquake zone. In 2001, an earthquake did serious damage to the Alaskan Way Viaduct—a major artery that runs through the city. Inspectors discovered earth subsidence of as much as five inches beneath the structure, a situation that fore-tells disaster if left unchecked. Options for repair remain mired in red tape. In the meantime, the seismic clock keeps ticking.

Chicago, Illinois

Traffic woes add mightily to Chicago's infrastructure head-ache. Considered the nation's third most congested, the Circle Interchange slows traffic to a crawl due to its outdated, tightly curved ramps. This produces an estimated 25 million hours of delays per year. The problem has yet to be addressed.

"Stadiums rise with tax dollars; schools and clinics crumble, in the same city. Grotesque!"

—RALPH NADER

Basic Laws of the Richter Scale

In 1935, Charles F. Richter developed a way to measure an earthquake's magnitude based on the seismic waves that radiate from it. Because most big earthquakes are followed by smaller quakes called aftershocks, the Richter scale can indicate the size of these potential secondary tremors.

✳   ✳   ✳   ✳

Magnitude 2.0 and below: You usually can't feel the effects of a quake this size, and the majority of the world's earthquakes have a magnitude of 2.5 or lower. During the earthquake "swarm" in Arkansas in 1982, there were 88 earthquakes between June 24 and July 5. From then until 1985, there were 40,000 quakes of this magnitude in the state.

Magnitude 2.0–2.9: Known as "very minor," earthquakes of magnitude 2.0–2.9 are recorded, though they're generally not felt. Worldwide, there are on average 1.3 million of these per year.

Magnitude 3.0–3.9: Called a "minor" earthquake, rumblings of magnitude 3.0–3.9 are often felt, but they rarely cause damage. In 1983, Lake Charles, Louisiana, shook from a magnitude 3.8 earthquake, and there are about 130,000 quakes of this magnitude per year worldwide.

Magnitude 4.0–4.9: Often felt but seldom damaging, occurrences of these "light" earthquakes average about 13,000 per year worldwide. In 1947, Michigan had a magnitude 4.4 earthquake, and in 1986, a 4.9 quake occurred in Ohio, with aftershocks felt in 11 states.

Magnitude 5.0–5.9: Known as "moderate" earthquakes, these can cause major damage to poorly constructed buildings but present little threat to sturdy structures. There are about 1,300 of these per year worldwide. Kentucky had a 5.1 magnitude earthquake in 1980; New Brunswick, Canada, had a 5.7 in 1982; Indiana had a 5.9 in 1983; and in 2008, Illinois had a 5.2 quake.

Magnitude 6.0–6.9: There are approximately 135 "strong" earthquakes in the world each year. They can be destructive to areas as far as 60 miles from the epicenter. One of the most notable earthquakes in recent years was a 6.9 shocker that hit near Santa Cruz, California, just as the 1989 World Series was getting underway in nearby Candlestick Park.

Magnitude 7.0–7.9: These "major" earthquakes can cause serious damage over larger areas, and there are about 17 such quakes each year worldwide. In 1811 and 1812, New Madrid, Missouri, endured three earthquakes estimated to have been between 7.2 and 8.3, with 203 aftershocks. But the most noteworthy of earthquakes in the magnitude 7 range was on April 18, 1906, in downtown San Francisco. Estimated at magnitude 7.8, this quake and the subsequent fire left more than 225,000 people homeless and 3,000 dead.

Magnitude 8.0–8.9: The earth averages one "great" earthquake per year. These can cause serious damage in areas several hundred miles from the epicenter. In February 1965, a magnitude 8.7 quake shook the Aleutian Islands in the northern Pacific, west of Alaska. One of the deadliest earthquakes of all time—an estimated 8.7 magnitude—struck Lisbon, Portugal, in 1755, killing nearly 70,000 people.

Magnitude 9.0 and above: Also known as "great" earthquakes, the planet endures one of these monster quakes about every 33 years. They can cause devastation several thousands of miles from the epicenter. In 1964, the Good Friday Earthquake rocked Prince William Sound, Alaska, at a whopping 9.2 magnitude, making it the largest North American earthquake on record. Chile holds the record for the strongest earthquake in the twentieth century: A massive 9.5 magnitude quake struck on May 22, 1960.

The Old-School JELL-O Belt: The State of Deseret

The "JELL-O Belt" (yes, so-called due to the abundance of JELL-O found at today's Latter-day Saints church functions) runs through the U.S. Mountain West. But founder Brigham Young's ideas ran a bit bigger than JELL-O salad.

✳   ✳   ✳   ✳

Pioneers

IN 1846, BRIGHAM Young led a large group of Mormons (almost all of them, in fact) west across America to what is now Utah, with the hope of being left alone to build their own society. (You may recall another American group that description once fit: the Pilgrims.) The Latter-day Saints (LDS), as they called themselves, had grown sick of persecution. They also expected a cataclysmic wipeout of the wicked, sinful world, and they didn't care to be in the path of the spiritual cyclone.

Modern Utahans call these early settlers the Pioneers, and they're a key part of LDS cultural lore. But, cataclysm or no, in 1848, the treaty that ended the Mexican War ceded the Pioneers' turf (along with most of the modern Southwest) to the United States. Young's Pioneers had gotten busy setting up a functional government, but now they would have to come to terms with Washington.

Politics

In 1849, Young proposed that the U.S. Congress admit to the Union the State of Deseret. The name came from a term in the Book of Mormon meaning *honeybee*, which symbolized hard work. The name fit well because the Pioneers had been working very hard to gain ground against unfamiliar and frustrating conditions: icy winters, frosty springs, foreign soil, hungry crickets, and other headaches.

Young's suggested state would have included nearly all of modern Nevada and Utah; small parts of southern Oregon and southern Idaho; big pieces of western Wyoming, Colorado, and New Mexico; most of Arizona; and much of southern California—a total area significantly larger than modern France.

But the Mormons had underestimated national anti-LDS prejudice, especially against the practice of polygamy. In hindsight, it's rather astonishing that they thought they'd get their way, especially after being persecuted and even assaulted all across the Ohio Valley until a lynch mob murdered their founder, Joseph Smith, in 1844. By 1849, American opinion firmly opposed the notion of a state run by the LDS Church. In 1850, California gained statehood, and a far smaller portion of proposed Deseret became the Utah Territory. The name was something of an in-your-face by the U.S. government, given the conflicts the Pioneers had experienced with Ute Indians.

This Isn't Over

Young's Pioneers weren't going to give up on Deseret so easily.

They maintained an active Deseret Legislature and a sort of shadow government, mainly run by the same people governing the territory. Mormon leaders bucked U.S. sovereignty. An armed Mormon militia wasn't always kind to non-LDS people passing through, as evidenced by some violent incidents and the very ugly 1857 Mountain Meadows massacre.

In 1857, President Buchanan sent the U.S. Army to apply some pressure to the Mormons of Deseret. The Pioneers' militia readied for action, and Young swore to burn the Temple in Salt Lake City rather than see it occupied by the heathens. But in the end, the "Utah War" saw very little armed conflict. It also put the kibosh on the State of Deseret idea, though the shadow government remained until well after the Civil War.

Legacy

It took 46 years for Utah to go from territory to state (1896). Neighboring Nevada had been admitted in 1864, Colorado in 1876. If you suspect that this long delay had much to do with the LDS practice of plural marriage, you paid attention. The practice was discontinued in 1890, and the modern LDS Church utterly disavows it.

Even today, however, Utah is known as the Beehive State, and its state highway signs and highway patrol cars depict a beehive. Its second-largest daily newspaper goes by the name of *Deseret News*.

A New Land

It took a little more than 40 years, but the Inuit of Canada finally saw their dream come true. Their new territory was the biggest change to the map of North America since Alaska and Hawaii became U.S. states in 1959.

✳ ✳ ✳ ✳

O N APRIL 1, 1999, the Canadian territory of Nunavut was born. Nunavut (the word means "our land" in Inuktitut) spans the eastern half of Canada's rugged northland. Roughly the size of Western Europe, it is the least populated and largest of the territories of Canada, with fewer than 30 isolated towns scattered across its vast region. The capital, Iqaluit (formally Frobisher Bay), is home to 5,000 people, or almost 20 percent of the territory's population.

Nunavut is the first full-fledged political region in North America governed by aboriginal peoples. Though its new boundaries were created in 1993 when the Nunavut Land Claims Agreement Act was officially passed, it took five more years to properly abolish the previous Northwest Territorial districts and set up a working government. The 19 members of the unicameral Legislative Assembly do not belong to political parties, and the legislature works on a consensus model. The head of the government, the premier of Nunavut, is elected by the members of the Legislative Assembly.

Baby, It's Cold Outside

Documents reveal that the Inuit have lived in this area for more than 4,000 years. With the average winter temperature hovering around 22 degrees Fahrenheit, the aboriginal peoples have adapted superbly to their environment. They rely on animals—fish, sea mammals, and those on land—for almost all their needs: food, shelter, clothing, and more. Their fortunes have risen and fallen over the centuries, but their success was once based on trading furs and letting whalers hunt the Arctic waters for bowhead whales to harvest their oil and baleen.

When Europeans landed on their shores, the Inuit helped the ill-equipped foreigners survive the harsh conditions of the Arctic by serving as hunters, interpreters, and guides. They traded their services for guns, cloth, metal, tools, alcohol, and tobacco. But by the 1920s, things took a turn for the worse: Exploration was nearly complete, fur prices were fluctuating, and bowhead whales were rare. Sadly, the Inuit had been decimated by many new diseases that the Europeans brought with them from their home countries.

Nearly a century later, however, Canada's Inuit have proven resilient as ever, continuing to flourish and grow. As a community, they make a point to meld traditional ways as smoothly as possible with modern technology; as individuals, they tend to stay close to home and Mother Nature.

Pejoratively Speaking

The Inuit, or Eskimos, make up 85 percent of the 30,000 people living in these vast regions of tundra, pine forests, and ice fields in and around the Arctic Circle. It has become politically incorrect to call the Inuit Eskimos, although all Inuit in Canada and Greenland are Eskimos (not all of the Yupik and Inupiat in Alaska are). For some reason, a false but widely held belief is that the word *Eskimo* means "eaters of raw meat." Etymologists at the Smithsonian Institute say that the word *Eskimo* means "snowshoe netters." Linguists from the Innu-Montagnais (the language from which the word originates) reported in 1978 that the word *Eskimo* means "people who speak a different language."

You Can Call Me Al

A funny thing happened when Nunavut officially became a new territory. The remaining Northwest Territories decided that perhaps they should also change their name to stay more in touch with their culture and identity. So the premier asked the deputy premier to draw up a list of possibilities for the next session of the legislative assembly. Pranksters, however, hijacked the process, with "Bob" becoming the second-most-popular choice. Since then, the debate has faded somewhat.

An Alabama First!

Christmas is an international holiday, but Alabama was the first state to grant it legal status.

✳ ✳ ✳ ✳

IT'S COMMONLY BELIEVED that Christmas has been a legal holiday in the United States since the nation was established, but that's not correct. While the birth of Christ has been celebrated worldwide for nearly two millennia, no mention of it appears anywhere in the establishing documents created by our country's founders.

As a result, it wasn't until 1836 that Christmas was finally granted legal recognition in the United States. The first state to do so? Alabama!

By 1890, all the remaining states and territories, plus the District of Columbia, had followed Alabama's lead in establishing Christmas as a legal holiday. Interestingly, Christmas is also the only religious holiday to receive this kind of official secular recognition in America.

No Cause for Celebration

Despite this historic first step, Alabama celebrates Christmas pretty much like all the other states; nothing special is done to observe the Yellowhammer State's foresight in making Christmas something more than just a religious observance. But that shouldn't stop those who know about the first-of-its-kind legislation from feeling just a little superior.

The Christmas holiday aside, Alabama has hosted many other important achievements over the years. Among them:

* Alabama introduced Mardi Gras to the Western world. (Sorry, New Orleans!)
* Montgomery established the nation's first electric trolley system. It premiered in 1886.
* The first open-heart surgery in the Western Hemisphere was performed by Dr. Luther Leonidas Hill of Montgomery in 1902. He saved a boy's life by suturing a stab wound in the youngster's heart.

Clipperton Island

Clipperton Island, an isolated Pacific island 700 miles southwest of Mexico, provided refuge for pirate John Clipperton in the 1700s and whaling ships in the 1800s. In 1897, ownership switched from France to Mexico; it went back to France in 1935. In 1914, approximately 100 people were living on the island when provisions from the mainland ceased because of the Mexican Revolution. Many of these people were dead by the following year, when the U.S. warship *Lexington* offered to evacuate the survivors. The Mexican governor refused, forcing the survivors to continue to fend for themselves.

By 1917, only one man remained alive on the island, lighthouse keeper Victoriano Álvarez. He had proclaimed himself the island's ruler, beating, raping, enslaving, and in some cases murdering the remaining women. On July 18, 1917, while searching for enemy Germans, the USS *Yorktown* landed on Clipperton. The crew found only three women, eight children, and the body of Victoriano Álvarez, who had just been killed by one of the women.

In 1981, oceanographer Jacques Cousteau made the documentary *Clipperton: The Island Time Forgot,* bringing last survivor Ramon Arnaud, who was one of the children rescued in 1917, back to Clipperton Island, where he gave his account of Álvarez's killing.

A Tornado Runs Through It

Residents in communities across the United States believe they are safe from the threat of tornadoes because of their proximity to a river.

✳ ✳ ✳ ✳

UNFORTUNATELY, THIS LOCAL legend has done more damage than good when tornadoes have hit. A Native American belief long held by residents of Waco, Texas, was that the area was protected from tornadoes by the bluffs of the nearby Brazos River. In 1953, however, the community was forced to reevaluate its disaster-preparedness plans when a tornado tore through the city, killing 114 people.

Tornadoes cross rivers, lakes, ravines, and all manner of water. The deadliest tornado in history—the 1925 Tri-State tornado that ripped through Missouri, Illinois, and Indiana—killed 695 people and crossed the Mississippi River. In some cases, tornadoes can become even stronger when they come in contact with water. A tornado twisting through a narrow gully or canyon wall will spin increasingly faster, regardless of the rivers and streams that flow through these corridors.

Secede? Seriously?

Texas, the only state to have previously been its own republic, has already left the United States once. Is it so surprising that some in the state periodically call for an amicable separation?

✳   ✳   ✳   ✳

IN MANY WAYS Texas is a reluctant member of the United States. Before joining the Union, Texas was an independent country, and the affection for independence has never gone away. The ten years of sovereign Texas were filled with war, political strife, and some seriously overdue bills, but independence is independence.

Leave the Union!

One upsurge in secession talk arose in the late 1990s, and the most notorious voice at that time may have belonged to Richard McLaren, a founding member of the militia-allied group the Republic of Texas. Initially, McLaren was simply an opponent of taxation, but in a strange leap into the bizarre, he spent a little too much time reading arcane legal history and concluded that the United States never got the paperwork right when it annexed Texas.

McLaren claimed that because there was no treaty in place between the United States and Texas before annexation (as he interpreted international law to require), the whole state situation was null and void. Set aside for a moment that no one complained about this back when it would have actually mattered—in 1845. McLaren was able to convince a small group of people that his argument was actually a legitimate enough claim for them to assert themselves as the Republic of Texas. The early months of the ROT (an unfortunate acronym if there ever was one) were filled with the usual work of statecraft: figuring out how to get the money to keep things going.

ROT Forever!

McLaren elected himself ambassador and chief legal counsel, and he started issuing liens, judgments for trillions of dollars, and even his own license plates. He lobbied the United Nations for recognition as a sovereign country. He tied up courts for months with "paper warfare" to slow down real estate transactions across the state. To top it all off, he wrote millions of dollars' worth of bad checks, strangely echoing the financial turmoil of the historical independent Texas.

By 1997, the ROT had split into two factions, with McLaren in charge of the smaller and more violent group. On the opposing faction's website, the more peaceful members noted that McLaren had "gone off the deep end."

The "Republic" Falls Apart

Things at the ROT began to melt down completely when McLaren decided it was time for a modern version of the Alamo. The group kidnapped two of its neighbors, Margaret Ann and Joe Rowe, reportedly in retaliation for the arrest of two ROT members who were driving without state license plates.

Having recently added armed guards to his staff, McLaren also ordered members of his militia to begin "picking up federal judges, legislators, and IRS agents for immediate deportation." This was the last straw for Texas law enforcement. Almost 300 state troopers and Texas Rangers descended on and laid siege to the ROT in the mountain community of Ft. Davis. One member of the ROT was killed, and a hostage was wounded in the standoff. McLaren was sentenced to 99 years in prison for the kidnapping and standoff and an additional 12 years for 26 counts of mail and bank fraud and conspiracy.

Some People Still Have Ideas

Since then, supporters of the idea of an independent and sovereign Texas are still around, although there are fewer attempts to "fire" officials who impose state and federal laws. However, in a strange twist of the kind that could only happen in Texas, one of the state's most prominent officials brought up secession in 2009. At a "tea party" tax protest, Governor Rick Perry addressed shouts from the crowd calling on him to secede.

"There's a lot of different scenarios," said the governor. "We've got a great union. There's absolutely no reason to dissolve it. But if Washington continues to thumb their nose at the American people, you know, who knows what might come out of that. But Texas is a very unique place, and we're a pretty independent lot to boot."

Maybe the door isn't closed on this issue.

Freedom of Speech

Now a sparkling jewel of the Gold Coast, Washington Square Park was once a haven for great thinkers, poets, and kooks.

✳ ✳ ✳ ✳

LONG BEFORE WE could express ourselves by leaving obnoxious comments on internet message boards, people sought out "open forums" (parks and cafés) to debate the events of the day. In the 1920s, there were dozens of such "forums" around Chicago. The most famous, however, was Bughouse Square, the park officially known as Washington Square Park that still sits at the corner of Clark and Chestnut. In its prime, some people said it was the most educational place in town. Others likened it to an outdoor mental ward. People of both opinions, however, agreed that it was top-notch entertainment.

According to legend, when Orasmus Bushnell left the patch of land to the city in 1842 for use as a park, he included two stipulations. One was that the city had to build a wall around the park (which, in true Chicago fashion, the city got around by putting up about eight inches of limestone). The other condition was that anyone who wished had to be allowed to make a speech in the park at any time. Making a speech in the park became a popular pastime.

Well into the mid-twentieth century, one could find several people making speeches on soapboxes in Bughouse Square any night when the weather was decent. Some nights, as many as 3,000 people would crowd into the park to heckle the speakers. In those days, the Near North Side was the bohemian capital of the Midwest, and Bughouse Square was a favorite gathering place.

Drunken Hecklers Didn't Stand a Chance

Some of the great speakers and thinkers of the day made Bughouse Square a regular stop when they came through Chicago, but it was the weirdos and cranks who made the park famous. One regular was Herbert "The Cosmic Kid" Shaw, who was known for taking his audience on "philosophic flights into empyrean realms of thought." "Weird Mary" was just one of several cranks who often harangued the audience on the subject of religion. "One-Armed Charlie" Wendorf had the Constitution memorized. Since he could—and did—debate such famous lawyers as Clarence Darrow, Wendorf had no problem with drunken hecklers. "If brains were bug juice," he said to one, "you couldn't drown a gnat!"

Daily News columnist Mike Royko believed that the weirdos made the park a perfect stop for suburbanites. After one night there, they could go back to their quiet neighborhoods and tell all their friends they'd seen a crazy man give a speech about free love—right out in public!

Today, the Whole World Is Bughouse Square

By the 1970s, the neighborhood around Bughouse Square had gone badly downhill. Clark Street had always been known for squalor, but it had gotten too dangerous for any but the bravest to venture to Bughouse Square at night. And, anyway, by then everyone had a television set to entertain themselves after dark. Open forums had gone out of style. In 1969, Royko noted that he had just walked by the park and had not seen a single soapbox orator.

But the loss was hardly lamented. When Jack Sheridan, a former regular who had presided over a Druidic funeral in the park when The Cosmic Kid died, was asked in 1971 whether he missed the park, he chuckled and said, "Don't need to. The whole world is Bughouse Square now!"

Today, Bughouse Square is a quiet Gold Coast park. But once every summer, the nearby Newberry Library sponsors the Bughouse Square Debates. On those days, the weirdos, cranks and poets of the city head back to the park, just as they did back in the day.

Topics at recent Bughouse Square Debates have ranged from immigration to *foie gras* to the Family and Medical Leave Act.

Gems Along the Shore

Chicago boasts one of the longest stretches of freshwater shoreline of any city in the world, and, despite its potential real estate value, much of it is has been set aside as public space. The list below highlights some notable spots.

✳   ✳   ✳   ✳

* **South Shore Cultural Center:** Formerly a private lakefront country club, the South Shore Cultural Center at 70th and South Shore Drive is now a part of the city's massive public parks system. The 58-acre site hosts a nine-hole golf course, tennis courts, stables, an art gallery, and a lavish 100-year-old clubhouse that is often rented for private parties—including Barack and Michelle Obama's 1992 wedding reception.

* **Promontory Point:** Jutting out into Lake Michigan at South 55th Street, Promontory Point is a park first conceived as part of Burnham and Bennett's 1909 Plan of Chicago. The artificial structure, which was built in the 1920s and 1930s using innovative landfill techniques, allows visitors to stroll some 6,000 feet out onto the lake itself.

* **Northerly Island:** This manmade island just south of downtown was used as a main exhibition area for the 1933 Century of Progress exposition. Though it once housed the Meigs Field landing strip for small planes, much of the island is now set aside as a nature reserve, though it does include one of the city's major concert venues as well.

* **Chicago Harbor Light:** The Chicago Harbor Lighthouse dramatically marks the entrance to the city's main marine port. Built in 1893, it is one of the oldest existing lighthouses in Illinois. The structure has become a symbol of Chicago's role as a maritime shipping hub connecting the East Coast to the South via the Great Lakes and the Mississippi River. Its bright white tower and red-roofed outbuildings can easily be seen from the shore.

* **Buckingham Fountain:** Commissioned by Chicago philanthropist Kate Buckingham, Buckingham Fountain was donated to the city in 1927. One of the largest outdoor fountains in the world, the massive structure on Congress Avenue and Columbus Drive holds 1.5 million gallons of water and shoots geysers bathed in colored light as high as 150 feet.

* **Navy Pier:** This mile-and-a-half-long pier was opened in 1916 at the point where the Chicago River flows into Lake Michigan. Originally conceived as both a commercial marine facility and an entertainment venue, the pier was renovated in the mid-1990s and has become a center for public life in the city. The site offers boat tour excursions, various restaurants and shops, a towering Ferris wheel, live theater, an IMAX theater, and a children's museum.

* **Oak Street Beach:** Located off Lake Shore Drive just north of the Magnificent Mile, Oak Street beach is *the* place for Chicago's young and beautiful sun worshippers to gather during the sweltering summer months. The beach was created in the 1890s as part of a massive breakwater project designed to protect Lake Shore Drive from erosion.

* **Theater on the Lake:** Situated in sprawling Lincoln Park, the Theater on the Lake is housed in a simple brick building that offers views of Lake Michigan as well as low-priced live theater. Operated by the Chicago Park District, the theater has been in continuous operation since the 1940s. It offers various productions every summer, from family friendly performances to Shakespeare.

* **Montrose Point Bird Sanctuary:** Located near Montrose Beach, one of the city's favorite family beaches, the bird sanctuary provides food, water, and shelter to the more than 300 species of migratory birds that pass through the Chicago area. The 15-acre site was created in the 1950s as a buffer around an army installation. It became so popular with the feathered crowd that it was designated a protected nature area after the army left in the 1970s.

Bitter Onions or Striped Skunk?

Many know Chicago's name derives from an indigenous name for the Chicago River. And it has something, they might add, to do with "bitter onions." But few modern Chicagoans know that the origins of their beloved town's famous name may be lost in the notebook of a seventeenth-century explorer, that the word is as French as it is Native American, and, most important, that the great debate over its origin is far from over.

✳   ✳   ✳   ✳

RECORDS OF THE language of the Illinois and Miami Native Americans, who inhabited the area and presumably named many landmarks in the region, only date back to the end of the seventeenth century, when beleaguered Jesuits and French explorers recorded thousands of words and suggested certain overly practical origins.

It's true that many place names in the Midwest were based on descriptions of the terrain and that the stinky onions that pep-pered the riverbanks may have been the region's most salient botanical novelty. But it's also true that many explorers were translating the language into a kind of crude French, and their methods were often rooted in trial, error, and complacency.

It appears that the name of the river was first recorded by René-Robert Cavelier, Sieur de La Salle, whose own exhaust-ing moniker suggests a predilection for complicated language. In his notes, La Salle used "8," the Arabic numeral, as a kind of shorthand to stand in for the last syllable of the word that would become "Chicago." Historians have argued that the "8" stands in for an *A*, an *OU*, a *WA*, though they insist it couldn't be an *O*, as it is now.

More recently, scholars have noted that the locals' supposed fixation on onions is as apocryphal as it sounds, the error based on a mistranslation of La Salle's hastily written notes. Now it seems likely that the word Chicago is most closely linked to *sikaakwa* or *sikaakonki*, which relate not to "bitter onions," but "striped skunk"—perhaps a sign that, linguistics aside, Chicago has never been known for pleasant aromas.

Hull House: Chicago's Most Famous Haunted House

When Charles Hull passed away in 1889, he was a wealthy man who had helped build Chicago from a mud puddle to a metropolis. To Helen Culver—his cousin and business associate— he left an estate worth millions of dollars.

✳   ✳   ✳   ✳

HELEN CULVER TOOK her responsibilities as an heir very seriously. One of her first acts was to allow Jane Addams (a pioneer in the field of social work) to turn Hull's Halsted Street mansion into a settlement house—a place where the people in the neighborhood (who were mostly very poor immigrants) could go to get medical care or a meal, learn English and other skills, and otherwise work to improve their chances of success in their new country.

Records are spotty, but two or three members of Charles Hull's family may have died in the house, after which he abandoned living in it altogether: His wife died in her bedroom, and his sons Louis and Charley are thought to have died in the house, as well.

After Hull moved out of the mansion, the area around it became the worst neighborhood in the city; some said that it was more vile than Five Points in New York City, which Charles Dickens proclaimed to be one of the worst places he'd ever seen. Crime, corruption, drugs, alcoholism, gambling, and prostitution ran rampant, and most residents were living in overcrowded, unsanitary tenements.

Skeptical of Spooks?

In 1889, when Addams moved into the mansion, the house was already rumored to be haunted. Addams noticed that the staff placed buckets of water at the top of the stairs; she came to realize that they were there to keep ghosts away. After all, at the time, it was commonly thought that ghosts could not cross over water.

Jane Addams was a bit skeptical about the ghosts, but after moving into Mrs. Hull's old bedroom, she was often awakened by the sound of footsteps near her bed. After one of Addams's friends stayed in the room, the friend reported the same thing. Thereafter, whenever a dignitary visited Hull House, they would half-jokingly be invited to spend a night in "the haunted room." Most accepted the offer; many not only heard footsteps, but some also caught a glimpse of a ghostly woman looking down at them in the middle of the night.

The Devil's Spawn?

The work Addams did for the poor made her famous, and Hull House grew rapidly. To allow the facility to expand, the buildings that flanked the mansion were torn down, along with many crumbling tenements. At its height, Hull House covered an entire city block.

But for all the great works that Jane Addams accomplished at Hull House, it is still best remembered for the rumor that, in 1913, a "devil baby" had been born and was left there.

Stories of how a child with horns, hooves, scaly red skin, and a tail came to exist varied wildly. Among the more common explanations was that a Catholic woman had married an atheist, became pregnant, and placed a picture of the Virgin Mary on the wall. The husband flew into a rage, ripped the picture in two, and said, "I would rather have the devil in this house than a picture of that woman!" Another tale said that a woman had given birth to seven daughters, and upon learning that she was pregnant again, her husband said, "I would rather the next be the devil than another girl!"

All of the stories ended the same way: The child was born looking like a miniature devil, and in some versions, he could speak fluent Latin. Legend has it that when the father brought the baby to Hull House and approached a priest, the infant jumped from the man's arms, stole the priest's cigar, and began to smoke it while cursing the priest and displaying a forked tongue. The story may sound outrageous, but Hull House was mobbed with visitors wanting to see the baby.

Where the story came from is anyone's guess. Some speculate that a neighborhood baby may have been born with harlequin ichthyosis, a disease that causes humans to be born with red, scaly skin. Addams suggested that perhaps a deformed baby had been born somewhere on the West Side, but she also noted that the story could have been a thousand years old; in fact, one variation of the origin is identical to the story of the Jersey Devil. If such a child did exist, it was never brought to—and was certainly never exhibited at—Hull House.

But that didn't stop hundreds of curious spectators from lining up at Hull House, demanding to see the devil baby, and offering to pay any cost to do so. "To see the way otherwise intelligent people let themselves be carried away by this ridiculous story is simply astonishing," Addams told the *Chicago Examiner.* "If I gave you the names of some of the professional people—including clergymen—who have asked about it, you simply would not believe me!"

Addams eventually came to see the episode as a great sociological phenomenon. Many of the neighborhood immigrants had only recently realized that the stories they'd been taught as facts in their home country were regarded as superstitions everywhere else, so they were looking for something that would help them cling to their old beliefs. Others were women with very little control over their lives who wanted to tell their husbands, "I have seen that devil baby. If you don't start treating me better, the same could happen to us!"

The story eventually died down, and in 1931, Addams became the first American woman to win the Nobel Peace Prize. In the

1960s, Hull House moved its operations elsewhere, and the buildings—except for the dining hall and the original house, which became museums—were torn down to make room for the expansion of the University of Illinois at Chicago.

Hauntings Persist

But the stories of the hauntings that predated Addams persisted, and in the 1970s, Hull House became a popular stop on the first ghost tours in Chicago. While a few people still claim to see the Devil Baby, among the most common sightings are the spirits of Mrs. Hull and a young girl whose identity is not known. Children frequently report seeing a woman in a white bonnet in one of the windows.

Stranger still are the many photos that have been taken of spectral men in hooded robes. No one knows who these ghosts were in life because Hull House was certainly never a monastery.

As with many allegedly haunted houses, dozens of bizarre stories without any basis in fact have circulated about Hull House over the years, causing some ghost hunters to avoid the place altogether. But it is difficult to ignore the fact that even these skeptical investigators continue to report sightings of a spectral older woman and a young girl—the same ghosts that have been spotted there for 150 years.

Marshall Field: A Chicago Institution

It's hard to imagine what Chicago would be like today if Marshall Field hadn't lived there.

✳   ✳   ✳   ✳

ASIDE FROM THE legendary flagship store that bore his name for 125 years, Marshall Field's credits to the city of Chicago include: the Field Museum, the Museum of Science and Industry, the John G. Shedd Aquarium, and the University of Chicago. That's quite an influence to wield over a single city, all due to Field's generosity and philanthropy.

The Man Behind the Legendary Clock

Born in Conway, Massachusetts, Field moved to Chicago when he was 21 and started working at a dry-goods merchant. Within ten years, he became a senior partner at his own establishment, Field, Palmer, Leiter & Co. In 1881, Field bought out his business partners and changed the store's name to Marshall Field and Company.

Field changed the face of shopping to reflect the extravagance of the gilded age in the late 1800s. Returns accepted and refunds issued with a smile are just a couple of the ideas that he established.

The department store café developed after a clerk shared her lunch with a tired shopper. Immediately, Field thought of opening a tearoom so shoppers wouldn't have to leave to eat. Traditional dishes join new favorites today at the Walnut Room.

Field's also started the first bridal registry and revolving credit and was the first store to use escalators. Marshall Field's book department pioneered the concept of the book signing, and Christmas at Field's became legendary, with its downtown windows filled with sparkling animated displays. The phrases "Give the lady what she wants" and "The customer is always right" are slogans attributed to Field and his colleague, Harry Gordon Selfridge.

An Era Ends

In 2005, Federated Department Stores acquired Marshall Field's and changed the name in 2006 to Macy's Department Store. His name may be gone, but Field's legacy in the retail business will carry on.

The Lost City of Atlantis

Ever since Plato first mentioned the ancient civilization of Atlantis in his dialogues Timaeus and Critias, academic analysts have debated the existence of the lost continent. Was the prophetic philosopher fabricating a tale or indicating valuable information?

According to Plato, the ancient civilization of Atlantis was a colossal naval power that conquered many parts of Western Europe and Africa more than 9,000 years before the time of Solon, or approximately 9500 B.C. After a failed attempt to invade Athens, the entire continent collapsed into the ocean "in a single day and night of misfortune." Since Plato never bothered to divulge the manner of demise, historians have been left to argue over the authenticity of the alleged Atlantis. The skeptical side of the ledger contends that Plato was using his creative leverage to force his readers to both examine and question the limitations and logistics of greed, government, and power. Simply put, Plato's message was that power corrupts and the price paid is high.

Wanna Buy a Bridge?

The Brooklyn Bridge is one of the most famous suspension bridges in the world. And it costs nothing to cross.

✳   ✳   ✳   ✳

YOU DON'T HAVE to live in New York City to love the architecturally stunning Brooklyn Bridge. Completed in 1883, it's one of the Big Apple's best-known landmarks and is currently crossed by an estimated 131,500 commuters each day to traverse the East River between Manhattan and Brooklyn.

Over the years, a number of myths have sprung up regarding the Brooklyn Bridge. Among them:

* Several bodies were entombed in the structure during construction. This myth is also commonly said of Nevada Hoover Dam and is untrue on both counts. It is true that between 20 and 50 workers perished during the construction of the bridge, but none were entombed there.

* Gullible rubes have actually tried to purchase the Brooklyn Bridge. This hoary tale has been around almost as long as the bridge itself, but there is no proven account of anyone actually being tricked into purchasing the bridge, which is public property.

* The bridge was designed by John Augustus Roebling and Wilhelm Hildenbrand. Roebling died before construction began; his son, Washington, took over the project.

* Construction of the bridge spanned 13 years and cost $15.1 million. It has a total length of 5,989 feet.

* President Chester Arthur and New York Governor Grover Cleveland attended the bridge's dedication on May 23, 1883. Washington Roebling's wife, Emily, took the first ride across the bridge with a rooster in her lap, a symbol of victory.

* On its dedication day, the Brooklyn Bridge charged a toll of one penny, and three cents thereafter. Today, it's free.

The Statue of Suez?

Evidence suggests Lady Liberty has origins in a design originally intended for the Suez Canal.

✳   ✳   ✳   ✳

IN 1865, FRENCH sculptor Frédéric-Auguste Bartholdi (1834–1904) learned of his country's plan to create a gift for the United States. The present was intended to cement Franco-American friendship and commemorate the 100th anniversary of America's independence—still more than a decade away. The sculptor couldn't know it then, but he would go on to design this gift—now known as the Statue of Liberty. Surprisingly, evidence suggests Bartholdi's inspiration for the project came not from anything found in America, but rather from the Suez

Canal, an engineering marvel that was in the works at the time.

A Grand Idea

Bartholdi's interest in the waterway came when he met fellow Frenchman Ferdinand-Marie, Vicomte de Lesseps, in Egypt. Bartholdi loved grand ideas, and de Lesseps's ambitious (or laughable, depending on your perspective) plan to channel through the desert from the Mediterranean Sea to the Red Sea was deliciously dramatic. With such shared passions fueling their friendship, the pair would become lifelong comrades.

By 1869, when the "laughable" Suez Canal was nearing completion, Bartholdi drew up plans for a commemorative statue. He envisioned a robed figure standing beside the canal's entrance, the lights within her headband and her torch guiding ships much like a lighthouse. Bartholdi deemed the figure "Progress," and presented his plans to Egyptian ruler Isma'il Pasha for funding. To his disappointment, the project was never commissioned.

Plan B

Soon thereafter, Bartholdi designed the Statue of Liberty, a great gift to America. It was erected on Bedloe's Island (later to become Liberty Island) just south of Manhattan and has since welcomed millions of immigrants to the New World.

Although Bartholdi denied any connection between Progress and Liberty, the uncanny similarities between the two are hard to ignore. Even so, the truth behind Liberty's lineage is mostly moot. This grande-dame symbol of freedom and acceptance has been doing yeoman's duty in New York Harbor since 1886. The rest is just details.

Fun Facts About Lady Liberty

* The statue's real name is "Liberty Enlightening the World."

* Alexandre Gustave Eiffel was the structural engineer.

* A quarter-scale bronze replica of Lady Liberty was erected in Paris in 1889 as a gift from Americans living in the city. The statue stands about 35 feet tall and is located on a small island in the River Seine, about a mile south of the Eiffel Tower.

* There are 25 windows and 7 spikes in Lady Liberty's crown. The spikes are said to symbolize the seven seas.

* Lady Liberty is 152 feet, 2 inches tall from base to torch and 305 feet, 1 inch tall from the ground to the tip of her torch.

* There are 192 steps from the ground to the top of the pedestal and 354 steps from the pedestal to the crown.

* *The statue functioned as an actual lighthouse from 1886 to 1902. There was an electric plant on the island to generate power for the light, which could be seen 24 miles away.

* The Statue of Liberty underwent a multimillion-dollar renovation in the mid-1980s before being rededicated on July 4, 1986. During the renovation, Lady Liberty received a new torch because the old one was corroded beyond repair.

Bridges of the East River

Henry Hornbostel, who worked on both the Williamsburg and Queensboro bridges, died in 1961 at age 94. He was the last living of the East River bridge designers.

The following are New York City's East River bridges and their designers:

* The Brooklyn Bridge, built from 1870 to 1883; designed by John Augustus Roebling (1806–69) and completed by his son, Washington Roebling (1837–1926)

* The Manhattan Bridge, completed in 1909; designed by

Leon Moisseiff (1872–1943)

* The Williamsburg Bridge, completed in 1903; designed by Leffert L. Buck (1837–1909) and Henry Hornbostel (1867–1961)

* The Queensboro Bridge, completed in 1909; designed by Gustav Lindenthal (1850–1935) and Henry Hornbostel (1867–1961)

The Literary Village

Greenwich Village has always welcomed the offbeat. Here are a few of the great writers who once called these streets their own.

✻ ✻ ✻ ✻

S TORYTELLING SEEMS TO come easily in this part of town, with its cozy tangle of small streets. It's tempting to conjure up the vision of Washington Irving ensconced at his sister's home at 11 Commerce Street circa 1819, possibly writing "The Legend of Sleepy Hollow." Up the block at #38 is the Cherry Lane Theatre, established in 1924 by poet Edna St. Vincent Millay. She lived around the corner at 75 Bedford Street in "the narrowest house in New York"—still a highly coveted domicile, despite the fact that it measures just 9.5 feet at its widest. Originally constructed in 1873, the house's 1930s inhabitants included *New Yorker* cartoonist and *Shrek* creator William Steig, his first wife, and her sister, anthropologist Margaret Mead.

Down by the River

On the West Side, a couple of blocks east of the Hudson River, stands St. Luke in the Fields (487 Hudson Street), founded in part by church warden Clement Clark Moore, who wrote 1822's beloved "A Visit from St. Nicholas" ("'Twas the night before Christmas..."). A bit farther north, at 567 Hudson and 11th Street, the White Horse Tavern occupies a wooden structure that dates to the mid-1600s. The tavern has served everyone from Jack Kerouac (who used to be thrown out on a regular basis) to John F. Kennedy Jr., but it is primarily known for the legend that Welsh poet Dylan Thomas drank himself to death here by downing 18 whiskeys in one go. In truth, Thomas imbibed a few beers at the tavern on November 9, 1953; he was already feeling ill and died a few days later at nearby St. Vincent's Hospital.

John Lennon to Emma Lazarus

Sinclair Lewis lived at 69 Charles Street for three years, beginning in 1910; Woody Guthrie had a brief 1942–43 tenancy at #74 (and wrote "This Land Is Your Land" while living on 14th Street—the northernmost border of the Village). Maurice Sendak (*Where the Wild Things Are*) is thought to have lived at #92. In 1971, John Lennon and Yoko Ono moved into their first New York apartment together a few blocks north at 105 Bank Street.

Not all the Village's famous alumni actually *lived* here. Thomas Paine, the author of "Common Sense," passed away in 1809 at 59 Grove Street, off Seventh Avenue. The original building is long gone, but a plaque on the present structure notes its significance.

A few steps west of Tenth Street and Sixth Avenue is the little gated alley called Patchin Place, which at one point or another was home to poet e.e. cummings (for 40 years), critic Djuna Barnes, journalist John Reed (*Ten Days That Shook the World*), and writer Theodore Dreiser. Across Sixth, just west of Fifth Avenue is 14 West Tenth Street, where Mark Twain is said to haunt the stairwell—even though he spent only a year here in 1901, enjoying far more time at 21 Fifth Avenue. Emma Lazarus dwelled a few doors down at #18; her 1883 sonnet "The New Colossus" ("Give me your tired, your poor") is immortalized on a bronze plaque at the Statue of Liberty.

Mid-Village

To the southeast lies Washington Square Park, hotbed of 1950s bohemia and 1960s rebellion. Henry James's 1880 *Washington Square* was inspired by visiting his grandmother at what was then 19 Washington Square North (the numbering system has changed). In 1882, James's friend Edith Wharton moved in a few steps away, with her mother, at #7. Wharton's keen observations of latter nineteenth-century New York society informed her 1920 novel *The Age of Innocence*, making her the first female recipient of a Pulitzer Prize.

Master of the Macabre—and Moving

Although Edgar Allan Poe spent his final New York years in a cottage in the Bronx, he was also a Village habitué. When living at Sixth Avenue and Waverly Place in 1837, Poe visited the Northern Dispensary—still at Waverly and Christopher Street—to treat a head cold. He later moved to 113 Carmine Street, 130 Greenwich Street, 15 Amity Street (now 15 West Third Street), 154 Greenwich Street, 195 East Broadway, and finally—in the fall of 1845—85 Amity Street (now 85 West Third), where he began "The Cask of Amontillado" while revising "The Raven" and other poems. Preservationists were horrified when owner New York University, originally intent on demolishing the 1835 three-story town house, came up with a compromise "interpretive reconstruction" in the early twenty-first century that destroyed the original brick facade and moved the original site a half-block away. Northeast of Washington Square Park, at Broadway and East Tenth, is the Gothic-revival Grace Church, thought to have inspired "The Bells"; Poe was visiting family friends nearby when he wrote the first draft.

Across the Park

South of Washington Square Park, on MacDougal Street between West Fourth and Bleecker, is Caffe Reggio, the first place to serve cappuccino in the United States when it opened in 1927. Louisa May Alcott probably could have used a coffee

break 60 years earlier, while she wrote *Little Women* across the
street at 130–132, in the row houses belonging to her uncle.
Down the street at 113 MacDougal and Minetta Lane, the
Minetta Tavern has been reinvented as an upscale bistro, but
back in 1923, when *The Reader's Digest* was founded in the
basement, this was a hangout for e.e. cummings, Ezra Pound,
and playwright Eugene O'Neill, whose boarding house was on
Washington Square South.

Heading East

Around the corner on Bleecker Street, the long-closed
San Remo Café (#189) played host to the Beats: Kerouac,
Burroughs, Corso, and Ginsberg. In the '70s, longtime Villager
Ginsberg moved northeast to 437 East 12th Street, where he
stayed for over 20 years; his neighbors included author/punk
rocker Richard Hell.

After immigrating to New York in 1981, lavender-coiffed
British transplant Quentin Crisp (*The Naked Civil Servant*)
made his home at 46 East Third Street and Second Avenue—
not far from Bill Burroughs's 222 Bowery "bunker," a window-
less apartment in a former YMCA where the *Naked Lunch*
author lived from 1974 to 1980.

What Used to Be Here?

*New York has been so intensely modified, shaped, demoed, burnt,
rebuilt, filled, and drilled that there is a past city modern residents
barely know.*

✳   ✳   ✳   ✳

Beekman's Swamp is a roughly 30-acre bog in Lower
Manhattan just south of the modern Brooklyn Bridge. Beekman
Street would border its south edge if Southbridge Towers wasn't
built smack on the spot. The swamp was drained in 1734.

Collect Pond was a 48-acre lake in Lower Manhattan (modern

Foley Square) until about 1800. It was fed by groundwater and drained to the Hudson. The Pond was the city's water supply until people literally trashed it. By 1811, it was filled in completely.

Eastern Park was home to the Brooklyn Grooms/Bridegrooms during 1891–97, and the spot where the Trolley Dodger name (later the "Dodgers") originated. The park stood between Pitkin and Sutter avenues and between Van Sinderen Avenue and Powell Street in East New York. The team left the Eastern in 1897 for another, cheaper venue, and the park was demolished within a few years.

Ebbets Field was the Dodgers' last real home, and fewer and fewer fans are left who remember the Marble Rotunda in this fabled place at 55 Sullivan Place, Flatbush. Its team gone after the 1957 season, it succumbed to the wrecking ball in 1960, leaving only memories and some high-rise apartments.

Five Points resulted from a haphazard fill job on Manhattan's Collect Pond that left a smelly, miasmal area near modern Worth and Baxter streets. Five Points was the archetypical Victorian den of urban squalor and crime. Cleanup began in the 1890s, and today the area houses municipal buildings.

Fort Amsterdam was a square fortress in Lower Manhattan in modern Bowling Green Park. From above it would have looked like a square ninja-throwing star. Finished in 1625, it was dismantled in 1790—probably due to decrepitude.

Hilltop Park was where the first Yankees—who were called the Highlanders—played from 1903 to 1912. It stood in Washington Heights between 165th and 168th streets, between Fort Washington Avenue and Broadway. After the team departed, Hilltop was purchased by investors and was razed in 1914.

Lenape Villages stood near modern City Hall, east of Chinatown, on the Lower East Side and in Chelsea. These

American Indian dwellings were extant when Dutch settlers arrived, with the biggest concentrations found in Inwood along the Harlem River and in Washington Heights near the I-95 bridge's west base.

Lower Manhattan Waterfront roughly followed Greenwich Street; the eastern followed Pearl Street. The southernmost tip was just south of Water and State Streets. The waterfront landfill process that erased LMW has taken centuries.

Pennsylvania Station was a magnificent neoclassical structure at the corner of West 34th Street and Eighth Avenue. Wait, you're thinking, you go into Penn Station at Seventh and 32nd. And you'd be right—but that's the new, unimproved Penn Station. The original was built in 1910 on the site of today's Madison Square Garden. Among its many grand features was a glass-and-steel vaulted ceiling that rose 150 feet above the tracks. It was demolished in 1963.

Polo Grounds housed the Gothams/Giants between 1883 and '88. It stood between Fifth and Sixth avenues and 110th and 112th streets. In 1888, the city confiscated the land adjoining Central Park and tore down the Polo Grounds shortly thereafter. Today, 111th Street runs right through the old outfield.

Polo Grounds II/III/IV were "home" for many New York sports teams, and saw many great moments, from 1889 to 1963. These venues actually comprised two different Manhattan parks, both located between Edgecombe Avenue and the Harlem River, and 155th and 159th streets. They were flattened in 1964 to build apartments.

Shea Stadium opened in 1964 as the Mets' new home in Flushing, at 126th Street and Roosevelt Avenue; the Jets played here, as well, until 1983. The Mets stayed through the 2008 season, after which Shea was pulled down to provide parking for the new Citi Field.

Stadt Huys, Manhattan's first city hall, was also a tavern. It stood where 85 Broad Street is today, between South William Street and Pearl Street. Built in 1642, it was city hall for the Dutch until 1667 and continued as such for the English until 1699. During its glory years, it was fronted by stocks that provided public punishments to wrongdoers. Stadt Huys evidently fell apart around 1700.

Wall Street Bastions was the original Dutch wall along "Het Cingle" (now Wall Street). It had two north-extending stone bastions, one just east of Broadway, the other just west of the American International Building. The bastions and the entire wall came down in 1699.

Washington Park I/II/III were early homes of the Brooklyn Atlantics and the Trolley Dodgers, 1884–1912, and then housed the Federal League's Brooklyn Tip-Tops. The venue was comprised of two different parks in adjoining lots, both between First and Fifth streets and Third and Fifth avenues. Remnants of the final park can still be seen today on Third Avenue between First and Third streets. The wall of the Con Edison yard is part of the old clubhouse wall.

The World Trade Center, actually multiple buildings in Lower Manhattan dominated by a pair of enormous, peg-like skyscrapers, was in Lower Manhattan. Construction wrapped in 1973. Until both towers were brought down by the terrorist attack of September 11, 2001, the so-called Twin Towers were iconic parts of the newer NYC skyline.

Yankee Stadium I/II was "The House That Ruth Built," opening during the glory year of 1923, just south of the current incarnation at East 161st Street and River Avenue in the Bronx. The park was closed for renovation following the 1973 season and opened for the '76 campaign. Yankee Stadium closed for good at the end of the Yankees' 2008 season.

Washington Square Is for Everybody

Just south of Eighth Street at the foot of Fifth Avenue lies "the beating heart of Greenwich Village," better known as Washington Square Park. Its main claim to fame might be as the public gathering place that hosted the 1950s and 1960s folk music revival. But Washington Square Park has a much longer and more fascinating history.

✳ ✳ ✳ ✳

IN THE EARLY 1600s, the now-covered Minetta Brook— once a favorite trout stream—cut through the area that is now Washington Square Park, dividing Manhattan Island from the north to the East River. New Amsterdam then had a population of around 200. The Dutch—having driven Native Americans off this land—wanted to turn the duck marsh into viable farmland and also protect it from reclamation by the natives. So in 1644, in return for acting as a buffer against Indian attacks, as well as surrendering an annual share of their crop yield, 11 African slaves were given ownership of a two-mile strip of land that included the park area. They also received their freedom (but not that of their descendants). For the following two decades, this area was known as "The Land of the Blacks."

Caution: Dead Underground

The area continued as farmland until 1797, when the city's Common Council acquired it as a potter's field (a burial ground for the unknown or poor), which is what it remained until 1825 or 1826. To this day, most park visitors don't realize that they are walking over 20,000 bodies interred underfoot.

However, the legend that the park was a public execution ground is uncertain. The only recorded hanging took place in

1820, when Rose Butler was put to death for arson—and even the two eyewitness accounts to that event differ over exactly where it happened. A 300-year-old English elm (the oldest known living tree in Manhattan) at the northwest corner of the park is still referred to as the "Hanging Tree."

Fashionable Living

In 1826, the square briefly became the Washington Military Parade Ground, where volunteer militia trained; the following year, it was dedicated as a public park. Between 1829 and 1833, a row of Greek-Revival red-brick townhouses that still stand were built on the north side of the square. The wealthy inhabitants would eventually serve as inspiration for novelists such as Henry James and Edith Wharton. Interestingly, though, land south of the park—just a few blocks away—was home to poor immigrants who were jammed into miserable tenements known as "rookeries."

In 1889, a plaster-and-wood arch was erected to commemorate the centennial of George Washington's inauguration; it proved so popular that a permanent marble structure, designed by renowned architect Stanford White after Paris's *Arc de Triomphe*, was put up in 1892. Interestingly enough, excavations uncovered human remains, coffins, and at least one headstone.

Battleground I

Beginning in 1935, New York Parks commissioner Robert Moses fought to route traffic either through or around the park according to plans that Moses never bothered to run past the locals. His schemes were finally defeated in 1963 after a long battle led by residents such as urbanologist Jane Jacobs and former First Lady Eleanor Roosevelt, when Fifth Avenue was cut short at Washington Square Arch and the park became a pedestrian-only zone. It now offers playgrounds, a much-loved chess and scrabble playing area at the southwest corner, commemorative statuary, and two popular dog runs (for little and larger canines).

The first fountain, in the center of the park (but not aligned with the entrance under the arch), was completed in 1852. A redesign in 2009 brought it in line with the arch—despite fervent protest by Village residents, who are almost always in conflict with nearby New York University, which owns much of the area.

Battleground II

Artists have always been part of the Village, but the park's open space particularly lends itself to musicians, who have gathered there on Sundays since at least 1947. As the late Mary Travers, of Peter, Paul & Mary, who grew up in the Village, once reminisced: "It was writers, sculptors, painters, whatever, listening to Woody Guthrie, Pete Seeger, the Weavers. People sang in Washington Square Park on Sundays, and you really did not have to have a lot of talent."

Even those with plenty of talent were drawn to the park. During the brief period in 1958 when Buddy Holly lived with his bride Maria Elena two blocks north, he came to the park incognito in sun-glasses almost every morning to strum his Gibson guitar. His widow remembers that Buddy would "just sit there, and all these other young musicians—a lot of folksingers—used to come and talk with him . . . He'd advise them, 'Look at anything you see here in the park and then write something about that—that's how you compose.'"

But the city soon began to require permits for public performances, and by the early 1960s a crackdown had begun on music in the park. On April 9, 1961, Folklore Music Center founder Izzy Young led a few thousand supporters in a march through the park that ended with ten people being arrested; one local newspaper reported the clash as a "beatnik riot." But the ban on music was soon lifted, and Bob Dylan and other aspiring folksingers began calling the park their own. By the time the 1960s were in full swing, the park had become de rigueur as a hippie hangout.

A Dada-esque Declaration

During the 1970s and 1980s, the park fell into disrepair, attracting drug dealers and other disreputable types. The situation led the local citizenry to complain—and stay away. Concerted efforts by neighbors and law enforcement eventually managed to turn the tide, and the park has once more become a comfortable gathering place for students and professors; musicians and artists; lovers and dog-lovers; parents and children, and tourists and locals alike.

One final interesting footnote: On the snowy night of January 23, 1917, Surrealist/Dada artist Marcel Duchamp and several friends got into the interior stairway of the marble arch and climbed the spiral staircase to the roof. From that lofty perch, a local poet playfully announced the Village's secession from the United States, designating the land below as the "Free and Independent Republic of Washington Square." What foresight those irreverent pranksters had!

Local Legends

It's no secret that New York City includes a reasonably sizable homeless population. According to the Coalition for the Homeless, for instance, every night of March 2010 saw more than 38,000 homeless people sleeping in municipal shelters. Thousands more were forced to sleep outdoors in parks, on the streets, and in the subway system.

✳   ✳   ✳   ✳

Wait a minute—the subway system? One legend involving the city's have-nots remains a mystery. The labyrinthine tunnels of the subway system contain an awful lot of empty space. Sure, it's dark, dirty, and dangerous, but settlers in the area generally don't have their turf invaded. And some tunnels even have free electricity.

The homeless population inhabiting the subway tunnels is

sometimes referred to as "the mole people," and years of study and a lot of speculation have yielded few facts about them. For starters, no one is sure how many homeless people live underground. Some say hundreds; others, thousands. The lore surrounding the mole people can get quite bizarre. Some of the more creative urban legends purport that underground dwellers have evolved webbed feet to navigate the mucky terrain and are cannibals preying on unobservant commuters.

In 1993, journalist Jennifer Toth published *The Mole People: Life in the Tunnels Beneath New York City*, a controversial book in which she claims to have visited mole people in the tunnels. The book details a complex underground society with a justice system and official governing powers. But many people, including public transportation experts, smelled a rat. Details didn't all add up, especially Toth's architectural descriptions of the tunnel networks.

So here's what we do know: Some homeless people live underground in the subway tunnels, especially around the transportation hubs of Penn Station and Grand Central Station. It can't be confirmed whether these people are living independently or if they've established hierarchical underground cities. But don't worry—if you doze off on the train, you're far more likely to miss your stop or get your wallet stolen than you are to be eaten.

A Continent or an Island?

Why is Australia considered a continent instead of an island?

✳ ✳ ✳ ✳

IN GRAMMAR SCHOOL, some of us were far more interested in the "social" aspect of social studies than the "studies" part. Nevertheless, everyone can recite the continents: Africa, Asia, Europe, South America, North America, Australia, and... some other one.

What gives with Australia? Why is it a continent? Shouldn't it be an island?

It most certainly is an island (the world's largest) and so much more. Australia is the only land mass on Earth to be considered an island, a country, and a continent.

Australia is by far the smallest continent, leading one to wonder why it is labeled a continent at all when other large islands, such as Greenland, are not. The answer lies in plate tectonics, the geologic theory explaining how Earth's land masses got to where they are today. According to plate tectonic theory, all of Earth's continents once formed a giant land mass known as Pangaea. Though Pangaea was one mass, it actually comprised several distinct pieces of land known as plates.

Over millions of years, at roughly the speed of your hair growth, these plates shifted, drifting apart from one another until they reached their current positions. Some plates stayed connected, such as South America and North America, while others moved off into a remote corner like a punished child, such as Australia. (It's no wonder Australia was first used by the British as a prison colony.) Because Australia is one of these plates—while Greenland is part of the North American plate—it gets the honor of being called a continent.

All of this debate might ultimately seem rather silly. Some geologists maintain that in 250 million years, the continents will move back into one large mass called Pangaea Ultima. Australia will merge with Southeast Asia—and social studies tests will get a whole lot easier.

Fresh Mountain Air

Why are you colder on a mountain, even though you're closer to the sun?

✳ ✳ ✳ ✳

THIS QUESTION ASSUMES you might think that the only factor influencing temperature is proximity to that fireball in the sky. In other words, this question assumes you might be an idiot. It's much more complicated than proximity.

It has to be, or else the lowest nighttime temperatures on Mercury, which is two-and-a-half times closer to the sun than Earth is, wouldn't be −297 degrees Fahrenheit. And the moon, which is sometimes 240,000 miles closer to the sun than Earth is, wouldn't get as cold as −280 degrees Fahrenheit.

The reason it's colder on a mountaintop is because at that altitude, the atmosphere is different. Specifically, the air pressure is lower. The pressure at the top of Mount Everest, which is five-and-a-half miles above sea level, is less than a third of what it is at sea level.

During July—the warmest month on Everest—the average temperature hovers around −2 degrees Fahrenheit. It doesn't get above freezing up there, ever.

In simplest terms, when air is put under more pressure, it gets warmer. When the pressure lessens, it gets colder. That's why a bicycle pump warms up when you pump up a tire—in addition to the friction that's caused by the piston inside, the pump creates air pressure. It's also why an aerosol can gets downright cold if you spray it too long—air pressure escapes from the can.

When you think about all this, you realize how many scientific factors combine to make Earth hospitable for life. The moon has no atmosphere whatsoever; Mercury has a minute amount of it. The precise combination of gases that make up our atmosphere accounts for the air we breathe, the way the sun warms it, the color of the sky, and myriad other factors that explain life as we know it.

In fact, the cold temperatures at the top of a mountain are pretty minor when it comes to the miraculous—but scientifically logical—realities that are related to atmosphere.

Bethlehem

Perhaps the biblical place best known for its association with Jesus, Bethlehem was ancient by his time.

✳ ✳ ✳ ✳

In Biblical Times

BETHLEHEM HAS MORE Old Testament mentions than New. It was David's city and the burial place of Rachel (Genesis 48). Non-biblical sources reference it as early as the Amarna letters (1400 B.C.). It did not flourish greatly after Christ's time but did not die out. The Samaritans sacked Bethlehem in A.D. 529; Islamic troops captured it in A.D. 637.

Jesus' Connection

The story of Jesus begins in Bethlehem. It does not stay there long, however. In Matthew 2, wise men "from the East" (possibly Persian and possibly astrologers) were drawn to the town by a star. When they found the infant, they gave him gifts. Unfortunately for Joseph's family, King Herod was madder than a hornet. He didn't know the baby Jesus by sight, but he figured to kill him by killing every Bethlehem-area child under age two. Joseph took his family to Egypt for safety; how times had changed for Jews, to be trying to enter Egypt rather than escape it! When the vengeful king died in 4 B.C., the family returned but settled in Nazareth.

Bethlehem Today

Modern Bethlehem (Hebrew, Bait-lechem, "house of bread"; Arabic, Bayt lam, "house of meat") is a predominantly but not overwhelmingly Arab and Muslim city in the West Bank, governed by the Palestinian Authority. It stands six miles almost due south of Jerusalem. Its population is about 30,000, probably far more than in biblical times. The city houses one of the world's oldest continuous Christian populations; the city's law requires its mayor to be a Christian. Pilgrims flock to the Church of the Nativity, built over the site where tradition holds

Christ was born. In addition to tourism, Bethlehem survives on sales and exports of hand-crafted items.

Nazareth

Christ was, of course, a Nazarene. So what was, and is, the town of Nazareth?

✳ ✳ ✳ ✳

In Biblical Times

NAZARETH'S SITE WOULD seem a very attractive place to live, to go by its history of occupation. The earliest archaeological finds in the immediate area have been dated to the late Stone Age. By Christ's time, Nazareth was a small farming town; it could even be considered, in our lingo, somewhat podunk. In John 1, Nathanael responded to Philip's word of Jesus by asking, "Can anything good come out of Nazareth?" Luke describes it as the site of the Annunciation. It had a significant Jewish population until about A.D. 630, when the Eastern Roman Empire ran them out. Soon thereafter, Islamic forces captured the town.

Jesus' Connection

After King Herod died, Joseph brought his family to Palestine from Egypt. After a vision from an angel, Joseph settled in Nazareth, Galilee. Young Jesus grew to maturity there, and then he went out to minister. When he returned to Nazareth, he didn't get much respect. In Luke, he attended Shabbat at synagogue in Nazareth and tried to preach but was rejected and almost thrown off a cliff. Mark also refers to this episode. Christ took it philosophically, authoring the famous sentence: "Prophets are not without honor, except in their home town, and among their own kin, and in their own house." Scripture does not record Jesus returning to Nazareth.

Nazareth Today

Modern Nazareth (the Hebrew name is Natzrat or Natzeret; in Arabic it's An-Nasira), the "Arab capital of Israel," is some 16 miles west southwest of the Sea of Galilee. Over 60,000 people live in Nazareth proper, predominantly Arabs, who are roughly two-thirds Muslim and one-third Christian. It is part of a greater metro area with nearly 200,000 people. The chief modern attraction is the Church of the Annunciation, built over the spot where tradition says Gabriel appeared to Mary.

Jerusalem

It's one of the most storied cities in the world, pivotal in Christ's life: Golden Jerusalem, as it is called in Hebrew.

✳   ✳   ✳   ✳

In Biblical Times

JERUSALEM WAS GREATLY ancient even by the time of Christ, with known habitation at least back to 3000 B.C. Here King David reigned and Solomon built the temple. It had already been fought over, conquered, destroyed, and rebuilt numerous times. It was one of the Holy Land's most cosmopolitan cities and a center of Roman administration: in Latin it was called Hierosolyma. Its permanent population was somewhere between 30,000–50,000, with perhaps an equal number of pilgrims at any given time. Interestingly, guess who had restored the grandeur of the city with massive building projects? The hated King Herod.

Jesus' Connection

Jerusalem is thoroughly bound up with the life of Jesus. He went there for Passover, where to his disgust, a flea market was operating in the temple. He threw a fit, turning the tables over, and running out customers and vendors alike. Scripture recorded that his ministry would take him to Jerusalem several times. On his final visit, he prophesied its destruction. It was the site of the Last Supper, Jesus' sorrow as he prepared for the worst—his arrest, trial, and crucifixion.

Jerusalem Today

Incredibly, by A.D. 1800, Jerusalem had less than 10,000 people. How times change! Today, with nearly 800,000 residents, it is the capital of the state of Israel. It houses the Western (Wailing) Wall, the Church of the Holy Sepulchre, the Dome of the Rock, and Al-Aqsa Mosque.

One of the world's most important religious sites for all three faiths of the book, it's also a fairly modern city. Government employment and administration rank alongside tourism as the keys to modern Jerusalem's economics. It is 37 miles from the Mediterranean Sea. As Jerusalem is the major cause of disagreement between Muslims and Jews, the Arab-Israeli dilemma isn't going away until the Jerusalem issue is resolved.

Chapter 6

The Past, Present, & Future of Technology

The Face of the Future?

Are you on Facebook? Odds are pretty good that your coworkers, your mom or dad, your kids, or your best friends from grade school are.

✳   ✳   ✳   ✳

HARVARD UNIVERSITY IS well known for its innovators. Adding his name to that esteemed number, Mark Zuckerberg (class of 2006) put together a website on February 4, 2004, that afforded students an opportunity to communicate en masse. Buzz about the website spread across the campus as quickly as talk of a free keg party. (Well, maybe not *that* fast!) Soon, Stanford and Yale universities joined the new, funky site. Realizing that he had tapped into something big, Zuckerberg dropped out of college (sorry, mom and dad; I'll make you proud regardless) and took the idea to the national level. Facebook was on its way.

Although it is considered one of the more user-friendly social networking sites, Facebook is actually staggeringly complex. But what else would you expect from a website featuring more than 300 million users in total, half of whom log on to the site every day? Of course, these figures only scratch the surface of Facebook's story.

Surprisingly, the fastest growing demographic on Facebook does *not* include teens or those in their 20s—even though these age groups are renowned for their keen interest in technology. In fact, it is the over-35 crowd (backhandedly referred to as "dinosaurs" by cyber-snobs) who are logging on in unprecedented numbers. Can you possibly believe it?

As is plain to see, there is nothing trivial about Facebook. Nevertheless, the website does harbor its quirky facts. According to *Forbes* magazine, founder Mark Zuckerberg is America's youngest billionaire (the Harvard dropout turned a ripe 26 in 2010), and his website ranks as the third largest in the world—bettered only by Google and Yahoo. Facebook also features its share of controversy. In 2008, Zuckerberg dished out $65 million as a final settlement to a long-running legal battle. The claim? That it was Zuckerberg's former roommate who actually invented the Facebook concept. Yikes!

Facebook sustains itself with U.S. offices in Atlanta, Chicago, Dallas, Detroit, New York, Venice Beach, and Palo Alto. Its international offices are located in Toronto, Sydney, Dublin, London, and Paris. The average Facebook user is said to have 130 friends in their personal network. More than 70 language translations are available on the site. This is especially handy since 70 percent of Facebook users are located outside of the United States. Who knew?

Finally, what self-respecting web giant would be complete without a bona-fide behavioral disorder named after it? Facebook Addiction Disorder (FAD) is said to be a legitimate problem that can strike anyone who doesn't use Facebook judiciously. No, we're not kidding. Actually, this isn't too surprising. In a world where 130 cyber friends are as accessible as one's fingertips, the Facebook-driven disorder was bound to gain ground. Particularly in those trendy coffee shops.

Facebook by the Numbers

3 billion: the number of photos uploaded to Facebook each month

14 million: the number of videos uploaded each month

35 million: the number of status updates posted each day

6 billion: the collective number of minutes Facebook users spend (waste?) on the site each day

---

Pocket Egotism

It might be narcissistic and slightly voyeuristic, but so what? Where there's a photo booth, there's fun. Read on for the story behind those beloved self-portraits.

✳   ✳   ✳   ✳

If You Build It, They Will Insert Coins

IN 1926, A young Siberian immigrant and inventor named Anatol Josepho created his Photomaton machine, a large booth that could take a photographic image of a person and automatically develop it while he or she waited. Josepho placed his creation in seedy-but-thrilling New York's Times Square. For a quarter, a person received eight photos of themselves within minutes. No one had seen anything like it and word got around. Immediately, the photo booth was a sensation.

People lined up around the block to get their photos taken. In 1932, a Photomaton station opened on Broadway and 47th. Despite the fact that Americans were within the depths of the Great Depression, people gladly forked over a quarter for pictures of family, friends, and even pets.

The photo booth craze continued to rage on; in the 1950s, visual artists such as Andre Breton, Salvador Dali, and Luis Bunuel all took artistic advantage of the photo booth's small and affordable images. Later, pop artist Andy Warhol would also frequent Times Square photo booths.

Keep On Clickin'

The chemical-dipped, eight-picture photo booths are no longer manufactured, but there are still many working, old-fashioned photo booths in bars, on fairgrounds, and in various unlikely places around the country. But the photo booth isn't fading away—it's just growing up. If you've been in almost any shopping mall in the past few years, you've probably seen digital photo booths set up in heavy traffic areas. Here, subjects can pick colorful backgrounds and add captions.

Like jazz, baseball, and the quilt, photo booths are a staple of American culture.

Technology of the Future

In case you've grown bored with the advances in technology over the past couple of decades, brace yourself for some of the breakthroughs to come.

✳ ✳ ✳ ✳

* **Photo Tourism:** Billions of photos will be combined online so you can see objects and places in 3D from any angle in panorama. Existing software can collect images from all the different photo-sharing pages on the web, and it's just a matter of time before it all comes together for sightseeing via computer.

* **Virtual Earth:** Real-imaging Global Positioning Systems will enable you to access any location at any time. Soon you will be able to pull up a 3D map of San Francisco, for example, made of 10 million images, including 50,000 aerial photographs as well as shots taken at street level. Unlike Google Maps, this imaging will combine the street-level

pictures with aerial photos.

* **Smart Clothing:** The Laboratory on Emerging Technologies is refining the ability to package computer processors into washable clothing, thereby offering personal access to information, connectivity, and entertainment.

* **Smart Thinking:** Remote computing using brainwaves is the high-tech hit of the future. Just slide on an electrode headband and it will translate the electrical impulses from your brain into keystrokes. Once you're in sync with your computer, all you have to do is imagine moving your hands, feet, or any object, and the corresponding action will take place on the screen.

* **Virtual Keyboard:** A tiny Bluetooth laser the size of a matchbook can project a keyboard on any flat surface and make it functional! For those of us attached to our physical keyboards, it even makes simulated clicking sounds when we type.

* **Surface Computing:** This technology has been introduced by Microsoft and will soon allow us to use a touch-based, visual computer on tables, countertops, and even floors.

The Origins of the Couch Potato

We couldn't remotely imagine watching TV without our trusty remote controls, but believe it or not, American families used to do just that.

* * * *

THESE DAYS, REMOTE controls are a key part of the television viewing experience. In fact, virtually 100 percent of the televisions sold in this country come with a remote control. But when TVs started cropping up in living rooms across the United States in the late 1940s, viewing programs required a lot of up and down activity. As families gathered together to catch the latest variety shows, countless children of that generation became begrudgingly accustomed to the order to "get up and change the channel."

Taking Control

In 1950, Zenith became the first television manufacturer to offer a remote control for its product. The Lazy Bones device allowed viewers to turn the channel up or down and switch the TV on or off, but it was a wired device and the 20-foot cable strung across the living room floor was such a nuisance that few customers used it. Seeking to eliminate the cord, Zenith engineers came up with the Flashmatic, which was essentially a bulky flashlight that sent a signal to light receptors in one of the four corners of the screen to control the television. This system also had its shortcomings: The receptors in the screen could also be activated accidentally by other light sources.

Things Start to Click

Zenith engineer Robert Adler hit on the idea of using ultrasonic sound for the control mechanism. He and his team developed a system that used carefully tooled and cut aluminum rods inside the remote. When someone pressed a button on the remote, a hammer struck these rods. Each rod was cut to a slightly different length and vibrated at a slightly different frequency, making each produce a distinct ultrasonic sound. A complex array of receptors in the set recognized the sounds, performing a different action for each one. One remarkable aspect of Adler's device, which was called the Space Command, was that it was entirely mechanical. The remote operated without batteries or any other power source. Some factions at Zenith objected to the idea of a battery-powered remote because they actually feared that if the batteries went dead, customers would assume their television was broken. One serious shortcoming of the Space Command, though, was that it increased the cost of a set by 30 percent.

The company began manufacturing Adler's Space Command

remote in 1956, and the ultrasonic technology remained in use in virtually all remotes for the next 25 years, though in the 1960s the devices switched from the mechanical design to one that relied on transistors.

Visualizing a Better Life

In advocating for animal welfare and individuals with autism, Temple Grandin pictures a better world.

✳ ✳ ✳ ✳

"I THINK IN pictures," writes Dr. Temple Grandin, in the opening chapter of her book, *Thinking in Pictures*. "Words are like a second language to me. I translate both spoken and written words into full-color movies, complete with sound, which run like a VCR tape in my head." Throughout her life, this visual thinker has sought to explain what it is like to live with autism. Born in 1947, she was diagnosed with the developmental disorder in 1950. By sharing her perspective and experiences, she hopes that she will enlighten and empower others.

Grandin is also a Professor of Animal Science, a world-renowned advocate for animal welfare, and a prolific author. She also has had considerable influence in the livestock industry, where she has helped design more humane facilities, served as a consultant for firms such as McDonald's and Burger King, and educated people about proper animal handling. These accomplishments earned her such nicknames as "The Woman Who Thinks Like a Cow." She has said that "using animals for food is an ethical thing to do," but that it requires respect: "We've got to do it right. We've got to give those animals a decent life and we've got to give them a painless death."

The Squeeze Machine

As is common with autistic children, Grandin did not speak until age three and a half. Instead, she would communicate via screaming or humming. She was also highly sensitive to touch and sound. Doctors told her parents that she should be placed in an institution, but Grandin remained in school. Although she often endured ridicule from classmates, she was an imaginative thinker and developed her own strategies for coping with stress and anxiety. In one of her more profound instances of "thinking like a cow," in 1992, Grandin developed something called the squeeze machine or hug box for those with autism. Modeled after the squeeze chutes used to restrain cattle while they're being given veterinary treatment, this machine applies deep pressure stimulation (similar to a firm and long-lasting hug) to the person using it. "As a little kid, I wanted to experience the nice feeling of being held, but it was just too much overwhelming stimulation," Grandin said in a BBC documentary about her life, *The Woman Who Thinks Like a Cow*. Using the machine gives her more control of the situation, which allows her to relax and enjoy the feeling.

Other Innovations

Another one of Grandin's groundbreaking inventions is a curved chute or race system for corralling cattle. Designed to lower stress and fear in the animals, the curved chutes are more efficient than straight chutes, because, Grandin explains, "they take advantage of the natural behavior of cattle." (Cows have a natural tendency to return to where they came from.) Now processing plants throughout the world—businesses that slaughter millions of cattle and pigs for human consumption—use this type of corralling method. Grandin also developed an objective scoring system to assess how well cattle and pigs are handled at these plants. In addition, she has studied bull fertility, stunning methods for cattle and pigs, and cattle temperament. Grandin credits her strong visual thinking skills for her sensitivity to animals' experiences and ability to come up with humane treatment solutions.

Telling Her Story

In addition to working as a consultant to the livestock industry and teaching courses on livestock behavior and facility design, Grandin is the author of a number of bestselling books, including, *Emergence: Labeled Autistic, Animals in Translation: Using the Mysteries of Autism to Decode Animal Behavior,* and *Animals Make Us Human: Creating the Best Life for Animals.* She has also written articles for numerous magazines and is a go-to expert on most things cow-related. The neurologist Oliver Sacks wrote about her in his book, *An Anthropologist on Mars.* In sharing her experiences, Grandin aims to provide hope and insight to individuals on the autism spectrum.

Technology 101

Some folks swim in the tide of technology; others flounder and wave their arms for help or simply stay on shore. These questions were posed on behalf of technological landlubbers.

Q: What's virtual reality?

A: The fine art of having a computer mock up a realistic environment. *Virtual* just means "fake." Someday there may be electronically created virtual worlds where one sits in the equivalent of a sensory deprivation tank and experiences artificial touch, smell, sight, taste, and hearing. For now, a good (if less comprehensive) example is the pilot-training simulator. To the extent that they involve the simulation of flight, these approach virtual reality.

Q: What is a neural network?

A: Depends what kind you mean. A biological neural network has to do with actual brain function, the connections between one's neurons. An artificial neural network creates artificial intelligence using computer software. If you can program all the natural reactions of a deer to its environment, for example, perhaps you can make a virtual deer behave realistically using an artificial neural network.

Q: Is it true that the original computer bug was a literal insect?

A: It is. Before we had transistors and diodes—we now cram many millions of transistors on a single chip—we had vacuum tubes, which looked and worked somewhat like dim incandescent lightbulbs. If a moth got in, attracted by the heat and glow of the tubes, it messed up the tubes, just as a drop of water on a hot lightbulb will shatter it. This actually happened in 1945, when U.S. Navy Captain Grace Murray Hopper was working on a primitive computer at Harvard University. Though the moth story was thought by many to be a myth, Hopper was able to produce the page of the log she kept at the time, to which she had taped the offending moth.

A Cure for Bedroom Blues

Viagra began as a suprising breakthrough and ultimately became a genuine pharmaceutical phenomenon. Not since the birth control pill has a drug had such an astounding social impact.

✳   ✳   ✳   ✳

PFIZER'S "LITTLE BLUE pill" has brought relief to millions of men worldwide who suffer from erectile dysfunction, which is defined as an inability to maintain an erection. But that wasn't what its developers originally had in mind.

Sildenafil citrate, the active ingredient in Viagra, was originally designed as a heart drug. Because it acts as a vasodilator (a drug that helps blood vessels dilate), researchers thought it would be an effective treatment for high blood pressure and conditions such as angina.

However, sildenafil had an unusual side effect: The drug made it easier for men—especially those with erectile dysfunction—

to get an erection. Pfizer, knowing a lucrative breakthrough when it saw one, changed direction and began studying sildenafil as a treatment for one of the most common sexual problems in the world. The rest, as they say, is history.

The response to Viagra has been phenomenal. Nearly 570,000 prescriptions were written during the drug's first month on the market in early 1998. Viagra remains one of the world's most frequently prescribed drugs and in recent years has been joined by competitors like Cialis (tadalafil) and Levitra (vardenafil).

Viagra works by boosting blood flow to the penis, blocking an enzyme known as phosphodiesterase type 5 (PDE5). Approximately 70 percent of men who take Viagra for erection problems with a physical cause report success, noting that their erections develop faster, are harder, and last longer.

But Viagra is not perfect: Potential side effects include headache, a blue tint to vision, facial flushing, indigestion, and dizziness. Satisfied users say it's a small price to pay for a big boost in the bedroom.

Soap Floats

Ivory Soap's buoyancy doesn't have anything to do with purity. Here's the lowdown on one of America's favorite bars of soap.

❋   ❋   ❋   ❋

PERHAPS ONE OF the most memorable lines in commercial advertising is the following: "It's 99 and $^{44}/_{100}$ percent pure!" Whenever viewers heard this line uttered on television, they knew a pure-white bar of Ivory Soap would soon make an appearance, its distinctive etched lettering positioned for maximum impact. Print ads also capitalized on the soap's purity with the tagline "Ivory Soap. It floats."

Of course, a more discriminating viewer—let's call him "I. M.

Sinical"—might sometimes watch TV with his wife Jane, with a decidedly different reaction. "What is this soap trying to hide?" the curmudgeon would demand. "I want to know what's in the $^{56}/_{100}$ percent! And what's with this 'so pure it floats' malarkey? Dog droppings sometimes float, and I'm not about to bathe in them!"

The Pure Truth?

As the story goes, in 1879, a "White Soap" producer at Procter & Gamble neglected to turn off his mixing machine at lunchtime. Fearing punishment, he allowed the air-enriched batch of soap to be shipped. Soon, customers were asking for more "soap that floats," a fun by-product of the error. The worker came clean, company officials complied, and Ivory Soap was born.

It's a great story. But it isn't true. In 2004, Procter & Gamble discovered records dating back to 1863, which indicated that the floating soap was indeed intentional. Anyone who has ever lost a bar of soap while taking a bath can see why the company thought floating soap might be a good idea.

To conclude, we'll answer Mr. Sinical's probing questions with established facts: It is air that makes Ivory Soap float, *not* purity. And the composition of the suspect $^{56}/_{100}$ths? Uncombined alkali, carbonates, and mineral matter—each an *impurity*. How's that for truth in advertising?

The Hoxsey Cancer Clinics

Sick people have always sought alternatives to mainstream health and medical counsel. Some alternatives are more successful than others.

✳   ✳   ✳   ✳

IN 1924, TEXAN Harry Hoxsey opened his first clinic, claiming that a cure for cancer lay in herbal remedies—an internal tonic and two salves—concocted by his Quaker great-grandfather, who had seen a dying horse revived by eating certain medicinal weeds. By the 1950s, Hoxsey had clinics in 17 states, making his the largest alternative-medicine movement in American history.

Not So Fast

The American Cancer Society continues to condemn Hoxsey, while admitting that, "In some animal studies, a few of the herbs contained in the treatment showed some anti-cancer activity." Hoxsey was considered a quack, and although he was arrested more times than any other person in medical history, all charges of practicing medicine without a license were thrown out of court. Morris Fishbein, then-editor of the prestigious *Journal of the American Medical Association*, led the charge by continually filing suit against Hoxsey.

Closing Down Shop

Hoxsey, who had made his fortune in oil, claimed that Fishbein's efforts were revenge for Hoxsey's rebuff when Fishbein tried to buy the Hoxsey formulae. However, herbal treatments cannot be patented, so no company could have made significant profits from mass production. After the U.S. Food and Drug Administration banned the sale of Hoxsey treatments in 1960, Hoxsey was forced to close all of his clinics, although one was relocated to Tijuana, Mexico, where it continues to operate, using the name Bio-Medical Center.

In 1967, Hoxsey discovered that he had prostate cancer, but unfortunately neither his own medicine nor conventional surgery helped, and he died in 1974. A report by the National Institutes of Health has since urged further investigation of the Hoxsey treatments due to "several noteworthy cases of survival."

The New Technology Culture

Wait! Don't buy that new gadget yet—there might just be an even newer version of it coming tomorrow. Versions 2.0 and beyond of products show up in what seems to be a continuous loop, especially now that technology has become a pervasive element in most people's everyday lives. But what's the point of buying a newer version of something you already have?

✳ ✳ ✳ ✳

Necessity

A QUICK CHECK OF history and culture tells us that some things demand improvement. Take, for example, refrigeration. In its initial stages, refrigeration essentially involved the use of ice and snow to cool food down to a temperature at which it could be kept safely and wouldn't spoil. Later, the first cellars were developed: Holes in the ground were lined with wood or straw and packed with snow and ice. Eventually, machines were developed to cool food. But these used toxic gases, and leaking refrigerators caused fatal accidents. Researchers tried to find a different way to refrigerate, ultimately settling on the use of Freon, which became standard for almost all home kitchens. Unfortunately, the chlorofluorocarbons were destroying the ozone layer, so further developments in refrigeration were necessary.

The same process goes for medicines or vehicles. Medical research is constantly coming up with new versions of old antidotes, building both on the need for new solutions and the availability of technology to research and develop them. The bicycle was invented because Karl von Drais wanted to find an alternative to the horse during a time when crop failure was causing starvation and death. The needs of a culture or society often demand that kind of improvement of old methods, which often leads to the discovery of completely new devices or processes.

Desire

Of course, some versions of technology, machines, and vehicles are improved upon even without a desperate need. Because, let's face it, sometimes people just want cooler products. For instance, the iPod, Apple's portable media player, was regenerated through quite a number of versions just to perfect its usability. Developed initially to compete against the big and clunky or the small and mostly useless digital music players on the market, Apple concocted a cool-looking device that fit a ton of music in its user's pocket. Subsequent improvements included an upgraded interface, upgraded technology, and upgraded storage. Were these really necessary to make it more user-friendly? Did customers really need a touch-sensitive wheel when a scroll wheel performed precisely the same function? Maybe, maybe not. But it can't be denied that consumers jumped at the newer versions, so more than likely, Apple would have been hard-pressed to come up with any reason not to improve their product.

Competition

Whether society needs or demands a new and improved product is sometimes incidental to the fact that companies are going to offer their "new and improved" products no matter what. Especially with technology—video game consoles, iPods, cell phones, even household appliances, cars, and televisions— improvements come fast and furious, at rates that may seem mind-boggling to the individual consumer. Many companies need to get ahead of their competition in the marketplace, so it's out with the old and in with the new before the old actually has time to age. Some companies even follow an itinerary of planned obsolescence for their devices, targeting a certain life span for the product and then coming out with a new version. Sometimes they'll even go so far as to stop providing technical support for older models. Proponents believe this stimulates economic involvement in a market economy. Skeptics say it's a cheesy way to scam consumers and it also creates waste that affects the environment. Regardless, as the old adage says, "The more things change, the more things stay the same."

The Most Watched City on Earth

If you ever get that feeling that there's a pair of eyes on you, try walking around in the shoes of a Londoner.

✳ ✳ ✳ ✳

THE PEOPLE OF London, England, are photographed 300 times a day by closed-circuit television cameras (CCTVs). The UK is home to an estimated five million surveillance cameras: 1 for every 12 citizens.

Big Brother Is Watching—and Listening and Talking

It seems the CCTVs are dissatisfied with merely watching; now some of them talk, too. The mysterious men and women behind the camera wait until a Londoner does something naughty and then politely chastise the offending party. For example, a woman who leaves a bottle on a park bench will suddenly hear a voice from above, asking her to throw it away.

No, this is not a scene from a science-fiction novel—a handful of such cameras have already been installed, and there are more to come. Police have also started putting cameras in their helmets.

The surveillance shenanigans don't stop there. Radio Frequency Identification Technology (RFID), which uses radio waves to detect small implanted chips, is already used in English passports and in the travel cards Londoners swipe when using public transit. With these chips, people can easily be tracked. Experts fear that the technology will soon be used to monitor purchases and employees. They may even be implanted in all citizens. RFID chips are commonly implanted in European pets.

Government officials and the corporations that produce these technologies claim that surveillance is in the interest of security. During the 1990s, the English Home Office, which is involved in law enforcement, spent 78 percent of its budget on CCTVs. Many studies have shown that these cameras do not actually reduce crime. However, studies have found that adding more streetlights reduces crime by 20 percent. If only there was a larger profit margin in light bulbs.

Faster, and Slower, than the Speed of Light

Albert Einstein taught us that the speed of light is constant at 186,282 miles per second. An unbending, iron law of nature, right? Wrong.

❋ ❋ ❋ ❋

FOR YEARS, DILIGENT laboratory scientists have sped up, and greatly slowed down, the components of light. They have actually made light travel many times faster than the speed of light. And they've decelerated light to a plodding pace that wouldn't merit a speeding ticket.

Speed it Up!

At New York's University of Rochester in 2006, scientists led by optics professor Robert W. Boyd fired a laser into an optical glass fiber. The fiber had been laced with the rare metal erbium, which amplified the signal it produced—by a lot. Before the entire pulse even entered the fiber, part of it appeared at the fiber's end and then raced backward faster than the speed of light. The process was attributed to the erbium, which gave extra energy to the light. Professor Boyd said, with some understatement, "I find it nifty."

Slow it Down!

The University of Rochester team has also taken the opposite tack and slowed down light. In 2003, Boyd's crew shone a green laser through a tiny ruby in an attempt to saturate the chromium atoms that give the gem its reddish tint. When a second green laser zapped the jewel, its light slowed to 127 miles per hour, which is 5.3 million times slower than the light of the first laser. In 1999, scientists at Harvard University slowed laser light to 38 mph, a speed slower than the legal vehicular limit on most interstates. They did this by shooting a laser through matter that was supercooled to 459 degrees below zero—a temperature at which atoms, or particles of light, practically freeze in their tracks.

Voluptuous Velvet

Velvet offerings range from the sublime to the ridiculous. Members of European royalty were fond of it, Santa Claus's suit is said to be made of it, and Elvis has been immortalized on it. Here's the story behind this super-soft and shiny fabric.

✳ ✳ ✳ ✳

✳ Velvet is a closely woven fabric with a thick, short pile on one side. The highest-quality velvet, made from silk, is luxuriously soft and beautiful and can be used for apparel, home fashions, and as a canvas for paint, as well as for numerous other purposes.

✳ The first evidence of velvet weaving comes from the Far East, sometime in the fourteenth century, but velvet really made a name for itself when medieval Italians began using it. By doubling the pile and weaving in brocade and other ornaments, artisans of the time created rich tapestries that hang in museums today.

✳ The word velvet comes from the ancient French *veluotte*, and *velouté* is a term in French cooking that describes a smooth, silky texture, typically a rich white sauce thickened with cream and egg yolks.

✳ A velvet canvas takes paint surprisingly well. Most artists use black velvet, which allows the paint colors to "pop" from the background. From the 1950s to the 1970s, velvet paintings gained popularity for their kitsch factor, reflected in the many velvet paintings that feature dogs playing poker or likenesses of Elvis Presley.

* Is it velvet or velour? Authentic velvet is made from silk. Velour (popularly used in "fashionable" track suits) is a fabric with a similar feel, but it's made from cotton, not silk.

* Developed in the eighteenth century, corduroy was originally known as the poor man's velvet. The warp of this heavy cotton fabric is higher than its weft, producing a look similar to velvet but at a significantly lower price.

* To avoid permanent creases in this delicate fabric, velvet should be hung when stored rather than folded.

How It All Began

Plastic Panache

In the late 1940s, George Lerner was a well-known inventor with visions of fruits and vegetables. His idea? To create plastic mouths, eyes, and noses that could be pushed into pieces of produce to make funny faces.

Toy companies pooh-poohed the idea: In conservation-minded post-World War II America, the thought of turning food into a toy seemed wasteful. Eventually, a cereal company decided Lerner's pieces would make a good box prize and bought his idea for $5,000.

In 1951, Lerner met with Rhode Island toymakers and brothers Henry and Merrill Hassenfeld, who ran a small family-owned company eventually known as Hasbro. They loved his idea, and a deal was struck so that the Hassenfelds held the rights to the toys.

On April 30, 1952, the Mr. Potato Head Funny Face kit debuted. It sold for just under $1 and, as the first toy advertised on TV, it became an instant success, with sales hitting more than $4 million the first year.

Steel Boom

If playing with plastic produce is fun, why not a steel coil? In 1943, Philadelphia-based naval engineer Richard James accidentally knocked a torsion spring off his desk and watched it bounce around his office. Seeing potential for a toy, he set to work developing a steel formula that would allow the spring to walk down stairs. Richard's wife, Betty, searched the dictionary for a word to aptly describe the spring's movement. She ultimately landed on slinky, the Swedish word for "stealthy, sleek, and sinuous."

With a $500 loan, the Jameses produced a small number of Slinkys, which didn't sell until Gimbels department store agreed to let Richard do a demo shortly before Christmas 1945. It was a hit: All 400 Slinkys sold out in 90 minutes. To keep up with the growing demand, Richard devised a machine that could produce a Slinky every ten seconds.

In 1960, Richard left the company to follow a religious cult to Bolivia, leaving Betty with six children to raise and a business to run. Undaunted, Betty continued growing the company to the multimillion-dollar industry it is today. She eventually moved production to her hometown of Hollidaysburg, where the Slinky—now the state toy of Pennsylvania—is still produced.

The First General Purpose Computer

In 1946, John Mauchly and J. Presper Eckert of the University of Pennsylvania completed development of the first general-purpose digital computer, the ENIAC. Funded during World War II by the U.S. Army to calculate ordnance trajectories, the ENIAC offered a thousandfold speed increase over electromechanical computers because it worked by sending electrons through semiconductors. One might liken it to the difference between e-mail and a typed, mailed letter.

The ENIAC could perform complicated equations some 50,000 times faster than a human being and had numerous practical applications going beyond military science. It weighed 27 tons, occupied 680 square feet, and gulped 150 kilowatts of juice. (It is a myth, however, that its power draw dimmed the lights in Philly.)

Accidental Inventions

We tend to hold inventors in high esteem, but many of their discoveries are the result of an accident or twist of fate. This is true for a surprising number of everyday items, including those that follow.

✳ ✳ ✳ ✳

Play-Doh

ONE SMELL MOST people remember from childhood is the aroma of Play-Doh, the brightly colored, nontoxic modeling clay. Play-Doh was accidentally invented in 1955 by Joseph and Noah McVicker while trying to make a wallpaper cleaner. It was marketed a year later by toy manufacturer Rainbow Crafts. More than 900 million pounds of Play-Doh have been sold since then, but the recipe remains a secret.

Fireworks

Fireworks originated in China some 2,000 years ago, and legend has it that they were accidentally invented by a cook who mixed together charcoal, sulfur, and saltpeter—items commonly found in kitchens in those days. The mixture burned, and when compressed in a bamboo tube, it exploded. There's no record of whether it was the cook's last day on the job.

Potato Chips

If you can't eat just one potato chip (and who can?), blame it on chef George Crum. He reportedly created the salty snack in 1853 at Moon's Lake House near Saratoga Springs, New York. Fed up with a customer who continuously sent his fried potatoes back, complaining that they were soggy and not crunchy enough, Crum sliced the potatoes as thin as possible, fried them in hot grease, then doused them with salt. The customer loved them, and "Saratoga Chips" quickly became a popular item at the lodge and throughout New England. Eventually, the chips were mass-produced for home consumption, but since they were stored in barrels or tins, they quickly went stale. Then, in the 1920s, Laura Scudder invented the airtight bag by ironing together two pieces of waxed paper, thus keeping the chips fresh longer. Today, chips are packaged in plastic or foil bags or cardboard containers and come in a variety of flavors, including sour cream and onion, barbecue, and salt and vinegar.

Saccharin

Saccharin, the oldest artificial sweetener, was accidentally discovered in 1879 by researcher Constantine Fahlberg, who was working at Johns Hopkins University in the laboratory of professor Ira Remsen. Fahlberg's discovery came after he forgot to wash his hands before lunch. He had spilled a chemical on his hands, and it caused the bread he ate to taste unusually sweet. In 1880, the two scientists jointly published the discovery, but in 1884, Fahlberg obtained a patent and began massproducing saccharin without Remsen. The use of saccharin did not become widespread until sugar was rationed during World War I, and its popularity increased during the 1960s and 1970s with the manufacture of Sweet'N Low and diet soft drinks.

Post-it Notes

A Post-it Note is a small piece of paper with a strip of low-tack adhesive on the back that allows it to temporarily be attached to documents, walls, computer monitors, and just about anyplace else. The idea for the Post-it Note was conceived in

1974 by Arthur Fry as a way of holding bookmarks in his hymnal while singing in the church choir. He was aware of an adhesive accidentally developed in 1968 by fellow 3M employee Spencer Silver. No application for the lightly sticky stuff was apparent until Fry's idea.

A Clean Slate: The Cutting Edge in Classroom Technology

The introduction of the blackboard revolutionized teaching practices. Chalk it up to a Scottish teacher's desire to get the word out.

✳ ✳ ✳ ✳

FEW THINGS SEEM as mundane or uninspiring as a classroom blackboard: a slate surface covered in dusty, white text detailing tonight's reading assignment or the date of next week's test. What could be less revolutionary?

But when James Pillans, headmaster of the Old High School of Edinburgh, Scotland, began using one in his classroom in 1801, he sent ripples of excitement throughout the educational world.

Before that time, teachers had no way of displaying written material to an entire class; they also had no way of mechanically reproducing copies of material written on paper. Consequently, teachers spent a considerable amount of time writing out assignments, dictating them to the class, or painstakingly copying them down on each student's small slate.

The Writing Is on the Wall

Pillans's innovation was considered a revolutionary piece of technology that would—and did—transform the educational experience. In fact, in 1841, Josiah F. Bumstead, a writer and educator, said that the inventor of the blackboard "deserves to be ranked among the best contributors to learning and science, if not among the greatest benefactors of mankind." Teachers could now work out equations, diagram sentences, and write out the week's new spelling words for the entire class at one time. And students could now experience the dread of going up to the board to work out those impossible math problems while the whole class watched!

The first recorded use of the blackboard in the United States was likely by George Baron at the United States Military Academy at West Point in 1801. By the mid-1800s, a blackboard could be found in virtually every schoolroom in America—even the isolated one-room schoolhouses that dotted the Western frontier.

New Changes Afoot

Of course, many of today's classrooms have since replaced their chalkboards with whiteboards. Teachers are also increasingly relying on digital technologies that enable them to pass out and collect assignments electronically. Pillans's innovation may be on its way out, but there is no denying that it served teachers and students well for more than 200 years. Its impact won't be erased anytime soon.

The Ultimate Power Grab

One of the greatest U.S. inventors gets charged up over some competition and tries to short-circuit another promising innovator's career.

✳   ✳   ✳   ✳

RIVALRY CAN BRING out the best in people, but it can also bring out the worst. Too often, it seems the latter is the case for otherwise grounded individuals. Consider Thomas Alva Edison during the famous War of the Currents waged over electricity during the 1890s. Edison put all his energy into discrediting the system discovered by Yugoslavia-born inventor

Nikola Tesla even though Tesla's was the superior setup.

By the late nineteenth century, the United States' ever-increasing demands for energy required a revamped power-delivery system. Edison's direct current (DC) method had worked up to this point, but it suffered from inherent weaknesses: The system was cumbersome, could not easily be switched between high and low voltages, and would suffer great power losses when transmitted over long distances. It was then that Edison's former employee, Tesla, devised a system for alternating current (AC). Point for point, it answered all the problems that Edison's system presented and was more economical to boot. With the full financial backing of industrialist George Westinghouse, Tesla quietly presented his system to the public. Edison, however, was not so demure—the war was on.

In an effort to smear the science behind Tesla's invention, Edison spread spurious information about fatal AC accidents and staged public executions of animals using "dangerous" AC.

The smear campaign backfired on Edison. Alternating current replaced direct current as the central station power choice across the world, and Tesla's theories were proven correct. Years later, Edison would admit that he should have listened to Tesla and embraced alternating current. Amen to that.

Enlivening the Lunch Box

By adding Mickey Mouse, Hopalong Cassidy, and other licensed characters, manufacturers of school lunch pails thought outside the box.

✳ ✳ ✳ ✳

IN THE MID-1900S, many factory workers and laborers carried lunch with them to work in a covered pail. Parents of that era often sent their children off to school with a midday meal packed in an old tobacco or cookie tin. That all changed shortly after the thermos bottle appeared on the market in

1906—thanks to British inventor James Dewar—but the story just begins there. A few years later, the American Thermos Company started manufacturing and selling a workman's lunch pail to hold its thermoses and the user's accompanying noon-time repast.

By 1920, American Thermos began offering a version for schoolkids, but parents still tended to rely on a paper sack or a reused tin. Even after Mickey Mouse became the first licensed character to appear on a school lunch kit in 1935, most families weren't willing to spend the extra money on a store-bought item, and most kids didn't seem to mind.

Then television entered the American home in the 1950s, and a school lunch box suddenly became a must-have item. Chicago-based Aladdin Industries secured licensing rights for the *Hopalong Cassidy Show* in 1950 and sold 600,000 lunch boxes adorned with the famous cowboy hero. American Thermos countered with Roy Rogers three years later, and over the next two decades, every cartoon character, television star, sports hero, or other popular children's icon was slapped onto a rect-angular, latching steel box. The character lunch box has become such a universally remembered piece of kitschy Americana that the Smithsonian Institution created an exhibit in its honor.

The Trampoline: A New Sport Springs to Life

The trampoline has become a fixture in backyards and gymnasiums as a source of recreation. But can its origin really be traced to Alaska?

✳   ✳   ✳   ✳

IF POSTCARDS SOLD in the Anchorage, Alaska, airport are to be believed, the genesis of the trampoline can be traced all the way to the Arctic Circle. The tourist tokens show Eskimos stretching a piece of walrus skin and using the taut tarp to toss each other in the air. It's a good story, but it's not true.

It was actually an athlete and coach from the University of Iowa who created the first manufactured version of the rebounding rig known as the trampoline. During the winter of 1934, George Nissen, a tumbler on the college gymnastics team, and Larry Griswold, his assistant coach, were discussing ways to add some flair to their rather staid sport. The two men were intrigued by the possibilities presented by the buoyant nature of the safety nets used by trapeze artists. Griswold and Nissen constructed an iron frame and covered it with a large canvas, using springs to connect the cloth to the frame. The apparatus was an effective training device and a popular attraction among the kids who flocked to the local YMCA to watch Nissen perform his routines. The pair of co-creators eventually formed the Griswold-Nissen Trampoline & Tumbling Company and started producing the first commercially available and affordable trampolines.

Nissen can also claim fame for attaching a name to his pliant production. While on a tour of Mexico in the late 1930s, Nissen discovered the Spanish word for springboard was *el trampolin*. Intrigued by the sound of the word, he anglicized the spelling, and the trampoline was born. In 2000, trampolining graduated from acrobatic activity to athletic achievement when it was officially recognized as a medal-worthy Olympic sport.

The Fountain Pen:
Mightier Than, at Least, the Quill

The story of how an inconvenient mess ended up making a mark on history.

✳   ✳   ✳   ✳

RUMORS OF A writing instrument that had a reservoir for ink go all the way back to the tenth century, but we'll stick to the more recent past. The first truly operable fountain pen, which had a leak-proof reservoir, a steady writing nib, and a reliable ink flow, didn't come about until 1884, well after the invention of two critical components: hard rubber and iridium.

From Ink Stain to Invention

As the story goes, New Yorker Lewis Waterman, an insurance broker, had been using pens of a lesser quality for years when he lost an enormous contract to a competing broker, all because of a massive blot from his writing instrument. In a gesture that might have been accompanied by outraged screaming, he vowed to create his own pen—one that wouldn't leak. In 1884, after years of experimentation, he patented a pen that held ink in a reservoir, allowing it to flow at a conservative rate through a gold-and-iridium nib. Waterman's pen was far less complicated than earlier pens had been, consisting of only four parts made entirely of hard rubber.

The "Write" Stuff

Four short years later, another American, George Parker, a professor of telegraphy in Janesville, Wisconsin, encouraged all of his students to buy fountain pens, but he found himself consistently having to improve or repair these writing implements. Parker decided to invent and sell his own line of pens, which rapidly began to outsell those offered by Waterman's New York company.

By the early 1900s, many improvements were on the horizon: W. A. Scheaffer, a jeweler, created a pen that could be filled by raising and lowering a lever on the shaft of the pen, eliminating any need to dirty one's fingers. Meanwhile, the German ink company Pelikan introduced the piston feed, which allowed users to rotate a cap at the end of the shaft and fill the pen that way.

Waterman did not keep up with the times and fell rapidly behind in sales, but in a twist of history, Sanford, a Midwestern company that started out in the ink and glue business, now distributes both Parker and Waterman writing instruments.

Ink has been around almost 6,000 years. Ballpoint pens were invented less than 150 years ago.

John J. Loud patented the ballpoint pen in 1888, but since he used it only to mark leather, he neglected to consider its wider commercial possibilities. In later legal skirmishes over the right to claim the invention, his limited patent was ignored.

Patent Wars

So you think the origins of some things—the sewing machine, the modern airplane, the cotton gin, office chairs—ought to be pretty clear-cut? Think again: Patent wars have been around almost as long as the patents system itself.

✳ ✳ ✳ ✳

The Wright Brothers vs. Glenn Curtiss: Even Alexander Graham Bell got involved in this battle over the invention of a critical piece of airplane machinery. Graham Bell's company, the Aerial Experiment Association, hired aeronaut Glenn H. Curtiss to create an airplane. Despite being warned off by Wilbur and Orville Wright, Curtiss went ahead with his design, which led the Wrights to file several lawsuits against him and his company. Curtiss eventually lost the case; his company, the Curtiss Aeroplane & Motor Company, Ltd., merged with the Wright Aeronautical Corporation just before Curtiss's death in 1930.

Elias Howe vs. Isaac Singer: Something as small as a needle's eye was the lynchpin to this case. Isaac Singer's sewing machine was the first commercially successful sewing machine. However, his machine used the same stitch as Elias Howe's sewing machine, and Howe sued Singer for use of the stitch. Howe won the case, and Singer was forced to pay him a per-use royalty fee.

Netflix vs. Blockbuster: While customers of Netflix and Blockbuster were busy enjoying the fact that both companies offered home delivery of movies, the two were duking it out in court. Netflix challenged Blockbuster for patent infringement of its system; Blockbuster claimed that the former had never patented the method by which it would lease out its movies. The argument eventually fizzled out less than a year later: Both companies agreed to settle out of court.

Herman Miller vs. Teknion: Herman Miller's Aeron chair, which was designed in the mid-1990s, has made a lot of office workers very comfortable, and it has made Herman Miller a lot of money. Ergonomic chairs became practically *de rigueur* in the workplace, and other companies were quick to jump on the bandwagon. But Herman Miller didn't become an industry leader for nothing: When Teknion, a Japanese company that also makes office furniture, introduced their own version of the Aeron, Herman Miller was quick to sue over a long list of design-oriented patents. The suit was settled in 2007.

The Beta Wars

When videotape recorders entered the consumer market, formatting differences between Betamax and VHS didn't exactly spark a shooting war, but in some quarters they could have.

❋   ❋   ❋   ❋

O N FIRST HEARING about high-definition television, comedian Paula Poundstone said that she wasn't buying into another system until she was certain that it was the *last* system. It was a complaint that most Americans understood.

The question of media formatting goes back at least to the days when the printing press replaced hand-lettered manuscripts, but it became a matter of open, partisan warfare in 1975 when videotape was introduced as a mass medium. Sony introduced the Betamax video system, which was followed a year later by JVC's totally incompatible VHS. It was eight-tracks and cassette tapes all over again.

Quality Versus Price and Convenience

There is little disagreement that Sony's Betamax was a technically superior system, but JVC's VHS (which stood for Video Helical Scan) was marketed intensively. Its players were cheaper and easier to make, and other manufacturers started to adopt the VHS format. Additionally, Beta featured only one-hour tapes—not long enough to record a movie—while VHS had two-hour tapes. By the time Beta developed B-II (two-hour) and B-III (three-hour) formats, VHS had a four-hour format. Eventually, Beta achieved five hours, and VHS reached 10.6 hours.

In 1985, Sony introduced SuperBeta; JVC countered with Super-VHS. As the systems tried to outdo each other, Beta was never quite able to catch up. Major studios released fewer movies on Beta. Then, in a 1989 episode of *Married . . . with Children*, the Bundys were described as "the last family on earth with Beta." That offhand comment was the kiss of death.

VHS ruled the roost. At least, that is, until DVDs came along.

Feel the Burn:
The Active Denial System

The U.S. Air Force and the Department of Defense, paired with corporate weapons contractors, have developed a new non-lethal weapon called the Active Denial System (ADS).

While this weapon has the potential to save lives, some worry about the potential for abuse.

✳   ✳   ✳   ✳

The Pain Ray

THE STORY BEHIND the Active Denial System reads like a sci-fi thriller: Academics discover the power of invisible rays, and the government harnesses that technology for the forces of good and evil, all against the backdrop of a controversial war.

In the 1980s, scientists discovered that a wavelength of energy called a "millimeter wave," which registers somewhere between an X-ray and a microwave, causes intense pain when directed on human skin. At a frequency of 94 to 95 gigahertz, the energy penetrates $1/64$ of an inch below the skin, causing the water molecules located there to heat rapidly. This technology was named "Active Denial" for its potential to actively deny potential intrusions or assaults—in this case, "active denial" is a euphemism for "causes perpetrator to retreat in spasms of pain." In fact, the media sometimes refers to ADS as the "pain ray."

Beginning in 2000, the Air Force Research Laboratory, in partnership with the Department of Defense's Joint Non-Lethal Weapons Directorate, created prototype weapons that harnessed this technology. Large-scale tests were done on human subjects, and the weapon was used in simulated military scenarios. The ADS looks like a satellite dish with a long arm that directs the invisible beam of millimeter energy onto a target. The device is operated by software that controls the strength of the beam, the duration of the beam's shot, and the distance the beam travels to reach the target. Ideally, when the beam hits a person, they'll run away in pain.

Putting ADS to Use

Now that ADS technology has been tested and developed, the question remains about its use. In 2003, generals in the Iraq war requested ADS units in hopes that its crowd-dispersal potential would limit Iraqi civilian deaths, but ADS testing wasn't complete until 2007. The government began using ADS units in military operations in 2010. Generals in Iraq are not the only anticipated buyers. Another version of ADS technology is being developed by the Justice Department in the hope that one day these painful beams will emit from small handheld devices, sort of like high-tech mace. The weapons contractor corporation Raytheon, which was involved with the military's development of ADS, is developing and marketing the technology for law enforcement and private security use.

Potential Problems

While ADS technology certainly doesn't have the apocalyptic potentials of past developments like the atomic bomb, some red flags have been raised. During trials, a small number of subjects sustained burn blisters after exposure; one test subject suffered from second-degree burns. The trial tests were ambiguous concerning how the intensity of the beam is calibrated to the distance of the target. Another issue is whether victims will really get out of the way before they are seriously injured. This concern was referred to in a 2007 report as the "safety margin between the repel response and injury." Another worry is that the method's "crowd dispersal" potential will be used to limit civil liberties and peaceful protests.

While most information on ADS testing has been released to the public, some information still remains classified, including the system's operational range (i.e., how far the beam can shoot), and its potential use for "unconventional countermeasures" (whatever that means). As ADS technology continues to proliferate, one can only hope that it will be used for its stated purposes of saving, rather than taking, human lives.

Chapter 7

Tragedies & Disasters

Titanic: The Journey of an Iceberg

Most North Atlantic icebergs calve (detach) from the Greenland ice sheets. From the Greenland coast, the Labrador Current carries them south, where they may calve growlers (mini-icebergs) and bergy bits (big ice chunks). When they hit the Gulf Stream (roughly New Jersey's latitude), they melt.

In a typical year in the early 1900s, six to eight ships would hit icebergs. Most collisions occurred off Newfoundland's rugged coast, far north of *Titanic's* path. The luxury liner was right along the southern edge of the danger zone, and maritime scuttlebutt had it that the 'bergs were further south than usual.

The disaster inspired the foundation of the International Ice Patrol (IIP), which first experimented with naval gunfire to destroy the icebergs. When the targets proved indestructible, the IIP did a far more practical thing: find and track icebergs, keeping mariners apprised by radio.

Titanic: The Rescue Operation

After the *Titanic* hit the fatal iceberg, the RMS *Carpathia* came to its aid. Unlike the "mystery ship," *Carpathia* was helpful. *Carpathia's* alert radio operator relayed *Titanic's* distress call to Captain Arthur Rostron, who twice clarified the message because he was shocked to receive such a call from the *Titanic*. Now he would learn just what sort of ship and crew he had. Defying the obvious risk of an iceberg strike, the *Carpathia* raced to the site of *Titanic's* last bearings while the crew readied everything from hot drinks to blankets to rescue gear. In forlorn optimism (they expected to find *Titanic* afloat), they prepared to load baggage and mail.

When the ship arrived, there was no *Titanic. Carpathia's* crew began a five-hour operation, retrieving lifeboats and comforting stricken survivors. If it hadn't been for these rescuers, most might have died of hypothermia. Rostron later received plentiful well-deserved accolades, including induction as a Knight Commander of the Order of the British Empire and a U.S. Congressional Gold Medal.

* The last survivor of the rescue operation was 15-year-old apprentice Herbert Johnston. He helped pull survivors onto the *Carpathia.* Johnston later served in both world wars and died in South Africa in 2002 at age 104.

* The International Ice Patrol was merely one of the safety strides brought on by *Titanic's* loss. Passenger ships would now monitor the radio 24 hours a day and 7 days a week. Ships increased their lifeboat complements. New liners reflected design lessons gleaned from the disaster: longer rudders (for improved maneuvering), double hulls, and improved riveting (icy waters had made *Titanic's* rivets brittle).

The Peshtigo Fire

On October 8, 1871, North America's worst forest fire occurred in northeastern Wisconsin and Michigan's Upper Peninsula. About 1,500 people died, including 800 of the 2,500 residents of Peshtigo, Wisconsin. The city was totally destroyed in an hour, leaving the nearby Peshtigo River as the only place of safety. Poor logging practices and an exceptionally dry summer were blamed for the fire. Augusta Wegner Bruce was the last living survivor of the conflagration. She died on

February 10, 1974, at age 104.

Coincidentally, the great Chicago Fire erupted the very same evening as the conflagration at Peshtigo. Although the Chicago fire was smaller and its death toll a mere fraction of the Peshtigo tragedy, the brouhaha made over the Chicago blaze would serve to obscure the worst forest fire in North American history. It's not too surprising.

The Chicago fire took place in a highly populated, major American city. This ensured reams of newspaper coverage featuring hair-raising, first-person accounts. Since Chicago was a major player in national and world commerce, this too factored into the fire's notoriety.

Perhaps the greatest reason for the Chicago fire's fame was the story about "Mrs. O'Leary's Cow." Blamed for kicking over a lantern and starting the Chicago blaze, the controversial tale was long regarded as factual. Today, it's considered dubious at best. Because of such sensationalism, the Peshtigo fire has been dubbed the "forgotten fire." Too bad Peshtigo didn't have its own cow story to tell.

The Peshtigo Fire: What Caused the Flames?

Like many great conflagrations, the cause of North America's worst forest fire is open to conjecture. Factors such as a prolonged and widespread drought provide reasons for the epic disaster but stop short of pinpointing its origin. What is certain is that the enormous fire (which was 10 miles wide and 40 miles long) burned for two days and claimed the lives of approximately 1,500 people. When the fire reached the waters of Green Bay, it lost its fuel source, and its storm-like winds diminished. A rainstorm delivered the blaze its final deathblow. A poem published in the *Marinette Eagle* captures the tragedy's essence:

On swept the tornado, with maddening rush,

Uprooting the trees o'er the plain, thro' the brush,

And the sky-leaping flames, with hot, scorching breath,

Gathered parents and children to the harvest of death.

As years roll along and the ages have sped

O'er the charred, blackened bones of the Peshtigo dead,

And the story is told by the pen of the sage,

In letters immortal on history's page,

No fancy can compass the horror and fright,

The anguish and woe of that terrible night.

San Francisco 1906: The Fire

The quake was bad—but not catastrophic by itself. The serious devastation began when the tremors upended numerous oil lamps, igniting dozens of fires. Matters got even worse when the gas mains ruptured. Even this might have been contained, but the water mains also broke. To complete the melancholy recipe, the initial quake mortally injured the fire chief—a devastating loss of leadership.

The blaze quickly overwhelmed firefighting efforts in the downtown core. Fire caused about 90 percent of the total destruction. Short of water, desperate firefighters dynamited buildings to create firebreaks. Had experts done this, it might have helped; done by relative amateurs, it more often started new fires. So did property owners: Many were insured against fire but not earthquake damage. A little timely arson assured eventual payment.

Inadequate as the dynamite method may have been, it did eventually halt the spreading flames—more than 500 incinerated city blocks later.

New York City's Worst Catastrophes

The city presents itself like Rocky: It can take a punch and keep swinging. Given that New York remains standing after the following haymakers, the image is deserved.

✳   ✳   ✳   ✳

Yellow Fever Epidemics: The city was struck by the mosquito-borne virus in 1668, 1702, 1794–95, 1798, 1803, 1819, and 1822. Some of the outbreaks killed hundreds; others killed thousands. The outbreak of 1798, with more than 2,000 deaths, was the worst.

Great Fire of New York: This conflagration that consumed the west side of southern Manhattan started on September 21, 1776, probably in a waterfront tavern, during the colonial defense of the city against the British. Some 400 to 500 buildings were destroyed.

Chatham Street Fire: On May 19, 1811, high winds gusting to gale force turned a factory blaze into a pyre for 100 buildings. A general shortage of water available to firefighters was an early wake-up call about the city's future needs.

Long Island Hurricane: The first major hurricane in the city's history hit at Jamaica Bay on September 3, 1821. The 13-foot storm surge flooded Battery Park and lower Manhattan as far as Canal Street. While damaging, the flood caused few deaths.

Cholera Epidemics: In 1832, 1848–49, and 1866, cholera outbreaks killed thousands at a time. Indelicately put, the ailment killed with diarrhea that led to irreversible fluid loss. Early treatments included opium suppositories and tobacco enemas—neither of which is recommended for home treatment today!

Great Financial District Fire: On December 16–17, 1835, city firefighters discovered that water is very hard to pump when the air temperature is 17 degrees Fahrenheit. This largely unchecked blaze incinerated 500 buildings around Wall Street, including most of the few remaining Dutch-era structures.

Civil War Draft Riots: Resentment over Civil War conscription became a pretext for 1863 rioting against war profiteers and African Americans. During July 13–16, at least 119 people died (many at the hands of murderers), and thousands were injured. Property damage was extensive.

***Westfield II* Ferry Explosion:** The boiler of this Staten Island steamer blew up at Manhattan dockside on July 30, 1871, killing 125 and injuring about 140.

Brooklyn Theatre Fire: On December 5, 1876, theatergoers who had gathered to see a popular French melodrama, *The Two Orphans*, were sent into panic when fire broke out at the Brooklyn Theatre. Many of the 278 dead were children in the cheap seats, where fire-escape provisions were inadequate.

Great Blizzard of 1888: New York tried to absorb snowdrifts of 20 feet or more and winds in excess of 45 mph, when a late-winter storm slammed the Atlantic coast from Maryland to Maine. Two hundred of the storm's 400 deaths occurred in New York City.

Heat Wave of 1896: During the long span of August 5–13, sustained temperatures above 90 degrees Fahrenheit scorched people in tenements, sometimes lethally. In the end, 420 or more people died, mostly in the overcrowded squalor of the Lower East Side.

***General Slocum* Disaster:** Until September 11, 2001, June 15, 1904, was New York's deadliest day. During a church picnic aboard a chartered steamboat in the East River, more than 1,000 people, most of them German-American women and children, died when the triple-deck, wooden ship caught fire.

Triangle Shirtwaist Fire: On March 25, 1911, a carelessly tossed match or cigarette started a fast-spreading fire inside Max Blanck and Isaac Harris's shirtwaist (blouse) sweatshop, which occupied the eighth, ninth, and tenth floors of Manhattan's Asch Building. Grossly inadequate fire exit provisions, plus locked inner doors, spelled disaster. Most of the 146 dead were immigrant women, mainly Jewish. Those that did not burn to death died of smoke inhalation or from injuries sustained when they leapt from windows.

Wall Street Bombing: Was it a car bomb that exploded in the financial district on September 16, 1920? No, it was a horse-drawn wagon bomb carrying 100 pounds of dynamite and hundreds of pounds of iron that went up in front of 23 Wall Street. The massive explosion killed 38 people and wounded more than 300. No perpetrator was ever found, but authorities unofficially blamed two popular bogeymen of the day: anarchists and Communists.

1943 Harlem Riots: When a black G.I. who tried to prevent a white police officer from manhandling a black woman was shot, simmering racial tensions ignited. It was August 1, 1943, and throughout the night and into the following day, rioters destroyed property across Harlem. Six African Americans died, and hundreds of people (including 40 cops) were injured. At least 500 people were arrested.

Holland Tunnel Fire: New York City officials have good reasons for banning highly explosive carbon disulfide from being driven through the Holland Tunnel. On Friday, May 13, 1949, a 55-gallon drum of the solvent fell off a truck and caught fire. The blaze spread quickly, engulfing many of the 125 vehicles that were in the tunnel at the time, and ravaging the structure's ceiling and walls. An FDNY battalion chief was felled by smoke and died four months later. Sixty-six people were injured.

TWA Flight 266/United Flight 826: Snow, rain, and fog, plus pilot error, precipitated the December 16, 1960, midair collision of a TWA Constellation and a United DC-8 some 5,200 feet above the city. United Flight 826 had been badly off course. The DC-8 fell onto Brooklyn's Park Slope neighborhood, killing six people on the ground. The Constellation disintegrated on impact and crashed at Miller Field on Staten Island. All 128 people on the two planes perished, although an 11-year-old boy aboard the DC-8 survived long enough to describe the crash to authorities.

Eastern Airlines Flight 66: June 24, 1975, a Boeing 727 attempting to land at JFK International Airport was knocked to earth short of the runway by freak wind shear caused by a thunderstorm. Seven passengers and two flight attendants survived; the other 115 passengers and crew did not.

1977 Blackout: Except for south Queens, all of NYC lost power on July 13–14, 1977, when a lightning strike sent electrical grids into a tizzy. Unlike the famed 1965 blackout, which was notable for its peaceful nature, this one encouraged widespread looting, arson, and vandalism. More than 3,700 people were arrested, and hundreds of police were injured.

World Trade Center Garage Bombing: On February 26, 1993, Islamic terrorists detonated 1,500 pounds of explosives in a lower-level garage, killing six people. Over 1,000 were injured, mostly during the towers' frantic evacuation.

TWA Flight 800: A Boeing 747 out of JFK Airport with 230 people aboard blew up south of Long Island on July 17, 1996. There were no survivors, but numerous conspiracy theories made the rounds. The FBI found no evidence of a criminal act, and the NTSB attributed the crash to an electrical spark that ignited fuel vapors in a wing tank.

World Trade Center Attacks: September 11, 2001, will live in infamy as the nation's worst terrorist attack. Two airliners hijacked by Islamic extremists were flown into Manhattan, where each of the planes struck one of the twin towers of the World Trade Center, which ultimately collapsed. A total of

2,751 died, and over 6,000 were injured—many of the casualties were police and firefighters. (On the same morning, another hijacked airliner crashed into the Pentagon, and a fourth crashed in rural Pennsylvania.)

American Flight 587: Freak physics and some operator overreaction were the causes of the November 12, 2001, crash of an Airbus A300 just minutes out of JFK International Airport. The American Airlines flight took off in a wake of intense turbulence left by a larger 747. The pilots' struggle with the rudder led to catastrophic structural failure: The vertical stabilizer sheared off, followed by both engines. What remained of the plane went down in the Belle Harbor neighborhood of Queens, demolishing houses and killing five people. In all, 265 people lost their lives.

The Sago Mine

Coal mining has long been a dangerous and thankless profession, and in many ways it is defined by the conflict between the working-class laborers who toil underground and the huge companies that pay them to do so. No incident in recent memory has better illustrated that history than the Sago mine disaster of January 2, 2006, in Upshur County, West Virginia.

In the early morning of January 2, 2006, two work crews entered the Sago mine about 15 minutes apart. Shortly thereafter, a pocket of methane gas in an abandoned area of the mine exploded, rupturing the seals that divided it from active mining areas and flooding the mine with smoke and carbon monoxide.

One of the 13 workers in the first crew was killed in the explosion and the other 12 were trapped more than 250 feet below ground. Sixteen other workers who had been stationed above the point of the explosion immediately made their way toward the trapped miners but were forced back to the surface due to dangerous levels of toxic gas.

Mass Confusion and Miscommunication

Amid a blizzard of media coverage, rescue workers spent the next day and a half working to reach the trapped workers, whose families waited anxiously in a nearby church. Just after midnight on January 4, word came from the rescue command center that all but one of them had been found alive. The families celebrated their seeming good fortune as various media outlets trumpeted the miraculous news. But three hours later, to the outrage of the families, a mining company spokesman revealed that there had been a tragic miscommunication. Only one miner—Randal McCloy Jr.—had actually survived.

Investigators determined that the trapped laborers had attempted to clear the wreckage blocking their escape but were driven back by smoke and fumes. Following standard procedure, they retreated to an area of relatively clean air deeper in the mine and constructed a makeshift barrier to keep the deadly carbon monoxide out. Each person had been equipped with an emergency breathing apparatus, but they were forced to share their limited supplies of oxygen when four of the emergency breathing apparatuses failed to work.

Eventually, their refuge was flooded with toxic gas and 11 of those trapped perished. McCloy was likely only minutes from death when rescuers reached him 44 hours after the explosion. He suffered from carbon monoxide poisoning, a collapsed lung, brain hemorrhaging, and limited heart function. He remained in a coma for three weeks and was unable to speak for several days after regaining consciousness.

Following months of treatment and intensive therapy, the lucky miner was released from the hospital and returned to his home on a street renamed Miracle Road in his honor. McCloy made a full recovery, and in 2008, he celebrated his 29th birthday with his wife and three children.

The Sago Mine: The Grieving Continues

Various groups conducted investigations into the tragedy, including labor organizations, state and federal agencies, and both houses of the U.S. Congress. Many were outraged to learn that the mine's owner, International Coal Group, had received more than 200 violation notices from state and federal regulators in the year before the disaster, though most of them were for minor infractions not directly related to safety. The cause of the explosion was never definitively determined, but most investigators attributed it to a lightning strike that occurred near the entrance to the mine.

Within weeks of the disaster, new state and federal laws aimed at improving mining safety were passed. The new regulations required better communication systems for both miners and rescuers, as well as additional survival equipment for miners. Many felt it was too little, too late. Months after the disaster, the tragedy claimed more victims. Two workers who had been in the mine the day of the explosion committed suicide in 2006—one in August, and one in October.

The Fort Dearborn Tragedy

Delays and indecision result in an 1812 massacre.

❋ ❋ ❋ ❋

FORT DEARBORN, WHICH was situated near the current intersection of Wacker Drive and Michigan Avenue, was a major strategic site because of its access to waterways, trails, and forests. The fort had few residents until 1810, when Captain Nathan Heald was put in charge of a small garrison due to rising conflict with the British. When the War of 1812 broke out, there were approximately 100 men, women, and children living at the fort.

In July 1812 the garrison on Michigan's Mackinac Island was captured by the British army. Shortly thereafter, many Native

Americans began joining with the British forces to attack U.S. forts and outposts. It quickly became clear to the U.S. forces that the Brits' next stop would be Fort Dearborn. With that in mind, U.S. General William Hull sent word to Captain Heald to evacuate the fort. He told Heald to remove the people, leave everything else behind, and head toward safer territory in Fort Wayne, Indiana.

A Fatal Delay

Unfortunately, Heald did not immediately follow Hull's command. As a result of this delay, the Potawatomi had time to gather and position themselves around the fort. On the morning of August 15, 1812, Heald realized that simply abandoning the fort was no longer an option. The only way to get out would be to reach some sort of agreement with the Potawatomi.

Heald requested a meeting with the Potawatomi council, and his request was granted. An agreement was reached in which Heald and his people would be allowed to leave the fort unharmed. In exchange, Heald promised they would leave all their extra provisions, including ammunition and weapons, inside the fort.

After Heald returned to the fort and gave the order to evacuate, some residents expressed concern that any weapons left behind might be used against them. At that point, it was decided that all the extra guns and ammunition would be disposed of in an old, abandoned well on the fort property. Unbeknownst to the people of the fort, Potawatomi scouts observed them doing this; they reported back to their leaders, who became furious.

Walking to the Slaughter

While all of this was going on, Captain William Wells arrived from Fort Wayne, Indiana, and was put in charge of helping relocate the Fort Dearborn residents. When all the arrangements were made, the soldiers, women, and children began walking south. Less than two miles from the fort (near today's intersection of 18th and Calumet), the Potawatomi turned on the group, lashing out violently. By the time the massacre ended, most of the 100 people who left the fort had been killed. A few managed to escape into the wilderness, but most of the survivors were taken prisoner and sold to the British army as slaves. However, upon hearing of the massacre, the British released all the survivors.

Grim Reminders

As news of the massacre spread across the United States, people began avoiding the Fort Dearborn area altogether. In fact, no one returned there until the War of 1812 ended. Those who went back discovered the skeletal remains of the massacre victims, who had simply been left where they had fallen. All of the victims were eventually given proper burials. Years later a small plaque and a relief panel were placed near the site of the former fort to commemorate the massacre.

When the Chicago flag was created in 1915, it featured four red stars, the first of which represents Fort Dearborn. With that, many people felt the horrible events were finally put to rest. However, in the 1980s construction workers unearthed skeletal remains that were later determined to have been from victims of the Fort Dearborn tragedy. Those remains were relocated to a nearby cemetery, but the event caused a stir. Shortly thereafter, people started reporting seeing figures dressed in period clothing wandering around in a small field near the site of the massacre. Some of the figures appeared to be screaming, although no noise was ever heard. It seemed that for a few brief moments, a portal to another era opened up, and the events of that day in August 1812 were being replayed.

A Liner Capsizes on the River

One of the most tragic events in Chicago history took place on July 24, 1915. On that overcast summer afternoon, hundreds of people died in the Chicago River when the Eastland *capsized just a few feet from the dock.*

* * * *

JULY 24 WAS GOING to be a special day for thousands of Chicagoans. It was reserved for the Western Electric Company annual summer picnic, which was to be held across Lake Michigan in Michigan City, Indiana. And although officials at the utility company had encouraged workers to bring along friends and relatives, they were surprised when more than 7,000 people arrived to be ferried across the lake on the five excursion boats chartered for the day. Three of the steamers—the *Theodore Roosevelt*, the *Petoskey*, and the *Eastland*—were docked on the Chicago River near Clark Street.

On this fateful morning, the *Eastland*, a steamer owned by the St. Joseph-Chicago Steamship Company, was filled to its limit. The boat had a reputation for top-heaviness and instability, and the new federal Seaman's Act, which was passed in 1915 as a result of the RMS *Titanic* disaster, required more lifeboats than previous regulations did. All of this resulted in the ship being even more unstable than it already was. In essence, it was a recipe for disaster.

The Ship Overturns

As passengers boarded the *Eastland*, it began listing back and forth. This had happened on the ship before, so the crew emptied the ballast compartments to provide more stability. As the boat was preparing to depart, some passengers went below deck, hoping to warm up on the cool, cloudy morning, but many on the overcrowded steamer jammed their way onto one side of the deck to wave to onlookers on shore. The *Eastland* tilted once again, but this time more severely; passengers began to panic. Moments later, the *Eastland* rolled to her side, coming to rest at the bottom of the river, which was just 18 feet below the surface. One side of the boat's hull was actually above the water's surface in some spots.

Passengers on deck were tossed into the river. The overturned ship created a current that pulled some of the floundering swimmers to their doom, while many of the women's dresses snagged on the ship, tugging them down to the bottom.

Those inside were thrown to one side of the ship when it capsized. The heavy furniture onboard crushed some passengers, and those who were not killed drowned when water rushed inside moments later. A few managed to escape, but most didn't. Their bodies were later found trapped in a tangled heap on the lowest side of the *Eastland*.

Firefighters, rescue workers, and volunteers soon arrived and tried to help people escape through portholes. They also cut holes in the portion of the ship's hull that was above the water line. Approximately 1,660 passengers survived the disaster.

In the end, 844 people died, many of them young women and children. Officially, no clear explanation was given for why the vessel capsized, and the St. Joseph-Chicago Steamship Company was not held accountable for the disaster.

The bodies of those who perished in the tragedy were wrapped in sheets and placed on the *Theodore Roosevelt* or lined up along the docks. Marshall Field's and other large stores sent wagons to carry the dead to hospitals, funeral homes, and a makeshift morgue, the Second Regiment Armory, where more than 200 bodies were sent.

After the ship was removed from the river, it was sold and later became a U.S. warship as the gunboat U.S.S. *Wilmette*. The ship never saw any action but was used as a training ship during World War II. After the war, it was decommissioned and eventually scrapped in 1947.

Lingering Spirits

At the time of the *Eastland* disaster, the Second Regiment Armory (located on the Near West Side) was the only public building large enough to be used as a temporary morgue. Chicagoans with missing loved ones filed through, searching for familiar faces. In 22 cases, there was no one left to identify them—those families were completely wiped out. The names of these victims were learned from neighbors who came searching for their friends. The weeping, crying, and moaning of the bereaved echoed off the walls of the armory for days.

As years passed, the armory building went through several incarnations, including a stable and a bowling alley, before Harpo Studios, the production company owned by talk-show maven Oprah Winfrey, purchased it. A number of *The Oprah Winfrey Show* staff members, security guards, and maintenance workers claim that the studio is haunted by the spirits of those who tragically lost their lives on the *Eastland*. Many employees have experienced unexplained phenomena, including the sighting of a woman in a long gray dress who walks the corridors and then mysteriously vanishes into the wall. Some believe she is the spirit of a mourner who came to the armory looking for her family and left a bit of herself behind at a place where she felt her greatest sense of loss. Staff members have also witnessed doors opening and closing on their own and heard sobbing sounds and phantom footsteps on the lobby staircase.

Chicago River Ghosts

In the same way that the former armory seems to have been impressed with a ghostly recording of past events, the Chicago River seems haunted too. For years, people walking on the Clark Street Bridge have heard crying and moaning sounds coming from the river. Some have witnessed the apparitions of victims splashing in the water. On several occasions, some witnesses have called the police for help. One man even jumped into the river to save what he thought was a person drowning. When he returned to the surface, he discovered that he was in the water alone. He had no explanation for what he'd seen, other than to admit that it might have been a ghost.

So it seems that the horror of the *Eastland* disaster has left an imprint on these spots and continues to replay itself, ensuring that the *Eastland* victims will never be forgotten.

The Flood of 1913

On March 23, 1913, a rainfall began that did not cease for three days. The lives of 467 people were claimed, and 40,000 homes were flooded in what is still considered Ohio's worst natural disaster.

✳ ✳ ✳ ✳

THE RESIDENTS OF Dayton always knew their city was a flood disaster waiting to happen. Dayton was built where the Great Miami River converges with three separate tributaries: Stillwater River, Mad River, and Wolf Creek. In the late 1700s, local Native Americans warned that the area was victim to frequent floods. Nevertheless, the city built itself up, and its frequent floods were buffered by dams and canals in the meantime. On the eve of the disaster in 1913, detailed blueprints for a sophisticated flood prevention system were in the works. This turned out to be too little, too late.

The Storms Begin

The rain began on Good Friday. It fell on ground that had frozen the day before, meaning 90 percent of the precipitation ran off right into the Great Miami and its many tributaries. The rains continued throughout Monday, and the citizens watched in fear as the river rose. At midnight on Easter Sunday, March 23, warning sirens went off throughout Dayton. The waters overflowed into the streets, and by the next day, water crests 20 feet deep were exploding through downtown Dayton. Much of central Ohio lost all power and transportation services, and the rest of the nation tried desperately to reach an area that seemed to have blacked out entirely.

The floods affected all of Ohio, but the worst toll was in Dayton, where 123 people were killed. Another 100 deaths were tolled in nearby Hamilton, and 100 died in Columbus where the Sciota River reached record levels. Even communities that had never experienced flooding in the past were overcome. While the devastation was incalculable, there was an unexpected rainbow at the end of this storm: The gargantuan rescue and future flood prevention efforts showed an unusual level of organization and generosity.

Cash to the Rescue

Due to high water on railroad tracks, help did not reach the most affected areas until several days after the rain began. The American Red Cross sent 268 nurses and 43 community relief units in their largest relief effort ever. The Ohio National Guard arrived on the scene, and those who had escaped onto attics, rooftops, and trees were rescued by boat. But perhaps the most significant contribution came from a single private citizen.

John H. Patterson of Dayton was the founder and president of the National Cash Register Company. The company's factory rested on a hill that was unaffected by the floods. Patterson opened up his factory to the public, and it became an emergency center for the displaced community of Dayton. Under the direction of Patterson, National Cash Register employees constructed 300 boats and assisted the National Guard in rescue efforts. At least one child born during this time period was later named "Cash."

Remember the Promises

Three weeks after the flood, Patterson organized a meeting to raise funds for flood prevention efforts throughout Ohio. A sign outside the meeting read: "Remember the Promises You Made in the Attic—Flood Prevention Fund." Patterson opened the meeting by pledging $400,000. By the end of the night, $2 million had been raised. Although Theodore Roosevelt vowed to provide federal funds for improved flood prevention in Ohio, the state did not want to wait. The Miami Conservancy District was created, and plans were set in motion to build a system of levees and dams throughout the state. The project was completed in 1922 at a cost of $30 million.

All funds were raised by private donations or state-sponsored agencies. The system has since protected Ohio from flooding more than 1,500 times, adding a final note of good fortune and community spirit to Ohio's greatest tragedy.

Christmas Disasters!

A lot of train wrecks seem to occur around the Christmas holidays. Thank goodness Santa rides a sleigh.

✳   ✳   ✳   ✳

BE CAUTIOUS WHEN taking the train around Christmas time. Historically, that's when a lot of accidents occur. According to experts, a variety of factors contribute to the high number of train disasters, including poor weather conditions, driver fatigue, and the stress of trying to stay on schedule over the holidays.

Here's a rundown of the most devastating yuletide train wrecks over the past century:

* **December 26, 1902:** In Wanstead, Ontario, a miscommunication places two trains on the same track, resulting in a head-on collision. A total of 28 people are killed.

* **December 29, 1906:** An express train strikes the back of another train during a blizzard in Elliot Junction, Scotland, killing 22.

* **December 24, 1910:** Six separate train accidents occurred worldwide. They include two collisions in England, three in France, and one in Upper Sandusky, Ohio. The following day, a seventh accident involving a train and a horse-drawn carriage occurred in Chateaudun, France, killing six.

* **December 23, 1933:** A train accident in France occurs when the nation's largest steam-engine locomotive, traveling at 60 miles per hour, plows into a stopped train at the Lagny-Pomponne station. The standing train is reduced to

splinters; 230 people are killed and 300 are injured.

* **December 24, 1938:** A troop train and a local train collide head-on when accidentally directed to the same track in Etulia, Romania. A total of 93 people are killed and 147 injured.

* **December 27, 1941:** The Berlin-Warsaw express rear-ends a stationary train at the Frankfurt, Germany, station, killing 38.

* **December 28, 1941:** Fifty-six people are killed and another 50 are injured when a collision occurs on the Nantes-La Roche-sur-Yon line in La Gourge, France.

* **December 30, 1941:** Two days later, France experiences another train disaster when 50 people are killed in an accident near Hazebrouck.

* **December 27, 1942:** In Almonte, Ontario, 36 people are killed and more than 200 injured when a troop train strikes the rear of a passenger train as it is pulling out of the Almonte station.

* **January 1, 1946:** Freezing weather and a misread danger signal cause a fish train to ram the rear of a local passenger train as it waits at the station in Lichfield, England; 20 people are killed and 22 injured.

* **December 24, 1953:** The eruption of Mt. Ruapehu, a volcano near Walouru, New Zealand, destroys a traveling train, killing 151 people.

* **December 25, 1953:** The Prague-Bratislava express train, traveling at high speed, plows into the back of a local train waiting at the station in Sakvice, Czechoslovakia. A total of 186 people are killed.

* **January 1, 1958:** More than 30 people are killed and 85 injured when foggy conditions cause a collision between

the Delhi- Pathankot express and a local train at the station in Mohri, India.

* **December 24, 1963:** An error on the part of an engineer results in a collision between two trains in Szolnok, Hungary. The negligent driver is sentenced to 11 years in prison for the accident, which kills 45 people.

* **December 31, 1969:** A collision between a freight train and a passenger train results in the deaths of 20 people in Theis, Senegal.

* **December 31, 1987:** Guerilla fighters ambush a train carrying 1,500 migrant workers in Mozambique. The assailants use a land mine to derail the train, killing more than 22 people, then they open fire with guns. Several passengers are kidnapped.

Flight 255

In August 1987, a Northwest Airlines jet crashed into a highway after takeoff from Detroit Metropolitan Airport. The flaps were not correctly set for takeoff, and the plane stalled shortly afterward.

Of the 154 people aboard, all died except Cecelia Cichan, then four years old. Cecelia's parents and six-year-old brother were killed in the crash. Understandably, Cecelia experienced an outpouring of attention after the tragedy, but some child psychologists speculated that her newfound celebrity might hinder the little girl's ability to recover from the trauma she had experienced. At the request of her extended family, the judge overseeing the civil suit for the accident sealed her records to protect her privacy. A maternal aunt and uncle from Birmingham, Alabama, accepted custody of young Cecelia and carefully shielded her throughout her childhood. Cecelia graduated from college and got married, and the firefighter who discovered her in the wreckage attended her wedding. She remains an intensely private person, though she occasionally posts updates and comments through a website that has been set up as a memorial to the victims of the crash of Flight 255.

Flight 225: Pilot Error or System Malfunction

Witnesses say that at takeoff, Flight 255 struggled to get off the ground and began to dip sharply from side to side once it became airborne. About half a mile from the runway, the left wing struck a light pole and the plane plummeted downward, bursting into flames as it skidded across the ground.

Investigators suspected that the plane's wing flaps, which provide stability and lift, had not been properly set for takeoff. Flight data recorders and analysis of the wreckage confirmed the theory. The National Transportation Safety Board determined that the pilot had not properly set the flaps and that an electrical short prevented an onboard alarm system from warning of the error. The plane's manufacturer now recommends that the alarm system be tested before every takeoff, but investigators of a similar crash of a Spanish airliner in 2008 found that that plane's alarm system had failed as well.

The New Orient Coal Mine Explosion

On December 21, 1951, a massive explosion occurred at the New Orient Coal Mine in West Frankfort, Illinois. Some 120 workers were inside the mine at the time of the explosion, but only one would live to tell of it.

✳   ✳   ✳   ✳

WITH 12 MILES OF tunnels, the New Orient Mine was considered the biggest shaft coal mine in the world. It had suffered its share of small explosions—which are nearly unavoidable in coal mining—but never anything as sizable as this blast.

Sole survivor Cecil Sanders managed to live through the horror for 60 hours before being rescued. "We tried to put up canvas curtains so the gas would go around us," said Sanders in describing the plight of his group, "but the gas current was so strong it caught us between two air courses. We knew the only thing to do was find a hole and hope the gas would go over us." Sanders eventually lost consciousness, coming to only after a rescuer's flashlight jarred him back to reality.

Although the cause of the explosion was never confirmed, the mine had a dismal safety record with 21 safety code violations cited at a previous inspection. In 1952, Congress amended and strengthened the Coal Mine Health and Safety Act. It gave federal mine inspectors the power to close any mine that they deemed unsafe.

No Mercy for Those Aboard the *Ceramic*

On December 6, 1942, the British liner SS *Ceramic* was torpedoed by a German U-boat as it moved through the Azores. The Australia-bound craft, transporting soldiers and civilians, met its fate at the hands of submarine *U-515* commanded by Werner Henke. The sub picked up only one survivor, leaving the rest to die.

Three months before the *Ceramic's* ill-fated voyage, the German *U-156* torpedoed and sank the ocean liner RMS *Laconia*. When the U-boat approached the sinking liner to search for senior military personnel among the survivors in the water, *U-156* Lieutenant Commander Werner Hartenstein realized many of the survivors were civilians and Italian prisoners of war. At that point, *U-156* and three other submarines plucked survivors from the sea and, in some cases, draped Red Cross flags on their decks to indicate nonthreatening cargo. During the rescue operation, a U.S. Army B-24 *Liberator* spotted the U-boat and received orders to attack. The U-boats, now under full attack from the American bomber, would escape only after cutting tow lines to lifeboats containing rescued survivors. Because of the incident, the German Navy handed down the Laconia Order, which would halt all rescue efforts associated with sunken vessels and would directly affect the future sinking of the SS *Ceramic*.

Observing the new orders, sub *U-515* was no longer interested in lifesaving measures. After it launched its torpedoes, it watched the *Ceramic* slip beneath the waves, moving toward the ship hours later only in hopes of rescuing its captain for interrogation. When stormy seas precluded an in-depth search of the site, the *U-515* fished out the closest survivor. Royal Engineer Eric Munday would be vigorously interrogated but lived to tell the tale.

The disaster would commit more than 650 people to an early grave and land Munday in a prisoner of war camp, where he remained until war's end. The book *SS Ceramic: The Untold Story* would later document Munday's harrowing experience.

Ceramic: Henke's Fate

When *U-515* Commander Werner Henke refused to rescue survivors from the SS *Ceramic*, he invited retaliatory measures. Allied propaganda reports declared Henke a war criminal and claimed Henke had "machine-gunned" helpless survivors of the *Ceramic*. Authorities threatened to bring Henke to trial at war's end and hang him for crimes against humanity. Henke caught wind of some of these broadcasts, though in his mind the threats against him came specifically from Britain, rather than from the Allies in general.

Although Henke was following orders when he fled the scene of the *Ceramic* sinking, it was later reported that Henke felt haunted for abandoning survivors during the *Ceramic* incident. Perhaps because of this, the commander later defied the Laconia Order and rescued survivors from the SS *California*

Star and SS *Phemius* after sinking them in 1943. Nevertheless, the supposed British threats loomed very real in the back of Henke's mind.

On April 19, 1944, a group of U.S. ships—the USS *Guadalcanal* among them—left Casablanca with a specific mission to find and sink U-boats. The American ships were equipped with sophisticated detection equipment that enabled them to locate *U-515*. After a dramatic chase, *U-515* was sunk by the American forces.

Henke survived the sinking and was held in the United States as a prisoner of war. In June 1944, he was transferred to Canada. Knowing that Canada held strong British ties, Henke believed his execution was a certainty. The commander decided to deny his captors their chance. On June 15, Henke scaled a prison fence. After disobeying repeated shouts of "Halt," the German U-boat commander was shot dead. Henke is buried at Ft. Meade, Maryland.

Tragedy at the Millfield Mine

The Millfield disaster of November 5, 1930, was Ohio's worst mining accident, killing 82 at the Sunday Creek Coal Company's #6 mine. At 11:45 A.M. a rockfall at the back of #6 ruptured a cable, arcing electricity into a pocket of firedamp (mostly methane). *Whoosh!* The blast twisted I-beams like pipe cleaners, made instant kindling of shoring timbers, mangled rail cars into instant train wrecks, tore up 760 feet of track, and scorched equipment more than 1,500 feet from the blast. To worsen matters, the explosion filled the mine with afterdamp: lethal concentrations of carbon monoxide mixed with carbon dioxide and nitrogen.

When it was over, 138 miners had survived the disaster. Some escaped early; others described forlorn, desperate searches for safe air and a clear path out. Many could only sit tight and await rescue. Fatalities included Sunday Creek Coal's president, four other executives, and four visitors. Sad but ironic: They were inspecting such recent safety improvements as steel I-beam supports, brickwork, electric lighting, and a new ventilation shaft to vent flammable or toxic gases.

The son of a Hungarian immigrant who also worked in #6, young Sigmund Kozma toiled in the mine hooking up coal cars. Shortly after they felt the explosion, he recalls his dad hurrying to rig a barrier with brattice cloth, protecting their room from the deadly afterdamp. They waited three hours before heading for the exit, with Sigmund Jr. carrying a wounded man to safety. Kozma died in 2009 at age 97.

Millfield Mine: A Heroic Effort

Alert Sunday Creek Coal supervisor John Dean saved himself and 18 others with timely action. After the explosion, Dean instructed his miners to brattice themselves into a room, lest the afterdamp get them.

Two disregarded his suggestion and made a run for the entrance, then cried out for help. Dean went after them, but he found them overcome by afterdamp. Too weakened to carry them, he dragged himself back to the bratticed room. Once inside, he collapsed. Dean was one mine boss who barely survived his own valor.

Nome Diphtheria Epidemic

Dr. Curtis Welch served as a Public Health Service physician in Nome, Alaska. In January 1925, a severe illness began spreading among Nome's children. When fatalities began, Welch realized it was diphtheria—a highly infectious disease battled with antitoxin (also called serum).

Nome's supply of diphtheria serum was small and stale. If fresh serum didn't arrive within two weeks, Welch would need to order child-size coffins instead. Welch radioed a plea for help.

There were no roads to Nome in the wintertime. Serum could travel by rail as far north as Nenana, but it would have to go the last 674 miles by the dogsled mail route, which usually took 25 days. A team of 20 (mostly Native; some Russian, and Scandinavian) mushers with 150 dogs positioned their sleds to relay the serum through the mid-winter snow and -50 degree Fahrenheit.

The first sled left Nenana on January 27. On February 2 an exhausted Norwegian banged on Welch's door carrying the precious package. Several mushers sustained severe frostbite en route, and many dogs gave their lives. Not one vial was broken, however. Thanks to the serum, only a handful of Nome's people died. Today, the world-famous annual Iditarod race commemorates this event.

What Is Diphtheria?

As late as the 1920s, the United States had more than 100,000 diphtheria cases annually, with a mortality rate near 10 percent (heavily concentrated in children). Diphtheria is now rare in the industrialized world. In developing nations, however, the disease is more common.

Diphtheria symptoms usually begin with a sore throat, fatigue, and fever. The bacteria attack the upper respiratory tract, producing a potentially lethal toxin. Because the toxin phase comes very swiftly, every minute counts when starting treatment.

Antitoxins combat illness, whereas vaccines prevent them. The serum sent to Nome in such valiant haste functioned by neutralizing the bacteria's deadly toxin, much like snake antivenin. The first diphtheria vaccine was developed in 1913, but the diphtheria toxoid-containing vaccine (invented 1929) ranks alongside the polio and smallpox vaccines as one of history's great public health strides. Where vaccine is unavailable, diphtheria outbreaks still take lives.

Honda Point Incident: A Seven-Destroyer Pileup

Shortly after nightfall on September 8, 1923, seven of fourteen ships of the U.S. Navy's Destroyer Squadron 11 ran aground near Santa Barbara, California. The accident would claim the lives of 20 sailors from the USS Young and three more from the flagship USS Delphy. Its occurrence is representative of the crude navigation methods that prevailed during the era.

✳ ✳ ✳ ✳

AT THE TIME of the incident, Captain Edward H. Watson was piloting the *Delphy*. After check- ing his charts against bearings supplied by a radio direction finding (RDF) station at Point Arquello, the captain was satisfied that he was at the Santa Barbara Channel and initiated his turn into the water- way. He was dead wrong. In reality, the *Delphy*—and by exten- sion all of Squadron 11—was at Honda Point, several miles north and further east than Watson believed. When a sickening crunch indicated his ship had run aground, the captain realized his error and sounded the ship's siren.

In short order, six more ships from the squadron ran aground, but none more devastatingly than the USS *Young*. After ripping its hull open on submerged rocks, the vessel rolled over onto its starboard side.

Earlier that day, the mail steamship *Cuba* had also run aground off Honda Point. It was surmised that this grounding and the ones that followed may have resulted from unusual currents produced by a recent earthquake in Tokyo. This theory was never proven, however.

Honda Point Incident:
A Jump Into Treacherous Waters

When the armada of ships grounded one by one, the USS *Young* took the mightiest hit. As the ship foundered on its starboard side in a turbulent, rock-strewn sea, a number of valiant acts ensured the survival of most of its crew.

Due to the *Young's* extreme list, its lifeboats could not be deployed. Understanding this, commanding officer William L. Calhoun ordered his crew to the port side of the vessel to await rescue. When the USS *Chauncey* grounded upright just 75 yards from the *Young*, a stepping-stone to salvation was created. Without hesitation, Chief Boatswain's Mate Arthur Peterson dove into the churning sea to join the two ships with a line. Once accomplished, a series of raft shuttles delivered all 70 of the *Young's* surviving sailors to safety aboard the *Chauncey*.

For such efforts, well-deserved commendations were made. Lieutenant Commander Calhoun was cited for "coolness, intelligence, and seamanlike ability" directly responsible for the tragedy's "greatly reduced loss of life." Chief Boatswain's Mate Peterson would be commended for "extraordinary heroism" for his courageous swim.

Other players aboard the *Young* would also receive mention. These included a Lieutenant E. C. Herzinger for "especially meritorious conduct," and Fireman First Class J. T. Scott, for his heroic attempt to close down the ship's master oil valve to stave off an explosion.

✳ Captain Watson of the *Delphy* received a court martial for his navigational blunder, but he wasn't the only one held responsible. Varying degrees of blame were placed on those commanders who had also grounded their vessels. With this move, the Navy was following a tradition that holds captains responsible for the safety of their ships, even when they are sailing in formation.

* Navigational methods have greatly improved since Honda Point. Breakthroughs such as the global positioning system (GPS) and enhanced radar/sonar have rendered manual plotting methods such as "dead reckoning" nearly obsolete. A ship's crew can now pinpoint its position down to a few feet and can "see" underwater protrusions that may cause it harm. Although solid-state navigation has taken the luster off of manual plotting, many captains believe that the safest setup involves knowledge of both methods. Electronics can and do fail, after all.

The Steamboat *Columbia*

On July 5, 1918, the South Side Athletic Club of Pekin, Illinois, chartered the steamboat *Columbia* for an evening cruise along the Illinois River. The destination was the upriver Al Fresco Amusement Park in Peoria, an agreeable spot where partiers could escape their troubles and enjoy a fun-filled evening. As the club's largest annual event, the cruise drew some 500 people, mostly from the towns of Pekin and neighboring Kingston Mines, Illinois.

On its return voyage *Columbia* suddenly found itself mired in fog. While moving uncertainly through the murky conditions, the vessel wandered too close to shore and struck a submerged tree stump. The resulting wound proved fatal. Due to the river's shallow depth, however, the ship would only partially sink. Despite such luck, 87 people would die as a result of a ceiling collapse triggered by the forceful collision.

The Dag Hammarskjöld Crash

On the night of September 17, 1961, United Nations Secretary-General Dag Hammarskjöld of Sweden and 15 others took off from an airport in Leopoldville (former Belgian Congo). Their airplane crashed just before reaching its landing point in Northern Rhodesia.

After learning that violence had erupted between troops in the Katanga province of the Congo and noncombatant forces of the United Nations, Hammarskjöld had arranged for a conference with President Moise Tshombe of Katanga. Any hopes of brokering peace were instantly dashed when the Secretary-General's DC-6 violently crashed through a stand of trees and disintegrated.

The craft had been under orders to fly only at night to avert risks posed by Katangan jet fighters. After the crash, investigators suspected foul play and advanced their investigations accordingly. In the end, no evidence of anything other than a "controlled crash into terrain" was ever uncovered, but conspiracy theories persisted. The most popular of these involved onboard bombs and surface-to-air missile attack. Burmese diplomat U Thant was chosen to succeed Hammarskjöld as Secretary-General, and the official crash investigation drew to a close. The only survivor of the tragedy, American security officer Harold Julian, died several days later from injuries sustained in the crash.

The Thredbo Landslide

On the night of Wednesday, July 30, 1997, a landslide roared down an embankment near the village of Thredbo in New South Wales, Australia. It first swept away the Brindabella Ski Club's lodge, Carinya, and then followed with a parking garage. The massive wall of earth, rock, concrete, and vehicles continued down the slope, finally slamming into the staff quarters of the Bimbadeen ski lodge, completely destroying that four-story structure.

Although this happened at the height of the area's ski season, only one person was in the Carinya lodge that night, and 18 people were in the Bimbadeen staff quarters. Rescue workers shortly arrived on the scene, but operations were hampered by cold weather, the unstable arrangement of the rubble, and the threat of a leaking gas main. They recovered one body on Thursday and three more on Friday; by Friday night, rescuers had given up any real hope of finding any survivors.

The Thredbo Landslide: A Cause for Hope
Early on Saturday morning, however, they discovered ski instructor Stuart Diver pinned beneath three slabs of concrete next to the lifeless body of his wife. The couple had been in their first-floor bedroom of the Bimbadeen lodge at the time of the disaster, and the entire building had collapsed upon them. Rescuers rigged a system to deliver liquid nourishment to Diver and to blow warm air over him, hoping to curb the effects of malnourishment and exposure to the frigid winter air. After ten hours of careful digging, they pulled Diver, suffering from lacerations and mild hypothermia, from the rubble.

Investigators later determined that a leaking water main had eroded the embankment of a mountain road above the lodges, and caused the landslide. The government agencies responsible for maintaining infrastructure in the area were held accountable and paid some $40 million in settlements. Diver later opened his own bed-and-breakfast hotel in the Thredbo area and remarried in 2002.

The Explosion of the *Sultana*

A mysterious ship explosion took the lives of hundreds on board, including many Union soldiers on their way back home after the South had surrendered.

✳   ✳   ✳   ✳

IT SHOULD HAVE been a voyage of joy for many of the Union soldiers on the steamship *Sultana*. On April 27, 1865, the war was over, and they had finally been released from Andersonville and other prison camps. They were hungry and fatigued, and they simply wanted to go home. Passing the time on the two-day voyage north up the Mississippi, they played cards, slept, and told stories of the war recently concluded. They didn't know that, although the war was over, their ordeal was not.

Heavy Load

The *Sultana* had only been in service for two years. A side-wheel steamboat of 1,700 tons, it was overcrowded as it left the port of Memphis at around midnight on its way to Cairo, Illinois. At least 2,300 people crowded the decks, far more than the boat's capacity of at least 400. In addition to its soldiers, refugees, and civilians, the boat had also taken on more than 1,500 horses, cows, pigs, and other animals.

Boiling Point

Nate Wintringer, the *Sultana*'s chief engineer, had been dealing with a leak in the ship's boiler since the start of the voyage in Vicksburg, Mississippi. Wintringer and his crew were doing the best they could to patch the boiler with plugs and iron straps. He knew the boiler needed major work, but his experience told him the machine would hold out until they reached their final destination.

At about 2:00 A.M., as the ship was passing Paddy's Old Hen and Chickens islands just north of Memphis, a huge explosion shook the vessel. Passengers scrambled to escape the flaming wreckage, but the disaster claimed about 1,700 lives—because the precise number of passengers is unknown, so is the number who died, but it was more than died on the *Titanic*. Many of the hundreds who did make it off later died from the wounds they had sustained. Only one woman escaped: Anna Annis. Her husband—Union Lieutenant Harvey Annis—her child, and her sister all perished in the tragedy.

Conspiracy Theory

An official inquiry blamed the explosion on the leaking boiler, although leaking equipment such as that was not known to explode. Theories abounded that it was a guerrilla attack, which would not have been unheard of at the time.

Confederate sympathizers continued to harass Union ships and troops, even after the official surrender had been signed. In fact, just before the *Sultana* sailed, a communications ship named *Greyhound* had been sabotaged when explosives were placed in the coal bunkers.

The belief that the explosion was not an accident was given new life in 1888 when William Streetor, formerly a Union prison clerk, claimed that Robert Lowden, a known Confederate operative, had destroyed the *Sultana*. Streetor said that Lowden had told him how he smuggled a bomb disguised as a lump of coal onto the ship and placed it in the coal pile. When that bomb was shoveled into the furnace, the theory goes, the ship exploded.

Sunken Treasure

Following the explosion, the charred hulk of the ship would remain in the Mississippi mud. When the river was low, bones, skulls, and personal articles could be seen on the ship. Some of the items would occasionally wash to shore to be grabbed by morbid souvenir hunters.

The Cleveland Gas Explosion

In 1942, the East Ohio Gas Company constructed a tank farm for liquefied natural gas (LNG) near Lake Erie. Placed in a mixed-use section of Cleveland, it provided natural gas to local war industries. In 1944, however, one of those tanks ruptured, setting in motion a chain of events that would cause massive loss of life and property.

✳ ✳ ✳ ✳

ON THE AFTERNOON of October 20, 1944, a leak developed in a storage tank holding more than 650 million gallons of liquefied natural gas. The winds blowing off Lake Erie pushed the white vapor into the Cleveland sewer system, where the gas mixed with air and became explosive. The blast created a fireball towering more than half a mile high—it was visible more than seven miles away. Jets of flame blasted out of the sewers, propelling manhole covers into the air. Later, one of the manhole covers from the affected area would be found several miles away.

All Clear—or Not

After the first explosion, area residents assumed that the incident had been handled by the fire department and returned to their homes. Unfortunately, not much later, a second storage tank exploded. Pockets of natural gas persisted in the sewer system and exploded throughout the afternoon, trapping residents in their homes and businesses. The full chain of events resulted in an inferno that engulfed more than a square mile and caused the evacuation of more than 10,000 people, leaving almost 700 homeless.

The cost of the resulting fires in terms of casualties and property damage was staggering: The incident claimed 130 lives, including 55 employees of the East Ohio Gas Company. More than 200 people were injured. Two factories and 79 houses were destroyed. Property losses also included more than 200 automobiles and tractors, as well as damage to streets and underground utility installations. In addition to the physical structures destroyed by the fire, many residents kept significant amounts of cash, as well as stock and bond certificates, in their homes, all of which were lost to the fire. In total, the loss of property was estimated somewhere between the present-day equivalent of $80 and $172 million.

Corner-Cutting Causes

Because the United States was in the midst of World War II, the public initially suspected that the explosion was the work of a German saboteur. However, the subsequent investigation determined that the nickel content of the steel LNG tank had been the primary cause of the leak. Nickel is added to steel to increase its strength. During the war, however, rationing for various metals was in effect, and the tank was constructed of steel that had too small an amount of nickel. The temperatures required for LNG storage, generally between 120 and 170 degrees Celsius, made the steel composing the tank very brittle. Today, the standard nickel content for steel used in LNG applications is nearly three times what was in the steel of the leaking tank. Additionally, the tanks at the East Ohio storage facility lacked a means of secondary containment in case of leakage. That's required today for all above-ground LNG storage tanks.

The Cleveland disaster changed the way natural gas is transported and prompted a migration to underground storage. The East Ohio Gas Company ultimately paid more than $3 million to residents and another $500,000 to families of the 55 employees killed in the blast. About 50 percent of those who died in the fires that day are buried in Cleveland's Highland Park Cemetery, including all those who were never identified.

A Superior Tragedy:
The Edmund Fitzgerald

Many ships have been lost to the Great Lakes, but few incidents have fascinated the world like the sinking of the Edmund Fitzgerald off the shores of northern Michigan on November 10, 1975. The mysterious circumstances of the tragedy, which took 29 lives—all memorialized in a 1976 song by Gordon Lightfoot—have kept the story fresh to this day. The fateful journey began in Wisconsin.

✳ ✳ ✳ ✳

Least Likely to Sink

THE 729-FOOT-LONG EDMUND *Fitzgerald* was considered as unsinkable as any steamer. At its christening in June 1958, it was the Great Lakes' largest and most expensive freighter. Its name honored Edmund Fitzgerald, the president of

Northwestern Mutual Insurance Company of Milwaukee, who commissioned the boat.

During the christening, a few incidents occurred that some saw as bad omens. As a crowd of more than 10,000 watched, it took Mrs. Fitzgerald three tries to shatter the bottle of champagne. Then, when the ship was released into the water, it hit the surface at the wrong angle, causing a wave that splattered the entire ceremonial area with lake water and knocking the ship into a nearby dock. One spectator died on the spot of a heart attack.

The Last Launch

The weather was unseasonably pleasant the morning of November 9, 1975, so much so that the crew of 29 men who set sail from Superior, Wisconsin, that day were unlikely to have been concerned about their routine trip to Zug Island on the Detroit River. But the captain, Ernest McSorley, knew a storm was in the forecast.

McSorley, a 44-year veteran of the lakes, had captained the *Fitzgerald* since 1972. He paid close attention to the gale warnings issued that afternoon, but no one suspected they would yield a "once-in-a-lifetime storm." However, when the weather report was upgraded to a full storm warning, McSorley changed course to follow a safer route closer to the Canadian shore.

Following the *Fitzgerald* was another freighter, the *Arthur Anderson*. The two captains stayed in touch as they traveled through winds measuring up to 50 knots (about 58 miles per hour) with waves 12 feet or higher. On November 10, around 1:00 P.M., McSorley told Captain Cooper of the *Anderson* that the *Fitzgerald* was "rolling." By about 2:45 P.M., as the *Anderson* moved to avoid a dangerous shoal near Caribou Island, a crewman sighted the *Fitzgerald* about 16 miles ahead, closer to the shoal than Cooper thought safe.

About 3:30 P.M., McSorley reported to Cooper that the *Fitzgerald* had sustained some minor damage and was beginning to roll to one side. The ships were still 16 to 17 miles apart. At 4:10 P.M., with waves now 18 feet high, McSorley radioed that his ship had lost radar. The two ships stayed in radio contact until about 7:00 P.M. when the *Fitzgerald* crew told the Anderson they were "holding [their] own." After that, radio contact was lost, and the *Fitzgerald* dropped off the radar. Around 8:30 P.M., Cooper told the Coast Guard at Sault Ste. Marie that the *Fitzgerald* seemed to be missing.

Evidently, the *Fitzgerald* sank sometime after 7:10 P.M., just 17 miles from the shore of Whitefish Point, Michigan. Despite a massive search effort, it wasn't until November 14 that a navy flyer detected a magnetic anomaly that turned out to be the wreck. The only other evidence of the disaster to surface was a handful of lifeboats, life jackets, and some oars, tools, and propane tanks. A robotic vehicle was used to thoroughly photograph the wreck in May 1976.

One Mysterious Body

One odd aspect of the tragedy was that no bodies were found. In most temperate waters, corpses rise to the surface as decomposition forms gas. But the Great Lakes are so cold that decomposition is inhibited, causing bodies to stay on the bottom.

In 1994, a Michigan businessman named Frederick Shannon took a submarine equipped with a full array of modern surveillance equipment to the site, hoping to film a documentary about the ship. His crew discovered a body on the lake bottom near the bow of the wreck, covered by cork sections of a decayed canvas life vest. However, this body may not be associated with the *Fitzgerald*. Two French vessels were lost nearby in 1918, and none of those bodies had been recovered either. A sailor from one of them could have been preserved by the lake's frigid water and heavy pressure.

What Sank the Mighty Fitz?

One theory is that the *Fitzgerald* got too close to the dangerous Six-Fathom Shoal near Caribou Island and scraped over it, damaging the hull. Another is that the ship's hatch covers were either faulty or improperly clamped, which allowed water in. Wave height may also have played a part, with the storm producing a series of huge swells known as the "Three Sisters"—a trio of lightning-fast waves that pound a vessel—the first washes over the deck, the second hits the deck again so fast that the first has not had time to clear itself, and the third quickly adds another heavy wash, piling thousands of gallons of water on the ship. Few ships can withstand this.

For Whom the Bell Tolls...

On July 4, 1995, the bell of the *Edmund Fitzgerald* was retrieved and laid to rest in the Great Lakes Shipwreck Historical Museum in Whitefish Bay, Michigan. A replica bell, symbolizing the ship's "spirit," was left with the wreckage. Every year on November 10, during a memorial service, the original, 200-pound bronze bell is rung 29 times—once for each crewmember who perished.

The SS *Normandie* Goes Up in Flames

Luxurious liners don't always reach majestic ends.

❋ ❋ ❋ ❋

A HUGE, PROUD VESSEL that cut through the sea hardly making a wave, the SS *Normandie* was a French ocean liner that many considered the finest ever built. Dedicated in 1932, it was the star of a new class of liners designed for wealthy tourists rather than poor immigrants like most of its predecessors.

Dominating the Competition

No detail was too minor in the construction, and the vessel gave new meaning to the term luxury liner. Upon its maiden voyage in 1935, the *Normandie* set many new seafaring standards. At a weight of more than 79,000 gross tons, it was the heaviest ship on the seas. It was also the longest, exceeding 1,000 feet. Even more impressive was its speed: During its maiden voyage, the *Normandie* averaged nearly 30 knots in its westbound journey across the Atlantic. During its return voyage, the grand liner averaged more than 30 knots.

The combination of speed and luxury made the *Normandie* the pride of France. Before transatlantic flight, ocean liners were the only means of travel from Europe to the United States. England and Italy had grand ships, including the RMS *Majestic* and the SS *Rex*, but the *Normandie* outdid its peers in terms of both size and speed. Its Art Deco interior was a marvel of design and luxury. The first-class dining room, at more than 300 feet in length and featuring a 20-foot-high bronze entryway, was like that of no other liner in existence. The vessel boasted the work of the era's finest designers and dazzled passengers with its lavish accommodations and facilities, including both indoor and outdoor pools, a theater, and a chapel.

War Changes Everything

Despite its accolades, the *Normandie* was not destined for lengthy service. Upon arriving in New York in late August 1939, officials decided to keep the *Normandie* in harbor due to the escalation of World War II. It had just completed its 139th Atlantic crossing. After France fell to Nazi Germany in June 1940, the U.S. Maritime Commission and then the navy took custody of the ship. Hitler tried to lay claim to the liner, but the United States refused to release it. After the Japanese attack at Pearl Harbor, the U.S. War Department began converting the *Normandie* for service as a troopship, rechristening it the USS *Lafayette* in honor of the French Marquis de Lafayette, a key

American ally during the Revolutionary War.

Never Work Near an Open Flame

On February 9, 1942, the final stages of the conversion process were underway when a massive fire broke out, sending billowing clouds of smoke across New York City. Unfortunately, the ship's onboard fire-protection system had been dismantled during the conversion, so fire brigades were dispatched. As the firefighters began spraying copious amounts of water at the vessel in an attempt to extinguish the raging blaze, the mighty ship listed heavily and eventually capsized.

With Pearl Harbor a fresh memory, a skittish American public initially feared that the fire was a result of Nazi sabotage, but the real cause of the blaze was an errant spark from a welding torch. Regardless of the cause, the once-majestic luxury liner lay on its side in the harbor in the inferno's aftermath. The ship was eventually set to right, but it was a total loss. The once majestic Normandie was ultimately sold for scrap.

The Saga of the *Boston*

As a new, fully green crew member aboard the American trading ship *Boston* in 1803, Englishman John Jewitt was coping with the difficulties of sea life. In addition to having to learn just about everything connected with sailing, Jewitt, an armorer (weapons maker) who had apprenticed under his father, was trying his best to head off repeated bouts of seasickness. Although he couldn't possibly know it, stomach distress was soon to become the least of his problems.

Everything centered on an outburst the ship's captain had in front of Chief Maquina, a Nootka tribal leader, while docked at Nootka Sound, Vancouver Island. When Chief Maquina returned a broken firearm and told the captain that the gun was *peshak* (bad), the captain launched into a volley of insults and slurs, calling the chief a liar. Since he was speaking English, a language that the chief supposedly didn't understand, the captain thought he could do this with impunity. He was wrong. The powerful chief knew only too well what some of the key words meant and silently declared war on the *Boston*.

The day before the ship was to go out to sea, Maquina and his men attacked the *Boston*. The attack came swiftly, while Jewitt was below deck. He heard a commotion and ascended, only to be struck a glancing blow by an ax. Maquina saved Jewitt from further injury because he knew Jewitt's weapon-making skills would be useful. All but one of his crewmates were brutally massacred. (The other survivor, John Thompson, was found hours later; Jewitt was able to convince Maquina to spare Thompson's life by falsely claiming that Thompson was his father.)

From that point on, Jewitt and Thompson were slaves. When they arrived at the chief's village on Friendly Cove, how-ever, the villagers greeted Jewitt with an outpouring of unex-pected affection. Even the chief now showed a genuine affinity for his captive.

At one point, Maquina arranged a marriage between Jewitt and one of the women in his tribe (though she eventually went back to live with her family). Despite such unexpected treatment, it was understood that should Jewitt or Thompson try to escape, "daggers would come." Clearly, however, this wasn't a typical master/slave relationship.

This situation would continue until 1805, when the ship *Lydia* rescued the captives. During his time in captivity, Jewitt kept a journal. In 1815, he recounted his bizarre tale in *A Narrative of the Adventures and Sufferings of John R. Jewitt*. The book brought Jewitt a measure of notoriety, and he lived out his days playing the captive in plays and singing his signa-ture song, "The Poor Armourer Boy." Jewitt spent the latter part of his life in New England and died in Hartford, Connecticut, on January 7, 1821.

The Sinking of the *Duncan Dunbar*

When the clipper ship *Duncan Dunbar* slammed against a reef off Australia in August 1857, a heavy toll was exacted from Sydney. In a few short hours, 63 passengers and 58 crew members making the journey there from London were committed to a watery grave.

Thousands of the living would begin their grieving process, for the ship was not full of strangers—it was full of Sydney locals returning after visiting friends and family in England. Word of the wreck quickly spread, and the towns people hurried to the shore to inquire about loved ones. When they came upon the wreckage and saw the bodies floating in the water, they were heartbroken. The only survivor of the disaster was seaman James Johnson, who was rescued more than a day later from the ledge of a cliff.

Newtown's St. Steven's Cemetery staged a mass funeral for the victims and later erected a monument in their honor. During the September 24 ceremony, 20,000 mourners lined George Street to view the seven hearses and more than 100 carriages that held the victims. In deference to the tragedy, scores of bankers and shopkeepers closed their businesses, bringing commerce in the city to a virtual halt.

Today, the Hornby Lighthouse is situated near the fated site at the tip of South Head. It stands as a brick-and-mortar reminder of the perilous hazards found just beneath the waves, and as a final legacy to those doomed souls aboard the *Duncan Dunbar*.

In later years, James Johnson became a lighthouse keeper at the entrance to Newcastle Harbor, where on July 12, 1866, he helped rescue Frederick Hedges, the lone survivor of the 60 men and women on the *Cawarra* when it sank. On April 13, 1915, Johnson died in Sydney at age 78.

The Johnstown Flood

On May 31, 1889, a catastrophic breach of Western Pennsylvania's South Fork Dam delivered unimaginable destruction to gritty Johnstown, a steel company town in a valley 14 miles below. With 2,209 deaths attributable to the dam break, the tragedy ranks among the worst in American history. As if such loss of life weren't unsettling enough, subsequent reports of improper dam maintenance and outright neglect led to a startling conclusion: The Johnstown Flood could have been avoided.

During the Gilded Era (1845–1916), the South Fork Fishing and Hunting Club membership roster read like a veritable "Who's Who" of wealthy industrialists. Such magnates as Andrew Carnegie and Henry Clay Frick would summer at the fishing and boating oasis at Lake Conemaugh, conveniently located just a short train ride from Pittsburgh.

But there was a problem brewing beneath the lake's surface. Since the club had acquired the property, dam maintenance had gone by the wayside. Worse still, members had lowered the dam's height and installed fish traps in the spillway to prevent stocked fish from escaping. These screens would at times collect debris and render the spillway almost useless. In addition, critical discharge pipes had been removed and never replaced. Despite warnings and recommendations from dam inspector Daniel Morrell, the members maintained this dangerous status quo. The stage was set.

Johnstown Flood: A Spectacular Downpour

When the rains came on May 31, 1889, they came with a vengeance. The U.S. Army Signal Corps estimated that six to ten inches of rain fell over the region in a 24-hour period. Just after 4:00 P.M., things turned ominous at the South Fork Dam. A "whooshing" noise signaled the dam's unceremonious end, and untold horrors were about to unfold.

A 36-foot wall of water and debris slammed into Johnstown with a roar. It lifted all objects in its path, even freight cars. In an instant, entire families were obliterated and others were fractured, leaving large numbers of widows and orphans.

In the flood's aftermath, lawsuits against the wealthy club members went nowhere because the court viewed the catastrophe as an "act of God."

Last *Lusitania* Survivor

On May 7, 1915, during the height of World War I, a German U-boat torpedoed the luxury liner RMS Lusitania as it steamed across the Atlantic toward Liverpool, England. The vessel sank with alarming haste, taking almost 1,200 people along with it.

✳ ✳ ✳ ✳

JUST ONE WEEK before the fateful journey, Germany issued a warning to "vessels flying the flag of Great Britain, or any of her allies" planning voyages through waters adjacent to the British Isles. Since a number of British merchant ships had already been destroyed by German U-boats, *Lusitania's* Captain William Turner understood full well that these Teutonic forces meant business.

Despite such dangers, the *Lusitania* departed New York Harbor on May 1, 1915, bound for Liverpool with approximately 2,000 passengers on board. In theory, the captain's avoidance strategy should have been straightforward. He would use the *Lusitania's* superior speed to sidestep enemy attacks while adhering to a set of evasive directives prescribed by the British Admiralty. In reality, he did neither. For reasons still shrouded in mystery, the *Lusitania* actually slowed when it reached enemy waters, sailing close enough to shore to present a tempting target. When a lurking U-boat fired its torpedoes, the resulting explosion sealed *Lusitania's* fate. A second blast, now believed to have come from disturbed coal dust (Germany would later claim this as being onboard munitions) completed the job.

Audrey Lawson-Johnston of Bedfordshire, England, is the last survivor of the sinking. She died in 2011 at age 95, she was a mere infant at the time of the tragedy. She went on to marry Hugh Lawson-Johnston, whose grandfather had developed the beef-extract product Bovril. The last survivor who claimed to remember the sinking was American Barbara McDermott of Connecticut. She was 95 when she passed away in April 2008.

Rescue Efforts of the *Lusitania*

Although the *Lusitania* sank less than 15 miles off the shores of southwestern Ireland, rescue steamers and tugs needed some two hours to reach the ship. In a scenario where every minute counted, the nearby fishing vessel *Wanderer* rushed to *Lusitania's* aid after seeing the liner suddenly list. "Go for her, be British!" came the urgent cry from the *Wanderer's* captain as the tiny vessel made its way to the floundering liner and set about the business of rescuing its survivors.

The *Wanderer*, strained with a heavy payload of humanity, rendezvoused with the tug *Flying Fish* some two miles off the coast of Kinsale, Ireland. The tug's captain, Thomas Brierly, organized a shuttle system with the *Wanderer* that would transport survivors from the site of the tragedy to Queenstown (now Cobh), Ireland. Making several such perilous journeys, the team is credited with saving some 200 people.

The *General Slocum*

As the sidewheel steamer *General Slocum* cast off into New York's East River on the morning of June 15, 1904, the band played "A Mighty Fortress Is Our God." A local Lutheran congregation had chartered Slocum for its annual Sunday School picnic on Long Island. Some 1,330 people, mainly immigrant German women and children from the Lower East Side, bubbled with anticipation.

Any parishioner who knew Slocum's history was demonstrating serene faith. In 13 years of paddling about New York, the ship had racked up several vessel collisions and numerous groundings. Corrupt federal inspectors had recently certified its life preservers (the life preservers proved to be useless—if not lethal—which gives an indication of how inept the inspectors were). The same inspectors did not even bother to check the lifeboats and fire hose.

❋ ❋ ❋ ❋

A Voyage Through Hells Gate

Slocum's course lay through a stony, swirly shoal called Hell Gate. Approximately forty minutes into the trip, as Captain William H. Van Schaick focused on navigating the hazard, a boy yelled up to the pilothouse: "Hey, Mister! The ship's on fire!" Presuming a bad practical joke, Van Schaick swore, "Get the hell out of here!"

Crew members soon echoed the warning. Van Schaick looked outside and saw two causes for concern: flames consuming the steamer's port side and passengers leaping overboard. The crew deployed the fire hose; it fell apart, rotten. Passengers clawed for life preservers, many of which disintegrated into useless rags and cork dust. The crew was not trained in fire procedures and had never dislodged a lifeboat. Nor could they have on this journey, for the *Slocum*'s boats were wired and painted to the deck.

Van Schaick didn't like his chances on the nearby shore because of the rocks and the lumberyards and oil tanks beyond, so he gritted his teeth and floored it for North Brother Island, a mile away. *Slocum* left a wake of drowning and burnt passengers as the rapid passage fanned the flames. The ship shoaled just short of North Brother. Numerous swimmers and small craft hurried to the rescue, often risking their own lives.

Appalling contemporary photos show dozens of corpses

washed ashore. The grim human accounting was 1,031 dead, including two of the crew of 30. Van Schaick suffered burns and a broken ankle. Officials blamed the fire on crew carelessness in the lamp room. Only Van Schaick paid a legal penalty, doing three-and-a-half years in Sing Sing Prison before his pardon by President William Howard Taft.

The public outcry had a lasting effect, as every excursion boat in New York underwent inspection in earnest. Many failed as badly as *Slocum* should have. Many well-dressed rear ends were chewed, the U.S. Steamboat Inspection Service swabbed its decks, and higher safety standards came in force. Many survivors moved away from their Lower East Side neighborhood, where they felt haunted by memories of the friends they had lost in the fire.

The Trials

When a thousand people die, someone must pay. *Slocum* owner Frank Barnaby did everything possible to avoid being that someone. He hurried to counterfeit safety records, then blamed the whole mess on corrupt federal inspectors (fair) and panicked passengers (ridiculous).

A grand jury saw it otherwise, indicting Van Schaick, Barnaby, the inspector, and eight others for manslaughter by criminal negligence. When three hung juries failed to convict the inspector, thus sinking most of the other indictments (including Barnaby's), prosecutors decided to try only Van Schaick. By tradition and law, a vessel's master is responsible for the safety of the passengers and crew. Van Schaick made the easiest scapegoat, and the jury faulted him for ultimate negligence. Under the Seaman's Manslaughter Act of 1838, he got the maximum sentence: ten years.

Chapter 8

Language, Literature, & Its Practitioners

The Story Behind Storytelling

We all have stories to tell. Whether it's recounting a favorite childhood memory, reminiscing over a wedding day, or remembering a difficult struggle, everyone wants to share their own version of the human experience with others. This desire is so universal that it transcends the boundaries of countries, cultures, and time itself. So what is the story behind storytelling?

✳ ✳ ✳ ✳

ALTHOUGH NO ONE can pinpoint the exact moment that humans began telling stories, it's likely that stories were being told even before humans developed language. Early humans may have used pantomime, or props like stones, sticks, and leaves, to get their point across. Humans also learned to draw and create picture stories. An example was discovered in 1940 at the Lascaux Caves in southern France. Estimated to be around twenty thousand years old, the cave drawings depict many different types of animals. Researchers believe that the pictures perhaps tell a simple story about hunting practices or rituals of the day.

The Oral Tradition

Once spoken language was developed, stories were told as a record of information. Since no one knew how to write, these verbal storytellers were revered members of their societies. People wanted others to know of their great feats—battles fought, kingdoms conquered, enemies vanquished—and stories made these accomplishments sound even more grand than they already were.

The first great work of written literature is often considered to be the *Epic of Gilgamesh,* a poem from ancient Mesopotamia that dates to around 2100 B.C. Written on tablets in the extinct cuneiform language of Akkadian, the story describes the adventures and journey of a demigod named Gilgamesh. Scholars theorize that Gilgamesh may have been an actual person—most likely a Sumerian king who ruled sometime between 2800 and 2500 B.C.—and the story was written as an homage to his greatness.

But even after the invention of written language, the practice of passing down oral stories continued; most people would still be illiterate for centuries to come. The power of the oral tradition can be seen in examples like Aesop's famous fables. Aesop, who died in 564 B.C., never wrote down a single page of his stories. But people recited his fables so often that they were able to compile and print collections of his tales hundreds of years later. Likewise, much of what was written in the Bible occurred long before any of it was written down. Humans passed anecdotes and parables along from generation to generation, until they ultimately could record them in written form. In fact, the ritual of passing along spoken stories is so well-loved that many cultures—such as the Cherokee in America or poets called "griots" in West Africa—still today consider the practice an important part of their lifestyles.

The Written Tradition

Once the tradition began moving from oral stories to written stories, books were often used to convey what were considered historical truths. Even books of mythology—works like Homer's *Iliad* and *Odyssey*—were used as tools to give meaning to the human existence. Stories explained natural phenomenon, described the origins of life, and pondered the afterlife. Many people only saw books in churches, when priests would read from scarcely available Bibles. But by the twelfth century, storytelling began to take on a new life with works of fiction. Instead of composing stories for practical reasons such as to record a historical event or to calm people's fears of the unknown, stories were told purely for entertainment. Perhaps one of the most famous early examples is Geoffrey Chaucer's *The Canterbury Tales*, which was written in the late 1300s. Chaucer's book revolves around a group of pilgrims who travel together to the shrine of Saint Thomas Becket at Canterbury Cathedral. On their way, they have a storytelling contest. Chaucer wrote each section of the book as a different character telling a story—so in effect, *The Canterbury Tales* is storytelling about storytelling!

God's Word Straight off the Presses

In the 1440s, Johannes Gutenberg created his movable type printing press and written storytelling was transformed. The people who had only seen books in churches—Bibles that had been painstakingly handwritten by scribes—could now possess their own copies of the scriptures and other books. The printing press led to an increase in literacy, since books were now more readily available to everyone, and not just the wealthy. This, in turn, led to a stronger middle class during Renaissance times, when the literate elite no longer had a stronghold on education.

Even so, in the time of William Shakespeare, many people were still unable to read. But Shakespeare was clever—he wrote his prose to appease the well-educated readers in his audience, but made sure to include plenty of violence, humor, and action to appeal to those who were unable to read his stories but attended the theatrical productions of his works. He was also extremely versatile—while many writers chose to stick with one genre, Shakespeare tackled comedy, drama, adventure, historical tales, and love stories. And his influence was so great that not only do we often quote him without even realizing it ("love is blind," "bated breath," or "kill with kindness," for instance), but his works have stood the test of time and have been adapted many times over. Shakespeare's storytelling has inspired a wealth of new stories!

Everyone Has a Story and a Means to Tell It

The printing press, the advent of cheaper paper, and a rise in literacy all contributed to the increasing popularity of the novel. Although early examples of novels can be found as far back as two thousand years ago, the modern novel—especially realistic fiction—didn't achieve popularity until the eighteenth century. These stories were often inspired by current events of the times, and their prose reflects struggles like military conflicts, political strife, crime, fear of the government, or visions of the unknown future.

In the early twentieth century, technology presented us with a brand-new way to tell stories in the form of radio, television, and movies. Storytellers were now able to connect with multitudes of people simultaneously. But there was a catch to this form of expression: it cost a lot of money. Shows and movies required money to produce, and advertisers—who also tell short "stories" about their products—paid money to have their stories heard. So while the general public loved hearing and seeing the stories produced by these new mediums, only those with large amounts of money could get their stories out to the masses.

Enter the digital age: the advent of the internet has radically changed the way we tell stories. The average person no longer needs money to tell a story that hundreds, thousands, or even millions of people can hear. We live in a connected world, where a person in Tokyo can tell their story and someone in Miami can hear about it nearly instantaneously. Sharing our stories through social media, blogs, and message boards has made it possible to reach a worldwide audience, and given us a chance to learn about other points of view and cultures. But it's also brought up questions about how much information is too much, and whether telling so many stories is worth a decline in personal privacy.

Regardless of where the world heads in the future, one thing is certain: we have yet to see "the end" of the evolution of storytelling.

The National Book Awards

The National Book Foundation sponsors the National Book Awards. In 1950, the first year of the awards, three people were honored. Nelson Algren won the Fiction Award for *The Man with the Golden Arm*.

Algren's manuscript examined the tumultuous life of a back-alley card dealer with a morphine monkey on his back. The book, later made into a film starring Frank Sinatra, master-fully depicted the disintegration of the lead character against a gritty urban backdrop. Algren was well within his element with this subtext. The budding writer grew up in a poor immigrant neighborhood on Chicago's South Side; he witnessed the seedy side of life every day. With the prize-winning *The Man with the Golden Arm*, he conveyed firsthand experiences of such a world to an audience stunned by its bleakness.

Stories of the downtrodden struck a particular chord with Algren, as did exposés on corruption. *A Walk on the Wild Side* (1956) and *Chicago, City on the Make* (1951) illustrate the author's longing for fair play in a largely unfair world. Cataloging the life of a Depression-era drifter, *A Walk on the Wild Side* was hailed as a masterpiece by critics. "The book asks why lost people sometimes develop into greater human beings than those who have never been lost in their whole lives," explained Algren.

Algren's personal life mirrored this philosophy. Hospitalized on several occasions for depression, the author attempted suicide after *A Walk on the Wild Side* was first released. He wrote numerous books, many to rave reviews, before his career ended. Nelson Algren was the last survivor of the first three National Book Award winners when he passed away on May 9, 1981.

The following were the other recipients of the 1950 National Book Awards:

✳ **Ralph L. Rusk (1888–1962) received the Nonfiction Award for** *Ralph Waldo Emerson.*

✳ **William Carlos Williams (1883–1963) received the Poetry Award for** *Paterson: Book III and Selected Poems.*

The Pulitzers

Joseph Pulitzer was born near Budapest, Hungary, in 1847. His father died when he was still just a child, and the family fell on hard times. As a teenager, Pulitzer tried to enlist in the Austrian army but was denied because of his poor eyesight. Pulitzer then tried joining the armies of several other European countries, but he was rejected each time. Because civil war had broken out in the United States, Pulitzer decided to try to enlist there.

Pulitzer arrived penniless at Castle Garden in New York City in 1864. He spoke very little English and at times had to resort to sleeping on park benches. However, he was finally able to enlist. He joined the Union Army First Regiment, New York (Lincoln) Cavalry in September 1864 and was discharged the following year. Next, he traveled to the western United States with an Austrian who had been his friend in the army; they could afford to travel as far as St. Louis. Once there, Pulitzer took any job he could find. He worked on a ferry and then as an undertaker during a cholera epidemic. He studied law and was admitted to the bar in 1868. He did not enjoy law, however, and started searching elsewhere for a job that held more interest for him.

When he began working as a reporter for a German newspaper, he knew he had found his calling. He rose to city editor, then managing editor, and then became part owner of the paper. In 1878, the *St. Louis Evening Dispatch* was offered at auction; Pulitzer bought it and soon took over the *Evening Post* as well. In this way, the *St. Louis Post-Dispatch* came into being.

Joseph Pulitzer died on his yacht near Charleston, South Carolina, in 1911. His will had a provision for the establishment of prizes that would encourage and reward excellence in the field of journalism. The first prizes were awarded in 1917. Herbert Bayard Swope, who died in 1958, was the last surviving recipient of the first Pulitzers. Swope received the Reporting prize for the *New York World* series of articles entitled "Inside the German Empire."

The following individuals also received Pulitzers in 1917:

* French Ambassador J. J. Jusserand (1855–1932) won the History prize for his book *With Americans of Past and Present Days.*

* Laura E. Richards (1850–1943) and Maude Howe Elliott (1854–1948) shared the Biography/Autography prize for their book *Julia Ward Howe.*

Evil in the Ink: The Story of EC Comics

Comic books were hugely popular in the 1950s. Plenty of publishers offered material that might politely be termed objectionable, but one outfit created the darkest, most unsettling comics of all—which remain influential today.

✳   ✳   ✳   ✳

NEWSPAPER COMIC STRIPS became popular at the end of the nineteenth century and the beginning of the twentieth, and comic books came into their current form in the mid-1930s. In the late 1930s and early 1940s, superheroes such as Superman, Batman, Captain America, and Wonder Woman burst onto the scene, enticing America's kids to bury their noses in colorfully illustrated worlds of action and adventure. GIs picked up the comics habit while they were overseas, and shortly after the end of World War II, comic book publishers were printing nearly 80 million copies every month.

One of these publishers was Max Gaines, who had a line of innocuous books the likes of *Tiny Tot Comics*, *Dandy Comics*, *Saddle Romances*, and *Picture Stories from the Bible*—all under the banner of Educational Comics, called "EC Comics" for short.

A New Direction

Gaines's son, William, took the reins of EC Comics in 1947, following Max's death in a freak boating accident. Bill Gaines was a soft-spoken young man with a chemistry degree. He'd never thought much about the family business, but his mother convinced him to step into his dad's shoes. With a new staff headed by editor-writer-artist Al Feldstein, Gaines developed a so-so line of romance, Western, and crime comics. Significantly, because both he and Feldstein had been fans of "spook" radio shows such as *Lights Out* and *Inner Sanctum*, horror tales began to sneak into EC's crime titles. By 1950, the company was committed to building what Gaines called the "New Trend" in comics: unusually intelligent tales of horror, science fiction, war, crime, and suspense. Gaines had changed the meaning of the *E* in EC Comics from "Educational" to "Entertaining" in 1947, and now the company really lived up to its name, introducing titles such as:

Tales from the Crypt: The lead artist on this title was Jack Davis, whose declarative, rough-hewn style was ideal for chilling tales of gross, often rural horror and revenge—all hosted by the queasily ironic Crypt Keeper.

Vault of Horror: Mainstay artist Johnny Craig brought a smart, crisply illustrative style to unnerving stories about cheating, murderous spouses and the gruesomely rough justice meted out by those they had betrayed. The manic Vault Keeper—his hideous open-mouthed grin burnished by ropes of saliva—introduced the tales in this title.

Haunt of Fear: The third in the triumvirate of EC horror comics, Haunt featured the artwork of Graham Ingels, a quiet man with a warped, spidery style that was perfect for sick stories about vengeful corpses, homicidal senior citizens, and awful goings-on inside mausoleums and ramshackle old houses. The "fear fables" were hosted by the wall-eyed Old Witch.

EC's Horror Stories AreComically Absurd

A chicken king who murders his partner ends up Southern fried; a fellow who renders his friend into a bar of soap gets his comeuppance when the soap clogs the shower drain and causes him to drown; a baseball star who murders another player is later gutted and dismembered, his intestines used to mark the baselines, his head used as the ball. Gaahhh!

Gaines and Feldstein brainstormed and wrote a story a day, not just for the horror titles but for a line that also included *Weird Science* and *Weird Fantasy*, and *Shock SuspenStories* and *Crime SuspenStories*. Another editor-writer-artist, Harvey Kurtzman, managed *Frontline Combat* and a general adventure title, *Two-Fisted Tales*.

In addition to hiring skilled artists, Gaines paid top industry rates to top comics talent that included Wally Wood, Al Williamson, George Evans, John Severin—even the legendary Frank Frazetta. Science-fiction writer Ray Bradbury was so impressed with EC's unauthorized rip-off of his work that he arranged a deal that gave the company permission to adapt other Bradbury stories for use in the horror and sci-fi titles. EC Comics became the industry's leading innovator, not simply with literate, darkly funny stories and eye-filling artwork, but with a liberal social conscience that revealed itself in hard-hitting stories of racism, misguided patriotism, bad cops, mob violence, and other controversial issues.

A Bubbling Cauldron of Trouble

The success of Bill Gaines's EC Comics was unfortunately short-lived. A worrisome uptick in juvenile crime happened to coincide with cutthroat competition among comics publishers for rack space in the early 1950s. Companies' very survivals were at stake, and many fly-by-night outfits—and even EC—unwisely took shock to unprecedented levels. All of this, plus politicians' claims that a weakened moral fiber of American youth would encourage communism, focused a harshly negative light on the comics industry. The anti-comics bias of Bellevue child psychiatrist Dr. Fredric Wertham was expressed in his 1954 book, *Seduction of the Innocent*, a well-meaning but laughably argued study of the effects of comics on America's youth. In the course of his psychiatric work, Wertham saw only troubled youth: Those kids read comics; ergo, they had been corrupted by comics. Partly because it took parents off the hook, *Seduction of the Innocent* sold briskly and brought comics under government scrutiny. The State of New York and the U.S. Senate quickly held separate hearings investigating the purported link between comics and juvenile delinquency. In one of the worst decisions of his life, Gaines voluntarily testified to a Senate subcommittee, engaging Tennessee Democrat Estes Kefauver in a fruitless debate about the aesthetics of horror comics.

Fallout from the various investigations forced the comics industry to agree to the development of a censorship body to be called the Comics Code Authority. A stamp with the CCA seal (A for *approved*) appeared on the covers of comics that had been scrutinized and passed by the CCA's cadre of volunteer housewives. The symbol assured parents (and warned kids) that, henceforth, comic books would be as safe and as bland as oatmeal. It also assured the demise of Gaines's innovative and exciting line of EC Comics.

All Except One

Gaines had one title that took an anarchic, wickedly satirical look at American culture and the world. And, because Gaines had the foresight to change the format from a comic book to a magazine, it survived the purge of comics in late 1954. In fact, it can still be purchased and enjoyed today. The title? *MAD* magazine.

Comics Get Marvel-ous in the 60s

The Marvel Comics team changed the face of comic books with characters that had real flaws, human problems, and timely quandaries.

❋   ❋   ❋   ❋

FROM THE 1930S through the 1950s, comic book superheroes were as simple and straightforward as the stories they inhabited. Good was good, and it always triumphed over evil. Superman and Batman led honest and uncomplicated lives. But the mounting threat of atomic weapons and the Cold War created a newly complex world that seemed unsuited for simple comics heroes. Enter Stan Lee.

Parents of the Modern Superhero

At only 17 years old, writer and editor Stan Lee began working for Timely Comics in 1939. It was the beginning of what would become known as the Golden Age of Comics. Some 22 years later, Lee was the editor in chief at Timely's successor, Marvel.

Artist Jack Kirby joined Timely in late 1940 with writing partner Joe Simon. Together, they created Captain America, a great icon of patriotism, just in time for America's entry into World War II. Kirby had an amazingly exciting style of illustrating action. He worked at a number of comic book companies, with Simon and without. He was again doing material for Timely (now called Atlas) in the late 1950s.

Around that same time, artist Steve Ditko, an illustration school grad, was drawing for Marvel's science fiction titles such as *Journey Into Mystery* and *Amazing Adventures*. Ditko's work was admired for its clean, angular appearance and style. A collaborative spirit was brewing between Ditko, Kirby, and Lee that would change the face of comics forever.

Changing the Paradigm

The comic industry usually focused on whatever was the rage in films across America. If Westerns were big, the industry sold Western comics. If war was big, then war comics were on the stands. In the early 1960s, science fiction and monsters were the "in" thing. Marvel's publisher noticed that superhero teams were in vogue and urged Lee to put together a team for Marvel.

But Lee wanted to avoid the one-dimensional characters that until then had seemed the norm—Superman was so super, almost nothing could stop him. Batman's alter ego, Bruce Wayne, was rich and successful—if anything got really sticky, he just threw money and expensive gadgets at it. Lee thought readers could relate to superheroes with realistic, human problems.

A Fantastic Start

Working with Kirby, Lee created a comic book that he would enjoy as a reader. The characters would have shortcomings and bad habits. They would have feet of clay. They would have real relationships. And they would not have secret identities.

With those guidelines, Lee and Kirby introduced *Fantastic Four* in November 1961. Exposed to cosmic radiation, a group of space travelers return to Earth with strange powers. Here, Lee and Kirby used two of the biggest and most mysterious concerns of the day—radiation and space exploration—to profitable effect.

The Fantastic Four were a quirky bunch. Reed Richards could stretch his body like a rubber band. His fiancée, Sue Storm, had the gift of invisibility. Her kid brother, Johnny, could turn into a flaming, flying projectile. Pilot Ben Grimm had become enormously strong, but he had also become enormously ugly, like a walking brick wall. *Fantastic Four* was a tremendous hit at the newsstands.

Enlisting Ditko in August 1962, Lee introduced another innovative character in *Amazing Fantasy #15.* A high school science nerd named Peter Parker gets bitten by a radioactive spider and voilà—he is blessed (and cursed) with the powers of an arachnid. *The Amazing Spider-Man* was born, both as a character and as its own comic book.

Keeping It Up

Marvel had hit its stride, launching characters such as the shunned and brawny Incredible Hulk, the high-tech Iron Man, the mysterious Dr. Strange, the blind and acrobatic Daredevil, and the mythic Mighty Thor, among many others. Stan Lee, with Jack Kirby, Steve Ditko, and the rest of the "Marvel Bullpen," had created super-heroes that seemed a bit closer to the ground than previous ones.

Totally Tintin

Anyone serious about graphic novels and comics should get to know Tintin, whose stories broke the genre's mold worldwide.

✳   ✳   ✳   ✳

IN HIS NATIVE Europe he is more popular than Mickey Mouse. In Canada he is as familiar as Superman. Since his first appearance in 1929, his fans have included luminaries such as Madame Chiang Kai-shek and Andy Warhol. French President Charles DeGaulle cited him as his only international rival. More importantly, millions of children throughout the world have grown up avidly following the adventures of Tintin, the 14-year-old reporter; his faithful dog, Snowy (Milou in French); the coarse, hard-drinking, but eminently lovable Captain Haddock; and their colorful collection of enemies and friends.

A Tintin Primer

Tintin, who sports a distinctive slightly-curled spike of blonde hair atop his head and a pair of knickers, was the creation of Belgian artist Hergé (the nom de plume of Georges Prosper Remi), who pioneered the art deco-derived *ligne claire* (clear line) style of drawing that has since influenced several generations of artists.

The Tintin comic series draws its inspiration from the spirit of Jules Verne's fantastical stories as well as *National Geographic's* detail-oriented imagery.

Readers enjoy a cavalcade of exotic locales, subtle humor, captivating technology, political intrigue, plot twists, and plenty of cliff-hanging action. Titles included such tantalizing fare as *The Crab with the Golden Claws*, *Explorers on the Moon*, and, considered by many to be Hergé's masterpiece work, *Tintin in Tibet*.

So, Who Likes Tintin?

Aside from hundreds of millions of fans around the world and a growing number in America, Tintin's friends include director and producer Steven Spielberg, who directed the film, *The Adventures of Tintin: Secret of the Unicorn*. Before Spielberg, however, other directors, including Walt Disney and Roman Polanski were interested in filming the boy reporter's exploits. Spielberg's enormously popular Indiana Jones series of films also drew inspiration from Tintin's tales.

Who Didn't Like Tintin?

Villains: In the course of his adventures, Tintin meets up with plenty of bad guys, including several American capitalists and a character named Musstler, who, as a thinly disguised amalgam of Hitler and Mussolini, led the evil nation of Borduria (an obvious stand-in for Nazi Germany) in 1938's *King Ottokar's Scepter.*

Anti-fascists: At the start of World War II, Hergé, on leave from the Belgian army, fled to Paris ahead of the Nazis but returned to Belgium after King Léopold III appealed to his subjects to return to work. During the occupation, Hergé abandoned political issues in his Tintin books and concentrated entirely upon exotic scenarios intended to entertain a downtrodden populace. After the war, Hergé was briefly imprisoned for working under the occupation. Though quickly released, he was blacklisted for many years.

The American consumer: The 1950s were a tumultuous time for the American comic book industry. Despite being wildly popular with children (or perhaps because of it), comics were viewed by educators as anathema to learning and morally debased. In 1955, comics were banned by the New York Senate panel. Tintin's American debut was carefully orchestrated to present comics in a different light. Even London's *The Times Literary Supplement* had high praise for the books, celebrating the comics as "works of high quality and even beauty... brimming over with intelligence and life." Figuring people would believe a work of beauty would cost more than a lowly comic, the American publisher produced high-quality issues of Tintin at $1.95 each (whereas most comics cost 20 cents). Unaccustomed to the concept of comics as serious literature and deterred by the high price tag, American consumers balked. The first four titles sold a combined 32,000 copies over the 1959 holidays. Meanwhile, Europeans were purchasing about 250,000 Tintin books every week.

The Gold of Little Golden Books

Little Golden Books first hit the literary world in 1942. Back then, the books cost just 25 cents each and were an instant hit—more than 1.5 million copies were printed in their first five months. By the time Little Golden Books celebrated its 60th birthday in 2002, more than two billion of them had found their way to children and their parents. So which are the best and brightest titles? And which are just a little weird? You'll have to read on to find out.

※　※　※　※

The Poky Little Puppy—This remains the best-selling Little Golden Book of all time. The odds are good that you read this book when you were a child; more than 15 million copies of *The Poky Little Puppy* have been sold since the book was first published in September 1942 as part of the original 12 Little Golden Books. The story itself is a classic: A puppy who dawdles on his way home is consistently rewarded despite his meandering ways, getting extra treats such as custard even after he arrives home long after his fellow dogs. But in the end, the puppy's bad habit finally catches up to him: The dog has to go to bed without any strawberry shortcake. Even worse, his fellow puppies fill their stomachs with the treat before they head off to sleep.

The Little Red Hen—This book was also part of the first set of Little Golden Books released in 1942. The story is a classic tale about the benefits of hard work. The hen of the title busies herself making a loaf of bread. But none of her animal friends are willing to help pick the wheat, travel to the mill, or bake the bread. Once the delicious bread is baked, though, the hen has the last laugh. She asks the lazy animals if any of them would like to help her eat the bread. They all volunteer this time, but the hen refuses their help and eats the bread alone with her chicks.

Doctor Dan, The Bandage Man—Many Little Golden Books

have been used to teach children not to be afraid of medical professionals. *Doctor Dan, The Bandage Man* was one of the more unusual. Released in 1951, the book came with Johnson & Johnson Band-Aids glued to the right side of its title page. The book made history as one of the first examples of a joint effort between a corporation and a publishing company. It sold 1.75 million copies in its first printing.

Little Lulu and Her Magic Tricks—This book, released in 1954, had a huge first printing of 2.25 million copies. Part of the appeal was the small package of tissues attached to its front cover. The book explained how children could make toys from the tissues. Lulu even made it on *The Arthur Godfrey Show*, a popular television show, during its first month of release.

Scooby-Doo: The Haunted Carnival—Several top-selling Little Golden Books have featured popular television or cartoon characters. Scooby-Doo is no exception. In 2000, *Scooby-Doo: The Haunted Carnival* ranked as the third best-selling hardcover children's title of the year, according to *Publishers Weekly*.

Seven Little Postmen—Little Golden Books highlighting different professions have always been popular. The books have featured firefighters, police officers, and doctors, of course. But one of the most popular profession-focused books is *Seven Little Postmen*, published in 1952. This popular book tells the tale of how seven hardworking postmen deliver a letter from a little boy to his grandmother.

The Original Dozen

The first 12 Little Golden Books, published in 1942, were:

1. *Three Little Kittens*
2. *Bedtime Stories*
3. *Mother Goose*
4. *Prayers for Little Children*
5. *The Little Red Hen*
6. *The Alphabet A–Z*
7. *Nursery Songs*
8. *The Poky Little Puppy*
9. *The Golden Book of Fairy Tales*
10. *Baby's Book*
11. *The Animals of Farmer Jones*
12. *This Little Piggy*

Lewis Carroll's Little Girls

Maurice Chevalier famously sang "Thank Heaven for Little Girls," but it was Lewis Carroll who got the bad rap.

✳ ✳ ✳ ✳

CHARLES LUTWIDGE DODGSON (1832–98) was the author of *Alice's Adventures in Wonderland*, although he is better known by his pen name of Lewis Carroll. Even though Alice and her fantasyland have become much beloved, Dodgson/Carroll's life and work have been tainted ever since a 1933 article suggested that his fascination with little girls hid a secret pedophilia. The truth of the matter is, of course, somewhat more complicated.

Friendly and Engaging

Dodgson was the son of a country parson, the third of 11 children. Homeschooled, he later held a professor's post in mathematics for more than 25 years at his father's alma mater, Christ Church at Oxford University. He was also a logician, a keen amateur photographer (dating from the inception of the art, circa 1856), and despite his stammer, quite a gregarious fellow. Dodgson was a gifted writer who had short stories published in 1855 and 1856. With an eye toward extra income, he had considered ideas for children's books, including a Christmas book and an instructional manual about marionettes.

In 1856, a new dean, Henry Liddell, arrived at Oxford with his wife and four children: Harry, Ina, Alice, and Edith. Dodgson originally befriended Harry, and later he would take all of the children (with their governess) on picnics and lake outings, where he told them fanciful stories and photographed them. In 1862, after 11-year-old Alice implored him to write down the story with her namesake at its center, Dodgson realized its possible commercial potential and began his masterwork.

Trouble in Paradise

There was, however, a sudden, mysterious break between Dodgson and the Liddell family in June 1863. The Liddells never spoke of it publicly, and the page that related to June 27–29, 1863, which might have shed light on the matter, was cut from Dodgson's diaries. In fact, all of Dodgson's diaries from April 18, 1858, through May 8, 1862, are missing, likely destroyed by his nieces, the heirs to his estate. The estate's executor, Dodgson's brother Wilfred, is also known to have burned quantities of personal papers after Dodgson's death.

The general assumption about the issue is that Mrs. Liddell was concerned about the amount of time Dodgson was spending in the company of little Alice. However, in 1996, after dogged research, Dodgson defender and author Karoline Leach discovered a note thought to have been written by Dodgson's niece Violet, allegedly summarizing the missing diary page. According to the letter, Mrs. Liddell had accused Dodgson of using the children as a cover for wooing their governess—and suggested that perhaps he was interested in the Liddells' eldest daughter, Ina. Ina was tall and well-developed, 14 to Alice's 11; girls were then legally marriageable at 12, and both daughters had already spent far too much time (by the standards of the day) in the company of this adult bachelor. Tongues were probably already wagging. Then again, the authorship of the note is far from certain. Dodgson did pay the family a visit in December 1863, but the friendship would never be rekindled.

Even "curiouser"—as Alice might say—Liddell inexplicably broke college rules to allow Dodgson to stay at Christ Church, where instructors needed to have taken holy orders, despite Dodgson's rejection of the priesthood after a battle with a mysterious psychological torment in the early 1860s (the exact nature of his pain remains a mystery, as well, thanks to the disappeared diaries).

A Figment of the Imagination

Adding to the confusion, although the name "Alice" was borrowed from Liddell, Dodgson stressed that his "Alice" was entirely imaginary. Nor did Sir John Tenniel draw inspiration for his famed illustrations from Dodgson's photographs of Alice. Dodgson's own drawings for the original manuscript (then entitled *Alice's Adventures Under Ground*) bear little resemblance to the real Alice.

While Dodgson's obsession with photographing young Alice certainly seems, at the very least, somewhat kinky to modern minds, it needs to be seen through the lens of the Victorian era, when upper-class children were widely romanticized (while their poorer counterparts were most cruelly used). Dodgson became intrigued by the new art of photography because he saw in it a means to re-create a more innocent time.

The Diaries Did Him In

Dodgson was—according to Leach—effectively thrown to the Freudian wolves by Roger Lancelyn Green, editor of Dodgson's expurgated diaries. (Leach contends that between Green and Dodgson's nieces, more than half of the entries were eliminated.) Leach, in a work prepared in the United Kingdom, accused Green of concealing evidence of Dodgson's sexual interest in adult women in favor of his own Carroll construct, a wistful man-child who was a paragon of Victorian sanctity. "I suspect he had decided, at least on a subconscious level," Leach wrote, "that a soft-focus, gentle, quasi-paedophile 'Carroll' was easier for him to accept than the real, spiky, mysterious and deep Charles Dodgson."

In any case, after the immediate and extraordinary success of *Alice in Wonderland* following its publication in 1865, Dodgson became a very busy man. Even as his wealth and fame grew, he continued to teach at Christ Church until he died. He— or rather, his alter ego Lewis Carroll—published *Through the Looking Glass and What Alice Found There* in 1872; *The Hunting of the Snark* in 1876; and a two-volume novel, *Sylvie and Bruno*, in 1889 and 1893, respectively. He published mathematical papers (as Dodgson) and journeyed throughout Europe and Russia in 1867. During the 1870s, he was an active campaigner against vivisection and became a member of the Society for Psychical Research at its 1882 inception. He died suddenly of severe pneumonia in his Guildford home in January 1898.

As for Alice Liddell, she has become immortal, as generation after generation rediscover the dreamland that Carroll created for her. Charles Dodgson passed away more than a century ago, but Lewis Carroll lives on.

Oxford English Dictionary

One of the English language's most esteemed reference books has links to madness.

✳   ✳   ✳   ✳

THERE'S NO DISPUTING that dictionaries are valuable tools. But did you ever stop to wonder who originally compiled the words in these syllabic storehouses? Certainly, anyone vying to be the authoritative word on, well, words, would need credentials above reproach. Right?

Wrong. The decidedly highbrow *Oxford English Dictionary* (*OED*)—the reference book of note that many turn to when they wish to mimic the King's English—was created in part by a murderer. In fact, this madman was one of the book's most prolific contributors. Who knew?

Inititally called the *New English Dictionary* (*NED*), the compendium was a project initiated by the Philological Society of London in 1857. It was a daunting task by any yardstick. From 1879 (the year real work on the *NED* began) until its 1928 completion, tens of thousands of definitions would be culled from a small army of donors. One of these contributors was Dr. William Chester Minor, a retired American surgeon who had served the Union Army during the Civil War. During his military stint, the surgeon would witness horrible atrocities at the famed Battle of the Wilderness. This experience, along with other horrifying wartime encounters, would inflict emotional scars that would eventually drive the good doctor completely over the brink.

Answering an ad seeking literary contributions, Minor first came to the attention of Professor James Murray, the *NED*'s chief editor from 1879 until his death in 1915. Impressed by the neat, well-researched quotes that Minor had mailed to him, Murray accepted the material for inclusion in the dictionary.

As a sensationalized account of the story goes, after a few such go-rounds, Professor Murray asked the man to meet him in Oxford so they could discuss future work. Each time the editor made the gesture, he was politely rebuffed. This baffled Murray. He knew that Minor was located just 50 miles away at the Broadmoor Criminal Lunatic Asylum and had assumed that he was one of their doctors. Surely the physician could take a brief leave from his duties to discuss the dictionary in person?

But Minor wasn't part of Broadmoor's staff. He was a patient whose grip on reality was tenuous at best. Minor killed a laborer whom he thought meant him harm and was consequently judged insane and permanently confined to the asylum.

Eventually, Minor relented and allowed Murray to meet him at the facility. One can only imagine the editor's shock when he arrived to discover that his prized contributor was a homicidal madman. After allowing the truth to gel, Murray was undeterred. It was obvious that Minor, despite his demons, was meticulous in his research and gifted in his application. It was also obvious that he could use a friend.

Murray would continue to accept Minor's dictionary contributions and visit him regularly until 1910, the year the troubled man was relocated to the United States. In the end, Minor was one of the most prolific contributors to the *NED*. Why had Murray been so keen to accept contributions from a stark, raving madman? As any seasoned editor will tell you, ability is where you find it—and when you find it, you hang on tight. Minor had the stuff, and Murray knew it. And, as it now happens, so do you.

✳ The 1928 version of the *NED*, published under the title *A New English Dictionary on Historical Principles*, contained more than 400,000 words and was divided into ten volumes.

✳ The *New English Dictionary* became the *Oxford English Dictionary* in 1933.

Mad About *MAD* Magazine

For those who know it only by reputation, MAD is a satire magazine that makes fun (of the PG-13 variety) of anyone or anything, from Saddam Hussein to pop culture to the British royal family. It's a thick-skinned reader's hoot and a touchy reader's cerebral hemorrhage.

✳ ✳ ✳ ✳

*M*AD HAS BEEN *MAD* since the early 1950s, but its prehistory extends back to the darkest days of the Great Depression. Its emblem, Alfred E. Neuman, dates back even further.

Contrary to popular belief, iconic publisher William "Bill" Gaines didn't invent *MAD*. His father, Max Gaines, pioneered newsstand comic books in the mid-1930s as cheap, commercially viable amusement for children. Son Bill was an eccentric prankster, the type of kid peers might label "Most Likely to Publish an Iconoclastic Satire Mag." Upon his father's tragic death in 1947, Bill inherited the family comic book business, Educational Comics (EC). He steered EC to stand for Entertaining Comics: a publisher of garish horror comics veering into sardonic social commentary.

In 1952, Bill's early collaborator Harvey Kurtzman proposed a new comic called *MAD*, which would poke fun at just about anything. Kurtzman's brainchild was a success, and in 1955 Bill allowed Kurtzman to convert *MAD* from comic book to magazine. Kurtzman left EC shortly thereafter, but their creation still thrives more than a half century later.

Two Types of *MAD*

✳ As a comic book: #1 (October–November 1952) through #23 (May 1955)

✳ As a magazine: #24 (July 1955) to the present

MAD Mascot Alfred E. Neuman

✳ Motto: "What, me worry?"

✳ First appearance in *MAD*: #21, March 1955

✳ First cover to prominently feature Alfred's face: #30, December 1956

✳ First artist to draw Alfred: Norman Mingo

✳ Ten other artists who have drawn Alfred for the cover: Kelly Freas, Jack Rickard, Jack Davis, Mort Drucker, Mort Kuntzler, Bob Jones, Al Jaffee, Sergio Aragones, Richard Williams

From Cover to Cover

✳ Only president since 1960 *not* to be featured on the cover: Gerald Ford

✳ Pop star with the most cover appearances: Michael Jackson (five appearances in four issues: #251, #277, #420, #438)

✳ Most controversial cover: #166 (April 1974). Featured a hand giving the middle finger. Angry retailers refused to stock it, and the issue was returned by the box load. It is now a rare collector's item.

✳ Only cover drawn by an ape: #38 (March 1958), painted by celebrity chimp J. Fred Muggs.

MAD Magazine and *Star Wars*

✳ Number of covers to feature the *Star Wars* franchise: 9.

✳ Between them, George Lucas and Steven Spielberg have purchased the original art to 11 *MAD* covers featuring their movies.

✳ An attorney for Lucas Films once sent Bill Gaines a threatening letter following a parody of one of the *Star Wars* films.

At the same time, Gaines received a letter from George Lucas praising the same parody. An amused Gaines settled the issue by sending a photocopy of Lucas's letter to the attorney with a note reading: "Take it up with your boss."

✳ Number of *MAD* editors who have worked for Lucas Films: 1 (Jonathan Bresman)

The Real "Spy vs. Spy"

People love a good story involving intrigue and conflict. One enduring tale has run for over 40 years in the form of a much-beloved comic strip called "Spy vs. Spy."

✳ ✳ ✳ ✳

Hidden Meanings

❚❚SPY VS. SPY" was the brainchild of Cuban political cartoonist Antonio Prohias. The artist came up with the idea for the wordless strip during the late 1950s as a means of expressing his political views and to call attention to the rapidly escalating Cold War.

In the strip, two spies—who look identical, except one is all dressed all in black and the other all in white—portray two opposing (though never stated) agendas and constantly attempt to sabotage each other through a series of creative schemes and inventions. Prohias never really informed his readers whom the characters represented, leaving fans free to figure it out for themselves. Occasionally the strip will introduce a third, grey-clad female spy (thus becoming "Spy vs. Spy vs. Spy"), who inevitably becomes the central point of the conflict as the two suitors battle for her affection.

The Man Behind the *MAD* Comic

Prohias began drawing the "Spy vs. Spy" comic shortly after he fled his native Cuba for the United States in 1960. After Cuban dictator Fidel Castro took over the last "free press," Prohias feared that his days were numbered. He spent his days working in a garment sweatshop and drew the strip in his kitchen at night. The wacked-out *MAD* magazine picked up the continuing series; soon Prohias was able to devote all of his time to drawing comics and honing his technique. Still, he was always aware of the comic's origins. In a clever nod to his underground days, he would sign "By Prohias" in Morse code underneath the title: -* * * -* —* —* * -* —.* * * * * * -* * * .

After creating over 500 comics, Prohias relinquished the project to the *MAD* magazine staffers in 1990. He died on February 24, 1998. But his work lives on: Although the Cold War has ended, fans of the strip still continue to enjoy the antics of Prohias's two hapless spies.

Without Question, a Useful Punctuation Mark

What goes at the end of this sentence, and where would we be without it?

✳   ✳   ✳   ✳

PUNCTUATION IS THE bane of many an elementary school student, but reading printed text without it would be a terrible chore. Here, give it a try:

forcenturiesmostwrittenlanguagesusedneitherpunctuation-marksnorspacesbetweenwordsreadingwasatediousinterpretive-affairleftlargelytospecialists

The text above isn't very easy to read without punctuation, is it? Here it is again: For centuries, most written languages used neither punctuation marks nor spaces between words. Reading was a tedious, interpretive affair left largely to specialists. And that was just fine, until Latin was adopted as a common language for scholars and clerics throughout Europe in the first century. The practice of reading and writing boomed, as intellectuals from different countries who spoke different languages could now communicate with each other in written text.

Even then, authors and scribes did not use punctuation of any kind, but people who did public readings of texts began marking them up to indicate pauses, bringing rhythm to their presentations and giving themselves a chance to catch their breath. Readers relied on a variety of marks but generally used them to indicate three things—a brief pause, like the modern comma; a middle pause, like the modern semicolon; and a full pause, like the modern period. In the seventh century, Isidore of Seville expanded on this practice by creating a formal punctuation system that not only indicated pauses but also helped clarify meaning. It was only then that authors began to use punctuation as they wrote.

And what about the question mark? Some say ancient Egyptians created it and that they patterned it after the shape a cat's tail made when the feline was perplexed. It's a cute story, but there's absolutely no truth to it. The question mark debuted in Europe in the ninth century; back then, it took the shape of a dot followed by a squiggly line. The modern version—a sickle shape resting atop a dot—was adopted after the invention of the printing press for the convenience of typesetters.

Origins of Standard Symbols

Removing a colon is pretty serious business—whether you're a surgeon or a copy editor. You use punctuation marks and other symbols on your computer keyboard every day, but have you ever considered their origins?

✳   ✳   ✳   ✳

¶—THE PILCROW IS a typographical character used to indicate a new paragraph. The name may have come from *pylcraft*, a derivation of the word *paragraph*, and the symbol that resembles a backward *P* may have originated as a C for "chapter," or to represent a new train of thought.

!—Usually used to indicate strong feeling, the exclamation mark is a pictographic device believed to have originated in the Roman empire. Its resemblance to a pen over a dot was thought to represent a mark a writer might make when surprised or overjoyed at completing a long writing project.

*—The asterisk gets its name from *astrum*, the Latin word for "star", which the asterisk is also called. It is not an "asterix"— that's the name of the star of a French cartoon. The asterisk was created in feudal times when the printers of family trees needed a symbol to indicate date of birth, which may explain why it's shaped like the branches of a tree.

;—The semicolon was invented by an Italian printer for two main purposes: to bind two sentences that run on in meaning and to act as a "super comma" in a sentence that already contains lots of commas. Excessive use of the semicolon is considered showy by many writers, especially when employed to create long, multisegmented sentences. Author Kurt Vonnegut once said, "Do not use semicolons. All they do is show you've been to college."

?—What is the origin of the question mark? The symbol is generally thought to originate from the Latin *quaestio*, meaning "question," which was abbreviated to *Qo*, with the uppercase *Q* written above the lowercase *o*. The question mark replaces the period at the end of an interrogative sentence. There's a superstition in Hollywood that movies or television shows with a question mark in the title do poorly at the box office. That may explain the mark's absence in the title of the game show *Who Wants to Be a Millionaire*, a program that would not exist without questions!

&—The ampersand, used to replace the word *and*, has been found on ancient Roman sources dating to the 100 A.D. It was formed by joining the letters in *et*, which is Latin for "and." Through the nineteenth century, the ampersand was actually considered the twenty-seventh letter of the English alphabet.

%—The percent sign is the symbol used to indicate a percentage, meaning that the number preceding it is divided by 100. The symbol appeared around 1425 as a representation of the abbreviation of *P cento,* meaning "for a hundred" in Italian.

=—The equal sign is a mathematical symbol used to indicate equality and was invented in 1557 by Welsh mathematician Robert Recorde. In his book *The Whetstone of Witte,* Recorde explains that he invented it "to avoid the tedious repetition of these words: 'is equal to.'" Recorde's invention is commemorated with a plaque in St. Mary's Church in his hometown of Tenby, Wales.

Abbreviation Originations

Abbreviations save time—and we're not talking about the LOLs and OMGs found on the web. Here's a look at how some of our language's most common (and legitimate) abbreviations came to be.

✳   ✳   ✳   ✳

Prescription: Rx

WE MAY UNDERSTAND that *Rx* stands for "prescription," but what do the letters stand for? The abbreviation comes from the Latin term *recipe,* which means to "take" or "receive." The *x,* most accounts indicate, was initially written as a slash on the *R* itself. Of course, some people also swear that the symbol is a derivation of Jupiter's astrological sign, so take your pick.

Pound: lb.

This two-letter statement of weight may look strange to native English speakers, and it's no wonder: This abbreviation is also derived from Latin. The abbreviation *lb.* is actually short for *libra pondo,* a Latin phrase meaning, "a pound by weight." Over time, the phrase was shortened from *libra pondo* to pound. Despite the change, the original two-letter abbreviation stuck.

Missus: Mrs.

Wondering why the abbreviation for *missus* has that mysterious *R* in the middle? It's because it used to stand for something else. *Mrs.* was developed as a bunched-up version of *mistress*, which, back in the old days, didn't used to have the saucy connotation it does now. (It simply meant "wife.") Once again, this is a case of the language evolving, but the abbreviation staying the same.

Baseball Strikeout: K

A little sports history can teach you a lot about *K*, the common abbreviation for a strikeout in the game of baseball. Back in the late 1800s, a strikeout was referred to as having struck. Since the letter *S* was already taken in the box score as shorthand for *sacrifice*, the next logical choice for *struck* was its last letter.

Double Negatives: Not (Necessarily) Ungrammatical

Despite the rallying cries of grammarians to banish the double negative, many people see the construction as a logical and vital part of the English language.

✳   ✳   ✳   ✳

THE GRAMMAR RULES enforced by grade-school teachers can stick in the brain as reflexive laws that must be followed: It is incorrect to start a sentence with "but" or end one with "of"; make sure your subjects and verbs agree; double negatives are illogical, etc. But many matters in grammar are not straightforward, and the double negative is a good example.

Not a Mathematical Matter

The common objection to the double negative goes something like this: Using logic analogous to algebra, two negatives make a positive. Therefore, saying, "I am not unhappy" is logically equivalent to saying, "I'm happy." The problem is that words convey meaning, and in most cases this meaning is not simply negative or positive. The double negative is used in languages worldwide to convey the many nuances between *yes* and *no*.

There are several types of double negatives, and most respected grammar books accept some grudgingly and reject others outright. One kind uses the double negative to express a weak affirmative, or to stealthily affirm something without coming right out and saying it. Referred to as the rhetorical figure litotes, these constructions convey understatement by denying the contrary, and they're often used to avoid an overstrong presentation. Examples include "I don't dislike him" or the aforementioned "I am not unhappy."

Don't Be So Negative!

The double negative that provokes strong negative reactions is the type that uses two or more negatives to convey a nuanced or emphatic negative meaning. Examples include "I'm not going nowhere," "You ain't heard nothing yet," and "We don't need no stinking education." Using the double negative in this way follows consistent rules of grammar, yet this particular usage has fallen out of favor. In this case, words such as *no* and *nothing* serve as the logical equivalents to *any* and *anything*, transforming the previous sentences into "I'm not going anywhere," "You haven't heard anything yet," and "We don't need any stinking education." In most languages, two negatives are preferred to the "negative-plus-any" construction. Yet, according to the "two negatives equals a positive" argument of grammarians, the sentences would translate roughly as "I'm going somewhere," "You've heard something," and "We need a stinking education."

Old and New Opinions

The double negative fell out of favor in the eighteenth century, when English and American academics attempted to create a standardized language that could be used in writing. Although the double negative had long been treasured as a powerful rhetoric device—Erasmus once deemed it "graceful" and "elegant"—many came to see the double negative as either illogical or vulgar; George Orwell felt it should be "laughed out of existence." The double negative of the "don't need no" variety came to be associated with the lower classes and was condemned as illogical. The "not unhappy" variety, which was still used by many in the upper classes, was permitted.

Double negatives in English are alive and thriving today, and according to linguist Jenny Cheshire, "They're used in all the dialects, whether rural or urban, Southern Hemisphere or Northern Hemisphere; they occur in African-American English and in all the English Creoles. It is only in the standard variety of English that double negatives have fallen out of favor." It would probably be a bad idea to use the double negative in a college application essay, but as far as the logic of the double negative is concerned, it's not incorrect to say it's okay.

"Now, correct me if I'm incorrect, but was I not told it's untrue that the people of Springfield have no faith? Was I not misinformed?" —Brother Faith, in *The Simpsons* episode "Faith Off"

Riddles in Rhymes

A 2004 English study found ten times more violence in nursery rhymes than on prime-time television. Just look at what happened to Jack and Jill or Humpty Dumpty: contusions and possible murder. Learn more about the origins of some famous nursery rhymes.

✳ ✳ ✳ ✳

Who Said That?

THE ORIGINS OF many nursery rhymes can be found in historic references, which often had to be subtle because overt ridicule or criticism could have cost the composer his or her life. Some of these include:

✳ "Baa Baa Black Sheep"—A medieval peasant's protest against crippling taxation.

✳ "A Frog He Would Awooing Go"—A derisive objection to the relationship between Queen Elizabeth I and France's

Duc d'Alencon.

* "Jack Horner"—A description of a land swindle perpetrated during the time of King Henry VIII.

* "Wee Willie Winkie"—In its earliest form, this was a tongue-in-cheek dissing of King William III.

Rating the Rhymes

Some nursery rhymes would likely deserve a PG rating today. "Ride a Cock Horse to Banbury Cross" (or Coventry) is said to refer to Lady Godiva's famous ride in the buff. Meanwhile, "Little Jumping Joan" was a brief paean about a celebrated bawd. Other rhymes such as "Goosey Goosey Gander" and "Mary, Mary Quite Contrary" display religious intolerance, while "Tom Tom of Islington" and "Punch and Judy" spotlight spousal abuse.

The most gruesome nursery rhymes may be "Ring Around the Rosy" and "London Bridge." The former makes light of the horrors surrounding the Black Death, as a (rosy) red rash was one of the symptoms of the plague. "London Bridge" alludes to the legend of live children interred in the bridge's foundation to ensure the bridge didn't fall down.

Alvin Schwartz's Terrifying Tales

Peruse any bookstore's Young Adult section or any school library in North America and you'll probably locate at least one of Alvin Schwartz's Scary Stories to Tell in the Dark books. But are they too scary for their own good?

* * * *

Building a Book of Frights

WHEN ALVIN SCHWARTZ was a kid, he liked all kinds of stories, but he had a particular fondness for being spooked. Years later, he began writing to supplement his family's income. The first books he published were lighthearted reads full of folklore, riddles, and poems. But Schwartz knew that all of us—especially kids—love scary stories; as his writing career developed, the first *Scary Stories* book began to take shape.

The yarns Schwartz wrote were aimed at a young-adult audience and were largely based on traditional tales of fear and the unknown. "The Golden Arm" is a classic scary story that even Mark Twain used to tell when he gave public performances. "The Wendigo" is based on a Native American tale. Schwartz also took inspiration from Shakespeare, the Greeks, classic poetry, and folklore from all corners of the world. At the end of each book, Schwartz included pages of notes and source information, though for most of his juvenile readers, this wasn't necessary.

As scary as these early stories were, Schwartz knew that the level of fear could be kicked up a notch, so he went in search of an illustrator.

Author + Illustrator = *AAGGGGHHH!*

Artist Stephen Gammell began his career doing commercial freelance work, but by the 1970s, his interest in illustrating children's books had been piqued. His use of watercolor and other media was unique, and it caught Alvin Schwartz's eye. Gammell wasn't the only artist to work on the first *Scary Stories* book—artists Luis Erique and Daniel Urena contributed as well—but it was Gammell's aesthetic that shaped the truly terrifying images in the *Scary Stories* books that followed.

Haunting, gruesome depictions of oozing ghouls, rotting corpses, and furious witches filled the pages. No one had seen illustrations like these before—certainly not in the Young Adult section of the library. Kids squealed and screamed with a mix of terror and delight when the first *Scary Stories to Tell in the Dark* was published in 1981. But not everyone was happy.

How Scary Is Too Scary?

As more and more kids brought home *Scary Stories to Tell in the Dark,* more and more parents raised an eyebrow. Plenty of people thought that the books were great; after all, kids were reading, talking about what they were reading, and using their imaginations. But some of the tales and accompanying images were causing problems. *The New York Times* said that the stories were "the stuff nightmares are made of," and, sure enough, plenty of kids were having frightening dreams after reading them.

Some parents, teachers, and child advocacy groups demanded that the books be removed from school libraries, stating that occult overtones could be found in the stories. Some went so far as to say that the books were satanic in tone, while others argued that the themes were simply too dark for children. Either way, the books disappeared from library shelves in many areas of the country. However, the popularity of what Schwartz and the artists had created couldn't be denied: *More Scary Stories to Tell in the Dark* was released in 1984 and *Scary Stories 3: More Tales to Chill Your Bones* followed in 1991. Still, the American Library Association reports that for more than 20 years now, Schwartz's *Scary Stories* books have been among the most challenged titles in libraries across the country.

In 2010, a tamer version of *Scary Stories* was released; it featured illustrations by Brett Helquist that were deemed more "kid-friendly." We'll never know how Schwartz feels about this watered-down version of his collection—he passed away in 1992 at age 64.

Russian Revelation

Karl Marx was a philosopher, political thinker, and the father of communism. But he was not Russian. In fact, he was never known to set foot in the country whose history he would so indelibly influence.

✳ ✳ ✳ ✳

K ARL MARX WAS born a Jew in Germany, but his father had the family convert to Christianity so he could keep his job as a lawyer. As an adult, however, Marx maintained no religious beliefs, famously saying, "Religion is the opium of the people" (frequently misquoted as "Religion is the opiate of the masses"). At the age of 25, Marx left Germany for Paris, where he met his lifelong collaborator, Friedrich Engels. Just a year later, he was expelled from the French capital. He lived in Brussels for three years before finally settling in London, where he lived until his death on March 14, 1883.

In 1848, Marx penned *The Communist Manifesto* with the opening line, "The history of all hitherto existing society is the history of class struggles." The first volume of his most famous work, *Das Kapital*, was published in 1867, but Marx lived much of his life in poverty and relative obscurity. He even supplemented his income during the 1850s by serving as a foreign correspondent for the *New York Herald Tribune*.

Marx's Influence

Marx believed that wealth should be distributed "from each according to his abilities, to each according to his needs" and that communism was the inevitable next evolutionary step after capitalism. More than three decades after his death, these ideas formed the basis of the 1917 Bolshevik Revolution in Russia. A wave of communism followed, and in the early 1980s, at its peak, almost one-third of the world's population lived under communist rule. However, these oppressive regimes have badly misrepresented much of Marx's philosophy.

Lost Sources of the Bible

When the biblical authors sat down to write their books, what did they have to go on? Did they rely solely on memory? Or did they refer to earlier writings as modern historians do? The Bible itself tells us that the authors of the historical books of the Old Testament did indeed rely on earlier sources. Some of them are even named in the Bible itself, though sadly they are now lost.

✳   ✳   ✳   ✳

M ANY OF THE stories in the Old Testament books, especially those covering the time before King David, were probably passed along verbally from generation to generation by professional storytellers. Most of the material was transmitted in the form of simple prose tales, but often major historical events were immortalized in poetry. Both prose and verse accounts were later incorporated into the Bible—and occasionally the Bible refers to these sources by title.

Royal Records

When David established his capital in Jerusalem, he championed literacy and began keeping court records. Along with statistics and inventories, these records included annals or chronicles of what was done by the individual kings from David on. The annals provided an invaluable source for the authors of 1 and 2 Kings and Nehemiah, who cite them. Because the biblical authors were concerned with examining the relationship that existed between Yahweh and the king, they often left out material that would ordinarily be included in a history. To compensate for what was missing, the authors of these books often end their accounts of a king by stating that other (secular) information on that ruler can be found in the book of the Acts of Solomon (1 Kings 11:41) or, more frequently, in the annals of the Kings of Israel or Judah. For example, 1 Kings 14:19 reads: "Now the rest of the acts of Jeroboam, how he warred and how he reigned, are written in the Book of the Annals of the Kings of Israel." Because of these references, we know the biblical authors consulted the court records, undoubtedly using them as research materials.

The author of the books of Chronicles used the books of Samuel and Kings to retell and update Israel's history— although he seems to have used a different version of those books than the one in the Bible today. The chronicler also cites the court records plus accounts of the words and actions of various prophets. Finally, in 2 Chronicles 24:27, he cites the commentary on the Book of the Kings. Even though its title suggests an interpretive volume, this otherwise unknown book may be the court records under another name.

Early Poetry

Two poetic works constitute the most interesting of all the cited source material in the Old Testament. The first of these is either a long poem or a collection of poems about the wars fought by the Israelites when they took possession of the Promised Land of Canaan. Numbers 21:14–15 cites two lines from the poem and identifies the verses as coming from the book of the *Wars of the Lord*. The archaic nature of the language in the cited passage suggests that the poem may have originated around the time of the war. Although they are difficult to translate, the verses seem to describe Yahweh as he leads the Israelite warriors into battle against the Canaanites.

The other poetic source is the book of Jashar, which is first cited in Joshua 10:12–13 as the source of Joshua's prayer for the sun to stand still long enough for him to win the battle at Gibeon. After giving the text of the short poem, the author asks: "Is this not written in the Book of Jashar?" In 2 Samuel 1:18 the book of Jashar is again given as a source—for David's lament over the deaths of Saul and Jonathan, which contains the refrain, "How the mighty have fallen!" The rest of the book of Jashar is lost to us, but if the other poems in the book were of as high quality as the two we have, the loss is great indeed.

A Monstrous Myth!

Frankenstein's monster is usually portrayed as a shambling, dumb brute who growls and terrorizes fearful villagers. But that's an entirely inaccurate representation.

❋ ❋ ❋ ❋

RANKENSTEIN'S MONSTER IS one of the best-known fictional fiends ever created. But in the 1818 novel *Frankenstein,* by Mary Wollstonecraft Shelley, the monster is at first gentle, almost childlike—and much more eloquent than the beast played by Boris Karloff in the 1931 movie of the same name.

Indeed, Victor Frankenstein's creation is initially an object of pity who is given life and then abandoned and disavowed by his horrified creator. Uncertain who or what he is, he wanders the countryside and eventually learns to speak by spying on a peasant family as they try to teach English to a relative. And he learns to speak remarkably well!

A Monster by Any Other Name...

In chapter 11, for example, the creature (who is never given a name but is alternately referred to as a fiend, demon, wretch, zombie, devil, and ogre) describes for Victor Frankenstein his recollections of his own birth: "It is with considerable difficulty that I remember the original era of my being. All the events of that period appear confused and indistinct. A strange multiplicity of sensation seized me, and I saw, felt, heard, and smelt at the same time and it was, indeed, a long time before I learned to distinguish between the operations of my various senses..." He's definitely a monster who has a way with words.

Of Stage and Screen

Interestingly, the novel, which Shelley wrote when she was a teenager, was an instant hit that resulted in numerous adaptations for the stage. *Presumption; or the Fate of Frankenstein* premiered in London in 1823, just five years after the book's initial publication. The first movie version was a ten-minute short produced in 1910 by Thomas Edison's film company. It starred Charles Ogle as the pitiful monster and was long listed by the American Film Institute as one of the "most culturally and historically significant lost films."

The 1931 Universal Studios version—undoubtedly the best known to moviegoers—was based more on a 1927 theatrical adaptation by Peggy Webling than on Mary Shelley's book. Almost all subsequent film versions continued to portray the monster as an inarticulate brute. Only a handful have made an attempt to stay true to the novel in portraying the creature as intelligent and sensitive.

Curious Adaptations

Over the years, the story of Frankenstein's mad science project has been the source material for hundreds of movies. The monster duked it out with a werewolf in *Frankenstein Meets the Wolfman* (1943), yukked it up with comedians in *Abbott and Costello Meet Frankenstein* (1948), and even encountered cartoon varmints in *Alvin and the Chipmunks Meet Frankenstein* (1999). Peter Boyle played the creature for laughs in Mel Brooks's *Young Frankenstein* (1974), which was later adapted into a successful Broadway play.

Although Boris Karloff's portrayal of Frankenstein's monster is considered a cinematic classic, the character suffered mightily in a slew of less prestigious productions. In the 1965 Japanese monster epic *Frankenstein Conquers the World*, for example, the creature's heart is transplanted in a young Japanese boy who then grows to 20 feet tall and battles a huge prehistoric monster. Other awkward adaptations include *I Was a Teenage Frankenstein* (1957), *Frankenstein Meets the Space Monster* (1965), *Jesse James Meets Frankenstein's Daughter* (1966), and *Blackenstein* (1973).

Turning the Page

Frankenstein's monster has become an ubiquitous feature in American popular culture. But if you want to enjoy the story in its purest form, read Shelley's novel. You'll find it a less horrific experience than many of the aforementioned movies.

The Vagabond Beat Generation

A group of artists, poets, and writers became the first generation of postwar nonconformists to influence those that came after them.

✳   ✳   ✳   ✳

THE "BEAT GENERATION" is the name given to a generation of poets, writers, artists, and activists during the 1940s and 1950s. The name originated in 1948 when Jack Kerouac, the most famous novelist among the Beats, told a magazine interviewer that his generation was "beat, man." Kerouac later said "beat" was short for "beatific."

Kerouac's novel *On the Road* (written in 1951 but published in 1957) became the Beat Generation's defining document. It was a thinly disguised autobiographical novel with many references to Kerouac's friends and fellow writers and poets Allen Ginsberg, William Burroughs, Gregory Corso, and Gary Snyder. According to some sources, Kerouac, to preserve his spontaneity, typed *On the Road* on a long roll of telegraph paper in one "take" with no corrections. His editor supposedly pleaded with him, "Jack, even Shakespeare made corrections— and Jack, you ain't Shakespeare!" The novel's central character, Dean Moriarty, was based on Neal Cassady, who didn't write much himself but became an avatar of the free life for his writer friends. Cassady wound up as the driver of author Ken Kesey's famous painted bus, "Further," during the 1960s.

The Beats' two other significant works were Ginsberg's long poem "Howl" (1956), which chronicled the adventures and misadventures of the same circle, and Burroughs's novel *Naked Lunch*, written in hallucinatory prose and banned for obscenity in several states for a time. Experiences chronicled by the Beats included drug use, free sex, homosexuality, crime, and stints in mental institutions and prison.

The Beats held San Francisco and New York in high regard. The Beat phenomenon coincided with the 1950's "San Francisco Renaissance" of poetry and art. San Francisco Beat poet Lawrence Ferlinghetti opened his famous bookstore and publishing company, City Lights, in 1953. Ferlinghetti was prosecuted for publishing "Howl" in a landmark obscenity trial. Ferlinghetti's partner, Peter Martin (who left after two years), named the bookstore after Charlie Chaplin's film. It was the first all-paperback bookstore in the United States. Kenneth Rexroth, a slightly older San Francisco poet and cultural critic, was close to many Beats. He lived a similarly unconventional life, wrote about the Beats, and promoted them on a radio show he hosted in San Francisco.

Despite its nonconformity, the Beat Generation became a cultural phenomenon. By the late 1950s, the stereotype of the bearded, turtlenecked, beret-wearing, "beatnik" (and the black-leotard-and-sandal-wearing, unsmiling "beat chick") became ensconced in popular culture. In a letter to *The New York Times*, Ginsberg complained, "If beatniks and not illuminated Beat poets overrun this country, they will have been created not by Kerouac but by industries of mass communication which continue to brainwash man." Hollywood producer Albert Zugsmith actually copyrighted the term "Beat Generation" in order to make his 1959 film *The Beat Generation*, which was derided by many as a campy exploitation flick.

Heart of the Beat Generation: The Death of Joan Vollmer

The accidental death of Joan Vollmer, wife of writer William S. Burroughs, proved to be the catalyst of a literary movement.

✳ ✳ ✳ ✳

The Beginnings of Beat

WHEN WRITERS JACK Kerouac, Allen Ginsberg, and William S. Burroughs first became friends in New York in the 1940s, they used to meet at an apartment on the upper west side of Manhattan, the home of Joan Vollmer and Edie Parker. Vollmer was a brilliant student at Barnard, an attractive woman in her early 20s, and well versed in philosophy and literature.

Vollmer also hosted amphetamine-fueled parties at the apartment and nurtured the literary revolution that became known as the Beat Generation. Her roommate, Edie Parker, was briefly married to Kerouac. Meanwhile, Vollmer became the common-law wife of the predominantly homosexual William Burroughs.

Benzedrine and Tequila Cocktails

By 1951, Vollmer and Burroughs were living in Mexico City with their young son and Vollmer's daughter from a previous marriage. Burroughs had left the United States to escape marijuana possession charges. It didn't help matters that both he and Vollmer had huge drug appetites. Vollmer was hooked on the amphetamine Benzedrine and consumed a copious amount of tequila every day. She was also suffering from a recurrence of childhood polio. The cumulative effect left her with swollen features, hair that was falling out, and a profound limp when she walked. At age 27, Vollmer's physical appearance was a long way from that of the bright young beauty who first acted as muse for some of the most gifted American writers of the twentieth century.

On September 6, Vollmer's life tragically ended in what many believe was a drunken attempt to replicate the feat of William Tell, the legendary bowman who shot an apple from the top of his son's head. Vollmer and Burroughs were at a party where plenty of drugs and alcohol were being passed around. There, an allegedly drunk Vollmer agreed to allow an equally drunk Burroughs to place a glass on the top of her head and let him shoot it off with a .38 caliber handgun. Unlike Tell, Burroughs was not successful: He missed and the bullet pierced his young wife's forehead. Vollmer died at the Red Cross Hospital in Colonia Roma.

Burroughs was arrested and charged with homicide. He allegedly admitted to police that he was attempting to shoot the glass off Vollmer's head, but later, after conferring with his lawyer, claimed that the gun had accidentally gone off. In a 1965 interview with *The Paris Review*, Burroughs said, "I had a revolver that I was planning to sell to a friend. I was checking it over and it went off—killed her." He also called the William Tell rumor "absurd and false."

The Mexican judge agreed and ruled the shooting an accident. Having served just 13 days in jail, Burroughs was freed.

Joan Vollmer's Legacy

Whether it was merely an accident or a ridiculous drug-fueled stunt gone wrong, the death of Vollmer proved a pivotal moment in both the life of Burroughs and in the history of American literature. During his trial, Burroughs began to write his first novel, *Junkie*. By 1958, he had written the wildly imaginative *Naked Lunch*, a book that in 2005 *TIME* magazine listed as one of the best 100 English language novels written since 1923. Perhaps if Vollmer hadn't died, Burroughs might never have written it. "I am forced to the appalling conclusion," he wrote in the introduction to his book *Queer*, "that I would never have become a writer but for Joan's death."

Vollmer's death similarly influenced Allen Ginsberg, who wrote his most famous poem, *Howl*, after dreaming about his deceased friend. Jack Kerouac also drew upon Joan and her Benzedrine addiction to write passages of his 1957 classic novel, *On the Road*.

T. S. Eliot's *The Waste Land*

Genuine poetry can communicate before it is understood.

—T. S. ELIOT

Thomas Stearns Eliot was born in 1888 to a wealthy St. Louis, Missouri, family. He attended Harvard University and eventually settled in England, where he studied philosophy and literature. Eliot has often been described as an unusually intellectual poet, an epithet that is particularly suited—Eliot studied Latin, Greek, French, German, and Sanskrit; he was an expert on the religions and cultures of the world; and he was a philosopher and literary critic extraordinaire. Yes, that all sounds pretty intellectual. In fact, Eliot's intimidating mind may help to explain why his works often received a frigid reception from literary critics.

European Classicism via American Poet

On the other hand, perhaps people were simply perplexed by what some have perceived to have been Eliot's identity cries. In 1927, Eliot officially converted to English Anglicanism and dropped his American citizenship to become a British subject. In 1928, he described himself as a "classicist in literature, royalist in politics, and Anglo-Catholic in religion."

Universality via Specificity

Eliot may have transformed himself from a rugged American into a cross-bearing, king-hailing Brit, but through poetry he sought to express the universal beauty and tragedy of the human condition. He did this by way of intentional confusion, contradiction, irony, and obscurity. If this seems paradoxical, take heart, and read on.

Eliot's most famous poem, *The Waste Land,* is a perfect example of his delicious illusiveness. It's dense and difficult to understand. The five-part, 433-line poem was written between 1919 and 1922. Most of it was composed in Switzerland, where Eliot was "resting" after a nervous breakdown.

The poem is traditionally analyzed as an ode to the disillusionment that followed World War I. Indeed, much of *The Waste Land* contrasts the chaos and physical ugliness of modernity with the beauty and principled glory of the classical and medieval past. The poem alludes to or directly quotes such antiquated figures as Homer, Virgil, Ovid, and Dante, as well as such modern figures as Joseph Conrad, Aldous Huxley, and Walt Whitman. But the analysis of the poem as an affirmation of modern hopelessness is disputed by many scholars.

Despite the poem's references to specific people and ideas, Eliot never intended a direct relationship between signified and signifier. Rather, he hoped to use his labyrinth of layered language to evoke a feeling that is greater than the sum of his words. *The Waste Land* was not a straightforward slogan for the disillusionment of a generation. Eliot once quipped, "I may have expressed for them their own illusion of being disillusioned, but that did not form part of my intention."

Clarity via Ambiguity

So, if *The Waste Land* resists its classical interpretations, then what exactly is it about? It turns out that this question may not have an answer. Frustrated critics have accused Eliot of intentionally creating an impenetrable poem. Eliot did include notes at the end of the poem to explain his bottomless grab bag of allusions, quotes, and references. Yet, he slyly neglected to footnote many allusions, and in some cases made his explanatory notes more confusing than the citation they were meant to elucidate.

Eliot saw poetry as a tool that could partially uncover the true order of the universe. But he also knew that words are imperfect. In *The Waste Land*, Eliot resorted to surface contradiction, unexpected changes in voice, jumps in time, intentionally misplaced satire, shifts into foreign languages, and half-understood allusion, believing that these devices were ironically the only way one could achieve poetic depth and clarity. Avid fans of *The Waste Land* profess that even if they don't quite get the poem in its entirety, they value the strong feelings that its words conjure. The intent of *The Waste Land* is best described by the author himself, who once famously stated, "Poetry may make us from time to time a little more aware of the deeper, unnamed feelings which form the substratum of our being, to which we rarely penetrate."

Inspire Me

To the Lighthouse

Virginia Woolf's modernist masterpiece *To the Lighthouse* was certainly inspired by a vast ocean of influences. But the primary influence behind the novel's second part, entitled "Time Passes," was good old-fashioned competition—literati style.

Woolf belonged to a wildly talented but intellectually snobbish group of English modernist writers, which included James Joyce, Katherine Mansfield, D. H. Lawrence, and E. M. Forster, all of whom sought to stretch language to its limits by representing reality as it is really experienced. One of the hallmarks of modernist literature is a technique called disjointed time. Time, as humans experience it, is illogical. Sometimes a single moment feels like a lifetime, while several years seem to pass in the blink of an eye. How can a writer use language to accurately capture this peculiarity of the human experience?

Virginia Woolf's diaries reveal that she was in competition with other modernists to depict the experience of time. Mansfield often experimented with time, and Woolf deemed her "the only writer I have ever been jealous of." Woolf was determined to take up the ultimate challenge: To represent the passage of time in the absence of humans. While other modernist writers succeeded in highlighting the paradoxical lengthiness of short periods of time—James Joyce's epic novel *Ulysses* takes place during a single day—Woolf sought to alternate the human experience of time with time as it really passes. Woolf once wrote, "The real novelist can somehow convey both sorts of being . . . I have never been able to do both."

But eventually she succeeded. *To the Lighthouse* is composed of three sections. The first covers one day in the life of a family. The third covers another day in the life of the same family. But the second section, "Time Passes," represents the ten years that elapse between these two days. The section takes place inside a house that gradually decays in the absence of its previous inhabitants. There is no plot or action in the traditional sense. Yet the section is unexpectedly beautiful and captivating. Only by contrasting "human time" with "real time" could Woolf successfully reveal the magnificence and strangeness of time as we know it. Or, in the words of Woolf herself: "Suddenly one hears a clock tick. We who had been immersed in this world became aware of another. It is painful."

Star-Crossed Lovers: Sylvia Plath and Ted Hughes

An icon to troubled teenage girls everywhere, poet Sylvia Plath killed herself and became immortal.

✳   ✳   ✳   ✳

S HE WAS A young American studying at England's Cambridge University on a Fulbright scholarship. He was an aspiring poet from a remote British mining town who had variously worked as a zoo attendant, a night guard, and a gardener. When they first met at a party in 1956, she bit so deeply into his cheek that she drew blood; he tore off her headband to ensure that they would meet again. They wed four months

later, and that union—or rather, its shocking denouement—
has been a fixture of gossip and literature ever since.

The Players

She was Sylvia Plath; he, Ted Hughes. They ultimately had two
children (a girl born in 1960, a boy in 1962) during a tempestuous marriage that ended circa 1962, after he left her for
Assia Wevill, a married family friend. But Wevill was more of a
symptom than a cause.

When Hughes's book *The Hawk in the Rain* was published
shortly after his marriage to Plath, he was hailed as one of the
most important poets of his generation. Plath had been a pre-
cocious poet herself, first published at age 8, and much praised
at Smith College. At the time of her marriage, however, her
work was not gaining recognition, despite manic bursts in the
wee hours that could produce two or three poems at a time. On
top of professional angst, Plath suffered through raging argu-
ments, crying babies, and Hughes's infidelity.

Plath's Final Statement

On February 11, 1963, 30-year-old Plath put milk and bread
at her children's bedsides. She sealed her flat's kitchen with wet
rags, put her head into the oven upon a neatly folded cloth,
and turned on the gas. With this action, Plath became forever
enshrined in the pantheon of brilliant-but-victimized women.
It was a drastic final solution seen as a fabulous career move
by Plath's contemporary, poet Anne Sexton: "That death was
mine." As Sexton foresaw, Plath was celebrated as an unsung
heroine by the burgeoning women's liberation movement,
despite her delight in household chores such as washing and
ironing (mundane domestic acts she deemed "celestial" in letters to her mother) and her willing subjugation to a "genius"
husband, which made her feel "very feminine and admiring."
Nonetheless, Plath came to be viewed by many young women
as a proto-feminist who had hoped in vain to have it all: an
adoring husband, marvelous children, and a glamorous career.

Acclaim Too Late

Some of Plath's final poems appeared in the American magazine *Encounter* to great acclaim eight months after her death. Her poetry was also splashed across *Time* magazine, and her slightly fictionalized autobiography-as-novel, *The Bell Jar*—which among other things described her shock treatment for depression and a previous suicide attempt—caused a sensation when published in the United States in 1971 (it had been released under a pseudonym in England a month before her death). Plath's collected works, edited by Hughes, won her a posthumous Pulitzer Prize and helped make her one of the world's best-selling female poets.

But as the executor of Plath's estate, Hughes exercised what some saw as a jealous control over his late wife's writings, and he was even suspected of doctoring them as he saw fit. That he claimed to have destroyed some of her journal material (because, reportedly, it might hurt the children's feelings) was proof to many of his complicity in his wife's death. Hughes's bad reputation became writ in stone in 1969 when Wevill duplicated Plath's suicide-by-oven, taking their four-year-old daughter, Shura, with her. Yet Hughes declined to defend himself, even as crowds jeered him as a killer, and Plath's Yorkshire grave perpetually had his name chipped off by her angry fans. However, ongoing resentment toward Hughes failed to prevent his 1984 appointment to the esteemed post of Britain's Poet Laureate.

Another Point of View

Hughes finally told his side of the story in the 1998 book *Birthday Letters*, which was mostly written in the form of letters to Plath on each of her birthdays since her suicide. He claimed that she would push him away only to plead for his return, in a seemingly endless cycle of rejection and need. Worse, nothing he did was ever enough to exorcise the ghost of Plath's father, who died when Sylvia was only ten (this has the ring of truth, as Plath's most famous poem is the furious "Daddy"). As one of Hughes's friends summed up: "Long before he walked out of the house to be with someone else, it was already pretty clear that Plath had left him for her father," adding that Hughes had been at least as much a victim as Plath ever was. "His story has dovetailed with a particular moment in feminist thinking, a surge of political correctness and the tendency of people to read poems as life transcripts ... [The book] makes you feel that he never stopped loving her."

The case for rehabilitating Hughes's battered image was also helped by recent critical reappraisals of the situation. A professor and biographer of both Anne Sexton and Plath declared that "depression [had] killed" the latter, while another pundit announced that "the very source of Sylvia Plath's creative energy was her self-destructiveness." Even Plath's own mother sadly wrote: "Her physical energies had been depleted by illness, anxiety and overwork ... some darker day than usual had temporarily made it seem impossible to pursue." Indeed, until recently, no one seems to have considered postpartum depression as a factor; after all, Plath's son was scarcely more than a year old at the time of her death.

As for Hughes, although he may have found a measure of contentment in a second marriage while ushering his children by Plath into adulthood, any sympathy that may have been engendered by *Birthday Letters* came too little, too late: Almost simultaneously with its publication, Hughes died at age 68.

No Regrets: The Life of American Poet Hart Crane

I am not ready for repentance;
Nor to match regrets. For the moth
Bends no more than the still
Imploring flame.

✳ ✳ ✳ ✳

A T FIRST GLANCE, the opening words of "Legend"—an early poem by Hart Crane—could almost be read as a challenge. Review the lines again, and the sadness that permeates them offers a glimpse into the troubled psyche of a young man who apparently felt more than just a little out of step with the rest of the world. In some ways, they might almost be considered the suicide note he never left when, at age 32, he leaped from the deck of a steamship into the Gulf of Mexico.

Although he died young, Crane succeeded in his life's goal of being remembered as a poet. While the amount of work he produced may have been small in comparison to others, students of American literature have expressed new interest in both his life and his writing in recent years—in Crane's case, the two were virtually inseparable. While every artist's work is influenced by his lifestyle, in many respects Hart Crane seemed to embody both the best and the worst aspects of his generation.

Understanding the Man

Harold Hart Crane was born on July 21, 1899, in the village of Garrettsville, Ohio, a tiny 2.5-square-mile town that today is home to a little more than 2,000 residents. His love of words was evident at an early age, but his father, a successful businessman, tried to turn Hart's attention toward more practical matters. When he wasn't focused on trying to change his son, the elder Crane was busy fighting with his wife, a devout Christian Scientist. As a result, Crane spent much of his childhood at his grandparents' home in Cleveland.

The aspiring writer discovered at an early age that he was homosexual—not something readily accepted by the world at that time. Crane felt that this was just another aspect of his personality that set him apart. Although he tried to comply with his father's wishes to fit in, after his parents divorced in 1916, he dropped out of school and fled to New York. Still determined to be a poet, Crane devoured the work of other wordsmiths in an effort to learn his craft. Although he lived in a garret and was forced to sell ads for poetry magazines to support himself, he knew that he was among kindred spirits. He spent every spare moment at the home of Margaret Anderson, founder and editor of *The Little Review*, who first recognized the talent of Ezra Pound and Robert Frost.

Testing the Waters

Crane grew discouraged when his own work went unappreciated—and climbed aboard an emotional roller coaster that he rode for the rest of his short life. He returned to Cleveland in 1922, where he spent his days writing advertising slogans. In his spare time, he wrote "My Grandmother's Love Letters," a charming poem that was soon accepted by a literary magazine. Encouraged, Crane returned to New York, where he relied on the generosity of friends, including playwright Eugene O'Neill and photographer Walker Evans, for necessities such as food and rent. Finally free of mundane concerns, he focused on his work. A year later, Crane completed "For the Marriage of Faustus and Helen," his first major poem.

Unlike some of his contemporaries who were breaking away from traditional forms, Crane didn't use free verse. He modeled his work on that composed by classic authors such as John Donne and modern poets such as Walt Whitman. His stanzas were rich with obscure imagery that at the same time evoked a sense of immediacy. Although the average reader may not have always been able to easily understand him, Crane was seeking new ways to use formal language to describe the frenetic fury of the Jazz Age.

Building a Reputation

Crane moved into a boardinghouse overlooking the Brooklyn Bridge, a view that would become as much an inspiration for him as it had for so many other artists and writers. His work started to appear in significant literary magazines, and he attracted a small audience that seemed to appreciate his poems. Although his personal life seemed filled with a growing sense of alienation, he was attempting to create a landscape of hope with his words. He played the role of social outcast to the hilt, however—besides flaunting his sexuality, he was frequently drunk and violent and was sometimes beaten up by the partners he chose for one-night stands.

His first volume of poems, *White Buildings*, was published in 1926. It contained some of his best work, including erotic poems that he collectively titled *Voyages*. This success convinced Crane that it was time for him to follow in Whitman's footsteps by creating an epic poem about American life, using the Brooklyn Bridge as his focal point. Published in 1930, *The Bridge* was not well received, and that sent Crane into another downward emotional spiral. His drinking grew worse, and he spent his nights prowling waterfront bars trying to pick up men.

In an effort to escape his demons, Crane began to travel. After receiving a Guggenheim Fellowship in 1931, he went to Mexico, where he had an affair—reputedly his first heterosexual affair—with Peggy Cowley, the wife of his friend, Malcolm Cowley.

The End Comes

Crane's voice was stilled a short time later when, just before noon on April 27, 1932, he threw himself off of the steamship carrying him back to New York from Mexico. Since his body vanished beneath the waves and was never recovered, his life is commemorated by a marker on his father's tombstone in Garrettsville that reads simply "Harold Hart Crane 1899–1932 Lost at Sea," and by a handful of poems, which proclaim that Crane lived by his own standards.

Machiavelli, the Party Guy

It turns out that sixteenth-century philosopher Niccolò Machiavelli was much more interested in having fun than in gaining power through treachery.

✳ ✳ ✳ ✳

Powerful or Playful?

BASED ON MACHIAVELLI's name alone, you might expect that he was quite an unpleasant person. After all, the term "Machiavellian" is often used to describe craftiness and deceit. The philosopher's most famous work, *The Prince*—a guidebook on achieving and maintaining power—justifies evil as a means to an end and advises leaders that cruelty will get them further than love. In it he writes, "It must be understood that a prince ... cannot observe all of those vitues for which men are reputed good, because it is often necessary to act against mercy, against faith, against humanity, against frankness, against religion, in order to preserve the state."

It is then understandable that one would assume that Machiavelli himself was ruthless and power-hungry. In fact, this was not the case. He was generous, witty, and always ready to play a practical joke. Machiavelli was, by all accounts, the life of the party.

Man of Many Talents

A contemporary of Leonardo da Vinci, Machiavelli was a true Renaissance man, living his life through the political turmoil of Florence in the early 1500s. He was a painter, engineer, diplomat, playwright, philosopher, and poet. In his day, he was not known for his political treatises. Instead, his lighthearted songs and bawdy plays were his claim to fame. *La Mandragola* (The Mandrake), a raunchy comedy that made fun of (among other things) the clergy, had plenty of off-color humor and was one of his biggest hits. True to character, Machiavelli wrote the play while in exile for allegedly plotting against Medici.

Social Butterfly

Between his work as a diplomat, which sent him all over Europe, and his engineering endeavors (he collaborated with da Vinci on a failed attempt to divert the Arno River), Machiavelli somehow managed to find time to relax. He spent most of his evenings with friends in the taverns and alleys of Florence, gambling, drinking, and telling stories. He is known to have fallen in love twice (neither time with his wife) and was a regular customer of the city's brothels. His intellectual stimulation seemed to come from a group that he called his "noontime friends," a collection of writers, poets, and scholars of some repute. Although they most certainly discussed weighty issues of philosophy, it appears that they also spent a good deal of time drinking and making up carnival songs.

Blame *The Prince*

The Prince, which Machiavelli wrote to gain the favor of the ruling Medici family, was poorly received and was not even published during his lifetime. Twenty-five years after its publication, the Catholic Church banned it because of its perceived anti-Christian sentiments. The ban greatly contributed to its author's increasing unpopularity. Soon, the caricature of Machiavelli as evil incarnate began to take hold. It is said that Shakespeare based many of his most villainous characters on Machiavellian traits. Machiavelli's reputation has not been helped by the fact that some of history's most diabolical figures were fans of his work. Hitler, Napoleon, and even organized crime figure John Gotti are said to have studied it. Full of contradictions, and controversial to this day, Machiavelli's political writings seem to have something for everyone. Feminists, communists, and Christians have all found positive aspects in his work.

A Pleasing Personality

Machiavelli spent his lifetime aspiring to please, courting the favor of whomever was in charge of Florence at the time (and landing in exile or even the torture chamber when he happened to end up on the wrong side). Through all of this, poetry interested him much more than politics. He remained lighthearted even on his deathbed, where it is said he entertained his friends by telling jokes.

Samuel Clemens's Psychic Dream

One night in the late 1850s, Samuel Clemens—better known as Mark Twain—woke up clutching the sheets on his bed; his palms were sweaty and his heart was pounding. It had been so real, he thought ... so vivid. Had it really been just a dream, or did it actually happen? And if it was indeed a dream, it was more like a nightmare.

✻   ✻   ✻   ✻

IN THE LATE 1850s—before he was world-renowned author and humorist Mark Twain—Samuel Clemens worked as an apprentice riverboat pilot on the *Pennsylvania*. His younger brother Henry also worked on the vessel as a "mud clerk"—a hard and dreary job that was barely one step above indentured servitude. But Henry stuck with it, perhaps enticed by the possibility of a promotion to a superior position on the steamboat.

While the ship was docked in St. Louis, Samuel stayed with his sister and brother-in-law, who lived in town, and Henry would often drop by to visit before returning to his shipboard duties. In May 1858, Henry was unusually solemn as he prepared to return to the *Pennsylvania*; it was not like him to be so somber.

Did That Really Just Happen?

That night, Samuel saw images in a dream that was frighteningly realistic. He saw Henry lying in a coffin that was balanced on two chairs in the sitting room of their sister's house. Henry was wearing a suit of Samuel's, and in his hands—which were folded on his chest—he held a bouquet of white roses with one red rose in the middle.

When Samuel awoke, he didn't know whether he had just had

a dream or if the events were real. Was his brother dead? His mind spun; he decided that he must find out. Samuel leaped out of bed and charged into the sitting room where he had seen the coffin during his dream. To his relief, the room was empty.

Later that day, as he piloted the *Pennsylvania* down the Mississippi River to New Orleans, Samuel couldn't get the dream out of his mind. Unfortunately, on the trip downriver, Samuel got into an argument with the owner of the steamer and was relieved of his duties when the *Pennsylvania* reached New Orleans; however, Henry remained on board.

A Nightmare Becomes Reality

Several days later, the *Pennsylvania* left on its return trip to St. Louis. As it approached Memphis, the boat's boilers exploded with a titanic roar. Dozens of people on board were killed and wounded.

Samuel heard about the horrible accident and quickly made his way to Memphis. After he arrived, he searched high and low for his brother until he found him on a mattress in a warehouse that had been turned into a hospital to treat the accident victims. Henry had inhaled red-hot steam and was not expected to live. But somehow he fought back, and his condition slowly improved.

One night, the agonizing screams of those in the makeshift hospital were getting the best of Henry, so a physician ordered a small dose of morphine to help him sleep. But the person who administered the drug gave Henry too much: He overdosed and died before morning broke. The body of Henry Clemens was dressed in one of Samuel's suits, placed in a coffin, and displayed in a viewing room at the makeshift hospital. As Samuel was mourning near his brother's casket, a woman placed a bouquet of white roses with one red rose in the center in his dead brother's hands. Samuel was stunned. His chilling dream—or rather nightmare—had come true.

Henry's coffin was sent back to his sister's house in St. Louis. Samuel arrived there just before the coffin was placed in the sitting room. There, two chairs sat spaced apart, waiting to receive the coffin. It was the final detail of Samuel's psychic dream to come true.

Samuel Clemens was so deeply affected by his prophetic dream that foreshadowed his brother's death that 24 years later, he joined the Society for Psychical Research, a British group of supporters of paranormal studies.

The Best Laid Plans

Go ahead, plan all you want—but don't forget what happens to the field mouse's nest when plowing begins!

✳ ✳ ✳ ✳

John Steinbeck is often given credit for the saying "The best laid plans of mice and men often go astray." The title of his classic novella *Of Mice and Men* automatically brings this piece of wisdom to mind. But Steinbeck did not dream up the title; rather, he borrowed it from a poem.

Anyone particularly knowledgeable about literature should correctly cite the source of this saying as Robert Burns's 1785 poem "To a Mouse." There was a time back in the early twentieth century—the era in which Steinbeck grew up—when every schoolchild in the United States was required to memorize poems. "To a Mouse" was a favorite selection, and Steinbeck would have been familiar with it, as would have most of his contemporaries.

"To a Mouse" describes Burns's sadness at having destroyed a mouse's nest with his plow. He empathizes with the mouse, which had spent so much time and care building its house, only to have it ruined in an instant. Burns writes (in the Scottish dialect): "The best laid schemes o' mice an' men gang aft a-gley," which translates as "The best laid schemes of mice and men go oft astray." Steinbeck's choice of a title for his novella reflects the story's plot. Two hard-luck Depression-era migrant workers do everything they can to improve their lot in life, only to have their plans struck down by circumstances out of their control. The message of the story is that dreams are fragile and plans can be futile. Robert Burns's life turned out to be proof of this sentiment. Having spent most of his adult years as an unsuccessful farmer, Scotland's National Poet died in poverty at the age of 37.

The Greatest Authors of Nineteenth-Century Concord, Massachusetts

The last of the great nineteenth-century authors who lived in Concord, Massachusetts, was Louisa May Alcott (1832–88), author of *Little Women* and *Little Men*. Alcott was educated by her father, Bronson Alcott, a transcendentalist philosopher. Louisa enjoyed writing from a young age. She kept a journal and would often write plays that she and her sisters would perform.

When Louisa was in her teens, her family was struggling financially. Louisa began working but was frustrated by the few job opportunities available to women at the time. She worked various jobs—servant, seamstress, teacher, and governess. During this time in her life, Louisa wrote *Work: A Story of Experience*.

In the years preceding the Civil War, Louisa was writing articles for the *Atlantic Monthly*. Once war broke out, however, she signed up to work as a volunteer nurse. This took her to Washington, D.C., where she worked at Union Hospital. Unfortunately, Louisa contracted typhoid fever there, and the treatment she received (which involved mercury) led to health problems later in her life.

After the war, Louisa's publisher asked her to write a book for girls. This prompted Louisa to begin working on her master-piece, *Little Women*.

The following are other well-known authors from Concord, Massachusetts:

* Henry David Thoreau (1817–62) wrote *Walden*.

* Nathaniel Hawthorne (1804–64) wrote *The Scarlet Letter* and *The House of Seven Gables*.

* Ralph Waldo Emerson (1803–82) wrote such essays and poems as "Self-Reliance" and "The Rhodora."

The Adventures of Saul Bellow

This wanderer's observations produced numerous splendid stories.

❋   ❋   ❋   ❋

"I AM AN American, Chicago born—Chicago, that somber city—and go at things as I have taught myself, free-style, and will make the record in my own way..." So says the protagonist of Saul Bellow's *The Adventures of Augie March* (1953). Bellow's free-spirited characters wandered the urban landscape looking for answers to life's questions, and Chicago was the backdrop for many of Bellow's stories.

Literature from a Scientific Mind

Bellow was born in Quebec in 1915. His Russian-Jewish family relocated to Chicago's Humboldt Park neighborhood in 1924. Bellow enrolled at the University of Chicago in 1933 but later transferred to the more economical Northwestern University to study anthropology and sociology. After beginning graduate studies in Wisconsin and then getting married, he decided to pursue writing. During the Depression, he participated in the WPA Writers' Project.

While serving in the Merchant Marines during World War II, Bellow wrote his first novel, *Dangling Man* (1944), about a young man's search for meaning as he waits to be drafted. A few years later, while living in Paris and elsewhere, he wrote *Augie March*. The book established his literary reputation, and he earned a National Book Award for the novel in 1954. Bellow's other works, many of which explore modern urban dilemmas, include *Herzog* (1964) and *Humboldt's Gift* (1975). Bellow won the National Book Award three times—the first writer to do so. He was also awarded a Pulitzer in 1975 and a Nobel in 1976.

Although he traveled extensively, Bellow identified first and foremost with Chicago—a city where, although he did not find all the answers, he certainly found inspiration.

Suspicious Spell

When the bewitched women in Shakespeare's Scottish tragedy Macbeth *gathered around the cauldron to summon up a spell or two, they did not dispatch their dirge with the phrase, "Bubble, bubble, toil and trouble."*

✳   ✳   ✳   ✳

No one should ever confuse the musings of quirky quacker Scrooge McDuck with the wise and witty writings of William Shakespeare, but that's exactly what occurred when the peculiar pen of Walt Disney and his stable of scribes met the beautiful balladry of the Bard. In the opening scene of Act 4 of Shakespeare's play *Macbeth*, three witches stand around a steaming kettle and warble the famous phrase, "Double, double, toil and trouble, Fire burn and cauldron bubble." The poetic punch of that couplet remained untainted until we were presented with Disney's classic cartoon "Much Ado About Scrooge," a jocular jaunt that parodies Shakespeare's classic tragedy. In the wonderful world of Disney, the trio of ducks reverses the words in Will's rhyming scheme, declaring, "Bubble, bubble, toil and trouble, Leave this island on the double." From that moment on, things were never the same in

Stratford-upon-Avon, as countless schoolchildren were convinced that McDuck's verse was right and the *Macbeth* rhyme was wrong. English teachers around the country could only wring their hands and hang their heads.

The trend continued into the modern age of television when, in 1991, the comedy series *Home Improvement*, which would later become a number-one-rated program, presented an episode titled, you guessed it, "Bubble, Bubble, Toil and Trouble." The plot revolved around a whirlpool and a botched bathroom renovation. It goes without saying that *Tool Time* in prime time didn't do Shakespeare any favors.

The Vandals' Bad Rap

It is generally believed that the word vandalism derives from the barbarian Vandals who sacked Rome in A.D. *455. In reality, the word has a more civilized origin.*

✳   ✳   ✳   ✳

THE VANDALS WERE a Germanic barbarian tribe that made quite a name for themselves in the Mediterranean during the fifth century. Over 30 years, the Vandals romped from Poland westward through Europe, the Iberian peninsula, and North Africa, eventually establishing the Kingdom of the Vandals in modern-day Tunisia and Algeria after vanquishing Carthage in A.D. 439.

Have Pity for the Vandals

Why? Because their reputation as conquering warriors is not the one they have today. Instead, thanks to their plundering of Rome in A.D. 455, the Vandals are credited with inspiring the term that describes an act of malicious destruction.

The Vandals were only one of many barbarian hordes during the Dark Ages that ravaged the Western Roman Empire until its fall in A.D. 476. But they weren't any more barbaric than others, nor were they even the first to pillage Rome. Their German cousins, the Visigoths, had turned that trick 45 years earlier.

After a diplomatic falling-out between the two Mediterranean powers, the Vandals headed to Rome, where they plundered the city for two weeks. But even that was considered to be a relatively civilized affair, because the Vandals graciously refrained from wanton burning and violence.

A Bad Rap

So if the Vandals weren't all that vandalistic, where did the word *vandalism* originate? The answer is France, during the French Revolution. As that great experiment in civil liberty and equality began to descend into chaos, the bishop of Blois, Henri Grégoire, denounced what he termed the *vandalisme* of unruly mobs that went around destroying churches and private property.

"Keeping up With the Joneses"

On the surface, keeping up with the Joneses may seem to be a cultural cliché about competing with one's neighbors, but its origin is far more literal.

✳   ✳   ✳   ✳

❙❙KEEPING UP WITH the Joneses" refers to the need to be considered as good as one's neighbors, contemporaries, or coworkers, using the accumulation of material goods as a measuring stick.

Although the popularity of the phrase is usually credited to a popular comic strip of the same name that was created by cartoonist Arthur R. "Pop" Momand, its origin can be traced to a column in the February 15, 1894, edition of a New Philadelphia, Ohio, newspaper called *Ohio Democrat*. In a report on common surnames in the area, the paper reported "The New Philadelphia Directory shows the names of 30 Smiths, 30 Millers, 29 Joneses, and 28 Kniselys. This is a pretty good showing for the Millers and the Kniselys, when they can keep up with the Smiths and the Joneses."

The *Keeping Up With the Joneses* comic strip created by Momand ran in *The New York World* newspaper from 1913 until the early 1940s. Mr. Momand said the strip was based on his observations of life in Cedarhurst, New York, where he and his wife had lived "far beyond their means" in a vain effort to keep pace with "the well-to-do class." The main characters in the strip were the McGinis family—dad Aloysius, mom Clarice, daughter Julie, and housemaid Belladonna. Interestingly, the Joneses of the title were often mentioned in the strip but never seen, which added to their allure.

In the 1950s, *The Daily Mirror* newspaper, the British daily that spawned the popular *Andy Capp* cartoon, also ran a strip called *Keeping Up with the Joneses*, but it had no relation to Pop Momand's creation beyond the title.

Pariahs: A People Apart

A word that originally described the cultural function of a social group came to denote the most despised members of a society.

✳   ✳   ✳   ✳

THE WORD PARIAH (or a variation thereof) appears in a number of European languages, including English, French, and Portuguese, but it comes from the Tamil culture of southern India. Most Tamil people are Hindu, although some are Christians, Muslims, or Jains. It is within the Hindu caste system that the term acquired its most potent meaning of "outcast"—something or someone to be despised and shunned.

The word is derived from the Tamil *paraiyan*, or "drummer." In ancient times, members of this group were known as sorcerers and drummers who played at ritual occasions. However, pariahs also worked as laborers or menial servants. Eventually, the group was absorbed into the category known as "untouchables," the bottom tier of Hindu society.

Pariah appeared in Western languages in the seventeenth century. In 1498, the Portuguese were the first to trade in India, and other countries soon followed. The Dutch East India Company was formed in 1602 to protect Holland's trading rights in the east. England was an active presence in India by the end of the seventeenth century, and Queen Victoria was crowned empress of India in 1876. The word probably entered popular conversation through its frequent appearance in late eighteenth-century French novels.

In some contexts, the word *pariah* has become a gentler epithet. Formerly the pariah dog was any stray or undomesticated dog; now the term designates a primitive breed of dogs—but not a mixed breed or mongrel—that shares particular characteristics wherever it is found in the world.

Synonyms for *pariah* also include *leper* and *exile*. The word is most commonly used to describe people deliberately isolated from society—victims of antiquated social attitudes and prejudice.

Dead as a Doornail?
Perish the Thought!

Shakespeare scripted it and Dickens popularized it, but people have been using the phrase "dead as a doornail" as a description for demise for as long as words have been printed on paper.

❋   ❋   ❋   ❋

ALTHOUGH THE ORIGIN of the phrase "dead as a doornail" is not entirely known, its meaning is certain. To be "dead as a doornail" is to be truly and without question expired, passed on, totally bereft of life, and pushing up daises. The phrase was used in the poem "The Vision of Piers Plowman," which was written by William Langland sometime in the late 1300s. And in Act IV, Scene X of his epic play *Henry VI, Part 2*, William Shakespeare also scripted the slogan. The character John Cade utters this threat, "... if I do not leave you all as dead/as a door-nail, I pray God I may never eat grass more."

Okay, so the dead part is clear enough; it's the doornail part that leaves most scholars scratching their heads. Charles Dickens popularized the parlance in the opening lines of his iconic novel *A Christmas Carol* when the narrator states emphatically that Old Marley is dead as a door-nail, but just a few lines later, the narrator continues: "Mind! I don't mean to say that I know, of my own knowledge, what there is particularly dead about a door-nail."

Some astute authorities in the diction of demise have decided the most logical conclusion relates to carpentry. If you hammer a nail through a piece of timber, such as a door, and bend the end over on the other side so it cannot be removed—a technique called *clinching*—the nail is said to be *dead*, because it can't be used again.

"Kick the Bucket"

We bet you're just dying to know how the phrase "kick the bucket" originated.

✳   ✳   ✳   ✳

WHILE THE MEANING of "kick the bucket" has always been clear, the relationship between death and kicking the old kettle or booting the big bucket is murky at best.

The first known reference to the phrase can be found in the 1785 edition of Captain Francis Grose's *Dictionary of the Vulgar Tongue*, described by *Encyclopaedia Britannica* as "reflecting well the low life of the eighteenth century." Grose's entry—fittingly placed below *kicks* (breeches) and before *kickerapoo* (interestingly, another slang term for death)—reads: "To Kick the Bucket: to die. *He kicked the bucket one day; he died one day.*" Mr. Grose fails to make any connection between croaking and kicking, a mistake that was corrected in the 1811 edition of his classic tome—without Mr. Grose's knowledge, one assumes, seeing as how the old captain went to meet his own maker in 1791. In the updated publication, an important clarification was added. The refined entry reads: "To KICK THE BUCKET. To die. *He kicked the bucket one day: he died one day. To kick the clouds before the hotel door; i.e. to be hanged.*"

From this entry, one might conclude that the phrase means putting noose to neck, standing on a bucket and kicking the bucket away, thereby reaching out to the great beyond by one's own hand. Still, there is room for debate. *Cassell's Dictionary of Slang*, published in 2006, claims that the expression comes from an old method of slaughtering a pig by hanging the animal on a "bucket" or beam by its hind legs. As it dies, the pierced porker literally kicks the bucket.

Forged Jury

The skills of the blacksmith are not usually equated with speed, so it may seem ironic that the term "strike while the iron is hot" was forged to describe swift and timely action.

❋   ❋   ❋   ❋

THE PHRASE "STRIKE while the iron is hot" is a reference to acting quickly, moving swiftly, and forging ahead with an idea, plan, or opportunity while conditions are favorable for success. In other words, snooze and you lose, go in and you win. It's similar to the old adage "make hay while the sun shines." The proverb's roots are decidedly European, with its first recorded use occurring in the fourteenth century. The saying itself refers to the act of forging and shaping iron in a blacksmith's shop. The blacksmith would heat a piece of iron in the fire until the tip of the rod became red-hot. After removing the tongs from the flames, the smith had to hammer or strike the iron into the desired shape and mold it while it was still hot. Once the metal cooled, it became brittle and was impossible to manipulate. So, speed, precision, a steady hand, and a keen eye are key ingredients for success, whether one is forging iron or pursuing a potentially prosperous path in life or business.

The phrase is used to describe any number of situations—be it politics, real estate, or the stock market. Bands and artists such as Kenny Neal, the Vigilantes of Love, and Orange and Lemons have written songs using the phrase, and the group Born Hammers borrowed the maxim as the title of their 2003 album. The jury is still out on the quality of these recordings.

Misfire Caught Fire— as a Metaphor

The expression "flash in the pan" ignited from a weapon known for its frequent malfunction.

✳   ✳   ✳   ✳

THE ORIGIN OF the expression "flash in the pan" is most frequently traced to the flintlock musket. This firearm was introduced around 1610 and was last used by U.S. soldiers in the early days of the Civil War. Pulling the trigger on a flintlock sparked a small charge of gunpowder, which ignited a flame. The flame would then shoot up a touchhole and ignite a more significant charge of gunpowder. It was this charge that fired the lead ball ammunition. But if the flame failed to create enough of a spark to fire the ball—because of wet gunpowder, too little gunpowder, or for some other reason—the result would be nothing more than a flash in the pan. Literally.

As an expression, "flash in the pan" suggests the disappointment of expecting a result that does not materialize. It is often used to describe a promising career that goes nowhere or a hopeful start to a project that doesn't deliver.

You'll sometimes see the phrase traced to other origins, such as the California gold rush, where it is said to refer to a flash of gold in a pan. But the flintlock origin is the most plausible and is well documented.

Oll Korrect!

"OK" may be America's most successful export—it has the distinction of being the most understood word on Earth.

✳ ✳ ✳ ✳

THERE SEEMS TO be no limit of probable explanations for OK's origins. The Finnish word for *correct* is *oikea*. School papers used to be marked with the Latin *Omnis Korrecta* (OK). A telegraph symbol that meant "open key" was often abbreviated to "OK." Alas, none of these theories are accepted as OK. When etymologists study word meanings, they follow strict guidelines to authenticate a word's source. It isn't enough to say a word was once used in a certain way. It must be found in writing and in the correct context.

An 1830s craze for wordplay in New York and Boston ultimately provided the written proof needed to establish OK's origin. Long before the age of text messaging, this fad had people intentionally misspelling words and stringing initials together to form comical acronyms. (Examples include "N.C." for *nuff ced* and "K.Y." for *know yuse*.) OK was first found in print in 1839. A Boston newspaper story about the anti-bell ringing society (A.B.R.S.) used O.K. as an acronym for the intentionally misspelled "oll korrect." Its use spread a year later in the 1840 presidential campaign. The incumbent Martin Van Buren's nickname was "Old Kinderhook" (based on the name of his birthplace: Kinderhook, New York). Van Buren's supporters began forming "Democratic O.K." clubs and used "OK" as an insider's campaign slogan.

X Marks the Spot

Born in an era of peaceful paranoia, the offspring of the Cold War period of prosperity have been described as "underemployed, overeducated, intensely private, and unpredictable." However, the generation is best known by a single letter: X.

✳ ✳ ✳ ✳

IN MATHEMATICS, THE letter X is used to represent a value that is unknown and unpredictable. The variable was easily transposed to indicate the uncertain characteristics of the generation of post–Baby Boomers brought into this world between 1965 and 1982.

The term "Generation X" actually dates to the December 1952 edition of a now-defunct travelogue magazine called *Holiday*. But it wasn't until 1964 that the phrase first started gaining steam. British author Jane Deverson was commissioned by *Woman's Own* magazine to conduct a series of interviews with teenagers of the time. Her study ascertained that the current generation of teenagers, dubbed "Generation X," slept together before they were married, didn't believe in God, disliked the Queen, and didn't respect their parents—conclusions the publishers deemed too controversial for use in their magazine. Deverson, with the cooperation and support of Hollywood correspondent Charles Hamblett, decided to publish her findings in book form. Their novel, titled *Generation X*, was a lively description of the trials and tribulations of a select group of children who would come of age in the 1960s and 1970s. Of course, today we know this generation as the Baby Boomers.

Although Deverson and Hamblett's book was published in 1964, the term Generation X didn't achieve worldwide acclaim until 1991 when author Douglas Coupland wrote his own novel entitled *Generation X: Tales for an Accelerated Culture*. Coupland's version is a fictional account of three strangers who distance themselves from society to get a better sense of who and what they are. Coupland describes the characters as "underemployed, overeducated, intensely private, and unpredictable." It was at this point that Generation X came to describe the generation born between 1965 and 1982.

A Dark and Stormy Night

On a searingly bright, sunny, and radiant day that could only hold gently forth the promise of good things to come, an incredibly overdressed, overthinking Victorian baron named Edward George Bulwer-Lytton started his novel Paul Clifford with these words: "It was a dark and stormy night." The rest, as they say, is history.

✳   ✳   ✳   ✳

A MORE DISCRIMINATING MODERN editor might have argued that stormy nights are usually dark and, therefore, summarily thrown Bulwer-Lytton's book into the reject—or, at least, rewrite—pile. Bulwer-Lytton apparently didn't have that kind of working partner: His novels and plays were published intact—florid prose, overwrought descriptors, and all.

Nevertheless, "It was a dark and stormy night" is likely the most famous opening line in the world, perhaps on par with Herman Melville's "Call me Ishmael." It's also the key to Bulwer-Lytton's lasting but questionable reputation: His name is now synonymous with bad writing, as is evidenced by a California university's annual Bulwer-Lytton Fiction contest in which "wretched writers are welcome," and a judging panel collects and scrutinizes tremendously bad writing. Winners and especially noteworthy contestants are immortalized in a widely available book.

Perhaps a better illustration of Bulwer-Lytton's legacy is the fact that his line has been appropriated by two world-famous authors. Children's novelist Madeleine L'Engle started her book *A Wrinkle in Time* with "It was a dark and stormy night," and comic fans may remember that Snoopy's novel, which he was forever writing from his workstation on his doghouse roof, began the exact same way. L'Engle's book went on to win the Newbery Medal and had sold more than six million copies at the time of her death in 2007.

Ju Idealisma Origino da Esperanto

"What we've got here is failure to communicate."

—*COOL HAND LUKE,* **1967**

It's been the world's lament, but one man was certain he had a solution.

✳ ✳ ✳ ✳

What Do Words Say?

A S A BOY living in Bialystok in Russian-controlled Poland in the 1860s and 1870s, Ludwik L. Zamenhof was keenly aware of the endless bickering that preoccupied neighborhood kids and grown-ups. Everybody talked, and if they listened at all, they only grew angrier because nobody could understand what the others were saying. That was because Bialystok was dominated by three groups: Jews, who spoke mainly Yiddish; white Russians, who spoke Belarusian; and Germans, who spoke, well, German. This central inefficiency of local communication was aggravated because the language of government administration was Russian. Young Ludwik may have appreciated the small mercy that Person A likely never realized that Person B had just let loose with a withering insult, but he had no doubt that sometimes language isn't an advantage, but an awful impediment.

As Zamenhof grew into young adulthood, he became an ophthalmologist and perfected his understanding of Russian, Yiddish, and German. He also immersed himself in Latin, English, French, Hebrew, and Greek. His thoughts soon turned to the creation of a universal language that could easily be learned, spoken, and written, eliminating the enormous linguistic barriers that impaired relationships not just in Poland, but across the globe. Zamenhof reasoned that without such a language, civilization would forever be defined by endless ethnic strife and war.

In 1887, when Zamenhof was just 28, he published *Lingvo Internacia*, the first textbook of his new language, which he called Esperanto ("hopeful one"). The book's primary text was written in Russian, and authorship was attributed to "Dr. Esperanto."

How It Works

Although Esperanto was designed to be culturally neutral, it shares qualities with European languages—no surprise, given Zamenhof's background. What sets Esperanto apart is its internal consistency. The alphabet has 28 letters. There are no silent letters and no variations in pronunciation. All words put stress on the next-to-last syllable: "ess-per-AHN-toe." The language functions with only 16 rules—no exceptions. Suffixes identify parts of speech: All nouns end in *O*, all adjectives in *A*, adverbs in *E*. The letter *J* forms the plural and *N* indicates a direct object.

Zamenhof gave up all claims to ownership of Esperanto, making it his gift to humanity. This is unvarnished idealism, so Zamenhof was greatly disappointed when the Russian tsar banned Esperanto as a tool of sedition. Even so, freethinkers and linguists across Europe, particularly in France and Germany, became excited about Esperanto. Many famous works were translated into the new language, and 1889 brought the first magazine written entirely in Esperanto, *La Esperantistto*. Zamenhof himself published the first Esperanto dictionary in 1894.

The first World Esperanto Congress attracted 688 linguists and other enthusiasts to Boulogne, France, in 1905. Three years later, the Universal Esperanto Association was established.

Tragedy and Triumph

Ludwik Zamenhof died in 1917; his wife, Klara, passed away in 1924. A decade later, Hitler outlawed Esperanto across the Third Reich, claiming it was part of the imaginary world Jewish conspiracy. In a particularly ugly irony, all three Zamenhof children were ensnared in the web of Hitler's Holocaust and killed.

Esperanto has outlived its detractors. Across Europe and the Middle East, plaques, busts, and street names honor Zamenhof. A minor planet discovered in 1938 is called Zamenhof.

Since it was first embraced by enthusiasts, Esperanto has been regularly spoken by anywhere from 100,000 to 2 million persons. All dialogue in *Incubus*, a 1965 movie starring William Shatner, is in Esperanto. British comic Spike Milligan famously remarked, "I can speak Esperanto like a native." Conventions and publications are common, and the language's proponents now lobby for its adoption as the official language of the European Union.

The Proof of the Pudding Is in the Meaning

During any argument in which one party makes generalizations and the other contradicts them, someone eventually yells, "The exception proves the rule!" Is this claim ironclad logic, or is it a rhetorical device as sophisticated as "I'm rubber and you're glue"?

✳   ✳   ✳   ✳

THE PHRASE "THE exception proves the rule" began appearing in English in the seventeenth century and has been misused ever since. Even the great lexicographer H. W. Fowler admitted to being uncertain about its meaning. The two most common interpretations of the phrase argue that the item that breaks the rule is actually what shows the rule to be true, which, of course, makes no logical sense.

Exceptions Make the Rule Stronger

The first misuse suggests that a rule is valid specifically because it doesn't apply to all cases. This tactic is particularly brilliant in that it can be used to justify any argument that otherwise flies in the face of reason and logic. Often, it's used to deflate an opponent's argument when there isn't a fact-based leg on which to stand. For example, John argues that all butterflies are blue. Mary points out that Monarch butterflies are not blue, to which John responds that Monarchs are the exception that prove the rule. John is content, sticking to his belief that all butterflies but for those pesky Monarchs are blue (conveniently ignoring all the other non-blue butterflies). Meanwhile, Mary thinks John is a chucklehead. Despite its popular use, this clearly is not a logical argument.

Except in This Case

The second misuse of the proverb uses a different meaning of the word *prove*, but it's wrong nonetheless. In interpreting the word prove as "to test or check" (as in "proving grounds" or "mathematical proofs") rather than as "to show as true," it is explained that having an exception actually helps test the validity of the rule. But in John's all-butterflies-are-blue argument, the Monarch exception would not help him test the strength of his rule because it in fact pokes a gigantic hole in it. This usage, therefore, is also illogical.

Proverbial Prosecution

The proverb was originally based upon a point of Latin law. In 56 B.C., Cicero was charged with defending Lucius Cornelius Balbus against accusations of having gained Roman citizenship illegally. The prosecution argued that treaties with some non-Roman tribes actually prohibited granting them citizenship, which should be then treated as the standard, to which Cicero replied, "*Quod si exceptio facit ne liceat, ubi <non sit exceptum, ibi> necesse est licere.*" For those who may have missed that day in Latin class, he was arguing, "If the exception makes such an action unlawful, where there is no exception the action must necessarily be lawful." Point and match to Cicero.

Who Made Up Theses Rules, Anyway?

The misunderstanding of the English phrase began in interpreting the word *exception* as an object (something to be excluded) rather than an action (the act of making something a special case). The proverb actually says that by spelling out an exception to a rule, one implicitly acknowledges that a rule exists in the first place. The exception gives authority and strength to the original rule. We all understand that "Free Parking on Sundays" means we'd better be cramming quarters into the meters all other days of the week.

Whether you're listening to someone loudly claim that exceptions only make his or her argument stronger, or that all rules need exceptions to be true, you have a choice: You could smile, take the high road, and walk away, or you could enthusiastically offer the correct use of the phrase, explaining that while you can have a rule without an exception, you cannot have an exception without a rule. But understand that the latter choice involves a considerable commitment of time and patience.

All That Glitters

If there was ever an adage for the ages, it is "All that glitters is not gold." This phrase is commonly attributed to Shakespeare, but he wasn't the first to write it.

As far back as 600 B.C., Aesop was warning against the danger of being distracted by shiny outward appearances. In his fable *The Hen and the Golden Eggs*, a farmer has a hen that lays—you guessed it—golden eggs. Thinking that the hen must be filled with gold, he slaughters it, only to find that it's just an ordinary hen. The twelfth-century philosopher Alain de l'Isle advised: "Do not hold everything that shines like gold." Two hundred years later, Chaucer introduced this proverb in *The Canterbury*

Tales: "But all thing which that schyneth as the gold Ne is no gold, as I have herd it told."

Shakespeare knew a good line when he saw one and adapted the expression for his play *The Merchant of Venice.* The heroine, Portia, instructs her suitors that they must choose which of three caskets contains her picture. One of the caskets is made of lead, one of silver, and one of gold. The first suitor makes the mistake of choosing the one that appears the most valuable— the golden casket. Instead of finding the prize of Portia's picture, he finds a scroll with a poem that begins, "All that glisters is not gold" (and he loses the bid for Portia's hand). The word *glister* comes from the German *glistern,* which translates to "sparkle." In modern English, *glitter* has the same meaning.

Shakespeare's version of this saying has been misquoted countless times. Even the venerated rock band Led Zeppelin put its own twist on the proverb: "There's a lady who's sure all that glitters is gold, and she's buying a stairway to heaven."

Viva the Chauvinist

Most people today would define a chauvinist as a man who believes that women are inferior beings. But a look at the origins of the word reveals a different meaning.

✳   ✳   ✳   ✳

WHEN PEOPLE USE the word *chauvinist,* it's usually in reference to an ignorant bigot who believes that women are inferior to men. Originally, though, the word had nothing to do with gender. Instead, it was used to describe someone who has an ardent loyalty to a nation or group. The term is derived from a legendary French soldier, Nicolas Chauvin, who was wounded 17 times and severely disabled while serving under Napoleon Bonaparte. The deposed emperor of France was a hugely unpopular figure in that country after the Napoleonic Wars in the early nineteenth century, but Chauvin bucked popular opinion and remained a dedicated supporter of Bonapartism. Like other Bonapartists, Chauvin refused to acknowledge the French defeat at Waterloo or the Congress of Vienna, which redrew the political map of Europe following Napoleon's defeat.

Chauvin's name entered the public lexicon when he was featured as a character in the satirical French play *La Cocarde Tricolore* in 1831 and in Emmuska Orczy's 1903 novel *The Scarlet Pimpernel*. The word *chauvinism* was coined to describe blind nationalism, and in the French language, at least, it retains that meaning.

In the English-speaking world, however, *chauvinist* was adopted by the women's liberation movement of the 1960s and was used to describe men who view women as being inferior due to their gender. Initially, the term used was "male chauvinist" or even "male chauvinist pig." Over time the "male" became obsolete, and the word *chauvinist* was used to describe a bigoted man who wasn't afraid to express his sexist (rather than patriotic) views in either word or deed.

Don't Fence Me In

The saying "Good fences make good neighbors" can be used for a variety of purposes—so many that few people are clear on its true intention. Should we be outfitting our property lines with chain link or picketing our neighbor's pickets?

✳ ✳ ✳ ✳

THE LINE IS lifted from Robert Frost's poem "Mending Wall" (1914), in which two men walk their property lines together, repairing the stone wall that separates them. The narrator wonders at the wall's purpose, as neither of them owns livestock, and the wall separates one type of tree from another. The neighbor, repeating what he firmly believes, twice states, "Good fences make good neighbors."

A Matter of Interpretation

Some people use this saying to mean its opposite—that fences make terrible neighbors. The poem's narrator is clearly against his neighbor's belief in boundaries. He points out that the wall keeps nothing in or out, that a wall could give offense, and the yearly damage shows that a wall goes against nature itself. He even compares the neighbor to a "savage." To many, if the narrator said it, then Frost said it, and therefore it must be true. Walls are bad, end of story.

Another use of this phrase emphasizes the quality of the fence, as if that were the issue rather than the existence of the fence. If you're going to have a fence, it should be a good fence. It is not neighborly to allow your wall to fall into disrepair so that your dog ends up soiling your neighbor's yard.

Still others use this phrase to advocate metaphorical distance from other people as a way to be happy. The 1960 musical *The Fantasticks* tells the story of two scheming fathers who build a wall between their properties so that their children will have an obstacle to overcome and, thus, fall in love.

Give Me My Space

Folks in the United States are fond of fences—more than 3 million people live in gated communities. Some towns are entirely surrounded by fences, and there is a fence along portions of the country's southern border. Many people believe that private property is sacrosanct. No flesh-and-blood neighbor could ever be as pleasant as a barrier demarcating yours and mine. Just as early pioneers would move when they saw smoke from a neighbor's chimney, Americans love wide open spaces and plenty of room between neighbors. Although the open frontier no longer exists, a fence creates that elbow room, much the same way an invisible line drawn down a car's backseat separates squabbling siblings.

This sentiment is not limited to people in the United States. Proverbs from around the world suggest that a little separation is a good thing. From the medieval Latin *Bonum est erigere dumos cum vicinis* ("It is good to erect hedges with the neighbors") to the Japanese "Build a fence even between intimate friends" to the Norwegian "There must be a fence between good neighbors," variations exist in many cultures and religions.

A recent study by scientists at Brandeis University and the New England Complex Systems Institute show that there is some truth to this idea. In places occupied by more than one cultural group, clearly defined boundaries such as fences can help ease ethnic or cultural tensions. Another study by University of California research economists found that every 10 percent decline in population density results in a 10 percent increase in neighborly communication and a 15 percent increase in community involvement.

Mysterious Lexicon

Encore: Although many people might expect an appreciative French crowd to yell this word at the end of a performance, the French actually call out *"bis bis!"* to show their desire for more. In fact, the word *encore* means "another" in French, which is why English speakers use it to request more of a performance.

Economist: This word first appears in the late sixteenth century and was used strictly in reference to housekeepers. It did not acquire its modern (and arguably loftier) meaning until centuries later.

Stripteaser: First recorded in 1938, this relatively recent addition to the world's lexicon describes a profession that goes back much further in human history. In 1940, the famous stripteaser Georgia Sothern asked linguist H. L. Mencken to coin a word to describe her profession; the result was *ecdysiast*, which refers to the process of molting undergone by insects. Many dancers, including the premiere stripper of her time, Gypsy Rose Lee, balked at being compared to an insect, and the word never gained popular footing. This explains why the seedier sections of town are not littered with Ecdysiast Clubs.

Googol: Around 1940, when mathematician Dr. Edward Kasner needed a word to describe the number one followed by a hundred zeroes, he turned to his nine-year-old nephew. The child responded with "google," which has since become as a great internet users who use the popular search engine Google.

Zipper: The inventor of this revolutionary fastening device, Whitcomb L. Judson, first introduced the zipper to the public in 1893 as the "Universal Fastener." It was an executive at the B. F. Goodrich Company who coined the term by which we know it today.

Payola: Referring to the practice of record companies paying radio deejays to play their artists' songs, the term "payola" is a combination of *pay* and *Victrola*—one of the largest manufacturers of turntables in America when the word was first used in the 1960s.

Abyss: One of the few words in the English language of Sumerian origin, it refers to the Abzu, the primordial sea of Sumerian tradition.

The Not-So-Sweet Story of *Candy*

A sensual tale jumped through countless legal hoops on its road to cult-classic status, making it one of the most beleaguered and scandalized pieces of fiction in contemporary history.

✳   ✳   ✳   ✳

The saga of the novel *Candy* is legendary in the literary world. First published in 1958, the erotic story tells of Candy Christian, a sweet, innocent, but incredibly curious young girl who travels the world in search of adventure. Yet more interesting than the plot, perhaps, is the backstory surrounding the novel's writing and publishing—and publishing, and more publishing...

Let's Start at the Very Beginning

Many young American writers came out of World War II wondering what they could do with their wordy talents. Texan Terry Southern and New Yorker Mason Hoffenberg, both veterans, chose to take their GI Bill benefits and attend the Sorbonne in Paris in 1948. They became fast friends and were early examples of Beat artists such as Jack Kerouac (who was close with Southern and Hoffenberg in Paris). The duo spent evenings in jazz clubs drinking a thick, syrupy, anise-flavored liqueur called Pernod and smoking hashish. Occasionally one or the other would sell an article to a little-read literary magazine, while success and satisfaction eluded them.

Enter the Publisher

A man named Maurice Girodias ran Obelisk Press, a risqué book company in Paris that he had inherited from his father before the war. When one of France's largest publishers bought out the company in 1952, Girodias set out on his own with Olympia Press. He quickly made his mark by publishing English-language versions of forbidden erotic books by authors such as Henry Miller. In 1955, he made history by publishing Vladimir Nabokov's *Lolita*, only to see it banned by French censors. The publisher brought a lawsuit against the censors and won, earning the right to continue printing the story of a grown man who obsesses over a 12-year-old girl. Girodias also embraced many of the young American writers in Paris, including Southern and Hoffenberg. He encouraged many female writers as well, many of whom wrote what were simply called "dirty books," or "DBs," under male pseudonyms.

Meanwhile, Hoffenberg returned to New York City—more specifically, to the bohemian neighborhood of Greenwich Village—where he acquired a dangerous affinity for heroin. Southern remained in Paris, where he got the notion to create a modern satire of Voltaire's 18th-century novel *Candide*. Southern described the outline of this novella to Girodias in a letter dated December 1956, telling of a young Midwestern girl who is party to a series of erotic adventures with men from all walks of life. The publisher was quite intrigued and encouraged Southern to extend the book into a full-length novel.

Writing under the pen name Maxwell Kenton, Southern began to flesh out Candy, writing at least two pages every day. But the task quickly became tedious and, even with the encouragement of his wife, Carol, he began missing deadlines to his publisher. The frustrated author contacted Hoffenberg in New York City and asked him to contribute to the story. The two writers wrote and exchanged pages of *Candy* for nearly two years, continuing after Hoffenberg moved back to Europe.

Like Taking Candy from a Baby

Girodias paid Southern and Hoffenberg only a few hundred dollars for their finished manuscript. As soon as he printed and distributed 5,000 copies of *Candy* in France, the French vice squad confiscated them as immoral. Girodias would not be dissuaded. He merely changed the title and cover and rewrote the first few pages; the police were none the wiser. Girodias's "new" novel, *Lollipop*, was exported to England as well as peddled by local Parisian booksellers. He was back in business. The authors, however, received nothing from this "new" publication.

Southern continued to ply his craft, writing for magazines including popular titles such as Esquire. Hoffenberg, on the other hand, was a poet at heart who was also fighting a seesaw battle with his addiction to heroin. In 1962, Girodias reprinted *Candy* with a caveat that it was "not to be sold in the USA or the UK." At the same time, Southern, who continued to gain credibility as an author and screenwriter (working with director Stanley Kubrick on the *Dr. Strangelove* script), had renowned literary agent Sterling Lord working to publish *Candy* in the United States. The task was not easy, as Lord was representing a book the authors did not own.

A fault in international copyright laws at the time complicated matters by depriving the writers of the royalties owed them. Works written outside the United States were not protected by a U.S. copyright unless an interim copyright was filed in America. Neither Southern nor Hoffenberg (and certainly not Girodias) ever made the application, allowing dozens of unauthorized, pirate editions of *Candy* to hit bookshelves in the 1960s. The authors did not receive a dime of the hundreds of thousands of dollars that might otherwise have been owed to them.

Despite all of this, the editor in chief at G. P. Putnam's Sons Books was keenly interested in *Candy*, having fought the censorship battle by successfully publishing the best-selling American edition of *Lolita* in 1958. He signed a royalty contract with Southern and Hoffenberg (who ironically had possession of Girodias's pen to sign it) and an American hardcover edition of *Candy* appeared in May 1964.

America Likes Its Candy

To say the novel was a best seller is an understatement of enormous proportions. Putnam sold more than 10,000 copies in the first two days, with 14,000 copies sold in the first week. Although not without its share of decency lawsuits, *Candy* was a landmark publication. If *Lolita* had been the first nail in the coffin of print censorship in America, then *Candy* was the sound of it sealing shut.

Yet, sadly, *Candy*'s success led to the acrimonious parting of Southern and Hoffenberg as friends. Hoffenberg became envious of Southern's success; Hoffenberg's drug addiction had made him persona non grata on the book's publicity trail. As far as the public could see, Terry Southern was the author of the nation's number-two best seller of 1964.

A Happy Ending?

A final agreement was signed in early 1967 establishing Southern and Hoffenberg as the sole copyright owners. Maurice Girodias was allowed to keep the money he had made on the book and could negotiate publishing rights in Britain. All parties consented to legally pursue the myriad pirate editions together.

By the year's end, a movie version of *Candy* was under way, although Hollywood had yet to adjust its rules of censorship the way the literary world had done. Many wondered how the film could possibly be made. Hoffenberg had left the situation entirely, and Southern, miffed when he heard the book's famous "hunchback encounter" would not be included, left the screenplay writing to hired hand Buck Henry.

The 1968 film was ultimately a disaster; stars such as Marlon Brando, Richard Burton, Ringo Starr, James Coburn, and Walter Matthau couldn't save it. The movie may have been doomed from the start when a Swedish girl named Ewa Aulin—who spoke no English—was cast to play the pivotal all-American title role.

Southern's writing career continued to grow exponentially, as he went on to international acclaim for such highly influential books as *The Magic Christian*, *Blue Movie*, and *Flash and Filigree*, as well as for the scripts of some of the most emblematic films of their eras, such as *The Cincinnati Kid*, *Casino Royale*, and *Barbarella*. He even did some television work, writing for *Saturday Night Live* in the early 1980s. By the time of his death from stomach cancer in 1995, Southern was known as a great literary satirist, lambasting Hollywood, pop culture at large, and the human libido. Hoffenberg, however, managed to write two other little-read books alongside a smattering of poetry and is mostly remembered as a shadow in the sometimes sweet, often bitter *Candy* saga.

Chapter 9

Myths, Mysteries, & Clandestine Workings

The Myth of the 24-Hour Flu

If you're sitting on or kneeling in front of the porcelain throne, what you're suffering from is not the flu.

✳ ✳ ✳ ✳

EVERY FLU SEASON, millions of people who get their flu shots still come down with a nasty stomach bug that puts them in bed for up to 48 hours. The cause of their suffering is not the flu, which is a respiratory disease transmitted by airborne viruses that can survive up to a month and cause severe or even life-threatening illness. Chances are it's a case of gastro-enteritis, an inflammation of the stomach and intestines caused by ingesting a virus or microbe. The associated nausea, vomiting, diarrhea, and stomach cramps often subside within a day.

The likely culprit is the highly contagious *norovirus*, which accounts for half of food-borne diseases, according to the Centers for Disease Control. *Norovirus* infection often causes large outbreaks and on occasion has sent the majority of passengers on cruise ships to their sick beds for a day or two. The vomit and stools of those infected are highly contagious, and the virus can linger on the surface of objects for weeks. Approximately 30 percent of stomach bugs are caused by two similar viruses, the *rotavirus* and the *astrovirus*.

Other stomach bugs are triggered by bacteria, including *salmonella, shigella, staphylococcus, clostridium,* and *E. coli.* Exposure usually occurs through the consumption of contaminated food or water. Most people don't associate their illness with something they ate or drank, though, because 24 to 72 hours usually pass before they feel sick.

Now They Have to Kill Us: The Bavarian Illuminati

Before delving into the intricacies of the Illuminati's origin, we'd recommend donning a tinfoil hat. It will protect you against the New World Order conspiracy.

❋ ❋ ❋ ❋

Q: What does Illuminati actually mean?

A: "The Enlightened." Like many religious faiths and secret societies, the original Bavarian Illuminati were founded in search of enlightenment. Prior groups with similar ideas used similar names.

Q: Did earlier Illuminati groups evolve into the Bavarian Illuminati?

A: Well, let's examine some earlier groups. Spain's Alumbrados ("enlightened") dated to the time of Columbus (1490s), suffered from the Inquisition, and developed a following in France (as the Illuminés) that endured until the late 1700s, when the French Revolution sat on them. The Rosicrucians started in Germany in the early 1600s, claiming lineage from the Knights Templar; by the late 1770s, their theme was becoming increasingly Egyptian. Many Rosicrucians were also Freemasons, a group with unbroken lineage to the present day.

They all had ideas in common with the Bavarian Illuminati; however, the Bavarian Illuminati sprang from the fertile mind of an iconoclastic law professor, not from a previous group. At most, the Bavarian group experienced some cross-pollination with other similar groups (notably Freemasonry), but that doesn't equal ancestral continuity.

Q: How'd the Bavarian group get going?

A: It began in Ingolstadt, Bavaria, with a German 20-something named Adam Weishaupt. In 1775, Weishaupt accepted a natural and canon law professorship at the University of Ingolstadt that had recently been vacated by an ejected Jesuit. Weishaupt was a maverick prone to anticlerical utterances: the anti-Jesuit, if you will. He soon managed to convince himself, without irony, that he was destined to lead humanity out of superstition toward enlightenment. Unsurprisingly, the Jesuits hated his guts.

Evidently, Weishaupt couldn't afford the Masons' fees, so he launched the Perfectibilists (later the Bavarian Illuminati) on May 1, 1776 (this would later fuel plentiful conspiracy theories about May Day celebrations). Fascinated with Egyptian stuff, he assigned his society a pyramid as its symbol.

Q: Did this group extend tentacles into business, government, and church?

A: To extend tentacles, one must first possess some. The Illuminati concerned themselves mostly with secret degrees and titles, plus absolute obedience to the chain of command with Weishaupt at the top. There is no evidence the group ever controlled anything. Illuminati were supposed to spurn superstition and strive toward rationalism to help perfect each other's mentalities. The meta-goal was clearing the earth of inhumanity and stupidity. It actually sounds more than a little like modern Scientology, at least in terms of stated goals (as opposed to reality).

Q: That sounds like the vision of a new world order, doesn't it?

A: It does. The modern conspiracy question rests not in the nature of the original Bavarian Illuminati, which is well documented, but rather to what degree it has survived to exert control over modern affairs. As any nightly news broadcast will show, their work didn't make a lasting dent in either inhumanity or stupidity.

Q: Why not?

A: Because inhumanity and stupidity are so very human, perhaps? Think of the Illuminati as a die intended to mint enlightened persons. This die possessed one fundamental crack: Its concept of enlightenment categorically discouraged questioning the autocratic leader. That's no way to run a freethinkers' group. In such groups, true freethinkers drift away, leaving only quasi-freethinkers who don't argue with the Maximum Leader.

Q: But the organization still grew. Why?

A: It only grew for a brief time, and that had much to do with the work of Baron Adolph Knigge, who joined in the 1780s. Knigge was both well-known and a capable administrator who gave the Illuminati a great deal of practical Masonic wisdom, helping sort out Weishaupt's rather rinky-dink organization. By its peak in 1784, it had several thousand members.

Q: What sent it downhill?

A: First there was the inevitable squabble between Weishaupt and Knigge, which ended with Knigge telling Weishaupt where to shove his little fiefdom. It's tempting to blame the whole thing on Weishaupt, but the evidence indicates that Knigge had an ego to match Weishaupt's and could be just as great a horse's posterior. The deathblow came when Duke Karl Theodor of Bavaria banned all unauthorized secret societies.

Q: Did that simply shatter the organism into many pieces that grew independently?

A: Evidence suggests that the ban, plus police raids, shattered the Illuminati into dying pieces rather than living ones. Sacked from teaching, Weishaupt fled to a neighboring state and died in obscurity. Others tried to keep Illuminati islets alive, without evident success. Like witchcraft of an earlier age, the actual practice became far rarer than the accusation—and official paranoia over secret societies and sedition kept the term Illuminati cropping up.

Q: So, why does the intrigue linger?

A: Perhaps for the same reason the Freemasons, Knights Templar, and so forth keep showing up in conspiracy theories: When someone wants to point to a potential conspiracy, he or she can usually find some bit of circumstantial evidence hinting a connection to one of the above. Those who disagree, of course, must be toadies of the conspiracy! It's an argument that can't end.

But insofar as we are guided by actual evidence, the Bavarian Illuminati did end. Whatever world conspiracies there might be today, it's doubtful any descend directly from Weishaupt's ideological tree-house club.

Say It Ain't So

Myth: Penguins, attempting to watch airplanes flying overhead, will fall over backwards in efforts to keep their eyes on the soaring sight.

Truth: One could easily envision the waddle-prone creatures toppling over onto their backs while excitedly eyeballing the whir of an airplane overhead. However, there is no truth at all to this silly penguin myth. Penguins, the nervous-nellies that they are, will typically run and hide from the frightening, loud noises of a plane in flight.

Myth: Drivers of red automobiles receive more speeding tickets than do drivers of any other color car.

Truth: Actually, white car owners typically receive the most tickets. Statistically, white cars make up a greater share of the car population, so the heightened instances of white car pullovers would make sense. Red car pullover rates, too, run proportional to the red car share of the car population. It is actually gray cars that, proportional to their share of the overall car population, are pulled over at surprisingly high rates.

Myth: Be careful of cats. They will suck the breath right out of babies!

Truth: As many cat owners can attest, some feline pets do seem inexplicably drawn to their owners' faces in the bedtime hours. Waking up with a cat-hat is commonplace for many kitty parents. However, no instances of cat-on-child suffocation have ever proven true. Still, cats have sometimes been blamed for crib death. In one such 2000 case, the death of an infant was initially blamed on a supposed baby-breath-sucking cat. The innocent cat was exonerated, however, when a pathologist eventually linked the sudden death to non-feline-related causes.

Myth: Poinsettias, the popular holiday flowers, are poisonous.

Truth: Allowing a supposedly toxic flower to become such a traditional component of the holiday season seems crazy, but this rumor persists, nonetheless. Perhaps it is due to the word poinsettia's auditory resemblance to poison, or maybe it's because of a few toxic plants that are in the poinsettia family tree. Whatever the reason, the myth of the poisonous flower has sent many a protective mom into a Christmastime tizzy.

The Mysterious Death of Thelma Todd

Old Hollywood has more than its fill of secrets. Here's another one.

✳   ✳   ✳   ✳

O N DECEMBER 16, 1935, at about 10:30 A.M., actor Thelma Todd was found dead behind the wheel of her Lincoln Phaeton convertible. Her maid, Mae Whitehead, had come to clean the luxurious apartment Todd lived in above her rollicking roadhouse, Thelma Todd's Sidewalk Café. The maid discovered Thelma in a nearby garage. Some sources claim the ignition of her car was still turned on and the garage door was opened a crack. An obvious suicide? Not quite.

Humble Beginnings

Thelma Todd was born in Lawrence, Massachusetts, on July 29, 1905 or 1906, depending on the source. She was an academically gifted girl who went on to attend college, but her mother pushed her to use her physical assets as well as her intellectual gifts. She made a name for herself in local beauty pageants, winning the title "Miss Massachusetts" in 1925. Though she did not take the top prize in the Miss America pageant, she was discovered by a talent agent and soon began appearing in the short one- and two-reel comedy films of producer/director Hal Roach.

Before Thelma knew it, she was starring with big names, including Gary Cooper and William Powell, and working at an exhausting pace on as many as 16 pictures a year. Her forte was comedy, however, and she found her biggest success as a sidekick to such legends as the Marx Brothers and Laurel and Hardy. Around Hollywood, she was known as "The Ice Cream Blonde" or "Hot Toddy" (a nickname she assigned to herself). But Thelma knew that fame was fleeting, and she decided to invest in a nightclub/restaurant with her sometimes boyfriend, director Roland West. The upscale gin joint became a favorite with Hollywood's hard-partying, fast set.

A Complicated Girl

To say that Thelma's love life was messy would be an understatement. Her marriage to playboy Pasquale "Pat" DiCicco (from 1932 to 1934) was a disaster, filled with domestic abuse.

She turned to West after her divorce but was reportedly also seeing mobster Charles "Lucky" Luciano on the side. It was said that Luciano wanted a room at the Sidewalk Café for his gambling operation, and he was willing to go to great lengths to get it. The rumor was that even after he got Thelma hooked on amphetamines, she was still of sound enough mind to refuse. Supposedly, the couple got into a huge screaming match about the subject one night at another restaurant, The Brown Derby, and various threats were exchanged.

So, Who Did It?

All the romantic drama and hard living came to a head on the evening of December 14, 1935. Thelma had been invited to a party involving a good friend of hers, Ida Lupino, and she was driven there by her chauffeur, Ernest Peters. Unfortunately for Thelma, her ex-husband showed up with another woman and made a scene. After a nasty argument, DiCicco left with his date, and a drunken Thelma informed Lupino that there was a new man in her life, a rich businessman from San Francisco.

Thelma was dropped back at her apartment by Peters at around 3:30 A.M. on December 15. She apparently couldn't get into the building and instead retreated to the garage, perhaps to sleep there. She might have turned on the car for warmth, not paying attention to the carbon monoxide. The Los Angeles County determined the time of death had been between 5:00 and 8:00 A.M.

Making the circumstances even more mysterious is the fact that, although Thelma was determined to have died early on Sunday morning, December 15, her body was not found until Monday morning. There were uncorroborated reports that she had been seen during the day on Sunday in Beverly Hills. Is it possible that Thelma actually died 24 hours later than was reported?

The coroner's report listed carbon monoxide asphyxiation as the cause of death and ruled it a suicide, but Thelma's crazy life led many to dismiss that verdict. With so many intriguing suspects—the violent ex-husband, the jealous boyfriend, the ruthless gangster lover, and the mysterious out-of-town paramour—who could blame them? That initial report was reconsidered and overturned, with the ruling changed to accidental death, but some observers believe the incident was never investigated thoroughly.

Hey, It's The Freemasons!

For many, talk of Freemasonry conjures up images of intricate handshakes, strange rituals, and harsh punishment for revealing secrets about either. In actuality, the roots of the order are brotherhood and generosity. Throughout the ages, Masons have been known to fiercely protect their members and the unique features of their society.

✳   ✳   ✳   ✳

THE FANTASTICALLY NAMED Most Ancient and Honorable Society of Free and Accepted Masons began like other guilds; it was a collection of artisans brought together by their common trade, in this case, stone cutting and crafting. (There are many speculations as to when the society first began. Some believe it dates back to when King Solomon's temple was built. Others believe the guild first formed in Scotland in the sixteenth century.) The Freemasons made the welfare of their members a priority. Group elders devised strict work regulations for masons, whose skills were always in demand and were sometimes taken advantage of.

Organized Freemasonry emerged in Great Britain in the mid-seventeenth century with the firm establishment of Grand Lodges and smaller, local Lodges. (No one overarching body governs Freemasonry as a whole, though lodges worldwide are usually linked either to England or France.) In 1730, transplanted Englishmen established the first American Lodge in Virginia, followed in 1733 by the continent's first chartered and opened Grand Lodge in Massachusetts. Boasting early American members including George Washington, Benjamin Franklin, and John Hancock, Freemasonry played a part in the growth of the young nation in ways that gradually attracted curiosity, speculation, and concern.

The source of the organization's mysterious reputation lay partly in its secrecy: Masons were prohibited from revealing secrets (some believed Masons would be violently punished if they revealed secrets, though the Masons deny such rumors). The Masonic bond also emphasized a commitment to one another. Outsiders feared the exclusivity smacked of conspiracy and compromised the motives of Masons appointed to juries or elected to public office. And nonmembers wondered about the meanings of the Freemasons' peculiar traditions (such as code words and other secretive forms of recognition between members) and symbolism (often geometric shapes or tools, such as the square and compass). Design elements of the one-dollar bill, including the Great Seal and the "all-seeing eye," have been credited to founding fathers such as Charles Thomson and other Masons.

Freemasonry in the United States suffered a serious blow in September 1826 when New York Masons abducted a former "brother" named William Morgan. Morgan was about to publish a book of Masonic secrets, but before he could, he was instead ushered north to the Canadian border and, in all likelihood, thrown into the Niagara River. His disappearance led to the arrest and conviction of three men on kidnapping charges (Morgan's body was never found)—scant penalties, locals said, for crimes that surely included murder. The affair increased widespread suspicion of the brotherhood, spawning an American Anti-Mason movement and even a new political party dedicated to keeping Freemasons out of national office.

In the decades following the Civil War, men were again drawn to brotherhood and fellowship as they searched for answers in a changing age, and Freemasonry slowly regained popularity. Today, Freemasonry remains an order devoted to its own members, charitable causes, and the betterment of society. It has a worldwide membership of at least five million. Its members are traditionally male, though certain associations now permit women. Despite the name, most members are not stonemasons. They are, however, required to have faith in a supreme being, but not necessarily the Christian god (Mohammed, Buddha, and so forth are all acceptable).

From The Vaults of History

Superstition Everywhere

Superstition is a common phenomenon among both ordinary folk as well as the rich and famous. Queen Elizabeth II of England was so afraid of severing the "ties of friendship" that she insisted on paying a halfpenny after being presented with a gift of cutlery. According to lore at the time, there was a superstition that said to accept a knife without some form of payment risked cutting the bonds of friendship with those who are close to you.

Writer Somerset Maugham warded off bad vibes by having the "evil eye" symbol carved into his fireplace mantel. Although British Prime Minister Winston Churchill was brilliant, he also struggled with his share of superstitions. He believed that Fridays were unlucky and avoided traveling on those days. Another famous figure who avoided traveling on Fridays was U.S. President Franklin D. Roosevelt. Also, if asked to sit at a table that accommodated 13 people, he would move to another table. To ensure a successful event, entertainer Al Jolson wore old clothes to open a new show. Grammy Award-winning singer and songwriter Missy "Misdemeanor" Elliott will actually turn around and go back home if a black cat crosses her path, regardless of her destination or purpose.

Wagons Ho!

If you were a child addicted to spending Saturday afternoon munching on popcorn and watching westerns, you probably thrilled at the scenes of wagon trains laboring across the open prairie. There would be an Indian attack, and the wagon master would scream at the top of his lungs, "Circle the wagons!" In reality, circling the wagons to defend against attacking Indians never really happened, and it was largely the invention of twentieth-century movie directors. The act of slowing down the horses and turning the wagons inward into a circle took far too long to be a defensive tactic. While it's true that travelers did circle their wagons at night when they camped, it was usually designed to corral the animals—not to guard against travelers getting scalped.

The Judith Coplon Case

How one beautiful American spied for the Russians and used promiscuity, patience, and the U.S. Constitution to best the FBI at the start of the Cold War.

✳ ✳ ✳ ✳

A Mother's Sorrow

IN THE SPRING of 1949, Mrs. Rebecca Coplon sat in a New York courtroom sobbing into a handkerchief. The cause of Mrs. Coplon's grief: Her beautiful and talented 27-year-old daughter Judith was on trial for international espionage.

Judith Coplon had come from a respectable family in upstate New York. Her father, a retired toy merchant, was known as the "Santa Claus of the Adirondacks" for his yuletide generosity to needy children. Judith herself had shown great promise at New York City's Barnard College and, more recently, as an analyst for the Department of Justice in Washington, D.C.

Sadly, Mr. Coplon died of a cerebral hemorrhage shortly after hearing of his daughter's arrest. Mrs. Coplon was completely unnerved by both her daughter's arrest and her husband's sudden demise. She could only sit sadly on the sidelines of one of the most sensational trials of the twentieth century.

A Sloppy Arrest

Judith Coplon had been arrested in New York City, ostensibly on her way to visit her family. In her possession were confidential documents that had been fed to her by FBI agents. The FBI suspected that Russian engineer and U.N. liaison Valentin Gubitchev, whom Coplon met with regularly, was more than he appeared to be. In fact, Coplon began gathering information for the Soviet Union in her college days, with Gubitchev acting as her case manager in the newly formed New York bureau of the KGB. Moreover, Coplon and Gubitchev were lovers.

The FBI already knew all of this. Following information gleaned from a secret decryption project codenamed "Verona," they conducted extensive wiretapping and surveillance of the pair to gain further information. However, the FBI arrested Coplon before she had actually handed the confidential documents to Gubitchev. What's more, they failed to obtain a warrant for her arrest, despite having had ample time to do so.

A Burlesque Trial

For her trial in Washington, D.C., Coplon hired the first lawyer she could find who agreed to work pro bono—the inexperienced, comedic, and essentially inept Archie Palmer. Despite his professional shortcomings, Archie turned out to be a genius at creating an aura of sensational wrongdoing and soon won public sympathy for Coplon's cause. The FBI alleged that, in addition to Gubitchev, Coplon was involved in a sexual relationship with a lawyer (who would end up serving as one of the prosecutors in a second trial in New York). However, Palmer's courtroom clowning and Coplon's hedged denials effectively downplayed the issue. Palmer sneered, laughed, and sarcastically poked holes in the FBI's case. He argued that the "confidential source" named by the FBI was nothing more than an illegal wiretap, which was true. One FBI agent even admitted that the details of the meeting between Coplon and Gubitchev were only known because of tapped phone conversations.

America's Evil Darling

The lurid details of Coplon's promiscuous and traitorous life made their way to the front pages and gossip columns of newspapers and magazines across the United States. The public was entranced by stories of the so-called "sexy spy," who giggled throughout her trial, and by the antics of her sensationalistic lawyer. Nevertheless, the juries in both the Washington, D.C., and New York trials found Coplon guilty. Both cases were appealed. The dubious legality of the wiretaps and the lack of an arrest warrant created a legal quagmire. As a result, Coplon never served a day in jail and lived to see both cases against her dismissed.

Tamanend, Chief of the Lenni Lenape

One statue that immortalizes Chief Tamanend stands in Philadelphia. Its inscription reveals the beloved leader's vision that English colonists and members of his tribe "live in peace as long as the waters run through the rivers and creeks and the stars and moon endure."

❋   ❋   ❋   ❋

Was There Really a Tamanend?

YES. HE WAS chief of the Native American Lenni Lenape tribe, also known as the Delaware, in the 1680s. His tribe was a member of the Unami, or Turtle clan, that lived in the Delaware River region. The name Tamanend means "pleasant," "polite," or "easy to talk to." Given these traits, it's not surprising that a missionary once described Tamanend as a long-revered figure among his people. He also allegedly sold a portion of what would become Pennsylvania to William Penn in 1683.

In keeping with his name, he swore to live in peace with Penn's people forever.

What Has Kept His Name Alive?

In addition to his own people, Tamanend made a strong impression on European colonists in America. By the time of the American Revolution, people celebrated the first of May as "Saint Tammany's Day." This holiday was a time for feasting and companionship that essentially replaced the May Day traditions of Europe. Though he was never an official saint, early Americans considered Tamanend, or "Tammany," to be a secular "patron saint" of their new home.

Who Else Used the Name "Tammany?"

In the 1770s, the Society of St. Tammany was formed, and chapters opened across the northeast. New York City's chapter would morph into the Tammany Hall political machine, the model for government corruption and influence peddling. Tammany Hall manipulated New York City politics and patronage beginning in the 1840s until it faded away in the 1960s.

The Myth About Brain Matter

Contrary to popular belief, adults can grow new brain cells.

✳   ✳   ✳   ✳

Science for the Birds

ODDLY ENOUGH, SOME of the first people to recognize that brains are not set in stone were crooked canary sellers. Because male canaries sing and female canaries usually do not, only male canaries fetch a handsome price at pet stores. In the 1940s and 1950s, enterprising bird importers took to injecting female canaries with testosterone in hopes of giving them the gift of song. The scam worked: The masculinized female canaries sang just long enough to be sold as males to hoodwinked pet-store owners and their unsuspecting customers.

Elevated Research

In the mid-1970s, when scientists at Rockefeller University repeated the canary sellers' testosterone experiments, they discovered that the region of the brain responsible for singing was much larger in male canaries than in females. The injected female birds generated glial cells (which give structural support to the brain) and new neurons in that region. Subsequent research at Cornell University confirmed that this was not just stuff for the birds: All vertebrate brains, whether canary or human, house precursor cells, which can be stimulated to develop into new neurons, just as they would during embryonic development. Adult neurogenesis holds the tantalizing promise of rebuilding brain cells destroyed by injury, stroke, or degenerative diseases such as Alzheimer's or Parkinson's—a goal long considered to be the Holy Grail of medical research.

Horsing Around

According to folk wisdom, the position of a horse's hooves on an equestrian statue—specifically, a statue of a military figure on horseback—reveals the way in which the rider died. It's an interesting theory, but it's not always accurate.

✳   ✳   ✳   ✳

ACCORDING TO THE most common version of the legend, if one hoof is raised, the rider was wounded in battle and may or may not have died from his wounds; two raised hooves means the rider died in battle; four hooves on the ground means the rider survived all of his battles without injury.

A good place to test this theory is Washington, D.C., which has more equestrian statues than any other city in the United States. A quick examination shows that many of the statues there follow this convention. For example, the horse in the statue commemorating Ulysses S. Grant has four hooves on the ground, and of course Grant survived the Civil War unharmed and went on to become the nation's eighteenth president. The statue commemorating Major General John A. Logan has one hoof raised, and Logan was twice wounded in battle but survived.

However, a great many other equestrian statues around the city do not accurately reflect the legend. For example, the statue of General Simon Bolivar features a horse with one hoof raised, yet Bolivar sustained no battle wounds and died of tuberculosis in peacetime. And the statue honoring Major General Andrew Jackson features a horse with two hooves raised, yet Jackson also died in peacetime long after he'd left military service.

Gettysburg's Ghosts

The Battle of Gettysburg holds a unique and tragic place in the annals of American history. It was the turning point of the Civil War and its bloodiest battle. From July 1 through July 3, 1863, both the Union and Confederate armies amassed a total of more than 50,000 casualties (including dead, wounded, and missing) at the Battle of Gettysburg. All that bloodshed and suffering is said to have permanently stained Gettysburg and left the entire area brimming with ghosts. It is often cited as one of the most haunted places in America.

✳ ✳ ✳ ✳

First Ghostly Sighting

FEW PEOPLE REALIZE that the first sighting of a ghost at Gettysburg allegedly took place before the battle was over. As the story goes, Union reinforcements from the 20th Maine Infantry were nearing Gettysburg but became lost as they traveled in the dark. As the regiment reached a fork in the road, they were greeted by a man wearing a three-cornered hat, who was sitting atop a horse. Both the man and his horse appeared to be glowing. The man, who bore a striking resemblance to George Washington, motioned for the regiment to follow. Believing the man to be a Union general, Colonel Joshua

Chamberlain ordered his regiment to follow the man. Just about the time Chamberlain starting thinking there was something odd about the helpful stranger, the man simply vanished.

As the regiment searched for him, they suddenly realized they had been led to Little Round Top—the very spot where, the following day, the 20th Maine Infantry would repel a Confederate advance in one of the turning points of the Battle of Gettysburg. To his dying day, Chamberlain, as well as the roughly 100 men who saw the spectral figure that night, believed that they had been led to Little Round Top by the ghost of George Washington himself.

Devil's Den

At the base of Little Round Top and across a barren field lies an outcropping of rocks known as Devil's Den. It was from this location that Confederate sharpshooters took up positions and fired at the Union soldiers stationed along Little Round Top. Eventually, Union soldiers followed the telltale sign of gun smoke and picked off the sharpshooters one by one.

After Devil's Den was secured by Union forces, famous Civil War photographer Alexander Gardner was allowed to come in and take photos of the area. One of his most famous pictures, "A Sharpshooter's Last Sleep," was taken at Devil's Den and shows a Confederate sharpshooter lying dead near the rocks. There was only one problem: The photograph was staged. Gardner apparently dragged a dead Confederate soldier over from another location and positioned the body himself. Legend has it that the ghost of the Confederate soldier was unhappy with how his body was treated, so his ghost often causes cameras in Devil's Den to malfunction.

Pickett's Charge

On July 3, the final day of the battle, Confederate General Robert E. Lee felt the battle slipping away from him, and in what many saw as an act of desperation, ordered 12,000 Confederate soldiers to attack the Union forces who were firmly entrenched on Cemetery Ridge. During the attack, known as Pickett's Charge, the Confederates slowly and methodically marched across open fields toward the heavily fortified Union lines. The attack failed miserably, with more than 6,000 Confederate soldiers killed or wounded before they retreated. The defeat essentially signaled the beginning of the end of the Civil War.

Today, it is said that if you stand on top of Cemetery Ridge and look out across the field, you might catch a glimpse of row after ghostly row of Confederate soldiers slowly marching toward their doom at the hands of Union soldiers.

Jennie Wade

While the battle was raging near Cemetery Ridge, 20-year-old Mary Virginia "Ginnie" Wade (also known as Jennie Wade) was at her sister's house baking bread for the Union troops stationed nearby. Without warning, a stray bullet flew through the house, struck the young woman, and killed her instantly, making her the only civilian known to die during the Battle of Gettysburg. Visitors to the historical landmark known as the Jennie Wade house often report catching a whiff of freshly baked bread. Jennie's spirit is also felt throughout the house, especially in the basement, where her body was placed until relatives could bury her when there was a break in the fighting.

Farnsworth House

Though it was next to impossible to determine who fired the shot that killed Jennie Wade, it is believed that it came from the attic of the Farnsworth house. Now operating as a bed-and-breakfast, during the Battle of Gettysburg the building was taken over by Confederate sharpshooters. One in particular, the one who may have fired the shot that killed Jennie Wade, is said to have holed himself up in the attic. No one knows for sure because the sharpshooter didn't survive the battle, but judging by the dozens of bullet holes and scars along the sides of the Farnsworth house, he didn't go down without a fight. Perhaps that's why his ghost is still lingering—to let us know what really happened in the Farnsworth attic. Passersby often report looking up at the attic window facing the Jennie Wade house and seeing a ghostly figure looking down at them.

Spangler's Spring

As soon as the Battle of Gettysburg was over, soldiers began relating their personal experiences to local newspapers. One story that spread quickly centered on the cooling waters of Spangler's Spring. It was said that at various times during the fierce fighting, both sides agreed to periodic ceasefires so that Union and Confederate soldiers could stand side-by-side and drink from the spring. It's a touching story, but in all likelihood, it never actually happened. Even if it did, it doesn't explain the ghostly woman in a white dress who is seen at the spring. Some claim that the "Woman in White" is the spirit of a woman who lost her lover during the Battle of Gettysburg. Another theory is that she was a young woman who took her own life after breaking up with her lover years after the war ended.

Pennsylvania Hall at Gettysburg College

One of the most frightening ghost stories associated with the Battle of Gettysburg was originally told to author Mark Nesbitt. The story centers around Gettysburg College's Pennsylvania Hall, which was taken over during the battle by Confederate forces, who turned the basement into a makeshift hospital. Late one night in the early 1980s, two men who were working on an upper floor got on the elevator and pushed the button for the first floor. But as the elevator descended, it passed the first floor and continued to the basement. Upon reaching the basement, the elevator doors opened. One look was all the workers needed to realize that they had some-how managed to travel back in time. The familiar surround-ings of the basement had been replaced by bloody, screaming Confederate soldiers on stretchers. Doctors stood over the soldiers, feverishly trying to save their lives. Blood and gore were everywhere.

As the two men started frantically pushing the elevator buttons, some of the doctors began walking toward them. Without a second to spare, the elevator doors closed just as the ghostly figures reached them. This time the elevator rose to the first floor and opened, revealing modern-day furnishings. Despite repeated return visits to the basement, nothing out of the ordinary has ever been reported again.

Myth Conceptions

Myth: If you shave hair on the face, legs, neck, etc., it will grow back thicker.

Fact: Nope. Shaving is simply the act of cutting the hair at the skin surface and has no effect on the part of the hair where growth and pigmentation occur—that happens way below the skin's surface.

Myth: Casino owners pump oxygen into their casinos to keep patrons awake, gambling, and giddy.

Fact: This is a myth. No casinos use this made-up method.

Myth: Sugar makes adults—and especially kids—hyper.

Fact: No evidence currently exists that shows feeding children a high-sugar diet will induce hyperactivity. In fact, some people get lethargic and tired after eating sugar.

Myth: Reading in dim light will ruin your eyesight.

Fact: There is no evidence to support this, though it is true that eyes have to work harder to see in dim light. Still, reading *War and Peace* at bedtime won't make you go blind—it might just make you sleepier.

Myth: Decaf coffee has no caffeine.

Fact: International standards say decaffeinated coffee must be 97 percent caffeine free.

Myth: You can tell what sex a baby will be by the height and position of the mother's belly.

Fact: This is purely an old wives' tale. There's no scientific proof that you can tell the sex of a baby until the baby's sex can be clearly seen.

Myth: You can cure a hangover with _____.

Fact: If you have a hangover, it's because you drank too much alcohol. No "hair of the dog that bit you" (i.e., more liquor), miracle pill, or strong coffee is going to help. Only time and proper hydration will cure what ails you.

Myth: Elephants are afraid of mice.

Truth: Who hasn't come across an image of a great elephant cowering in fear from the mere sight of a skittering mouse? This myth couldn't be further from the truth, because elephants— among the most fearless of all animals—barely notice mice, much less fear them. On occasion, an elephant will encounter a noise it cannot identify, in which case, it might demonstrate some nervousness. However, the squeak of a mouse does not typically send an elephant running for the hills, as folklore might suggest.

Myth: Henry Kissinger was the last person in Harvard history to graduate with straight A's.

Truth: While former national security advisor, secretary of state, and Nobel Peace Prize laureate Henry Kissinger was, in fact, a stellar student, since his 1950 graduation a few Harvard alums have managed to pick up their diplomas with a stream of straight A's behind them. Besides, although Kissinger most certainly did graduate summa cum laude, his record of straight A's wasn't quite as perfect as the myth implies. It was apparently slightly tarnished by one pesky little B in a philosophy course.

Myth: Yreka, a small town in Siskiyou County near the Oregon border in northern California, was so named for a poorly made canvas sign at the town's bakeshop that transmitted the word bakery without the b and backward.

Truth: Mark Twain furthered this rumor in his autobiography, relaying the explanation as he had heard it. According to his understanding, soon after the town's settling, visitors to the small community saw a freshly painted bakery sign upon entering town. The *B* had not yet been painted on, so the sign appeared to read *yreka*. The community had not yet been named, so when the visitors began calling it by this odd name, the community supposedly picked up on it, too. In truth, the story of the bakery sign is just a clever legend. The name *Yreka* actually comes from a Native American word meaning "white mountain," after the nearby Mount Shasta.

Under a Raging Moon

Does a full moon really influence people's behavior?

✳   ✳   ✳   ✳

EVERYONE KNOWS THAT crazy things happen during a full moon. Or do they? Folklore regarding the connection has long, deep roots. In fact, the word lunatic derives from the Latin *luna*, or "moon." Recently, studies have been performed to establish a tie between human behavior and the phases of the moon. These tests have focused on such things as homicides, common crimes, even post-surgical crises during lunar phases. Like the full moon itself, the results have proved illuminating.

In one prominent study, University of Miami psychologist Arnold Lieber zeroed in on homicides. During a 15-year period, his team collected murder data from Dade County, Florida. The researchers found that of the 1,887 recorded murders during the period, the incident rate uncannily rose and fell based upon phases of the moon. Simply put, as a full moon or a new moon approached, murders rose sharply. Conversely, homicides dropped off significantly during the moon's first and

last quarters. A previous study performed by the American Institute of Medical Climatology had similar findings. That test revealed a correlation between the full moon and peaks in psychotically oriented crimes such as arson and murder. But criminal impulses aren't the only things mirroring phases of the moon. A study of 1,000 tonsillectomies listed in the *Journal of the Florida Medical Association* revealed that 82 percent of postoperative bleeding crises occurred nearest the full moon, even though fewer tonsillectomies were performed during that period.

While such findings certainly sound definitive, scientists are reluctant to pronounce a direct connection until a physical model becomes accepted. As for theories that explain *why* the moon might have an influence over human behavior, Dr. Lieber speculates that a human being's water composition may undergo a "biological tide" that wreaks havoc with emotions and body processes. But the fact is that no one can say for certain if the human/lunar connection is real or just so much howling at the moon. Stay tuned.

Christmas Myths!

Be careful what you believe—the Christmas holidays are rife with urban legends, very few of which are true.

✻ ✻ ✻ ✻

CHRISTMAS HAS SPAWNED a variety of urban legends over the years, myths and incredible stories that, upon closer examination, almost always prove to be false. Here is a sampling of the most popular:

1. Myth: The number of suicides jumps dramatically over the Christmas holidays.

Fact: Proponents of this urban legend believe that the joy of the Christmas season exacerbates the hopelessness felt by many, causing them to take their own lives. However, numerous studies have found this not to be true. One of the most compelling was a Mayo Clinic survey of suicides over a 35-year period that failed to find even a small spike in self-inflicted deaths before, during, or after the Christmas holidays.

2. Myth: "The Twelve Days of Christmas" was written as a coded reference to Catholicism during a period in British history when the religion was illegal.

Fact: According to this myth, "The Twelve Days of Christmas" is a catechism song chock full of hidden meaning. "Two turtle doves," for example, refers to the Old and New Testaments of the Bible, and "three French hens" means the theological virtues of faith, hope, and charity. However, there is absolutely no historical evidence that this claim, which dates back only to the 1990s, is true. At best, it's mere speculation.

3. Myth: Salvation Army bell ringers get to keep a portion of the money placed in their kettles.

Fact: This is absolutely untrue, Salvation Army officials state. Most bell-ringers are volunteers, though some are paid seasonal employees, often recruited from homeless shelters and the Salvation Army's own retirement homes when volunteers are in short supply. Those hired receive a straight salary, while all of the money dropped into their kettles goes toward a variety of charitable endeavors.

4. Myth: A dad who was supposed to miss Christmas because he was on a business trip decided to cancel the trip at the last minute and surprise his kids by dressing up as St. Nick and sliding down the chimney. Unfortunately, the man became stuck and died of asphyxiation. His family knew nothing about his plans … until they lit a fire in the fireplace.

Fact: This is one of the oldest and most oft-repeated holiday urban legends to make the rounds. It's certainly a great story, but a single real-life case has yet to be verified. You can find a variation on this urban legend in the movie *Gremlins* (1984); it's how Phoebe Cates's character lost her dad.

5. Myth: The common abbreviation for Christmas—Xmas—is a disrespectful attempt to remove Christ from the holiday.

Fact: Everyone needs to calm down. The use of "Xmas" as an abbreviation for Christmas is eons old and based on the fact that the Greek word for Christ begins with the letter *chi*, which is represented in the modern Roman alphabet by a symbol that closely resembles an *X*.

6. Myth: The candy cane was invented as a tribute to Jesus. The shape represents the letter *J* and the red and white stripes symbolize purity and the blood of Christ.

Fact: A variation on this urban legend also suggests that candy canes were created as a form of secret identification among Christians during a period of persecution; both stories are false. The truth is that this popular Christmas candy has been around at least since the late seventeenth century (when there was little persecution of Christians in Europe), but the color striping is strictly a twentieth century invention developed for decoration and flavor.

Thirsty for Knowledge

Medical experts have been warning people for years: If you wait until you're thirsty to drink, it may be too late because dehydration may have already set in. This topic still generates controversy, but here are the prevailing thoughts on thirst.

✳ ✳ ✳ ✳

To DRINK OR not to drink before you're thirsty: That's the question some physicians, nutritionists, and athletes still debate. Although many people worry about becoming dehydrated, most experts believe that if you drink when you're thirsty, you'll be well hydrated.

Kidney expert Heinz Valtin, M.D., of Dartmouth Medical School, disputes the idea that people are already dehydrated by the time they are thirsty. He believes thirst begins when the concentration of blood (an accurate indicator of our state of hydration) has risen by less than 2 percent. However, other experts define dehydration as beginning when that concentration has risen by at least 5 percent.

How did the thirst-dehydration debate start? It could have simply been the result of a successful marketing campaign. Look at all the products devoted to continuous water intake—spring water, demineralized water, fancy water-bottle holders, and water tubes for athletes, just to name a few.

Dr. Valtin thinks the notion may have begun when the Food and Nutrition Board of the National Research Council recommended approximately "one milliliter of water for each calorie of food," which would amount to roughly two to two and a half quarts per day (64 to 80 ounces). The council also said most of that amount is contained in prepared foods, but that fact likely was missed or misinterpreted, leading to the "8×8" rule—8 eight-ounce glasses of water per day. To consume that amount, you would obviously have to drink before you were thirsty.

So unless you need lots of water to prevent kidney stones, or for running marathons or living in a hot, dry climate, listen to your body: Drink when you're thirsty.

Priority Seating

Most people who fly on planes have little choice about where they sit. If they did, a popular misconception might have the majority of passengers clamoring for the back of the plane rather than the first-class section.

❋ ❋ ❋ ❋

ANY TRAVELER WILL tell you that sitting at the back of an airplane is just a stifling sound track of engine roars punctuated by toilet flushes. But you'd be surprised at the number of people who will weather the annoyances because they are convinced that the back of the plane is a much safer place to sit than the front. After all, they reason, a debilitated plane plunges nose first, so those seated in front would at least be first to redeem their lifetime air miles for a pair of angel wings.

Some aviation experts say the back of a plane is statistically safer by about 10 percent over business class—a small consolation. But others insist that the seats over the wings are the safest ones to occupy, because the structure of the wing section can absorb more impact damage. The prevailing wisdom, however, is that the seats closest to the emergency exits are your best bet.

When most people think of aviation accidents, they conjure up catastrophic midflight events in which mechanical malfunctions send a plane plummeting to the ground or into a mountainside. The fact is that nearly 95 percent of all airplane mishaps take place either at takeoff or during landing, which means the high-altitude cruise is actually the safest part of the journey.

Misquote Gains Momentum

According to bumper stickers and T-shirts worldwide, Thomas Jefferson believed that "Dissent is the highest form of patriotism." The problem is that this quote didn't exist ten years ago, let alone in the eighteenth century.

✳ ✳ ✳ ✳

Thomas Jefferson would be impressed by the wildfire spread of his latest alleged sound bite. Tracing this misquote's proliferation is like watching somebody trip in slow motion—you see it happening but aren't sure if the person's reflexes are a match for the inevitability of gravity.

During an interview on July 3, 2002, American historian and social scientist Howard Zinn defended his opposition to the war on terror by arguing that "Dissent is the highest form of patriotism. In fact, if patriotism means being true to the principles for which your country is supposed to stand, then certainly the right to dissent is one of those principles." Zinn appears to be the originator of this quote, and it quickly popped up in political speeches and newspaper articles as a defense for opposition to the war in Iraq.

That would have been the end of it, had the quote not become a nexus for Republican versus Democrat warfare. Republican bloggers picked up on the quote's false source and attacked Senator John Kerry for misattributing it to Jefferson in a 2006 antiwar speech. Since then, so many journalists have debunked the misquote that it just may eventually be salvaged and properly sourced as a Zinn quote. As for Jefferson, he would have wanted nothing to do with the affair, as he explained in a letter he wrote in 1797: "So many persons have of late found an interest or a passion gratified by imputing to me sayings and writings which I never said or wrote ... that I have found it necessary for my quiet and my other pursuits to leave them in full possession of the field.

Howlin' at the Moon

One of the most romanticized images of the wild is that of a lone wolf howling against the backdrop of a full moon. The light of the moon usually gets our attention, but it's doubtful that a wolf cares what's happening in the night sky.

✳ ✳ ✳ ✳

WHEN SHAKESPEARE WROTE, "Now the hungry lion roars and the wolf behowls the moon," he was referring to the long-held belief that wolves are more likely to howl when the moon is full. In fact, wolves howl at all times, and the moon itself doesn't trigger any special reaction from them. When any animal howls, it extends its neck upward, but this is to project sound rather than to target a specific object.

The notion that wolves howl at the moon is probably common among people because *they* are attracted to a full moon, not because wolves are. Moonlight draws people outdoors, which increases the chances that they will hear the sounds of wildlife at night. Anecdotal reports that wolves howl more during a full moon are not backed by scientific observation.

Wolves howl for a variety of reasons. The alpha wolf will howl to gather pack members for a hunt, and a wolf that has been separated from its pack will howl to try to regain contact. The most haunting sound is when a group of wolves howl in a chorus to claim a stretch of territory. By shifting the pitch of their howls, the pack makes itself sound larger than it is. Wolves will howl in this manner through an entire night and can be heard for miles. These are the scary sounds that punctuate the scenes of countless horror movies, serving to cement in our consciousness the connection between wolves and a full moon.

Shhh! It's A Secret Society

Though documentation proves this secret organization to preserve the Southern cause did indeed exist, many mysteries remain about the Knights of the Golden Circle.

✳ ✳ ✳ ✳

THE KNIGHTS OF the Golden Circle was a pro-South organization that operated out of the Deep South, the border states, the Midwest, and even parts of the North both before and during the Civil War. Much of its history is unknown due to its underground nature, but it is known that this secret society, bound by passwords, rituals, and handshakes, intended to preserve Southern culture and states' rights. Its precise origin, membership, and purpose are documented in a handful of primary sources, including the club's handbook, an exposé published in 1861, and a wartime government report that revealed the K.G.C. to be a serious threat to the federal government and its effort to quash the rebellion and maintain the Union.

Some historians trace the organization of the Knights of the Golden Circle back to the 1830s, though the name did not surface publicly until 1855. According to a report by the U.S. government in 1864, the organization included as many as 500,000 members in the North alone and had "castles," or local chapters, spread across the country. Members included everyone from notable politicians to the rank and file, all prepared to rise up against federal coercion as they saw their rights to slavery slipping away.

What's in a Name?

The group's name referred to a geographic "Golden Circle" that surrounded the Deep South. Its boundaries were the border states on the north, America's western territories, Mexico, Central America, and even Cuba. Southern leaders and organization members hoped to gain control of these lands to create a strong, agrarian economy dependent on slavery and plantations.

This would either balance the numbers of slave states to free states in the federal government or provide a distinct nation that could separate from the Union. The proslavery leader John C. Calhoun of South Carolina was the group's intellectual mentor, although the K.G.C. didn't likely achieve great numbers before his death in 1850. The 1864 government report cited that members initially used nuohlac, Calhoun spelled backward, as a password.

Adding Fuel to the Fire

Once the Civil War began, the K.G.C. became a concern for both state and federal governments. The most obvious public figure associated with the K.G.C. was Dr. George Bickley, an eccentric pamphleteer of questionable character. He is credited with organizing the first castle of the Knights of the Golden Circle in his hometown of Cincinnati. He also sent an open letter to the Kentucky legislature declaring that his organization had 8,000 members in the state, with representatives in every county. The legislature called for a committee to investigate the organization, which had begun to menace that state's effort to remain neutral by importing arms and ammunition for the secession cause. Federal officers arrested Bickley in New Albany, Indiana, in 1863 with a copy of the society's Rules, Regulations, and Principles of the K.G.C. and other regalia on his person. He was held in the Ohio state prison until late 1865. Bickley died two years later, never having been formally charged with a crime.

Methods and Tactics

The underground group used subversive tactics to thwart the Lincoln administration's effort once the war began. A telegram between a Union colonel and Secretary of War Edwin Stanton states how the "Holy Brotherhood" sought to encourage Union soldiers to desert and to paint the conflict as a war in favor of abolition. Some of the government's more questionable wartime tactics, such as the suspension of habeas corpus and the quelling of some aspects of a free press, were rallying points in the Midwest, and they were issues that surely connected northern dissidents such as Copperheads with the Knights in spirit if not in reality. When antiwar sentiment and Peace Democrats influenced populations in Indiana, a U.S. court subpoenaed witnesses for a grand jury to learn more about the organization. The grand jury claimed the secret organization had recruited 15,000 members in Indiana alone and indicted 60 people in August 1862. The Union army attempted to infiltrate the organization and expose its subversive operations by sending new recruits back home to join the K.G.C.

Political Ties

Nationally known political leaders were also allegedly tied to the group. The 1861 exposé referred to a certain "Mr. V—of Ohio" as one of the few reliable members among prominent Northern politicians. It would likely have been assumed that this referred to leading Copperhead and Ohio Representative Clement Vallandigham, who decried abolition before the war and criticized Republicans in Congress and the administration. Union officers arrested Vallandigham, and a military court exiled him to the South. Another possible member was John C. Breckenridge, vice president under James Buchanan and a presidential candidate in 1860. Even former President Franklin Pierce was accused of having an affiliation with the organization.

Assassination Conspiracy

Some also believe that the K.G.C. had a hand in the assassination of Abraham Lincoln. The contemporary exposé stated, "Some one of them is to distinguish himself for—if he can, that is—the assassination of the 'Abolition' President." According to a later anonymous account, Lincoln's assassin, John Wilkes Booth, took the oath of the society in a Baltimore castle in the fall of 1860.

Myth Conceptions

Myth: Swallowing gum is dangerous because it will stay in your system for seven years.

Fact: Actually, gum doesn't just hang out in your guts. The gum will pass through your system and will likely come out the other end looking just like it did while you were chewing it. Ick.

Myth: Dried fruit isn't as good for you as fresh fruit.

Fact: Actually, ounce for ounce, dried fruit has the nutrients and vitamins that fresh fruit have, just less vitamin C. Stay away from dried fruit that has added sugar, but otherwise, eat all you want and rest easy knowing you got your fruit for the day.

Myth: If you don't dress warmly in the winter, you'll catch a cold.

Fact: Viruses, which cause the common cold, have no response to the temperature. People tend to get more colds in wintertime because they spend more time indoors with other people and viruses pass most easily between other humans.

Myth: Fingerprints are there to help you grip stuff.

Fact: Nope. Scientists in 2009 tested this age-old hypothesis and found that fingerprints don't improve a grip's friction. Why? Because fingerprints reduce our skin's contact with objects that we hold—and can actually loosen our grip in some circumstances. The actual reason for our fingerprints remains a bit of a mystery.

Myth: The trucks that collect recycling end up burning more energy and produce more pollution, making recycling pointless.

Fact: No way. It does take a lot of energy to recycle—in fact, it takes up about half of a recycling program's budget—but it's still worth it. It takes a lot less energy to convert something that already exists as, say, plastic, than to create plastic from raw materials. So keep recycling, kids.

Myth: Healthy folks poop once a day.

Fact: Though moving your bowels regularly helps keep away discomfort and constipation, studies show perfectly healthy people don't necessarily poop every day. You're not officially constipated until you've gone three days without a bowel movement.

Does the Ghost of Aaron Burr Take the Subway?

A particular gentleman has been seen hanging out in a café and at a romantic restaurant in Greenwich Village, wandering the halls of a historic mansion in Washington Heights, and gazing at New York Harbor from Battery Park. He's even been spotted at a historic inn in Pennsylvania and a cemetery in New Jersey. The problem is that he's been dead for nearly 200 years. The spirit of Aaron Burr is a ghost that gets around.

✳ ✳ ✳ ✳

Burr's Long Life Leads to an Even Longer Afterlife

ALTHOUGH AARON BURR might be most famous for killing Alexander Hamilton in a duel, this incident was not the only part of his life that might have caused his soul to remain earthbound. Born in 1756, Burr was a brilliant lawyer who served under George Washington during the Revolutionary War. He was chosen as a senator from New York in 1791 and was nearly elected President of the United States in 1800; instead, he served as Thomas Jefferson's vice president.

By the summer of 1804, near the end of Burr's term as V.P., it was clear that he would not be on the ballot for reelection. Instead, he decided to run for governor of New York, but much political intrigue ensued, which led to his fateful duel with Hamilton on July 11, 1804. Despite the fact that dueling was illegal in New Jersey (where the fatal encounter took place),

Burr never stood trial for murder, and all charges against him were eventually dropped.

After finishing his term as vice president, Burr headed west, where he met up with a friend from the Revolutionary War who turned out to be a spy for Spain. As a result, Burr was accused of plotting to invade Mexico and was tried for treason. He was found not guilty, but to avoid creditors, he traveled to Europe shortly thereafter. In France, Burr attempted to enlist Napoleon in a plot to invade Florida, but the emperor declined to get involved. In 1812, Burr returned to New York to practice law. He died in 1836 in Staten Island—although that is one of the few places his ghost has *not* been seen—and was buried in Princeton, New Jersey, where his specter has been spotted several times.

A Ghost that Gets Around

In the early 1960s, Burr's apparition was seen in a building in Greenwich Village that, back in his time, would have abutted the stables of his estate, Richmond Hill. In July 1961, the owner of the Café Bizarre entered the building to pick up a package that she'd left behind earlier in the day. Although it was very late at night and the place was closed, she sensed that she was not alone. In a dark corner, she saw a man with piercing black eyes who was wearing a ruffled white shirt. When she demanded to know who he was, he remained silent and seemed to smile. Previously, a waiter had quit immediately after seeing this same spectral figure. In 1962, a psychic confirmed that someone with the initials "A. B." was connected to the site.

A few years later, Burr's ghost spoke to a young girl as she walked by the café; he wanted her to find information that would prove that he was not treasonous. In 1967, a psychic spoke with a spirit that declared that he was not a traitor or a murderer and called out for "Theo," Burr's pet name for his daughter Theodosia.

The psychics who conducted this séance hoped that it would allow Burr's spirit to rest, but unfortunately, it did not. Patrons and staff at the restaurant One If By Land, Two If By Sea on Barrow Street in Manhattan have also experienced Burr-related paranormal activity. They've had chairs pulled out from under them and witnessed dishes thrown by invisible hands. Many women sitting at the bar find their earrings mysteriously removed, and a maître d' quit after being shoved repeatedly by an unseen force. These unexplained acts have been attributed to the restless spirits of Aaron Burr and his beloved daughter, Theodosia Burr Alston, who have apparently been reunited in the afterlife at the site of what was originally part of Richmond Hill. (Theo's ghost has also been spotted near Huntington Beach State Park in Nags Head, North Carolina, where her ship disappeared or was captured by pirates. It is rumored that Theo was forced to walk the plank, which perhaps explains the angry pushing and throwing that takes place at the restaurant.)

Eight miles north of the former Café Bizarre and One If By Land, Two If By Sea, Burr has also been known to greet guests at the Morris-Jumel Mansion in Washington Heights, where he lived with his second wife, Eliza Jumel. As one might expect given that it is the oldest house in Manhattan, Aaron Burr is not the only spirit that resides there: The specters of a servant girl who committed suicide at the mansion, a Revolutionary War soldier, and Eliza Jumel also wander the property.

Burr has also been seen standing by the American Merchant Marine Memorial at Battery Park, which is located at the southern end of Manhattan. Many have surmised that he waits in perpetuity for Theo to arrive. Only a few blocks away, Alexander Hamilton is buried at Trinity Church. Perhaps Burr seeks another chance to set the record straight about what really happened during their infamous duel.

Breaking Out of the Big Apple

Burr is not content to haunt various neighborhoods in Manhattan, however. After the duel with Hamilton, Burr hid for at least a week at a residence in New Hope, Pennsylvania. Today, his spirit continues to seek refuge there, although the building is now known as the Wedgewood Inn. One woman saw a male figure in Colonial clothing standing behind her as she wiped steam off the bathroom mirror; when she turned to face him, no one was there. Other guests have reported feeling someone staring at them from behind. Known as "Burr's sightless stare," the phenomenon tends to occur on the second floor and in the stairwell leading to the basement, but it has been known to happen throughout the house.

Even before Burr's ghost was reported in Manhattan, the staff at Lindenwald—Martin Van Buren's childhood home in Kinderhook, New York—knew that he was not resting peacefully. After killing Hamilton, Burr spent three years at Lindenwald, and after his death, strange sounds—such as footsteps of a man pacing back and forth—were heard inside the house. Burr—dressed in a burgundy coat with lace cuffs—also presented his spectral self to servants outside the house.

Many historians feel that Aaron Burr was a misunderstood patriot whose enemies destroyed his reputation and career. Whether or not this is the case, his restless wanderings are as extensive in death as they were in life.

Vanished: The Lost Colony of Roanoke Island

Twenty years before England established its first successful colony in the New World, an entire village of English colonists disappeared in what would later be known as North Carolina. Did these pioneers all perish? Did Native Americans capture them? Did they join a friendly tribe?

* * * *

Timing Is Everything

TALK ABOUT BAD timing. As far as John White was concerned, England couldn't have picked a worse time to go to war. It was November 1587, and White had just arrived in England from the New World. He intended to gather relief supplies and immediately sail back to Roanoke Island, where he had left more than 100 colonists who were running short of food. Unfortunately, the English were gearing up to fight Spain. Every seaworthy ship, including White's, was pressed into naval service. Not a one could be spared for his return voyage to America.

Nobody Home

When John White finally returned to North America three years later, he was dismayed to discover that the colonists he had left behind were nowhere to be found. Instead, he stumbled upon a mystery—one that has never been solved.

The village that White and company had founded in 1587 on Roanoke Island lay completely deserted. Houses had been dismantled (as if someone planned to move them), but the pieces lay in the long grass along with iron tools and farming equipment. A stout stockade made of logs stood empty.

White found no sign of his daughter Eleanor, her husband Ananias, or their daughter Virginia Dare—the first English child born in America. None of the 87 men, 17 women, and 11 children remained. No bodies or obvious gravesites offered clues to their fate. The only clues—if they were clues—that White could find were the letters CRO carved into a tree trunk and the word CROATOAN carved into a log of the abandoned fort.

No Forwarding Address

All White could do was hope that the colonists had been taken in by friendly natives.

Croatoan—also spelled "Croatan"—was the name of a barrier island to the south and also the name of a tribe of Native Americans that lived on that island. Unlike other area tribes, the Croatoans had been friendly to English newcomers, and one of them, Manteo, had traveled to England with earlier explorers and returned to act as interpreter for the Roanoke colony. Had the colonists, with Manteo's help, moved to Croatoan? Were they safe among friends?

White tried to find out, but his timing was rotten once again. He had arrived on the Carolina coast as a hurricane bore down on the region. The storm hit before he could mount a search. His ship was blown past Croatoan Island and out to sea. Although the ship and crew survived the storm and made it back to England, White was stuck again. He tried repeatedly but failed to raise money for another search party.

No one has ever learned the fate of the Roanoke Island colonists, but there is no shortage of theories as to what happened to them. A small sailing vessel and other boats that White had left with them were gone when he returned. It's possible that the colonists used the vessels to travel to another island or to the mainland. White had talked with others before he left about possibly moving the settlement to a more secure location inland. It's even possible that the colonists tired of waiting for White's return and tried to sail back to England. If so, they would have perished at sea. Yet there are at least a few shreds of hearsay evidence that the colonists survived in America.

Rumors of Survivors

In 1607, Captain John Smith and company established the first successful English settlement in North America at Jamestown, Virginia. The colony's secretary, William Strachey, wrote four years later about hearing a report of four English men, two boys, and one young woman who had been sighted south of Jamestown at a settlement of the Eno tribe, where they were being used as slaves.

If the report was true, who else could these English have been but Roanoke survivors? For more than a century after the colonists' disappearance, stories emerged of gray-eyed Native Americans and English-speaking villages in North Carolina and Virginia. In 1709, an English surveyor said members of the Hatteras tribe living on North Carolina's Outer Banks—some of them with light-colored eyes—claimed to be descendants of white people. It's possible that the Hatteras were the same people that the 1587 colonists called Croatoan.

In the intervening centuries, many of the individual tribes of the region have disappeared. Some died out. Others were absorbed into larger groups such as the Tuscarora. One surviving group, the Lumbee, has also been called Croatoan. The Lumbee, who still live in North Carolina, often have Caucasian features. Could they be descendants of Roanoke colonists? Many among the Lumbee dismiss the notion as fanciful, but the tribe has long been thought to be of mixed heritage and has been speaking English so long that none among them know what language preceded it.

Red Eyes Over Point Pleasant: The Mysterious Mothman

In 1942, the U.S. government took control of several thousand acres of land just north of Point Pleasant, West Virginia. The purpose was to build a secret facility capable of creating and storing TNT that could be used during World War II. For the next three years, the facility cranked out massive amounts of TNT, shipping it out or storing it in one of the numerous concrete "igloo" structures that dotted the area. In 1945, the facility was shut down and eventually abandoned, but it was here that an enigmatic flying creature with glowing red eyes made its home years later.

✳   ✳   ✳   ✳

"Red Eyes on the Right"

O N THE EVENING of November 15, 1966, Linda and Roger Scarberry were out driving with another couple, Mary and Steve Mallette. As they drove, they decided to take a detour that took them past the abandoned TNT factory.

As they neared the gate of the old factory, they noticed two red lights up ahead. When Roger stopped the car, the couples were horrified to find that the red lights appeared to be two glowing red eyes. What's more, those eyes belonged to a creature standing more than seven feet tall with giant wings folded behind it. That was all Roger needed to see before he hit the gas pedal and sped off. In response, the creature calmly unfolded its wings and flew toward the car. Incredibly, even though Roger raced along at speeds close to 100 miles per hour, the red-eyed creature was able to keep up with them without much effort.

Upon reaching Point Pleasant, the two couples ran from their car to the Mason County Courthouse and alerted Deputy Millard Halstead of their terrifying encounter. Halstead couldn't be sure exactly what the two couples had seen, but whatever it was, it had clearly frightened them. In an attempt to calm them down, Halstead agreed to accompany them to the TNT factory. As his patrol car neared the entrance, the police radio suddenly emitted a strange, whining noise. Other than that, despite a thorough search of the area, nothing out of the ordinary was found.

More Encounters

Needless to say, once word got around Point Pleasant that a giant winged creature with glowing red eyes was roaming around the area, everyone had to see it for themselves. The creature didn't disappoint. Dubbed Mothman by the local press, the creature was spotted flying overhead, hiding, and even lurking on front porches. In fact, in the last few weeks of November, dozens of witnesses encountered the winged beast. But Mothman wasn't the only game in town. It seems that around the same time that he showed up, local residents started noticing strange lights in the evening sky, some of which hovered silently over the abandoned TNT factory. Of course, this led some to believe that Mothman and the UFOs were somehow connected. One such person was Mary Hyre of *The Athens Messenger*, who had been reporting on the strange activities in Point Pleasant since they started. Perhaps that's why she became the first target.

Beware the Men in Black

One day, while Mary Hyre was at work, several strange men visited her office and began asking questions about the lights in the sky. Normally, she didn't mind talking to people about the UFO sightings and Mothman. But there was something peculiar about these guys. For instance, they all dressed exactly the same: black suits, black ties, black hats, and dark sunglasses. They also spoke in a strange monotone and seemed confused by ordinary objects such as ballpoint pens. As the men left, Hyre wondered whether they had been from another planet. Either way, she had an up-close-and-personal encounter with the legendary Men in Black.

Mary Hyre was not the only person to have a run-in with the Men in Black. As the summer of 1967 rolled around, dozens of people were interrogated by them. In most cases, the men showed up unannounced at the homes of people who had recently witnessed a Mothman or UFO sighting. For the most part, the men simply wanted to know what the witnesses had seen. But sometimes, the men went to great lengths to convince the witnesses that they were mistaken and had not seen anything out of the ordinary. Other times, the men threatened witnesses. Each time the Men in Black left a witness's house, they drove away in a black, unmarked sedan. Despite numerous attempts to determine who these men were and where they came from, their identity remained a secret.

The Silver Bridge Tragedy

Erected in 1928, the Silver Bridge was a gorgeous chain suspension bridge that spanned the Ohio River, connecting Point Pleasant with Ohio. On December 15, 1967, the bridge was busy with holiday shoppers bustling back and forth between West Virginia and Ohio. As the day wore on, more and more cars started filling the bridge until shortly before 5:00 P.M., when traffic on the bridge came to a standstill. For several minutes, none of the cars budged. Suddenly, there was a loud popping noise and then the unthinkable happened: The Silver Bridge collapsed, sending dozens of cars and their passengers into the freezing water below.

Over the next few days, local authorities and residents searched the river hoping to find survivors, but in the end, 46 people lost their lives in the bridge collapse. A thorough investigation determined that a manufacturing flaw in one of the bridge's supporting bars caused the collapse. But there are others who claim that in the days and weeks leading up to the collapse, they saw the Mothman and even the Men in Black around, on, and even under the bridge. Further witnesses state that while most of Point Pleasant was watching the Silver Bridge collapse, bright lights and strange objects were flying out of the area and disappearing into the winter sky. Perhaps that had nothing to do with the collapse of the Silver Bridge, but the Mothman has not been seen since...or has he?

Mothman Lives!

There are reports that the Mothman is still alive and well and has moved on to other areas of the United States. There are even those who claim that he was spotted flying near the Twin Towers on September 11, 2001, leading to speculation that Mothman is a portent of doom and only appears when disasters are imminent. Some believe Mothman was a visitor from another planet who returned home shortly after the Silver Bridge fell. Still others think the creature was the result of the toxic chemicals eventually discovered in the area near the TNT factory.

Say It Ain't So

Myth: Suck on a penny to beat a breathalyzer test.

Truth: Pennies have no magical control over boozy breath. From the early 1980s on, pennies have been made mostly of zinc with a thin copper exterior. Neither zinc nor copper has any known power to ward off the long arm of the law.

Myth: Turkeys are so stupid they will drown themselves while admiring a downpour of rain.

Truth: Perhaps Thanksgiving Day enthusiasts invented this lame-brained myth to make themselves feel better about rampant feasting on dim-witted turkeys once a year, but there is no truth to this odd idea. Turkeys, although never seen working their way through a tricky crossword puzzle, are no more mentally challenged than any other bird. Besides, turkeys are not even physically capable of staring up at the falling rain as described in this myth. Turkeys' eyes are set on opposite sides of their noggins so, at best, were they so mesmerized by the rain, only one eye at a time could view its fall.

Myth: Geraldo Rivera changed his name from the more Anglo Jerry Rivers to draw in Latino fans.

Truth: Although calling talk show icon Geraldo Rivera a journalist might, according to some, be a misnomer, calling him Mr. Rivera is not. His grandparents came from Puerto Rico and brought the Rivera surname with them. Born Gerald Rivera to a Latin dad and a Jewish mom, Geraldo's only name change came with the addition of a somewhat subtle o, not a full-fledged switch from Jerry Rivers as has oft been claimed.

Myth: Opossums swing upside down on trees, hanging only by their tails.

Truth: Opossums, the only North American marsupial, do not hang from trees by their tails, but they are extremely adept tree crawlers. The sturdy tail provides leverage in scaling trees and— thanks to a pair of opposable thumbs on their hind feet—opossums can easily grasp branches and such for optimal scrambling. However, erase the image of upside-down, dangling opossums, because tail swinging isn't the norm.

An Overture to William Tell

Most of us learned about the controversial legend as children. This should help answer any lingering questions.

✳   ✳   ✳   ✳

Let's go over the legend again. In 1307, Austria's Hapsburgs wanted to clamp down on the Swiss. An Austrian official named Hermann Gessler put his hat atop a pole and then made a petty, ridiculous rule: All passersby had to bow to his hat. An expert crossbowman named William Tell refused to bow, so Gessler's police arrested him. But Gessler wasn't satisfied with that.

In a fit of sadistic illogic, Gessler made a deal with Tell. If Tell could shoot an apple off Tell's son Walter's head with the crossbow, both would be free. If Tell whiffed, or nailed his son, Gessler would execute him. Tell hit the apple but couldn't resist a snarky comment to Gessler. The latter, not renowned for his *joie de vivre*, got mad and threw Tell in jail. Eventually, Tell escaped and assassinated Gessler. This touched off a rebellion that led to the Swiss Confederation (which is still in business today, operating banks and ski lifts).

Where's the controversy? To begin with, there is no contemporary historical evidence for Tell or Gessler. The legend first appeared in the late 1400s, and no one can explain the delay. What's more, the motif of an archer shooting a target off his son's head, then slaying a tyrant, appears in diverse Germanic literature predating 1307. It's not that the William Tell legend is necessarily false, because we can't prove it. The combination of faults—lack of evidence, duplication of older legends—makes the William Tell story a tough sell as history.

How do the Swiss feel about it? It wasn't easy for Swiss patriots to carve out and hold their own country with all the warlike tides of Europe buffeting them. The multilingual Swiss have built and maintained a prosperous Confederation that avoids warfare from a position of strength. William Tell symbolizes Swiss love of freedom and disdain for tyrants, domestic or foreign.

Steel-Driving John Henry

"But John Henry drove his steel sixteen feet…an' the steam drill drove only nine." So the song goes. We'd like to believe in John Henry. Two different towns claim him, but who's right?

✳   ✳   ✳   ✳

Retelling the legend. It's a great one. They say that John Henry was born and raised a slave, perhaps in the 1840s. He grew up into a fortress of a man, a mighty worker, and after slavery ended he went to work for a railroad. In order to blast railroad tunnels, someone had to hammer a long steel stake deep into the rock, creating a hole where others could slide in dynamite. After workers cleared away the blasted rock, the "steel-driving men" got busy pounding more stakes. Henry was the best in the business. One day someone brought in a newfangled steam drill or steam hammer, probably suggesting in scornful tones that Henry's skill was now obsolete. John challenged the steam drill to a contest, outdrove it almost two to one, then keeled over from a heart attack.

The trouble with that story? It's a lack of evidence or conflicting evidence. No one doubts that a mighty ex-slave worked on railroad-construction gangs; many thousands of freedmen did, and it wasn't a job for the weak. It's plausible that one such man, full of heart and pride, challenged a steam drill and lost. But where and when did this happen? "John Henry" was a common enough name, appearing often in railroad employment records.

Different accounts, none well corroborated, place the event in different states. If big John lived, it's unfortunate for his memory that people didn't bother keeping detailed records. But we can't make the story true by wishing it so.

Where does this scant evidence place John? Some believe that the steam drill challenge occurred at Talcott, West Virginia. Others place it near Leeds, Alabama. One historian argues that Henry was a prisoner leased out by the warden (a legal practice in those days). We don't know for sure, though both towns commemorate John Henry. All of the claims can't be right; possibly none are.

So we can say nothing with authority? Actually, we can say a great deal. John Henry, fictional or real, reminds us of much undisputed history and human nature. Any person, even if illiterate and raised in slavery, has personal pride that should never be laughed away. For many, and especially freedmen, manual labor paid ridiculously low wages for dangerous, difficult work. As the twentieth century approached, machines took over more and more jobs. A man with a hammer, defying the boss and his job-stealing machine, is an evocative symbol of labor. And whether he lived or not, John Henry represents the mighty part played by every African-American cowhand, rail worker, blacksmith, homemaker, and millhand as the United States expanded west. That's worth remembering.

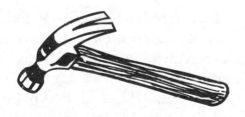

High John the Conqueror, African-American Legend

Africans brought a great deal to America, including vastly rich folklore. It's been said that High John the Conqueror arrived with an unbridled spirit that no person or peril could break.

✳ ✳ ✳ ✳

Who Was He?

Most likely, High John the Conqueror was a mythical creation, but his myth offers excellent insight into history. African-American culture first developed under slavery, mixing the customs of the new, African-born captives with that of their American-born counterparts. This synthesis created a diverse ethnic identity that has long retained traces of the ancestral homeland.

Many African-American folktales are believed to have origins in Africa, including the stories of High John the Conqueror. He is often portrayed as an ingenious individual who was captured in Africa and brought to America, where his new masters attempted to put him to work as a slave. However, he never embraced his new position and rebelled in a number of clever ways. In some versions of the legend, the slave owner's barn mysteriously burned down, or John's mule team "accidentally" trampled the cotton. John always remained above his master's suspicion, yet every slave knew what had really happened.

Why Were His Stories So Popular?

The everyday life of a slave was one of many commands and few personal decisions. Anything, including family, could be taken away at any time. The one safe place that was fully sheltered from authority was within the mind. Tales of High John the Conqueror, and of the unnamed slaves whose real-life defiance and clever deeds probably built the legend, reminded slaves of their humanity and intelligence, the very traits that their masters hoped to suppress. John was a spark of individuality and creativity in a strictly controlled world.

Too Big to Be True

Made famous by French writer Francois Rabelais as a symbol of insatiable appetites, Gargantua was said to belong to a race of giants.

✳   ✳   ✳   ✳

ARGANTUA IS AN icon of gluttonous hunger. According to myth, he was born from the ear of his mother, Gargamelle, and had a hunger so voracious that he consumed the milk of 17,813 cows every day. In a later adventure, he swallowed five people on religious pilgrimage, tossing these pilgrims and their staves into a salad. He was also the father of a lusty young giant named Pantagruel.

How did this myth spread? The son of a lord from Touraine, France, made this story famous. Francois Rabelais (c. 1494–1553) was educated in monasteries and at the universities at Paris and Lyon. He was trained as a physician and was a scholar of ancient Greek. Rabelais also published parodies of the predictions of astrology.

In 1532, Rabelais published the first of a series of books based on these characters, which he borrowed from an unknown author. *The Very Frightful Life of the Grand Gargantua* appeared in 1534. Thanks to the invention of movable type in 1450, Rabelais's books enjoyed wide readership and enormous popularity; among his greatest admirers was King Francis I of France. After the death of Francis I in 1547, however, literary praise for Rabelais's wit and satire turned to social condemnation. Rabelais left Paris for Metz and then went to Rome. He later became a curate in the town of Meudon, where he lived quietly and died in relative obscurity.

Superstition: Three on a Match

Almost everyone is superstitious in their own way, whether they knock on wood, refuse to walk under ladders, or steer clear of black cats. Many people, especially smokers, also consider it unlucky to light three cigarettes on a single match.

✳   ✳   ✳   ✳

THE ORIGINS OF the "three on a match" superstition is thought to have its modern-day genesis in the military but could be rooted in older taboos regarding the use of one taper to light three candles or lamps. And like many superstitions, it is also based partially in reality: On a dark battlefield, a prolonged match flame can easily draw the attention of enemy snipers. Therefore, to light one cigarette is dangerous; to light three is to invite disaster.

Some historians believe this superstition started during the Boer War (1899–1902), when careless British soldiers became easy targets for Dutch sharpshooters by lighting up in the trenches. To be the third man in line for a light was extremely dangerous because you were likely already in the enemy's crosshairs by then.

Others believe that "three on a match" was started by Swedish match manufacturer Ivar Kreuger, who supposedly conceived the myth as a way of increasing sales during wartime. Kreuger certainly would have profited from this superstition, but there is very little evidence to suggest that the story is true.

What is true is that the history of superstition among soldiers dates back thousands of years, to the very first armed conflicts. "War is a situation in which you do everything possible to avoid being killed or your buddies being hurt, but so many things are out of your control," explains Dr. Stuart Vyse, author of *Believing in Magic: The Psychology of Superstition.* "Superstition gives service-members the feeling that they are doing something that might have an effect—that they are taking some action to control a situation that is by definition uncontrollable. And that gives them comfort."

Say It Ain't So

Myth: The word *news* was created by joining the cardinal directions of north, east, west and south.

Truth: Although this myth would be a tidy fit, unfortunately there is no truth to it. Describing current events as news is simply revealing what is going on that is new. Pluralize the word new, and plain and simple, you get news.

Myth: So grateful for their success in online dating, a couple from Romania chose the name Yahoo for their newborn son.

Truth: In many parts of the world, parents traditionally choose names in honor of ancestors or events. Sometimes, as would be the case in this mythical instance, names even recall a serendipitous occurrence such as finding love online. In this example, though, a baby named Yahoo turned out to be the result of a fabricating news reporter, not internet-loving parents.

Myth: Dr. Benjamin Spock, the renowned child-care expert and author of several books, was father to a son who took his own life.

Truth: The now deceased Dr. Spock fathered two sons during his first marriage. Both sons, Michael and John, were successful in their chosen professions (in the museum and construction fields, respectively) and outlived their father, who died in 1998. Sadly, however, this rumor may have been based on the fact that Spock's grandson did kill himself. On Christmas Day, 1983, Peter Spock, the son of Michael, plummeted to his death from atop the Boston Children's Museum. He was only 22 years old.

Myth: Nine months after September 11th, hospitals around the country experienced an unusual surge of births.

Truth: Although the phenomenon of "blackout babies" has been well documented in other periods of devastation, couples were apparently not sticking close to home base, engaging in activities that are most often conducted with the lights off, in the time soon after the September 11th attacks.

Good Knights and Good Luck

Don't believe everything you see in the movies. Hollywood might have you believe that the Knights Templar were the guardians of hidden treasures and spectacular secrets. But whether the Christian military order ever really found the Holy Grail, knew the location of the Ark of the Covenant, or had the inside track on whether Jesus Christ survived his crucifixion is lost to the ages.

✳   ✳   ✳   ✳

THE TRUTH IS, the Templars had a power that rivaled the kingdoms of Europe. For two centuries, they were an extremely powerful order, both militarily and economically. Today, the Templars are remembered as crusader knights of the Christian cause, but the Knights Templar also acted as medieval bankers with official Papal sanction—at a time when the lending of money was generally considered a sin.

Defending the Faithful

It was the Crusades in the Holy Land that led to the rise—and, ironically, the eventual fall—of the Knights Templar. On July 15, 1099, the First Crusade stormed Jerusalem and slaughtered everyone in sight—Jews, Muslims, Christians—didn't matter. This unleashed a wave of pilgrimage, as European Christians flocked to now-accessible Palestine and its holy sites. Though Jerusalem's loss was a blow to Islam, it was a bonanza for the region's thieves, from Saracens to lapsed Crusaders: a steady stream of naive pilgrims to rob.

French knight Hugues de Payen, with eight chivalrous comrades, swore to guard the travelers. In 1119, they gathered at the Church of the Holy Sepulchre and pledged their lives to poverty, chastity, and obedience before King Baldwin II of Jerusalem. The Order of Poor Knights of the Temple of Solomon took up headquarters in said Temple.

Going Mainstream

The Templars did their work well, and in 1127 Baldwin sent a Templar embassy to Europe to secure a marriage that would ensure the royal succession in Jerusalem. Not only did they succeed, they became rock stars of sorts. Influential nobles showered the Order with money and real estate, the foundation of its future wealth. With this growth came a formal code of rules. Some highlights include:

* Templars could not desert the battlefield or leave a castle by stealth.

* They had to wear white habits, except for sergeants and squires who could wear black.

* They had to tonsure (shave) their crowns and wear beards.

* They had to dine in communal silence, broken only by Scriptural readings.

* They had to be chaste, except for married men joining with their wives' consent.

A Law Unto Themselves—and Never Mind That Pesky "Poverty" Part

Now with offices in Europe to manage the Order's growing assets, the Templars returned to Palestine to join in the Kingdom's ongoing defense. In 1139, Pope Innocent II decreed the Order answerable only to the Holy See. Now exempt from the tithe, the Order was entitled to accept tithes! The Knights Templar had come far.

By the mid-1100s, the Templars had become a church within a church, a nation within a nation, and a major banking concern. Templar keeps were well-defended depositories, and the Order became financiers to the crowned heads of Europe—even to the Papacy. Their reputation for meticulous bookkeeping and secure transactions underpinned Europe's financial markets, even as their soldiers kept fighting for the faith in the Holy Land.

Downfall

Templar prowess notwithstanding, the Crusaders couldn't hold the Holy Land. In 1187, Saladin the Kurd retook Jerusalem, martyring 230 captured Templars. Factional fighting between Christians sped the collapse as the 1200s wore on. In 1291, the last Crusader outpost at Acre fell to the Mamelukes of Egypt. Though the Templars had taken a hosing along with the other Christian forces, their troubles had just begun.

King Philip IV of France owed the Order a lot of money, and they made him more nervous at home than they did fighting in Palestine. In 1307, Philip ordered the arrest of all Templars in France. They stood accused of apostasy, devil worship, sodomy, desecration, and greed. Hideous torture produced piles of confessions, much like those of the later Inquisition. The Order was looted, shattered, and officially dissolved. In March 1314, Jacques de Molay, the last Grand Master of the Knights Templar, was burned at the stake.

Whither the Templars?

Many Templar assets passed to the Knights Hospitallers. The Order survived in Portugal as the Order of Christ, where it exists to this day in form similar to British knightly orders. A Templar fleet escaped from La Rochelle and vanished; it may have reached Scotland. Swiss folktales suggest that some Templars took their loot and expertise to Switzerland, possibly laying the groundwork for what would one day become the Swiss banking industry.

The Elevator Incident

In most urban legends, the story being told never happened to the person telling the story. Instead, it's usually traced to "the second cousin of my great-uncle's pool-cleaning guy." Here's the basic version of one such tale.

✳ ✳ ✳ ✳

THREE ELDERLY WOMEN are visiting the imposing metropolis of New York City for the first time. They have been warned to "not mess around with muggers—do whatever they say." Entering the elevator of their hotel, they are joined by an African American man and his dog on a leash. When the man shouts, "Sit!" the paranoid and terrified women quickly sit down on the floor of the elevator. The man offers his apologies, telling the ladies he was addressing his pet. He leaves with his dog when the car reaches the main floor. Later, as the women dine, they are offered a bottle of champagne from their waitperson, who tells them, "This is compliments of Mr. (famous black celebrity) who, along with his dog, completely enjoyed meeting you in the elevator today."

This story has origins in the early 1980s, when newspaper reporters told the story and named Baseball Hall of Fame slugger Reggie Jackson as the protagonist of the tale (despite his repeated denials.) Over the years, the characters have changed—they have included hoops icon Michael Jordan, boxing champ Larry Holmes, the Reverend Jesse Jackson, Sr., and actor Eddie Murphy. The locations have also been noted as Las Vegas and Los Angeles.

The real source of the story may be the 1970s sitcom *The Bob Newhart Show*. In one episode, a black man tries to control his unruly white dog in a dentist's office. When the man says, "Sit, Whitey!" the dentist obediently plops down on his desk. Of course, what may have happened is that the urban legend served as inspiration for the sitcom script.

Gone Without a Trace

While we all watch in amazement as magicians make everything from small coins to giant buildings disappear, in our hearts, we all know it's a trick. Things don't just disappear, especially not people. Or do they?

✳   ✳   ✳   ✳

Louis Le Prince

THE NAME LOUIS Aimé Augustin Le Prince doesn't mean much to most people, but some believe he was the first person to record moving images on film, a good seven years before Thomas Edison. Whether or not he did so is open to debate, as is what happened to him on September 16, 1890. On that day, Le Prince's brother accompanied him to the train station in Dijon, France, where he was scheduled to take the express train to Paris. When the train reached Paris, however, Le Prince and his luggage were nowhere to be found. The train was searched, as were the tracks between Dijon and Paris, but no sign of Le Prince or his luggage was ever found. Theories about his disappearance range from his being murdered for trying to fight Edison over the patent of the first motion picture to his family forcing him to go into hiding to keep him safe from people who wanted his patents for themselves. Others believe that Le Prince took his own life because he was nearly bankrupt.

Jimmy Hoffa

On the afternoon of July 30, 1975, Jimmy Hoffa, former president of the International Brotherhood of Teamsters, stepped onto the parking lot of the Manchus Red Fox Restaurant near Detroit and into history. Scheduled to meet with known mobsters from New Jersey and New York, Hoffa vanished and was never seen or heard from again. Since that day, wild theories involving mob hits and political assassinations have run rampant. But despite hundreds of anonymous tips, confessions from mob hitmen, and even the wife of a former mobster accusing her husband of the hit, it is still unknown what happened to Hoffa or where he's buried, and the case officially remains open. As recently as May 2006, FBI agents were still following leads and digging up yards in Michigan trying to find out what happened to Hoffa.

Dorothy Arnold

After spending most of December 12, 1910, shopping in Manhattan, American socialite Dorothy Arnold told a friend she was planning to walk home through Central Park. She never made it. Fearing their daughter had eloped with her one-time boyfriend George Griscom, Jr., the Arnolds immediately hired the Pinkerton Detective Agency, although they did not report her missing to police until almost a month later. Once the press heard the news, theories spread like wildfire, most of them pointing the finger at Griscom. Some believed he had murdered Arnold, but others thought she had died as the result of a botched abortion. Still others felt her family had banished her to Switzerland and then used her disappearance as a cover-up. No evidence was ever found to formally charge Griscom, and Arnold's disappearance remains unsolved.

D. B. Cooper

On the evening of November 24, 1971, a man calling himself Dan Cooper (later known as D. B. Cooper) hijacked an airplane, and demanded $200,000 and four parachutes, which he received when the plane landed in Seattle. Cooper allowed the plane's passengers to disembark but then ordered the pilot to fly to Mexico. Once the plane had gained enough altitude, somewhere over the Cascade Mountains near Woodland, Washington, Cooper jumped from the plane and fell into history. Despite a massive manhunt, no trace of him has ever been found. In 1980, an eight-year-old boy found nearly $6,000 in rotting $20 bills lying along the banks of the Columbia River. A check of their serial numbers found that they were part of the ransom money given to Cooper, but what became of the rest of the money, and Cooper, is a mystery to this day.

Frederick Valentich

To vanish without a trace is rather unusual. But to vanish in an airplane while chasing a UFO—now that's unique. Yet that's exactly what happened to 20-year-old pilot Frederick Valentich on the night of October 21, 1978. Shortly after 7:00 P.M., while flying a Cessna 182L to King Island, Australia, Valentich radioed that an "unidentified craft" was hovering over his plane. For the next several minutes, he attempted to describe the object, which had blinking lights and was "not an aircraft." At approximately 7:12 P.M., Valentich stated that he was having engine trouble. Immediately after that, the flight tower picked up 17 seconds of "metallic, scraping sounds." Then all was silent. A search began immediately, but no trace of Valentich or his plane was ever found. Strangely enough, the evening Valentich disappeared, there were numerous reports of UFOs seen all over the skies of Australia.

Frank Morris, John Anglin, and Clarence Anglin

Officially, records show that there was never a successful escape from Alcatraz Prison while it was in operation. Of course, those records leave out the part that three men *might* have made it, but they disappeared in the process.

After spending two years planning their escape, inmates Frank Morris and brothers Clarence and John Anglin placed homemade dummies in their bunks, crawled through hand-dug tunnels, and made their way to the prison roof. Then they apparently climbed down, hopped aboard homemade rafts, and made their way out into San Francisco Bay.

The next day, one of the largest manhunts in history began. Pieces of a raft and a life preserver were found floating in the bay, as well as a bag containing personal items from the escapees, but that was all. The official report stated that in all likelihood, the men drowned. However, a 2003 episode of *Mythbusters* determined that the men may have survived.

Welcome to Ohio: Don't Lose Your Head!

Sure, New York has its Headless Horseman, but Ohio can do that one better: a headless motorcycle ghost. And not just one, either. It's been said that the state of Ohio has more headless motorcycle ghosts per capita than any other state.

* * * *

CONSIDERED THE FATHER of all Ohio headless motorcycle ghosts, the legend of the Elmore Rider became popular in the 1950s and may have existed even further back. As the story goes, a young motorcycle enthusiast from Elmore was forced to leave his true love behind when he went to serve his country in World War I. Upon his return on the evening of March 21, the first thing the soldier did was hop on his motorcycle and race off to reunite with her. Imagine the man's shock and horror when, arriving at her home, he found her in the arms of another man. Full of rage, the young man jumped on his motorcycle and sped off into the night. As he crossed a bridge, he lost control of his bike and crashed, decapitating himself in the process. Today, it is said that if the curious go out to the bridge on March 21, the anniversary of the young man's death, and flash their lights three times, the ghostly light from a phantom motorcycle will begin coming toward them. As soon as the light crosses the bridge, it vanishes.

Calling out the Rider

Having heard about the Elmore Rider for years, a man named Richard Gill decided to try a series of experiments to test the tale's validity. In 1968, Gill and a friend visited that bridge on March 21 to catch a glimpse of the headless ghost. Armed with video and still cameras, the pair sat in Gill's car and flashed the headlights three times. Almost immediately, they saw a single white light come down the hill toward the bridge. As the pair looked on in amazement, the light crossed the bridge and vanished into thin air. Believing they were on to something, Gill and his friend strung a piece of string across the road and flashed their lights again. Almost on cue, the light appeared, came down the hill, and promptly disappeared when it reached the other side of the bridge. Amazingly, when Gill checked the string, it was still intact—even though the light had appeared to go right through it.

As a final experiment, Gill managed to convince his friend to stand in the middle of the road, directly in the path of the phantom headlight. Gill went to the car and flashed the lights three times, summoning the ghost. The light appeared and, from Gill's viewpoint, looked like it went right through his friend before disappearing. Running onto the bridge, Gill found that his friend was no longer there. He was lying in a ditch alongside the road, unconscious. When he came to, the friend remembered nothing. Weirdly, the video and audio tapes revealed nothing except a strange whining noise, without so much as a flicker of light visible.

So ended Gill's experiments. But even the threat of bodily harm hasn't stopped people from showing up in droves every March 21, hoping to see a real-life ghost . . . or at least its headlight.

The Oxford Motorcycle Ghost

Having only been around since the 1980s, the headless motor-cycle ghost of Oxford could be considered the newcomer. But the legend is unique in that it contains an explanation as to why people have to flash their lights three times to get the ghost to appear.

The Oxford story begins with a young couple, both of whom were living on Oxford-Milford Road while falling madly in love with each other. There was only one problem: The girl's parents didn't approve of the fact that the boy rode a motorcycle, and they forbade her from seeing him. The lovestruck girl secretly disobeyed her parents, and the couple devised a plan. As soon as the girl's parents were fast asleep, she would flash her front porch light three times. Upon seeing the light, the boy would push his motorcycle over to the girl's house, located around a sharp bend. Once he got there, the girl would creep out, and they would push the motorcycle back down the road before racing off. The plan worked fine until one fateful night when the boy fell asleep waiting for his girlfriend to flash the porch light. Some say he grew tired because he had been in town drinking earlier that night. Regardless, when he woke up, he saw that his girlfriend had been frantically flashing the porch light over and over. Not wanting to keep her waiting a minute longer, he cranked up his motorcycle and sped toward her house. In too much of a hurry, he was unable to navigate the sharp bend, and he crashed through a barbed wire fence, coming out the other side minus his head.

It is said that even today, the headless ghost still rides his motorcycle down Oxford-Milford Road. The girlfriend's house is long gone, but if ghost chasers go to the spot near the sharp curve where it once stood and flash their lights three times, the ghost will come speeding down the road. The light will then go barreling off the road when it reaches the bend.

A Chicago Connection to the Boston Tea Party?

Is the last surviving participant of the Boston Tea Party buried in Lincoln Park?

✳   ✳   ✳   ✳

THE PLACE NOW occupied by Lincoln Park used to be City Cemetery. While the gravestones were moved in the 1870s, many of the bodies remained. In the 1890s, a memorial boulder was set up to mark the burial spot of one of Chicago's earliest heroes: David Kennison, the last surviving participant of the Boston Tea Party. The boulder is still in place, despite the fact that we now know that Kennison is probably buried about a block from the spot...and that Kennison was full of it.

Before his death in 1852, Kennison claimed that he had reached 115 years of age. He would regularly regale Chicagoans with stories of the Revolution and the War of 1812, both of which he claimed to have fought in. He even donated a vial of tea leaves that he claimed were from the Boston Tea Party to the Chicago Historical Society. The institution (which now calls itself the Chicago History Museum) still has them, even though historians no longer believe Kennison's story. Genealogists today have determined that Kennison was at least 30 years younger than he claimed to be, making him only about six years old at the time of the Boston Tea Party. Historians do believe he served in the War of 1812, however.

While his stories were outrageous, if people in Chicago doubted him in his day, they never said so. He became one of the first heroes of the fledgling city, and, when he died, he was granted a full military funeral. A marching band—his favorite kind of band—followed the casket from a Clark Street church up to City Cemetery. He may have been a liar, but he inspired a generation of Chicagoans.

Remember the Alamo!

Many myths abound regarding the Alamo and its legendary fighters. What's true, and what's not?

✳   ✳   ✳   ✳

THE STORY OF the Alamo is known to every student of American history, and 2.5 million visitors tour the original structure in downtown San Antonio every year. With any epic conflict, the tales of bravery and the details of the battle become embellished over time, and the facts surrounding the Battle of the Alamo are no exception. In fact, much of what you think you know about that battle may be wrong.

Not What People Think

One of the most common myths about the battle, which was fought in 1836, is that there were no survivors. In truth, close to 20 women and children who were under siege during the conflict survived to return to their homes. William Travis's personal slave and about 14 pro-Texan Hispanics were also among the survivors.

There are two sides to every fight, and that is true of the Alamo. The event has often been simplified to paint the Texans as the good guys and the Mexicans as the bad guys, but each side had its own reasons for entering the battle. The Mexicans were fighting to defend their country, and the Texans were seeking changes to Mexican laws. Many of the Americans entering Texas were slaveholders, and there was much sentiment toward abolition in the Mexican government. In addition to seeking their independence, the Texans fighting at the Alamo wanted to make sure they kept the right to own slaves.

What Really Happened?

Myths also surround the most memorable figures in the battle: Davy Crockett and Jim Bowie. Many have heard the tale of how Davy Crockett heroically died clutching his favorite rifle, "Old Betsy," in his hands and leaving a swath of dead Mexicans in his wake. Although accounts vary, many historians agree that Crockett was captured along with the other surviving combatants and was most likely quickly executed.

Jim Bowie has come to symbolize the dedication of the Texans to their cause. According to legend, William Travis drew a line in the courtyard and challenged the soldiers who wished to stay and continue fighting to cross the line. Bowie, who was ill, is said to have asked for his cot to be carried across the line. Historians, however, have been unable to find records to support this account.

The story of the line in the sand led to another myth that the volunteers could have left at any time. Technically this is true, but these citizen soldiers had signed an oath of allegiance to the provisional government of Texas, and they chose to remain true to their oath.

William Travis, the leader of the freedom fighters, is often portrayed as pompous and disliked by the men who served with him. This myth has been supported by the fact that the volunteer fighters refused to take orders from him and instead elected Jim Bowie as their leader. But that decision wasn't based on personalities; Travis was respected by both the soldiers and the volunteers and was often described as gregarious and honorable. The only reason the volunteers elected Bowie was because they didn't want to take orders from an officer.

Another myth is that the flag of Texas proudly flew over the Alamo for the duration of the battle, but conflicting records suggest that the flag flown may actually have been that of the Louisiana Grays or even the Mexican flag. Most historians now conclude that it was the tricolor *Tejas y Coahuila* flag that hung over the embattled compound.

Did They Know Their Influence?

Perhaps the greatest patriotic myth is that the freedom fighters died without knowing that Texas had gained independence. The truth is that even though the garrison members were killed before hearing that the Declaration was signed, they fully expected it to happen and had sent delegates to the convention prior to the battle.

Even when these myths are dispelled, it is clear that the battle of the Alamo was a pivotal event in Texas history and that the players on both sides performed admirably under horrific conditions.

Biblical Urban Legends

Many wild stories involving the Bible have popped up in recent years. Though fascinating, few of them are true.

✳ ✳ ✳ ✳

URBAN LEGENDS ARE as American as apple pie. Traditionally passed along from person to person and usually involving "a friend of a friend," this fascinating aspect of American folklore really picked up steam with the growth of the internet, which made it possible to transmit urban legends around the world with the click of a mouse.

Urban legends cover a broad array of topics, so it should come as no surprise that many have a biblical angle. Though fun to read, most fall apart under scrutiny and very few are actually true. Here's a sampling of some of the more popular biblical urban legends:

Myth: An unburned Bible was found in the charred rubble of the Pentagon after the terrorist attack on September 11th.

Fact: A total of 189 people perished when American Airlines Flight 77, which had been commandeered by terrorists, crashed into the southwest section of the Pentagon. According to a popular urban legend, a Bible miraculously survived the fiery carnage, a fact many attributed to divine intervention. In truth, a book was found undisturbed by rescue workers, but it was a "bible" of a different kind: a dictionary.

A Gift from the Gideons

Myth: Christians often leave money in Gideon Bibles to reward the next person who turns to the book for solace.

Fact: This legend has been making the rounds for decades, and many people eagerly rifle through the Bibles in their hotel rooms immediately upon check-in hoping to find financial treasure. However, there are few if any verifiable accounts of money being found in a Bible. In truth, it's the Bibles themselves that altruistic evangelists leave—not money within them.

Myth: A father left his only son a spectacular gift within a Bible, but the son, angry at his father's miserly ways, didn't find it until his father's death.

Fact: According to this supposedly true legend, which has circulated for years, the son of a wealthy man wanted only a fancy sports car for his college graduation gift and was angry and upset when he received a gorgeous leather-bound Bible instead. He cast the book aside without looking at it and didn't see it again until he was called home upon his father's passing. While going through his father's possessions, the young man found the Bible still in its gift box. Paging through the book, he found that his father had underlined Matthew 7:11: "And if ye, being evil, know how to give good gifts to your children, how much more shall your Heavenly Father which is in Heaven, give to those who ask Him?" As the son read the words, a car key fell from the back of the Bible. On the tag was the date of his graduation and the words "Paid in Full."

Avoiding the Beast, End Times, and Missing Sun

Myth: Because the book of Revelation states that 666 is the Mark of the Beast, or Antichrist, Christian shoppers often add a small item to their purchases so the total is never $6.66.

Fact: According to store clerks, this one is true—superstitious people often do add a package of gum or other item to change their total if it comes out to $6.66. In fact, it apparently happens quite often.

Myth: Airlines will not pair Christian pilots and copilots out of fear that the Rapture will take them away, leaving the plane without someone to land it.

Fact: Many Christians believe in the Rapture—a time when Jesus will return and call all believers up to heaven, leaving nonbelievers on earth. This belief is based on a passage in

1 Thessalonians, which concludes, "Then we which are alive and remain shall be caught up together with them in the clouds, to meet the Lord in the air: and so we shall be with the Lord."

Are airlines comparing pilots' religious beliefs when making assignments, just to be on the safe side? Not according to FAA officials, who told a reporter, "The FAA does not have any regulations referencing religious beliefs." The nonexistence of such a regulation was also confirmed by a representative of American Airlines.

Myth: NASA scientists have discovered a "missing" day in time that corresponds with biblical accounts of the sun standing still in the sky.

Fact: According to this urban legend, NASA researchers were checking where the sun, moon, and planets would be positioned 100 years and 1,000 years in the future. While running the measurements through a computer, the machine screeched to a halt. While servicing the computer, technicians found a day missing in space in elapsed time, which coincided with a biblical account of the sun standing still. This is a great story, especially if you are a Christian looking for scientific proof of scripture. But according to NASA Public Affairs, it never happened.

Determining a Biblical Center

Myth: The true center of the Bible is Psalm 118.

Fact: Located between the shortest chapter of the Bible and the longest, Psalm 118 is often noted as being the absolute center of the Bible because there are 594 chapters before it, and 594 chapters after it. Add those up, believers say, and you get 1188, or Psalm 118:8, which states what many believe to be the Bible's most important concept: "It is better to take refuge in the Lord than to put confidence in man." The problem is that the math doesn't work for all Bibles, only the one used by most Protestant denominations. So if you're Jewish or Catholic, no such luck.

Chapter 10

The Goings-On Behind the Screen

I Want My MTV!

Screaming out of about a half-million televisions on August 1, 1981, was something most people hadn't seen before: an entire cable channel dedicated to broadcasting music videos. The channel was named, aptly, Music Television, or MTV.

✳   ✳   ✳   ✳

USING A MONTAGE of images from the *Apollo 11* moon landing, MTV kicked off its birthday at 12:01 A.M. with the introduction, "Ladies and gentlemen, rock and roll." The first video played? "Video Killed the Radio Star" by The Buggles. During its early days, MTV's format was similar to that of Top 40 radio at the time—hosts introduced song after song, but instead of playing a song on the radio, the hosts played a video on cable. The first hosts, called VJs for video jockeys, were Nina Blackwood, Mark Goodman, Alan Hunter, J. J. Jackson, and Martha Quinn.

The Evolution

Early programming on MTV consisted almost entirely of videos made for cheap or cut together from other sources, such as concerts. As MTV started to stake its claim in popular culture, however, videos started to become more slick and developed. Record companies soon realized the marketing potential that came with having a video on MTV, so they began to finance the creation of individual artists' videos. Videos became more elaborate and highly stylized, often including story lines and character development. Many directors who would later find success directing feature films started their careers directing music videos. Many rock groups who were just starting out hit it big with videos that ultimately gained a huge following among the MTV audience. Eventually, programming at MTV branched out into award shows, animated shows, and reality shows, gradually moving away from music videos.

In the mid-1980s, Viacom bought MTV (among other channels) and created MTV Networks. Shows hosted by VJs slowly lost airtime in lieu of more conventionally formatted programs. Features such as *MTV News* and *MTV Unplugged,* which showcased acoustic performances, were worked into the lineup. In the early 1990s, more animated shows, including *Beavis and Butthead* and *Celebrity Deathmatch,* were introduced. By 2001, reality programming, such as *MTV's Fear* and *The Osbournes,* was placed on the schedule. Almost all of MTV's music programming had been moved to other channels. In addition, the network had launched channels around the globe, taking over airwaves in Europe, Japan, India, and Australia.

The Youth

MTV's audience has always been a young group—people between 12 and 24 years old. *MTV Generation* became a term to define those growing up in the 1980s. But as that generation aged, the channel continued to change its programming and identity to match the interests of the next group of 12- to 24-year-olds. As a result, videos were gradually replaced with reality shows. Series such as *The Real World* and *Road Rules* became staples in MTV's rotation. But as MTV continued to gain popularity and became a huge dictator of taste for the youth generation, it also came under fire for its influence on culture.

Groups such as the Parents Television Council and the American Family Association have criticized MTV frequently, arguing that the channel advocates inappropriate behavior and lacks moral responsibility for its careless programming targeted at kids. Of course, MTV hasn't always been its own best advocate, as seen in controversies such as the 2004 MTV-produced Super Bowl halftime show, in which Justin Timberlake tore off part of Janet Jackson's wardrobe and exposed her (pierced) breast; as well as MTV's problematic coverage in July 2005 of the Live 8 benefit concert, when the network cut to commercials during live performances and MTV's hosts repeatedly referred to the show by anything but its actual name. Given that they were broadcasting the show to the very fans who wanted to see the Live 8 bands they were interrupting, this may have marked a milestone in cultural politics, where the typically liberal youth culture was just as annoyed with the channel as the conservative groups were.

Social Activism

While full recovery from such snafus is probably unlikely, MTV has tried to respond to criticism about its programming. The network has a long history of promoting social, political, and environmental activism in young people. During election years, the network has invited presidential candidates to discuss their platforms. MTV has also initiated annual campaigns addressing a variety of issues affecting the youth culture, including hate crimes, drug use, and violence. In addition, MTV started branching out into various social activities, illustrated most notably by the Rock the Vote campaign, which encouraged young people to vote.

The Meaning

MTV's effect on popular culture has been enormous. Some believe MTV is a reflection of what's happening in the youth culture today, but others say it dictates what is happening now and what will happen in the future. Still, for all its bravado regarding its youth and flexibility, MTV has stayed the course like any solid corporation. Its mission has always been to appeal to youth culture. So, while the gradual decline in the airing of music videos may be bemoaned by older viewers who enjoyed them during MTV's infancy, the young people in the twenty-first century prefer reality shows about rich people who live in Southern California. The target demographic has stayed the same, but the people in that demographic have changed.

One critique the network can't seem to dodge, though, is its effect on the music industry itself. First, MTV has a tendency to remember only its own history as opposed to musical history in general. Older artists influential in the creation of genres and styles are oddly left out of the MTV world, despite the fact that so many artists on MTV are quite obviously in debt to them. Second, by playing only those artists who fit into a prescribed image and are backed by big money from music companies, the network has had the net effect of aiding the consolidation of the music industry and narrowing the choices to which consumers are exposed. As it was in 1981, MTV is still screaming out from televisions around the world. But now, the network is doing so in a highly stylized, profit-making way—and doing so from *billions* of television sets around the world.

The Real-Life Explorers Who Made *King Kong*

Long before Jurassic Park, The Blob, or even Godzilla terrorized big-screen audiences, a prehistoric gorilla by the name of Kong served up its own enormous case of king-size quivers to the moviegoing masses.

✳   ✳   ✳   ✳

MONKEYS ARE A mainstay of zoos today, but in the early twentieth century, when Merian C. Cooper's original *King Kong* came out, few zoos held displays of the entertaining and excitable creatures. Capitalizing on that void and incorporating his own anthropological background, Cooper coupled with fellow filmmaker and friend Ernest B. Schoedsack to parlay their nature documentary into a feature film. Little did they know at the time how their "creature feature epic," the first of its kind, would change the landscape of cinematic and pop culture.

Thrilling Adventure

Cooper lived an exciting life before creating one of the most adventurous epics of all time. As a U.S. Army officer and bomber pilot in World War I, he traveled the globe and was a prisoner of war. His initial filmmaking career was devoted to creating nature documentaries for Paramount Pictures. As such, much of his time was spent exploring exotic locales. Always the innovator, even with these documentaries, he incorporated technological techniques to ensure that action-packed sequences were the main features of his works. Unlike the typical nature documentary, Cooper always insisted that stage-set action sequences accompany the nature footage to ensure just the right feel of excitement.

Schoedsack, too, was an ardent fan of technological advancements in filmmaking. Schoedsack and Cooper met while both were providing military service in Ukraine. Upon their return to the United States, they forged a working relationship that combined their mutual interests in nature, adventure, and filmmaking innovations. Their initial collaborations continued their previously established work in the documentary genre, but their united efforts on *King Kong* put Cooper and Schoedsack on the cinematic map.

It's All in the Script

From the start, the filming of *King Kong* was riddled with odd and unexpected roadblocks. The original scriptwriter commissioned by Cooper fell ill and died before producing a workable text. Even though scriptwriter Edgar Wallace is credited as a writer on the film, Cooper, Schoedsack's wife, Ruth Rose, and

James Ashmore Creelman were forced to quickly rework the entire script to get it done in time for production. Creelman was hired to reconstruct Wallace's unedited draft to Cooper's liking. Although Creelman's changes were pleasing to the perfectionist Cooper, he still thought that the script lacked snap. Thus, Rose was asked to jump into the screenwriting process. Cooper was pleased with her adjustments but, of course, felt compelled to imprint his own voice, as well.

Another marked change in the film's production revolved around its name. *King Kong* went through several name changes before its release. The movie went by *Kong, King Ape, The Beast, The Ape,* and *The Eighth Wonder* before finally being released as *King Kong.* In fact, even as press release packets were being sent out in anticipation of the release, the film was referred to as *The Eighth Wonder.* Only one known pamphlet—which brought $11,000 at auction in 2005—exists with this designation.

Pushing Film Technique Forward

Several technologically innovative methods were employed in *King Kong*'s production. One technique, stop-motion, was a new trick in which objects were filmed at different locations and positions in many frames to mimic movement. This animation method was utilized to create special effects involving the film's prehistoric creatures—dinosaurs and the ape himself. By today's standards, the choppiness of the technique might appear hokey, but at the time, stop-motion was a cutting-edge means to meet the movie's needs.

Another method employed, rear-projection, was combined with the magic of stop-motion to create the illusion that Kong was tromping through scenes alongside the live actors. To achieve this technique, a camera projects a previously recorded background onto the scene's backdrop while live action takes place in front of it. This technique was not a first choice—in fact, multiple alternate routes were explored fully. However, just as filming was scheduled to start, an advanced version of rear-projection was discovered, and Cooper jumped on the innovation.

Although some have suggested that Kong was, at times, portrayed by a man in an ape suit, all scenes with the prehistoric beast were made utilizing stop-motion, rear-projection, and other special effects with one of the four Kong models crafted in various sizes. Although the differing dimensions could not produce a consistently accurate Kong, whether the gigantic ape terrorized at 18 feet or the 24 feet he appeared to be while menacing Manhattan, each rendition was produced by a miniature model made from crude materials including aluminum, rubber, and wire.

Boffo Box Office

King Kong, released in 1933, had the biggest opening weekend of its time. It became the highest-grossing film of the year and the fifth of the entire decade. Not bad considering that 1933 was, by many accounts, the lowest point of the Great Depression. The film's great success brought the production company that carried it, RKO (Radio-Keith-Orpheum), back from the brink of bankruptcy.

Critics and the public were in love with the mammoth gorilla. In fact, the film was so popular that it was rereleased three more times in the next 20 years. But with each new showing, the strong arm of censorship took its toll. Through the years, various images deemed too horrifying were cut out, piece by piece. For instance, scenes featuring the giant gorilla taking a few nibbles of a New Yorker and causing a person to plummet to his death were removed. By modern standards, these scenes might seem fairly tame, but such gruesomeness was uncommon then. In 1971, however, the original film was pieced back together and rereleased, yet again, in its entire form.

Since *King Kong* popped into pop culture, countless monster movies have been created, including those manufactured during the great giant monster genre surge in the 1950s. But it was the great Kong and the technological ambitiousness of its creators, Cooper and Schoedsack, that set the stage for the special effects and terrifying monsters that scare audiences right out of their seats today.

Inspiration Station

A (Really) Big Idea: Stan Lee's Incredible Hulk

Everyone's favorite green superhero, the Incredible Hulk, was inspired by two of literature's most famous monsters: Frankenstein and the dualistic personality of Dr. Jekyll and Mr. Hyde. By combining the two characters, says creator Stan Lee, "I got myself the monster I wanted, who was really good, but nobody knew it"—much like the monster in Mary Shelly's classic novel, *Frankenstein*. "He was also somebody who could change from a normal man into a monster," Lee said, which was the case for Dr. Jekyll in the famous story by Robert Louis Stevenson. The whole green skin thing was less an inspired idea and more of a fluke, however; the printer of the comic couldn't achieve the shade of gray that Lee had originally desired. Lee okayed the Hulk's color change to green.

Inspiration, Muppet Style

Genius entertainer and puppeteer Jim Henson dreamed up a Muppet rock band as far back as 1951. The inspiration for what would become The Electric Mayhem came directly from musicians in the world of rock 'n' roll. Muppet bass guitarist Sgt. Floyd Pepper is an obvious reference to the Beatles album, *Sgt. Pepper's Lonely Hearts Club Band*. Pepper is also a nod to Pink Floyd, since he's pink in color, and well, named Floyd. Janice, the lanky-haired sometime vocalist and lead guitar player is named after Janis Joplin, although rumors abound that both her appearance and character were inspired by Joni Mitchell. Blues musician Dr. John directly inspired Mayhem bandleader Dr. Teeth. And although Henson never confirmed it, manic drummer Animal is said to have been inspired by

Keith Moon of The Who. Some say the rumor is substantiated by the fact that Henson named one of his *Fraggle Rock* characters Wembley, which happens to be the town in which Moon was born.

"Life's like a movie, write your own ending. Keep believing, keep pretending."

—JIM HENSON

Behind the Films of Our Times

The Graduate

Robert Redford and Doris Day were originally considered to play young Benjamin and the seductive Mrs. Robinson before those roles in this 1967 film went to Dustin Hoffman and Anne Bancroft instead. Director Mike Nichols showed great intuition in only his second feature film—great enough to win the Academy Award for Best Director. When Benjamin and Elaine hop the bus to end the film, they have no clue as to their future together or what they'll do next, and the actors weren't quite sure how to play the scene. Nichols was able to coax the appropriate "performance" from actors Hoffman and Katharine Ross by keeping the cameras running long after the shot was supposed to be over. As actors, they didn't have any idea what they were supposed to do next—perfectly reflecting the same predicament faced by their characters.

The Blob

This 1958 monster movie, featuring an oozing and growing mass of who-knows-what, was the first starring role for 28-year-old Steve McQueen, who played a character nearly ten years younger. His movie girlfriend, Aneta Corsaut, went on to play teacher Helen Crump in TV's *The Andy Griffith Show* during the 1960s. Composer Burt Bacharach and lyricist Mack David wrote the film's theme song, "Beware of the Blob." It became a Top 40 hit, reaching number 33 on the charts for "The Five Blobs." This vocal "group," however, was actually just one performer, Bernie Nee.

Raiders of the Lost Ark

Released in 1981, this action and adventure film started out with nail-biting scenes that would have made for a great climax in most other films. Director Steven Spielberg had Harrison Ford, as thrill-seeker and archeologist Indiana Jones, open the flick by narrowly escaping being flattened by an enormous rolling boulder. Another famous scene came about through the star's frustration rather than creativity. Jones encounters a sword-slinging villain, and the script originally called for the hero to engage in a gripping duel, with Jones finally winning by snapping the weapon away from his foe with his trusty whip. But Ford was extremely ill with food poisoning and didn't want to perform such an extended sequence. He quickly ended the threat by simply pulling his pistol and shooting the bad guy.

A Crying Shame

A popular public-service campaign from the 1970s featured a Native American man named Iron Eyes Cody whose tearful visage implored people not to litter. In truth, his heritage was fabricated.

✳   ✳   ✳   ✳

❚❚ PEOPLE START POLLUTION; people can stop it." Although the public service campaign was one of the most successful ever created, Iron Eyes Cody's career encompassed much more than that particular spot. He appeared in an estimated 200 movies and dozens of television shows, typically playing a Native American. Off-screen, he worked faithfully and tirelessly on behalf of the Native American community. Throughout his adult life, Iron Eyes Cody claimed to be of Cherokee/Cree lineage. However, the assertion was a lie: Cody was, in fact, a full-blooded Italian.

Of Immigrants Born

His story began in the tiny town of Kaplan, Louisiana, where he was born Espera DeCorti in 1904. His parents, Antonio

DeCorti and Francesca Salpietra, had emigrated from Italy at the turn of the century. Espera—who went by the name Oscar—was the second eldest of the couple's four children.

Antonio abandoned his family in 1909 and moved to Texas. Francesca divorced him and married a man named Alton Abshire, with whom she bore five more children. While still in their teens, Oscar and his brothers, Joseph and Frank, joined their father in Texas and, like their father, shortened their last name to Corti. In 1924, following Antonio's death, the brothers moved to Hollywood, where they again changed their last name—this time to Cody—and started working in motion pictures.

Joseph and Frank managed to land a few jobs as movie extras but eventually gave up their acting dreams and moved on to other careers. Oscar, however, had found his niche. He quietly changed his name to Iron Eyes Cody and started passing himself off as a full-blooded Native American.

Who Knew?

At the time, no one had reason to challenge him. Cody had a distinctive Native American look, and he took great pains to embrace his new identity and false heritage. He married a Native American woman named Bertha Parker, and together they adopted several Native American children. Iron Eyes almost always wore his long hair in braids and dressed in Native American attire, including beaded moccasins.

In fact, it was Cody's appearance that made his anti-littering public service announcement such a success. Everyone who saw it assumed that Cody was a real Native American and thus felt tremendous sympathy for him when a bag of garbage was tossed at his feet. Many even thought the tear that ran down his cheek at the ad's conclusion was real, but it was really just a drop of glycerin.

The television ad made Cody a household name and brought

him quite a bit of attention. In the years that followed, he repeatedly denied nagging rumors that he was not what he claimed to be, and his story finally unraveled in the mid-1990s when his half-sister sent journalists proof that he was actually Italian. Several newspapers jumped on the story, eagerly pulling back the curtain to reveal the truth behind Cody's ancestral lie. But even in the face of overwhelming evidence (including his birth certificate), Cody stuck steadfastly to his story, which he maintained until his death.

Who Cared?

Ultimately, it didn't really matter to most Native Americans that Iron Eyes Cody had lied. He had spent decades working on their behalf, drawing international attention to their concerns. In 1995, Hollywood's Native American community honored him for his many charitable endeavors.

Iron Eyes Cody—perhaps the most famous Native American who never was—died on January 4, 1999, at the age of 94.

The Coogan Bill: A Law Child Actors Can Trust

Exploitation of a child star led to a protective law.

✳ ✳ ✳ ✳

THE COOGAN BILL is an interesting piece of legislation, and it all began with a child actor by the name of Jackie Coogan, who later played the role of huggable Uncle Fester in the 1960s television series *The Addams Family*. Although the baby boomer generation associates Coogan with that memorable role, film buffs may recall a pint-size actor who equaled any in popularity. In fact, Jackie Coogan (née John Leslie Coogan Jr.) was the first major child star churned out by the Hollywood celebrity machine. With a breakthrough role in *The Kid* (1921) and subsequent roles in a score of silent films, the boy with the pageboy haircut became one of Hollywood's highest paid performers.

Despite his overwhelming success, Coogan's financial state was far from secure. From the very beginning of his career, his mother and stepfather had complete control of his holdings, and tragically for Coogan, they refused to part with any of it.

In 1935, Coogan was injured in an automobile crash that claimed the life of his father, Jack Coogan Sr., and child actor Trent Bernard "Junior" Durkin. In 1938, the former child star sued his parents' production company to reclaim his money. He would recoup just $126,000—exactly half the remaining value of the firm that his irresponsible parents had overseen and neglected. It was only a fraction of the estimated $4 million that Coogan had earned.

Coogan became a poster boy for exploited child actors. In 1939, the state of California enacted a preventative law to address the problem. The *California Child Actor's Bill* (Coogan Bill) stated that a portion of a young actor's earnings would be directly deposited into a trust fund. The law came a bit late to benefit Coogan—his financial problems had already "festered" for years—but at least the star's loss wasn't in vain.

The Rumor of Oz

It's said that if you watch The Wizard of Oz closely enough, you'll see an actor who played one of the Munchkins commit suicide on the set. Or is that just an urban legend?

✳   ✳   ✳   ✳

IN ONE OF the most famous scenes in *The Wizard of Oz*, Dorothy links arms with the Scarecrow and the Tin Man and the three dance off along the yellow brick road singing, "We're off to see the wizard, the wonderful wizard of Oz." Almost as famous as the scene itself is the rumor that has long accompanied the classic 1939 movie. Take your eyes off the

central characters for a moment and you can clearly see something move in the background among the trees. Look closely
enough, some people say, and you'll see that the movement is
created by an actor, playing one of the Munchkins, as he hangs
himself. Apparently, the man in question was distraught over
being romantically rejected by a fellow Munchkin.

A Flap Over Nothing

Soon after the release of *The Wizard of Oz*, rumors began to
circulate about Munchkin unruliness on the set. The suicide
story, however, didn't gain ground until the movie was released
on video and viewers were able to pause and watch the scene
repeatedly in slow motion. Morbid imaginings aside, the movement is not a suicide in progress but the flapping wings of an
oversize bird.

To make the forest scenes seem more realistic, filmmakers borrowed large birds from the Los Angeles Zoo and allowed them
to roam around the set. The birds can be seen more clearly
in earlier scenes: As Dorothy and the Scarecrow are reviving
the Tin Man with oil outside his cabin, a peacock leisurely
strolls by. In the scene in question, however, the bird (either an
ostrich or a crane) is visible only as a blurry background image.
Furthermore, the forest scenes were filmed before those that
took place in Munchkinland, so no Munchkins would have
been on set at the time.

Casper the Friendly Ghost

A friendly ghost so doggone sweet that children run toward him?
What on earth were his creators thinking? Cha-ching! That's what
they were thinking.

✳   ✳   ✳   ✳

He's a Scream!

IN 1940, WRITER Seymour Reit and illustrator Joe Oriolo
proposed the idea of *Casper the Friendly Ghost* as a story-

book, but the project was tabled for unknown reasons. A few years later, Paramount Pictures Famous Studios (the studio's animated division) acquired the rights to the dormant project and debuted Casper not as a book but as part of its *Noveltoon* theatrical cartoon series. During this early period, Casper experienced requisite growing pains, found himself mired in existential uncertainty, and survived a brash suicide attempt. Yikes!

Gonzo Genealogy

Believe it or not, lovable Casper's family tree actually has some pretty dark roots. The very fact that Casper is a ghost suggests that he was once alive but died. But did he? While it's true that Casper was seen residing beside gravestones in his earliest cartoon strips, it's also true that later he mysteriously grew very humanlike feet and was often seen in the company of his two ghostly parents. Some say that such clues positively prove his mortality; others disagree, choosing instead to believe that Casper and his family were simply "born" as ghosts or were supernatural beings. While no definitive answer exists (fans debate Casper's origins to this very day), such ambiguity probably sprang from Paramount's concerns over keeping the "Friendly Ghost" friendly—especially to easily startled young viewers. After all, there'd be precious little sense in making Casper the ghost of a dead child if the goal was *not* to scare the wits out of American youngsters. On the other hand, it's difficult to explain Casper's existence any other way. Some things are just better left unknown.

A Suicidal New Yawker?

It may shock some to learn that Casper began his cartoon career at Paramount as a ghost-child from New York, but this was strongly suggested by his accent. It may also be surprising to learn that in "The Friendly Ghost," the very first Casper cartoon short produced by Paramount in 1944, the ghost-boy tried to end his "life" by lying across railroad tracks. Hey, if you were an existentially uncertain, amorphous white blob that scared almost everyone you met, wouldn't you consider the deep sleep? Thankfully, because Casper was already a ghost, the train passed right through him. The outcome pleased fans and spared writers the unenviable task of explaining how a ghost dies again.

Grown-Ups Don't Understand

Perhaps the most memorable part of the Casper experience was the theme song created for the TV cartoon series of the early 1950s. Written by Jerry Livingston and Mack David, the catchy ditty features lyrics that have etched themselves into the minds of baby boomers everywhere:

Grown-ups don't understand,
why children love him the most,
but kids all know that he loves them so
Casper, the friendly ghost

Young Casper fans were eager to jump on the bandwagon. It's no wonder that Casper lunch boxes, board games, Halloween costumes, and stuffed toys sold like hotcakes.

Still Friendly After All These Years

The Casper phenomenon has withstood the test of time. Over the years, the sweet specter has been featured in animated movies and cartoons, comic books, and even a live-action feature film (*Casper*, *1995*). It was in this vehicle that Casper's backstory was finally told ... Or was it? Viewers learned that he was really a 12-year-old boy named Casper McFadden, who entered the ghostly realm after dying of pneumonia. But in the follow-up films *Casper: A Spirited Beginning* (1997) and *Casper Meets Wendy* (1998), these ideas are contradicted, clouding the issue once again. With so much conflicting information making the rounds, we may never fully understand Casper. Then again, grown-ups aren't supposed to.

The Lady Is a Vamp

Meet Theda Bara—Hollywood's first "bad girl."

✳ ✳ ✳ ✳

Publicity Makeover

THEODOSIA BURR GOODMAN was born in Cincinnati in 1885, the eldest daughter of a prosperous Polish tailor and a Swiss-born wigmaker. Dullsville, right? However, when Goodman became known as film star Theda Bara, a more flamboyant bio was concocted to match Bara's exotic on-screen persona: the Egyptian-born daughter of a French actress and an Italian sculptor. Bara held press conferences in a steamy hotel room fashioned to resemble a Sultana's chambers. Never breaking character, she gave interviews in a sultry French accent. Bara's willingness to participate in such outlandish stunts helped propel her into stardom—she now ranks among the top silent film stars, trailing only Mary Pickford and Charlie Chaplin in popularity.

A Brief but Memorable Career

Bara landed her first screen role in 1914 as an extra when she was nearly 30 years old. Soon, a Fox film director lobbied for her to star in the 1915 vampire flick, *A Fool There Was.* The immortal catchphrase "Kiss me, my fool" helped propel her to stardom; suddenly, the good Jewish girl found her silver-screen niche as a blood-sucking femme fatale. When Bara took on the title role in her most famous film, *Cleopatra* (1917), her publicists hyped her alias, "Theda Bara," as an anagram for "Arab Death."

Her career flourished, but it ultimately went bust in 1919 after Fox began promoting flat-chested flappers over the buxom Bara. Unfortunately, Bara was unable to shake her vampy typecasting, which made it difficult to find work as censorship in Hollywood became stricter. She continued to make movies until 1926. Bara made more than 40 films, but sadly, all but three have been lost, giving her the highest percentage of lost work for someone with a star on the Hollywood Walk of Fame. Despite the film industry moving on without her, Bara remains one of the most memorable figures of early filmmaking.

Disney on Ice

When his family shared only sketchy details of Walt Disney's death and next-day funeral with the media, a rumor germinated: He'd been cryogenically frozen and was stashed under Pirates of the Caribbean at Disneyland.

✳ ✳ ✳ ✳

ACCORDING TO RECORDS at St. Joseph's Hospital in Burbank, California, Walter Elias Disney died of lung cancer on December 15, 1966. On December 16, his studios announced that the funeral had already taken place at the Little Church of the Flowers in Forest Lawn Memorial Park in Glendale, California. There was a small, private funeral, followed by cremation and entombment on December 17.

The speedy ceremony raised a few eyebrows. Disney's daughter Diane had written years earlier that her father was neurotic about death. But because he hated funerals and didn't want one, his family simply honored his wish with a private burial. Months later, when a California psychologist underwent the first cryonic preservation, rumors began to swirl that Disney himself had been frozen.

Disney, a wealthy technophile, certainly could have afforded the expense of early cryonic preservation, but there is no evidence that he was particularly interested in the procedure. Records reveal that Disney's estate paid $40,000 for his burial plot, and his ashes rest at Forest Lawn—at the ambient temperature.

✳ Another popular myth about Walt Disney is that just before he died, he prepared a videotaped presentation in which he advised top executives on how to keep his namesake business running profitably. However, this rumor presupposes that Disney actually ran his own corporation. In fact, he had little to do with business operations, leaving those details to his brother Roy.

Behind the Films of Our Time

* The name James Bond is believed to have come from a real-life ornithologist, or bird enthusiast, with the same name.

* The makers of *The Wizard of Oz* paid the dog portraying Toto $125 per week for appearing in the film.

* Tom Hanks's 1988 hit *Big* was originally written with a drastically different ending. In the film, Hanks plays a 12-year-old named Josh who inadvertently transforms himself into an adult by wishing on a carnival fortune-teller machine. The adult Josh develops a relationship with an adult woman named Susan, but in the end, of course, he becomes a kid again and leaves her behind. The original version, however, ended with a girl named Susan showing up at his school soon thereafter— in other words, the adult Susan visited the same carnival machine to wish herself a child so she could rejoin him. Apparently, test audiences didn't like it; the movie's makers cut it at the last minute.

* James Earl Jones, the man who gave *Star Wars*'s Darth Vader his signature deep, booming voice, never met the man who played the villain's body, David Prowse. In addition to Jones and Prowse, two people helped make the Vader character come to life: Sebastian Shaw played the unmasked face, and Ben Burtt, the film's sound designer, did the infamous breathing effects.

* The sound of E.T. walking, in the movie *E.T.: The Extra-Terrestrial*, was created by a crewmember playing with jelly in her hands.

* Some of the guts that spring out when the shark explodes in 1983's *Jaws 3-D* were actually made out of unsold E.T. dolls.

* Actor Jean-Claude Van Damme plays the costumed alien in parts of the Arnold Schwarzenegger hit *Predator*. Van Damme left filming early but is said to be in most of the climbing scenes.

A Cinematic Rebirth: Hollywood Grows Up in the '60s and '70s

Movie formulas had always served Hollywood studios well. Good guys wore white; bad guys wore black. The hero always walked (or rode) off into the sunset with the heroine in the end. The monster always wreaked havoc on the town, and there was always time during a crisis to break into song. But then it was time to grow up.

✳ ✳ ✳ ✳

HOLLYWOOD HAD BECOME quite rich and quite comfortable with its formulas of the 1930s, 1940s, and 1950s. But in the 1960s, American culture began to change, and television provided big competition. Social, political, and cultural norms in America were turned upside down. The president was assassinated, draft cards were burned, and the generation gap became a chasm. Suddenly, the formula wasn't enough for audiences . . . or for filmmakers. From the ashes of these tumultuous times rose a rebirth of American cinema. A new class of movies—many with directors who were schooled in classrooms rather than on soundstages—dared to go where no celluloid had gone before.

Bonnie and Clyde

If any one film marked the beginning of this rebirth, it was *Bonnie and Clyde*. Director Arthur Penn redefined the "cops and robbers" genre in 1967 with this fairy tale about two outlaws. Crime became glamorous, as the tagline for the film claimed, "They're young . . . they're in love . . . they rob banks." The violence was loud and graphic, the action was relentless, and the ending was brutal. The characters of Bonnie Parker and Clyde

Barrow, although portrayed as robbers and killers, became the standard for antiheroes in future films, including George Roy Hill's *Butch Cassidy and the Sundance Kid* and Brian De Palma's *Scarface*. Nominated for ten Oscars and winner of two, *Bonnie and Clyde* opened the door for Hollywood's new cinema.

M*A*S*H

This 1970 film was set during the Korean War, but it might as well have been set against America's ongoing conflict in Vietnam. Director Robert Altman created the ultimate in antiestablishment and antiwar attitudes in the main characters—army surgeons required to patch up wounded soldiers so they could go back to the front to get injured again or killed. *M*A*S*H* portrayed undisciplined and cynical doctors who were forced into the military. The result was the darkest of black comedies, one that allowed Altman to write his own ticket as a cutting-edge director. He prolifically helmed several outstanding features in the five-year period following *M*A*S*H*, including *Brewster McCloud, McCabe & Mrs. Miller, The Long Goodbye, California Split*, and *Nashville*.

The Last Picture Show

Director Peter Bogdanovich moved into the future by way of the past in this 1971 feature. A film writer for *Esquire* magazine, he followed the examples of French New Wave directors and decided to make his own movies. *The Last Picture Show*, based on the novel by Larry McMurtry, depicts life in a small, dusty, lonely Texas town in the early 1950s as two friends finish their senior year of high school. Frank sexual situations and nudity placed the film at the forefront of early-1970s cinema, but lush black-and-white cinematography made it feel like a throwback to the 1940s or 1950s. In fact, it was the first mainstream black-and-white movie to come out since the mid-1960s, and it proved that such a limited color palette could be a viable artistic choice. Bogdanovich continued to make films, releasing two more commercial blockbusters in the next two years. *What's Up, Doc?* in 1972 recalled Hollywood's great screwball comedies of the 1930s, and 1973's *Paper Moon* was another evocative black-and-white movie, this time set during the Great Depression.

American Graffiti

A graduate of the USC School of Cinema-Television, director George Lucas indulged his interest in fast cars and first loves with *American Graffiti* in 1973. Shot on a budget of less than one million dollars, the film eventually grossed $115 million, proving that this new breed of independent filmmaker could turn a profit for distributing studios. Somewhat autobiographic in nature, *American Graffiti* follows the adventures of Southern California teens on one night in 1962. Lucas later solidified his place in Hollywood history by becoming the creative force behind the immensely popular and successful *Star Wars* series.

The Godfather

A UCLA Film School alum, director Francis Ford Coppola cut his teeth working under low-budget producer Roger Corman in the 1960s. In 1972, Coppola took a best-selling novel by Mario Puzo and created a dark, sprawling saga of the Mafia in America, *The Godfather*. Gangsters in the movies had never been portrayed as three-dimensionally—or as brutally—as the Corleone family, which was headed by film icon Marlon Brando. Coppola's vision continued with 1974's *The Godfather: Part II*, which expanded the story and spanned a 60-year period. Both films were critical and box-office successes, but they are only part of Coppola's cinematic accomplishments, which also include 1974's *The Conversation* and 1979's *Apocalypse Now*.

Taxi Driver

Frequently called the greatest living American film director, Martin Scorsese graduated from the prestigious New York University Film School. Like many of his contemporaries, he drew heavily on his own experiences—in this case, growing up in the gritty neighborhoods of New York City. *Taxi Driver*

teamed Scorsese with edgy actor Robert De Niro—one
of their many pairings. Like other films of the era, *Taxi Driver*
painted its lead character as an antihero. Loner Travis Bickle
became a fully realized character, driving his cab through the
foul streets of the Big Apple, stalking a presidential candidate,
befriending a preteen prostitute (played by Jodie Foster), and
murdering several unsavory individuals. The bloody violence
and gritty real-life locations became trademarks for Scorsese,
who went on to direct other stark and compelling films, including *Raging Bull, Goodfellas, Casino*, and *The Departed*, for
which he won what many saw as a long-overdue Oscar for best
director.

French New-Wave Cinema? *Mais Oui*!

*A group of Parisian filmmakers changed the way the world
conceived of and made movies.*

✳   ✳   ✳   ✳

THE FILMMAKERS OF *La Nouvelle Vague*, or French New
Wave, in the late 1950s established the auteur theory of
making movies, wherein the director is considered the ultimate
creator of a film (*auteur* is French for "author"). These concepts about film initially appeared in a radical and influential
magazine called *Cahiers du Cinema*, founded by critic André
Bazin in the early '50s. Many of the writers in this journal
put their theories into practice and began making films themselves. Admiring highly individualized American mavericks
such as Orson Welles and John Ford as well as Briton Alfred
Hitchcock, New Wave directors sought to mark each of their
films with a personalized stamp. These movies broke new
ground, turning away from traditional narrative forms that
were the norm in post–World War II France. Directors such
as François Truffaut, Alain Resnais, and Jean-Luc Godard
thumbed their noses at the traditions ofFrench cinema.

Although short on technical skills and money, these renegade filmmakers actually turned their shortcomings into strengths and signature characteristics. New Wave films were known for handheld cameras, on-location shooting, improvised scenes and dialogue, natural lighting, long single takes, and jarring jump-cut editing. Originally dismissed as esoteric "art films," many French New Wave efforts, such as Truffaut's *The 400 Blows* and *Shoot the Piano Player*, Godard's *Breathless* and *Une femme est une femme*, and Resnais's *Hiroshima, Mon Amour*, became international hits. Their influence, particularly the idea that a director should be free to include what-ever nontraditional elements that he or she pleased, led to a fresh view of film. This can especially be seen in the "Hollywood Renaissance" of the late '60s and '70s.

The 400 Blows

Autobiographical in nature, this first feature by Truffaut tells of a troublesome 12-year-old boy, Antoine, who runs away from home to create his own world of petty crime and fantasy, only to end up being arrested. Its impact was immediate, winning Truffaut the Best Director award at the 1959 Cannes Film Festival. The final scene of the boy's escape from detention camp is, like much of New Wave cinema, ambiguous. After running for what seems to be forever, Antoine arrives at a peaceful but desolate beach. He turns and the frame freezes— is he free or has he been recaptured? From the look on his face, it's hard to tell.

Hiroshima, Mon Amour

This 1959 feature by Alain Resnais chronicles the brief affair of a married French actress and a married Japanese architect who meet while she is filming in Japan. Their love scenes are contrasted with horrific footage of the aftermath of Hiroshima's atomic bombing. Resnais uses liberal flashbacks and repetitive phrases throughout the film, keeping viewers off balance while the lovers recall moments from the war. *Hiroshima, Mon Amour* seems to focus simultaneously on two tragedies: the couple's impossible romance and the world's political turmoil. Resnais's story of lost love and rebuilding earned Oscar nominations and won critics' awards.

Weekend

Director Jean-Luc Godard once wrote in *Cahiers du Cinema*, "A film should become a reality within itself." The seemingly endless 360-degree pan, accompanied by a Mozart piano piece, that opens *Weekend* may have been part of Godard's reality, but it hardly belongs to the average viewer's world. This 1967 film still stands as one of the more experimental New Wave offerings. The plot involves a married couple's nightmarish weekend trip to visit family. A famous scene features a ceaseless din of blaring car horns, children playing next to a car accident, and a seven-minute-long tracking shot that reveals a most surreal traffic jam. Godard left his definitive statement about the medium itself by ending *Weekend* with two title cards: "End of Cinema," followed by "End of the World."

The Truth About Telethons

You turn on the television, hoping to tune in to your favorite sitcom—only to find that a telethon is airing in its place. And you wonder: How did the telethon get its start? And how long has it been around?

Q: How long have telethons been confounding viewers who had hoped to tune in to their regularly scheduled television show?

A: Telethons aren't a recent development; they have been a part of television since the 1940s. The first recognized telethon was a 1949 fund-raiser for New York's Damon Runyon Cancer Memorial Fund and was hosted by comedian Milton Berle, who had become one of the biggest names in television as the host of the wildly popular Texaco Star Theater.

For an incredible 16 straight hours, Berle—fueled by black

coffee and cold sandwiches—stood before the television camera performing his shtick and imploring viewers to donate. By the telethon's end, he had raised more than a million dollars.

Q: What does telethon mean, anyway?

A: The word telethon is a hybrid of "television" and "marathon" and very accurately describes these events, which can last from a few hours to a full week. They're a grueling way to raise money, but they keep airing because they work.

Q: When did Jerry Lewis become a name in telethons?

A: In 1950, Dean Martin and Jerry Lewis went before the cameras as the hosts of a telethon for the New York Cardiac Hospital and managed to raise a whopping $1 million. Two years later, singer Bing Crosby teamed with comedian Bob Hope to raise money to send the United States Olympic Team to the Helsinki Games. (This was long before deep-pocketed commercial sponsors came along.)

By the mid-1950s, telethons had become the fund-raiser of choice for a wide variety of charities and organizations. In 1955, Dean Martin and Jerry Lewis announced the biggest telethon yet, a massive appeal for the Muscular Dystrophy Association (MDA). The event, broadcast from WABD in New York, was scheduled to run from 10:00 A.M. on Friday, June 29, to 7:00 P.M. Saturday night. The undertaking was so large that Martin and Lewis brought in a complete television production team from Hollywood at their own expense.

Q: So, what happened to Dean Martin?

A: Dean Martin and Jerry Lewis broke up the following year, and Jerry Lewis became the sole host of the second MDA telethon, held between November 30 and December 1, 1957. In an attempt to make the event even more accessible to viewers, Lewis moved it from a television studio stage to the Grand Ballroom at New York's Roosevelt Hotel. According to *New*

York Herald Tribune writer Bob Salmaggi, the move gave the telethon "the air of a spontaneous party."

Q: Does the MDA Telethon still take place?

A: Yes. The Jerry Lewis MDA Telethon is a Labor Day tradition, televised worldwide and bringing in tens of millions of dollars for muscular dystrophy research. It has also proved beyond a doubt that telethons are a great way to make money quickly. Over the years, a wide variety of charities and organizations have jumped on the telethon bandwagon in some form or another, including St. Jude Children's Research Hospital, the Children's Miracle Network, and the Christian Broadcasting Network.

Q: Any other telethons I should know about?

A: National Public Radio and the Public Broadcasting Service use modified telethons (usually a few minutes of intense begging between features) as a way to help raise funds, and no less a body than the Democratic National Committee held three telethons between 1973 and 1975 to help pay off a $3.5-million debt.

Love 'em or hate 'em, telethons are probably here to stay. Critics often ridicule them (writer Cliff Jahr called them "institutionalized kitsch" in *New York* magazine), but the fact is, millions of people tune in to watch each year, many sticking around from beginning to end, and a good percentage of them are sufficiently moved to pledge a few bucks to a worthy cause.

Behind the TV Shows of Our Times
You're in the Picture

Jackie Gleason was often referred to as "The Great One." He had secured his place in TV history by playing always-trying-but-never-winning bus driver Ralph Kramden on *The Honeymooners* series in the 1950s. In January 1961, Gleason offered a game show to TV audiences called *You're in the*

Picture, in which celebrities stuck their heads through holes in prepainted pictures and had to guess the scene in which they were now involved. Gleason was the MC, egging them on. The premise doesn't sound promising, but it was actually much worse. With the abominable show ditched after its only airing, the network had a hole in its schedule. Gleason returned to the same time slot the following week and made an on-air apology—which many viewers said was much funnier and more appealing than *You're in the Picture.*

Life With Lucy

In the early days of TV, Lucille Ball distinguished herself as the "Queen of Comedy" on her hit show, *I Love Lucy*. Red-haired and wild-eyed, she defined female physical comedy, while engaging in a never-ending war of words with her Cuban bandleader husband, Ricky Ricardo—played by her real-life mate, Desi Arnaz. From that time on she was never far away from the small screen. But, apparently, the 35 years since her *I Love Lucy* debut made a difference. In 1986, Lucy bombed in an embarrassing comedy series called *Life with Lucy*. At 75, with a voice hoarsened by a lifetime of cigarette smoking, she struggled through eight episodes as a doting grandmother before ABC canceled the show.

Gunsmoke

Long before the days of reality shows, television was loaded with Westerns. Big, sprawling sagas of American expansion into the West, they were full of cowboys, Indians (before they were called Native Americans), horses, and gunfights. Like many early TV shows, *Gunsmoke* had previously appeared on the radio. It featured Marshal Matt Dillon, sworn to uphold law and order in Dodge City. When the TV show premiered in 1955, it featured a new actor as Dillon. Few people knew James Arness, who was replacing William Conrad from the radio. To introduce Arness to audiences, *Gunsmoke* producers chose the biggest Western star they could find—John Wayne.

Trouble for the Prince of Noir

Robert Mitchum was the original off-screen bad boy—before James Dean ever appeared on the scene. He defined cool before Hollywood knew the hip meaning of the word. He was rugged, handsome, and jaunty. A hobo turned actor, he was the antithesis of the typical movie hero—and he was on his way to becoming a star, primarily in film noir. Then it happened: A drug bust with a buxom blonde, and Mitchum was in the headlines in a way he never intended. Ironically, this incident accelerated his stardom.

✳ ✳ ✳ ✳

I N AUGUST 1948, Hollywood tabloids were emblazoned with headlines proclaiming the scandalous drug bust (for possession of marijuana) of actor Robert Mitchum, who was in the company of 20-year-old aspiring actress Lila Leeds. This was the era of the marijuana frenzy: The government was at war with cannabis users, and propaganda, entrapment, blatant lies, and excessive punishments were just a few of the weapons they used. Mitchum was the perfect whipping boy. The actor was no stranger to pot and hashish, having experimented with both as a teenage hobo riding the rails. He was also a fugitive from the law, having escaped from a Georgia chain gang after being arrested for vagrancy in Savannah at age 16. Despite hiring Jerry Giesler, Hollywood's hottest defense attorney, Mitchum was found guilty and was sentenced to 60 days on a prison farm. His "I don't give a damn" smirk when his sentence was pronounced would define the attitude of the drug culture that burst upon the scene as the 1940s came to a close.

A Career Ruined?

When Mitchum was sentenced, he was earning $3,000 a week—a princely sum at the time. He was married to his childhood sweetheart, Dorothy Spence, and was in the midst of a seven-year contract with RKO studios. When the tabloids ran a picture of inmate 91234 swabbing the jail corridors in prison attire, Mitchum anticipated it would be "the bitter end" of his career and his marriage. In reality, the publicity had the opposite effect. With the exception of becoming a small embarrassment to the studio and causing the cancellation of a speech Mitchum was scheduled to deliver to a youth group, the actor's off-screen bad-boy persona had little negative effect on his career or personal life. If anything, it only added to his counter-culture, tough-guy, antihero image.

Great PR

While Mitchum served his 60-day sentence on the honor farm (which he described as "Palm Springs without the riff-raff"), RKO released the already-completed film *Rachel and the Stranger* (1948). Not only did movie audiences stand and cheer when Mitchum appeared on the screen, the low-budget movie also became the studio's most successful film of the year.

In 1950, another judge reviewed Mitchum's conviction and reversed the earlier court decision because the arrest smelled of entrapment: Leeds's Laurel Canyon bungalow had been bugged by two overly ambitious narcotics agents. The judge changed Mitchum's plea to not guilty and expunged the conviction from his records—not that Mitchum appeared to care one way or the other. By then, he was a bona fide Hollywood star.

A Long and Successful Livelihood

Mitchum enjoyed an illustrious career, making more than 70 films, some to critical acclaim. He also enjoyed success as a songwriter and singer, with three songs hitting the best-seller charts. His marriage remained intact for 57 years, possibly a Hollywood record. He earned a star on the Hollywood Walk of Fame along with several other prestigious industry awards. Not a bad lifetime of achievements for a pot-smoking vagabond fugitive from a chain gang. Often seen with a cigarette dangling from his sensual lips, Mitchum died of lung cancer and emphysema on July 1, 1997, at his home in Santa Barbara, California. He was 79 years old.

The Great Train Robbery

At the turn of the twentieth century, short film clips were displayed in parlors, known as nickelodeons, on individual viewers called Kinetoscopes and Vitascopes. Customers stood in line to be thrilled by such seemingly mundane scenes as a train pulling into a station or a man and a woman kissing.

* * * *

PROLIFIC INVENTOR THOMAS Edison produced these clips in a studio in the exotic moviemaking locale of West Orange, New Jersey. Edison's camera operator, Edwin S. Porter, had a greater vision for movies. Believing the clips could tell complete stories, he produced and directed America's first "feature film"—1903's *The Great Train Robbery*—although it was only 12 minutes in length.

A Flurry of Firsts

Porter was a pioneer in location shooting, and he was the first to have one location stand in for another, using the northern New Jersey woods as a substitute for the Wild West. He was also the first to use a method of dynamic editing called crosscutting, in which the viewer's attention is focused on two separate but simultaneous scenes of action. In addition, Porter found a way to move the bulky camera so that it was mobile rather than stationary.

More importantly, his film had a beginning, a middle, and an end. Bandits stop a train, rob its passengers, and make their escape on horseback. A posse gives chase and guns down the bandits. Porter based the story on an 1896 stage play of the same name and the real-life adventures of outlaws Butch Cassidy and the Sundance Kid, who robbed a Wyoming train in 1899.

The director obviously knew the potential impact that moving pictures could have—he finished *The Great Train Robbery* with a scene of an outlaw firing his pistol right into the camera, caus-ing startled viewers to duck and recoil in surprise.

It wouldn't be the last time that happened in the movies.

Behind the Films of Our Times

Alien

Directed by Ridley Scott, 1979's *Alien* was considered a "haunted house in deep space" film. The nightmarish crea-ture, designed by imaginative artist H. R. Giger, was played by seven-foot-tall Bolaji Badejo. On the spaceship *Nostromo*, space traveler Kane, played by John Hurt, was infested by the alien and, to the utter shock of fellow crew members, his body ruptured. A baby alien puppet burst from Hurt's chest, spew-ing blood and guts across the faces of the unsuspecting actors in the scene. Veronica Cartwright's reaction of total shock was totally real.

Fargo

This compelling and quirky 1996 story about a kidnapping gone wrong came from the Coen Brothers. Set in frigid North Dakota and Minnesota, the film offered stellar performances from Frances McDormand, William H. Macy, and Steve Buscemi, among others. Opening titles indicate that *Fargo* is "a true story (that) took place in Minnesota in 1987." Interviews quoted the creators claiming the movie was "pretty close" to the facts. But news media reports offered no accounts of similar events, revealing this claim to be another practical joke from those crazy Coens.

The Fly

This 1958 horror film started as a short story that first appeared in *Playboy* magazine. Author James Clavell wrote the subsequent screenplay. Vincent Price liked to tell the story of how he and fellow actor Herbert Marshall nearly collapsed with laughter as they tried to shoot the scene in the garden where they are searching for the fly while a squeaky voice cried,

"Help me! Help me!" They finally got through an acceptable take by turning almost back-to-back and not looking at each other.

The Godfather

The title role in this sprawling story of organized crime was one of the most coveted in Hollywood history. Imagine any of the following as the gruff and crafty Vito Corleone—Frank Sinatra, Anthony Quinn, Ernest Borgnine, TV stars David Jansen (*The Fugitive*) and Vince Edwards (*Ben Casey*), entertainer Danny Thomas, and even aging crooner Rudy Vallee. They all sought the part, but writer Mario Puzo and director Francis Ford Coppola could only foresee two actors as the Don—Laurence Olivier or Marlon Brando. Brando got the nod—and an Oscar (which he refused).

Amazing Animation

Animation is almost as old as cinema itself. Here are five outstanding features that illustrate all that the genre has to offer.

✳ ✳ ✳ ✳

1. ***Snow White and the Seven Dwarfs* (1937)**—An undisputed classic, this take on the Grimm fairy tale is historic for being one of the world's first full-length animated features, as well as the first to be produced by Walt Disney. In 1939, Disney was given an honorary Academy Award for *Snow White*—an award made especially for him, consisting of one statuette and seven miniature statuettes.

2. ***Fantasia* (1940)**—A commercial failure at the time of its release (film critic Roger Ebert blames a World War II-era lack of whimsical spirit), this wondrous ode to classical music is now an acknowledged masterpiece that was well ahead of its time in both theme and execution.

3. ***Shrek* (2001)**—Based on the children's picture book by William Steig, the computer-animated *Shrek* stars Mike

Myers as the titular green ogre, Eddie Murphy as a wise-cracking donkey, and Cameron Diaz as Princess Fiona. This was the film that put DreamWorks on the map, as it pokes hilarious fun at popular culture (and all things Disney), with plenty of guffaws for children and adults alike.

4. *Spirited Away* (2001)—The Japanese consider animation a genuine art form, and Hayao Miyazaki, who wrote and directed this anime classic, is revered as one of the genre's masters. The story concerns Chihiro, a young girl who wanders into a bizarre world of spirits and monsters. *Spirited Away* (real name: *Sen to Chihiro no Kamikakushi*) won the Academy Award for Best Animated Feature in 2003. If you've never experienced Japanese animation, this is a great place to start.

5. *WALL-E* (2008)—The delightful story of an endearing (and industrious) little robot who falls in love, travels into space, and ultimately saves the world, *WALL-E* deservedly won the 2009 Academy Award for Best Animated Feature. It's the perfect blend of story, character, and eye-popping computer animation in one neat package. It might also make you shed a tear or two.

Errol Flynn and the *Cuban Rebel Girls*

Flynn's last film is a peculiar screen epitaph of a Hollywood legend.

✳ ✳ ✳ ✳

THE FINAL SCREEN appearance of virile Hollywood leading man Errol Flynn is a shocker. It seems inconceivable that the man who had starred in *The Adventures of Robin Hood* and *The Sea Hawk* should place himself in a no-budget 1959 picture called *Cuban Rebel Girls*—co-starring his real-life teenage girlfriend, no less. Not to mention Flynn's physical condition in the movie is more than disquieting—at barely 50 years old, he was lined, faintly bloated, and visibly drunk.

Screen Idol

Errol Flynn played swashbuckling heroes many times, but nowhere as effectively as in real life. Tall, athletic, and dashingly handsome, he exuded an easy, irreverent charm that won him fans and friends. An accomplished yachtsman, Flynn also was a novelist, memoirist, inveterate womanizer, and Olympian drinker. He was married three times, and after he beat a statutory rape charge in 1943, Americans began using the expression, "In like Flynn," to signify a person who beat the system, someone too cool for words.

Politically, Flynn leaned to the left—no surprise for a man who reveled in excess and answered to no one. While traveling in Cuba in 1958, Flynn became enchanted with Fidel Castro—or perhaps with the *idea* of Castro—and the final push to oust U.S.-supported dictator Fulgencio Batista.

The Actor, the Girl, and the Guerrilla

Accompanying Flynn in Cuba was 16-year-old Beverly Aadland, a baby-faced blonde whom he had chatted up when he met her a year or two prior at the Hollywood Professional School. With Aadland and a small film crew in tow, Flynn ventured into the Sierra Maestra mountains, where he arranged a face-to-face meeting with Castro and filmed the leader and his rebels.

One result of this was a not-bad 50-minute documentary called *Cuban Story*. Since documentaries didn't exactly draw big crowds in 1958, Flynn reasoned that he could cover his travel and production expenses if he spliced some of the real-life footage into a new, fictional story: *Cuban Rebel Girls*.

The Creative Muse

A small cast of unknowns was assembled. Flynn selected Barry Mahon to direct and, nominally, produce the picture. In earlier years, Flynn had worked with some of the best directors in the world, but Mahon's only prior credit was a wretched sci-fi thriller called *Rocket Attack USA*. (Mahon's resume would later include such triumphs as *Pagan Island*, *Nudes Inc.*, and *Prostitutes' Protective Society*.)

Flynn plays himself in *Cuban Rebel Girls*, but not simply as a movie star with a vague political agenda—no, he's a globetrotting adventurer hired by a news service to cover the revolution. As he makes his way deep into the mountains in the opening of this 68-minute "epic," he encounters Castro, and he chronicles the guerrillas' daily activities via a blend of fact and fabrication. The Cuban rebel girls—including the very-blonde Aadland—are just as convincing as one might imagine.

Fade to Black

In the film's woeful highlight, Flynn takes a (fake) bullet in the leg and is bandaged by Aadland. Our hero is very obviously and very amiably drunk in these scenes, unsteady on his feet, and unable to focus on Aadland or anything else. But star power seldom dies out completely; although Flynn appeared older than his years, he still was a good-looking man who managed to summon an ounce of the old sparkle.

Flynn did not live to see the brief theatrical run of *Cuban Rebel Girls*; he died of heart failure in Vancouver on October 14, 1959. An autopsy revealed that more than just Flynn's heart was worn out: Most of the rest of his body—particularly his poor, beleaguered liver—was shot. The doctor remarked that, internally, Flynn's 50-year-old body was that of an elderly man.

In *The Filmgoer's Companion*, film historian Leslie Halliwell praised Flynn "for living several lives in half of one, and almost getting away with it."

The Truth About Mighty Mouse

Which Mighty Mouse is your favorite? Do you like the classic opera-singing Mighty Mouse and his famous call "Here I come to save the day!" Or do you prefer the more modern Mighty Mouse who came with his own sidekick, Scrappy Mouse? Whichever mouse you like most, you're sure to be surprised by some of these forgotten facts regarding everyone's favorite flying mouse.

✳   ✳   ✳   ✳

1. Mighty Mouse was almost a housefly. When Terrytoons studio writer Izzy Klein first came up with the idea of a tiny super-powered creature, he designed a character called Superfly. Thankfully, cooler heads prevailed: Studio head Paul Terry changed our hero into a mouse. Good thing, too; no one likes flies. (As opposed to mice. We all love having a mouse for a houseguest, don't we?)

2. Even after he became a mouse, our hero still wasn't "Mighty." In his first two cartoon appearances, the flying mouse went by the name Super Mouse. Terrytoons changed the name to Mighty Mouse only after learning that a new comic book, Coo Coo Comics, had introduced its own Super Mouse character in 1943. Terrytoons renamed their mouse "Mighty Mouse" to avoid competition. The studio later altered Mighty Mouse's first two adventures upon re-release to reflect the change.

3. The first *Mighty Mouse* cartoon debuted in 1942. It was titled "The Mouse of Tomorrow."

4. Mighty Mouse's most famous villain is Oil Can Harry, a nasty cat. Oil Can, though, made his debut long before the flying mouse, starring in Terrytoons' 1933 cartoon "The Banker's Daughter." In that cartoon, he was a villainous human out to steal the virtuous Fanny Zilch from her stalwart lover, J. Leffingwell Strongheart.

5. During his early adventures, Mighty Mouse's girlfriend was the sweet Pearl Pureheart. Pearl usually managed to get captured by Oil Can Harry. The first *Mighty Mouse* cartoons were actually parodies of the silent-film serials that often featured heroines in peril with the requisite strong-chinned heroes rushing to their rescue. Many *Mighty Mouse* cartoons started with the mouse and Pearl already in some trap devised by the nefarious Oil Can—say, tied to railroad tracks as a locomotive steamed toward them.

6. Mighty Mouse is known for his operatic cartoons, in which characters sing their lines. The first operatic *Mighty Mouse* episode titled "Mighty Mouse and the Pirates" aired in January 1945.

7. For the most part, *Mighty Mouse* has been slighted by the Academy. Only one of his cartoons, "Gypsy Life" (1945), was nominated for an Oscar. It didn't win.

8. Some of the original *Mighty Mouse* cartoons, especially the operatic cartoons, were rather violent for kiddie fare. Mighty Mouse would often pummel his enemies, mostly cats of some sort, until they fled the scene.

9. In some cartoons, Mighty Mouse boasts telekinetic powers, making objects fly through the air. In one adventure, he even managed to turn back time.

10. *Mighty Mouse* cartoons first aired as animated shorts that ran before feature films in movie theaters. In 1955, CBS brought the character and his old adventures to television screens. The network then replayed the old shorts for 12 years on the *Mighty Mouse Playhouse*.

11. Famed animator Ralph Bakshi—who created the adult *Fritz the Cat*—created his own version of Mighty Mouse in the 1980s. Called *Mighty Mouse: The New Adventures*, the cartoon shared elements of the flying mouse's backstory with viewers. For instance, when he wasn't fighting crime,

Mighty Mouse posed as an ordinary mouse named Mike Mouse. He also gained a sidekick in this version, Scrappy Mouse.

12. The Bakshi version of the cartoon lasted only two seasons, but that was long enough for it to generate controversy. In one cartoon, Mighty Mouse sniffs a white powder. The Reverend Donald Wildmon, founder of the American Family Association, claimed the mouse was snorting cocaine. Bakshi denied this, saying the mouse was actually sniffing his lucky cheese. Later, Bakshi said Mighty Mouse was sniffing crushed flowers.

Five Good Reasons The Weather Channel Should Have Failed

In 2008, The Weather Channel, founded as the brainchild of Chicago weather forecaster John Coleman and media executive Frank Batten, was sold to NBC for the whopping sum of $3.5 billion. That somebody was willing to pay billions for a channel that broadcast nothing but weather information is only slightly less puzzling than the fact that somebody thought a channel devoted to overcast-with-a-chance-of-rain was a good idea to begin with. Here are five of the top reasons why The Weather Channel should have been rained out.

✳   ✳   ✳   ✳

1. **Weather is not a commodity:** Most television networks make money by providing what no other network can, whether that be through original programming, televised sporting events, or highly paid television personalities. Weather, though, is free to all. What's more, The Weather Channel (TWC) originally got its weather information through the National Weather Service—a government-run organization that was already providing its forecasts free through 24-hour radio broadcasts.

2. **Weather is boring:** Sure, tornadoes and hurricanes might be exciting, but your average everyday weather isn't exactly a pulse-throttler. Indeed, for most people, weather is a conversation piece of last resort, a signal that you have nothing of substance to say. Sounds like a great idea for a television network.

3. **Weather forecasts are notoriously inaccurate:** The fallibility of weather forecasts is woven into the fabric of popular culture. In fact, according to ForecastAdvisor.com, a website devoted to tracking the accuracy of weather forecasters, The Weather Channel hit the mark a mere 71 percent of the time in 2008—barely a passing grade. We're not sure whether the fact that The Weather Channel's abysmal showing led the weather forecasting pack reflects well on TWC or poorly on everybody else.

4. **The Weather Channel didn't provide anything new:** The Weather Channel initially provided little more than the average person could get by reading the morning paper, watching the evening news, or sticking their head out the window.

5. **It failed everywhere else:** Bolstered by their early popularity in the United States, Landmark Communications, the media company behind The Weather Channel, tried to start sister channels in other countries, most notably in the United Kingdom and Europe. These flopped miserably. Evidently Europeans have better things to do than sit around and watch television coverage of the weather!

"Conversation about the weather is the last refuge of the unimaginative."

—OSCAR WILDE

Gene Siskel: A Critical Myth

Contrary to a widespread rumor, famed film critic Gene Siskel did not insist that he be buried with his thumb pointing up.

✳   ✳   ✳   ✳

EW IN THE specialized field of film criticism have been
as well known or respected as Gene Siskel, who penned
countless movie reviews for the *Chicago Tribune* and later
teamed up with fellow critic Roger Ebert of the *Chicago Sun-Times* on the popular television show *At the Movies.*

The show was famous for its movie rating system of "thumbs
up–thumbs down," which became the duo's critical trademark.
Shortly after Siskel's death in 1999 from complications follow-ing brain surgery, a story started to circulate that, among other
provisions, Siskel's will stipulated that he be buried with his
thumb pointing skyward.

Siskel's thumbs had made him internationally renowned,
a legacy that he may have wanted to take to his grave. The
rumor raced through the internet in the form of a fake UPI
news story that noted Siskel's unusual request. It read, in part:
"According to public records filed in chancery court in Chicago,
Gene Siskel asked that he be buried with his thumb pointing
upward. The 'Thumbs Up' was the Siskel–Ebert trademark."

The story continued: "'Gene wanted to be remembered as a
thumbs-up kind of guy,' said Siskel's lawyer. 'It wasn't surpris-ing to me that he'd ask for that. I informed his family after his
death, but he didn't want it made public until after his will had
been read.'"

The faux article carries all of the marks of a typical urban
legend. Most telling is its failure to identify Siskel's attorney by
name, an omission that no legitimate news organization
would make.

The magazine *Time Out New York* investigated the rumor and set the record straight, reporting on July 15, 1999: "A glance at the will, now on file with a Chicago court, makes clear that there are no digit-placement requests in [Siskel's] last wishes."

The Real Legends of Hollywood

They say that truth is stranger than fiction. Nowhere is that more obvious than in Tinseltown, where legends are born . . . and some really great urban legends are, too!

✱   ✱   ✱   ✱

Three Men and a Baby...and a Ghost

According to legend, the ghost of a young boy who accidentally shot himself haunts the building where portions of *Three Men and a Baby* were filmed. Also, in one scene viewers can see the outline of a phantom shotgun in the window, then seconds later, the boy's ghost appears in the frame standing in front of the same window.

Those images do appear in the background of a scene, but producers claim the shotgun is just an optical illusion caused by light on the curtains. As for the ghostly boy, they say it's nothing more than a cardboard cutout of actor Ted Danson that was left in the scene by mistake. To further squash the ghost story, producers point out that the scenes were shot on a soundstage and not in an actual apartment building.

The Texas Chain Saw Massacre Is a True Story

When Tobe Hooper's *The Texas Chain Saw Massacre* first hit theaters in 1974, it was touted as being based on a true story, even using the line "It happened!" on movie posters. But the truth isn't so black and white. Hooper did base the character Leatherface on a real person—murderer and grave robber Ed Gein. But although Gein was a convicted killer who also fashioned human body parts into jewelry and furniture, there is no evidence that he offed anyone with a chain saw. And he lived in

Wisconsin, not Texas. Apparently *The Wisconsin Rifle-Shootin'*
Massacre wasn't as scintillating.

O. J. Simpson Was Considered for the Lead Role in *The Terminator*

Most people are familiar with the iconic image of Arnold
Schwarzenegger as the murderous Terminator cyborg. What
many people don't know, though, is that one of the actors
considered for the lead role was none other than O. J. Simpson.
Producers passed on Simpson because they felt he was too
"nice" and wouldn't be believable playing the role of a killer.
Although ironic, this tale appears to be true.

Disney's Snuff Film

In the 1958 Disney documentary *White Wilderness*, dozens
of lemmings are shown jumping to their deaths off a cliff into
the ocean as part of a bizarre suicide ritual. There was only
one glitch: Lemmings don't commit suicide en masse. When
principal photographer James R. Simon arrived in Alberta,
Canada to film, he was informed of this. But rather than scrap
the project, Simon had the lemmings herded up and forced off
the cliff while the cameras rolled. As the creatures struggled to
keep from drowning, the narrator delivered the disturbing and
all-too-telling line: "It's not given to man to understand all of
nature's mysteries."

Despite the film winning an Oscar for Best Documentary in
1959, once the truth about what happened on those cliffs was
revealed, it quickly and quietly was locked away, becoming one
of Disney's deep, dark secrets.

The Death of Actor Vic Morrow Can Be Seen in *Twilight Zone: The Movie*

In the early morning of July 23, 1982, actor Vic Morrow and
two children were recreating a Vietnam War battle scene—
complete with helicopters and explosions—for *Twilight Zone:*
The Movie.

The scene began fine, but then one of the helicopter pilots lost control and crashed, killing Morrow and the two child actors. Multiple cameras were rolling at the time and caught the carnage on film, but the footage was locked away. However, while the deaths don't appear in the *Twilight Zone* film, some of the tragic scenes appeared in the 1992 direct-to-video flick *Death Scenes 2.*

Poltergeist Movies Are Cursed

A series of strange, unexpected deaths surrounding actors who worked on the popular *Poltergeist* films have led many to believe that the supernatural theme of the movies has conjured up curses over those associated with them. There have been several untimely deaths, including 22-year-old Dominique Dunne, who played older daughter Dana Freeling in the original *Poltergeist*. She died in November 1982 as a result of injuries sustained when she was attacked by her abusive boyfriend. Little blonde Heather O'Rourke, who starred in all three movies as the perpetually haunted Carol Anne, died of septic shock on February 1, 1988, at age 12. Today, her grave site is a stop on the popular "Haunted Hollywood" tour.

Other cast member deaths were more expected. When Julian Beck, who played Kane in *Poltergeist II: The Other Side*, passed away in September 1985, he was 60 years old and had been battling stomach cancer for nearly two years. Similarly, Will Sampson, the lovable Native American guide from *Poltergeist II*, died from complications after receiving a heart and lung transplant. It's not apparent there's a *Poltergeist* curse, but there sure has been a lot of real-life tragedy.

Behind the TV Shows of Our Times
Password

In the world of TV game shows, *Password* was legend. With more than 2,500 episodes aired in the 1960s and 1970s, the game teamed a celebrity with a contestant, who competed against another such team to recognize words by giving only one-word clues. Play passed back and forth until someone guessed the correct word. Points went down as clues accumulated. It sometimes made strategic sense to pass the first clue to the other team rather than play it oneself. Host Allen Ludden started the show by saying, "Hi, doll." The story was often told of a large mannequin posed in front of his TV at home, assuring him that there would always be at least one face watching him every day. In reality, his greeting was directed to his mother-in-law—actor Betty White's mom. Ludden met White when she was a celebrity panelist on the show.

Turn-On

With the enormous success of *Rowan & Martin's Laugh-In* on NBC in 1968, copycat shows were sure to follow. *Turn-On* was a fast-paced ABC comedy also produced by *Laugh-In* producers George Schlatter and Ed Friendly. Success was not forthcoming for *Turn-On*, however—it was almost immediately canceled when ABC executives recognized that it was full of double entendres and secret implications. (It has even been rumored that the suits canceled the show before the first episode was over.) While the country was relaxing its moral values, it clearly wasn't ready to see a pregnant woman singing "I Got Rhythm" or a Catholic nun primping for a date. Some stations dumped the show during its first commercial break. Guest-hosted by Tim Conway, *Turn-On* is one of the shortest-running TV series ever broadcast.

Head of the Family

Comedian Carl Reiner was fresh from a successful run as a writer and second-banana performer on Sid Caesar's *Your Show of Shows* in the 1950s. Deciding to write a comedy show about a father and husband in the TV business, he starred in the pilot that broadcast as *Head of the Family* in the summer of 1960. It bombed badly, and friend and producer Sheldon Leonard knew why—Reiner was all wrong for the lead. They recast the show, and renamed it *The Dick Van Dyke Show* in 1961.

"I'm King of the World!"

How Hollywood director James Cameron ascended to his Titanic *throne.*

✳ ✳ ✳ ✳

IT'S RARE TO find a film with a title describing its own existence. There is, of course, no doubt that 1997's *Titanic* was precisely that. The brainchild of writer/director James Cameron was titanic in every sense of the word. With a $200-million budget, it became the most expensive film ever made up to that point. It stayed at the number-one spot at the box office for 15 continuous weeks—a record—and enjoyed a run of more than eight months. Raking in $600 million in American theaters and $1.8 billion in theaters worldwide, it broke U.S. and international records for the highest-grossing film in history. It garnered 14 Academy Award nominations—tying with 1950's *All About Eve* for the all-time lead in nominations. It won 11 of them, including Best Picture, Best Director, and Best Cinematography, tying with *Ben-Hur* and *Lord of the Rings: The Return of the King* for number of Oscars won. *Titanic* would lead Cameron and his crew to become international award-season royalty.

Ready to Roll

Cameron had the proper track record to take on a project of such magnitude. The filmmaker co-wrote and directed blockbuster hits such as *The Terminator* (1984), *Aliens* (1986), and *True Lies* (1994). These three films grossed more than $800 million worldwide, proving that Cameron could handle big budgets and bring big results.

He began his plan to shoot a film about the supposedly unsinkable ship more than ten years before the project's eventual release. Scientists found the wreckage of the storied steamship two-and-a-half miles under the Atlantic Ocean in 1985. Cameron's concept combined a fable set in 1912, the year the

RMS *Titanic* sank, with a present-day component including actual deep-sea footage of the hulking remains.

Cameron's script surrounds a search for sunken treasure from the *Titanic*, including a legendary diamond necklace. When a locked trunk thought to contain the necklace is brought up from the seabed, a sketch of a beautiful young woman named Rose is found instead. After a frantic search for her identity, the woman is found to be a 101-year-old survivor of the sinking. The crew brings her to the expedition in hopes of finding the necklace's whereabouts. Revealing her story in flashbacks, she tells about the maiden voyage of the *Titanic*, during which her engagement to a haughty suitor finally fails and she falls in love with a penniless artist named Jack. When the *Titanic* strikes an iceberg, she is left with Jack to survive in the icy arctic water. The young man succumbs to the sea, but Rose lives on. After finishing her story, she steals away to the stern of the exploration boat and drops the hunted necklace—a present worth millions from her former fiancé—into the sea. She had it all along but wishes it to rejoin the *Titanic* and her lost love. Throughout Rose's telling, the grandiose action is visually retold with larger-than-life detail and high drama.

Casting Off

A film of such ambition required the combined financing and resources of two major Hollywood studios. Paramount Pictures and Twentieth Century Fox partnered to bring *Titanic* to the screen.

Working closely with casting director Mali Finn to find the biggest stars in Hollywood, Cameron set out on a long mission to find what he would consider the perfect cast. Both Sean Connery and Gene Hackman were offered the role of treasure hunter Brock Lovett before it finally went to Cameron favorite Bill Paxton. (Ironically, Connery would be the one to hand Cameron the Best Picture Oscar at the awards ceremony.) Fox studios wanted a box-office guarantee such as Brad Pitt or Tom

Cruise for Jack's character before Cameron landed teen heart-throb Leonardo DiCaprio. They tested Gwyneth Paltrow and Claire Danes for young Rose before deciding on Kate Winslet. Fay Wray (1933's *King Kong*) and Ann Rutherford (the Andy Hardy series and 1939's *Gone With the Wind*) both turned down the role of the older Rose, and it went to 87-year-old Gloria Stuart. Cameron didn't think Stuart looked old enough for the part, so she wore latex makeup. Oscar-winner Kathy Bates was brought on as the "Unsinkable" Molly Brown, while young stud Billy Zane would play Rose's jilted beau.

Lights, Camera . . . Ocean!

The company that built the *Titanic*, Harland & Wolff, provided original blueprints that had not been publicly available for years. Combined with Cameron's extensive undersea exploration of the ship, these items gave production designers, set builders, prop makers, and even costumers the ability to remake every facet of the voyage in meticulous detail. Opulent dinnerware and lavish woodwork were perfectly replicated for every shot.

Creating an environment in which Cameron could shoot his epic also involved re-creating the water surrounding the ship. Fox purchased 40 acres of waterfront land on the Pacific Coast in Baja California, Mexico. A nearly full-size replica of the *Titanic* was built in a 17-million-gallon tank, with another 5-million-gallon tank assembled for interior shots. Gigantic hydraulic pistons allowed the ship to repeatedly break apart and sink on cue. Computer graphics allowed for a seamless combination of real people and digital effects.

A Temperamental Genius

Throughout the six-month "ordeal," as Kate Winslet once called the making of the picture, Cameron continued to cement his reputation as a brilliant yet difficult and demanding director. He was well known for yelling at his cast and his crew alike, as well as for running his sets like they were some sort of "a military campaign." Cameron admitted the need for rigorous control, for which he was not at all apologetic, citing logistical and safety concerns. Filming continued even when stunt performers broke bones and extras caught colds, the flu, and kidney infections from their waterlogged activities. Cameron acknowledged that he wasn't an easygoing director on this project. He once asked, "Where does it say that good stuff comes from easy working situations? I don't think it does." When the movie was done, Cameron pocketed an estimated $115 million for his efforts.

In the Final Reel

Much of the success and appeal of a film such as *Titanic* seems to arise from contrasting forces that surround both the celluloid and authentic stories. Notions such as these made Cameron, the crew, and the *Titanic* itself kings of the cinematic world.

A Star Is Born

A publicity stunt catapulted actress Florence Lawrence to fame as the first movie star. But her story doesn't have a happy ending.

✳ ✳ ✳ ✳

LONG BEFORE THE age of cinema, featured performers in theater, vaudeville, and even sports were recognized and admired as stars in the public eye. But it was the movie industry that would glamorize and exploit the concept of stardom to such a degree that film actors and actresses were ultimately turned into fantasy figures idolized by an adoring public. Ironically, the American film industry did not immediately employ a star system and was actually even slow to credit the actors who appeared in its movies.

In the early days, performing in front of the camera was not considered a special talent by many production companies, which often required their casts to also serve as crew members by building sets, making costumes, or helping with other chores. Despite the relative anonymity of movie actors, audiences wrote to production companies to express interest in certain performers whether they knew their names or not.

Around 1908–1909, production companies began to hold their performers in higher regard and consider them on par with theater actors. As a result, small-scale efforts to tout actors or at least identify them emerged. In January 1909, Kalem released a photo of their cast roster to the *New York Dramatic Mirror*, listing the actors' names beneath the photos; in the fall, the Edison Company became the first to announce the cast of their films onscreen. Both efforts were in response to the public's interest in their performers and were a bid to generate more attention.

The First Star and the First Major Publicity Stunt

Against this backdrop, an incident occurred that immediately boosted the popularity of one actress, propelling her into fullfledged stardom. Florence Lawrence had been a popular actress for American Biograph and was recognized by the public as the Biograph Girl, though her real name was unknown. In late 1909, she left Biograph and signed with a rival upstart, IMP Moving Picture Co., owned by Carl Laemmle.

Laemmle wanted audiences to know that the Biograph Girl now worked for IMP. In the December 1909 issue of *Moving Picture World*, a photo of Lawrence appeared in an ad for her film *Lest We Forget*. Written across her photo in bold was "She's an IMP!" Though the ad did not mention Lawrence by name, it traded on the public's recognition of her as the Biograph Girl and then mischievously let them know that IMP had snapped her up.

In March 1910, Laemmle escalated his publicity efforts. On March 12, he placed an ad in *Moving Picture World*, claiming that rival production companies had spread rumors in St. Louis, Missouri, newspapers that Florence Lawrence (the IMP Girl, formerly the Biograph Girl) had been killed in a streetcar accident. He lambasted his enemies for spreading lies and reassured the public that she was doing the best work of her career for IMP. Laemmle's claims regarding the newspaper article were probably false; no such article has ever been discovered. His goal was to direct attention to Lawrence in a large-scale way, reveal her real name to the public, and tout her films for IMP so that audiences would flock to see them.

This publicity stunt worked and became the archetype for promotion tactics of the future. It generated articles about Lawrence in major newspapers, and when the IMP Girl came to St. Louis the following month to appear at the premiere of her latest film, she was mobbed.

Lawrence did become the first movie star as a result of Laemmle's publicity stunt, though her fame was short-lived. After she was badly burned in a 1915 fire, her popularity was eclipsed by Mary Pickford, among others. Lawrence was relegated to bit parts and was soon forgotten. In 1938, she committed suicide—a victim of the star system she helped create.

Tune in Next Week...

What's on television tonight? Nowadays, this question might send you to the internet or to your cable network's on-screen guide. But once upon a time, viewers relied on the TV Guide to answer this age-old question.

✳   ✳   ✳   ✳

*T*V GUIDE IS the iconic American weekly magazine that lists television programming for the upcoming week. In addition to series listings, *TV Guide* includes feature articles, industry gossip, and interviews with television stars and behind-the-scenes personnel.

Launched in 1953, the magazine was the brainchild of Walter Annenberg, the owner and publisher of Triangle Publications. His goal was to provide a service for viewers, increase their enjoyment of the medium, and serve the television industry. Annenberg got the idea when he noticed *TV Digest*, which had been listing Philly's TV programming since 1948, as well as Chicago's *TV Forecast* and New York's *TV Guide*. He envisioned a larger-scale magazine that would provide the same information on a national level.

Annenberg purchased the *TV Digest*, *TV Forecast*, and *TV Guide*, and he contracted with TV magazine publishers in other cities to buy his nationally based guide. Annenberg quickly gained control of television-guide publishing, gathered staffs in each major city, and established his associate Merrill Panitt as the editorial director. What might have been a logistical nightmare for other publishers—gathering and organizing data in different time zones for different markets—was right up Triangle Publications' alley; it already published such data-driven guides as *The Daily Racing Form*, which listed every horse in every race at various tracks in different regions across the country.

The first issue of *TV Guide* featured Lucille Ball's new baby on the cover, commemorating one of the most popular events in television history. The handy 5-by-7$\frac{1}{2}$-inch guide sold one and a half million of the debut issue at fifteen cents per copy. By the 1960s, *TV Guide* was the most read and circulated magazine in the United States. With its familiar red-and-white logo immediately recognizable, the guide was sold at the counters of grocery stores, making it as accessible and indispensable as milk. The company was sold in 2008 for a single dollar—an amount less than the cost of a single issue.

Poor Marie Prevost

"She was a winner/that became a doggie's dinner." So goes the 1980s pop song written about Marie Prevost, the silent film star who once epitomized flapper chic. Prevost rose high and fell hard in the early days of Hollywood.

La Belle Canadienne

BEFORE SHE WAS Marie Prevost, she was Mary Bickford Dunn: an Ontario, Canada, native born on November 8, 1898, and educated in a Catholic convent. After her father's death, 17-year-old Mary moved with her mother and sister to Los Angeles, where the comely Mary found work as a stenographer. At age 18, her secretarial aspirations took a star turn when she tagged along with a girlfriend to meet producer (and fellow Canadian) Mack Sennett.

The curvy, dark-haired beauty captivated Sennett. He called her the "exotic French girl" and cast her as one of his Bathing Beauties under the stage name "Marie Prevost." As one of Sennett's Beauties, Prevost joined future Tinseltown royalty Gloria Swanson and Carole Lombard as the scantily clad eye candy in Sennett's silent slapstick comedies.

Star of the Silent Screen

By 1921, Prevost had graduated from bathing beauty to flirty flapper. Her looks were ideal: saucer eyes, trendy bob, and cupid's-bow lips. Prevost signed a contract with Universal to play coy party girls in a string of silent pictures.

Two years later, she abandoned Universal to become a leading lady, starring in the Warner Bros. film adaptation of F. Scott Fitzgerald's novel *The Beautiful and the Damned*. Fitzgerald denounced the film as the worst garbage he'd ever seen, but the movie proved box-office boon—due in no small part to the smoldering on- and off-screen chemistry of Prevost and her co-star, matinee hunk Kenneth Harlan. The two married soon afterward.

By 1926, Prevost had worked with nearly every big-name director of the day, including Frank Capra and Cecil B. DeMille. But at age 28, her career had already peaked; there was nowhere to go but downhill. Fast.

Beautiful and Damned, Indeed

That year, Prevost had just left Warner Bros. and was filming a new picture for Producers Distributing Corporation when she received word that her mother had been killed in a car accident. Prevost's marriage to Harlan was already on the skids after just two years; the tragedy pushed them over the edge, and they divorced the following year.

To cope, Prevost started hitting the bottle, which led to weight gain. At the same time, the movie business was undergoing a massive revolution, as "talkies" replaced silent films. Rumor has it Prevost's voice was nasal and unappealing for this new film format. True or not, by 1929, Prevost was overweight and out of work.

In the 1930s, Prevost slimmed down a bit thanks to a rigid alcohol-only diet, and she also had some success playing Rosie O'Donnell-type roles of the rotund, wisecracking friend. But parts were scarce: By now, Prevost was in her 30s; the best roles were going to the younger, fresher, and thinner talent. By 1936, her roles were reduced to uncredited parts with just a few speaking lines.

Dogged Demise

One night in January 1937, police were called to a dilapidated Hollywood apartment building after neighbors complained of a dog barking. Inside, they found Prevost dead, her arms and legs gnawed by her pet dachshund who'd tried to wake her. The cause of death was ruled a combination of malnutrition and starvation: Essentially, she had drunk herself to death.

Despite her early success, Prevost died with a paltry $300 to her name, which went to her sister and a friend. Fellow early flapper Joan Crawford allegedly paid for Prevost's no-frills funeral.

Before Hollywood Was Hollywood

For decades, the city of Hollywood, California, has been synonymous with the American film industry. But studios didn't take over this West Coast town until after World War I, and America had a thriving film industry for many years before that. So where did all those early films get shot?

✳ ✳ ✳ ✳

Movie Migration

F EW COMMUNITIES HAVE such an indelible association with a creative industry as Hollywood has had with American film. But in the early days of moviemaking, Tinseltown did not yet exist. Fledging film studios were scattered across the country, with many of them located in the large population centers of Chicago, New York City, and New Jersey.

These early film companies did not have the sprawling studios that would be built on the West Coast. Indeed, many relied heavily on location shooting, which was fine in late spring, summer, and early fall, but the heavy snows and bitter cold of the forbidding northern winters limited the ability to shoot year-round. As the demand for filmed entertainment grew in the early 1900s, studios began sending entire troupes to various parts of the South to work during the winter months. Florida quickly became a favored location. The "Sunshine State" was largely underdeveloped at this time, so land and labor were cheap. The state also offered a stunning array of landscapes— rolling hills in the Panhandle, open prairies in the central region, exotic swamplands in the south, and pristine beaches all around.

In 1908, the Kalem Company sent one of the first of these winter troupes to Jacksonville, Florida, and many other film companies soon followed. Located on the Atlantic coast, the growing community welcomed the high-profile industry—and the jobs it brought—with open arms. Local government offered tax breaks and smoothed the way for real estate transactions. Merchants embraced the studios as favorite customers, ensuring that they had ample supplies of paint, lumber, tools, and electrical materials. They even special-ordered unusual props for the studios. And the general public was thrilled to have a chance to see "flickers" being made firsthand.

Within a few short years, Jacksonville was the permanent home to a cluster of film studios, both established and new, that supplied the country with much of its filmed entertainment. Some of the era's biggest stars, including action star Kathlyn Williams and Western hero Tom Mix, worked in the area. Other performers who would eventually become household names also got their start in Florida, such as comedian Oliver Hardy. And the Norman Studios, one of the most prolific and successful producers of films with black actors for black audiences, called Jacksonville its home. The city seemed poised to become the film capital of America, and of the world, but alas, it was not meant to be.

Worn out Welcome

Jacksonville residents soon grew prickly over the inconsiderate practices of their new neighbors. Street closures for location shooting were a common and annoying occurrence. Filmmakers often worked on Sundays, when they could arrange access to banks and stores that were closed for the day. Even the city government got annoyed when unscrupulous filmmakers would call in false fire alarms in order to get free footage of fire trucks racing through the streets. In the mayoral election of 1917, a reform candidate ran and won on promises of reining in the studios, and Jacksonville soon became far less hospitable to the industry. Some Florida studios managed to hang on for a few years, but by the early 1920s, most had fled to the nation's new movie mecca on the West Coast, and Jacksonville was relegated to a little-remembered footnote in the history of American film.

Tutoring TV

By combining daring documentaries and captivating commentary with educational programming and inventive entertainment, PBS helped transform television from boob tube to brain train.

✳ ✳ ✳ ✳

THE ORIGIN OF the Public Broadcasting Service (PBS) can be traced to the very beginning of television. The network was originally founded as the Educational Television and Radio Center (ETRC) in November 1952, with funds provided by the Ford Foundation's Fund for Adult Education. The ETRC was originally intended to be a visual library of sorts, where educational programs produced by local television stations were exchanged and distributed to other stations. The network did not produce any material by itself.

In 1958, the network was renamed the National Educational Television and Radio Center (NETRC) and eventually increased its daily on-air broadcasting coverage from five to ten hours by adding programming that was originally produced by the BBC in England. In 1963, the network renamed itself National Educational Television (NET) and began airing controversial and biting documentaries and news programs, including its centerpiece show, the *NET Journal*. The network also provided a nationwide forum for innovative children's programming including *Mister Rogers' Neighborhood* (produced by WQED in Pittsburgh) and *Sesame Workshop* (produced by the Children's Television Network). However, the content of NET's more controversial programming and the expense of keeping the network operating caused the Ford Foundation to cut its funding, putting the future of the broadcaster in peril. In 1967, the U.S. government created the Corporation for Public Broadcasting, which eventually led to the creation of the PBS network on November 3, 1969. PBS began broadcasting on

October 5, 1970, with NET staples such as *Sesame Street* and *Mister Rogers* in their lineup.

Unlike America's other networks, PBS does not air commercials to help pay the bills. They rely on government funding, corporate sponsorship, and public donations to keep the cameras rolling and the viewers satisfied.

Classic vs Method Acting

Picture this: A solitary figure runs by you, sweat dripping from his brow as he labors beneath the searing sun. Undeterred by the burden, he pushes on in his quest, seemingly oblivious to any and all who observe him. Could this be a marathon runner embarking on a grueling training run? It could be. Then again, it might be a determined actor sufficiently preparing for an upcoming scene. "Method" actors often approach their roles with such immersion. Through the years, waves of method-trained actors have invaded Hollywood. And they've arrived to the shock and amazement of more traditional actors not so smitten by the technique.

✳ ✳ ✳ ✳

Method to the Madness

WHILE THE METHOD may sound mysterious and, when taken to extremes, can often appear bizarre, there's actually good solid theory behind it. Based on "the System," which was devised in the 1920s by Russian theater director Konstantin Stanislavski, the technique utilizes one's personal senses, memories, and experiences to better interpret a character. Examples are as varied as the roles being attempted. For instance, an actor hoping to exhibit grief might conjure up painful memories of personal loss and fold the physical aspects of human grief into his performance. Another looking to convey wonderment might recall an especially joyous occasion. Method techniques find actors signing on for boxing lessons before portraying fighters, conjuring a bad mood to help approximate sullen characters, and slipping into meditative states to express a character's sense of calm. While certain acting techniques can be clearly described and practiced, the Method cannot. It is as personal as each actor and role undertaken and, consequently, can be quite hard to teach.

Forming a Following

Since followers of method acting draw off tangible memories and practiced events to get inside their characters, you could say that the acting appears to be non-acting. The illusion is that actors actually become their characters. Method acting became prominent in film during the early 1950s with the emergence of the legendary Actors Studio—a Manhattan-based school founded by Elia Kazan, Cheryl Crawford, and Robert Lewis and operated under the tutelage of famed acting teacher Lee Strasberg from 1951 to 1982. Since the studio opened its doors in 1947, Hollywood heavyweights such as Al Pacino, Marlon Brando, Marilyn Monroe, James Dean, Robert De Niro, Paul Newman, and Joanne Woodward have gotten in touch with their inner voices, thus adding their names to the burgeoning ranks of method-trained stars. The Actors Studio became famous for developing the Method, but it's not the only training ground for this style of acting. Other proponents of this approach include Stella Adler and Richard Boleslavski, and still others offer a modified version of method techniques. This form of training has become so widespread that many of today's top actors, including Sean Penn and Johnny Depp, list method training on their résumés. For those actors captivated by the technique, there seems to be no other way to approach the art. Nevertheless, there are some actors not quite so swayed by the Method's charms.

Make Like a Tree . . . and *Leave!*

While filming *The Sheltering Sky* (1990), Academy Award nominee John Malkovich practiced a decidedly non-method acting approach. In between takes, Malkovich caught up on his needlepoint—a far cry from the search for "motivation" thought mandatory by method actors. When the cameras started to roll,

Malkovich suddenly transformed. His masterful performance went on to win him much critical acclaim.

Sir Laurence Olivier, considered by some to be the finest actor in the world, came straight to the point in regards to the Method: "All this talk about the Method. The Method! What method?" he demanded. "I thought each of us had our own method!" In keeping with his convictions, Olivier reportedly teased method actor Dustin Hoffman while the pair was filming *Marathon Man* in 1976. When a bedraggled, motivation-searching Hoffman arrived on the set without sleeping for two days (to prepare for a scene in which his character was physically tortured), Olivier was ready for him. "Why don't you just act?!" the veteran performer chided.

Steven Spielberg

One of the most commercially and critically successful directors in film history, Steven Spielberg has changed the way we see movies. Blending chills and thrills with moral messages and unforgettable stories, Spielberg films boldly announce themselves. Read on for more about this influential director's life and times and the films that helped shape cinema in the second half of the twentieth century.

✳ ✳ ✳ ✳

Spielberg Start-Up

AS A KID growing up in Cincinnati, Ohio, little Steven Spielberg (born in 1946) knew he wanted to work in the movies. He made his earliest films with his dad's 8mm camera and won his first filmmaking prize at age 13. By that time, Steven and his family had moved to Phoenix. Around age 17, Spielberg raised $500 to write and direct his first "feature" film, called *Firelight*. The picture, which was shown in his local movie theater, made a $100 profit and later inspired *Close Encounters of the Third Kind* (1977).

After high school, Spielberg applied to the University of Southern California to study in an acclaimed film program. He was turned down not one but three times. After a brief stint at California State University at Long Beach, Spielberg dropped out and moved to Hollywood.

Still in his early twenties, Spielberg found a chance to direct a few movies on his own, including the short film *Amblin'* (1968), which hinted at some of the interests that the director would later revisit: aliens, the desert, and the classic hero quest story line. *Amblin'* got the attention of a Universal bigwig, and Spielberg became the youngest director ever to sign a major long-term contract with a Hollywood studio.

His time with Universal and other studios throughout the late 1960s and early 1970s often resulted in television work. In 1970, Spielberg landed his first project as a director with part of the pilot for *Night Gallery*, which starred veteran movie star Joan Crawford. The high point of his television work was a 1971 made-for-TV movie titled *Duel*, about a mysterious trucker who pursues and terrorizes an average guy, played by Dennis Weaver. The theme was one Spielberg would return to again and again—an ordinary man caught up in extraordinary circumstances. It wasn't until 1974, however, that Spielberg's star truly began to rise. He directed Goldie Hawn in *The Sugarland Express*, a movie based on a true story about a husband and wife who take back their son and go on the run from the law. It was this film that made people in Hollywood sit up and take note; but it was the young director's next film that really grabbed the whole world's attention.

The B.D.O.C. (Biggest Director On Campus)

In 1975, movie audiences were introduced to a very big, very angry shark. In what would become what many consider the world's first blockbuster, *Jaws* terrorized filmgoers around the globe and became the first film in the United States to earn more than $100 million in first-run box-office receipts. This was largely due to the decision to give *Jaws* a wide release. Before this, movies were released slowly, a few cities at a time; *Jaws* opened in more than 400 theaters on the same day. All in all, Spielberg's hit grossed close to $490 million worldwide, was nominated for numerous Academy Awards (including Best Picture), won several of the coveted statuettes, and forever changed the way movies are marketed and distributed. It also put director Steven Spielberg on the map for good.

The auteur's next project was *Close Encounters of the Third Kind* (1977), a film that allowed him to explore one of his favorite subjects: alien visitors on Earth. The movie was a critical and commercial success and earned Spielberg his first Best Director nomination. Over the next few years, Spielberg experienced a few missteps: *1941* (1979), a World War II farce, was a big-time flop, but everyone would forgive him when he teamed up with George Lucas to bring a character named Indiana Jones to life on the big screen.

Raiders of the Lost Ark was unleashed in 1981 and, to this day, is considered by many to be *the* quintessential action-adventure film. Starring the handsome Harrison Ford as archeologist/adventurer Indiana Jones, *Raiders* paid homage to the cliff-hanger serials of a bygone Hollywood era. Audiences loved the film almost as much as Spielberg's next project: *E.T.: The Extra-Terrestrial* (1982).

The story of a young boy and his alien friend, *E.T.* stunned audiences around the world. The movie excited the imagination, offered humor and heart-wrenching drama, and, true to most Spielberg flicks, contained lots of really cool special effects. Nominated for buckets of awards, the film garnered critical praise from nearly all camps and surpassed *Star Wars* (1977) as the highest-grossing movie of all time—a record that would stand for nearly 15 years. If there was any doubt that Steven Spielberg was the most gifted director of the last half of the twentieth century, *E.T.* took care of that.

The next years for Spielberg were almost too dizzyingly successful to comprehend. A second *Indiana Jones* picture, *Indiana
Jones and the Temple of Doom*, was released in 1984, before
Spielberg moved on to producing mega-popular '80s movie
classics *Gremlins* (1984) and *The Goonies* (1985). Spielberg
gave audiences *The Color Purple* (1985), starring Oprah
Winfrey and Whoopi Goldberg, and *Empire of the Sun* (1987),
both successful book adaptations that were largely critically
acclaimed. In 1988, he produced the colossal hit *Who Framed
Roger Rabbit*, which earned more than $329.8 million at box
offices worldwide. In 1989, Spielberg nearly topped himself
when he directed and produced *Indiana Jones and the Last
Crusade* and served as executive producer on *Back to the Future
Part II*, both of which were blockbuster hits.

Spielberg in the 1990s: Does This Guy Ever Sleep?

Much of the early 1990s found this prolific director working in
television animation. He did a lot of producing in the animation genre (*Tiny Toons Adventures, Animaniacs, Pinky and the
Brain*, etc.), but in 1993, he returned to live-action filmmaking
with one of his most financially successful pictures ever: dino-
saur thriller *Jurassic Park*. That same year, Spielberg showed
his somber, serious side with *Schindler's List*, a lengthy, black-
and-white film based on a true story about the Holocaust.
Schindler's List won the director his first Best Picture and Best
Director awards. In 1994, Spielberg signed on to produce the
hugely popular television series *ER* and, along with David
Geffen and Jeffrey Katzenberg, founded DreamWorks, a production company responsible for more box-office wins than
we've got room to list.

Saving Private Ryan (1998), Spielberg's return to gripping,
historical drama, was an epic World War II search-and-rescue
story that earned him his second Best Director Oscar.

Looking to the Future

The first decade of the new millennium saw Spielberg bounce from movies based on true stories to sci-fi and other works of fiction. *Artificial Intelligence: AI* (2001), the story of a child-like android, whose programming allows him to feel love, came as a result of Spielberg's friendship with legendary filmmaker Stanley Kubrick, who had been developing the story since the early 1970s. Kubrick shared his ideas for the movie with Spielberg, and after Kubrick's death, Spielberg took on the project. Reviews were somewhat mixed, but no one could deny the director's unique vision.

Also in 2001, Spielberg revisited the topic of World War II, this time as an executive producer for the hugely successful television miniseries *Band of Brothers*. Spielberg has focused mostly on producing during the latter part of the decade, but he still directed some memorable films, including *Catch Me If You Can* (2002), *War of the Worlds* (2005), and *Munich* (2005), which was nominated for five Oscars for its depiction of the true story of 11 Israeli athletes who were murdered by a Palestinian terrorist group during the 1972 Olympics.

In 2008, Spielberg released the much anticipated fourth installment in the *Indiana Jones* series: *Indiana Jones and the Kingdom of the Crystal Skull*. It received generally favorable reviews, was nominated for several awards, and took in more than $700 million worldwide at the box office.

Steven Spielberg is not without his detractors. But it cannot be denied that the director's impact on the business of filmmaking is indelible or that millions have been moved, scared silly, or delighted by his work. Where Spielberg will go next with his career in film is anyone's guess. Though he and his partners sold DreamWorks in late 2005, we can bet that he'll revisit favorite themes. And the passion with which he approaches every project will likely keep us buying tickets to his movies for quite some time.

The Amazing Ackermonster

"If Forrest J Ackerman had not existed, it would have been necessary to invent him." —Anthony Boucher

✳   ✳   ✳   ✳

OR FORREST J Ackerman, life has been simply monstrous... and that's a good thing. Ackerman has spent his entire life passionately pursuing and promoting horror films. Not the modern ones, where buckets of blood substitute for terror, but the classics like *Frankenstein* and *Dracula*, where every creaky stair sends a chill down the spine.

Early Acker

Born in 1916, Ackerman saw his first fantasy film, *One Glorious Day*, at the tender age of five. He was immediately hooked. In 1926, Ackerman attained his first fantasy magazine (*Amazing Stories*) and became involved in the genre for the rest of his life, serving as literary agent for some of the greatest writers in the fantasy genre. He even coined the genre-forming term, "sci-fi," in 1954.

Monstrous Fame

But it was as the irreverent editor of the magazine *Famous Monsters of Filmland* that Ackerman (dubbed "Ackermonster") was to shine. It was first published in 1958, just as the classic horror films were beginning to reach television. The magazine influenced a generation of future filmmakers, including Steven Spielberg, who devoured Ackerman's slightly off-kilter accounts of the actors, films, and makeup secrets of popular horror films.

While in his 90s, Ackerman continued to give tours of his home in Los Angeles, dubbed "Son of Ackermansion" (he moved from the original 18-room Ackermansion in 2002), showing off his museum-worthy collection of movie monster memorabilia and sharing stories about the spooky side of the silver screen.

Alas, the Ackermonster passed on in December 2008. From those who share an appreciation for things that go bump in the black-and-white night, only one thing can be said for Ackerman: "Fangs for the memories, Forrest."

Hooray for Hollywood!

What is now the Hollywood Walk of Fame was conceived in 1958 as a permanent tribute to Hollywood's most celebrated personalities. A groundbreaking ceremony was held on February 9, 1960, and stars for the first 1,558 individuals were unveiled 16 months later. Administered by the Hollywood Chamber of Commerce, the Hollywood Walk of Fame was designated a cultural/historic landmark by the City of Los Angeles in 1978.

✳   ✳   ✳   ✳

A Star Is Born

THE WALK OF Fame is comprised of five acres of bronze stars, each embedded in pink terrazzo and surrounded by charcoal terrazzo squares. The recipient's name is engraved on his or her star, along with an emblem identifying the category for which he or she has been honored: motion pictures, television, radio, recording, or live theater.

The Hollywood Walk of Fame can be found on both sides of Hollywood Boulevard, from Gower to LaBrea, and on both sides of Vine Street, from Yucca Street to Sunset Boulevard.

When You Wish Upon a Star...

Receiving a star on the Hollywood Walk of Fame isn't as simple as just requesting one. There are strict criteria:

✳ Professional achievement

✳ Longevity of five years in the field of entertainment

✳ Contributions to the community

✳ An agreement to attend the dedication ceremony

Nominations, which are accepted by the Hollywood Chamber of Commerce during a specific 60-day nomination period, must be approved by the Walk of Fame Committee. Often, several annual nominations are required before a star is approved.

Walk of Fame Who's Who

Singing cowboy Gene Autry is the only personality to have a star dedicated to him in all five categories.

Singer John Denver was awarded a star in 1982. However, it had not been officially dedicated at the time of his death in 1997 because Denver had yet to schedule the required personal appearance.

Fictional personalities who have received a star on the Walk of Fame include Big Bird, Mickey Mouse, Bugs Bunny, the Simpsons, and Donald Duck.

The crew of Apollo 11, the first crewed mission to the moon, are honored with individual stars, all located at the intersection of Hollywood and Vine.

Ronald Reagan is one of only two California governors to be honored with a star on the Walk of Fame. The other is Arnold Schwarzenegger. Reagan is also the only U.S. president to be so honored.

Not all stars are located on a sidewalk. Boxing legend Muhammad Ali's star can be found mounted on a wall at the Kodak Theater because he insisted that he not be walked upon.

In 2004, Mary-Kate and Ashley Olsen, then 18, became the youngest recipients in any category to receive a star on the Walk of Fame.

Hollywood isn't the only city with a Walk of Fame; Palm Springs, California, boasts a "Walk of Stars" along Palm Canyon Drive. Approximately 300 movie stars and other notables are honored there, including Frank Sinatra, Elvis Presley, Marilyn Monroe, and Bob Hope.

Stop, Thief!

Over the years, four stars have been stolen from the Hollywood Walk of Fame. The stars of James Stewart and Kirk Douglas were swiped by an unscrupulous contractor after they had been removed during a construction project. One of Gene Autry's five stars was also absconded with during a construction project; it later turned up in Iowa. And in November 2005, thieves sawed Gregory Peck's star right out of the sidewalk. It was replaced in September 2006.

"Is Hollywood the cruelest city in the world? Well, it can be. New York can be that, too. You can be a Broadway star here one night, and something happens, and out—nobody knows you on the street. They forget you ever lived. It happens in Hollywood, too."

—BUSTER KEATON

Scorsese and De Niro

Hollywood has many tales of great actor-director pairs producing important films. But the collaborations between Martin Scorsese and Robert De Niro are truly unique, resulting in a remarkable collection of some of the greatest films and most unforgettable (and unpleasant) characters in Hollywood history.

✳ ✳ ✳ ✳

The Ultimate Antiheroes

ROBERT DE NIRO and Martin Scorsese both grew up as products of the tough streets of New York City in the 1940s and 1950s. When they were introduced by director Brian De Palma at a party in the early 1970s, they found they had much in common. Scorsese decided to cast De Niro in his next film *Mean Streets* (1973), which perfectly captured the gritty life of small-time criminals in New York City and launched both men on the path to superstardom. The two would go on to achieve remarkable accomplishments separately, and Scorsese would even pair up on multiple films with other actors, such as Harvey Keitel, Daniel Day-Lewis, and Leonardo

DiCaprio. But there is no question that some of Scorsese's finest work has come in the movies he's done with De Niro.

Scorsese and De Niro's second collaboration, *Taxi Driver* (1976), offered a chilling glimpse into the world of a disturbed New York City cabbie, who feels isolated and disgusted by the uncaring nature of his urban environment, so he commits a horrific act of violence. Scorsese's deft direction and De Niro's phenomenal portrayal combined to create one of the most complex and haunting protagonists ever to appear on film.

Raging Bull (1980), the biopic of New York boxer Jake La Motta, was a risky undertaking—shot in black and white and featuring a main character who was persistently repugnant. It performed poorly at the box office, but it earned De Niro an Academy Award and is now widely considered one of the greatest American films of all time. It also served to solidify the pair's place among the greatest actor-director combinations in film history.

The dark satire *The King of Comedy* (1982) also fared poorly on the financial front and was largely glossed over by critics. This peculiar character study focuses on Rupert Pupkin, a socially awkward misfit who clings pitifully to the dream of becoming a stand-up comedian and eventually resorts to kidnapping in pursuit of his shot at the big time. Pupkin engenders little sympathy for much of the film, until the final scene in which the audience finally hears his self-revealing comedy routine.

The Characters

By the mid-1980s, a consistent pattern had been established for Scorsese–De Niro protagonists. The featured characters were, to put it mildly, difficult to like or identify with. In fact, many bordered on being repulsive. A great many other films, of course, focus on dark, complex characters or flawed antiheroes who reflect the shortcomings of the societies in which they live. But *Taxi Driver*'s Travis Bickle, *The King of Comedy*'s Rupert Pupkin, *Cape Fear*'s Max Cady, and the gangsters in *GoodFellas*

(1990) and *Casino* (1995) represent some of the darkest and most wrenching explorations of the human psyche ever offered in the guise of popular entertainment.

Scorsese consistently explores the nature of the Hollywood hero, who often uses violence to resolve conflict. Because we identify with traditional heroes, we accept the violence when an attractive, morally upright protagonist uses it, even if he commits an illegal act. However, when Scorsese's protagonists commit similar acts of violence, we are repulsed by them. In this subtle way, the director forces us to think about our acceptance of violence through identification with movie heroes.

Scorsese and De Niro Filmography

Mean Streets (1973)

Taxi Driver (1976)

New York, New York (1977)

Raging Bull (1980)

The King of Comedy (1982)

GoodFellas (1990)

Cape Fear (1991)

Casino (1995)

Behind the Scenes of
Back to the Future

The *Back to the Future* films are cinematic classics, but the time-traveling trilogy had to overcome countless challenges in its quest to capture audiences worldwide.

❋   ❋   ❋   ❋

The Beginning

If Robert Zemeckis really could go back in time, he'd probably avoid a lot of the headaches that came with creating the *Back to the Future* films. The movies that brought us Doc Brown and Marty McFly faced more than their share of issues—and the problems started before the first part had even been cast.

Zemeckis and cowriter and producer Bob Gale struggled to get the idea for *Back to the Future* off the ground. The two were turned down by every studio they approached and for nearly every reason imaginable. For example, Disney thought the plot and its Freudian undertones were too risqué. Other studios said the family-friendly jokes weren't risqué enough.

Zemeckis has said that the commercial failure of his 1980 film *Used Cars* made selling the *Back to the Future* script even more difficult. It wasn't until 1984, with the success of his film *Romancing the Stone*, that studios were willing to revisit the concept and take a gamble on his proposal.

The Leading Man

Once Back to the Future finally got the green light from Steven Spielberg's Amblin Entertainment, Zemeckis and Gale discovered that they couldn't get the leading man they wanted. Michael J. Fox was their ideal guy for Marty McFly, but his work with the TV series *Family Ties* conflicted with the movie's production schedule, so they cast Eric Stoltz in the role instead.

Within weeks, though, it became clear that something wasn't

right. Even though they'd shot numerous scenes with Stoltz, Zemeckis and Gale convinced the studio to let them recast the part. With some careful negotiations, they were able to secure Fox for the role and resume filming.

Fox may have been perfect for Marty, but he brought with him his own set of challenges. Because Fox was still starring on *Family Ties*, Zemeckis and his crew had to work around his hectic schedule and film most of his scenes overnight. At times, production workers went to great lengths to accomplish this, dividing scenes into a number of shots and then filming Fox's shots separately and lighting locations to create the illusion of daylight while shooting at night.

The Title

Even with all of the pieces in place, Zemeckis and Gale found themselves fighting to keep their film's title. The head of Universal Studios told the two that no one would want to see a movie with the word future in the title and suggested that they call it *Spaceman from Pluto* instead. The ill-fated inspiration came from the scene in which Marty poses as an alien to convince his teenage father to ask Marty's future mother to the dance.

Executive producer Steven Spielberg solved the title trouble by sending a memo back to the Universal exec in which he thanked him for the "joke" and acted as if everyone thought the idea was a hoax. The exec, seemingly wanting to save face, never brought it up again.

Back to the Future's mix of adolescent humor and nostalgia for the 1950s was a surefire formula for a hit, and the film became the highest-grossing film of the year, raking in $208 million. But the success was bittersweet for Fox: He went from television actor to movie star, but, unfortunately, he was typecast in high-concept comedies as the young man on the cusp of manhood, as in *The Secret of My Success* (1987). When Fox tried to transition to dramas, his association with adolescent comedies combined with his short stature and youthful face doomed him to failure in more serious fare.

The Sequel

Contrary to popular belief, Zemeckis and Gale never intended for *Back to the Future* to be a series—they barely thought the first movie would get made! And even though the first film ends with Marty and Jennifer going to the future with Doc to see about their children, it was only meant for laughs, not to set the stage for a sequel.

In fact, the two say they wrote themselves into a corner by having Jennifer get into the car with Doc and Marty. Having her knocked out within the first moments of *Back to the Future Part II* was the only way they could come up with that made her presence work and still allowed for the story they wanted to tell.

The Missing Actor

Crispin Glover, who portrayed George McFly in the original Back to the Future film, created plenty of challenges for the creative team. Now widely known for his oft-eccentric behavior, Glover wanted to portray George in some unusual ways. In the DVD commentary, Zemeckis and Gale said they had to bend over backwards to get him to wear some of the wardrobe they'd selected for the character and to follow the direction they'd laid out for the part.

The biggest hurdle of all, though, came with the start of the second installment. According to Zemeckis and Gale, Glover made unreasonable demands when negotiating his return to the role. When he wouldn't budge, the filmmakers had no choice but to move forward on the film without him.

With the absence of such a recognizable character, the pair had to take steps to ensure that the movie still made sense. That's why George was dead for part of the movie and was wearing a futuristic upside-down back brace in the segments when he did appear. Zemeckis and Gale figured audiences would be less likely to notice the change in actors with the added distraction.

The second film did, however, use some archived footage of Glover in scenes meant to depict the past. Glover ended up suing Spielberg and received a settlement for the unauthorized use of his likeness.

The success of Part II led to *Back to the Future Part III*, in which Doc and Marty wind up in the Wild West. In the end, of course, the numerous challenges didn't keep the *Back to the Future* trilogy from soaring to success. Overall, Marty McFly's catchphrase may be the best way to sum up the adventure: "Whoa...that was heavy."

Woody Allen: The Gifted Neurotic

In 1951, a skinny Jewish kid from Brooklyn began a career in entertainment that would eventually make him one of Hollywood's biggest stars. His contributions as an actor, producer, and director have made Allen Stewart Konigsberg a household name—although you probably know him better as Woody Allen.

✳   ✳   ✳   ✳

Write On, Kid

As a teenager, Allen began selling jokes to newspaper columnists and stand-up comics who liked his clever, "woe-is-me" style. When Allen left home, he enrolled at NYU to study film but eventually dropped out of the program. There didn't seem to be much point in spending all his time studying when he was able to make good money writing bits for humorist Herb Shriner and, before long, comedy sketches for *The Ed Sullivan Show*, *The Tonight Show*, and the short-lived but critically acclaimed *Caesar's Hour*.

By the time he reached his twenties, Allen was also writing stage plays, some of which later became films. He also began crafting material for himself, and in the early 1960s, he became a stand-up comedian, presenting himself as a neurotic, self-obsessed therapy junkie with a voracious sexual appetite—a character that wasn't much different from Allen himself. It worked, and he landed gigs on television and in prominent nightclubs and, by 1969, he'd been featured on the cover of *Life* magazine.

Roll Camera

It seemed a natural progression for Allen to work in film, so he tried his hand as a screenwriter and actor. But his first screen-writing job, *What's New Pussycat?* (1965), left a bad taste in his mouth; between directorial cuts, the diva-like demands of actor Warren Beatty (who eventually quit the film because of "artistic differences"), and fights with meddling producers, moviemak-ing didn't seem like anything Allen wanted to be a part of—unless he could be in charge.

Once the rookie filmmaker got a hold of the reins, however, Hollywood was his oyster. The first project that gave him complete artistic control was a critical success: American International Pictures purchased the rights to a low-budget Japanese spy film and asked Allen to write the dialogue for the English dub. *What's Up, Tiger Lily?* (1966) was a spy spoof laden with one-liners and self-conscious parody. A string of successful, uniquely Woody Allen pictures began in 1969 with *Take the Money and Run* and continued throughout the early 1970s with hits such as *Bananas* (1971), *Everything You Always Wanted to Know About Sex* (*But Were Afraid to Ask)* (1972), and *Sleeper* (1973).

Allen had made a name for himself, but his tour de force came in 1977 with *Annie Hall*, which won the Oscar for Best Picture. The movie, Allen's deliberate twist on the romantic comedy genre, chronicles the rise and fall of the sweet, funny, and poignant relationship between Alvie (played by Allen) and Annie (Diane Keaton). Keaton won a Best Actress Oscar for the role.

Prolific, Terrific (and Not-So-Terrific)

After the riotous success of *Annie Hall*, Allen produced the Ingmar Bergman-inspired drama *Interiors* (1978) and then *Manhattan* (1979), another picture starring himself and Diane Keaton, as well as a young Mariel Hemingway. The film, Allen's so-called "love letter to New York," was well received. Woody Allen was officially a sophisticated, significant auteur, clearly influenced by Bergman and Federico Fellini. That's what the critics said, anyway—most people just went to his films to be entertained.

And they were entertained throughout the 1980s, though the stories Allen told increasingly combined both comic and tragic themes, as in *Stardust Memories (1980), Broadway Danny Rose (1984), Hannah and Her Sisters (1986), Crimes and Misdemeanors (1989),* and *The Purple Rose of Cairo* (1985), the last of which stars Allen's then-partner actress Mia Farrow and is considered one of his best films. Allen's work grew increasingly autobiographical, and he became more interested in parodying and deconstructing film conventions and genres.

The 1990s brought more success for Allen, including hits such as *Shadows and Fog* (1991), *Husbands and Wives* (1992), *Bullets Over Broadway* (1994), and *Mighty Aphrodite* (1995). The Academy was generous with Oscar nominations (and a few wins) for Allen and the actresses who appeared in his films, and Woody continued to have his pick of Hollywood's finest actors for his projects. Part of his appeal to actors is his reputation, and part of it is his low-key directorial style that allows actors to discover their characters and interpret them.

The Soon-Yi Thing

Since 1980, Allen had been in a serious relationship with actress Mia Farrow, who starred in many of his films. The two never married, but they adopted two children together and had a son of their own. Farrow also brought several children to the relationship, including some from her previous marriage to

Andre Previn, though Allen never formally adopted them. In 1992, when Farrow found nude photographs of her 21-year-old adopted daughter, Soon-Yi Previn, in Allen's possession, she separated from him at once. Allen and Soon-Yi revealed that they were in a relationship (despite a 35-year age difference). They were married in 1997 and have two children together.

Woody Returns

At the turn of the twenty-first century, the director's popularity—and, some would say, his comic style and attention to detail—waned. Was it because of the Soon-Yi scandal? Perhaps. Films such as *The Curse of the Jade Scorpion* (2001), *Hollywood Ending* (2002), and *Melinda and Melinda* (2004) were critical and commercial disappointments.

Then, in 2005, Allen directed *Match Point*, a drama that adapted the moral themes of Dostoevsky to a modern setting. *Match Point* was a success at the box office and with critics, too. The film grossed $23 million in its initial release—more than any Allen film of the previous 20 years—and earned even more abroad. Allen's next success came in 2008 with *Vicky Cristina Barcelona*, a sensual comedy starring Scarlett Johansson (a recent favorite of Allen's) and Penelope Cruz, who won an Oscar for Best Supporting Actress.

Now in his 70s, Woody Allen doesn't seem to be slowing down. His talent for wearing numerous hats within the motion picture industry has left an indelible mark on the art form.

The Film School Generation

The 1960s was a tumultuous time for the American film industry, as the old Hollywood studios lost their ironclad grip over it. At the same time, a new generation of edgy, provocative filmmakers moved in and shook things up, bringing an artistic vision that produced some of America's most remarkable films. These trendsetters were known as the Film School Generation.

* * * *

URING THE 1930S and 1940s, the Hollywood film industry operated under what would become known as the
studio system. A handful of studios dominated the industry,
holding stars under long-term contracts and employing armies
of writers, costumers, camera operators, and other professionals to crank out films using a factory-like system as their model.
Producers had creative control of films, overseeing every decision from casting to script approval to set design. And although
the system produced some of the most memorable movies
the world has ever seen, it began to crumble in the 1950s.
Competition from television hurt the studios, as did court rul-
ings that weakened the studios' grip over the marketplace and
gave a boost to the growing ranks of independent filmmakers.
Censorship standards were also loosening, so that the generally wholesome fare that had been Hollywood's standard began
to seem unsophisticated. By the 1960s, the studio system was
essentially gone, and Hollywood turned to a new breed of filmmaker. The Film School Generation had arrived.

The New Filmmakers

Actors such as Jack Nicholson, Dustin Hoffman, Warren
Beatty, and Faye Dunaway and directors such as Woody Allen,
Roman Polanski, Martin Scorsese, Mike Nichols, and William
Friedkin brought a unique frankness and realism to film. They
arrived at a time when new technologies allowed for more
location shooting and freer movement of the camera, and they
used this to give their work a distinctly new look. As a group,
they shared two things that Golden Age filmmakers lacked—a
counterculture sensibility and a formal university education
in film. The former trait led them to create films that tackled
sensitive social issues head-on, while criticizing the institutions
and values that old-school Hollywood films often reinforced.
Their study of film history in an academic setting gave them an
abiding respect for and deep knowledge of the techniques and
accomplishments of the great filmmakers that preceded them.

In fact, one of the hallmarks of the Film School Generation is that they frequently include tributes to earlier films in their work—they might duplicate the imagery, props, or camera angles of a specific shot or use the name of a character from an old film.

The 1960s saw the Film School Generation create seminal films such as *Bonnie and Clyde* (1967), *The Graduate* (1967), *Midnight Cowboy* (1969), and *Easy Rider* (1969), which offered gritty anti-heroes and frank treatments of sex and violence. In the 1970s, Francis Ford Coppola became one of the group's most accomplished directors with his masterworks *The Godfather* (1972) and *Apocalypse Now* (1979). Similarly, Robert De Niro became a leading actor of his time through his frequent collaborations with Martin Scorsese in films such as *Taxi Driver* (1976) and *Raging Bull* (1980).

Reining Them In

The successes of these filmmakers allowed them to command more creative control over their films than directors from previous generations were typically allowed. Studios may have been uneasy with the new direction in which they were being taken, but there was no denying that the work was artful, and more importantly, it made money. Any lingering questions about that were laid to rest when Steven Spielberg virtually invented the blockbuster with his 1975 film *Jaws*.

Some directors took their pursuit of artistry a bit too far, however, letting schedules and budgets spiral out of control in the name of achieving their vision. After a number of high-profile financial failures, most notably Michael Cimino's *Heaven's Gate* (1980), studios began requiring more accountability and control over their projects and the era of the Film School Generation essentially came to an end. While many of these filmmakers remain active today, they no longer enjoy the autonomy they had at the peak of their power.

Alfred Hitchcock

Born in London in 1899, Alfred Joseph Hitchcock became the most recognizable director in Hollywood history, not only for his commanding presence but also in regard to his cinematic style. Known as "The Master of Suspense," he made, on average, about one movie per year in a career that spanned more than 50 years. His influence in the world of cinema is unparalleled. Here's a little more about everyone's favorite Hitch.

✳ ✳ ✳ ✳

Hitch: The Younger Years

HITCHCOCK'S FILMS WERE largely suspense-filled, psychological thrillers with gallows humor that attracted audiences with their subject matter and dark visual imagery. He had a gift for transforming familiar characters and ordinary-looking locations into frightening stories about the moral failings that lurk in all of us and the evil hidden in the everyday world.

The son of a greengrocer in a working-class London neighborhood, Alfred was the only child of strict parents. When Hitch left school, he pursued a career as a draftsman, but became increasingly interested in movies. In 1920, with some experience as a designer under his belt, he got a job doing title cards (the intertitles that contain the dialogue and text between the scenes of a silent film) for a Hollywood studio called Famous Players–Lasky, which had an office in London. It was the beginning of his illustrious film career.

Stepping Up

Hitch put in time doing art direction work and quickly climbed his way up the ranks at the studio, becoming an assistant director in 1922. After some uncredited work, he got his first directorial assignment with *The Pleasure Garden* (1925). Sadly, none of the initial projects embarked upon by the fledgling director took off. It wasn't until 1927 that he had a hit—*The Lodger: A Story of the London Fog* was a commercial success and put

Hitch on the map. Two years later, he directed Britain's first "talkie," a thriller called *Blackmail*. The story of a woman who suffers pangs of guilt for killing a would-be rapist, *Blackmail* foreshadowed Hitchcock's mature style.

In 1934, Hitchcock garnered international attention with *The Man Who Knew Too Much*, followed by *The 39 Steps* the next year. His approach to the thriller was established by this time, and he became adept at using a plot device he liked to call the MacGuffin—the thing in the story that the characters are concerned with (important papers, secret microfilm, uranium) but the audience doesn't really care about because they are wrapped up in the suspense and the motivations of the characters.

By the end of the 1930s, the rotund English director had made quite the name for himself as a significant auteur. It was time to take on Hollywood.

Hollywood Loves Hitchcock

In 1939, mega-producer David O. Selznick offered Hitchcock a deal. Selznick had just made cinematic history producing the record-breaking, Oscar-winning epic *Gone with the Wind*. It gave the producer even more power, so when he offered Hitch a seven-year contract, it was clear that Selznick would have a significant amount of control over the director's work, which was par for the course in Hollywood at the time. It was not an arrangement that sat well with Hitch, but he agreed to the terms; he finally had Hollywood money with which to make his movies.

The first picture of the partnership was *Rebecca* (1940), a Gothic melodrama that starred Sir Laurence Olivier and Joan Fontaine. The movie was a critical and commercial hit, and when Oscar time rolled around, *Rebecca* won Best Picture. Hitch didn't win for Best Director, but it secured his reputation in Hollywood.

Hitch's Heyday

Throughout the 1940s, Hitchcock worked tirelessly, making movies that used familiar filmmaking techniques and typical conventions. Yet with his exquisite craftsmanship, the films were like works of art. He also toyed with audience expectations in regard to the casting, using leading man Cary Grant in a sinister role in *Suspicion* (1941), for example. Classic Hitch titles such as *Lifeboat* (1944) and—the director's personal favorite—*Shadow of a Doubt* (1943) were made during this time, complete with his expressive use of light and shadows, carefully worked-out compositions, and oblique angles.

But if Hitch had a golden age, it was the 1950s. The list of films he made reads like a "best of" list: *Dial M for Murder* (1954), *Rear Window* (1954), *To Catch a Thief* (1955), a remake of *The Man Who Knew Too Much* (1956), and *Vertigo* (1958). Hitch worked multiple times with Jimmy Stewart and Cary Grant as well as leading lady Grace Kelly. His favorite female archetype was the cool, sophisticated blonde, whom he often used as the lead character and even the protagonist. These films featured his key themes: the presence of evil in the everyday world, the deceptive nature of appearances, and the idea that we are all guilty of something. Hitchcock's most famous plotline—the story of the falsely accused man—was epitomized by the film that topped the decade, *North by Northwest* (1959).

By the 1950s, color film was the norm. Hitchcock used it to his advantage when it suited him, but he still had a fondness for the expressive nature of black and white, which was evidenced by one of his major masterpieces: *Psycho* (1960).

Later Years

Considered his most famous films, *Psycho* and *The Birds* (1963) mixed suspense with anxiety-inducing soundtracks by legendary composer Bernard Herrmann. *The Birds* chronicles an infestation of avian creatures that are terrorizing a California town, while *Psycho* offers a warning about the darkness that exists in all of us through the character of Norman Bates. As Norman says, "We all go a little mad sometimes ... haven't you?"

Hitch made two more significant works, *Marnie* (1964) and *Frenzy* (1972), but when his health started to decline, his output began to suffer. In 1976, the undisputed "Master of Suspense" made his last film, *Family Plot*, before dying of kidney failure in 1980.

Down for the Count: The Sad Life of Bela Lugosi

The man who once thrilled millions of moviegoers with his sexual magnetism, catlike movements, and creepy portrayals died a wizened, nearly penniless, recovering drug addict.

✳ ✳ ✳ ✳

Hungarian Heartthrob

BELA LUGOSI WAS born Bela Ferenc Dezso Blasko on October 20, 1882, near the western border of Transylvania, then a part of Hungary. The youngest of four children, he was raised in the town of Lugos, the name he would eventually adopt. Never fond of school, Lugosi left home in 1894 to pursue his dream of acting. By 1907, he was a leading figure on the Hungarian stage, going on to become a featured performer with the National Theatre in 1913. Although National Theater actors were exempt from military service, Lugosi enlisted in the army at the start of World War I. He returned to find his country politically unstable. Targeted for his activism, he fled Budapest in 1919, barely escaping with his life.

In 1921, Lugosi came to the United States. Six years later, he was awarded the lead role in the New York stage version of *Dracula*. The play was a smash, running for 500 performances. Yet Lugosi only received the role in Universal Studios'

1931 film version of *Dracula* because of the untimely death of silent-movie superstar Lon Chaney. Lugosi signed on for a meager $500 a week; in fact, he only made $3,500 from *Dracula*, one of the most successful pictures in movie history. Lugosi infused the otherwise turgid movie with energy, and in the process he created one of history's most iconic screen characters. Yet the moment of his greatest artistic triumph was also the beginning of his downward spiral.

Always the Monster, Never the Evil Genius

Universal planned for Lugosi to succeed Chaney as their next "Man of a Thousand Faces." However, creative differences scuttled his participation as the monster in the follow-up film *Frankenstein*. Lugosi's lost opportunity opened the door for the man who would eclipse him as a horror star: Boris Karloff.

Although Lugosi hoped to capitalize on his *Dracula* fame with good roles, he discovered that he was now irrevocably typecast as a horror actor. He spent much of the remainder of the 1930s starring in forgettable potboilers such as *Island of Lost Souls*.

Occasionally he was given decent material; he worked to rise above the travails of typecasting, such as in *Son of Frankenstein*, in which he played the grizzled Ygor. However, as the 1940s progressed, Lugosi's films were increasingly low budget. Even when he got a decent part, something bad always seemed to happen. In 1943, Lugosi finally had the opportunity to play the monster in *Frankenstein Meets the Wolf Man*. But Universal executives panicked at the idea of the monster with a Hungarian accent. They cut all of Lugosi's dialogue, as well as the much-needed explanation that the character was blind. On-screen, Lugosi's shuffling, lurching performance made no sense, and the film was resolutely panned.

Ed Wood and Addiction

In 1948, his film career virtually over, Lugosi played Dracula for only the second time on-screen in the daffy *Abbott and Costello Meet Frankenstein*. By then he had become increasingly dependent on morphine—an addiction that had begun when he first received the drug to relieve back pain. As work grew scarce and finances tight, his drug use increased.

In the early 1950s Lugosi's desperate need for paying work led him to work with eccentric film producer Ed Wood, who had a reputation for creating extremely low-budget schlock (see: rubber octopuses and bouncing tombstones). Finally, in 1955, a gaunt, shrunken Lugosi voluntarily committed himself to a hospital because of his drug use. Three months later he emerged and returned to Wood for work.

Lugosi died on August 16, 1956, while working on Wood's *Plan 9 From Outer Space*—popularly considered the worst movie ever. The man who played the most iconic vampire was buried in one of his Dracula capes.

The Rise and Fall of Fatty Arbuckle

As the saying goes, "The bigger they are, the harder they fall." And when it comes to early Hollywood scandals, no star was bigger or fell harder than Roscoe "Fatty" Arbuckle.

✳ ✳ ✳ ✳

THE SCURRILOUS AFFAIR that engulfed Roscoe "Fatty" Arbuckle (1887–1933) in 1921 remains one of the biggest Hollywood scandals of all time because of its repercussions on the film industry. (It was instrumental in the creation of organized film censorship in Hollywood.) The Fatty Arbuckle scandal rocked the world when it broke, and though few people today know the details, in 2007, *Time* magazine ranked it fourth on its list of the Top 25 crimes of the past 100 years.

As one of Hollywood's first headline-grabbing scandals, it contained all the elements that make a scandal juicy—drunkenness, debauchery, and death. But what made the tawdry tale big was Arbuckle, who himself was big in size (nearly 300 pounds), big in popularity, and, as Tinseltown's highest paid comedian, one of the biggest stars in the Hollywood galaxy at the time.

The Rise

Arbuckle began his career as a child, performing in minstrel shows and sing-alongs. The young entertainer already carried a noticeable girth, but his remarkable singing voice, acrobatic agility, and knack for comedy made him a rising star on the vaudeville circuit.

In 1913, Arbuckle got his big break in film when Mack Sennett hired him on at Keystone Film Company. Arbuckle initially rollicked as one of Sennett's Keystone Cops, but he was soon developing his unique comic persona as the lovable fat man and honing his own slapstick specialties based on the seeming contradiction between his size and graceful agility. By 1914, Arbuckle was teamed with comedienne Mabel Normand for the extremely successful "Fatty and Mabel" shorts, in which the pair offered humorous interpretations of romantic rituals. Arbuckle's charming persona ensured that he always got the girl. He became so adept at working out the duo's physical gags for the camera that he soon took over direction of the films.

In 1917, Arbuckle formed Comique Film Corporation with Hollywood mogul Joseph Schenck, who offered Arbuckle creative control and an astounding paycheck. At Comique, Arbuckle launched the screen career of the great Buster Keaton, who played the rotund actor's sidekick in classic silent comedies such as *Coney Island* (1917), *Good Night, Nurse!* (1918), and *The Garage* (1920).

In 1919, Arbuckle reached unprecedented heights when Paramount Pictures handed him a monstrous three-year $3 million contract to make several feature-length films. But Hollywood's first million-dollar man would have to work like a dog to meet production schedules. So on Labor Day weekend in 1921, a worn out Arbuckle headed to San Francisco for some rest and relaxation.

The Scandal

For the large-living, heavy-drinking Arbuckle, R & R meant a weekend-long bash at the St. Francis Hotel. On September 5, several people joined Arbuckle for a party, including a 26-year-old actress named Virginia Rappe and her friend Maude Delmont. Much has been exaggerated about the sexual exploits of Rappe, but her bad reputation was largely the product of the sensationalized press of the day. However, Delmont was a convicted extortionist known for her penchant for blackmail.

Around 3:00 A.M., Arbuckle left the party for his suite. Shortly thereafter, screams emanated from his room. According to press accounts of the day, several guests rushed in to find Rappe's clothing torn. She hysterically shouted at Arbuckle to stay away from her, supposedly uttering, "Roscoe did this to me." Though very dramatic, Rappe's accusation was most likely untrue and was probably invented to sell newspapers.

The story goes that the shaken Rappe was placed in a cold bath to calm her down and was later put to bed when a doctor diagnosed her as intoxicated. The next day, the hotel doctor gave her morphine and catheterized her when Delmont mentioned that Rappe hadn't urinated in some time.

Delmont later called a doctor friend to examine Rappe, saying that Arbuckle had raped her. He found no evidence of rape but treated Rappe to help her urinate. Four days later Delmont took Rappe to the hospital, where she died of peritonitis caused by a ruptured bladder. Delmont called the police, and on September 11, Arbuckle was arrested for murder.

The Fall

Arbuckle told police—and would contend all along—that he entered his room and found Rappe lying on the bathroom floor. He said he picked her up, placed her on the bed, and rubbed ice on her stomach when she complained of abdominal pain.

Delmont told police that Arbuckle used the ice as a sexual stimulant, and years later, rumors circulated that Arbuckle had raped Rappe with a soda or champagne bottle. Yet, there was no mention of this in the press during the arrest and trial. Instead, police alleged that Arbuckle's immense weight caused Rappe's bladder to rupture as he raped her. But contemporary research speculates that Rappe was probably struck hard in the abdomen, not raped. Whatever the cause, the public—enraged by the extremely sensationalized reports in the newspapers— wanted Arbuckle hanged.

Over the next seven months, Arbuckle was tried three times for the death of Virginia Rappe. The first two ended with hung juries. In the final trial, the jury deliberated for six minutes before declaring Arbuckle not guilty and offering a written apology for the injustice placed upon him.

Arbuckle was exonerated, but the damage was done. In April 1922, the Hays Office, the motion picture industry's censorship organization, which was established in the wake of the scandal, banned Arbuckle's movies and barred him from filmmaking. Although the blacklisting was lifted in December 1922, it would be several years before Arbuckle resumed his Hollywood career. A few years after his acquittal, Arbuckle began directing under the name William Goodrich, and in the early 1930s, RKO hired him to direct a series of comic shorts. In 1933, Vitaphone—part of Warner Bros.— hired Arbuckle to appear in front of the camera again in a series of six sync-sound shorts shot in Brooklyn.

But his revitalized career was short-lived. On June 29, 1933, one day after finishing the sixth film and signing a long-term contract with Warner Bros., Arbuckle died of a heart attack at age 46. Nearly eight decades later, Arbuckle is sadly remembered more for a crime that he *didn't* commit than as the comedic genius he was.

How Does It Really End?

Think you know everything about your favorite films? Think again. Movie studios often preview new movies with test audiences who can help producers and directors predict whether or not they've got a hit on their hands. After getting feedback, changes to the film are made—anything from small tweaks to total overhauls. Read on for some cases of big changes that were made at the eleventh hour. Consider this your official spoiler alert.

✳ ✳ ✳ ✳

Little Shop of Horrors

THE BROADWAY VERSION of this story goes something like this: Boy meets girl, boy and girl fall in love, boy and girl get eaten by carnivorous plant. Audiences were traumatized by Frank Oz's movie version of *Little Shop*, so the boy and girl live happily ever after on the big screen.

Fatal Attraction

Crazy Alex Forrest, the jilted lover brilliantly played by Glenn Close, was originally supposed to commit suicide and frame Michael Douglas's character for it. Test audiences didn't want the nasty lady to get off so easy, though; instead, Close's character was shot by Douglas's wife.

E.T.: The Extra-Terrestrial

In the original script, the lovable alien E.T. dies. This didn't sit well with children, so director Steven Spielberg gave in and allowed the little guy to make it home.

I Am Legend

This film adaptation, starring Will Smith in Richard Matheson's classic horror novella, is all about role reversals. Well, that and vampires. In the book, the mean, nasty vampires are actually revealed to be compassionate creatures only out to protect their own. It becomes clear that Smith's character is their enemy, just as much as they seem to be his. Well, this cautionary tale didn't fly with test audiences, so the main theme of Matheson's book was scrapped. Instead, Smith's character in the movie just blows everybody up.

The Wizard of Oz

The first audiences for this ultra-classic film thought Dorothy's classic "Over the Rainbow" number slowed down the story. It was kept in at the last minute.

Blade Runner

Ridley Scott, the Oscar-winning director who adapted Philip K. Dick's sci-fi classic to film, loved the dark tone of the story. The studio, however, didn't love it as much. In the original version of the film, the intense protagonist (played by heart-throb Harrison Ford) decides to harbor the renegade android he loves, even though she's doomed to short-circuit any second. Throughout the film, there are also allusions to the notion that Ford's character himself might be an android. The studio thought all this was a little too bleak, though, and decided to let the man and his android live happily ever after.

Pretty Woman

In the original version, Vivian, the prostitute with a heart of gold and legs for miles (played by Julia Roberts), rejects Richard Gere's character and goes on to seek her fortune. Test audiences cried foul, and the film ends with the couple together.

Butch Cassidy and the Sundance Kid

At the end of this timeless Western, Butch and Sundance are surrounded by what seems to be the entire Bolivian army. The film ends before the final gunfight, a clever way to leave it up to the audience to decide if the duo dies or manages to survive. The original version of the film showed their death, but test audiences preferred the alternate—more ambiguous (and less bloody)—ending.

Things You Don't Know (and Didn't Need to Know) About ... *The Simpsons*

The world's favorite yellow cartoon family, The Simpsons *made their television debut as an animated short on The Tracey Ullman Show on April 19, 1987. The dysfunctional quintet appeared in 48 episodes over three seasons before finally getting their own series. The first episode of* The Simpsons, *a Christmas episode titled "Simpsons Roasting on an Open Fire," aired on December 17, 1989.*

⁂ ⁂ ⁂ ⁂

Who Voices Whom?
Dan Castellaneta: Homer Simpson

Julie Kavner: Marge Simpson

Nancy Cartwright: Bart Simpson

Yeardley Smith: Lisa Simpson

A Man of Many Hats
Homer Simpson has held numerous jobs over the course of the series. They include: astronaut, boxer, butler, carny, conceptual artist, door-to-door sugar salesman, film producer, food critic, garbage commissioner, Kwik-E-Mart employee, missionary, monorail conductor, nuclear safety inspector, telemarketer, used car salesman, and village oaf.

Not Everyone Loves *The Simpsons*
Over the years, the writers of *The Simpsons* have managed to anger or offend a wide range of individuals, groups, cities, and nations. Among those most ticked off:

1. In 1990, as *The Simpsons* was becoming a national phenomenon, a principal in Ohio banned students from wearing *Simpsons* T-shirts declaring "Underachiever."

2. Riotur, the official tourism bureau of Rio de Janeiro, which threatened a civil lawsuit following an episode in which the Simpsons visit Brazil and find it rife with crime, slums, and child-consuming animals.

3. New Orleans, which took umbrage at an all-musical adaptation of *A Streetcar Named Desire* that portrayed the city as the "home of pirates, drunks, and whores." The following week, Bart made amends by writing on the blackboard: "I will not defame New Orleans."

4. Several Jewish groups, which protested the episode "Like Father, Like Clown," a parody of *The Jazz Singer* in which it was revealed that Krusty the Clown is Jewish and estranged from his rabbi dad, voiced by Jackie Mason.

5. The families of individuals with Tourette's Syndrome, who flooded the network with complaints following a 1992 episode in which Bart claims to have the condition in order to get out of taking a test. The reference was changed to rabies in reruns.

Movie Magic

Although any other mega-hit television series would have capitalized on its popularity with a hastily thrown-together motion picture, it took the creators of *The Simpsons* 18 years to come out with a Simpsons movie. Simply titled *The Simpsons Movie* (2007), it grossed more than $183 million in the United States alone.

Fun Facts

✳ In every script, Homer's trademark exclamation—D'oh!—is referred to only as "annoyed grunt."

✳ Nancy Cartwright, the voice of Bart Simpson, joined the Church of Scientology after reading the works of L. Ron Hubbard.

✳ Bart Simpson is left-handed.

✳ Matt Groening, the creator of *The Simpsons*, named the family after his own, except for Bart, which is an anagram for "brat."

The Simpsons by the Numbers

* **58:** the number of Emmy Award nominations the series has received

* **24:** the number of Emmy Awards the series has won

* **1:** the number of awards the show has received from the Gay & Lesbian Alliance Against Defamation (GLAAD), for the episode "Homer's Phobia"

* **21:** the number of series staff members who are Harvard University alums

* **8th:** where *The Simpsons* ranked in *TV Guide's* list of the 50 Greatest TV Shows of All Time

* **24th:** where the "Krusty Gets Kancelled" episode of *The Simpsons* ranked in *TV Guide's* list of the 100 Greatest Episodes of All Time

* **2:** the number of celebrities who have voiced a character on *The Simpsons* incognito: Michael Jackson (as John Jay Smith) and Dustin Hoffman (as Sam Etic)

Inside Pixar: The Makings of Modern Animation

Pixar has become a driving force in modern computer-based animation, creating hits such as Toy Story (1995), A Bug's Life (1998), and Finding Nemo (2003). The company that started as a small brainstorm by George Lucas has exploded into a blockbuster-producing giant. But it was hardly an overnight occurrence.

* * * *

Technical Beginnings

THESE DAYS, IT's hard not to know the name Pixar. The animation giant has enjoyed phenomenal success with films ranging from *Cars* (2006) to *WALL-E* (2008) and beyond. Long before the talking vehicles and rolling robots, however,

Pixar was just an idea in the mind of the guy behind *Star Wars* (1977). And it took some support from the guy behind Apple to really get things moving.

The first signs of Pixar popped up back in 1979, when George Lucas decided to start a computer-based graphics group to work within his existing Lucasfilm production house. He called it simply the Graphics Group. That same year, he met and hired computer scientist Ed Catmull, and the two hit it off. Both believed that, in the future, animation and special effects would be primarily computer generated. In 1986, Apple founder Steve Jobs paid $10 million to buy the division and spin it into its own company, which he called Pixar. Catmull came along with the deal, and animator John Lasseter was on board as creative leader.

Stepping into Animation

The Pixar team initially created and sold computer software and hardware, including the expensive Pixar Image Computer, which generated three-dimensional images. Animation was only a small part of the group's early work, and it was done primarily for showing off what the hardware and software could do. In fact, at this early juncture in Pixar's history, John Lasseter was the fledgling company's only animator.

The first film that Pixar released was a cartoon short called *Luxo Jr.* (1986). It was exhibited at a computer graphics conference, and it featured the hopping desk lamp that is still used in the Pixar logo today. *Luxo Jr.* was nominated for an Oscar, but it didn't win.

Fast-forward a couple of years, and Pixar's luck began to change dramatically. The next short that the company released, *Tin Toy* (1988), won an Oscar for Best Animated Short Film—and went on to provide the inspiration for the studio's first feature film.

The Leap to Feature Films

The move from *Tin Toy* to *Toy Story* wasn't instantaneous. Pixar spent several years using its animation techniques to create TV commercials for companies such as LifeSavers and Listerine. By the early 1990s, animation systems built by Pixar were being used to create intricate scenes within Disney hits such as *Beauty and the Beast* (1991), *Aladdin* (1992), and *The Lion King* (1994). Those successes led Pixar to the idea of producing its own feature film.

By 1995, *Toy Story* was ready to hit the big screen. The film took more than 100 computers to create, with some frames requiring as much as 13 hours to render. It took more than 400 computer models to make the film, with the help of 27 animators. It was a long way from *Luxo Jr.* As the world's first fully computer-generated feature film, *Toy Story* was the number-one film at the box office in 1995, and John Lasseter earned a special Academy Award for leading the Pixar creative team on the project.

The Story After *Toy Story*

Following the success of *Toy Story*, Pixar produced a number of other popular animated movies, including *Toy Story 2* (1999), *Monsters, Inc.* (2001), *Finding Nemo* (2003), *The Incredibles* (2004), *Cars* (2006), *Ratatouille* (2007), *WALL-E* (2008), and *Up* (2009).

✳ In 2006, the Walt Disney Company acquired Pixar for $7.4 billion, and the company is now officially a part of the Disney family.

✳ Since *A Bug's Life*, Pixar has created an animated short to go along with each of its feature films in the spirit of the Golden Age, when most features were accompanied by a short film or cartoon.

Chapter 11

The Arena of Sports

America's Game: 32 Teams, 1 Trophy

A fierce rivalry spawned the American sports world's biggest game.

✳   ✳   ✳   ✳

TODAY, SUPER BOWL Sunday is practically a national holiday. Fans and nonfans alike gather for huge meals and expensive commercial breaks. The championship game, which began in 1967, helped boost the popularity of American football.

Throughout its history, the National Football League (NFL) faced rival competing leagues. Each time, the NFL would emerge the victor. But that all changed with the creation of the American Football League (AFL). The upstart AFL successfully wooed players from the NFL and helped lay the foundation for modern American football.

The AFL got its start when the NFL rebuffed Lamar Hunt, the son of an oilman, in his bid for an expansion team. In response, Hunt went on to found the AFL and the Dallas Texans in 1960. The league consisted of eight teams and was bankrolled by other would-be owners who had been unable to procure expansion franchises in the NFL.

While the NFL tacitly enforced unwritten quotas for African American players, the AFL actively recruited them. The younger league also competed for top college talent, nabbing Heisman-winner Billy Cannon in 1959 and Joe Namath in 1964. In 1966, new AFL commissioner Al Davis actively wooed players from the NFL. This practice promoted bidding wars for players between teams in the two leagues.

Hunt and Dallas Cowboys President Texas "Tex" Schramm Jr. met privately to discuss the possibility of merging the two leagues. On January 15, 1967, the champion team of each league met in the AFL–NFL Championship Game to determine an all-around winner. Suggesting some consistency with the college "bowl" games (e.g., the Rose Bowl, the Orange Bowl) used to crown regional champions, Hunt recommended "Super Bowl," a reference to the Super Ball toy his kids enjoyed. The name stuck but was not officially used until Super Bowl III in 1969. (The 1967 and '68 championship games are only called Super Bowl I and II retroactively; at the time, they were called the AFL–NFL Championship Games). The Super Bowl trophy was named the Vince Lombardi Trophy following the legendary coach's death in 1970.

Gridiron Grammar

Football has always had a language all its own, and it has adopted many terms and truisms from commonplace sources outside of sports.

✳   ✳   ✳   ✳

Considering that the quarterback is often referred to as the "general" and his players are known as "troops," it's not surprising that many football terms, such as "blitz," "bomb," "trenches," and "gunners," have been borrowed from the military. In football, the blitz, like its wartime connotation, is a bombardment, but not from the air. It is an all-out frontal attack bolstered by 300-pound behemoths intent on planting the quarterback face-first into the turf. The football bomb is an aerial assault, but instead of an explosive-laden shell, this weapon is a perfectly delivered spiral carried triumphantly into the opposition's end zone. The trenches, much like their World War I counterparts, are pungent places, replete with sweat, spit, mud, and blood. Football's trenches are found along the line of scrimmage, where hand-to-hand combat determines who wins the day. Like their combative comrades, gridiron gunners are responsible for neutralizing the enemy and thwarting its attack. On the battle lines that are drawn between the boundaries, these gunners set their sights on the kickoff and punt-return specialists.

Whence Came the Knuckleball?

It's as hard to nail down the knuckler's origins as it is to pitch, catch, or hit a good one. Legend hands the credit to a guy named Toad, but does that hold up?

* * * *

THE FIRST KNUCKLEBALL pitcher was probably some unknown, creative sandlot kid in the 1800s who abandoned baseball in his teens. But alas, today we can only search for someone who gained notoriety from the pitch. Baseball lore indicates that Thomas H. "Toad" Ramsey, a pitcher hopping around the old American Association in the 1880s, threw the first knuckler.

The story goes that Toad was doing off-season masonry when he severed a tendon in his pitching index finger. (Until the 1970s, most ballplayers held off-season jobs.) Owing to this, Toad couldn't grip a baseball in the normal fashion. The basic fastball grip, for instance, requires two fingers to extend and grip the ball on top, with two other fingers curled into the palm. With a maimed index finger, Toad couldn't grip the ball quite right, so he curled the index finger down on the ball, leaving three fingers curled behind the ball and only one extended. Toad's pitch acted like a natural sinker, which makes sense if it was his index finger that was injured—Hall of Famer Mordecai "Three- Finger" Brown's missing index finger gave him a natural sinker. In 1886, Toad struck out 499 men pitching 589 innings for Louisville. That's impressive. Modern workhorses don't pitch half as many innings. As for strikeouts, since 1887 no one has fanned 400, let alone nearly 500.

Given that no two knuckleballers grip a baseball quite alike anyway, Toad's reputed grip could possibly have produced a knuckler. But there's reason to doubt that. The knuckleball isn't a cheap sinker; it's an anywhere pitch. The idea is to throw the ball slowly with very little spin at all, so that air resistance on the seams makes the ball dance. Neither pitcher, catcher, nor hitter knows for sure where it's going, making the pitch tough to hit. Thrown naturally, a fastball's fierce backspin enables it to fly straight. To throw a knuckleball, one must defeat that backspin, so the pitcher curls the fingers behind a seam and flicks them forward when throwing. Having fewer functional fingers is no asset here—just ask Hall of Fame hurler Phil Niekro, a knuckleball specialist who had perfect use of all five digits.

If done perfectly, the forward flick cancels the backspin. Accounts of Toad's pitch do not describe a maddeningly slow floater that bobbed toward the plate. They describe a sinker, or perhaps a knuckle curve—a topspin pitch.

If Toad wasn't throwing a real knuck, who did it first? Some credit Lew Moren, who may have developed it as a comeback pitch in 1906–07 with the Philadelphia Phillies. Others credit Eddie Cicotte, who has quite a history. He was almost certainly the first pitcher to throw a true knuckler for sustained success. Given his 208 lifetime wins and his career 2.38 ERA, you'd expect to see him in the Hall of Fame. You never will. Cicotte was one of the infamous eight members of the 1919 Chicago White Sox who conspired to throw the World Series to the Cincinnati Reds at the instigation of mobster Arnold Rothstein. When the news broke, the "Black Sox" received lifetime bans from baseball.

League of Dreams

Little League baseball has produced a parade of stars, but it's the everyday heroes that make it a success.

* * * *

OR NOLAN RYAN, Little League was the first stop on his way to the Hall of Fame and an important one on the journey through fatherhood. The latter, its founders might say, is precisely what Little League baseball was engineered to be.

Youth baseball leagues were formed in the United States as early as the 1880s. In 1938, Carl E. Stotz started a league for children in Williamsport, Pennsylvania, and devised rules and field dimensions for what would become, officially, Little League baseball. The next year, the first three teams— Lycoming Dairy, Lundy Lumber, and Jumbo Pretzel—took the field, with the parents who organized them forming the first Little League board of directors.

By 1946, there were 12 similar leagues, all in Pennsylvania. Three years later, there were more than 300 such leagues throughout the United States, and in 1951 Little League took hold in Canada. The league has now spread worldwide. Little League baseball is the world's largest organized youth sports program, with nearly 200,000 teams in more than 80 countries. Williamsport, though, has remained central. The Little League World Series (LLWS)—a truly international event—is played there each year, and it hit the national television airwaves in 1963.

Of these hundreds of thousands of teams, only 16 compete for the title of Little League World Series champion. To make it to the finals in Williamsport, teams of 11- and 12-year-olds must advance through the International Tournament—a process that requires more games worldwide than six full major-league seasons!

Eight teams from the United States battle for the U.S. championship as eight teams from other countries fight for the international crown in a ten-day tournament that culminates with the top international team and the winning U.S. squad battling for the LLWS title. Fans from all over the world pack hotels throughout central Pennsylvania each summer for the event. In 2004, the 32-game World Series drew 349,379 fans.

The format of the event has been tweaked through the years. As the young players have gotten better, the dimensions of the park have grown. From 1947 through 1958, the final was played at Original Field, where the outfield fences were all less than 200 feet from home plate. Beginning in 1996, a 205-foot blast was required to clear the fences in all fields. As of 2006, those fences stood at 225 feet.

Through all its growth, some things have remained pleasantly constant. For example, the World Series champions get invited to the White House. And Little League's founding goal remains this: to teach children the fundamental principles of sportsmanship, fair play, and teamwork, just as Stotz envisioned more than 70 years ago.

That those principles can help talented young players advance their baseball careers is a bonus Stotz may or may not have foreseen. Nolan Ryan's first organized sports experience was in Little League. "The first field in Alvin [Texas] was cleared and built by my dad and the other fathers of the kids in the program. I played Little League from the time I was nine years old until I was 13. Some of my fondest memories of baseball come from those years."

Little League remains a big deal in towns all over America. Ryan knows. Not only did he pitch a Little League no-hitter long before he threw seven of them in the majors, but he also helped coach his own sons' Little League teams. Less famous mothers and fathers do the same for their less famous sons and daughters on diamonds around the world.

Ryan, of course, graduated from Little League ball to the Hall of Fame, as did George Brett, Steve Carlton, Rollie Fingers, Catfish Hunter, Jim Palmer, Mike Schmidt, Tom Seaver, Don Sutton, Carl Yastrzemski, and Robin Yount. None of those greats ever played in the famed Little League World Series, but all were boosted by their organized baseball experience as youngsters, as were countless other major-league stars.

Only a small fraction of Little League players go on to the ranks of professional baseball, of course. But where would one be without dreams? And Little League baseball is about so much more than reaching the majors.

A Unique Set of College Mascots

Aggies (Texas A&M, New Mexico State, Utah State, and others): It's worth remembering that many land-grant schools initially taught mainly agriculture, so their students—and sometimes their teams—were called Farmers. "Aggies" grew as slang for this, and many of these schools now embrace the name proudly.

Banana Slugs (UC Santa Cruz): If a slug suggests a lethargic or reluctant team, that's just what students had in mind when they chose the image. The bright yellow banana slug lives amid the redwoods on campus and represents a mild protest of the highly competitive nature of most college sports.

Boll Weevils/Cotton Blossoms (University of Arkansas–Monticello, men/women): When cotton ruled Dixie, the boll weevil was more fearsome than any snake. Evidently, the women's teams didn't care to be named after an invasive insect, and who can blame them?

Cardinal (Stanford): It's the color, not the bird. That sounds odd until you consider the Harvard Crimson, Dartmouth Big Green, Syracuse Orange, and so forth. The university's overall symbol, however, is a redwood tree. A person actually dresses up as a redwood mascot, but the effect is more like a wilting Christmas tree than a regal conifer.

Crimson Tide (University of Alabama): The school's teams have always worn crimson, but the term "Crimson Tide" seems to have been popularized by sportswriters waxing poetic about epic struggles in mud and rain.

Eutectics (St. Louis College of Pharmacy, Missouri): *Eutectic* refers to the chemical process in which two solids become a liquid, representing the school's integration of competitive athletics and rigorous academic programs. ESPN recognized the Eutectic—a furry creature dressed in a lab coat—as one of the most esoteric mascots in the country.

Ichabods (Washburn University, Kansas, men): The university was established as Lincoln College, but it ran out of money. When philanthropist Ichabod Washburn bailed out Lincoln, the school renamed itself after Washburn.

Great War Withers Great Game

World War I moves manpower from diamond to trenches, and ballplayers are forced to struggle with their place in a war-torn society.

✳ ✳ ✳ ✳

DURING THE FOUR years World War I raged in Europe, the great American game endured several blows in the national consciousness, as people questioned baseball's role in the midst of global conflict. Was it important to keep baseball going as a way to boost civic morale? Or was this a questionable way for healthy young men to be occupied in a time of war?

Filling the Seats

The Federal League had started in 1914, just before the war began, but it disbanded after only two seasons. Some of those players later joined the American and National Leagues, but many wound up back in the minors or faded from the game along with the memory of the last upstart major league. Competition for the leisure dollar and public interest—thanks to the growing taste for boxing, horse racing, college football, and picture shows—was greater than it had ever been. Attendance for the AL and NL actually hit a five-year high in 1916—6.5 million total for the 16 teams—but that came after two years of depressed numbers because of the Federal League. In 1917, though, attendance dropped significantly, to 5.2 million paying customers. It fell 2.1 million more the following year.

Service and Sacrifice

The United States joined the war effort in 1917, and while American soldiers massed in Europe, baseball players fought the image that they were slackers unwilling to do their duty. The schedule was reduced from 154 to 140 games in 1918 (and again in 1919), and players performed pregame military drills to display their patriotism. But the military wasn't impressed. The May 1918 edict of "work or fight" required all men to be involved in "essential" war industry work by July 1 or risk induction. Baseball got an exemption through Labor Day, leading to the only September World Series in history. In all, nearly 250 major-leaguers joined a war industry or the service in 1918.

Future Hall of Famers Grover Cleveland Alexander and Christy Mathewson were wounded during the war. Alexander recovered, but thereafter suffered from seizures; Mathewson's exposure to poison gas led to his death in 1925. Three former players were killed. The best-known was Harvard grad and Giants third baseman Eddie Grant, a captain who was killed trying to reach the famous "Lost Battalion" in the Argonne Forest on October 5, 1918, five weeks before the end of the war. A plaque was placed in his honor at the Polo Grounds.

Raising the Country's Morale

The war also brought about a notable performance of "The Star-Spangled Banner." Although the song had been played a few times at ball games, it received popular approval during the seventh-inning stretch of Game 1 of the 1918 World Series. Its reception led to the song being played during each game of the Series by the Cubs and Red Sox, though it did not be come a regular pregame event until 1942, during America's next great war. In the intervening years, baseball would secure a higher spot in the national perception and be seen as vital to the country's morale.

Steve Dalkowski: The Best That Never Was

The most incredible pitcher no one's ever heard of.

✳   ✳   ✳   ✳

STATISTICS DON'T ALWAYS tell the whole story about a baseball player, but in the case of Steve Dalkowski—widely acknowledged as the fastest, wildest pitcher in history—they do a pretty good job.

Take 1960, for instance, when the left-hander was with the Stockton Ports, Class C affiliate of the Baltimore Orioles. In just 170 innings, he struck out 262 batters, walked another 262, and hit countless backsides and backstops throughout the California League. Or how about the 1957 game when he had 24 strikeouts and 18 walks? He had 39 wild pitches in 62 innings that year.

The picture is clear, even if the numbers are almost unfathomable. Dalkowski is the most incredible pitcher few people have ever heard of, simply because he never made the major leagues. His lifetime stats of 995 innings, 1,396 strikeouts, 1,354 walks, and a 46–80 record from 1957 to 1965 were compiled predominantly in the low minors, as the Orioles kept hoping he would harness his incredible gift.

Just 5'11" and about 170 pounds, with thick glasses and an easygoing manner, the New Britain, Connecticut, native couldn't fully explain how he threw a fastball an estimated 105–110 miles per hour—5 to 10 mph faster than anybody else. Dalkowski was never accurately timed in the pre–radar gun era; once, throwing at a makeshift device with a laser beam, he took about 40 minutes to hit the beam and clocked in at an exhausted 93.5.

Steve admitted his fondness for booze didn't help him any. He also suffered from over-tinkering, and with this in mind, minor-league manager Earl Weaver used a patient, simpler approach with Dalkowski during the 1962 season at Class A Elmira. Weaver sent him to major-league spring training in 1963, and "White Lightning" was dominating big-league batters when he felt a pop in his elbow during an exhibition game. The Orioles uniform he had been fitted for that same day would not be needed—then, or ever.

Bill Veeck: The Grand Hustler

One man seemed to have the magic touch when it came to boosting attendance, and doing it fast. That man was Bill Veeck, and he kept fans in stitches with gimmicks and goofiness for years.

✳ ✳ ✳ ✳

B ILL VEECK WAS literally born into baseball. His father was president of the Chicago Cubs. The junior Veeck grew up in the ballpark, working as everything from a soda-pop vendor and ticket taker to groundskeeper (he claimed to have planted the ivy on the outfield walls of Wrigley Field) before moving up to club treasurer while he took night courses in business, accounting, and engineering.

A Man of the People

In 1941, Veeck bought the American Association Milwaukee Brewers. He was just 27 years old, but he was already exploding with ideas. He never announced his promotions ahead of time, so folks would show up at the park with no idea what to expect. What they received were giveaways such as live lobsters, buckets of nails, or hosiery. They also got fireworks, live bands, and ballet. Anything could happen, and the fans loved it.

Veeck was unlike any other owner. While the other big-league moguls still wore steamed shirts and stickpins, Veeck never—ever—wore a tie. He much preferred the company of the bleacher fans to that of millionaires and movie stars. He spent his time during the games out in the stands, chatting with the fans, joining them for a beer, talking baseball. He asked the fans what they wanted, and he listened to their answers.

Taking Chances

As owner of the Cleveland Indians, Veeck had his greatest success. He integrated the American League by signing Larry Doby in 1947. (Veeck allegedly received 20,000 pieces of hate mail about the signing and replied to each one by hand.) When he persuaded living legend Satchel Paige to join his team in 1948, many called it a ridiculous publicity stunt. But it turned out to be anything but when Paige (at age 42, the oldest rookie in major-league history), went 6–1 in 72.2 innings, recorded an ERA of 2.48, and threw three complete games and two shutouts in his seven starts. The Indians won the pennant and the World Series in 1948, and fans came out in record numbers.

Make 'em Laugh

Veeck bought the St. Louis Browns in 1951, and that year he engineered a stunt designed to send the fans home chuckling and the baseball powers huffing and puffing in dismay. The fans were there to help celebrate the 50th anniversary of the American League; everyone received a slice of birthday cake as they entered the gate. Between games of the doubleheader, a fake birthday cake was rolled onto the field, and out of it jumped 3'7" Eddie Gaedel, wearing a Browns uniform with number $\frac{1}{8}$ on the back. His job was to crouch down and ensure he'd get a walk. He did, and the fans went crazy.

The Fans Have Their Say

Another memorable Veeck promotion was "Grandstand Managers' Day" on August 24, 1951, in which more than 1,000 St. Louis Browns fans decided on the game strategy while manager Zack Taylor sat alongside the dugout, propped up his feet, and drank an orange soda while he counted the fans' votes. The fans were given signs that said "YES" or "NO." Before the game, they held up these cards to select the Browns' starting lineup. During the game, they used these cards to vote on such questions as "Infield In?" or "Bunt?" The lineup choice was probably the fans' best decision. They replaced the regular starting catcher and first baseman with bench-sitters Sherm Lollar and Hank "Bow Wow" Arft. Each wound up with two RBI; Lollar had a homer and a double. The Browns, who had lost four of their previous five games, snapped the streak with a 5–3 crowd-managed win. Then they lost their next five.

In 1959, Veeck bought the Chicago White Sox and continued his fun-filled promotions. He created the exploding scoreboard that set off fireworks when a Sox player homered. And it was Veeck's idea to have Harry Caray lead the crowd in singing "Take Me Out to the Ball Game" during the seventh-inning stretch, a tradition that moved with Harry from Comiskey Park to Wrigley Field in 1982.

Versatile Veeck

Any attempt to categorize Bill Veeck will inevitably result in slamming into a few walls of contradictions. Was he simply a ruthless (self) promoter who delighted in blowing the buttons off stuffed shirts? Was he truly the fans' owner, the man who cared for them more than anything? Was he merely a hustler, a Barnum, primarily a con man?

From 1947 through 1964, the New York Yankees were toppled from their habitual perch atop the American League just three times—twice by a team Veeck owned (1948 Indians, 1959 White Sox) and once by a team he had built (1954 Indians). If Veeck didn't always know how to make money running a team, he knew how to make money selling it. Every deal he made showed substantial profits. His teams set attendance records in Cleveland and Chicago, and he quintupled attendance in St. Louis.

Even when Bill Veeck made a mistake, he turned it into good publicity (or at least a good laugh). But perhaps the trait that most clearly defined the huge and paradoxical style of Bill Veeck was his sheer lust for life. Despite living in severe pain (he was said to have had 36 different operations), he never let it hold him back. After he died, one of his obituaries noted that if a life is measured not by how long it is, but by how full it is, "the old rapscallion [Veeck] must have turned over the odometer a few times."

Bad Breaks and Bum Luck

A great deal of luck is needed to sustain a productive major-league career. Sometimes that luck eludes a young superstar.

✳   ✳   ✳   ✳

ONE OF THE heartbreaking elements of sport is that a player on his way to greatness can be derailed by something entirely out of his control. Three promising baseball stars who debuted between 1970 through 1980 were struck down by illness or injury, leaving their sad and disappointed fans to wonder what might have been.

J. R. Richard

At 6'8", J. R. Richard possessed the size of an NBA star. He chose baseball instead—a good choice, given that he possessed a right arm that could unleash fastballs at nearly 100 miles per hour and sliders almost as fast. In his major-league debut for the Houston Astros, on September 5, 1971, Richard dominated the potent attack of the San Francisco Giants, striking out 15 batters.

Despite his record-tying debut, Richard's success was not a given. He struggled with his control, three times leading the National League in walks. He also suffered from a lack of stamina, the result of throwing too hard too early in each game. By 1978, Richard had addressed some of those weaknesses: He still walked too many batters, but he led the league in strikeouts, becoming the first right-hander in NL history to reach 300 Ks in a single season. The following year, Richard led all NL starters with a tidy 2.71 ERA. Richard's high-powered pitching not only intimidated opposing hitters; it also frightened his own teammates. "I've never taken batting practice against him," Astros first baseman Bob Watson told *The Sporting News*, "and I never would. I have a family to think about." Richard continued his march toward stardom in 1980. While winning ten of his first 14 decisions, he posted an ERA of 1.90. It seemed as though Richard's career was on a Hall of Fame track. But in early July, Richard started complaining of a tired arm and said he wasn't feeling well. Some critics charged Richard with being lazy and unprofessional. Some fans and teammates even thought he had underlying motives for not wanting to play. But on July 30, Richard felt so nauseated during a light workout with former teammate Wilbur Howard that he had to lay down on the field. Within moments, he was rushed to the hospital.

Doctors had previously determined that Richard had developed a blood clot in his pitching shoulder that was blocking the flow of blood in a vessel near his ribs. When another clot formed in Richard's right carotid artery, a major stroke ensued. The stroke completely paralyzed the left side of his body.

Richard did his best to recuperate. He ran four miles a day and regained some of the zip on his fastball. In 1982, he attempted a comeback in the minor leagues, but he was hit hard and struggled badly with his control. Richard would never make it back to the major leagues.

Mark "The Bird" Fidrych

While Richard struck an intimidating pose, Mark "The Bird" Fidrych looked more like a character from *Sesame Street*. As a rookie with the Detroit Tigers in 1976, Fidrych brought a whole new attitude to the lagging team. When one of his infielders made a great defensive play, Fidrych openly applauded. After recording the third out of each inning, The Bird didn't walk off the mound—he *ran*, usually in full sprint. He liked to "landscape" the mound with his cleats. And then there was his most distinctive habit: Fidrych actually talked to the baseball. By doing so, he felt he could make his pitches move in the ways that he wanted. Although not quite sure what to make of his antics at first, observers and players soon realized that Fidrych was a genuinely joyful (and talented) person, and his goofy style of play won The Bird a large flock of fans.

Showing excellent control of his above-average fastball, the 22-year-old Fidrych won 19 games in 1976 and sported the American League's best ERA (2.34). After Fidrych's amazingly successful debut season (for which he earned the AL's Rookie of the Year Award), the Tigers eagerly awaited his encore. But during a spring training game in 1977, Fidrych hurt his knee chasing a pop-up. He also tore his rotator cuff, but the injury went undiagnosed until 1985. He tried to keep playing, but he never regained the brilliance he displayed in his debut year.

Joe Charboneau

Big, bad Joe Charboneau was just as colorful as Fidrych but without the down-home innocence. His ride to the majors was rocky. After being signed by the Philadelphia Phillies in 1976, Charboneau quit playing ball in his second minor-league season because of a dispute with management. He took up slow-pitch softball for a while before returning to the Phillies. He hit well in the California League, but his habit of barroom brawling led the Phillies to trade him to the Cleveland Indians organization. After hitting .352 at Double-A in 1979, Charboneau finally earned a promotion to the major leagues, where he promptly won the 1980 American League Rookie of the Year Award.

Charboneau became enormously popular in Cleveland— and not just for his lusty hitting. Nicknamed "Super Joe," Charboneau emerged as a cult figure because of his unusual habits. He ate cigarettes, opened beer bottles with his eye sockets (and drank the brew through a straw in his nose), and once rid himself of an unwanted tattoo by cutting it out with a razor blade. He even tried to fix his own broken nose by twisting it back into place with pliers. Apparently his penchant for pain rubbed off on his fans: In March 1980, one of them stabbed him with a pen as he waited for the team bus. But Charboneau's crazy behavior didn't keep him from shining on the field, where he had a .289 batting average and knocked out a team-leading 23 home runs, along with 87 RBI.

However, Charboneau's reckless ways seemed to foreshadow a short career; his intensity was bound to catch up with him. In 1981, he slumped so badly that the Indians demoted him to the minor leagues (making him the first-ever Rookie of the Year to play in the minors the following year). A back injury only made his situation worse, necessitating two operations, neither of which helped. By 1983, Charboneau was playing minor-league ball for Cleveland's affiliate in Buffalo. Struggling with a .200 batting average, he decided to give the hometown fans an "obscene salute." The gesture angered Indians management, which gave him his release. Only four years after it had begun, the legend of Super Joe had reached its final chapter.

Baseball—They Used to Be The…

What and where were some of today's major league baseball teams? Some borrowed the names of defunct teams but have no other continuity with the ghosts of old.

✳ ✳ ✳ ✳

Atlanta Braves (National Association/National League): formerly the Boston Red Caps and Red Stockings (1876–1882), then the Bean-eaters (until 1906), then Doves (to 1910), then Rustlers (for 1911). In 1912, they stopped the insanity, becoming the Boston Braves. After a 38–115 season in 1935, they played as the Boston Bees from 1936 to 1940. Just before the 1953 season, they lit out for Milwaukee and stayed 12 years, moving to Atlanta in 1966. In 1977, they began playing for owner Ted Turner.

Boston Red Sox (American League): founded as the Boston Americans in 1901, unconnected with the Boston Red Stockings, who became the modern Atlanta Braves. They've been playing as the Boston Red Sox since 1908. Other early names, such as Pilgrims, were in fact rarely used and not official.

Baltimore Orioles (AL): started play as the Milwaukee Brewers in 1901 (finishing last), then became the St. Louis Browns. Deciding that 52 years of bad baseball in one place would suffice, the team became the Baltimore Orioles in 1954—honoring a rough-and-tumble 1890s team by that name, though without direct succession.

Chicago Cubs (NA/NL): once the Chicago White Stockings (1876–1889), then Colts (1890–1897), then Orphans (1898–1901). In 1902, they finally settled on the name they still carry today.

Chicago White Sox (AL): grabbed the Cubs' old nickname (White Stockings) in 1901 on their founding, then took the official abbreviation of White Sox in 1904. If you want to have fun with Sox fans, just point out that their name is actually an old Cubs nickname.

Cincinnati Reds (American Association/NL): formerly the Red Stockings (1882–1889), then the Reds. During the McCarthy years (1954–1958), they quietly became the Cincinnati Redlegs, lest a team playing the American national pastime hint at a Bolshevik takeover. They soon resumed the nickname "Reds."

Cleveland Indians (AL): born the Cleveland Blues in 1901, called Broncos in 1902, then became the Naps in 1903 to honor star Nap Lajoie. After trading Lajoie in 1914, the team took its current name.

Los Angeles Angels (AL): began play in 1961, but in 1965 they became the California Angels, now playing in Anaheim. Thirty years later it was time for a change, so they became the Anaheim Angels. Since 2005, the team has officially been the Los Angeles Angels of Anaheim.

Los Angeles Dodgers (AA/NL): began as the Brooklyn Atlantics in 1884 and were often called the Trolley Dodgers. They would play as the Grays, Bridegrooms, Grooms, Superbas, Infants, and Dodgers—all before World War I! In 1914, they became the Robins (after manager Wilbert Robinson), then went back to Dodgers in 1932. After the 1957 season, their owner moved them to Los Angeles.

Milwaukee Brewers (AL/NL): started as the Seattle Pilots in 1969. After giving Emerald City ball fans a season of futile baseball in Sicks Stadium (today the spot is a hardware store), they fled to Milwaukee in haste for the 1970 season. When major league baseball expanded in 1998, a team had to switch leagues, and the Brew Crew moved to the National League.

Minnesota Twins (AL): began in the District of Columbia as the Washington Senators but were also periodically called the Nationals—from 1905 to 1906 the name even appeared on their jerseys. How could this nebulous situation be? Especially before

1920, nicknames were more fluid, and teams were often called by their city names: "The Bostons defeated the Detroits." In 1961, the Senators/sometime Nationals moved to their current Minneapolis home.

New York Yankees (AL): began (in 1901) as one of several Baltimore Orioles franchises in Major League Baseball. Moving to the Bronx in 1903, they became the New York Highlanders. The name Yankees gradually supplanted Highlanders, becoming official in 1913.

Oakland Athletics (AL): started play as the Philadelphia Athletics in 1901. In 1955 they became the Kansas City Athletics, a big-league team that seemd to act like an informal Yankee farm team by sending promising players to the Bronx in exchange for declining veterans. They moved to Oakland in 1968, then became a dynasty. They've also been called A's since they began.

Philadelphia Phillies (NL): started as the Philadelphia Quakers in 1883, but by 1890 the popular Phillies nickname was official. It has stayed that way except for 1943–1944, when they were called the Blue Jays.

Pittsburgh Pirates (AA/NL): Go Alleghenys! In 1882, that's how they were born—just Alleghenys, spelled thus, not Pittsburgh anything. Soon the Pittsburgh designation took over. Briefly called Innocents in 1890, they were then called Pirates for sup- posedly stealing a player from another team. That name sticks to this day.

St. Louis Cardinals (AA/NL): used to be the Brown Stockings (1882)—those were the days of flamboyant, creative, egoma- niacal owner Chris von der Ahe. The team quickly became the Browns. In 1899, someone decided to rename them the Perfectos, but that was too dumb to stick. The next year they became Cardinals.

Washington Nationals (NL): started in 1969 as les Expos de Montréal but never quite seemed to fit there. In 1977, they took bad baseball locations to the next level by moving to Stade Olympique, with its dysfunctional retractable roof. Local interest got so bad that from 2003 to 2004, they played some home games in Puerto Rico. The ownership disconnected the Expos from the Montreal respirator for the 2005 season, moving to D.C. and reviving the old Nationals name.

Overtime, in Time

Not every goal in sudden-death overtime has been scored in highlight-reel fashion, and not always has the hero been a household name. Here are a few of the weirdest and wackiest overtime markers in the history of the National Hockey League.

✳　✳　✳　✳

Slip-Sliding Away: Cam Connor, Montreal vs. Toronto, April 21, 1979

A JOURNEYMAN PLUGGER WHO spent much of the 1978–1979 season nailed to the bench, Cam Connor put his name in the NHL record books during Game 3 of the 1979 quarterfinal series between the Canadiens and the Maple Leafs. Early in the second overtime period of a 3–3 tie, Connor was given a rare shift and made the most of the opportunity. He broke into the clear and was loading up for a shot on goal when the puck slipped off his stick. The change of pace completely handcuffed Toronto goaltender Mike Palmateer, and the disc slowly slid through the compunctious crease cop's legs to give Montreal a 4–3 victory. It was the only goal Connor would ever score for the Montreal Canadiens.

From Doghouse to Penthouse: Petr Klima, Edmonton vs. Boston, May 15, 1990

Pinned to the pine for most of the opening game of the 1990 Stanley Cup Finals because of undisciplined play in the early stages of the contest, Petr Klima was finally unleashed from the doghouse by Oilers coach John Muckler late in the third overtime period. Seconds into his shift, Klima corralled a pass, slowly maneuvered into the Bruins' zone, and drifted a soft shot toward the Boston cage that somehow eluded Bruins goaltender Andy Moog to give the Oilers a 3–2 victory. It was the only overtime goal of Klima's career.

Eye in the Sky: Sergei Fedorov, Detroit vs. Minnesota, April 28, 1992

Late in the opening overtime stanza of a 0–0 game between the Red Wings and the North Stars, supersniper Sergei Fedorov slipped past Minnesota defender Chris Dahlquist and blasted a bullet that buzzed by goalie Jon Casey and appeared to carom off the iron behind the cage plumber. Play continued without a whistle for several minutes until an off-sides call stopped the action. Both teams retired to their respective benches for a well-needed respite while the video goal judge reviewed the play. Upon further examination, it was determined that Fedorov's shot had actually struck the back bar inside the net, giving Fedorov the first overtime goal of his career and the Wings a 1–0 win. It was the first time in league history a playoff game result was determined by a video review.

I Did What?: Tony Leswick, Montreal vs. Detroit, April 15, 1954

The 1954 Stanley Cup Finals between tempestuous rivals Montreal and Detroit marked only the second time in league history that overtime was required in a seventh and deciding contest. Early in the extra session, Detroit's Tony Leswick felt a moment of panic when he found the puck on his stick with a slew of Montreal attackers pursuing him. Leswick flipped the puck high into the air and retreated toward the Detroit zone. With his back turned to the play, he heard the Detroit Olympia faithful explode into a resounding roar. Leswick's little loft had deflected off the glove of Montreal's all-star defenseman Doug Harvey and floated over the shoulder of goalie Gerry McNeil, giving the Wings a 2–1 victory and the Stanley Cup.

Field of Dreams

Dubbed the eighth wonder of the world, the Houston Astrodome was renowned not only for its innovative design and remarkable roof but also for the artificial grass that covered its playing surface and forever changed the face of sports.

❋ ❋ ❋ ❋

THE SYNTHETIC SUBSTANCE that eventually became known as AstroTurf was originally designed as an urban playing surface meant to replace the concrete and brick that covered the recreation areas in city schoolyards. It was developed by employees of the Chemstrand Company, a subsidiary of Monsanto Industries, leading innovators in the development of synthetic fibers for use in carpeting. In 1962, Dr. Harold Gores, the first president of Ford Foundation's Educational Facilities Laboratories, commissioned Monsanto to create an artificial playing surface that was wear-resistant, cost-efficient, comfortably cushioned, and traction tested. Two years later, the company introduced a synthetic surface called ChemGrass and installed it at the Moses Brown School, a private educational facility in Providence, Rhode Island. The new product met each of Dr. Gores's criteria except one: It was expensive to produce and wasn't a viable substitute for cement on playgrounds. However, it soon found a new home and a new name.

In 1965, the Astrodome, the world's first domed stadium, opened in Houston, Texas, featuring a glass-covered roof that allowed real grass to grow inside the dome. However, the athletes that used the facility complained they couldn't follow the path of the ball because of the glare caused by the glass. Painting the glass killed both the glare and the grass, so the lifeless lawn was replaced in 1966 with the revolutionary ChemGrass, which was quickly dubbed AstroTurf. The new turf was a resounding success, and it soon became the desired surface for both indoor and outdoor stadiums.

Babe Ruth's Called Shot: Did He or Didn't He?

Whether Ruth called a home run in the 1932 World Series remains one of baseball's greatest mysteries.

✳ ✳ ✳ ✳

This much is known: The Yankees had already won the first two games of the 1932 fall classic when they met the Cubs at Wrigley Field for Game 3. Although Chicago players were understandably frustrated, there was bad blood between the teams that extended beyond the norm. In August, the Cubs had picked up former Yankee shortstop Mark Koenig from the Pacific Coast League to replace injured starter Billy Jurges, and Koenig hit .353 the rest of the season. Despite these heroics, his new teammates had only voted him a half-share of their World Series bonus money—a slight that enraged his old colleagues. The Yanks engaged in furious bench-jockeying with their "cheapskate" opponents the entire series, and Chicago players and fans shouted back, jeering that Ruth was old, fat, and washed-up.

Up to bat: When Ruth stepped up to bat in the fifth inning of Game 3, the taunts started as usual. A few people threw lemons at Babe from the stands, and he gestured toward the crowd before settling in at the plate. Charlie Root's first pitch was a called strike, and Ruth, looking over at the Chicago dugout, appeared to hold up one finger—as if to say, "That's only one." He did the same thing with two fingers after taking the second pitch, another strike. Then, some eyewitnesses recalled, he pointed toward dead center field. Others didn't remember this act, but there was no mistaking what happened next: Ruth slammed Root's third offering deep into the edge of the right-field bleachers. Onlookers recalled him laughing as he rounded the bases. And, as shown in a much-published photo, he and on-deck batter Lou Gehrig laughed and shook hands back at home plate.

What really happened?: Here is where the facts end and speculation begins. Those among the 49,986 fans on hand who noticed Ruth's display likely assumed it was just another round in the ongoing feud between the two clubs, and most sportswriters made nothing out of it in their accounts of New York's 7–5 victory. The homer was not a game-winner; it was just one (in fact, the last) of 15 home runs Ruth hit in World Series play during his career. He had already taken Root deep earlier in the same contest, and Gehrig also had two in the game. The Yanks finished their four-game sweep the next day.

This being Babe Ruth, however, it only took a few speculative accounts from among the many reporters present to get the ball rolling. "Ruth Calls Shot" read the headline in the next day's *New York World Telegram*, and soon sports fans everywhere were wondering. Gehrig claimed he heard Ruth yell to Root, "I'm going to knock the next one down your goddamned throat" before the fateful pitch, while Cubs catcher Gabby Hartnett recalled the remark as "It only takes one to hit." Root and Cubs second baseman Billy Herman denied any gesture to the outfield, and grainy film footage that surfaced in 1999 was unclear either way. Ever the diplomat, Ruth himself granted some interviews in which he substantiated the claim, and others in which he denied it.

So did he or didn't he?: We may never know for sure, but perhaps it's better that way. When the subject is Babe Ruth, facts are only half the fun.

Helmets Head On

For some players, wearing a helmet only at the plate is not enough.

✳ ✳ ✳ ✳

Since 1971, major-league batters have been required to wear helmets, but most fielders still opt for a soft cap. However, there have been a few players over the years who have wanted to protect their head at bat or in the field.

1953 Pittsburgh Pirates: During the 1953 season, the Pirates took the field wearing rather primitive fiberglass "miner's caps" at the mandate of general manager Branch Rickey, who owned stock in the company that produced the helmets. Though partially motivated by a desire to make money for his company, Rickey also understood the benefit of keeping his players healthy. Under Rickey's orders, the Pirate players had to wear the helmets both at bat and in the field. Even manager Fred Haney joined the helmet-wearing brigade, apparently to protect himself from banging his head against the top of the dugout when leaving it to visit the mound. The helmets became a permanent feature for Pirate hitters, but the fielders figured their chances of getting beaned in the head were so small, it wasn't worth putting up with the awkward, heavy headgear.

Richie Allen: Often a verbal target of fans in Philadelphia, Allen one day found himself bombarded by hundreds of pennies thrown by fans in the left-field stands at Connie Mack Stadium. The demonstration of violence convinced Allen to wear a helmet for the rest of his career, whether playing in left field or at first base. Even after being traded by Philadelphia, Allen continued the practice while playing in St. Louis, Los Angeles, Chicago, and Oakland.

George "Boomer" Scott: Like Allen, Scott began wearing a helmet in the field because of unruly fan reaction, but his decision came in response to actions of the road fans (who often threw things at him), not the hometown faithful at Fenway Park. The clunky helmet belied Scott's fielding grace; "Boomer" won eight Gold Gloves for the Red Sox and the Brewers.

Joe Ferguson: Primarily a catcher during his major-league career, Ferguson also played in right field from time to time. The time-sharing plan began early in his career with the Dodgers, who already had a fine defensive catcher in Steve Yeager but wanted to make room for the power-hitting Ferguson in their batting order. When the 200-pound Ferguson took to the outfield—a position he hated to play—he made sure to take his hard hat with him. This may have been due to his lack of confidence in catching the ball. Ferguson once lost two fly balls in the sun during the same game, making his head an easy target for a baseball dropping out of the sky. While Ferguson's fielding prowess in right field sometimes made his managers nervous, he didn't lack for ability in throwing the ball. Playing for the Dodgers during the 1974 World Series, Ferguson unleashed a 290-foot throw from right field to the catcher, taking a potential run off the board for the Oakland A's.

Dave Parker: It's easy to understand why "The Cobra" decided to start wearing a helmet in right field. On July 20, 1980, during the first game of a doubleheader against the Dodgers at Pittsburgh's Three Rivers Stadium, one particularly nasty hometown fan fired a nine-volt transistor battery at the beleaguered Parker, who had come under criticism for playing poorly while saddled with an injured knee. The battery barely missed Parker's head, whizzing by his ear before landing on the artificial turf. Stunned by the near miss, Parker walked off and didn't return to the outfield for the rest of the doubleheader. Amazingly, the battery episode wasn't the first time that Parker had found himself in the line of fan fire. Earlier in the 1980 season, another idiotic fan had hurled a bag of nuts and bolts in Parker's direction. (It also missed.)

John Olerud: While attending Washington State University in 1989, Olerud suffered a brain hemorrhage and an aneurysm during a morning workout. Though he recovered, doctors advised him to wear a protective batting helmet while playing first base or pitching (he was a two-position player in college). This would protect against line drives and collisions with baserunners that might result in contact with the skull.

An Ambassador and a Gentleman

When we think of baseball legends, we usually place them into one category: player, manager, or pioneer. But there are some icons who defy typecasting, and Buck O'Neil—one of baseball's greatest ambassadors—was one of them.

✷　✷　✷　✷

BUCK O'NEIL WAS a solid player in the Negro Leagues, with a career batting average of .288. The first baseman was a strong clutch hitter and had a league-leading .353 average in 1946; the next year he hit .358. He went on barnstorming tours with teammate Satchel Paige, played in the 1942 Black World Series, and was named to the East-West All-Star Game (the Negro Leagues' celebrated all-star game) in 1942, 1943, and 1949.

Yet there was so much more to Buck O'Neil than what he accomplished as a player. In 1948, he became manager of the Kansas City Monarchs. He won four Negro League pennants, led his clubs to two appearances in the Black World Series, and guided his teams to a perfect record of 4–0 in the East-West Game.

The Negro Leagues began to dissolve in the 1950s, and O'Neil segued into a career with the major leagues. Joining the Chicago Cubs as a scout, O'Neil played crucial roles in signing Hall of Famers Lou Brock and Ernie Banks and quality major-leaguers like Joe Carter and Oscar Gamble. O'Neil also became the first African-American coach in major-league history, joining the Cubs' "College of Coaches" (which unsuccessfully employed a group of managers rather than just one) in the early 1960s.

O'Neil's contributions to baseball reached far off the field. After leaving scouting and coaching, O'Neil probably did more than anyone else to promote the legacy of the Negro

Leagues. Whether charming audiences on Ken Burns' Baseball documentary or appearing on David Letterman's talk show, or through his work as a voting member of the Hall of Fame's Veterans Committee, O'Neil always did his best to praise the abilities and personalities of other Negro League stars. Ever modest about himself, he said that Oscar Charleston was the equal of Ty Cobb and praised Satchel Paige for bringing out the best in everyone—even the opposition.

O'Neil's storytelling greatly enhanced the public's knowledge and familiarity with the Negro Leagues, which had been largely overlooked until the 1990s. In 2000, O'Neil visited the Hall of Fame and discussed the ability that black players showed when they barnstormed against white teams featuring major-leaguers. "They [the major-leaguers] were just out there for a payday, but we wanted to prove a point that they weren't superior," O'Neil told the Cooperstown audience. "So we would stretch that single into a double, that double into a triple, that triple into a home run. This was Negro Leagues baseball, this was the baseball Jackie Robinson brought to the major leagues." O'Neil emerged as an unofficial ambassador for the sport, exposing younger generations to the rich culture of the Negro Leagues.

Even in Buck's final summer, he persisted in advancing the awareness of black baseball. He continued his work as the chair of the Negro Leagues Museum, which he had started through tireless promotional and fundraising efforts. At the Hall of Fame induction ceremony in July 2006, O'Neil stole the show with a humorous, lively, and uplifting speech. Then in August, he achieved an unusual place in baseball history when he became the oldest man—at 94 years of age—to take the plate in a professional game.

Unfortunately, the one thing O'Neil was not able to accomplish during his life was induction into Cooperstown. In 2006, he fell one vote short, which shocked his fans and supporters and certainly caused O'Neil a deeper disappointment than he ever let on. He passed away on October 6, 2006, at the age of 94.

In considering someone's candidacy for the Hall of Fame, most people feel it is not enough merely to focus on what one did as a player. Rather, the accomplishments of an entire career must be taken into consideration. In the case of O'Neil, his efforts as a manager, scout, coach, and ambassador raise his status, making him one of the most diverse and respected figures in baseball history. And it's the entirety of those accomplishments that should one day earn Buck O'Neil what he deserves—election and induction into baseball's Hall of Fame.

Inventors of Major Sports

Basketball is the only major team sport that is native to the United States. Also the most popular indoor team sport in the world, it was invented in Springfield, Massachusetts, by James Naismith (1861–1939), who arranged the first game in December 1891. Naismith played the game only twice because he felt he committed too many fouls (he believed this was because his extensive experience in wrestling and football made physical contact come naturally to him). In 1936, basketball was added as an Olympic sport. After many years as a professor of physical education at the University of Kansas, Naismith died in 1939.

The following were founders of other major American team sports:

❋ Baseball: Alexander Joy Cartwright (1820–92)

❋ American football: Walter Camp (1859–1925)

The Pirates of Pittsburgh

While watching a Pittsburgh Pirates baseball game, it's easy for fans to conjure up romantic images of Captain Kidd, Blackbeard, or Peg Leg. Here's the real connection between the team and those swaggering swashbucklers.

✳ ✳ ✳ ✳

THE CLUB LOGO features a pirate's head over crossed bats (in lieu of a skull and crossbones), so fans might be excused for yelling "Aye!" every time a player throws a strike, scores a run, or steals a base. Yet few people realize that the team's "Pirate" moniker was originally intended as a slur. In fact, calling a Pirate a pirate in 1890 was akin to a mutiny, and use of the epithet might brand the speaker a "dungbie" ("ass" in pirate-speak) by team loyalists. Here's how it came to pass.

The "Alleghenys" (with no reference to Pittsburgh whatsoever) originally formed in 1882 as charter members of the American Association. In 1887, the team transferred to the National League and changed its name to "Pittsburgh." In 1890, baseball was rocked by a players' revolt. Taking on established leagues of the day, the newly formed Players' League would last only one year but would bring forth many changes. After the league dissolved, most players went back to their original teams, provided the organizations had "reserved" them.

As a result of this peculiar loophole, one unattached star player—second baseman Lou Bierbauer, previously of the Philadelphia Athletics—ended up on Pittsburgh's roster. Like a shot fired across the bow, accusations of theft were immediately levied at these "pirates" by the Athletics. The put-down stuck. Eventually, in a classic "If you can't beat 'em, join 'em" move, the Pittsburgh squad adopted the name as its own. Since that day, baseball's pillagers have never looked back. So when you plunk down your doubloons to watch the Pirates play, understand that you are seeing the real deal.

The Heisman Curse

After being named best college football player in the nation, one's best position might be "fallback." Those who believe the Heisman Curse is just a sports myth should consider the following.

* * * *

D URING A FOOTBALL game in 1934, University of Chicago running back Jay Berwanger collided with University of Michigan defender Gerald Ford, bloodying the tackler's left cheek. The resulting scar on the future U.S. president would be permanent—as would, some say, the so-called Heisman Curse it begat.

A year later, Berwanger was awarded the first Heisman Trophy, emblematic of the best player in college football. Although he also became the first man ever drafted by the NFL, the "Genius of the Gridiron" never played another snap. Surprisingly few of the six dozen trophy recipients since have made more of an impact.

In recent years, the list of Heisman honorees has included several pro football busts, especially at the marquee quarterback position. Charlie Ward (1993), Eric Crouch (2001), and Jason White (2003) never played an NFL game. Danny Wuerffel (1996) earned just ten starts, and though Chris Weinke (2000) made 19, his team won just one of them.

Berwanger himself tacitly acknowledged that the Heisman wasn't worth the 25 pounds of bronze used to cast it. Until he eventually donated it to his alma mater, the trophy was displayed in his aunt's library—as a doorstop.

The Worst Team in Baseball History

Most teams experience an off-season. But in 1899, the Cleveland Spiders couldn't be more off their game.

✳   ✳   ✳   ✳

W HO WAS THE worst team in major league baseball history? The 1962 New York Mets and their record of 40–120? Ha! The 42–112 Pittsburgh Pirates of 1952? Please. The 2003 Detroit Tigers, who went 43–119? C'mon.

No, the worst team in professional baseball history was the 1899 Cleveland Spiders, whose record of 20–134 gave them a scintillating .130 winning percentage. They were good (or bad) enough to finish a mere 84 games out of first place. Yet just four years prior the Spiders had been the best team in baseball. What happened?

Along Came Some Spiders

The Cleveland Spiders, so called because of the skinny appearance of many of their players, began life in baseball's National League in 1889. In 1892, led by future pitching great Denton True "Cy" Young (who was bought by the team for $300 and a new suit), the Spiders finished second in the league. In 1895, the Spiders won the Temple Cup, the forerunner to the World Series.

However, despite the large crowds that would attend Sunday games, playing baseball on that day was still controversial. In 1897, the entire Spiders team was thrown into the pokey for playing baseball on the Sabbath. The following season, Cleveland was forced to shift most of their Sunday games to other cities. Attendance suffered, and the team stumbled to a record of 81–68.

Web Spinning

One other factor contributed to the Spiders' demise: Syndicate baseball. This meant that it was acceptable for owners of one National League team to own stock in another. Inevitably, the team with the better attendance and players drew most of the owner's attention and finances, while the lesser team suffered.

Syndicate baseball arrived in Cleveland in early 1899, when owner Frank Robison bought the St. Louis Browns at a sheriff's auction. He decided that St. Louis was a better market than Cleveland, and so he shipped all of the best Spiders there and renamed the new group—in case anyone missed the point—the Perfectos. Meanwhile, the absent Spiders were replaced by, well, anybody.

Robison's brother Stanley was put in charge of Cleveland. Stanley started off on the wrong foot with Cleveland fans by stating that he intended to operate the Spiders "as a sideshow." Faced with that encouraging news, less than 500 fans turned out for Cleveland's Opening Day double-header. Not surprisingly, the Spiders lost both games. The rout had begun.

And what a rout it was! After the first 38 games, the Spiders had 30 losses. Deciding that third baseman/manager Lave Cross was the problem, Robison sent him to St. Louis (which actually was a reward). With virtually no one showing up for the games, Stanley locked the Cleveland ballpark and announced that the Spiders would play their remaining "home" games on the road.

Woebegone Wanderers

The dismal team—now dubbed the "Wanderers," "Exiles," and "Foresakens"—won just 12 more games the entire season. At one point they lost 24 games straight, which is still a record. They were so bad that after the Spiders beat the Baltimore Orioles, the Orioles' pitcher was fined and suspended. In the midst of all this, Cleveland sportswriter Elmer Bates compiled a tongue-in-cheek list of reasons to follow the Spiders. Among them:

1. There is everything to hope for and nothing to fear.

2. Defeats do not disturb one's sleep.

3. There is no danger of any club passing you.

4. You are not [always] asked ..."What was the score?" People take it for granted that you lost.

On the last day of the season, a 19-year-old cigar stand clerk pitched for the Spiders; the team lost 19–3. After the game, the Spiders presented the team travel secretary with a diamond locket because, as the dedication said, he "had the misfortune to watch us in all our games." The following year Cleveland was dropped from the National League.

The Bellyache Heard Around the World

Let's face it, it wasn't exactly the "Shot Heard 'Round the World." But because it was Babe Ruth, the "Bellyache Heard Around the World" carried some importance. But what happened?

✳   ✳   ✳   ✳

Sultan of Swat

BABE RUTH WAS, and remains, one of the most famous baseball players in history. It was Ruth's prodigious slugging in the early 1920s that saved baseball from the Black Sox Scandal. It was also his presence on the New York Yankees—a formerly mediocre team—that turned them into a collection of world-beaters.

In his first few seasons with the Yankees, Ruth set home run records and drove the team into the World Series three years in a row (1921–1923). The Yankees won the series in 1923, and even though they missed out in 1924, there was every expectation that they'd be back in 1925—after all, they had Babe Ruth. But no one counted on the Bellyache Heard Around the World.

Hot Dogs and Fables

Although he was reportedly fighting the good exercise fight on his farm in Sudbury, Massachusetts, Ruth, who never met a meal he didn't eat, had ballooned to 245 pounds over the winter. Prior to spring training in early February 1925, Ruth went to Hot Springs, Arkansas, to get in shape for the coming season. Besides its therapeutic mineral baths, Hot Springs was also known as a pre-Vegas Vegas. Before long, Ruth was fully caught up in two of his favorite pastimes: sex and food. To combat his stomach's protests over the large amount of chow he was shoveling in, Ruth gulped bicarbonate soda to settle his belly. However, there was no such remedy for whatever sexual diseases were floating around. As contemporary sportswriter Fred Lieb noted: "One woman couldn't satisfy him. Frequently it took half a dozen."

Needless to say, Ruth was badly out of shape when spring training started in St. Petersburg, Florida. By late March he was struggling with "lame legs." But that hardly stopped the Ruthian caravan of food and sex. As teammate Joe Dugan later commented, "He was going day and night, broads and booze."

As the Yankees made their way north from spring training to start the season, Ruth got progressively worse. Finally, on April 7, Ruth collapsed at the train station in Asheville, North Carolina. Rumors spread like wildfire that the Sultan of Swat was dead; a London newspaper vividly reported the death scene. Ruth revived, only to collapse again in the train bathroom, smashing his head against the sink. When the train reached New York, the unconscious Ruth (estimated at 250–270 pounds) was hoisted out through the train window. At the hospital, Ruth was delirious and convulsing. On April 17, he had a very hush-hush operation.

So What the Heck Happened?

For decades, the story given to explain Ruth's illness was one invented by sportswriter W. O. McGeehan, which combined rambunctiousness with aw-shucks innocence: Ruth had simply eaten too many hot dogs, peanuts, and soda. That's just so All-American it has to be true, right?

There are other stories. Long after Ruth's death, his wife Claire wrote that he had suffered a groin injury. Perhaps, but groin injuries normally don't cause their subjects to become delirious. Another possibility is gonorrhea—a rumor believed by several teammates and even Yankee General Manager Ed Barrow. Yet while Ruth's liaisons with anything wearing a skirt could certainly have given him a STD, surgery would have been an unusual treatment.

This leaves the possibility that Ruth had what one of his physicians called an "intestinal abscess." Ruth biographer Marshall Smelser speculated that Ruth likely had an obstruction of the intestine, requiring a temporary colostomy. In those days, such a personal and private procedure would not have received mention in the press.

Most likely, we'll never know the full truth. That year was Ruth's worst season in baseball, but soon he was back to boozing and whoring. As his roommate "Ping" Bodie allegedly said when asked what it was like to room with Ruth, "I ain't rooming with Ruth. I room with his suitcase."

Lip's Quip

Long considered to be a placard for the passive and polite, the saying "Nice guys finish last" is credited to baseball manager Leo Durocher. For decades he sailed his ship on the wave created by that quote, but according to Durocher himself, he merely used the phrase best.

✳   ✳   ✳   ✳

K NOWN AS "THE Lip" during his lengthy major league career as a player and on-field manager, Leo Durocher was always quick with a quip and a colorful anecdote. On July 6, 1946, when he was bench boss of the Brooklyn Dodgers, Durocher was shooting the breeze with sports scribe Frank Graham about that afternoon's opponents, the crosstown-rival New York Giants. The Dodgers, known affectionately as "Da bums" by the Brooklyn faithful, were a motley crew of reprobates who played hard both on and off the field. When asked to describe the Giants, Durocher supposedly said: "Take a look at them. They're all nice guys, but they'll finish last. Nice guys. Finish last." In his summation of the conversation the following day, Graham shortened the quote to "Nice guys finish last." At the time, Durocher denied making the remark, and his account of the episode was substantiated by *New York Times* pundit Lou Effrat, who was adamant that the Lip had actually lamented, "Nice guys finish eighth," referring to the number of teams in the league.

In 1992, Ralph Keyes compiled a book of misquotes titled *Nice Guys Finish Seventh.* In his version of the events, Durocher said: "Why, they're the nicest guys in the world! And where are they? In seventh place." Which is where the Giants were in the standings when the Lip started flapping. Although no one can agree on what was actually said, Durocher nonetheless titled his 1975 best-selling autobiography—what else?—*Nice Guys Finish Last.*

The Hockey Hall of Fame— Where Legends Live On ... and On and On

The Hockey Hall of Fame in Toronto was created to showcase all things hockey: the best players, games, and coaches. It's no surprise that legends come alive there—it's a place where stars of the sport live on forever. So you probably wouldn't be surprised to find a ghost hanging around its hallowed halls, but you might be surprised to learn that she has absolutely nothing to do with hockey.

* * * *

Dorothy Who?

SITUATED ON THE corner of Yonge and Front Streets in downtown Toronto, the Hockey Hall of Fame resides in a beautiful old building that has the look of a cathedral, complete with a stained-glass dome. Built in 1885, the structure was home to the Bank of Montreal before it closed in 1982; the Hall moved into the building a decade later.

Over the years, there have been many theories regarding the building's resident ghost, Dorothy. As you can imagine, a lot of speculation has surrounded how the young woman died ... and why she stayed. Some thought that she was the victim of a robbery gone wrong. Others thought she was involved in an embezzling scheme and that she took her own life when the crime was uncovered. But most believed she was caught up in a tragic love affair. One version of the tale suggested that her boyfriend left to take "a job on the boats"; another told of her involvement with a married coworker.

In 2009, the *Toronto Star* conducted a thorough investigation of Dorothy and her mysterious demise. With that, the pieces started coming together.

In 1953, 19-year-old Dorothea Mae Elliott was working at the Bank of Montreal as a teller. She was a vivacious brunette, popular with coworkers and customers alike. Orphaned at nine years old, Dorothy didn't let her sad childhood get her down; in fact, friends and coworkers described her as "the most popular girl in the bank" and "the life of the party."

But on March 11, 1953, when Dorothy arrived at the bank, she appeared to be distressed and her clothing was disheveled. It would later be discovered that she had been involved in a romantic liaison with her bank manager—a married man—and when he chose to end the relationship, she was heartbroken. At some point, she discreetly removed the bank's .38-caliber revolver from a drawer and headed to the women's restroom on the second floor. At around 9 A.M., another female employee entered the room and began to scream: Dorothy had shot herself in the head and no one had even heard the gunshot. She died the next morning at a local hospital.

Cold Spots

Over the years, many employees, customers, and other visitors to the building have experienced odd phenomena, all of which have been attributed to Dorothy. Lights turn on and off on their own, and locked doors open by themselves when no one is around. People working in the building late at night have heard mysterious footsteps, and many have reported hearing moans and screams.

One worker who was setting up for an event witnessed a chair spinning around and around until it moved right into his hand. And while performing at an event in the building, harpist Joanna Jordan actually saw Dorothy's ghost along the second-floor ceiling. When she was invited to play there again, Jordan refused to venture onto that floor alone.

So attached was Dorothy to the old bank building that she remained there even after it was taken over by hockey fans and memorabilia. One young boy visiting the Hall also saw Dorothy's apparition; he screamed after glimpsing a woman with long dark hair gliding back and forth through the walls. Isn't there a penalty for that?

"There are some human beings who are dimly aware of their own deaths, yet have chosen to stay on in what used to be their homes, to be close to surroundings they once held dear."

—HANS HOLZER

Chapter 12

Food—From Fast to Gourmet

Moo Magic

Long dismissed as the beverage of the bland, milk got a boost from an astute ad agency that combined pop culture sensibility and a hip Hollywood director with a sexy stream of A-list celebrities to make sure everybody "got" milk.

✳ ✳ ✳ ✳

I**T'S NEARLY IMPOSSIBLE** to browse through a popular magazine or drive down a busy boulevard without seeing an ad or billboard of a Hollywood hotshot or superstar sports icon advocating the benefits of milk with a wink in their eye and a milk mustache on their lips. The Got Milk? advertising campaign revitalized the dairy industry and made cold milk cool.

The Got Milk? campaign was the brainchild of Goodby, Silverstein & Partners, a San Francisco ad agency that was just starting to compile a credible clientele. In 1993, the company was commissioned by the California Milk Processor Board to create an innovative and intriguing campaign that would encourage consumers to drink cow's milk.

The initial Got Milk? commercial, which was broadcast on TV for the first time in October 1993, featured a trivia buff who was given the opportunity to win a $10,000 prize if he knew who shot Alexander Hamilton in the famous duel. Although the knowledgeable nerd was an expert on the topic, his answer was unintelligible. He was marble-mouthed and crumb-clotted after eating a peanut butter sandwich because he didn't have any milk to wet his whistle. The ad's creative and comic approach, plus the high-style direction of Michael Bay—an MTV graduate who went on to helm a number of Hollywood blockbusters, including *Armageddon* and *Pearl Harbor*—helped put milk on the same playing field as soft drinks and other beverages. The "milk mustache" campaign, which began in 1995, is now seen as a gauge for measuring celebrity status.

A True Ad Pitch(er)

Could a pitcher with a face on it become an advertising icon for the ages? Oh yeah.

✳   ✳   ✳   ✳

BIG CORPORATIONS WILL use anything to sell product: Recall Mrs. Butterworth, the grandma of pancake syrup. Or Snap, Crackle, and Pop, the elves that live in your breakfast cereal.

Every once in a while, though, they get it right. In 1953, food giant General Foods bought Kool-Aid from inventor Edwin Perkins. Perkins's creation started out as a bottled liquid named Fruit-Smack, but the cost of bottle breakage and shipping forced Perkins to come up with a way to remove the liquid from his formula, resulting in a powdered concentrate that Perkins called Kool-Ade and later renamed Kool-Aid.

Legend has it that Marvin Potts, art director for General Food's advertising agency, was charged with coming up with a smart way to sell the powder. He had his best idea while watching his son draw smiley faces on a frosty window. It occurred to him that a friendly, frosty pitcher might be the perfect emblem for the drink. The smiley face is perhaps indicative of Perkins's good nature; during the Great Depression, he cut the cost of Kool-Aid in half so that everyone would be able to afford a tall glass of refreshment despite the dire economic circumstances.

The higher-ups at General Foods loved Potts's idea, and ads with a smiling pitcher started to hit the general public. It wasn't until 1975, though, when Kraft acquired General Foods, that the pitcher spouted arms and legs and donned some youthful blue jeans and sneakers.

The Kool-Aid Man has inspired so much loyalty that the town of Hastings, Nebraska, where Perkins launched his invention, hosts an annual Kool-Aid Days celebration. It is, after all, the official drink of Nebraska.

The Birth of Good Humor

There is surprising controversy behind this beloved slice of Americana.

✳ ✳ ✳ ✳

AMERICAN SUBURBIA: LAUGHING children, lemonade stands, sprinklers, and, of course, that ice-cream truck emitting its soothing jingle.

In 1920, Harry Burt, an ice-cream shop owner in small-town Ohio, invented the first ice-cream confection on a stick. His store was selling a lollipop called the Jolly Boy Sucker as well as an ice-cream bar covered in chocolate. Inserting a wooden stick into the ice-cream bar made it "the new, clean, convenient way to eat ice cream."

Burt quickly patented his manufacturing process and started promoting the "Good Humor" bar in accordance with the popular belief that one's palate affects one's mood. He then sent out a fleet of shiny white trucks, each stocked with a friendly Good Humor Man and all the ice-cream bars kids could eat. By 1961, 200 Good Humor ice-cream trucks wound their way through suburbia.

Not Without a Little Bad Humor

The ice cream on a stick suddenly found itself facing solid competition from other be-sticked frozen treats. First there was Citrus Products Company, champion of the frozen sucker. Then came Popsicle Corporation, home to the Popsicle. Good Humor took these companies to court, alleging that Good Humor's patent gave them exclusive rights to frozen snacks on a stick. Popsicle countered that Good Humor only owned the rights to ice cream on a stick, whereas Popsicles were flavored water. When Popsicle attempted to add milk to its recipe, a decade-long court battle ensued, centering on what precise percentages of milk constitute ice cream, sherbet, and flavored water.

Popsicle and Good Humor have settled their differences and are now owned by the same corporation. As for the Good Humor Man, he's endangered but not extinct. Good Humor stopped making its ice-cream trucks in 1976, but they are still owned by smaller distributors.

The Toll House Mystery

We know who invented the chocolate chip cookie, and we know when. But we're not exactly sure how.

* * * *

IN THE 1930S, Ruth Wakefield and her husband operated the Toll House Inn near Whitman, Massachusetts. Wakefield was a dietitian, cookbook author, popular food lecturer, and an excellent cook.

One day, she was mixing up a batch of Butter Drop cookies, a popular sugar cookie found in recipe books dating back to the colonial days.

According to oft-repeated legend, the recipe called for baker's chocolate, but Ruth didn't have any, so she used a bar of Nestlé semisweet chocolate instead. But why would a sugar cookie recipe include baker's chocolate? Who knows? In any event, Wakefield broke up the bar and added it to the dough.

Or did she? George Boucher, who was head chef at the Toll House Inn, told a different story. According to Boucher, the chocolate accidentally fell into the mixing bowl from a shelf just above it, knocked off by the vibrations of the electric mixer. Mrs. Wakefield was going to throw the batter out, but Boucher convinced her to try baking it, and the rest is cookie history. (Doubters might wonder why the chocolate would be sitting on a shelf unwrapped, just waiting to fall into the mix, but never mind them.)

The official Nestlé version of the story states that Wakefield expected the chocolate to melt and was surprised when it didn't. But as she was an experienced cook and knew her way around a kitchen, it seems more likely that she was intentionally trying to create a new recipe and added the semisweet chocolate on purpose.

Of this there is no doubt: In 1939, Nestlé invented chocolate chips specifically for the cookies and printed the recipe on the bag. Today, Toll House Cookies are perhaps the most popular cookie in history.

How It All Began

What's Black and White and Creamy in the Middle?

Oreo cookies have been a part of childhood in the West since 1912. In fact, by the time the Kraft company decided to bring their number-one product to the East, hundreds of billions of Oreos had already been consumed. Alas, since their introduction to China in 1996, the little black-and-white cookies failed to impress Chinese consumers, who thought the snacks were too sweet and expensive. For the first time in many decades, Oreos had to be taken off the assembly line and put back on the drawing board.

In 2006, Kraft reincarnated the Oreo in China as four sugar-reduced chocolate-coated wafer sticks with vanilla- and chocolate-cream filling. The traditional round chocolate cookies were still available for the few consumers who liked them. Also, by reducing the number of snacks in a box, Kraft was able to reduce the price. Between the two kinds of Oreo available, sales began to escalate.

Then, the Oreo aficionados in the Kraft research kitchens remembered a fundamental fact about the cookie: the delight in pulling apart the layers and licking off the filling. To solve this problem, the Krafty cooks came up with a cream-filled cylindrical wafer that, when the cream was sucked out of it, could be used as a milk straw until the wafer softened. The Oreo name stayed the same and so did the fun associated with eating the product. In 2007, Kraft saw their Oreo sales double in China and worldwide; according to Kraft and *The Wall Street Journal*, Oreo sales topped a billion dollars worldwide, making it the King of Cookies.

Of course, Oreo purists have groused about the new Chinese version—the cookies are supposed to be round, black, and white in the middle. But really, who cares as long as snackers young and old alike can enjoy them!

Memorable Fast-Food Mascots

The Big Boy

THE BIG BOY, a 12-foot statue of a chubby boy that stands outside Big Boy restaurants, is considered one of the first fast-food mascots. The grinning boy, with the words "Big Boy" stamped across his chest, sports red-and-white overalls and holds a triple-decker hamburger in his hand. No wonder he's so big.

Speedee

No, this isn't the Alka-Seltzer mascot. McDonald's originally had its own Speedee mascot, a chef with a hamburger for a head. McDonald's dropped Speedee to avoid any legal battles with Alka-Seltzer. The chain's new mascot, Ronald McDonald, has done pretty well: A poll once found that 96 percent of children recognized the burger-slinging clown.

The Taco Bell Chihuahua

You may not know that the Chihuahua that famously promoted Taco Bell products was named Gidget. You also may not know that Gidget passed away in July 2009 after suffering a stroke. She was 15.

Pizza Hut Chef

Many fast-food mascots have been discontinued because they were deemed insulting to different ethnic groups. Pizza Hut, for instance, once featured an Italian chef tossing a dough ball. The chef was replaced by the chain's "red roof" logo because PepsiCo, which had purchased Pizza Hut, was concerned that the mascot was too cartoonishly Italian.

Colonel Harland Sanders

Not many mascots are real people, but Harland Sanders, the mascot and founder of Kentucky Fried Chicken, is. Sanders lacked an advertising budget when starting his restaurant chain. To save money, he became his chain's own mascot.

Wimpy

Wimpy Grills, which closed in 1978, featured the hamburger-loving Wimpy character from the Popeye comic strip as its mascot. The restaurant, which had 1,500 outlets across the United States at one time, closed after the death of its founder, Edward Vale Gold. Gold had specified in his will that he wanted all Wimpy's outlets closed once he died.

The Tastee-Freez Twins

Female Tee and male Eff represent soft-serve ice-cream chain Tastee-Freez. The twins have ice cream running down their heads, with Tee sporting strawberry and Eff dripping chocolate.

Iam Hungry

If you blinked, you might have missed this fast-food mascot. Iam Hungry was a floating ball of fuzz with orange arms that tried desperately to mooch McDonald's meals from Ronald McDonald. McDonald's introduced the mascot in 1998 and dumped him in the early 2000s.

The Noid

The Noid, an odd creature with rabbit ears who wore a tight red latex suit, appeared in commercials for Domino's Pizza in the 1980s and 1990s. The creature only communicated with odd grunts and groans and ranks as one of the creepiest of fast-food mascots.

The Sleepy Mexican

Here is another example of a mascot that was dumped because it was racially offensive. Taco Bell used a Siesta-enjoying Mexican figure as its mascot until PepsiCo bought the chain. PepsiCo replaced the mascot with the now-familiar mission bell logo.

Gum Makes You Hungry

When hunger pangs strike, does chewing a piece of gum stave them off or stoke them? Scientists are still chewing on the answer, but prevailing research gives some clues.

✳ ✳ ✳ ✳

To Chew or Not to Chew?

DIETERS SOMETIMES SHUN gum because they fear it will exacerbate their feelings of deprivation and emptiness. They think—or feel—that chewing gum starts the gastric juices flowing by stimulating saliva in anticipation of some real food. When the juices find nothing to digest, it makes the person feel like devouring something.

Scientists have found evidence to the contrary, however. Stimulating saliva by chewing gum has not been shown to increase hunger. In fact, recent studies indicate that gum can *decrease* one's appetite. A study presented at the 2007 Annual Scientific Meeting of the Obesity Society found that chewing gum before an afternoon snack helped reduce hunger, diminish cravings, and promote fullness among people who were trying to limit their calorie intake.

That Adds Up!

The people who chewed gum before a snack consumed 25 fewer calories from that snack than the non-chewers. The study even touted the benefits of chewing gum for appetite control, saying that it is an easy, practical tool for weight management. If you think 25 calories is insignificant, here's a little weight-loss math: 2537 equals 175 calories per week; 2537352 equals 9,100 calories (or 2.6 pounds) per year.

Other research studies have shown that hunger and the desire to eat are significantly suppressed by chewing gum at one-, two-, and three-hour intervals after a meal.

If you're still convinced that chewing gum makes you hungry, consider whether boredom, habit, or stress are responsible instead. Until science discovers otherwise, chewing gum is a tasty alternative to an "unnecessary" meal.

Ten Rumors About Fast-Food Restaurants

Cow eyeballs, anyone? How about snakes with your fries? Rumors about fast-food parlors run the gamut from the mundane to the insane.

✳ ✳ ✳ ✳

Kentucky Fried Chicken and the Ku Klux Klan

THIS ONE WAS aimed squarely at KFC's founder, Colonel Harland Sanders. The rumor claimed that Sanders was a racial bigot who siphoned off 10 percent of his profits to the Ku Klux Klan. Intended to undermine the fast-food chain, the rumor gained little traction. With noses trained to smell a foul, Sanders's customers balked at the allegation, and the franchise suffered nary a bit.

Wendy's 25-Cent Hamburgers

More playful than many popular fast-food rumors, this 2008 untruth stated that in honor of Wendy's 60th anniversary, the chain would temporarily revert to founding-era pricing. This would mean that a hamburger would cost a quarter, French fries 15 cents, and so on. There were two problems with the story. First, Wendy's opened in 1969, making it just 39 years old in 2008. Second, the chain had absolutely no intention of altering its prices. Shucks!

McDonald's Uses Cow Eyeballs in Its Patties

A common rumor claims that substandard (read *cheaper*) ingredients are used to produce fast-food favorites. With McDonald's and cow eyeballs, rumormongers obviously weren't doing their math, since the orbs are actually more expensive than ground beef. It's doubtful that a national chain would spend *more* on production than it had to.

Jack in the Box Serves up Kangaroo Meat

Did you ever wonder what makes Jack spring up from his box? Could a kangaroo patty, *not* a hamburger, be responsible for Jack's jump? It's rather doubtful since kangaroo meat costs more than beef to produce. Nevertheless, the rumor gained some ground in the 1990s.

Arby's Liquid-Protein Alternative

Are Arby's roast beef sandwiches really made from pastes, gels, or other liquids? No. Well, not really. The truth is each roast beef patty is surrounded by a "self-basting" solution and packed inside an airtight bag. If viewed by the uninitiated, the product could appear to be completely liquid. One squeeze, however, will dispel such drippy notions.

McDonald's Shakes Are Made From Nonfood Items

Another bit from the seemingly endless mega-chain-cuts-corners rumor mill, this one alleges that McDonald's shakes are *not* made from the real thing. Here's the straight deal: Whole milk, cream, sugar, and corn syrup comprise the principal ingredients in a McDonald's shake. There are also a few food preservatives used in the mix. Bottom line? McDonald's shakes *are* made mostly from food items. Enough said.

Dunkin' Donuts Celebrates 9/11

This nasty rumor tells of Dunkin' Donuts storeowners/employees celebrating the September 11th attacks by burning American flags. The targeted shopkeepers, not too surprisingly, were ethnic, hailing from Pakistan, India, Portugal, and other lands. An investigation found absolutely no merit to the allegations, but the rumors persisted. In an effort to allay fears and stifle prejudices, storeowners took to displaying huge American flags on their buildings. Thankfully, things soon calmed down.

Taco Bell Stops Featuring Its Mascot Chihuahua After the Dog Dies

The real reason for ditching the doggie relates to the chain's bottom line, *not* the animal's flat line. Dwindling sales in 2000 prompted an advertising change and a decision to drop the canine. But Gidget (the dog's real name) had a starring role yet to come in *Legally Blonde 2*. The scrappy chihuahua reached 15 years of age in 2009 and then finally broke free of her leash, spiritually speaking. Rest in peace, girl.

In-N-Out Burger's Secret Menu

When is a rumor especially juicy? When it's based in fact and smothered in grease. In-N-Out Burger officially carries just four food items on its menu: a hamburger, a cheeseburger, a double-double, and French fries. But rumors (truths, as it turns out) continue to fly regarding a vast array of other food items. Samplings of these include the Flying Dutchman (two patties, two slices of cheese, nothing else) and Animal Style Fries (fries with special sauce, cheese, and onions). There are many more, but since the meal items are not advertised by name, a hungry patron must track each item down through word of mouth or internet surfing. Bon appétit.

Burger King Has Snakes in Its Play Pit

This macabre tale tells of a three-year-old boy who was playing inside Burger King's ball pit. Suddenly, the boy started whimpering. Hours later, he was dead. The cause? Baby rattlesnakes had infiltrated the pit and bitten the boy. Is it true? Worry not, moms and dads. This humdinger of a rumor is completely false and was likely cooked up for its shock value.

Things You Don't Know (and Didn't Need to Know) About... Pop-Tarts

Since the 1970s, rumors have been circulating about exploding Strawberry Pop-Tarts.

✳ ✳ ✳ ✳

✳ In 1994, computer scientist Patrick Michaud performed an experiment called "Strawberry Pop-Tart Blow-Torches." The study confirmed that the tarts were a potential fire hazard capable of causing flames of up to three feet high to shoot from the toaster if the Pop-Tart was left in too long. Read on to find out more than you ever wanted to know about Pop-Tarts.

✳ After examining sales data in the wake of Hurricane Charley in 2004, Wal-Mart executives discovered that Strawberry Pop-Tarts sold at seven times their normal rate in the days leading up to the hurricane. Even without hurricanes, Americans devour about two billion Pop-Tarts each year— enough to stretch halfway to the moon.

✳ Some lucky celebrities get to have a tart named after them. Back in 2005, Barbie had her very own flavor, Barbie Sparkleberry, with her picture stamped on the frosting. Other celebrity-themed tarts have included Indiana Jones Brown Sugar Cinnamon, American Idol Blue Raspberry, and Disney Princess Jewelberry.

✳ Kellogg's is always introducing new flavors. Over the years, the company has marketed Wild Watermelon, Guava Mango, and Chocolate Chip Cookie Dough.

✳ Frosted Strawberry is the favorite flavor of Bill Post of Glen Arbor, Michigan, the plant manager who invented Pop-Tarts back in 1963. He has "Pop-Tarts" engraved on his personalized license plate and sometimes drives over to the local supermarket just to hang out in the Pop-Tarts aisle. "I like to stand there and watch customers take them off the shelves," he told a reporter from Michigan's *Northern Express* on the tarts' 40th anniversary in 2003. Do his tarts ever catch fire in the toaster? No. He says he prefers to eat them raw.

Fun With Food

Hungry to know where your favorite foods originated? Take a bite out of this tasty treatise!

✳   ✳   ✳   ✳

Pizza

IT MIGHT BE considered American fast food today, but pizza originated in the South Italian region around Naples, where flat yeast-based bread topped with tomatoes was a local specialty. In 1889, baker Raffaele Esposito made pizzas for the visiting Italian King Umberto I and Queen Margherita. The queen's favorite was a pizza that featured the colors of the Italian flag—green basil leaves over white mozzarella cheese and red tomatoes. This dish soon became known as margherita pizza and was the taste of Italy around the world.

Sandwich

This lunchtime favorite likely dates back to the ancient Hebrews, who may have put meat and herbs between unleavened bread during Passover. But it was an eighteenth-century British noble that gave it its name. John Montagu, 4th Earl of Sandwich, was a keen card player and commonly ate meat between pieces of bread to keep from getting the cards greasy.

Pretzel

Monks in southern France or northern Italy, possibly dating back to the seventh century, can be credited with giving baked dough as a reward to children who learned their prayers, hence the shape, which is meant to resemble a person in prayer. The salty snacks gained popularity in southern Germany in the twelfth century, where folded, baked bread was called *Brezl*.

Caesar Salad

It is a salad fit for a Roman emperor, but it isn't named after Julius or even Augustus. It is the creation of Italian-born Mexican chef Caesar Cardini, who according to one story, whipped up the salad when faced with a shortage of ingredients for a Fourth of July celebration in 1924. Another tale attests that Cardini made it for a gourmet contest in Tijuana. Either way, the salad is worthy of his name!

Steak Tartare

The nomadic Tartar warrior tribe was known for eating raw meat, which was usually pressed underneath the saddle of a horse, but the raw meat dish today, which is usually chopped beef or horsemeat with a liberal amount of seasoning and spices, may take its name from the Italian word *tartari*, which means raw steak.

Ranch Dressing

One of the most popular salad dressings in the United States actually did start out on a ranch—a dude ranch in Santa Barbara, California. Opened in 1954 by Steve and Gayle Henson, the "Hidden Valley Ranch" served a special house dressing that was so popular visitors came just to buy it.

Pasty

The forerunner of the potpie was originally cooked up as a lunch meal by Cornish miners, who were unable to return to the surface to eat or even clean up. The pastry crust allowed the miners—as well as other laborers—the ability to eat the contents, which typically included meat, vegetables, and gravy, and then discard the shell.

TV Dinner

The advent of the microwave has changed the frozen food market, but in 1953, Swanson's TV Brand Frozen Dinner was a popular prime-time meal. However, it may come as a surprise that frozen dinners predated Swanson's by nearly a decade, when William L. Maxson devised a prepackaged frozen meal for airplanes in 1944. Still, clever marketing and better distribution ensured that the TV Dinner from Swanson became the nationally recognized leader in frozen food.

Taco

The handheld Mexican favorite can be considered one of the first "fusion" foods—and it is as much a mix of cultures as the Mexican people today. The native Nahuatl people ate fish served in the flat corn bread, but it was sixteenth-century Spanish explorers who gave the bread the name *tortilla* and began to fill it with beef and chicken as well.

Nachos

One of today's cheesiest snacks made its debut during World War II. When several U.S. soldiers stopped in at the Victory Club, just south of the Texas-Mexico border, chef Ignacio "Nacho" Anaya found he had little food to serve beyond tortillas and cheese. Cut into triangles and fried, the tortilla chips were served with the cheese. Over the next three decades, the dish spread throughout Texas until sportscaster Howard Cosell gave kudos to the dish during a taping of *Monday Night Football* in 1977.

Waffles

During the Middle Ages, a thin crisp cake was baked between wafer irons. Oftentimes, the irons included designs that helped advertise the kitchen that produced the waffle. Early waffles were made of barley and oats, but by the eighteenth century, the ingredients changed to the modern version of leaven flour.

Pop-Tarts

Kellogg's brand name for toaster pastries was actually developed in response to a product from Post Cereals that used a process initially used for dog food. Post had created a food-in-foil process for canine chow and then adapted it for a breakfast food the company introduced as "Country Squares." But Kellogg jumped on the bandwagon with its own sugary filling in a pastry crust, and thus Pop-Tarts won the battle of the toasters.

Ugly but Delicious: The Chocolate Truffle

Chocolate truffles may look like grubby little mushrooms, but that's where the resemblance ends.

✳   ✳   ✳   ✳

NAMED FOR THEIR physical resemblance to the fungus so treasured by chefs around the world, chocolate truffles have their origin in France, where chocolatiers originally set them out as Christmas-time goodies. Because of the high cream and butter content of the treats, and because refrigeration wasn't always de rigueur, truffles were only offered for a short time—typically during the winter months, when it'd be easier to keep them from spoiling.

Traditional truffles are made of chocolate paste (chocolate, cream, eggs, and butter) and then rolled in cocoa powder. They may be flavored with brandy, rum, vanilla, cinnamon, or coffee. Americans do it a little differently: We like ours in a hard chocolate shell and flavored with everything from ginger to jalapeño.

No one really knows where or how the truffle came into being, but we do know that pastry chef Alice Medrich, who first sampled a chocolate truffle when she was living in Paris in the

1960s, is largely credited with bringing this little treasure to the United States via her San Francisco store Cocolat. Now, *haut-chocolat* houses from coast to coast offer them: Vosges Haut-Chocolat, which offers retail locations in Chicago, New York, and Las Vegas, showcases savory flavors, while you can still find traditionally flavored truffles at Jacques Torres's Brooklyn, New York–based chocolate factory. Even middle-of-the-road chocolate companies offer their version of the truffle, although you won't find flavors such as "gold leaf" among their offerings.

How It All Began

The Bottled Water Craze

Bottled water is definitely trendy, but people have been hip to the healing powers of water from mineral springs since ancient times. By the late-eighteenth century, European nobles regularly headed to spas to bathe in and drink from the powerful waters (though not at the same time). By the mid-nineteenth century, railroads made it possible to ship bottled mineral water to middle-class consumers across Western Europe. In North America, Native Americans were sipping from springs in the mid-sixteenth century. White settlers discovered the springs' waters and soon jugs of the stuff were loaded onto western-bound wagon trains.

But by the twentieth century, municipal water systems had improved, thanks to the addition of chlorine, and bottled water fell out of fashion. That is, until the chairman of the French water company Perrier decided to try peddling his wares stateside in 1976.

Bottled Enthusiasm

Bruce Nevins was working for Pony athletic company when Perrier's Gustave Leven, an investor in Pony, suggested he sell the bottled carbonated water to U.S. consumers. Within two years, Nevins carved out a $20 million market for Perrier, emphasizing the water's exclusivity and, in particular, its healthfulness—a matter of interest to Americans in the 1970s and 1980s.

Impressed with Perrier's success, French company Danone International (known stateside as yogurt company Dannon) introduced Evian to America in 1984 as a plastic-bottled, noncarbonated water targeted to the gym crowd. By the end of the decade, it was Madonna's drink of choice and the hottest accessory for supermodels to be seen toting off the runway, touting its benefits as a complexion clearer and appetite suppressant. The 1990s health craze continued to keep the bottled water business afloat. Eventually, bottled water was everywhere from gas stations to gourmet restaurants as a portable—and potable!—cure-all.

Plastic Passion

The industry really took off, when—to counteract all the anti-soda health messaging—Pepsi and Coke jumped on the bandwagon, launching, respectively, Aquafina in 1994 and Dasani in 1999. Today, amid protests about the environmental waste of plastic water bottles, Americans collectively go through more than 25–50 million bottles of water a year.

Commendable Condiment

While an apple a day may keep the doctor away, taking something with a grain of salt will make that flavorful fruit—and any other advice that lurches on the ledge of logic—easier to swallow.

❋ ❋ ❋ ❋

UNLIKE MANY OF the phrases that originated in the era when recording history was lightly regarded and often ignored, the exact genesis of "take it with a grain of salt" has not been lost in the murky sands of time. Its meaning refers to administrating caution before accepting the validity of a claim, and its roots can be traced to first-century Rome, thanks to the well-documented works of scholar and naturalist Gaius Plinius Secundus, who is better known as Pliny the Elder.

His most famous offering was a comprehensive compilation entitled *Historia Naturalis*, an exhaustive encyclopedia completed in 77 A.D. and the largest tome of its type from the time of the Roman Empire to survive through the centuries.

Pliny's production consists of 37 books and includes virtually everything that the Romans knew about the natural world in the fields of mathematics, geography, anthropology, zoology, botany, pharmacology, mining, mineralogy, cosmology, astronomy, metallurgy, and agriculture. It also includes an ancient antidote for poison that states a person can survive poisoning if they combine the ingredients (walnuts, figs, and 20 leaves of rue) with a pinch of salt. Over the centuries, that advice was moderated to mean that a grain of salt can act as a measure of prevention against any injurious substance, be it poison or bad advice.

The Oxford English Dictionary dates the usage of the expression "with a grain of salt" to 1647.

Popcorn

A look at the development of pop-ular culture's favorite snack.

✳   ✳   ✳   ✳

✳ Aztec Indians of the sixteenth century used garlands of popped maize as a decoration in ceremonial dances. They were a symbol of goodwill and peace.

✳ Native American folklore speaks of spirits that live inside each kernel of corn. When heated, or "angered," the spirits explode in a "puff," often considered an omen of bad luck.

* The oldest ears of popcorn (the variety of corn grown for this particular purpose) were discovered in the Bat Cave (in Carlsbad Caverns National Park) in west central New Mexico in 1948.

* The physics of popping: Each kernel of corn contains a drop of water in a layer of soft starch. As the kernel heats up, the water expands, building pressure against the starch. Eventually, this hard surface cracks, exploding the kernel.

* Charles Cretors invented the popcorn machine in 1885, but that was really just a peanut-roasting apparatus that happened to also pop corn kernels. Eight years later, Cretors introduced the first mobile, steam-driven popcorn machine at the Chicago World's Fair.

* During the Great Depression, popcorn was ubiquitous on city streets because it was an inexpensive way to stave off hunger.

* In 1998, the National Popcorn Board was formed as a result of the Popcorn Promotion, Research, and Consumer Information Act signed in 1996 by President Bill Clinton, a big fan of the snack.

* More than 17 billion quarts of popcorn are consumed in the United States annually; that's about 56 quarts per person every year.

* "Old maids," the unpopped kernels at the bottom of a bag or bowl of popcorn, are likely the result of dehydration. A loss of three percent of the moisture in a popcorn kernel can render it unpoppable. Store popcorn in an airtight container to keep it from drying out before it's popped.

* There's been a slight downward trend in popcorn consumption in the United States recently, but its popularity has been steadily increasing in Europe, Asia, and South America.

* According to CalorieKing.com, the average large tub (20 cups) of buttered movie theater popcorn contains 1,657 calories and 134 grams of fat. Don't worry, though: You can burn it off by walking for about seven and a half hours.

* In October 2006, the World's Largest Popcorn Ball was created in Lake Forest, Illinois, to celebrate National Popcorn Month. It weighed 3,415 pounds, was 8 feet in diameter, and had a circumference of $24^1/_2$ feet.

* Colonial women poured sugar and cream on popcorn and served it for breakfast—likely the first "puffed" cereal! Some colonists popped corn in a type of cage that revolved on an axle and was positioned over a fire.

* According to the Popcorn Institute, popcorn is high in carbohydrates and has more protein and iron than potato chips, ice cream cones, pretzels, and soda crackers.

* By the time Europeans began settling in the New World, popcorn had spread to most Native American tribes in North and South America. More than 700 types of popcorn were being grown, elaborate poppers were being invented, and popcorn was sometimes worn in the hair and around the neck as jewelry. There was even a widely consumed popcorn beer.

* If you made a trail of popcorn from New York City to Los Angeles, you would need more than 352,028,160 popped kernels!

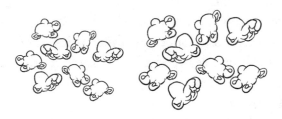

Fallacies & Facts: Junk Food

Fallacy: Fresh food is more healthful than processed food.

Fact: Food poisoning from such deadly bacteria as *E. coli* and *salmonella* (and transmission of some parasites) most often occurs when you eat fresh meat, poultry, or dairy products that are spoiled or undercooked. Heat treatments used in canning not only give canned goods long shelf lives, but they make them safe to eat without refrigeration. Irradiation kills bacteria in packaged meats, while pasteurization does the same for milk and fruit juices.

Fallacy: Processed foods are never as nutritious as fresh foods.

Fact: Some are just as nutritious, and some are even more so. Frozen vegetables are processed within hours of harvest, which preserves vitamins and minerals that can be lost in the days or weeks before fresh vegetables are eaten. Some processing techniques actually add nutrition to food. Vitamin D added to milk enhances calcium absorption and helps build strong bones. Separating bran from grain removes phytic acid, which improves iron absorption, and processing tomatoes into paste or sauce increases the amount of the antioxidant lycopene. New trends in "functional foods" add healthful vitamins, minerals, cholesterol-lowering fiber, and antioxidants to foods.

Fallacy: Additives and preservatives are artificial and largely unnecessary.

Fact: Many processors use laboratory-produced additives such as colors and sweeteners, but many other additives are derived from fruits and vegetables. Salt, sugar, and lemon juice are among the best-known food additives. Tartaric acid from fruit is used to give some foods a longer shelf life. Thickening agents extracted from seeds and seaweed add texture to foods. Vegetable oils and organic acids are used as emulsifiers in spreads such as jams and peanut butter.

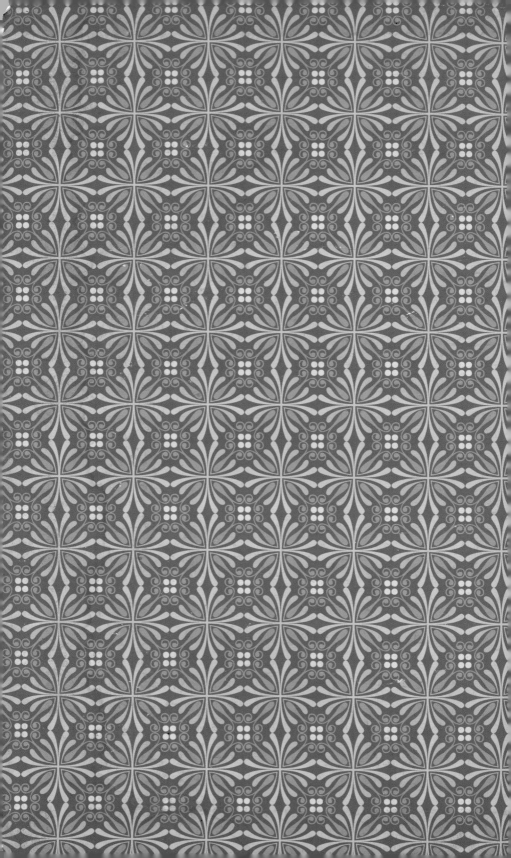